# Mastering Microso... ... ....

## Second Edition

MW00852030

Expert techniques to create interactive insights for
effective data analytics and business intelligence

**Greg Deckler**

**Brett Powell**

BIRMINGHAM—MUMBAI

# Mastering Microsoft Power BI
## Second Edition

Copyright © 2022 Packt Publishing

**Senior Publishing Product Manager:** Devika Battike

**Acquisition Editor – Peer Reviews:** Saby Dsilva

**Project Editor:** Amisha Vathare

**Content Development Editor:** Rebecca Robinson

**Copy Editor:** Safis Editing

**Technical Editor:** Aditya Sawant

**Proofreader:** Safis Editing

**Indexer:** Rekha Nair

**Presentation Designer:** Ganesh Bhadwalkar

First published: March 2018
Second edition: June 2022

Production reference: 3141022

Published by Packt Publishing Ltd.
Livery Place
35 Livery Street
Birmingham
B3 2PB, UK.

ISBN 978-1-80181-148-4

www.packt.com

# Foreword

Microsoft Power BI is the best analytics platform that empowers every employee to ask and explore questions, uncover insights, and gain intelligence through modern business intelligence tools. Power BI consists of cloud services, mobile applications, a data modeling and report authoring application, and other utilities, including the on-premises data gateway. Additionally, organizations can deploy Power BI reports on-premise via the Power BI Report Server and scale their deployments with Power BI Premium capacity.

This book provides an end-to-end analysis of Power BI tools and features, from planning a Power BI project to distributing Power BI apps to large groups of users. You will be familiarized with all the fundamental concepts and see how Power BI datasets, reports, and dashboards can be designed to deliver insights and rich, interactive experiences.

You'll also become knowledgeable about management and administration topics, such as the allocation of Power BI Premium capacities, Azure Active Directory security groups, conditional access policies, and staged deployments of Power BI content.

This book will inspire you to take advantage of these powerful features and follow consistent practices in deploying Power BI for your organization. I highly recommend this book to any new or existing Power BI users who want to learn what features and functionalities Power BI provides, as well as how they can quickly take advantage of their data.

*- Leon Gordon, Thought Leader at Forbes Technical Council, Microsoft Data Platform MVP and Partner at Pomerol Partners*

# Contributors

## About the authors

**Greg Deckler** is a Vice President at Fusion Alliance and has been a consulting services professional for over 27 years. Recognized as an expert in Power BI, Greg is a six-time Microsoft MVP for the Data Platform and an active member of the Power BI Community site with over 5,000 solutions authored and hundreds of Quick Measures Gallery submissions. Greg founded the Columbus Azure ML and Power BI User Group in Columbus, OH in 2016 and holds regular monthly meetings. Greg is also the author of numerous external tools for Power BI available for free on his gdeckler GitHub repository.

*I would like to deeply thank my family, son Rocket, my extended Fusion Alliance family, the dynamic and vibrant Power BI community as a whole and especially all of the Super Users as well as my user group members. A special thanks to Brett Powell for all of his support and guidance on this book as well as Power BI Cookbook, 2nd Edition.*

**Brett Powell** is a Microsoft business intelligence consultant and author. Brett has over 12 years of business intelligence experience across many industries as a developer, architect, and administrator. Although most known for his Insights Quest blog and the first editions of *the Microsoft Power BI Cookbook* and *Mastering Microsoft Power BI*, Brett primarily focuses on the needs of clients and project engagements though Frontline Analytics LLC, a Microsoft BI consultancy and Power BI partner.

*I give all glory and praise to my Lord and Savior Jesus Christ. I was alone and lost in sin, but Christ has forgiven me and granted me a new peace and purpose for my life.*

## About the reviewer

**Eugene Meidinger** has been working in business intelligence for over 8 years now, focusing heavily on business reporting. He speaks regularly at technical conferences, including Pass Summit and SQLBits. Eugene started his own company in 2018, SQLGene Training, and now produces training videos for Pluralsight and consults on Power BI.

*I would like to thank my husband Miles for supporting me during the nights and weekends I worked on reviewing this book.*

## Join our community on Discord

Join our community's Discord space for discussions with the author and other readers:

https://discord.gg/q6BPbHEPXp

# Table of Contents

## Chapter 3: Connecting to Sources and Transforming Data with M            83

# Preface

Microsoft Power BI is a leading business intelligence and analytics platform that supports both self-service data visualization and exploration as well as enterprise BI deployments. Power BI consists of cloud services, mobile applications, a data modeling and report authoring application, and other utilities, including the on-premises data gateway. Additionally, organizations can deploy Power BI reports on-premises via the Power BI Report Server and scale their deployments with Power BI Premium capacity.

This revised and expanded edition provides an end-to-end analysis of the latest Power BI tools and features, from planning a Power BI project to distributing Power BI apps to large groups of users. You'll be familiarized with all the fundamental concepts and see how Power BI datasets, reports, and dashboards can be designed to deliver insights and rich, interactive experiences. You'll also become knowledgeable about management and administration topics such as the allocation of Power BI Premium capacities, Azure Active Directory security groups, conditional access policies, and staged deployments of Power BI content. This book will encourage you to take advantage of these powerful features and follow thoughtful, consistent practices in deploying Power BI for your organization.

## Who this book is for

This book is intended for business intelligence professionals responsible for either the development of Power BI solutions or the management and administration of a Power BI deployment. BI developers can use this as a reference guide to features and techniques to enhance their solutions. Likewise, BI managers interested in a broad conceptual understanding, as well as processes and practices to inform their delivery of Power BI, will find this a useful resource. Experience in creating content using Power BI Desktop and sharing content on the Power BI service is helpful.

# What this book covers

*Chapter 1, Planning Power BI Projects*, discusses alternative deployment modes for Power BI, team and project roles, and licensing. Additionally, an example project template and its corresponding planning and dataset design processes are described.

*Chapter 2, Preparing Data Sources*, explains foundational concepts such as query folding, query design, data source preparation and important Power BI Desktop settings.

*Chapter 3, Connecting to Sources and Transforming Data with M*, depicts the data access layer supporting a Power BI dataset, including data sources and fact and dimension table queries. Concepts of the Power Query M language, such as parameters, are explained and examples of custom M queries involving conditional and dynamic logic are given.

*Chapter 4, Designing Import, DirectQuery, and Composite Data Models*, reviews the components of the data model layer and design techniques in support of usability, performance, and other objectives. These topics include relationship cross-filtering, custom sort orders, hierarchies, and metadata.

*Chapter 5, Developing DAX Measures and Security Roles*, covers the implementation of analysis expressions reflecting business definitions and common analysis requirements. Primary DAX functions, concepts, and use cases such as date intelligence, row-level security roles, and performance testing are examined.

*Chapter 6, Planning Power BI Reports*, describes a report planning process, data visualization practices, and report design fundamentals, including visual selection and filter scopes. In addition, it covers drillthrough report pages, visual interactions, bookmarks, and Live connections.

*Chapter 7, Creating and Formatting Visualizations*, reviews many standard visuals including slicers, single-number visuals, maps, waterfall charts, scatter charts, Power Platform visuals and Premium visuals, as well as how to format visuals, including the use of tooltips, conditional formatting, custom format strings, and sparklines.

*Chapter 8, Applying Advanced Analytics*, examines powerful interactive and analytical features, including AI visuals, R and Python visuals, ArcGIS Maps, custom visuals, animation, and the **Analytics** pane. Additionally, it covers Quick Insights and mobile optimized report pages.

*Chapter 9, Designing Dashboards*, provides guidance on visual selection, layout, and supporting tiles to drive effective dashboards. Alternative multi-dashboard architectures, such as an organizational dashboard architecture, are reviewed, as well as the configuration of dashboard tiles and mobile optimized dashboards.

*Chapter 10, Managing Workspaces and Content*, features the role and administration of workspaces in the context of Power BI solutions and staged deployments. Additionally, the Power BI REST API, content management features, and practices are reviewed, including field descriptions and version history.

*Chapter 11, Managing the On-Premises Data Gateway*, covers top gateway planning considerations, including alternative gateway architectures, workloads, and hardware requirements. Gateway administration processes and tools are described, such as the **manage gateways** portal, gateway log files, and PowerShell gateway commands.

*Chapter 12, Deploying Paginated Reports*, explains how to deploy and migrate paginated reports to the Power BI service and compares and contrasts the Power BI Report Server with the Power BI service and provides guidance on deployment topics such as licensing, reference topology, installation, upgrade cycles, and client applications.

*Chapter 13, Creating Power BI Apps and Content Distribution*, walks through the process of publishing and updating apps for groups of users. Additionally, other common distribution methods are covered, such as the sharing of reports and dashboards, email subscriptions, data-alert-driven emails, and embedding Power BI content in SharePoint Online, Teams, and custom applications.

*Chapter 14, Administering Power BI for an Organization*, highlights data governance for self-service and corporate BI, Azure Active Directory features such as Conditional Access policies, and the Power BI admin portal. Details are provided about configuring Power BI service tenant settings and the tools available to monitor Power BI activities.

*Chapter 15, Building Enterprise BI with Power BI Premium*, reviews the capabilities of Power BI Premium and alternative methods for allocating premium capacity. Additionally, administration and optimization topics are discussed as well as lifecycle management using the ALM Toolkit and SQL Server Management Studio.

# To get the most out of this book

A Power BI Pro license and access to the Power BI service is necessary to follow many of the topics and examples in this book. The assignment of the Power BI Service Administrator role within the Microsoft 365 admin center, as well as administrative access to an on-premises data gateway, would also be helpful. It's assumed that readers are familiar with the main user interfaces of Power BI Desktop and have some background in business intelligence or information technology.

The primary data source for the examples in this book was the AdventureWorks data warehouse sample database for SQL Server 2019. A SQL Server 2019 Developer Edition database engine instance was used to host the sample database. For the import mode dataset, an Excel workbook stored the sales plan data. For the DirectQuery dataset, the sales plan data was stored in the sample SQL Server database.

The original AdventureWorksDW2019 was customized by adding a schema and multiple views. The customized version of this database is included in the code bundle for this book as are the Power BI Desktop files and specific queries and scripts used.

## Download the example code files

The code bundle for the book is hosted on GitHub at `https://github.com/PacktPublishing/-Mastering-Microsoft-Power-BI-Second-Edition`. We also have other code bundles from our rich catalog of books and videos available at `https://github.com/PacktPublishing/`. Check them out!

## Download the color images

We also provide a PDF file that has color images of the screenshots/diagrams used in this book. You can download it here: `https://static.packt-cdn.com/downloads/9781801811484_ColorImages.pdf`

## Conventions used

There are a number of text conventions used throughout this book.

`CodeInText`: Indicates code words in text, database table names, folder names, filenames, file extensions, pathnames, dummy URLs, user input, and Twitter handles. For example; "Mount the downloaded `WebStorm-10*.dmg` disk image file as another disk in your system."

A block of code is set as follows:

```
let CalculateAge = (BirthDate as date) =>
        Date.Year(CurrentDayQuery) - Date.Year(BirthDate)
in CalculateAge
```

When we wish to draw your attention to a particular part of a code block, the relevant lines or items are highlighted:

```
let CalculateAge = (BirthDate as date) =>
```

```
        Date.Year(CurrentDayQuery) - Date.Year(BirthDate)
 in CalculateAge
```

Any command-line input or output is written as follows:

```
Install-Module MicrosoftPowerBIMgmt -Force
```

**Bold**: Indicates a new term, an important word, or words that you see on the screen, for example, in menus or dialog boxes, also appear in the text like this. For example: "All workspaces and content within those workspaces are provided a **globally unique identifier (GUID)**."

 Warnings or important notes appear like this.

 Tips and tricks appear like this.

# Get in touch

Feedback from our readers is always welcome.

**General feedback**: Email feedback@packtpub.com, and mention the book's title in the subject of your message. If you have questions about any aspect of this book, please email us at questions@packtpub.com.

**Errata**: Although we have taken every care to ensure the accuracy of our content, mistakes do happen. If you have found a mistake in this book we would be grateful if you would report this to us. Please visit, http://www.packtpub.com/submit-errata, selecting your book, clicking on the Errata Submission Form link, and entering the details.

**Piracy**: If you come across any illegal copies of our works in any form on the Internet, we would be grateful if you would provide us with the location address or website name. Please contact us at copyright@packtpub.com with a link to the material.

**If you are interested in becoming an author**: If there is a topic that you have expertise in and you are interested in either writing or contributing to a book, please visit http://authors.packtpub.com.

# Share your thoughts

Once you've read *Mastering Microsoft Power BI, Second Edition*, we'd love to hear your thoughts! Scan the QR code below to go straight to the Amazon review page for this book and share your feedback.

*https://packt.link/r/1801811482*

Your review is important to us and the tech community and will help us make sure we're delivering excellent quality content.

# Download a free PDF copy of this book

Thanks for purchasing this book!

Do you like to read on the go but are unable to carry your print books everywhere? Is your eBook purchase not compatible with the device of your choice?

Don't worry, now with every Packt book you get a DRM-free PDF version of that book at no cost.

Read anywhere, any place, on any device. Search, copy, and paste code from your favorite technical books directly into your application.

The perks don't stop there, you can get exclusive access to discounts, newsletters, and great free content in your inbox daily

Follow these simple steps to get the benefits:

1. Scan the QR code or visit the link below

https://packt.link/free-ebook/9781801811484

2. Submit your proof of purchase
3. That's it! We'll send your free PDF and other benefits to your email directly

# 1

# Planning Power BI Projects

Power BI is a robust, flexible business intelligence platform enabling organizations to deploy data analysis and reporting solutions according to their individual policies and use cases. Organizations can utilize Power BI to enable self-service data analytics and visualization for business analysts, as well as deploying enterprise-grade solutions involving technical expertise and advanced security and scalability features. Likewise, Power BI fully supports both cloud and on-premises data sources as well as all primary types of reports, ranging from interactive visualizations to pixel-perfect paginated reports to Excel-based reports.

While specific organizational goals, the data landscape, and specific resource responsibilities can vary greatly, the underlying concepts, deployment choices, roles, and planning processes for business intelligence projects remain the same. The long-term success or failure of most Power BI projects is most highly correlated to the planning, organization, and effective collaboration of the different stakeholders. Solutions that deliver the most value to the business over time are the result of thoughtful decisions around the people and processes involved in data governance, data quality, data modeling, and finally data visualization and distribution.

This chapter explores the various project planning decision topics, roles, and processes critical to the success of all Power BI projects.

In this chapter, we review the following topics:

- Power BI deployment modes
- Project discovery and ingestion
- Power BI project roles
- Power BI licenses
- Dataset design

- Data profiling
- Dataset planning

To begin, we first explore the different deployment modes for Power BI.

# Power BI deployment modes

Prior to the existence and adoption of BI tools capable of supporting self-service scenarios, business analysts were effectively relegated to the role of "end user" of solutions developed and maintained from end to end by their information technology department. While this top-down approach helped ensure that the solution would be secure, accurate, and resource-efficient, it was also relatively slow and inflexible to adjust to changing requirements.

As a consequence, business analysts commonly utilized the IT-owned solutions as merely a starting point or data source to their own MS Office-based solutions that business analysts could maintain. The perceived lack of flexibility and extended timelines sometimes associated with IT-owned solutions often frustrated business teams, resulting in a lack of adoption and "shadow IT" scenarios in which business users created their own solutions via Excel and other tools.

Modern business intelligence platforms such as Power BI provide increased opportunities for the business to participate in the creation and deployment of data assets for the organization. Organizations can deliver Power BI solutions that require the resources and technical expertise of a Corporate BI approach, as well as empowering business teams to leverage the self-service capabilities of the platform. This "self-service" can range widely from enabling teams to access and analyze certain certified Power BI datasets to empowering business analysts to create their own end-to-end solutions including their own data transformation workflows and semantic models.

In many scenarios, a combination of corporate IT resources, such as the on-premises data gateway and Power BI Premium capacity, can be combined with the business users' knowledge of requirements and familiarity with data analysis and visualization in order to increase the velocity of data asset development. More experienced organizations may even utilize multiple deployment modes depending on the distinct requirements and use cases for Power BI across different teams and projects.

For example, solutions involving highly sensitive data or targeted at executive leadership are generally owned from end to end by Corporate BI/IT personnel. However, in scenarios involving rapidly changing requirements where deep business knowledge is essential, business analysts familiar with the data are often empowered with sufficient Power BI licenses and resources to develop their own datasets and reports.

We refer to standard deployment mode as **Corporate BI**, a deployment mode where the IT department controls all aspects of the business intelligence platform. Alternative approaches are called **self-service**, where the business controls some or all aspects of the business intelligence platform.

Self-service approaches can benefit both IT and business teams, as self-service can reduce IT resource constraints and project timelines, and provide the business with greater flexibility and control as analytical needs change. Additionally, Power BI projects can be migrated across deployment modes over time as required skills and resources change. However, greater levels of self-service and shared ownership structures generally increase the risk of miscommunication and introduce issues of version control, quality, and consistency.

These deployment modes are summarized in *Figure 1.1*:

| Corporate BI | • Reports and dashboards owned by IT<br>• Datasets owned by IT |
|---|---|
| Self-Service Visualization | • Reports and dashboards owned by business<br>• Datasets owned by IT |
| Self-Service BI | • Reports and dashboards owned by business<br>• Datasets owned by business |

*Figure 1.1: Power BI deployment modes*

A Power BI dataset is a semantic data model primarily comprised of data source queries, relationships between fact and dimension tables, and measure calculations. A semantic data model adds meaning to the physical, underlying data by adding relationships between data entities, allowing organizations to extract truth and understanding from their data.

Datasets often contain hierarchies, row-level security roles, and often other metadata such as calculation groups, detailed row expressions, and other metadata that supports usability and analysis. Power BI datasets share the heritage and concepts of Analysis Services tabular mode models and are generally developed using Power BI Desktop, a Windows application.

Microsoft has now positioned Power BI Premium-hosted datasets as their flagship semantic modeling tool and a "superset" of Analysis Services models. As the "superset" term implies, Power BI Premium-hosted datasets now support all of the enterprise-grade modeling features of Analysis Services and there are a number of powerful modeling features, such as composite models and incremental refresh policies, that are only available via Power BI datasets. *Chapter 15, Building Enterprise BI with Power BI Premium*, covers Power BI Premium in more detail.

Now that deployment modes are understood at a high level, let's take a look at each of the three deployment modes in greater detail.

# Corporate BI

The Corporate BI delivery approach in which the BI team develops and maintains both the Power BI dataset (sometimes called a data model) and the required report visualizations is a common deployment option, particularly for large-scale projects and projects with executive-level sponsors or stakeholders. This is the approach followed in this chapter and throughout this book, as it offers maximum control over top BI objectives, such as version control, scalability, usability, and performance.

Corporate BI can be visualized as shown in *Figure 1.2*:

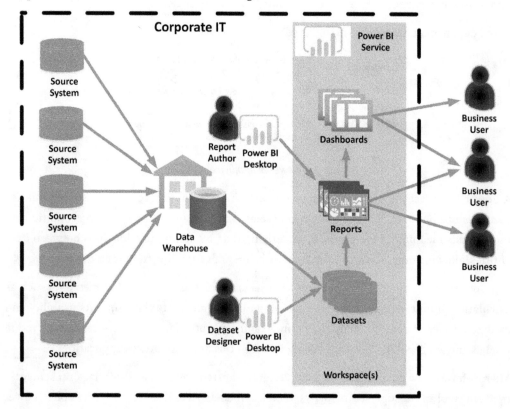

*Figure 1.2: Corporate BI*

As shown in *Figure 1.2*, all data and Power BI assets are owned by corporate IT and business users simply consume reports and dashboards published by corporate IT to the Power BI service.

Again, with the Corporate BI approach, business users are solely consumers of corporate business intelligence assets. Next, we compare this approach with self-service approaches where business users are more engaged with the creation and deployment of business intelligence assets.

# Self-Service Visualization

In the Self-Service Visualization approach, the dataset is created and maintained by the IT organization's BI team, but certain business users with Power BI Pro licenses create reports and dashboards for consumption by other users. In many scenarios, business analysts are already comfortable with authoring reports in Power BI Desktop (or, optionally, Excel) and can leverage their business knowledge to rapidly develop useful visualizations and insights.

With ownership of the dataset, the BI team can be confident that only curated data sources and standard metric definitions are used in reports and can ensure that the dataset remains available, performant, and updated or refreshed as per business requirements.

Self-Service Visualization is shown in *Figure 1.3*:

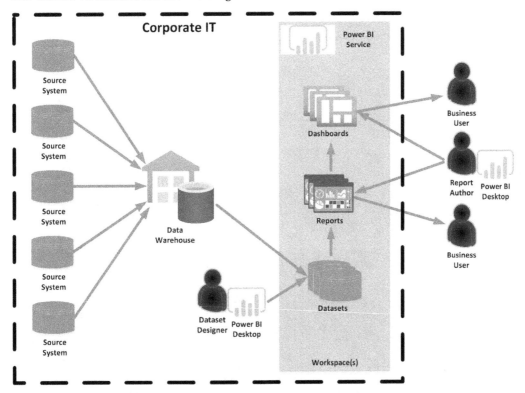

*Figure 1.3: Self-Service Visualization*

As shown in *Figure 1.3*, dataset designers within corporate IT still create and manage the Power BI datasets but business users author and publish reports and dashboards to the Power BI service. In the next section, we explore the Self-Service BI approach driven entirely by the business.

# Self-Service BI

In the Self-Service BI approach, the BI organization only contributes essential infrastructure and monitoring, such as the use of an on-premises data gateway and possibly Power BI Premium capacity to support the solution. Since the business team maintains control of both the datasets and the visualization layer, the business team has maximum flexibility to tailor its own solutions including data source retrieval, transformation, and modeling.

This flexibility, however, can be negated by a lack of technical coding skills and a lack of technical knowledge such as the relationships between tables in a database. Additionally, business-controlled datasets can introduce version conflicts with corporate semantic models and generally lack the resilience, performance, and scalability of IT-owned datasets. Self-Service BI can be visualized as shown in *Figure 1.4*:

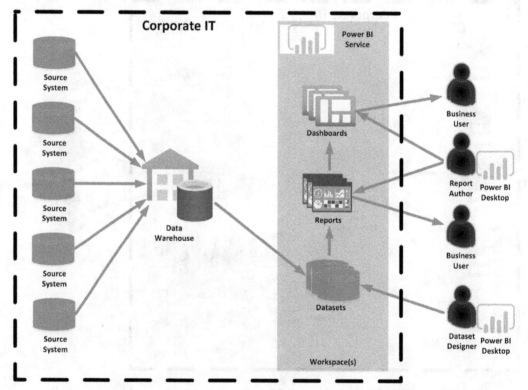

*Figure 1.4: Self-Service Visualization*

As shown in *Figure 1.4*, with a completely self-service approach to business intelligence with Power BI, the business, and not IT, performs all of the functions of dataset design and report authoring. Now that the three different deployment modes are understood in greater detail, next we cover choosing between them.

# Choosing a deployment mode

Organizations generally choose a standard deployment mode used throughout the business or choose a particular deployment mode based upon the unique requirements and goals of each individual Power BI project.

It's usually necessary or at least beneficial for Corporate BI organizations to own the Power BI datasets or at least the datasets that support important, widely distributed reports and dashboards. This is primarily due to the value of providing a single source of truth built on top of a curated data source such as a data warehouse as well as the technical skills involved in developing and managing large or complex datasets.

Additionally, BI organizations require control of datasets to implement security and to maintain version control. Security and version control often factor into corporate governance policies or are necessary to maintain compliance with regulations imposed by government agencies. Therefore, small datasets initially created by business teams are often migrated to the BI team and either integrated into larger models or rationalized given the equivalent functionality from an existing dataset.

Larger organizations with experience in deploying and managing Power BI often utilize a mix of deployment modes depending on the needs of the project and available resources. For example, a Corporate BI solution with a set of standard IT-developed reports and dashboards distributed via a Power BI app may be extended by assigning Power BI Pro licenses to certain business users who have experience or training in Power BI report design. These users could then leverage the existing data model and business definitions maintained by IT to create new reports and dashboards and distribute this content in a separate Power BI workspace and/or app.

A workspace is simply a container of datasets, reports, and dashboards in the Power BI cloud service that can be distributed to large groups of users. A Power BI app represents the published version of a workspace in the Power BI service and workspace. Members can choose which items in the workspace are included in the published Power BI app. See *Chapter 10, Managing Application Workspaces and Content*, and *Chapter 13, Creating Apps and Content Distribution*, for greater detail on app workspaces and apps, respectively.

Another common scenario is a **Proof of Concept (POC)**. A POC is a small-scale self-service solution developed by a business user or a team designed to be transitioned to a formal, IT-owned, and managed solution. Power BI Desktop's rich graphical interfaces at each layer of the application (query editor, data model, and report canvas) make it possible and often easy for users to create useful models and reports with minimal experience and little to no code.

It's much more difficult, of course, to deliver consistent insights across business functions (that is, finance, sales, and marketing) and at scale in a secure, governed environment. The IT organization can enhance the quality and analytical value of these assets, as well as providing robust governance and administrative controls to ensure that the right data is being accessed by the right people.

The following list of fundamental questions help guide a deployment mode decision:

1. Who will own the data model?

   Experienced dataset designers and other IT professionals are usually required to support complex data transformations, analytical data modeling, large data sizes, and security rules, such as RLS roles, as described in *Chapter 5, Developing DAX Measures and Security Roles*.

   If the required data model is relatively small and simple, or if the requirements are unclear, the business team may be best positioned to create at least the initial iterations of the model.

   The data model could be created with Analysis Services or Power BI Desktop.

2. Who will own the reports and dashboards?

   Experienced Power BI report developers with an understanding of corporate standards and data visualization best practices can deliver a consistent user experience.

   Business users can be trained on report design and development practices and are well positioned to manage the visualization layer, given their knowledge of business needs and questions.

3. How will the Power BI content be managed and distributed?

   A staged deployment across development, test, and production environments, as described in *Chapter 8, Managing Application Workspaces and Content*, helps to ensure that quality, validated content is published. This approach is generally exclusive to Corporate BI projects.

   Sufficient Power BI Premium capacity is required to support distribution to Power BI free users and either large datasets or demanding query workloads.

   Self-Service BI content can be assigned to Premium capacity, but organizations may wish to limit the scale or scope of these projects to ensure that provisioned capacity is being used efficiently.

As covered in this section, deployment modes represent the overall manner in which Power BI is used within an organization. Now that the different deployment modes for Power BI are fully understood, we next move on to covering the processes and roles for implementing individual Power BI projects.

# Project discovery and ingestion

An organization's business intelligence assets are the result of individual projects designed to accomplish a specific set of goals or answer a specific set of business questions. Thus, the successful initiation and execution of business intelligence projects is vital to all organizations.

Power BI projects often begin with answering a set of standard questions within a project template form. Business guidance on these questions informs the BI team of the high-level technical needs of the project and helps to promote a productive project kickoff. By reviewing the project template, the BI team can ask the project sponsor or relevant **Subject Matter Experts** (**SMEs**) targeted questions to better understand the current state and the goals of the project.

A sample Power BI project template is provided in the following section.

## Sample Power BI project template

The primary focus of the project planning template and the overall project planning stage is on the data sources and the scale and structure of the Power BI dataset required. The project sponsor or business users may only have an idea of several reports, dashboards, or metrics needed but, as a Corporate BI project, it's essential to focus on where the project fits within an overall BI architecture and the long-term **Return on Investment** (**ROI**) of the solution. For example, BI teams would look to leverage any existing Power BI datasets or Analysis Services tabular models applicable to the project and would be sensitive to version control issues.

The following section provides a completed template for a Power BI project.

## Sample template — Adventure Works BI

The template is comprised of two tables. The first table, *Table 1.1*, answers the essential who and when questions so that the project can be added to the BI team's backlog. The BI team can use this information to plan their engagements across multiple ongoing and requested Power BI projects and to respond to project stakeholders, such as Vickie Jacobs, VP of Group Sales, in this example:

| Date of Submission | 6/6/2022 |
|---|---|
| Project Sponsor | Vickie Jacobs, VP of Group Sales |
| Primary Stakeholders | Adventure Works Sales<br>Adventure Works Corp |
| Power BI Author(s) | Mark Langford, Sales Analytics Manager |

*Table 1.1: Project sponsors, stakeholders, and participants*

Identifying stakeholders is critical to the success of business intelligence projects. Stakeholders define the goals and requirements of the business intelligence project and ultimately determine success or failure in meeting identified goals. There are often multiple stakeholders for business intelligence projects and these stakeholders may even span multiple business domains. Start by identifying the business domains as stakeholders for the business intelligence project and then identify specific individuals within those domains who can provide the goals and requirements for the project.

It is always advantageous to identify a single individual as a special kind of stakeholder, a project sponsor. Project sponsors secure the funding and assist in the prioritization of resources for business intelligence projects.

The following table, *Table 1.2*, is a list of questions that describe the project's requirements and scope. It is critical to discover and answer as many of these questions as possible early on in a business intelligence project in order to set expectations in terms of the cost and duration of the project. For example, the number of users who are read-only consumers of Power BI reports and dashboards and the number of self-service users who need Power BI Pro licenses to create Power BI content largely impact the total cost of the project. Likewise, the amount of historical data to include in the dataset (2 years, 5 years?) can significantly impact performance scalability:

| Topic | # | Question | Business Input |
|---|---|---|---|
| Data sources | 1 | Can you describe the required data? (For example, sales, inventory, shipping) | Internet Sales, Reseller Sales, and the Sales and Margin Plan. We need to analyze total corporate sales, online and reseller sales, and compare these results to our plan. |
| Data sources | 2 | Is all of the data required for your project available in the data warehouse (SQL Server)? | No. |
| Data sources | 3 | What other data sources (if any) contain all or part of the required data (for example, Web, Oracle, Excel)? | The Sales and Margin Plan is maintained in Excel. |
| Security | 4 | Should certain users be prevented from viewing some or all of the data? | Yes, sales managers and associates should only see data for their sales territory group. VPs of sales, however, should have global access. |

| | | | |
|---|---|---|---|
| Security | 5 | Does the data contain any PCII, HIPAA, GDPR, or other sensitive data? | No, not that I'm aware of. |
| Scale | 6 | Approximately, how many years of historical data are needed? | 3-4. |
| Scale | 7 | Is it necessary to track the history of certain dimensions such as customers or products? For example, if a customer's address changes, is it necessary to store and report on both the prior address and the new address? | Yes, it would be helpful to track product history. |
| Data refresh | 8 | How often does the data need to be refreshed? | Daily. |
| Data refresh | 9 | Is there a need to view data in real time (as it changes)? | No. |
| Distribution | 10 | Approximately, how many users will need to view reports and dashboards? | 200. |
| Distribution | 11 | Approximately, how many users will need to create reports and dashboards? | 3-4. |
| Distribution | 12 | Will the users be viewing the reports and dashboards on mobile devices such as phones or tablets? | Yes, users need the ability to access the information on their phones. |
| Version control | 13 | Are there existing reports on the same data? If so, please describe. | Yes, there are daily and weekly sales snapshot reports available on the portal. Additionally, our team builds reports in Excel that compare actuals to the plan. |
| Version Control | 14 | Is the Power BI solution expected to replace these existing reports? | Yes, we would like to exclusively use Power BI going forward. |
| Version Control | 15 | Is there an existing Power BI dataset that targets the same business processes (fact tables)? | Not to our knowledge. |

*Table 1.2: Project questions regarding project's scope*

A business analyst inside the IT organization often partners with the business on completing the project ingestion template and reviews the current state in order to give greater context to the template. Prior to the project kickoff meeting, the business analyst usually meets with the BI team members to review the template and any additional findings or considerations.

Many questions with greater levels of detail are required as the project moves forward and therefore the template shouldn't attempt to be comprehensive or overwhelm business teams. The specific questions to include should use business-friendly language and serve to call out the top drivers of project resources and Corporate BI priorities, such as security and version control.

Now that you understand the process and requirements that drive project discovery and ingestion, we next cover the different roles involved in Power BI projects.

# Power BI project roles

Following the review of the project template and input from the business analyst, members of the Power BI team directly engage the project sponsor and other key stakeholders to officially engage in the project. These stakeholders include SMEs on the data source systems, business team members knowledgeable about the current state of reporting and analytics, and administrative or governance personnel with knowledge of organizational policies, available licenses, and current usage.

New Power BI projects of any significant scale and long-term adoption of Power BI within organizations require **Dataset Designers, Report Authors**, and **Power BI Admin(s)**, as illustrated in the following diagram:

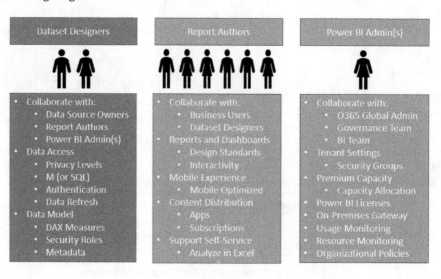

*Figure 1.5: Power BI team roles*

Each of the three Power BI project roles and perhaps longer-term roles as part of a business intelligence team entail a distinct set of skills and responsibilities. It can be advantageous in a short-term or POC scenario for a single user to serve as both a dataset designer and a report author. However, the Power BI platform and the multi-faceted nature of Corporate BI deployments are too broad and dynamic for a single BI professional to adequately fulfill both roles.

It's recommended that team members either self-select or are assigned distinct roles based on their existing skills and experience and that each member develops advanced and current knowledge relevant to their role. For example, individuals with a **user experience and user interface** (UX/UI) background are generally best suited to fulfill the **Report Author** role. Conversely, more technical developers with a background in coding and data modeling often fulfill the **Dataset Designer** role. A BI manager and/or a project manager can help facilitate effective communication across roles and between the BI team and other stakeholders, such as project sponsors.

Let's now take a closer look at each of the three roles involved in Power BI projects.

## Dataset designer

The dataset designer is responsible for the data access layer of the Power BI dataset, including the authentication to data sources and the M queries used to define the tables of the data model. Additionally, the dataset designer defines the relationships of the model and any required row-level security roles and develops the DAX measure expressions for use in reports, such as **year-to-date** (**YTD**) sales.

A Power BI dataset designer often has experience in developing Analysis Services models, particularly Analysis Services models in tabular mode, as this aligns with the semantic modeling engine used in Power BI. For organizations utilizing both Analysis Services and Power BI Desktop, this could be the same individual. Alternatively, business analysts experienced with Power Pivot for Excel or with the modeling features of Power BI Desktop may also prove to have the skills required of Power BI dataset designers for self-service scenarios.

Datasets (semantic models) have always been the heart of Power BI solutions as they serve as the data source responsible for rapidly resolving the report queries generated by reports and analysis sessions. Power BI datasets can be designed to import copies of data from multiple data sources into a compressed, in-memory cache, as well as merely passing report queries back to a data source system such as Azure Synapse Analytics. Additionally, Power BI dataset designers can mix both import (in-memory) and DirectQuery storage modes across different tables of a dataset thus balancing the tradeoffs between the two storage modes.

In addition to providing a performant and scalable data source that efficiently utilizes resources (CPU, RAM), datasets must provide a user-friendly interface for report authors and analysts to quickly produce effective content. Moreover, datasets also typically contain **Row-Level Security (RLS)** roles that limit what certain users or groups of users can see and can also contain complex logic to support certain business rules or report requirements. Datasets are therefore a critical component of Power BI projects and their design has tremendous implications regarding user experience, query performance, source system and Power BI resource utilization, and more.

Given the importance of Power BI datasets and the implications of dataset design decisions for entire environments, many organizations choose to dedicate one or multiple developer roles to Power BI datasets. These individuals are expected to have advanced- to expert-level knowledge of **Data Analysis eXpressions (DAX)** as well as experience with enterprise features such as aggregation tables, partitions and incremental refresh, and other supporting third-party tools such as ALM Toolkit. All of these topics are explained in later chapters.

Business analysts or "power users" can often independently learn or receive essential training to build basic Power BI datasets that meet the needs of their department. However, business analysts can also struggle to learn coding languages like M and DAX and can fail to appreciate other goals of a dataset such as resource usage. For this reason, organizations are well advised to regularly monitor the datasets developed by business teams/analysts and consider adopting a process for migrating ownership of these datasets from a business team to a Corporate BI team.

It can't be emphasized strongly enough that Power BI project teams should carefully distinguish between datasets and reports and maintain a goal of supporting many related reports and dashboards via high-quality, well-tested or certified datasets. This can be challenging as teams are generally tasked with developing reports regardless of the source dataset, thus creating a temptation to simply create a dataset dedicated to the needs of a single report. Over the long term this "report factory" approach results in both inefficient use of resources (CPU) as well as confusion and manageability issues with many datasets having slightly different logic and all needing to be maintained.

Dataset designers should regularly communicate with data source owners or SMEs, as well as report authors. For example, the dataset designer needs to be aware of changes to data sources so that data access queries can be revised accordingly, and report authors can advise of any additional measures or columns necessary to create new reports. Furthermore, the dataset designer should be aware of the performance and resource utilization of deployed datasets and should work with the Power BI admin on issues such as Power BI Premium capacity.

As per *Figure 1.5*, there are usually relatively few dataset designers in a team compared with the number of report authors. This is largely due to the organizational objectives of version control and reusability, which leads to a small number of large datasets. Additionally, robust dataset development requires knowledge of the M and DAX functional programming languages, dimensional modeling practices, and business intelligence. Database experience is also very helpful. If multiple dataset designers are on a team, they should look to standardize their development practices so that they can more easily learn and support each other's solutions.

With the crucial role of the dataset designer understood, we next explore the report author role.

## Report authors

Report authors interface directly with the consumers of reports and dashboards or a representative of this group. In a self-service deployment mode or a hybrid project (business and IT), a small number of report authors may themselves work within the business.

Above all else, report authors must have a clear understanding of the business questions to be answered and the measures and attributes (columns) needed to visually analyze and answer these questions. The report author should also be knowledgeable of visualization best practices, such as symmetry and minimalism, in addition to any corporate standards for report formatting and layout.

Power BI Desktop provides a rich set of formatting properties and analytical features, giving report authors granular control over the appearance and behavior of visualizations. Report authors should be very familiar with all standard capabilities, such as conditional formatting, drilldown, drillthrough, and cross-highlighting, as they often lead demonstrations or training sessions.

It's important for report authors to understand the use cases and essential features of the two alternative report types available in Power BI – paginated reports and Excel reports. For example, given the requirements to export or print detail-level data, a report author should be comfortable in building a paginated report via the Power BI Report Builder. Additionally, report authors should understand the organization's policies on custom visuals available in the MS Office store and the specific use cases for top or popular custom visuals.

It should be clear now that report authors have distinct responsibilities and skillsets compared to dataset designers. The ability to design intuitive reports and dashboards that are easily understood by the business is also of critical importance to the success of every Power BI project. Next, we look at the last critical role, the Power BI administrator.

# Power BI administrator

As Power BI has grown its capabilities and become a mission-critical tool for organizations, the role of a Power BI administrator (admin) has become increasingly common. Power BI administrators are responsible for ensuring Power BI is utilized effectively and according to the organization's policies. For example, Power BI administrators monitor and troubleshoot dataset refresh failures, performance issues, user access requests and issues, and the overall health of an organization's Premium capacities.

A Power BI administrator is assigned the Power BI administrator role in **Azure Active Directory**, the identity and access control service at the heart of Microsoft's cloud-based **Software as a Service (SaaS)** products. Assignment of the Power BI administrator role is done in the Microsoft 365 admin center and only **Global administrators** of Office 365 can assign users to the role.

Users assigned to the Power BI administrator role obtain access to the Power BI admin portal and the rights to configure Power BI tenant settings. The Power BI admin portal and tenant settings are used to enable or disable features, such as exporting data and printing reports and dashboards. BI and IT managers that oversee Power BI deployments are often assigned to this role, as the role also provides the ability to manage Power BI Premium capacities and access to standard monitoring and usage reporting.

The Power BI admin should have a clear understanding of the organizational policy on the various tenant settings, such as whether content can be shared with external users. For most tenant settings, the Power BI administrator can define rules in the Power BI admin portal to include or exclude specific security groups. For example, external sharing can be disabled for the entire organization except for a specific security group of users.

Power BI admins must also have a thorough knowledge of permissions, roles, sharing, and licensing of Power BI in order to resolve common issues related to access. For example, a Power BI admin would know that build permission to a dataset could be granted to a business analyst as a less permissive alternative to membership in the workspace of the source dataset.

Most organizations should assign two or more users to the Power BI administrator role and ensure these users are trained on the administration features specific to this role. *Chapter 14, Administering Power BI for an Organization*, contains details on the Power BI admin portal and other administrative topics.

While Power BI admins are not involved in the day-to-day activities of specific projects, the role is ultimately critical to the success of all projects, as is the overall collaboration between all project roles, which we cover in the next section.

# Project role collaboration

Communicating and documenting project role assignments during the planning stage promotes the efficient use of time during the development and operations phases. For organizations committed to the Power BI platform and perhaps migrating away from a legacy or different BI platform, project roles may become full-time positions.

For example, BI developers with experience in DAX and Analysis Services tabular models may transition to permanent dataset designer roles while BI developers experienced in data visualization and report development may become report authors:

| Name | Project role |
| --- | --- |
| Brett Powell | Dataset Designer |
| Jennifer Lawrence | Report Author |
| Anna Sanders | Power BI Administrator |
| Mark Langford | Report Author |
| Stacy Loeb | QA Tester |

*Table 1.3: Project role assignments*

It is important for the individuals within all of the various roles to work together and communicate effectively in order to deliver a successful project outcome. Proper communication and collaboration are important to all projects but are perhaps even more crucial within the realm of business intelligence given the distinct nature of the roles involved and the criticality of accurate, effective reporting to the success of organizations.

With project roles and responsibilities now understood, we next cover the various forms of licensing for Power BI deployments.

# Power BI licenses

Power BI provides a number of different licensing options that provide flexible and affordable pricing for individuals and organizations. These licensing options come in two primary categories:

- Shared capacity
- Dedicated capacity

Let us first have a look at shared capacity.

# Shared capacity

Shared capacity is like an apartment building. While each tenant in the building has their own personal living quarters accessible to only themselves, certain infrastructures such as plumbing, electrical wiring, and stairways are common to everyone in the building. Shared capacity for Power BI is similar. Each tenant within the Power BI service has its own area for publishing data and reporting assets but infrastructure such as memory and processing capacity are shared among the tenants. Thus, just like a noisy neighbor in an apartment building can affect other tenants, so too can tenants within shared capacity in the Power BI service impact the performance for other tenants.

Two licensing options exist for using shared capacity within the Power BI service:

- Free
- Pro

In the next two sections, we look at the differences between free and Pro licensing.

## Free

It is possible to use Power BI entirely for free. First, the Power BI Desktop application is always free to download and use. Licensing does not become a factor until one desires to use the Power BI service. However, there is a free version of the Power BI service license. The free license allows reports to be published to the Power BI service, however, there are significant limitations with this approach. *Figure 1.6* provides an overview of using Power BI free licensing.

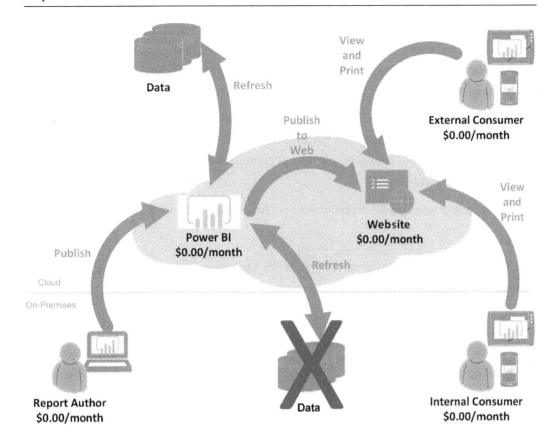

*Figure 1.6: Power BI free*

As shown in *Figure 1.6*, report authors can use Power BI Desktop to create datasets and reports and publish these assets to the Power BI service. However, datasets can only be refreshed from cloud sources and only from the user's personal workspace, **My Workspace**. Refreshing on-premises data sources is not supported. In addition, sharing content with other internal and external users is only possible through the **Publish to Web** feature.

It is important to understand that the Publish to Web feature does not provide any kind of security or authentication. Anyone that has the link to the report that has been published using the Publish to Web feature can access the report anonymously. There are many other features that cannot be used in the Power BI service as well, such as subscriptions and comments.

Once the limitations are understood, solely using the free license for Power BI has only limited uses. Mainly, it is used for testing or performing a proof of concept. However, the free Power BI service license can be coupled with Power BI Premium to provide a powerful and affordable solution for enterprises.

Now that the free licensing model is understood, let's compare it with the pro licensing model.

## Pro

The Pro licensing option for Power BI removes the limitations of free licensing when using the Power BI service. *Figure 1.7* presents an overview of Pro licensing.

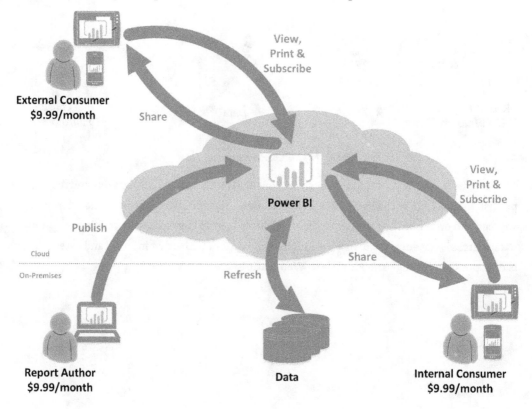

*Figure 1.7: Power BI Pro*

As shown in *Figure 1.7*, Pro licensing allows users to share reports with both internal and external users. However, those users also require a Pro license in order to access and view the reports and datasets. Essentially, anyone that collaborates (views, creates, edits) datasets, reports, and dashboards must have a Pro license.

Using a Pro license removes all of the restrictions of the free licensing structure and users are able to utilize the standard features of the Power BI service including the ability to create subscriptions, comment, create and use apps, and leverage the **Analyze in Excel** feature, which exports a report's underlying data to Excel in order to support further analysis.

Now that we have explored the free and Pro licensing options associated with shared capacity, we'll next look at the licensing models available for dedicated capacity.

# Dedicated capacity

In addition to shared capacity licenses, there are also dedicated capacity licenses available for Power BI. These licenses reserve memory and processing capacity solely for the use of a particular tenant. In addition, these licenses enable advanced features such as larger datasets, increased user quotas, more frequent dataset refreshes, paginated reports, goals, scorecards, pipelines, and embedding of content into corporate applications.

Three licensing options exist for using dedicated capacity within the Power BI service:

- Premium
- Premium Per User
- Embedded

We cover each of these licensing options in detail in the following sections.

## Premium

With Power BI Premium, users with Power BI free licenses are able to access and view Power BI apps of reports and dashboards that have been assigned to Premium capacities. This access includes consuming the content via the Power BI mobile application as well as fully interacting with standard Power BI service features such as using subscriptions and comments. Additionally, Power BI Pro users can share dashboards with Power BI free users if the dashboard is contained in a Premium workspace. Power BI Pro licenses are required for users that create or distribute Power BI content, such as connecting to published datasets from Power BI Desktop or Excel. *Figure 1.8* presents an overview of Premium licensing.

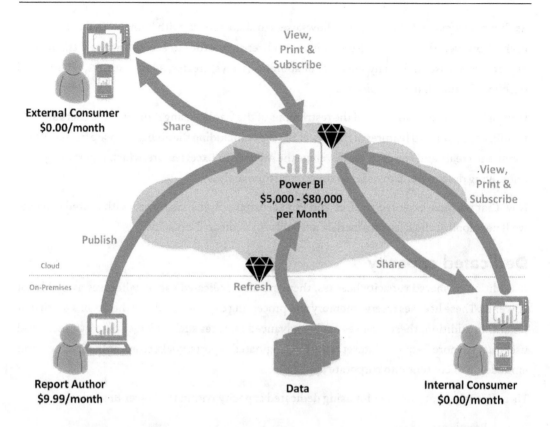

*Figure 1.8: Power BI Premium*

Power BI Premium is purchased in capacity units priced on a per-month basis. These capacity units are called node types and range in size from a P1 with 25 GB of RAM and eight virtual cores for $5,000/month to a P5 with 400 GB of RAM and 128 virtual cores for $80,000/month. It is important to understand that this is dedicated capacity and is charged on a per-month basis (not per minute or hour). Power BI Premium also includes a license for using Power BI Report Server on-premises.

An organization may choose to license Power BI Premium capacities for additional or separate reasons beyond the ability to distribute Power BI content to read-only users without incurring per-user license costs. Significantly, greater detail on Power BI Premium features and deployment considerations is included in *Chapter 15, Building Enterprise BI with Power BI Premium.*

With an entry price point for Power BI Premium of $5,000 per month, many mid-sized organizations were priced out of the ability to afford dedicated capacity. Thus, Microsoft recently introduced Premium Per User pricing, which we cover next.

# Premium Per User

**Premium Per User** (PPU) licensing effectively works identically to Pro licensing except that all users of a PPU workspace must have a PPU license. An overview of PPU licensing is shown in *Figure 1.9*.

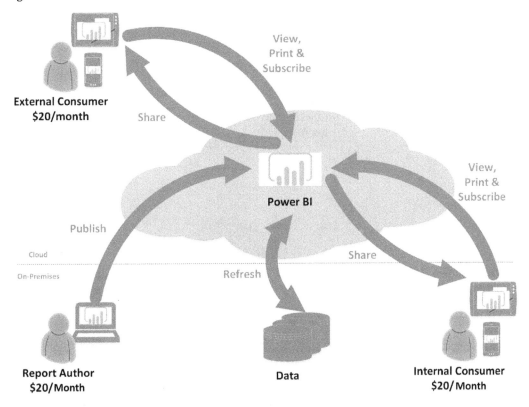

*Figure 1.9: Power BI Premium Per User*

As shown in *Figure 1.9*, PPU licensing works the same as Pro licensing except that PPU licensing adds the additional advanced features of Premium such as increased dataset sizes, increased refresh frequency, paginated reports, goals, scorecards, and pipelines.

Let's now take a look at the last dedicated capacity licensing option, Embedded.

# Embedded

Power BI Embedded is intended for use by developers and **Independent Software Vendors** (**ISVs**) that use APIs to embed Power BI visuals, reports, and dashboards within their custom web applications. These applications can then be accessed by external customers. *Figure 1.10* provides an overview of Power BI Embedded.

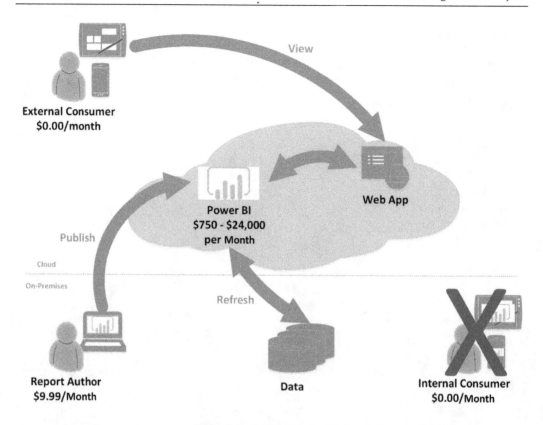

*Figure 1.10: Power BI Embedded*

Similar to Power BI Premium, capacity units or node types for Embedded range in size from an A1 with 3 GB of RAM and a single virtual core for $750 per month to an A6 with 100 GB of RAM and 32 virtual cores for $24,000 per month. However, different than Premium, Embedded is charged on a usage basis per minute versus a flat charge per month. The usage-based charge is attractive to developers and ISVs as this provides greater flexibility and less expense, particularly during development, since the service can be deprovisioned when development is not occurring.

With the basic licenses for Power BI understood, let's next consider how these different licenses are combined to provide a complete licensing scenario for an organization.

## Power BI license scenarios

The optimal mix of Power BI Pro and Power BI Premium licensing in terms of total cost varies based on the volume of users and the composition of those users between read-only consumers of content versus Self-Service BI users. In relatively small deployments, such as 200 total users, a Power BI Pro license can be assigned to each user regardless of self-service usage and Power BI Premium capacity can be avoided.

However, there are other benefits to licensing Power BI Premium capacity that may be necessary for certain deployments, such as larger datasets or more frequent data refreshes.

If an organization consists of 700 total users with 600 read-only users and 100 self-service users (content creators), it's more cost-effective to assign Power BI Pro licenses to the 100 self-service users and to provision Power BI Premium capacity to support the other 600 users. Likewise, for a larger organization with 5,000 total users and 4,000 self-service users, the most cost-effective licensing option is to assign Power Pro licenses to the 4,000 self-service users and to license Power BI Premium for the remaining 1,000 users.

Several factors drive the amount of Power BI Premium capacity to provision, such as the number of concurrent users, the complexity of the queries generated, and the number of Concurrent data refreshes. See *Chapter 14, Administering Power BI for an Organization*, and *Chapter 15, Building Enterprise BI with Power BI Premium*, for additional details on aligning Power BI licenses and resources with the needs of Power BI deployments.

In the sample project example introduced in the section *Sample template – Adventure Works BI*, Power BI Premium is being used. Therefore, only a few users need Power BI Pro licenses to create and share reports and dashboards.

Referencing *Table 1.3*, Mark Langford, a data analyst for the sales organization, requires a Pro license to analyze published datasets from Microsoft Excel. Jennifer Lawrence, a corporate BI developer and report author for this project, requires a Pro license to publish Power BI reports to app workspaces and distribute Power BI apps to users. Finally, Brett Powell as dataset designer also requires a Power BI Pro license to create and publish the underlying dataset.

Typically, a Power BI administrator is also assigned a Power BI Pro license. Per *Table 1.3*, Anna Sanders is the Power BI administrator. However, a Power BI Pro license is not required to be assigned to the Power BI administrator role.

The approximately 200 Adventure Works sales team users who only need to view the content can be assigned free licenses and consume the published content via Power BI apps associated with Power BI Premium capacity. Organizations can obtain more Power BI Pro licenses and Power BI Premium capacity (virtual cores, RAM) as usage and workloads increase.

We mentioned at the beginning of this chapter that Power BI is a robust, flexible business intelligence platform and the different licensing options and combinations are a reflection of that flexibility. In the following sections, we'll next cover the tools, processes, and overall design of datasets.

# Dataset design

Designing Power BI datasets is in many respects similar to designing data warehouses. Both datasets and data warehouses share concepts such as fact and dimension tables, star schemas, slowly changing dimensions, fact table granularity, and local and foreign keys for building relationships between tables.

This similarity allows us to use the same proven tools and processes for designing and building Power BI datasets as are used to design data warehouses. In this section, we cover the tools and processes used to design Power BI datasets, starting with the **data warehouse bus matrix**.

## Data warehouse bus matrix

The data warehouse bus matrix is a staple of the Ralph Kimball data warehouse architecture, which provides an incremental and integrated approach to data warehouse design. This architecture, as per *The Data Warehouse Toolkit (Third Edition)* by Ralph Kimball, allows for scalable data models, as multiple business teams or functions often require access to the same business process data and dimensions.

To promote reusability and project communication, a data warehouse bus matrix of business processes and shared dimensions is recommended. An example data warehouse bus matrix is shown in *Figure 1.11*:

| BUSINESS PROCESSES | Date | Customer | Product | Department | Promotion | Reseller | Sales Territory | Employee | Account | Organization |
|---|---|---|---|---|---|---|---|---|---|---|
| Internet Sales | ✓ | ✓ | ✓ | | ✓ | | ✓ | | | |
| Reseller Sales | ✓ | | ✓ | | ✓ | ✓ | ✓ | ✓ | | |
| Sales Plan | ✓ | | ✓ | | | | ✓ | | | |
| General Ledger | ✓ | | ✓ | ✓ | | | ✓ | | ✓ | ✓ |
| Inventory | ✓ | | ✓ | | | | | | | |
| Customer Surveys | ✓ | ✓ | | | | | | | | |
| Customer Service Calls | ✓ | ✓ | ✓ | | | | | ✓ | | |

*Figure 1.11: Data warehouse bus matrix*

Each row in *Figure 1.11* reflects an important and recurring business process, such as the monthly close of the general ledger, and each column represents a business entity, which may relate to one or several of the business processes. The shaded rows (**Internet Sales**, **Reseller Sales**, and **Sales Plan**) identify the business processes that will be implemented as their own star schemas for this project.

The bus matrix can be developed in collaboration with business stakeholders, such as the corporate finance manager, as well as source system and business intelligence or data warehouse SMEs.

The architecture of the dataset should support future BI and analytics projects of the organization involving the given business processes (fact tables) and business entities (dimension tables). For example, the same dataset containing **Internet Sales** data should support both an executive's sales and revenue dashboard as well a business analyst's ad hoc analysis via Excel PivotTables.

Additional business processes, such as maintaining product inventory levels, could potentially be added to the same Power BI dataset in a future project. Importantly, these future additions could leverage existing dimension tables, such as a product table, including its source query, column metadata, and any defined hierarchies.

Each Power BI report is usually tied to a single dataset. Given this 1:1 relationship and the analytical value of integrated reports across multiple business processes, such as **Inventory** and **Internet Sales**, it's important to design datasets that can scale to support multiple star schemas. Consolidating business processes into one or a few datasets also makes solutions more manageable and is a better use of source system resources, as common tables (for example, **Product, Customer**) are only refreshed once.

The data warehouse bus matrix is a proven tool used during the design process of data warehouses and is just as effective for designing Power BI datasets. We cover this design process in the next section.

## Dataset design process

With the data warehouse bus matrix as a guide, the business intelligence team can work with representatives from the relevant business teams and project sponsors to complete the following four-step dataset design process:

1. Select the business process
2. Declare the grain
3. Identify the dimensions
4. Define the facts

In the following sections, we cover each of these steps in detail, starting with selecting the business process.

# Select the business process

Ultimately, each business process is represented by a fact table with a star schema of many-to-one relationships to dimensions. In a discovery or requirements gathering process, it can be difficult to focus on a single business process in isolation as users regularly analyze multiple business processes simultaneously or need to.

Nonetheless, it's essential that the dataset being designed reflects low-level business activities (for example, receiving an online sales order) rather than consolidation or integration of distinct business processes such as a table with both online and reseller sales data:

- Confirm that the answer provided to the first question of the project template from *Table 1.2* regarding data sources is accurate.

- In this project, the required business processes are **Internet Sales**, **Reseller Sales**, and **Annual Sales** and **Margin Plan**.

- Each of the three business processes corresponds to a fact table to be included in the Power BI dataset.

- Obtain a high-level understanding of the top business questions for each business process. For example, "What are total sales relative to the **Annual Sales Plan** and relative to last year?".

- In this project, Internet Sales and Reseller Sales are combined into overall corporate sales and margin KPIs.

- Optionally, reference the data warehouse bus matrix of business processes and their related dimensions. For example, discuss the integration of inventory data and the insights this integration may provide.

- In many projects, a choice or compromise has to be made given the limited availability of certain business processes and the costs or timelines associated with preparing this data for production use.

- Additionally, business processes (fact tables) are the top drivers of the storage and processing costs of the dataset and thus should only be included if necessary.

A common anti-pattern (a response to a reoccurring problem that is generally ineffective and potentially counterproductive) to avoid in Power BI projects is the development of datasets for specific projects or teams rather than business processes. For example, developing a dataset exclusively for the marketing team and another dataset created for the sales organization. Assuming both teams require access to the same sales data, this approach naturally leads to a waste of resources, as the same sales data is queried and refreshed twice and both datasets consume storage resources in the Power BI service.

Additionally, this isolated approach leads to manageability and version control issues, as the datasets may contain variations in transformation or metric logic. Therefore, although the analytical needs of specific business users or teams are indeed the priority of BI projects, it's important to plan for sustainable solutions that can ultimately be shared across teams.

Let's now look at the next step in the process, declaring the grain.

## Declare the grain

The grain of fact tables ultimately governs the level of detail available for analytical queries as well as the amount of data to be accessed. Higher grains mean more detail while lower grains mean less detail.

All rows of a fact table should represent the individual business process from step 1 at a certain level of detail or grain such as the header level or line level of a purchase order. Therefore, each row should have the same meaning and thus contain values for the same key columns to dimensions and the same numeric columns.

During this step, determine what each row of the different business processes represents. For example, each row of the Internet Sales fact table represents the line of a sales order from a customer. Conversely, the rows of the Sales and Margin Plan are aggregated to the level of a Calendar Month, Products Subcategory, and Sales Territory region.

If it's necessary to apply filters or logic to treat certain rows of a fact table differently than others, the fact table likely contains multiple business processes (for example, shipments and orders). Although it's technically possible to build this logic into DAX measure expressions, well-designed fact tables benefit Power BI and other data projects and tools over the long term. Thus, in such circumstances, it is advisable to split the table into two separate tables.

When analyzing the grain of fact tables, consider the following:

- Review and discuss the implications of the chosen grain in terms of dimensionality and scale
- Higher granularities provide greater levels of dimensionality and thus detail but result in much larger fact tables
- If a high grain or the maximum grain is chosen, determine the row counts per year and the storage size of this table once loaded into Power BI datasets
- If a lower grain is chosen, ensure that project stakeholders understand the loss of dimensionalities, such as the inability to filter for specific products or customers

In general, a higher granularity is recommended for analytical power and sustainability. If a less granular design is chosen, such as the header level of a sales order, and this grain later proves to be insufficient to answer new business questions, then either a new fact table would have to be added to the dataset or the existing fact table and all of its measures and dependent reports would have to be replaced.

Once the grains of all fact tables are determined, it is time to move on to the next step and identify the dimensions.

## Identify the dimensions

Dimensions are a natural byproduct of the grain chosen in the previous design process step. A single sample row from the fact table should clearly indicate the business entities (dimensions) associated with the given process such as the customer who purchased an individual product on a certain date and at a certain time via a specific promotion.

Fact tables representing a lower grain have fewer dimensions. For example, a fact table representing the header level of a purchase order may identify the vendor but not the individual products purchased from the vendor.

When analyzing dimensions, consider the following:

- Identify and communicate the dimensions that can be used to filter (aka slice and dice) each business process.

- The foreign key columns based on the grain chosen in the previous step reference dimension tables.

- Review a sample of all critical dimension tables, such as **Product** or **Customer**, and ensure these tables contain the columns and values necessary or expected.

- Communicate which dimensions can be used to filter multiple business processes simultaneously. For example, in this project, the Product, Sales Territory, and Date dimensions can be used to filter all three fact tables.

- The data warehouse bus matrix referenced earlier can be helpful for this step.

- Look for any gap between the existing dimension tables and business questions or related reports.

- For example, existing IT-supported reports may contain embedded logic that creates columns via **Structured Query Language (SQL)** that are not stored in the data warehouse.

- Strive to maintain version control for dimension tables and the columns (attributes) within dimension tables.

- It may be necessary for project stakeholders to adapt or migrate from legacy reports or an internally maintained source to the Corporate BI source.

A significant challenge to the identity of the dimensions step can be a lack of **Master Data Management (MDM)** and alternative versions. MDM is a discipline practiced by organizations in order to ensure the accuracy, uniformity, semantic consistency, and stewardship of the official data assets.

For example, the sales organization may maintain its own dimension tables in Excel or Microsoft Access and its naming conventions and hierarchy structures may represent a conflict or gap with the existing data warehouse. Additionally, many corporate applications may store their own versions of common dimensions, such as products and customers.

These issues should be understood and, despite pressure to deliver BI value quickly or according to a specific business team's preferred version, the long-term value of a single definition for an entire organization as expressed via the bus matrix should not be sacrificed.

With dimensions identified, the final step is to define the fact tables.

## Define the facts

The facts represent the numeric columns included in the fact tables. While the dimension columns from step 3 are used for relationships to dimension tables, the fact columns are used in measures containing aggregation logic such as the sum of a quantity column and the average of a price column.

When defining the facts, consider the following:

- Define the business logic for each fact, represented by measures in the dataset. For example, gross sales is equal to the extended amount on a sales order, and net sales is equal to gross sales minus discounts.
- Any existing documentation or relevant technical metadata should be reviewed and validated.
- Similar to the dimensions, any conflicts between existing definitions should be addressed so that a single definition for a core set of metrics is understood and approved.
- Additionally, a baseline or target source should be identified to validate the accuracy of the metrics to be created. For example, several months following the project, it should be possible to compare the results of DAX measures from the Power BI dataset to an SSRS report or a SQL query.

- If no variance exists between the two sources, the DAX measures are valid and thus any doubt or reported discrepancy is due to some other factor

See *Chapter 2, Preparing Data Sources*, *Chapter 3, Connecting Sources and Transforming Data with M*, *Chapter 4, Designing Import and DirectQuery Data Models*, and *Chapter 5, Developing DAX Measures and Security Roles*, for details on the fact table columns to include in Power BI datasets (for import or DirectQuery) and the development of DAX metric expressions. The fact definitions from this step relate closely to the concept of base measures described in *Chapter 5, Developing DAX Measures and Security Roles*.

Ultimately, the DAX measures implemented have to tie to the approved definitions, but there are significant data processing, storage, and performance implications based on how this logic is computed. In many cases, the Power BI dataset can provide the same logic as an existing system but via an alternative methodology that better aligns with Power BI or the specific project need.

This concludes the dataset design process. Next, we cover another important topic related to datasets, data profiling.

## Data profiling

The four-step dataset design process can be immediately followed by a technical analysis of the source data for the required fact and dimension tables of the dataset. Technical metadata, including database diagrams and data profiling results, such as the existence of null values in source columns, are essential for the project planning stage. This information is used to ensure the Power BI dataset reflects the intended business definitions and is built on a sound and trusted source.

For example, *Figure 1.12* shows a database diagram that describes the schema for the reseller sales business process:

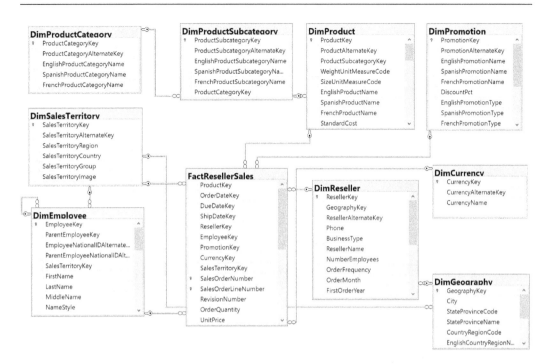

*Figure 1.12: SQL Server database diagram: reseller sales*

The foreign key constraints (the lines between the tables) identify the surrogate key columns used in the relationships of the Power BI dataset and the referential integrity of the source database. The columns used as keys are displayed in *Figure 1.12* with small key icons to the left of the column name.

In this schema, the product dimension is modeled as three separate dimension tables—DimProduct, DimProductSubcategory, and DimProductCategory. Given the priorities of usability, manageability, and query performance, a single denormalized product dimension table that includes essential Product Subcategory and Product Category columns is generally recommended. This reduces the volume of source queries, relationships, and tables in the data model and improves report query performance, as fewer relationships must be scanned by the dataset engine.

Clear visibility of the source system, including referential and data integrity constraints, data quality, and any MDM processes, is essential. Unlike other popular BI tools, Power BI is capable of addressing many data integration and quality issues, particularly with relational database sources that Power BI can leverage to execute data transformation operations. However, Power BI's **extract, transform, load (ETL)** capabilities are not a substitute for data warehouse architecture and enterprise ETL tools, such as **SQL Server Integration Services (SSIS)**.

For example, it's the responsibility of the data warehouse to support historical tracking with slowly changing dimension ETL processes that generate new rows and surrogate keys for a dimension when certain columns change. To illustrate a standard implementation of slowly changing dimensions, *Figure 1.13* shows the results of a query of the `DimProduct` table in the Adventure Works data warehouse returning three rows for one product (FR-M94B-38):

| ProductKey | ProductAlternateKey | EnglishProductName | StandardCost | ListPrice | DealerPrice | StartDate | EndDate | Status |
|---|---|---|---|---|---|---|---|---|
| 304 | FR-M94B-38 | HL Moutain Frame - Black, 38 | 617.0281 | 1191.1739 | 714.7043 | 2011-07-01 00:00:00.000 | 2007-12-28 00:00:00.000 | NULL |
| 305 | FR-M94B-38 | HL Moutain Frame - Black, 38 | 653.6971 | 1226.9091 | 736.1455 | 2012-07-01 00:00:00.000 | 2008-12-27 00:00:00.000 | NULL |
| 306 | FR-M94B-38 | HL Moutain Frame - Black, 38 | 739.041 | 1349.60 | 809.76 | 2013-07-01 00:00:00.000 | NULL | Current |

*Figure 1.13: Historical tracking of dimensions via slowly changing dimension ETL processes*

It's the responsibility of the Power BI team and particularly the dataset designer to accurately reflect this historical tracking via relationships and DAX measures, such as the count of distinct products not sold. Like historical tracking, the data warehouse should also reflect all master data management processes that serve to maintain accurate master data for essential dimensions, such as customers, products, and employees.

In other words, despite many line of business applications and **Enterprise Resource Planning (ERP)**, **Customer Relationship Management (CRM)**, **Human Resource Management (HRM)**, and other large corporate systems that store and process the same master data, the data warehouse should reflect the centrally governed and cleansed standard. Therefore, creating a Power BI dataset that only reflects one of these source systems may later introduce version control issues and, similar to choosing an incorrect granularity for a fact table, can ultimately require costly and invasive revisions.

Different tools are available with data profiling capabilities. If the data source is SQL Server, SSIS can be used to analyze source data intended for use in a project. In *Figure 1.14*, the **Data Profiling task** is used in an SSIS package to analyze the customer dimension table:

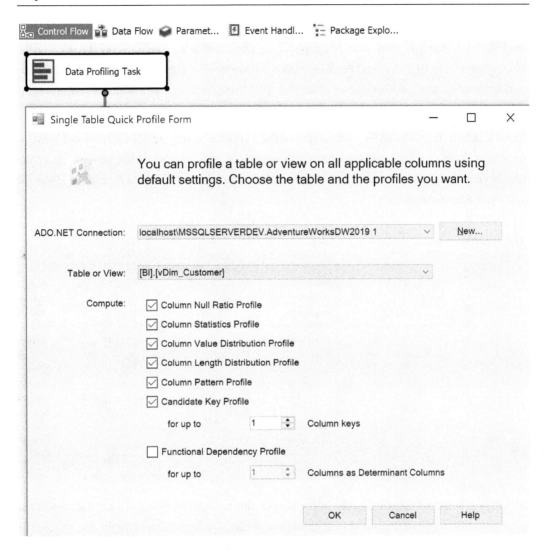

*Figure 1.14: Data Profiling task in SSIS*

The Data Profiling task requires an ADO.NET connection to the data source and can write its output to an XML file or an SSIS variable. In this example, the ADO.NET data source is the Adventure Works data warehouse database in SQL Server 2016 and the destination is an XML file (DataProfilingData.xml).

Once the task is executed, the XML file can be read via the SQL Server Data Profile Viewer as per the following example. Note that this application, Data Profile Viewer, requires the installation of SQL Server and that the Data Profiling task only works with SQL Server data sources. All fact and dimension table sources can be analyzed quickly for the count and distribution of unique values, the existence of null values, and other useful statistics.

Each Data Profiling task can be configured to write its results to an XML file on a network location for access via tools such as the Data Profile Viewer. In the example shown in *Figure 1.15*, the Data Profile Viewer is opened from within SSIS to analyze the output of the Data Profiling task for the customer dimension table:

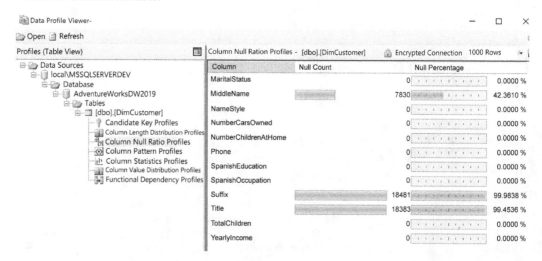

Figure 1.15: Data Profile Viewer: column null ratio profiles of DimCustomer table

Identifying and documenting issues in the source data via data profiling is a critical step in the planning process. For example, the cardinality or count of unique values largely determines the data size of a column in an import mode dataset. Similarly, the severity of data quality issues identified impacts whether a DirectQuery dataset is a feasible option.

In general, enterprise BI teams should utilize enterprise data profiling tools such as those included with SQL Server. However, basic data profiling tools are also available in Power BI Desktop, which we cover next.

## Data profiling with Power BI Desktop

Power BI Desktop includes simple data quality reporting within the Power Query Editor interface. The Power Query Editor is used to develop queries for connecting to and ingesting data from source systems and is covered in detail in *Chapter 2, Preparing Data Sources*.

To access the data quality reporting within Power Query Editor, use the **View** tab and check the boxes for **Column quality**, **Column distribution**, and **Column profile** as shown in *Figure 1.16*:

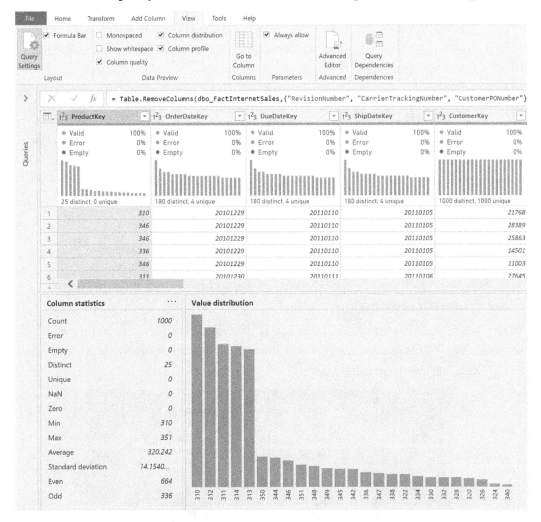

*Figure 1.16: Data quality in Power Query Editor*

As shown in *Figure 1.16*, activating the data quality reporting within Power Query Editor displays many important statistics such as the number of distinct values, the value distribution, and the percentage of valid values and errors.

While not as comprehensive as some enterprise data quality tools, the data quality reporting within Power Query Editor is useful as an additional data quality check for data accessed by Power BI Desktop.

Once source data is profiled, the next natural step is dataset planning as covered in the next section.

# Dataset planning

After the source data is profiled and evaluated against the requirements identified in the four-step dataset design process, the BI team can further analyze the implementation options for the dataset. In almost all Power BI projects, even with significant investments in enterprise data warehouse architecture and ETL tools and processes, some level of additional logic, integration, or transformation is needed to enhance the quality and value of the source data or to effectively support a business requirement.

A priority of the dataset planning stage is to determine how the identified data transformation issues are addressed to support the dataset. Additionally, based on all available information and requirements, the project team must determine whether to develop an import mode dataset, DirectQuery dataset, or composite dataset. Import, DirectQuery, and composite datasets are explained in the section *Import, DirectQuery, Live, and Composite Datasets*.

The initial step in the dataset planning process is planning for data transformations, which we'll review next.

## Data transformations

To help clarify the dataset planning process, a diagram such as *Figure 1.17* can be created that identifies the different layers of the data warehouse and Power BI dataset where transformation and business logic can be implemented:

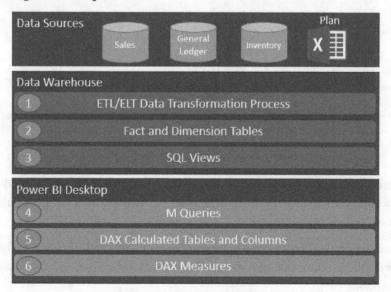

*Figure 1.17: Dataset planning architecture*

In some projects, minimal transformation logic is needed and can be easily included in the Power BI dataset or the SQL views accessed by the dataset. For example, if only a few additional columns are needed for a dimension table and there's straightforward guidance on how these columns should be computed, the IT organization may choose to implement these transformations within Power BI's Power Query (M) queries rather than revise the data warehouse, at least in the short term.

If a substantial gap between BI needs and the corporate data warehouse is allowed to persist and grow due to various factors, such as cost, project expediency, and available data warehouse skills, then Power BI datasets become more complex to build and maintain. Dataset designers should regularly analyze and communicate the implications of datasets assuming greater levels of complexity.

However, if the required transformation logic is complex or extensive with multiple join operations, row filters, and data type changes, then the IT organization may choose to implement essential changes in the data warehouse to support the new dataset and future BI projects. For example, a staging table and a SQL stored procedure may be needed to support a revised nightly update process, or the creation of an index may be needed to deliver improved query performance for a DirectQuery dataset.

Ideally, all required data transformation and shaping logic could be implemented in the source data warehouse and its ETL processes so that Power BI is exclusively used for analytics and visualization. However, in the reality of scarce IT resources and project delivery timelines, typically at least a portion of these issues must be handled through other means, such as SQL view objects or Power BI's M query functions.

A best practice is to implement data transformation operations within the data warehouse or source system. This minimizes the resources required to process an import mode dataset and, for DirectQuery datasets, can significantly improve query performance, as these operations would otherwise be executed during report queries.

For many common data sources, such as Oracle and Teradata, M query expressions are translated into equivalent SQL statements (if possible) and these statements are passed back to the source system via a process called query folding. See *Chapter 2*, *Preparing Data Sources*, for more details on query folding.

As per the dataset planning architecture diagram, a layer of SQL views should serve as the source objects to datasets created with Power BI Desktop. By creating a SQL view for each dimension and fact table of the dataset, the data source owner or administrator is able to identify the views as dependencies of the source tables and is therefore less likely to implement changes that would impact the dataset without first consulting the BI team.

Additionally, the SQL views improve the availability of the dataset, as modifications to the source tables are much less likely to cause the refresh process to fail.

As a general rule, the BI team and IT organization should avoid the use of DAX for data transformation and shaping logic, such as DAX calculated tables and calculated columns. The primary reason for this is that it weakens the link between the dataset and the data source, as these expressions are processed entirely by the Power BI dataset after source queries have been executed.

Additionally, the distribution of transformation logic across multiple layers of the solution (SQL, M, DAX) causes datasets to become less flexible and manageable. Moreover, tables and columns created via DAX do not benefit from the same compression algorithms applied to standard tables and columns and thus can represent both a waste of resources as well as a performance penalty for queries accessing these columns.

In the event that required data transformation logic cannot be implemented directly in the data warehouse or its ETL or **Extract-Load-Transform (ELT)** process, a second alternative is to build this logic into the layer of SQL views supporting the Power BI dataset. For example, a SQL view for the product dimension could be created that joins the Product, Product Subcategory, and Product Category dimension tables, and this view could be accessed by the Power BI dataset.

As a third option, M functions in the Power BI query expressions could be used to enhance or transform the data provided by the SQL views. See *Chapter 2, Preparing Data Sources*, for details on these functions and the Power BI data access layer generally.

Once data transformation planning is complete, the next step is to determine the mode of the dataset as explained in the next section.

## Import, DirectQuery, Live, and Composite datasets

A subsequent but closely related step in dataset planning is choosing between the default import mode, DirectQuery mode, Live mode, or composite mode. In some projects, this is a simple decision as only one option is feasible or realistic given the known requirements while other projects entail significant analysis of the pros and cons of either design.

If a data source is considered slow or ill-equipped to handle a high volume of analytical queries, then an import mode dataset is very likely the preferred option. Likewise, if near real-time visibility of a data source is an essential business requirement, then DirectQuery or Live mode are the only options.

The DirectQuery and Live modes are very similar to one another. Both methods do not store data within the dataset itself but rather query source systems directly to retrieve data based upon user interaction with reports and dashboards. However, Live mode is only supported for Power BI datasets, Analysis Services (both multi-dimensional and tabular), and Dataverse.

When DirectQuery/Live is a feasible option or can be made a feasible option via minimal modifications, organizations may be attracted to the prospect of leveraging investments in high-performance database and data warehouse systems. However, the overhead costs and version control concerns of import mode can be reduced via Power BI features, such as the dataset refresh APIs or pipelines discussed in *Chapter 10, Managing Application Workspaces and Content*, and incremental data refresh.

The following list of questions can help guide an import versus DirectQuery/Live decision:

1.  Is there a single data source for our dataset that Power BI supports as a DirectQuery/Live source?

    For example, each fact and dimension table needed by the dataset is stored in a single data warehouse database, such as Oracle, Teradata, SQL Server, or Azure SQL Database.

    The following URL identifies the data sources supported for DirectQuery/Live with Power BI, including sources that are currently only in beta: `http://bit.ly/2AcMp25`.

2.  If DirectQuery/Live is an option per question 1, is this source capable of supporting the analytical query workload of Power BI?

    For example, although Azure Synapse (formerly Azure SQL Data Warehouse) technically supports DirectQuery, it's not recommended to use Azure Synapse as a DirectQuery data source, given the limitations on the volume of concurrent queries supported and a lack of query plan caching.

    In many other scenarios, the data source may not be optimized for analytical queries, such as with star schema designs and indexes that target common BI/reporting queries. Additionally, if the database is utilized for **Online Transaction Processing** (OLTP) workloads and/or other BI/analytical tools, then it's necessary to evaluate any potential impact on these applications and the availability of resources.

3.  Is an import mode dataset feasible, given the size of the dataset and any requirements for near real-time visibility of the data source?

Currently, Power BI Premium supports import mode datasets up to 400 GB in size. However, the true limit for model sizes in Premium is limited to the total available amount of RAM within the capacity. In addition, PPU datasets are limited to 100 GB and Pro datasets are limited to 10 GB. Therefore, truly massive datasets must either use a DirectQuery data source or a Live connection to an Analysis Services model.

Additionally, Power BI Premium currently supports a maximum of 48 refreshes per day for import mode datasets. Therefore, if there's a need to view data source data for the last several minutes or seconds, an import mode dataset is not feasible.

4.  If the DirectQuery/Live source is capable of supporting a Power BI workload as per question 2, is the DirectQuery/Live connection more valuable than the additional performance and flexibility provided via the import mode?

5.  In other words, if an import mode dataset is feasible, as per question 3, then an organization should evaluate the trade-offs of the two modes. For example, since an import mode dataset is hosted in the Power BI service and in a compressed and columnar in-memory data store, it is likely to provide a performance advantage. This is particularly the case if the DirectQuery/Live source is hosted on-premises and thus queries from the Power BI cloud service must pass through the on-premises data gateway reviewed in *Chapter 11, Managing the On-Premises Data Gateway*.

    Additionally, any future data sources and most future data transformations need to be integrated into the DirectQuery/Live source. With an import mode dataset, the scheduled import process can include many data transformations and potentially other data sources without negatively impacting query performance.

For organizations that have invested in powerful data source systems for BI workloads, there's a strong motivation to leverage this system via DirectQuery/Live. In general, business intelligence teams and architects are averse to copying data into another data store and thus creating both another data movement and a source of reporting that must be supported.

Let's now take a more detailed look at each of the possible dataset modes.

## Import mode

An import mode dataset can include multiple data sources, such as SQL Server, Oracle, and an Excel file. Since a snapshot of the source data is loaded into the Power BI cloud service, in addition to its in-memory columnar compressed structure, query performance is usually good for most scenarios.

Another important advantage of import mode datasets is the ability to implement data transformations without negatively impacting query performance. Unlike DirectQuery/Live datasets, the operations of data source SQL views and the M queries of import datasets are executed during the scheduled data refresh process. The *Query design per dataset mode* section of *Chapter 2, Preparing Data Sources*, discusses this issue in greater detail.

Given the performance advantage of the in-memory mode relative to DirectQuery/Live, the ability to integrate multiple data sources, and the relatively few use cases where real-time visibility is required, most Power BI datasets are designed using import mode.

Next, we provide more detail about DirectQuery/Live mode.

## DirectQuery/Live mode

While DirectQuery and Live connections are different, as explained previously, they are similar to one another and share common traits, such as not storing data within the dataset itself but rather querying source systems directly to retrieve data based upon user interaction with reports and dashboards.

A DirectQuery/Live dataset is traditionally limited to a single data source and serves as merely a thin semantic layer or interface to simplify the report development and data exploration experience. DirectQuery/Live datasets translate report queries into compatible queries for the data source and leverage the data source for query processing, thus eliminating the need to store and refresh an additional copy of the source data.

A common use case of DirectQuery/Live is to provide near real-time visibility to changes in source data. For example, a manufacturer may want to monitor activities occurring on a manufacturing floor and potentially link this monitoring solution to notifications or alerts.

The performance of DirectQuery/Live datasets is strongly influenced by the design and resources available to the source system. Successful DirectQuery/Live datasets generally result from performance optimizations implemented in the source system such as via columnstore indexes, materialized views, and star schema designs that reduce the complexity of report queries.

With import and DirectQuery/Live modes understood, we next cover the relatively new composite mode.

## Composite mode

Composite mode is perhaps the most significant enhancement to Power BI in recent years as it enables table-level control over a table's storage mode (Import, DirectQuery, Dual).

Storage modes are covered in greater detail in *Chapter 2*, *Preparing Data Sources*. When designed effectively, a composite model can deliver the performance benefits of import (in-memory) models but also provide scalability for large DirectQuery source systems.

A common design pattern with composite models is to set the storage mode of a massive fact table to DirectQuery but configure a smaller, targeted aggregation table in import mode and related dimension tables in dual mode. Power BI automatically utilizes the in-memory aggregation table to resolve incoming report queries if the given aggregation table(s) and its related Dual mode dimension tables contain the necessary data.

Even more recently, Microsoft has unveiled DirectQuery for Power BI datasets and Azure Analysis Services. With DirectQuery for Power BI datasets and Azure Analysis Services, datasets developed and published to Power BI can be chained or extended to produce new datasets that incorporate additional import or DirectQuery sources.

With data transformation and data model storage mode decisions made, the dataset planning process is complete. Let's now take a look at how these planning processes and decisions apply to our sample project introduced earlier in this chapter.

## Sample project analysis

As per the data refresh questions from the project template (questions 7 and 8), the Power BI dataset only needs to be refreshed daily—there's not a need for real-time visibility of the data source. From a dataset design perspective, this means that the default import mode is sufficient for this project in terms of latency or data freshness.

The project template from *Table 1.2* also advises that an Excel file containing the **Annual Sales Plan** must be included in addition to the historical sales data in the SQL Server data warehouse. Therefore, unless the Annual Sales Plan data can be migrated to the same SQL Server database containing the Internet Sales and Reseller Sales data, an import mode dataset is the only option.

The data security requirements from the project template can be implemented via simple security roles and therefore do not materially impact the import or DirectQuery decision. DirectQuery datasets can support dynamic or user-based security models as well but, given restrictions on the DAX functions that can be used in security roles for DirectQuery datasets, import mode datasets can more easily support complex security requirements. However, depending on the data source and the security applied to that source relative to the requirements of the project, organizations may leverage existing data source security through a DirectQuery dataset via a single sign-on with Kerberos delegation.

Finally, the BI team must also consider the scale of the dataset relative to size limitations with import mode datasets. As per the project template in *Table 1.2 (#6)*, 3-4 years of sales history needs to be included, and thus the dataset designer needs to determine the size of the Power BI dataset that would store that data. For example, if Power BI Premium capacity is not available, the dataset is limited to a max size of 1 GB. If Power BI Premium capacity is available, large datasets (for example, 10 GB+) potentially containing hundreds of millions of rows can be published to the Power BI service.

The decision for this project is to develop an import mode dataset and to keep the Excel file containing the Annual Sales Plan on a secure network location. The BI team will develop a layer of views to retrieve the required dimension and fact tables from the SQL Server database as well as connectivity to the Excel file. The business is responsible for maintaining the following Annual Sales Plan Excel file in its current schema, including any row updates and the insertion of new rows for future plan years. An excerpt from this file is shown in *Figure 1.18*:

| Calendar | Sales Territory Region | Product Subcategory | Internet Net Sales | Internet Net Sales Margin % | Reseller Net Sales |
|---|---|---|---|---|---|
| 2018-Nov | Canada | Road Bikes | $22,429.387 | 0.35974584 | $87,240.4256 |
| 2018-Nov | Canada | Shorts | $371.8569 | 0.64355038 | $1,395.4774 |
| 2018-Nov | Canada | Socks | $22.404 | 0.70639074 | $75.053 |
| 2018-Nov | Canada | Tires and Tubes | $2,856.178 | 0.613382 | $4.7626 |
| 2018-Nov | Canada | Touring Bikes | $14,932.3292 | 0.33759492 | $18,242.4319 |
| 2018-Nov | Canada | Vests | $362.9342 | 0.574668 | $1,065.8653 |
| 2018-Oct | Canada | Bike Racks | $607.392 | 0.5674064 | $5,514.9595 |
| 2018-Oct | Canada | Bottles and Cages | $423.126 | 0.7341807 | $134.1574 |

*Figure 1.18: Annual Sales Plan in Excel data table*

By using the existing Excel file for the planned sales and margin data rather than integrating this data into the data warehouse, the project is able to start faster and maintain continuity for the business team responsible for this source. Similar to collaboration with all data source owners, the dataset designer could advise the business user or team responsible for the sales plan on the required structure and the rules for maintaining the data source to allow for integration into Power BI.

For example, the name and directory of the file, as well as the column names of the Excel data table, cannot be changed without first communicating these requested revisions. Additionally, the values of the Sales Territory Region, Product Subcategory, and Calendar Yr-Mo columns must remain aligned with those used in the data warehouse to support the required actual versus plan visualizations.

The sales plan includes multiple years and represents a granularity of the month, sales territory region, and product subcategories.

In other words, each row represents a unique combination of values from the `Calendar Yr-Mo`, `Sales Territory Region`, and `Product Subcategory` columns. The *Bridge tables* section in *Chapter 4, Designing Import and DirectQuery Data Models*, describes how these three columns are used in integrating the Sales Plan data into the dataset containing `Internet Sales` and `Reseller Sales` data.

This completes the sample project analysis and concludes this chapter.

## Summary

In this chapter, we've walked through the primary elements and considerations in planning a Power BI project. A standard and detailed planning process inclusive of the self-service capabilities needed or expected, project roles and responsibilities, and the design of the dataset can significantly reduce the time and cost to develop and maintain the solution. With a sound foundation of business requirements and technical analysis, a business intelligence team can confidently move forward into the development stage.

In the next chapter, the two data sources identified in this chapter (SQL Server and Excel) are accessed to begin the development of an import mode dataset. Source data is retrieved via Power BI's M language queries to retrieve the set of required fact and dimension tables. Additionally, several data transformations and query techniques are applied to enhance the analytical value of the data and the usability of the dataset.

## Join our community on Discord

Join our community's Discord space for discussions with the author and other readers:
`https://discord.gg/q6BPbHEPXp`

# 2

# Preparing Data Sources

This chapter follows on from the dataset planning process described in *Chapter 1, Planning BI Projects*, by providing guidance on how to prepare for connecting to and transforming data using **Power Query** (**M**) queries. Power Query queries are written in a data transformation language commonly called "M" or can be generated via the Power Query Editor user interface. These queries access data sources and optionally apply data transformation logic to prep the tables for the Power BI data model.

As mentioned in *Chapter 1, Planning BI Projects*, to the greatest extent possible data transformation processes should be implemented within data sources such as **Azure SQL** and **Azure Synapse SQL** rather than via Power BI's data transformation capabilities. The presence of significant data transformation logic (for example, joins, filters, and new columns) outside of an organization's primary data warehouse or "source of truth" makes these solutions more difficult to understand and support.

Prior to actually connecting to and transforming data, it is critical to understand a number of important concepts, design principles, data sources, and Power BI Desktop settings as well as source system preparation.

In this chapter, we cover the following topics:

- Query folding
- Query design per dataset mode
- Data sources
- SQL views

Before diving into detailed explanations about data sources, SQL views, and M, it is critical that the reader be familiar with the concept of query folding.

# Query folding

Query folding is one of the most powerful and important capabilities of the M language as it translates M expressions into equivalent query statements for the given source system to process. With query folding, Power Query (M) serves as a rich abstraction layer for defining both simple and complex data transformation processes while still leveraging the compute resources of the source system. When implementing any remaining logic or data transformations via M functions, a top priority of the dataset designer is to ensure that these operations are folded to the data source.

In the following M query shown in *Figure 2.1*, a Table.RemoveColumns() M function is applied against the SQL view for the **Internet Sales** fact table to exclude three columns that are not needed for the dataset:

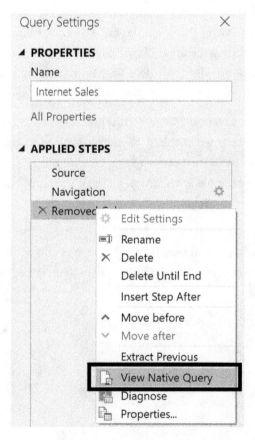

*Figure 2.1: Power Query Editor: View Native Query*

The additional step is translated to a SQL query that simply doesn't select the three columns. The specific SQL statement passed to the source system can be accessed by right-clicking the final step in the **Query Settings** pane and selecting **View Native Query** as shown in *Figure 2.1*. If the **View Native Query** option is grayed out, this indicates that the specific step or transformation is executed with local resources.

Most data sources that can be queried, such as relational databases (e.g. SQL Server, Oracle) support query folding. Data sources that lack any mechanism for understanding and resolving queries, such as Excel files and Azure blobs, naturally do not support query folding.. The M queries against these file sources use local M engine resources and thus the volume of data imported as well as the complexity of the query should be limited. Other sources, such as SharePoint lists, Active Directory, and Exchange, support some level of query folding, though significantly less than relational databases.

Queries may be completely folded to the source system or partially folded as explained in the next section.

## Partial query folding

Dataset designers should check the final step of each query in the dataset to ensure that query folding is occurring. If all required transformations or logic of an M query cannot be folded into a single SQL statement, the dataset designer should attempt to re-design the query to obtain as much query folding as possible.

For example, all common or simple transformations can be implemented in the first few steps of the query so that **View Native Query** is visible for as many steps as possible. The remaining logic can be added as the last step of the query and this locally executed step or transformation is applied against the results of the SQL statement generated from the last step in which **View Native Query** is active.

The Value.NativeQuery() M function can be used to pass a SQL statement to the data source. However, any further transformations applied to the results of this function in the M query exclusively use local resources. Therefore, if implemented, the SQL statement passed to the data source should either include all required logic for the query or return a small result set that can be further processed with local resources.

With the concept of query folding and its importance understood, we'll next explore the different designs and considerations for queries depending upon the mode of the dataset.

# Query design per dataset mode

As mentioned in *Chapter 1, Planning BI Projects*, to the greatest extent possible data transformation processes should be implemented within data sources such as Azure SQL and Azure Synapse Analytics rather than via Power BI's data transformation capabilities.

The presence of significant data transformation logic, such as joins, filters, and new columns, outside of an organization's primary data warehouse or "source of truth" makes these solutions more difficult to understand and support. In addition, source systems are generally provisioned with more compute resources to handle data transformations and often include secondary data structures, like indexes, that speed up certain operations such as filters and joins.

If resource or time constraints make it necessary to apply data transformations in Power BI rather than source systems, Power Query (M) should generally be favored over DAX calculated columns and tables. Additionally, the Power Query (M) transformations should be documented and communicated such that this logic or process can later be migrated to a source system.

With respect to query design per dataset mode, many common M queries are the same for both **import** and **DirectQuery** datasets. However, depending on the dataset mode, there can be widely different implications for the source system resource load (memory, CPU, and disk) and the performance of the queries from Power BI.

Therefore, it's essential that the dataset planning decisions regarding table storage mode (import, DirectQuery, Dual) are reflected in the M queries for the dataset. For example, a query that gets imported into memory only once a night is a much better candidate to implement data transformations than a query that is folded back to the source system during report interactions via DirectQuery.

The M queries supporting a Power BI dataset import mode should exclude, or possibly split, columns with many unique values, such as a `transaction number` column, as these columns consume relatively high levels of memory. A standard design technique for import mode models is to exclude derived fact table columns with relatively more unique values when these values can be computed via simple DAX measure expressions based on columns of the same table with fewer unique values.

In the following example, the `SUMX()` DAX function is used to compute the `Sales Amount` measure based on the `Order Quantity` and `Unit Price` columns of the `Internet Sales` fact table, thus avoiding the need to import the `Sales Amount` column:

```
Internet Sales Amount (Import) =
SUMX('Internet Sales','Internet Sales'[Order Quantity]*'Internet
Sales'[Unit Price])

Internet Sales Amount (DirectQuery) = SUM('Internet Sales'[Sales Amount])
```

As per the second measure, the Sales Amount column would be included in a DirectQuery data model and the DAX measure for the sales amount would exclusively utilize this column to generate a more efficient SQL query for the data source.

The import mode model is able to efficiently compute similar SUMX() expressions at scale with basic arithmetic operators (+, -, *, /) as these operations are supported by the multithreaded storage engine of the **xVelocity** in-memory analytics engine. For greater detail on DAX measures for import and DirectQuery datasets, see *Chapter 5, Developing DAX Measures and Security Roles*.

The M queries supporting a DirectQuery dataset should generally contain minimal to no transformation logic as the complexity of the resulting SQL statement may negatively impact the performance of Power BI report queries, as well as increasing the resource usage of the data source. This is especially important for the fact tables and any large dimension tables of the DirectQuery dataset. Given the central role of the data source for query performance and scalability of DirectQuery solutions, the Power BI dataset designer should closely collaborate with the data source owner or subject matter expert, such as a database administrator, to make the best use of available source system resources.

With composite models, individual tables are set with distinct storage modes (import, DirectQuery, Dual) in order to achieve a balance of the benefits of both import and DirectQuery modes. The most common use case for composite models involves very large fact tables with hundreds of millions or billions of rows. In a composite model, this large source table can be set as DirectQuery and a much smaller import mode aggregation table can be added to the model to resolve the most common or important report queries via compressed memory. Power BI composite models with aggregation tables can dynamically determine if report queries can be resolved by aggregation table(s), which are typically import mode tables, or if it's necessary to issue queries to the DirectQuery source tables.

As noted in the *To get the most out of this book* section of the *Preface*, an AdventureWorks data warehouse sample database (**AdventureWorksDW2019**) hosted on a local instance of the SQL Server 2019 database engine is the primary data source for the examples in this book. The PBIX files included in the code bundle reference **localhost\MSSQLSERVERDEV** as the name of the database server and **AdventureWorksDW2019** as the name of the database.

Therefore, any attempt to refresh the queries within these PBIX files or create new queries against this data source results in errors as the user doesn't have access to this source unless the same instance name and database name are used within the reader's own environment.

Additionally, certain objects of the **AdventureWorksDW2019** database used in this book, such as views, are not included in the original downloadable sample database from Microsoft. However, a backup of the database used for this book was created that includes the custom schema and views. This file is available in the code samples for this chapter. This file can be downloaded, unzipped, and the database restored to a local copy or other SQL Server and thus only requires that the query parameters be changed to point to the correct server and database.

Let's now take a look at design considerations for import mode dataset queries.

## Import mode dataset queries

All M queries of an import mode dataset, or import mode tables in a composite dataset, are executed once per dataset refresh. Therefore, if sufficient resources are available during the dataset refresh process, the M queries can contain more complex and resource-intensive operations without negatively impacting report query performance.

However, as mentioned in the previous section, as a Power BI dataset matures and particularly when a data warehouse system is available, it's considered a best practice to migrate M data transformation logic to the source view or table objects of the data warehouse. If migration of the data transformation logic to a data warehouse source system is not an option, a Power BI dataflow defined in the Power BI service might be a more robust alternative to a complex M query expression embedded within a dataset. This is particularly the case if the dataflow can utilize premium capacity and if other datasets may need to leverage the same data transformation workflow.

In this project example with an on-premises SQL Server database, the M queries can utilize the database server's resources during each refresh via a **query folding** process. Query folding simply means that the M query is translated into the native syntax of the source system and executed locally by the source system.

In the event that certain M expressions cannot be translated into an equivalent SQL statement for the given source, these expressions are instead evaluated by the **data gateway**. A data gateway is simply software installed on an on-premises server that serves as a bridge between the Power BI service and on-premises data sources. Data gateways are explored in depth in *Chapter 11, Managing the On-Premises Data Gateway*.

If the source database was in the cloud and not on-premises or within an **Infrastructure-as-a-Service (IaaS)** virtual machine, a gateway would not be required for the refresh, and resources in Power BI, such as Power BI Premium capacity hardware, would be used to execute any M expressions that can't query fold back to a source. Briefly, IaaS provides on-demand access to virtual and physical servers, storage, and networking. IaaS is distinct from **Platform as a Service (PaaS)** and **Software as a Service (SaaS)**, which provide on-demand access to ready-to-use services and software.

For import mode datasets, M queries can be partially folded such that a source database is used to execute only part of the required logic. For example, an M query may contain both simple transformation steps, such as filtering out rows, as well as more complex logic that references a custom M function. M functions are just like functions in other programming languages, blocks of code that perform specific tasks.

In the case of partial folding, a SQL statement is generated for the initial steps of the query, and the results of this SQL query are then used by the data gateway to process the remaining logic. All steps (variables) within an M query following a step that cannot be folded are also not folded. Likewise, any M step following a `Value.NativeQuery()` function that passes a SQL statement to a source system is also not folded. See the *Query folding* section earlier in this chapter for more details.

Next, we'll consider the designs of DirectQuery dataset queries.

## DirectQuery dataset queries

Similar to import mode dataset queries, there are also specific design considerations when dealing with DirectQuery dataset queries. For DirectQuery datasets or DirectQuery tables in a composite dataset, every M query is folded to exclusively utilize the resources of the data source. It should be noted that relatively few data source systems support DirectQuery. In addition, certain M functions and query logic that lack an equivalent translation for the given data source are not supported. In these scenarios, the dataset designer can develop alternative M queries that produce the same target data structure and are supported by the source system or implement the necessary logic within the source system, such as adding a layer of SQL views, to support the desired dataset.

An additional and fundamental limitation to the scope of M queries for DirectQuery datasets is the impact on query performance and user experience. Since the native statements representing M queries must be executed by the source system during report viewing sessions, common transformations such as converting data types and sorting tables can cause significant performance degradation.

Additionally, a high volume of sub-optimal native queries passed from Power BI reports can quickly drive up the resource usage of the source system. Therefore, although it's often technically possible to implement similar data transformation logic as import mode datasets using the native system and DirectQuery, the performance and resource implications of these transformations frequently prove unacceptable.

Dataset designers of DirectQuery datasets should document the native statements generated by their M queries. As shown in the *Query folding* section earlier in this chapter, these queries can be accessed from the **View Native Query** command within the **Applied Steps** pane of the Power Query Editor in Power BI Desktop. Sharing and reviewing these queries with the data source owner or a subject matter expert on the data source can often lead to new ideas to improve performance or data quality.

One powerful technique to optimize DirectQuery performance is via the dynamic Power Query (M) parameters feature. With dynamic Power Query parameters, the filter selections of the report user for a common dimension such as department or fiscal year are passed into a performance-optimized query such as the Where clause of a SQL statement.

Let's take a closer look at how DirectQuery operates during report execution.

## DirectQuery report execution

Because DirectQuery results in queries against the source system for each report interaction by users, it is important to fully understand the performance and operations of these queries.

In the database trace from SQL Server Profiler shown in *Figure 2.2*, a DirectQuery dataset has translated a Power BI report query into a SQL statement, which joins the SQL statements associated with the Reseller Sales, Reseller, and Date M queries:

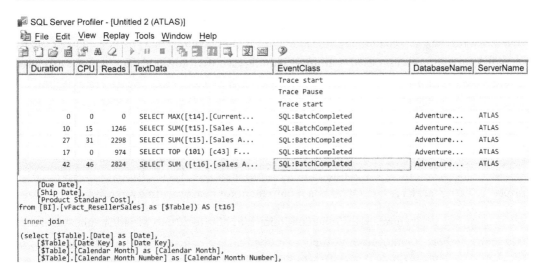

*Figure 2.2: SQL Server Profiler trace – Power BI DirectQuery report visualization*

For DirectQuery datasets, it's important to understand both the individual queries associated with each table of the model as well as how the data source is utilizing these queries in resolving report queries. In this example, the three table queries are used as derived tables to form the FROM clause of the outer SQL statement. Additionally, though not included in the trace image, the WHERE clause reflects a slicer (filter) selection for a specific calendar year in a Power BI report.

We'll now move on to query design considerations for composite datasets.

## Composite datasets

As described in *Chapter 1, Planning BI Projects*, composite datasets allow mixing DirectQuery mode tables from different sources and/or DirectQuery mode tables and import mode tables in a single dataset, such as having the reseller sales table in DirectQuery mode but the internet sales table in import (in-memory) mode.

With the release of the **DirectQuery for PBI datasets and AS** feature, multiple connections to Power BI datasets can be combined within a composite data model or a Power BI dataset can be modified through a process called **chaining**. Chaining involves a Power BI dataset that is extended through the creation of DAX columns and measures or by combining the dataset with import mode or other DirectQuery-mode tables.

The use of composite datasets should be considered carefully. Generally, whenever possible, it is best to design import mode datasets as they provide the best performance and the greatest amount of flexibility in terms of dataset design. Composite datasets can be useful, however, with respect to extremely large fact tables or a requirement for near real-time reporting.

When using composite models, the inherent limitations of DirectQuery are still applicable except that many of these limitations now apply to individual tables instead of the entire dataset. For example, a calculated column in a DirectQuery table can still only refer to other columns in the same table. Other DirectQuery limitations apply to the entire dataset if a single table within the dataset has a storage mode of DirectQuery, such as the unavailability of the **Quick Insights feature**. The Quick Insights feature is covered in *Chapter 8*, *Applying Advanced Analytics*.

With composite models, the concerns around data security and data privacy are extended to actually using a report versus solely during data refresh. Because the dataset contains multiple DirectQuery data sources or DirectQuery and import mode data sources, the underlying queries between tables can comingle the data from different sources. For example, sensitive information stored in a spreadsheet could be included in a query sent to a DirectQuery SQL Server relational database. Corporate security and privacy restrictions may not allow such interaction.

Dataset designers should be particularly cognizant of the encryption levels of data sources in composite models. It is unwise to allow information retrieved over an encrypted data source connection to be included in information sent to a data source accessed over an unencrypted connection.

There are also performance considerations when using composite datasets that are the same or similar to the performance concerns with pure DirectQuery datasets. However, composite datasets add an additional layer of performance considerations over simple DirectQuery datasets. This is because a single visual may send queries to multiple different data sources.

Consider that results from one query may be sent across to a second source via a subsequent query. This type of scenario can result in a DirectQuery SQL query containing a large number of literal values that becomes inefficient to include in a WHERE clause or results in multiple SQL queries involving one SQL query per group value.

Therefore, dataset designers must pay particularly close attention to the **cardinality** (number of unique values) of columns in such scenarios. Relatively low cardinality of a few thousand unique values should not impact performance but as cardinality increases, performance can be reduced or result in failure to execute the queries successfully.

In addition to the query design considerations for composite models covered thus far, composite models introduce additional table storage modes.

## Table storage modes

Composite models enable dataset creators to configure multiple storage modes across the different tables of a model thus balancing the benefits of both import (cached) data and DirectQuery. Typically, composite models also utilize hidden aggregation tables such that all common summary-level queries are resolved by either a relatively small use of memory or an optimized DirectQuery object but detailed queries are handled via a large-scale DirectQuery source system. Once a composite model is created, the Power BI dataset dynamically determines whether incoming report queries are resolved via imported in-memory cache or the source system via DirectQuery.

With composite models, there are four storage modes available for tables within the dataset. Of these four, we have already discussed import and DirectQuery modes. Two additional modes are added for non-calculated tables, **Dual** and **Hybrid**.

Dual mode tables are DirectQuery tables where a copy of the table is also kept in memory in order to support fast access and query performance as if the table were in import-only mode. Thus, Dual mode allows queries involving import mode-only tables to perform quickly when also requiring queries to the Dual mode table but still allow the table to participate in DirectQuery-only queries as well.

Consider a data model that involves fact tables using DirectQuery and imported dimension tables. In this scenario, the dimension tables should be set to Dual mode in order to support DirectQuery queries as well as fast performance with import mode queries.

Hybrid tables are tables that contain one or more import mode partitions as well as a single DirectQuery partition. Note that table partitions are simply a way to divide portions of data within the table. For example, incremental refresh adds additional table partitions so that the data within each incremental refresh partition can be processed separately from the initial load of the data.

This means that a single table can contain a large base load of data as well as data resulting from incremental refreshes. This data can be queried quickly because the data exists in memory within the dataset. However, the data within the table also supports near real-time visibility via its DirectQuery partition. Thus, queries against the table retrieve data from the one or more import mode partitions as well as the most recent data that has not been imported via DirectQuery.

Hybrid tables are a relatively new development but present an attractive design alternative where the dataset remains largely import but allows for near real-time data visibility as well. Hybrid tables should not be confused with Dual mode tables. Dual mode simply allows data model tables to be available for report visuals that may query both import and DirectQuery tables within the data model while Hybrid tables allow a single table to retrieve data from import mode partitions as well as via DirectQuery.

## Data sources

Data source connectivity is one of the strengths of Power BI, due to the vast list of standard data source connectors included in Power BI Desktop. In addition, numerous industry standards such as **Open Data Protocol (OData)**, **Open Database Connectivity (ODBC)**, and **Object Linking and Embedding Database (OLE DB)** are supported. The breadth of data connectivity options is further bolstered by the ability for developers to create custom Power BI data connectors for a specific application, service, or data source.

Although a Power BI dataset can connect to multiple sources ranging from Azure Synapse Analytics to a text file, solution architects and developers should strive to build solutions on a single, well-supported source such as a data warehouse database system that already contains the necessary data integrations as well as reflects data integrity constraints and quality processes. Power BI datasets that connect to several distinct sources, and particularly to less stable sources like files and folders, are much more prone to data quality and refresh errors and are more difficult to support.

Power BI's data connectors are consistently extended and improved with each monthly release of Power BI Desktop. New data sources are commonly added as a **preview** release feature (beta) and previous Preview connectors are moved from Preview to **general availability**. Generally available connectors are those that are considered fully functional and stable.

In the following example from the November 2021 release of Power BI Desktop, *Figure 2.3* shows that four new connectors have been released to **Preview** while three other connectors that are already generally available have been updated:

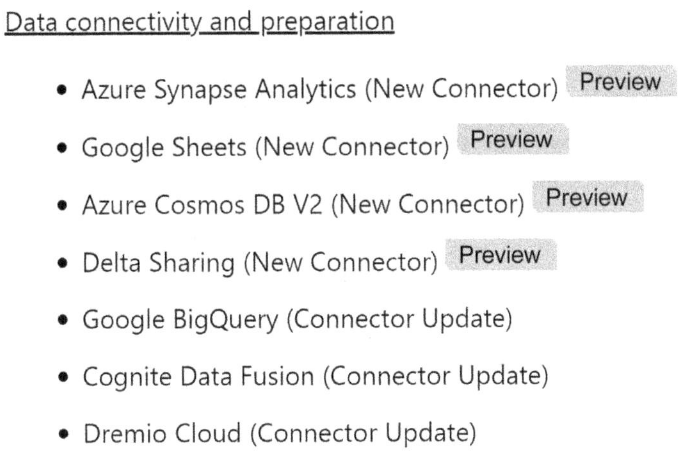

<u>Data connectivity and preparation</u>

- Azure Synapse Analytics (New Connector)  Preview
- Google Sheets (New Connector)  Preview
- Azure Cosmos DB V2 (New Connector)  Preview
- Delta Sharing (New Connector)  Preview
- Google BigQuery (Connector Update)
- Cognite Data Fusion (Connector Update)
- Dremio Cloud (Connector Update)

*Figure 2.3: Preview and generally available data connectors in Power BI Desktop*

Preview connectors should only be used for testing purposes, as differences between the preview release and the subsequent generally available connector may cause queries dependent on the preview version to fail.

Regardless of the data connector used, all data connectors share certain common elements within Power BI Desktop, including such things as authentication caching, data source settings, and privacy levels as covered in the following sections.

## Authentication

All data sources require some type of authentication, even if the authentication is simply **anonymous** such as publicly available web pages. Power BI Desktop saves a data source credential, or sign-in identity, for each data source connection used. These credentials and settings are not stored in the PBIX file but rather on the local computer specific to the given user.

Solution architects and developers should carefully consider which identity or principle is used to authenticate to the data source, which permissions have been granted to this account, and how this identity or credential is maintained. The main outcome of an authentication policy or process is to ensure that solutions utilize a system identity available to the IT/BI team and do not have a dependency on an individual user's account permissions.

For example, if SQL Server or Azure SQL Database is the source system, a BI team may create a SQL login and user with the minimal permissions necessary to read the objects within the scope of the solution. The password for this SQL login could be stored in Azure Key Vault and revised every 3-6 months by the IT/BI team.

An authentication dialog specific to the data source is rendered if the user hasn't accessed the data source before or if the user has removed existing permissions to the data source in Power BI Desktop's **Data source settings** menu. In the following example shown in *Figure 2.4*, a Sql. Database() M query function references the AdventureWorksDW2019 SQL Server database on the localhost\MSSQLSERVERDEV SQL Server instance.

In this scenario, the user has not previously accessed this data source (or has cleared existing source permissions), and thus executing this query prompts the user to configure the authentication to this source as shown in *Figure 2.4*:

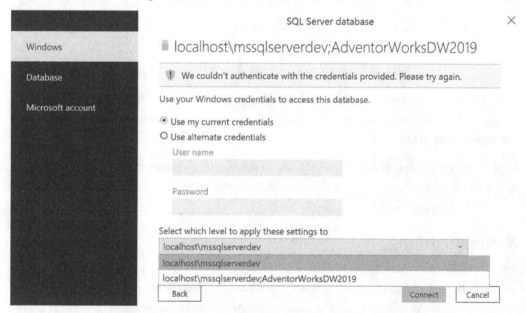

*Figure 2.4: Edit authentication credentials in Power BI Desktop*

Most relational database sources have similar authentication options. For SQL Server, the user can choose between the default **Windows** authentication (that is, **Use my current credentials**), **Database** authentication if the database is in **Mixed Mode** (SQL user or Windows authentication), or **Microsoft account** if SQL Server is running in Microsoft Azure.

Additionally, the credentials can be saved exclusively to the specific database or be reused for other databases on the same server as shown in *Figure 2.4* in the dropdown under **Select which level to apply these settings to**.

Once authentication is configured, the authentication settings for a data source can be accessed via the **Data source settings** menu within Power BI Desktop.

## Data source settings

The **Data source settings** menu provides access to the authentication and privacy levels configured for each data source within the current file and the saved permissions available to all of the user's Power BI Desktop files.

This menu can be accessed under the **Transform data** dropdown on the **Home** tab of Power BI Desktop's **Report view** or from the **Home** tab of the **Power Query Editor**, as shown in *Figure 2.5*:

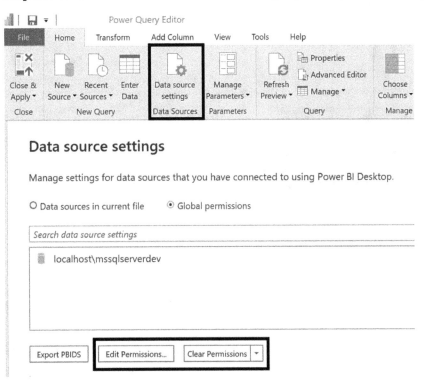

*Figure 2.5: Data source settings menu in Power Query Editor*

In this example, the user chose to save the Windows authentication to the SQL Server instance, **localhost\mssqlserverdev**, rather than the specific database (**AdventureWorksDW2019**) on the server. The **Edit Permissions…** command button provides the ability to revise the authentication, such as from **Windows** to **Database**, or to enter a new **User name** and **Password**.

The **Edit…** button of the **Edit Permissions** dialog, highlighted in *Figure 2.6*, prompts the same SQL Server credential menu used when originally configuring the method of authentication to the data source:

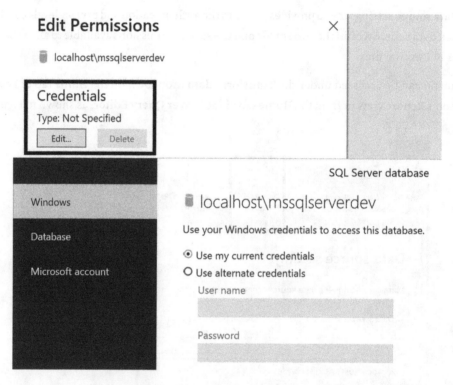

*Figure 2.6: Edit credentials accessed via Edit Permissions*

Many organizations set policies requiring users to regularly revise their usernames or passwords for certain data sources. Once these credentials are updated, the user should utilize the **Edit Permissions** menu to ensure that the updated credentials are used for M queries against the data source. Depending on the security policy of the data source, repeated failures to authenticate due to outdated credentials can cause the user's account to be temporarily locked out of the data source.

Having mentioned that the **Data source settings** menu also provides access to the privacy levels of data sources, we will explain these next.

# Privacy levels

In addition to the authentication method and user credentials, Power BI also stores a privacy level for each data source. Privacy levels define the isolation level of data sources and thus restrict the integration of data sources in M queries. For example, in the absence of privacy levels, an M query that merges a CSV file with a publicly available online database could result in the data from the CSV file being passed to the online database to execute the operation.

Although such behavior is preferable from a query performance and resource utilization standpoint, the CSV file may contain sensitive information that should never leave the organization or even an individual user's machine. Applying privacy levels, such as private for the CSV file and public for the online database, isolates the two sources during query execution, thus preventing unauthorized access to sensitive data.

The privacy level of a data source can be accessed from the same **Edit Permissions** dialog available in the **Data source settings** menu as shown in *Figure 2.7*:

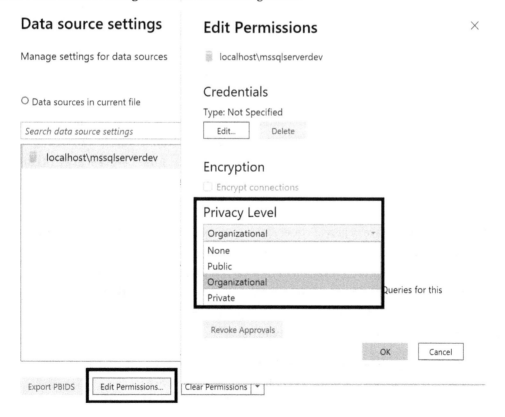

*Figure 2.7: Privacy Level options per data source*

The default **Privacy Level** for data sources is **None**. Therefore, dataset designers should revise privacy levels when first configuring data sources in Power BI Desktop based on the security policies for the given sources.

Four privacy levels are available:

- **None**: The privacy level applied is inherited from a separate data source, or not applied if the separate parent source has not been configured. For example, the privacy level for an Excel workbook stored on a network directory could be set to **None**, yet the isolation level of **Private** would be enforced if a data source for the root directory of the file is set to **Private**.

- **Public**: A public data source is not isolated from other public sources, but data transfer from organizational and private data sources to public data sources is prevented. Public source data can be transferred to an organizational data source but not to a private data source.

- **Organizational**: An organizational data source is isolated from all public data sources but is visible to other organizational data sources. For example, if a CSV file is marked as **Organizational**, then a query that integrates this source with an organizational SQL Server database can transfer this data to the database server to execute the query.

- **Private**: A **Private** data source is completely isolated from all other data sources. Data from the **Private** data source is not transferred to any other data sources, and data from public sources is not transferred to the **Private** source.

In this project, the Excel workbook containing the **Annual Sales Plan** is not merged with any queries accessing the SQL Server data warehouse and thus the privacy levels do not impact any queries. However, as with all other data security issues, such as **Row-Level Security (RLS)** roles, the dataset designer should be mindful of privacy levels and apply the appropriate setting per data source.

Restrictive privacy levels may prevent query folding from occurring and thus significantly reduce performance and reliability. For example, if an Excel workbook is isolated from a SQL Server data source due to a **Private** privacy level, then the local resources available to the M engine are used to execute this operation rather than the SQL Server database engine. If the source data retrieved from SQL Server is large enough, the resource requirements to load this data and then execute this operation locally could cause the query to fail.

With the essentials of data sources within Power BI understood, we'll next cover perhaps one of the most important data sources for Power BI, the Power BI service itself.

# Power BI as a data source

Dozens of cloud services are available to Power BI as data sources, such as Google Analytics and Dynamics 365. Most importantly for this project, the Power BI service is a fully supported data source enabling report development in Power BI Desktop against published datasets. As shown in *Figure 2.8*, the datasets contained in Power BI workspaces in which the user is a member are exposed as data sources:

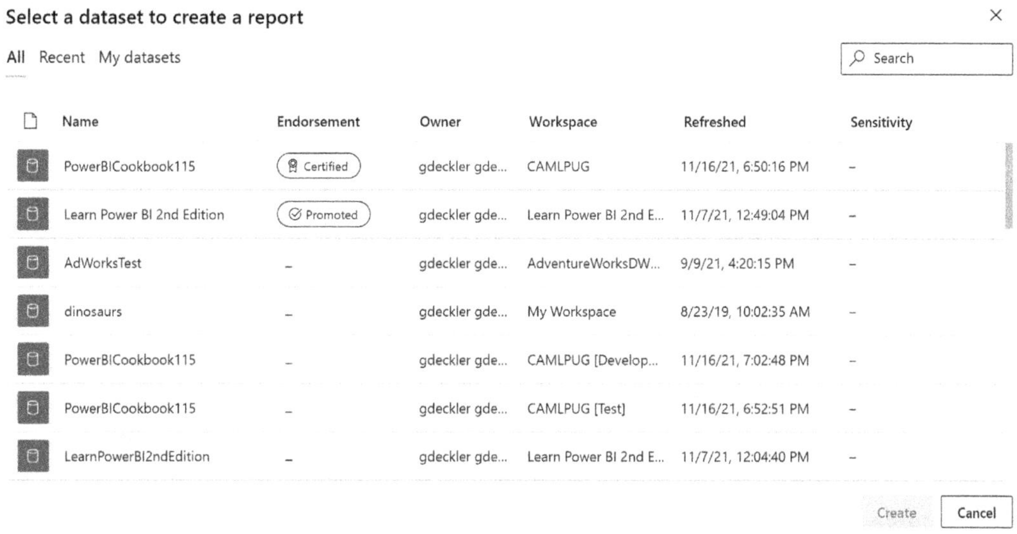

| | Name | Endorsement | Owner | Workspace | Refreshed | Sensitivity |
|---|---|---|---|---|---|---|
| | PowerBICookbook115 | ⚐ Certified | gdeckler gde... | CAMLPUG | 11/16/21, 6:50:16 PM | – |
| | Learn Power BI 2nd Edition | ⊘ Promoted | gdeckler gde... | Learn Power BI 2nd E... | 11/7/21, 12:49:04 PM | – |
| | AdWorksTest | – | gdeckler gde... | AdventureWorksDW... | 9/9/21, 4:20:15 PM | – |
| | dinosaurs | – | gdeckler gde... | My Workspace | 8/23/19, 10:02:35 AM | – |
| | PowerBICookbook115 | – | gdeckler gde... | CAMLPUG [Develop... | 11/16/21, 7:02:48 PM | – |
| | PowerBICookbook115 | – | gdeckler gde... | CAMLPUG [Test] | 11/16/21, 6:52:51 PM | – |
| | LearnPowerBI2ndEdition | – | gdeckler gde... | Learn Power BI 2nd E... | 11/7/21, 12:04:40 PM | – |

*Figure 2.8: Power BI service data connector in Power BI Desktop*

Connecting to a dataset published to Power BI establishes a live connection for the given report, just like connections to Analysis Services. With live connections, all data retrieval and modeling capabilities are disabled and the queries associated with report visualizations are executed against the source dataset.

In certain scenarios it's necessary or useful to integrate a portion of one Power BI dataset into a different dataset. In these cases, the XMLA endpoint can be used to connect to a Power BI dataset as though it's an Analysis Services database and pass a DAX query to support table(s) in the source dataset.

Additionally, the Power BI composite models feature now supports the ability to connect to multiple Power BI datasets and/or Analysis Services models from the same Power BI dataset. For example, if inventory and sales data is stored in separate PBI datasets and the requirement is to display inventory and sales visuals in the same report, connections to both datasets can be defined in Power BI Desktop and converted from Live connections to DirectQuery data sources. As shown in *Figure 2.8*, within the Power BI service, datasets can be endorsed as either **Certified** or **Promoted**.

Endorsed datasets are presented at the top of the dialog with **Certified** datasets displayed first and then **Promoted** datasets. Organizations should adopt a process of certifying datasets in order to distinguish enterprise data assets from other potentially less trustworthy data. Endorsing or featuring content is further discussed in *Chapter 14, Administering Power BI for an Organization*.

Leveraging published datasets as the sources for reports provides natural isolation between the dataset design and report development processes. For example, a dataset designer can implement changes to a local Power BI Desktop file, such as the creation of new DAX measures, and re-publish the dataset to make these measures available to report authors. Additionally, such connections provide report authors with visibility of the latest successful refresh of the dataset if the dataset is configured in import mode.

Before moving on from data sources, we'll next cover some important Power BI Desktop options that should be configured prior to starting query development.

## Power BI Desktop options

Dataset designers should be aware of the global and current file settings available in Power BI Desktop. Among other options, these settings include the implementation of the privacy levels described earlier, the DAX functions available to DirectQuery datasets, auto-recovery, preview features, and whether M queries are executed serially or in parallel.

Power BI Desktop options can be accessed from the **File** menu by doing the following:

1.  Choose **File** in the ribbon
2.  Choose **Options and settings**
3.  Choose **Options**

These steps open the **Options** dialog in Power BI Desktop. Choosing **Privacy** from the left navigation of the **Options** dialog presents the **Privacy Levels** options as shown in *Figure 2.9*:

# Options

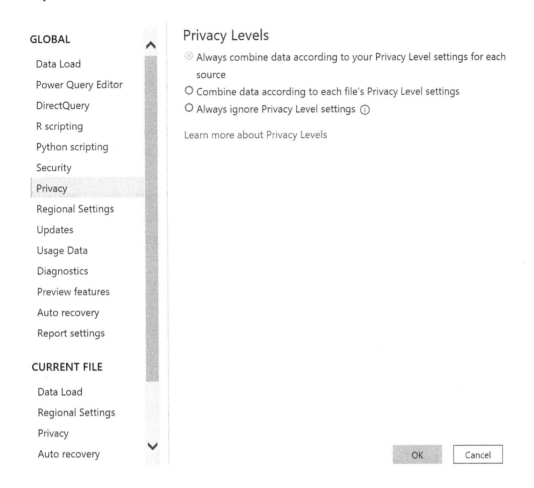

*Figure 2.9: Power BI Desktop options – GLOBAL| Privacy*

By setting the global **Privacy Levels** option to **Always combine data according to your Privacy Level settings for each source,** the current file privacy setting options are disabled. For all development and project activities, it's recommended to apply the privacy levels established per data source rather than each PBIX file's privacy settings (the second option) or to **Always ignore Privacy Level settings.**

It's outside the scope of this chapter to provide comprehensive details of every Power BI Desktop option, but the following two sections recommend settings that are relevant to dataset design. We start with global options (settings applied to all Power BI files).

## Global options

Global options only need to be set once and concern fundamental settings, including data source privacy levels and security:

1. For **Security**, under **Native Database Queries**, check the box for **Require user approval for new native database queries**. Under **ArcGIS for Power BI**, check the box for **Use ArcGIS Maps for Power BI**.

2. Set the **Privacy** option to **Always combine data according to your Privacy Level settings for each source**.

3. For **Power Query Editor** options, check the boxes for **Display the Query Settings pane** and **Display the Formula Bar**.

4. When finished, click the **OK** button in the bottom-right corner of the **Options** dialog to apply these settings.

Note that it may be necessary to restart Power BI Desktop for the revised settings to take effect. Next, we cover options that should be set for the current file.

## CURRENT FILE options

The CURRENT FILE options must be set per Power BI Desktop file and are particularly important when creating a new dataset:

1. Click on **Data Load** under **CURRENT FILE**

2. Under **Type Detection**, disable the option to **Detect column types and headers for unstructured sources**

3. Under **Relationships**, disable all options, including **Import of relationships from data sources on first load**, **Update or delete relationships when refreshing data**, and **Autodetect new relationships after data is loaded**

4. Under **Time intelligence**, disable the **Auto date/time** option

5. For larger import datasets with many queries, disable the checkbox for **Enable parallel loading of tables** under **Parallel loading of tables**

6. Click the **OK** button in the bottom-right corner of the **Options** dialog to apply these settings

Your **CURRENT FILE | Data Load** settings should look like *Figure 2.10*:

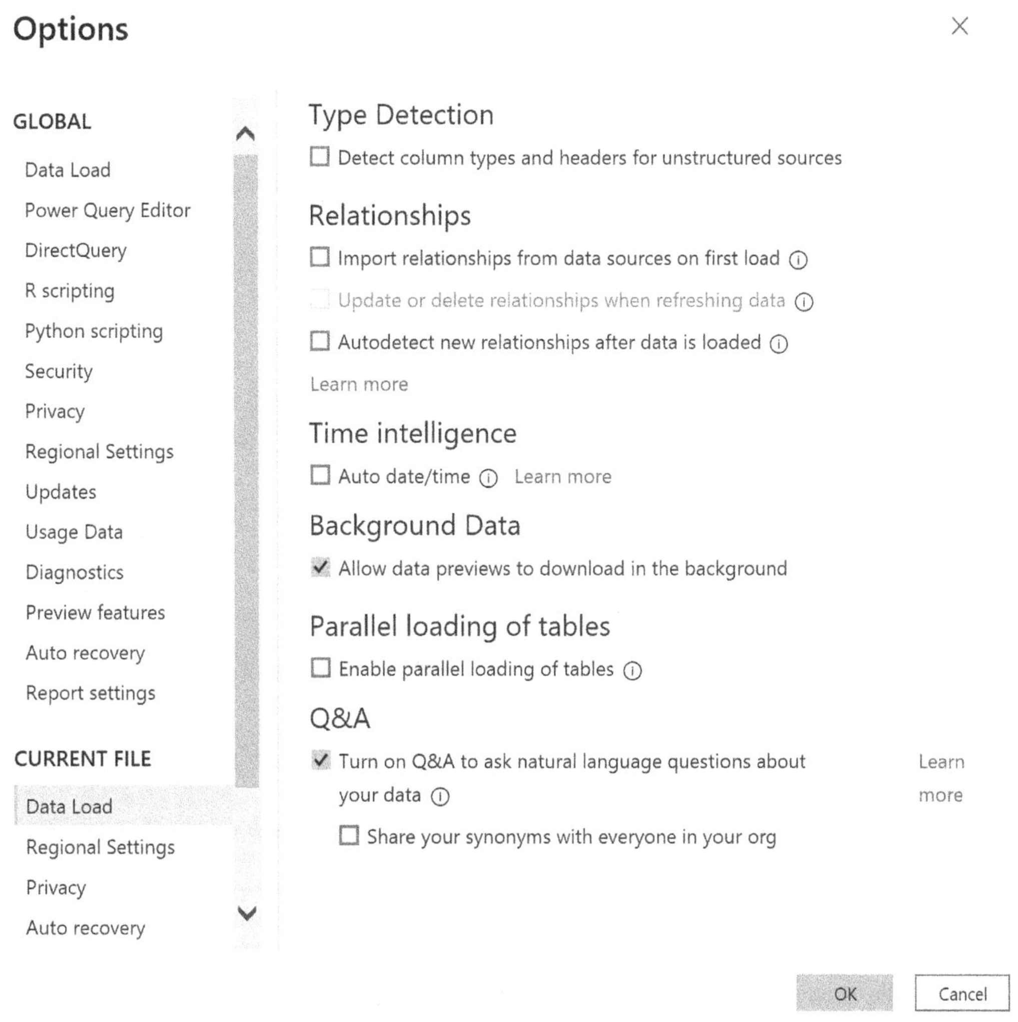

# Options                                                         ✕

GLOBAL

GLOBAL

Data Load

Power Query Editor

DirectQuery

R scripting

Python scripting

Security

Privacy

Regional Settings

Updates

Usage Data

Diagnostics

Preview features

Auto recovery

Report settings

**CURRENT FILE**

Data Load

Regional Settings

Privacy

Auto recovery

## Type Detection

☐ Detect column types and headers for unstructured sources

## Relationships

☐ Import relationships from data sources on first load ⓘ

☐ Update or delete relationships when refreshing data ⓘ

☐ Autodetect new relationships after data is loaded ⓘ

Learn more

## Time intelligence

☐ Auto date/time ⓘ   Learn more

## Background Data

☑ Allow data previews to download in the background

## Parallel loading of tables

☐ Enable parallel loading of tables ⓘ

## Q&A

☑ Turn on Q&A to ask natural language questions about       Learn
   your data ⓘ                                                    more

☐ Share your synonyms with everyone in your org

 

OK    Cancel

*Figure 2.10: Power BI Desktop Options – CURRENT FILE | Data Load settings*

Note that some of these same settings can be applied at the **GLOBAL** level as well, such as **Type Detection** and **Relationships** settings. The dataset designer should explicitly apply the appropriate data types within the M queries, accessing any unstructured sources, such as Excel files. Likewise, the dataset designer should have access to data source documentation or subject matter experts regarding table relationships.

Furthermore, the columns and hierarchies of the dataset's date dimension table can be used instead of the automatic internal date tables associated with the **Auto Date/Time** option. The creation of automatic date/time hierarchies for every date or date/time field within a dataset can significantly increase the size of import mode datasets due to the generally high cardinality of date and date/time columns.

Large Power BI datasets with multiple fact tables can contain many queries, which, if executed in parallel, can overwhelm the resources of the source system, resulting in a data refresh failure. Disabling the parallel loading of tables, therefore, improves the availability of the dataset and reduces the impact of the refresh process on the source server.

When Power BI Desktop is being used for report development rather than dataset development, the **Query reduction** settings in the **CURRENT FILE** options can benefit the user experience. These options, including the **Disabling of cross-highlighting/filtering by default** and enabling **Add an Apply button for each slicer to apply changes when you're ready** and **Add a single Apply button to the filter pane to apply changes at once**, result in fewer report queries being generated. Particularly for large and DirectQuery datasets, these options can contribute to more efficient and responsive self-service experiences with reports.

This concludes the overview of data sources and data source settings. We'll next move on to another important subject in data preparation prior to the creation of actual queries, SQL views.

## SQL views

As described in the *Dataset planning* section of *Chapter 1, Planning Power BI Projects*, a set of SQL views should be created within the data source and these SQL views, rather than the database tables, should be accessed by the Power BI dataset. SQL views are essentially virtual tables that provide an abstraction layer from the underlying database tables. SQL views can be used to merge database tables and to limit the number of columns, thus preventing such transformations from occurring within Power Query queries.

Each fact and dimension table required by the Power BI dataset should have its own SQL view and its own M query within the dataset that references this view. The SQL views should preferably be assigned to a dedicated database schema and identify the dimension or fact table represented as shown in *Figure 2.11*:

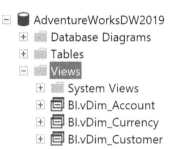

*Figure 2.11: Views assigned to BI schema in SQL Server*

A common practice is to create a database schema specific to the given dataset being created or to the specific set of reports and dashboards required for a project. However, as suggested in the *Data warehouse bus matrix* section of *Chapter 1, Planning Power BI Projects*, there shouldn't be multiple versions of dimensions and facts across separate datasets—version control is a top long-term deliverable for the BI team. Therefore, a single database schema with a generic name (BI in this example) is recommended.

The existence of SQL views declares a dependency to source tables that are visible to the data source owner. In the event that a change to the source tables of a view is needed or planned, the SQL view can be adjusted, thus avoiding any impact on the Power BI dataset, such as a refresh failure or an unexpected change in the data retrieved. As shown in *Figure 2.12*, a view (BI.vDim_Promotion) is identified as a dependent object of the DimPromotion dimension table:

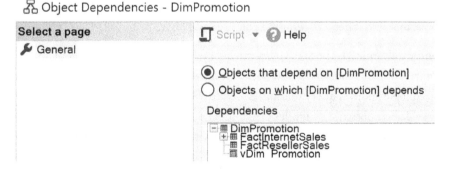

*Figure 2.12: SQL Server Object Dependencies*

For mature data warehouse sources, the simple query logic contained in each SQL view is sufficient to support the needs of the dataset. However, with Power BI (and Analysis Services tabular), BI teams can also leverage M functions to further enhance the value of this data. Such enhancements are covered in the *M query examples* section of *Chapter 3, Connecting to Sources and Transforming Data with M*. For now, we'll move on to the subject of the differences between using SQL views versus M queries for data transformation.

## SQL views versus M queries

A common question in Power BI projects specific to data retrieval is whether to implement any remaining transformation logic outside the data source in SQL views, within the M queries of the dataset, or both. For Analysis Services projects prior to SQL Server 2017, the layer of SQL views was the only option to implement any transformations and some BI teams may prefer this more familiar language and approach.

In some scenarios, the dataset author doesn't have the permissions necessary to create or alter SQL views in the source database. In other scenarios, the dataset author may be stronger or more comfortable with M queries relative to SQL. Additionally, given the expanded role of M queries in the Microsoft ecosystem, such as in Dataverse and **Azure Data Factory** (**ADF**) pipelines, other BI teams may see long-term value in M queries for lightweight data transformation needs.

Ideally, an organization's data warehouse already includes the necessary data transformations and thus minimal transformation is required within SQL or M. In this scenario, the M query for the table can simply reference the SQL view of the table, which itself contains minimal to no transformations, and inherit all required columns and logic.

As a secondary alternative, the SQL views can be modified to efficiently implement the required logic, thus isolating this code to the data source. As a third design option, M queries can implement the required logic and, via query folding, generate a SQL statement for execution by the source. Yet another design option, though less than ideal due to transformation logic existing in two different places and languages, is to implement part of the required logic in the SQL view and the remaining logic in the M query.

The guiding principle of the data retrieval process for the import mode dataset is to leverage the resources and architecture of the data source. The M queries of the Power BI dataset, which access the layer of SQL views in the source system, ultimately represent the fact and dimension tables of the data model exposed for report development and ad hoc analysis. This model should address all data transformation needs, thus avoiding the need for DAX-calculated columns and DAX-calculated tables.

Additionally, the data model in Power BI (or Analysis Services) should remain aligned with the architecture and definitions of the data warehouse. If a gap is created by embedding data transformation logic (for example, new columns) into the Power BI dataset that is not present in the data warehouse, plans should be made to eventually migrate this logic back to the data warehouse in order to restore alignment.

In other words, a user or tool should be able to return the same results of a Power BI report based on the Power BI dataset by issuing a SQL query against the source data warehouse. This is particularly essential in environments with other BI and reporting tools built on top of the data warehouse.

If it's necessary to use both SQL views and M functions to implement the data transformation logic, then both queries should be documented and, when possible, this logic should be consolidated closer to the data source.

As shown in *Figure 1.16, Dataset planning architecture*, from *Chapter 1, Planning Power BI Projects*, there are six layers in which data logic can be implemented. This figure is repeated as *Figure 2.13* for convenience:

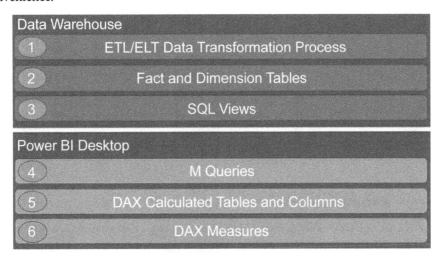

*Figure 2.13: Dataset planning architecture*

Data retrieval processes should strive to leverage the resources of data sources and avoid or minimize the use of local resources. For example, a derived column implemented within either **SQL Views** (layer 3) or **M Queries** (layer 4) that folds its logic to the data source is preferable to a column created by **DAX Calculated Tables and Columns** (layer 5).

Likewise, if data transformation logic is included within M queries (for example, joins or group by), it's important to ensure these operations are being executed by the source system as described in the *Query folding* section earlier in this chapter. These considerations are especially critical for large tables given the relatively limited resources (for example, CPU and memory) of a Power BI dataset or the data gateway if applicable.

Additionally, the dimension and fact tables of the Power BI dataset and any DAX measures created should represent a single version for the organization—not a customization for a specific team or project sponsor. Therefore, although the combination of SQL views and M queries provides significant flexibility for implementing data transformations and logic, over time this logic should be incorporated into corporate data warehouses and **Extract-Transform-Load** (**ETL**) processes so that all business intelligence tools have access to a common data source.

Incrementally migrate transformation logic closer to the corporate data warehouse over time. For example, a custom column that's originally created within an M query via the Table.AddColumn() function and a conditional expression (if...then) could subsequently be built into the SQL view supporting the table, thus eliminating the need for the M query logic.

In the second and final stage, the column could be added to the dimension or fact table of the corporate data warehouse and the conditional expression could be implemented within a standard data warehouse ETL package or stored procedure. This final migration stage would eliminate the need for the SQL view logic, improve the durability and performance of the data retrieval process, and in some scenarios also increase the feasibility of a DirectQuery dataset.

With the differences between SQL views and M queries understood, let's next explore some examples of SQL views.

## SQL view examples

As mentioned, the capabilities of source data systems, such as the creation of SQL views in SQL Server, should be leveraged when possible to transform data. Each SQL view should only retrieve the columns required for the dimension or fact table. If necessary, the views should apply business-friendly, unambiguous column aliases with spaces and proper casing.

Dimension table views should include the surrogate key used for the relationship-to-fact tables. As shown by the product dimension example later in this section, include the business or natural key column if historical tracking must be maintained.

Fact table views should include the foreign key columns for the relationships to the dimension tables, the fact columns needed for measures, and a WHERE clause to only retrieve the required rows, such as the prior three years. Given the size of many data warehouse fact tables and the differences in how this data can best be accessed, as per the *Query design per dataset mode* section earlier in this chapter, dataset designers should ensure that the corresponding SQL views are efficient and appropriate for the dataset.

A robust date dimension table is critical for almost all datasets and thus its SQL view and/or M query has a few unique requirements. For example, date dimension tables should include integer columns that can define the default sort order of weekdays as well as sequentially increasing integer columns to support date intelligence expressions.

The date table should also include a natural hierarchy of columns (that is, Year, Year-Qtr, Year-Mo, Year-Wk) for both the Gregorian (standard) calendar as well as any custom fiscal calendar. These columns enable simple drill-up/down experiences in Power BI and report visualizations at different date granularities that span multiple time periods, such as the prior two years by week.

Given the static nature of the date (and time) dimension tables, their minimal size, and their near-universal application in reports and dashboards, it's usually a good use of IT/BI resources to enhance the source date table in the data warehouse. This could include any derived columns currently supported via SQL views or M queries as well as columns uniquely valuable to the organization, such as company holidays.

Any dynamic columns, such as Calendar Month Status (Current Month, Prior Month), can be computed within a SQL-stored procedure or an ETL package and this processing can be scheduled to update the source date table daily.

For our first example, we take a look at building a date dimension view.

## Date dimension view

Nearly all data models include some sort of date table due to the importance of tracking metrics important to an organization over time. *Table 2.1* shows sample data from a date dimension SQL view that includes several columns needed by the Power BI dataset:

| Date | Calendar Year | Calendar Yr-Qtr | Cal-endar Yr-Mo | Calendar Yr-Wk | Calen-dar Year Month Number | Calendar Month Status | Calen-dar Year Status | Prior Calendar Year Date |
|------|---------|---------|---------|---------|---------|---------|---------|---------|
| 2/26/2022 | 2022 | 2022-Q1 | 2022-Feb | 2022-WK9 | 110 | Prior Calendar Month | Current Calendar Year | 2/26/2021 |
| 2/27/2022 | 2022 | 2022-Q1 | 2022-Feb | 2022-WK9 | 110 | Prior Calendar Month | Current Calendar Year | 2/27/2021 |
| 2/28/2022 | 2022 | 2022-Q1 | 2022-Feb | 2022-WK9 | 110 | Prior Calendar Month | Current Calendar Year | 2/28/2021 |
| 3/1/2022 | 2022 | 2022-Q1 | 2022-Mar | 2022-WK9 | 111 | Current Calendar Month | Current Calendar Year | 3/1/2021 |

*Table 2.1: Sample date dimension columns*

The `Calendar Year Month Number` column can be used to define the default sort order of the `Calendar Yr-Mo` column and can also support date intelligence DAX measure expressions that select a specific time frame, such as the trailing four months. Likewise, a `Prior Calendar Year Date` (or `prior fiscal year date`) column can be referenced in date intelligence measure expressions.

The `Calendar Month Status` and `Calendar Year Status` columns make it easy for report authors to define common filter conditions, such as the current and prior month or the current year excluding the current month.

Additionally, since the values for these columns are updated either by a daily job in the source database or computed within the SQL view for the date dimension, the filter conditions for these columns only need to be set once.

Power BI Desktop supports relative date filtering conditions for date columns by default. Similar to the `Calendar Month Status` and `Calendar Year Status` columns identified earlier, this feature is also useful in defining many common report filter conditions, such as the last 20 days. However, relative date filtering is not comprehensive in the conditions it supports and thus it often doesn't support specific report requirements.

Dataset developers should work with data warehouse developers and/or data engineers in the organization to ensure that the date dimension table contains the logical columns necessary to simplify report development and avoid the need for report authors to regularly update the date filters in their reports. As one example, an organization that runs on a fiscal calendar distinct from the standard Gregorian calendar can benefit from columns that can filter for the current fiscal period or the latest closed period. Additional details regarding relative date filtering are available in *Chapter 7, Creating and Formatting Visualizations*.

The following SQL statement from the date dimension view (`BI.vDim_Date`) leverages the CURRENT_ TIMESTAMP() function to compute two dynamic columns (Calendar Year Status and Calendar Month Status) and the DATEPART() function to retrieve the date rows from January 1st of three years ago through to the current date:

```
SELECT
  D.[FullDateAlternateKey]
,
  CASE
    WHEN YEAR(D.[FullDateAlternateKey]) = YEAR(CURRENT_TIMESTAMP) THEN
'Current Calendar Year'
    WHEN YEAR(D.[FullDateAlternateKey]) = YEAR(CURRENT_TIMESTAMP)-1 THEN
'Prior Calendar Year'
    WHEN YEAR(D.[FullDateAlternateKey]) = YEAR(CURRENT_TIMESTAMP)-2 THEN
'2 Yrs Prior Calendar Year'
    WHEN YEAR(D.[FullDateAlternateKey]) = YEAR(CURRENT_TIMESTAMP)-3 THEN
'3 Yrs Prior Calendar Year'
    ELSE 'Other Calendar Year'
  END AS [Calendar Year Status]
,
  CASE
    WHEN YEAR(D.[FullDateAlternateKey]) = YEAR(CURRENT_TIMESTAMP) AND
MONTH(D.[FullDateAlternateKey]) = MONTH(CURRENT_TIMESTAMP) THEN 'Current
Calendar Month'
    WHEN YEAR(D.[FullDateAlternateKey]) = YEAR(DATEADD(MONTH,-
1,CAST(CURRENT_TIMESTAMP AS date))) AND
    MONTH(D.[FullDateAlternateKey]) = MONTH(DATEADD(MONTH,-1,CAST(CURRENT_
TIMESTAMP AS date))) THEN 'Prior Calendar Month'
    WHEN YEAR(D.[FullDateAlternateKey]) = YEAR(DATEADD(MONTH,-
2,CAST(CURRENT_TIMESTAMP AS date))) AND
    MONTH(D.[FullDateAlternateKey]) = MONTH(DATEADD(MONTH,-2,CAST(CURRENT_
```

```
TIMESTAMP AS date))) THEN '2 Mo Prior Calendar Month'
    WHEN YEAR(D.[FullDateAlternateKey]) = YEAR(DATEADD(MONTH,-
3,CAST(CURRENT_TIMESTAMP AS date))) AND
    MONTH(D.[FullDateAlternateKey]) = MONTH(DATEADD(MONTH,-3,CAST(CURRENT_
TIMESTAMP AS date))) THEN '3 Mo Prior Calendar Month'
    ELSE 'Other Calendar Month'
  END AS [Calendar Month Status]
FROM
DBO.DimDate as D
WHERE
D.[CalendarYear] >= DATEPART(YEAR,CURRENT_TIMESTAMP)-3 AND
D.[FullDateAlternateKey] <= CAST(CURRENT_TIMESTAMP as date);
```

Provided that the scheduled refresh of the import mode dataset is successful, reports with filter conditions defined against the dynamic date columns, such as `Calendar Month Status`, are updated automatically.

If the date columns in the SQL Server data source are only available as integers in YYYYMMDD format, the following T-SQL expression can be used to produce a date data type within the SQL view:

```
CONVERT(date,CAST(F.OrderDateKey AS nvarchar(8)),112)
```

However, the **Mark as date table** feature can be used to leverage existing YYYYMMDD integer columns for date relationships, as described in the following section.

## Mark as date table

The DAX query language used by Power BI datasets comes with many time intelligence functions for creating analytical measures such as `DATESBETWEEN()`, `DATEADD()`, and `DATESYTD()`. In order to effectively utilize these functions, the dataset must have a table explicitly defined as a date table.

Most data warehouses store date columns as integers for query performance reasons. For example, an `Order Date Key` column on a fact table would store the `20180225` (YYYYMMDD) value as an integer data type to represent February 25th, 2018. Likewise, an existing date dimension table in the data warehouse usually also contains a YYYYMMDD date key column to support the join to these fact tables in SQL queries.

If this date dimension table also contains a date column and meets essential data integrity criteria, the **Mark as date table** feature in Power BI Desktop can be used to leverage existing integer/whole number columns representing dates for relationships.

In *Figure 2.14*, the **Date** table has been selected in the **Fields** list in Power BI Desktop and the **Mark as date table** icon has been selected from the **Table tools** tab of the ribbon:

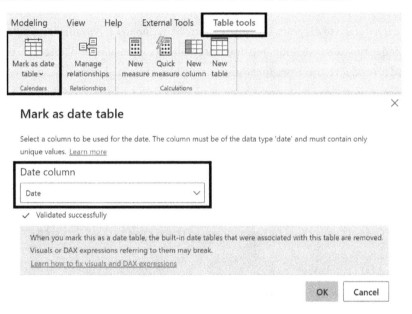

*Figure 2.14: Mark as Date Table*

As shown in *Figure 2.14*, the column named **Date**, which is stored as a **Date** data type, has been specified as the **Date column** to be used by the **Mark as date table** feature. Power BI validates that this column meets the required criteria to function properly.

In addition to relationships based on YYYYMMDD columns, this feature enables DAX time intelligence functions, such as SAMEPERIODLASTYEAR( ), to work properly. Power BI uses the date column specified by the model author in the **Mark as date table** setting in executing these expressions.

To utilize the **Mark as date table** feature, the **Date** column (**Date** data type) specified for the **Mark as date table** feature must meet the following criteria:

- No null values.
- No duplicate values.
- Contiguous date values:
  - There must be a single date value for each date from the earliest date to the latest date. In other words, there can't be any gaps or missing dates.
  - If a date/time column is used, the timestamp must be the same for each value of the column.

We'll now move on to a second SQL view example for the product dimension.

## Product dimension view

As shown in the database diagram schema referenced in *Chapter 1, Planning Power BI Projects*, it's recommended to provide a consolidated or de-normalized dimension for datasets. In the following view (BI.vDim_Product), three product dimension tables are joined and a logical column, Product Category Group, is created to support a common reporting and analysis need:

```
SELECT
  P.ProductKey as 'Product Key'
, P.ProductAlternateKey as 'Product Alternate Key'
, P.EnglishProductName AS 'Product Name'
, ISNULL(S.EnglishProductSubcategoryName, 'Undefined') 'Product
Subcategory'
, ISNULL(C.EnglishProductCategoryName, 'Undefined') AS 'Product Category'
, CASE
  WHEN C.EnglishProductCategoryName = 'Bikes' THEN 'Bikes'
  WHEN C.EnglishProductCategoryName IS NULL THEN 'Undefined'
  ELSE 'Non-Bikes'
  END AS 'Product Category Group'
FROM
DBO.DimProduct AS P
LEFT JOIN DBO.DimProductSubcategory AS S
ON P.ProductSubcategoryKey = S.ProductSubcategoryKey
LEFT JOIN DBO.DimProductCategory AS C
ON S.ProductCategoryKey = C.ProductCategoryKey
```

In this example, it's necessary to use LEFT JOIN since the product dimension table in the data warehouse allows for null values in the foreign key column (ProductSubcategoryKey). Retrieving the product rows that haven't yet been assigned a subcategory or category is necessary for certain reports that highlight future products. For these products, an ISNULL() function is used to replace null values with an undefined value. Additionally, similar to the Date view, a CASE expression is used to generate a column that groups the product rows into two categories (Bikes and Non-Bikes).

An additional aspect of the product dimension is that it is an example of a slowly changing dimension. The implications of slowly changing dimensions as related to SQL views and queries are covered in the following section.

# Slowly changing dimensions

As discussed in *Chapter 1, Planning Power BI Projects*, the historical tracking of core business entities, such as customers and products, via slowly changing dimension ETL processes is an essential requirement for data warehouses. While the ability to insert and update rows based on changes in specific columns is well outside the scope of this chapter, we do wish to cover slowly changing dimensions as related to the development of Power BI data queries.

The product dimension view retrieves both the surrogate key column used for relationships in the dataset as well as the business key that uniquely identifies the given product or customer, respectively. For example, as shown in *Table 2.2*, the same product (**FR-M94B-38**) is represented by three product dimension rows (**304, 305, 306**) due to changes in its list price over time:

| Product Key | Product Alternate Key | Product Name | Product List Price | Product Start Date | Product End Date | Product Status |
|---|---|---|---|---|---|---|
| 304 | FR-M94B-38 | HL Mountain Frame – Black, 38 | $1,191 | 7/1/2011 | 12/28/2011 | NULL |
| 305 | FR-M94B-38 | HL Mountain Frame – Black, 38 | $1,227 | 12/29/2011 | 12/27/2012 | NULL |
| 306 | FR-M94B-38 | HL Mountain Frame – Black, 38 | $1,350 | 12/28/2012 | NULL | Current |

*Table 2.2: Slowly changing dimension processing applied to product dimension*

DAX measures reference the business key or alternate key column of these dimension tables to compute the distinct count of these entities. For dimensions without slowly changing dimension processing applied, the foreign key column of the related fact table can be used to compute the distinct count of dimension values associated with the given fact or event. Greater detail on these measures is included in *Chapter 5, Developing DAX Measures and Security Roles*.

# Summary

In this chapter, we've covered a number of important concepts, design principles, data source settings, and source system preparation. This includes query folding, query design considerations per dataset mode, important Power BI Desktop configuration settings, data source privacy levels, and the layer of SQL views within a database source.

Understanding these concepts and properly preparing source systems greatly aids the process of connecting to and transforming data using Power BI.

In the next chapter, we'll leverage the prepared source systems and design techniques described in this chapter to connect to source systems and transform their data using Power Query (M).

## Join our community on Discord

Join our community's Discord space for discussions with the author and other readers:
`https://discord.gg/q6BPbHEPXp`

# 3

# Connecting to Sources and Transforming Data with M

This chapter follows the environment and data source preparation described in *Chapter 2, Preparing Data Sources*, by implementing **Power Query** (**M**) queries in a new Power BI Desktop file to retrieve the required fact and dimension tables. Power Query queries are written in a data transformation language commonly called "M" or can be generated via the **Power Query Editor** user interface. These queries access data sources and optionally apply data transformation logic to prep the tables for the Power BI data model.

Power Query (M) expressions are becoming ubiquitous throughout the entire Microsoft data platform. These expressions are used with dataflows, which are reusable by multiple Power BI datasets. They are also supported by **Azure Data Factory** (**ADF**) meaning that data mashup processes that begin in Power BI can be scaled up if necessary. Finally, M queries underpin dataflows within **Dataverse**, Microsoft's operational data store.

The M query language includes hundreds of functions and several books have been written regarding the language and its use. The greater purpose of this chapter is to understand M queries in the context of a corporate Power BI solution that primarily leverages an IT-managed data warehouse.

In this chapter, we use SQL Server and an Excel file as primary data sources for Power Query (M) queries. Parameters and variables are used to access a set of SQL views reflecting the data warehouse tables inside a SQL Server database and the Annual Sales Plan data contained in an Excel workbook.

Additional M queries are developed to support relationships between the sales plan and dimension tables and to promote greater usability and manageability of the dataset. Examples of implementing data transformations and logic within M queries, such as the creation of a dynamic customer history segment column, are included. Finally, reusable queries called dataflows are covered, as well as tools for editing and managing M queries, such as extensions for **Visual Studio** and **Visual Studio Code**.

In this chapter, we cover the following topics:

- Types of Power Query M queries
- Creating Power Query M queries
- Power Query M query examples
- Dataflows
- Power Query M query editing tools

Let's start by looking at the different types of M queries.

# Types of Power Query M queries

In *Chapter 2, Preparing Data Sources*, SQL views were created, data sources configured, and the Power BI Desktop environment options applied. With these tasks accomplished, the dataset designer can finally start developing the data retrieval queries and parameters of the dataset. Power Query (M) queries are the means by which data sources are connected to and data imported into Power BI datasets. M queries are necessary to connect to data sources such as SQL views and can also perform data transformation as required.

The Power Query M language is a functional coding language more formally called the Power Query Formula Language. M includes over 700 functions that are used to connect to data and perform transformations of that data. The lines of M code that connect to and transform data are called a query.

There are a number of different types of queries that serve different purposes, including:

- Data source parameters
- Staging queries
- Fact and dimension queries
- Parameter table queries
- Security table queries
- Custom function queries

This section explores each of these types of queries in detail. However, before delving into these different types of queries, it is important to understand how queries can be organized in order to achieve solutions that are more easily understood and maintained over time.

## Organizing queries

Within the **Power Query Editor** of Power BI Desktop, group folders are used to organize M queries into common categories such as **Data Source Parameters, Staging Queries, Parameter Tables, Fact Table Queries, Dimension Table Queries,** and **Bridge Table Queries** as shown in *Figure 3.1*:

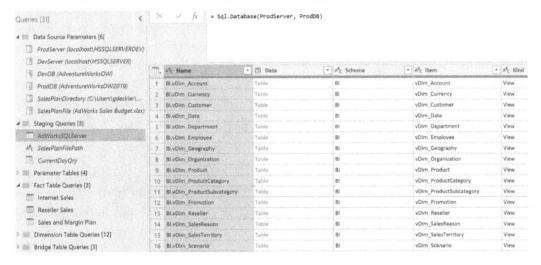

*Figure 3.1: Power Query Editor in Power BI Desktop with group folders*

New groups are created by right-clicking a query in the **Queries** pane and then choosing **Move To Group** and finally **New Group**. Once groups are created, queries can be moved between groups by dragging and dropping or by right-clicking the query, choosing **Move to Group**, and then selecting the desired group.

The parameters and queries displayed in italics are included in the refresh process of the dataset but not loaded to the dataset within Power BI Desktop. For example, the **AdWorksSQLServer** query displayed in *Figure 3.1* merely exposes the objects of the SQL Server database via the Sql. Database() M function for other queries to reference. This query, along with the data source parameters, is in italics and is used to streamline the data retrieval process such that a single change can be implemented to update many dependent queries.

Right-click a query or parameter in the **Queries** pane to expose the **Enable load** and **Include in report refresh** properties as shown in *Figure 3.2*:

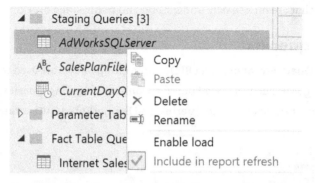

*Figure 3.2: Enable load and Include in report refresh*

For many datasets, the only queries that should be loaded to the data model are the dimension and fact table queries and certain parameter table queries. In addition, there may be instances where data within the source system is static, or unchanging. In these cases, there is no reason to refresh the data within the dataset after the initial load and thus the **Include in report refresh** option can be unchecked in order to save system resources and reduce refresh times.

We'll now take a detailed look at the different types of M queries, starting with data source parameters.

## Data source parameters

In the previous section, *Figure 3.1* displayed a group called **Data Source Parameters**. Parameters are special M queries that do not access an external data source and only return a scalar or individual value, such as a specific date, number, or string of text characters.

The primary use case for parameters is to centrally define a common and important value, such as a server name or the name of a database, and then reference that parameter value in multiple other queries. Like global variables, parameters improve the manageability of large datasets as the dataset designer can simply revise a single parameter's value rather than manually modify many queries individually.

Additionally, Power BI dataset authors can use parameters to only load a sample of a table's source data to the local Power BI Desktop file and later load the entire table to the published Power BI dataset. For example, starting and ending date parameters could be created and embedded in an M expression that applies a filter condition when loading a table.

The local Power BI Desktop file could use parameter values only representing a single month or year date range, but the published dataset could load multiple years based on revised starting and ending date parameter values. The dataset author or team can manipulate the parameter values manually in the Power BI service or a script could be used that modifies the parameters via the Power BI REST API. The Power BI REST API is described in the *Power BI REST API and PowerShell module* section of *Chapter 10, Managing Workspaces and Content*.

Query parameters can be created and modified via the **Manage Parameters** dialog available on the **Home** tab of the **Power Query Editor**. *Figure 3.3* shows the **Manage Parameters** dialog, which identifies the six parameters defined for the SQL Server database and the Microsoft Excel workbook:

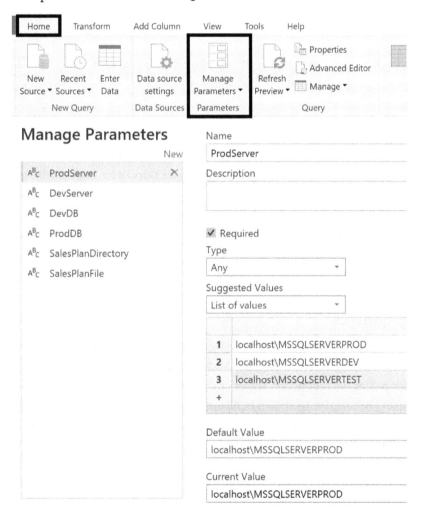

*Figure 3.3: Manage Parameters in Power Query Editor*

For this dataset, development and production environment database parameters (for example, **ProdServer** and **ProdDB**) are configured with a list of valid possible values to make it easy and error-free when switching data sources. For the same purpose, both the name of the Excel workbook containing the annual **Sales and Margin Plan** and its file directory are also stored as parameters.

The **Suggested Values** dropdown provides the option to allow any value to be entered manually, for a value to be selected from a hardcoded list of valid values, and for a query that returns a list (a value type in M, such as a table and a record) to dynamically populate a list of valid parameter values. Given the small number of valid server names in this example and the infrequency of changing production and development server names, the three suggested values have been entered manually.

Parameters are often used with **Power BI Template** files to enable business users to customize their own reports with pre-defined and pre-filtered queries and measures. For example, the user would open a template and select a specific department, and this selection would be used to filter the M queries of the dataset.

Additionally, parameters can be useful in defining the values used in the filtering conditions of queries, such as the starting and ending dates, and in the calculation logic used to create custom columns in M queries. Parameters are usually only used by other queries and thus not loaded (italic font in *Figure 3.3*) but they can be loaded to the data model as individual tables with a single column and a single row. If loaded, the parameters can be accessed by DAX expressions just like other tables in the model.

We'll now turn our attention to staging queries.

## Staging queries

With the data source parameters configured, staging queries are used to expose the data sources to the dimension and fact table queries of the dataset. For example, the **AdWorksSQLServer** staging query merely passes the production server and production database parameter values into the Sql.Database() M function as shown in *Figure 3.1*. This query results in a table containing the schemas and objects stored in the database, including the SQL views supporting the fact and dimension tables.

The **SalesPlanFilePath** staging query used for the Annual Sales Plan Excel workbook source is very similar in that it merely references the file name and file directory parameters to form a complete file path, as shown in *Figure 3.4*:

*Figure 3.4: Annual Sales Plan Staging Query—Excel Workbook*

The third and final staging query, **CurrentDateQry**, simply computes the current date as a date value as shown in *Figure 3.5*:

*Figure 3.5: Current date staging query*

Just like parameters, the results of staging queries, such as **CurrentDateQry**, can be referenced by other queries, such as the filtering condition of a fact table. In the following sample M query, the Table.SelectRows() function is used in the **Internet Sales** query to only retrieve rows where the Order Date column is less than or equal to the value of the **CurrentDateQry** (for example 12/29/2021):

```
let
    Source = AdWorksSQLServer,
    ISales = Source{[Schema = "BI", Item = "vFact_InternetSales"]}[Data],
    CurrentDateFilter = Table.SelectRows(ISales, each   [Order Date] <=
    CurrentDateQry)
in
    CurrentDateFilter
```

In this simple example, the same filter condition can easily be built into the SQL view (vFact_ InternetSales), supporting the fact table, and this approach would generally be preferable. However, it's important to note that the M engine is able to convert the final query variable (CurrentDateFilter), including the reference to the staging query (CurrentDateQry), into a single SQL statement via **query folding**.

In some data transformation scenarios, particularly with rapid iterations and agile project lifecycles, it may be preferable to at least temporarily utilize efficient M queries within the Power BI dataset (or Analysis Services model) rather than implement modifications to the data source (for example, data warehouse tables or views).

As covered in the *Query folding* section of *Chapter 2, Preparing Data Sources*, if it's necessary to use M to implement query transformations or logic, the dataset designer should be vigilant in ensuring this logic is folded into a SQL statement and thus executed by the source system. This is particularly important for large queries retrieving millions of rows, given the limited resources of the data gateway server (if applicable) or any provisioned capacities (hardware) with Power BI Premium.

Staging queries can also be used with DirectQuery queries.

## DirectQuery staging

It is possible to use staging queries even when working with DirectQuery. The database staging query for a DirectQuery dataset is slightly different than an import mode dataset. For this query, an additional variable is added to the let expression, as shown in the following example:

```
let
    Source = Sql.Database(ProdServer, ProdDB),
    DummyVariable = null
in
    Source
```

The additional variable (DummyVariable) is ignored by the query and the same Sql.Database() function that references the server and database parameters for the import mode dataset can also be used for the DirectQuery dataset.

With parameters and staging queries defined, we can now focus on the main data queries for our facts and dimensions.

# Fact and dimension queries

All of the work performed thus far has really been preparation work for creating the queries that connect to and import the data of interest, the tables for our facts and dimensions.

For import mode datasets, the M query is executed upon a scheduled refresh and the query results are loaded into a compressed, columnar format. DirectQuery mode datasets and import queries with the **Enable load** property disabled or not set (see the *Organizing queries* section in this chapter) only define the SQL statement representing the given dimension or fact tables. The DirectQuery data source utilizes these SQL statements to create SQL queries necessary to resolve report queries, such as joining the **Internet Sales** query with the **Product** query.

With proper preparation, most M queries should simply access a single SQL view, apply minimal to no transformations, and then expose the results of this query to the dataset as a dimension or fact table. Such queries are referred to as source reference-only queries.

## Source reference only

The following M query shown in *Figure 3.6* references the SQL view (BI.vDim_Customer) via the staging query (**AdWorksSQLServer**) and does not apply any further transformations:

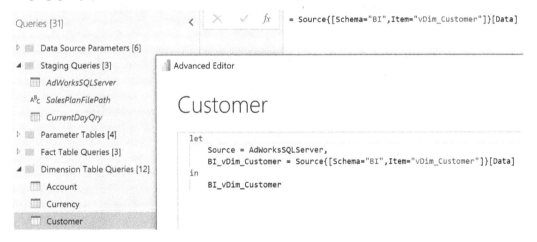

*Figure 3.6: Customer dimension query*

As shown in *Figure 3.6*, the **Customer** query accesses the unique M record associated with the schema (BI) and SQL view (vDim_Customer) from the table produced by the staging query (**AdWorksSQLServer**). This record contains all field names of the staging table query including the Data field that stores the SQL view. Referencing the Data field of the M record retrieves the results of the SQL view.

Since no M transformations are applied, the M query reflects the source SQL view, and changes to the SQL view such as the removal of a column are automatically carried over to the Power BI dataset upon the next refresh. The one-to-one relationship between the SQL view and the M query is one of the primary reasons to favor implementing, or migrating, data transformation logic to the data warehouse source rather than in the Power BI dataset.

Connecting to data warehouse databases such as Azure SQL Database or Azure SQL Managed Instance should generally result in simple M query expressions with little to no transformations required. Semi-structured and unstructured sources such as JSON and Excel files naturally require more transformations to prepare the data for analysis. We'll next look at a more complex query resulting from connecting to an unstructured data source, Microsoft Excel.

## Excel workbook – Annual Sales Plan

As demonstrated in the previous section, fact and dimension queries for structured data sources such as SQL Server should generally involve source reference-only queries. However, for the import mode dataset, the annual **Sales and Margin Plan** data is retrieved from a table object within an Excel workbook, an unstructured data source.

In the following fact table query shown in *Figure 3.7* (**Sales and Margin Plan**), the **SalesPlanFilePath** staging query is referenced within an `Excel.Workbook()` data access function:

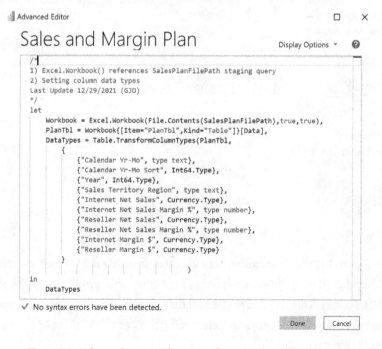

*Figure 3.7: Sales and Margin Plan query from Excel workbook source*

As covered in the *Power BI Desktop options* section in *Chapter 2, Preparing Data Sources*, the automatic data type detection option for unstructured sources should be disabled. Structured data sources such as SQL Server explicitly define the data types for columns. For unstructured data sources, the automatic data type detection feature attempts to analyze and determine the appropriate data type for each column.

With automatic data type detection disabled, it is necessary to explicitly define the appropriate data type for each column of the Excel table via the `Table.TransformColumnTypes()` function. The `Int64.Type`, `Currency.Type,` and `type number` arguments used in this function correspond to the **Whole Number**, **Fixed Decimal Number**, and **Decimal Number** data types, respectively.

For a DirectQuery dataset, the **Sales and Margin Plan** data would be retrieved from a SQL view within the same database as the other fact and dimension tables as shown in *Figure 3.8*:

Advanced Editor

## Sales and Margin Plan

```
let
    Source = AdWorksSQLServer,
    SalesMarginPlan = Source{[Schema = "BI", Item = "vFact_AdWorksSalesPlan"]}[Data]
in
    SalesMarginPlan
```

*Figure 3.8: Sales and Margin Plan M query for DirectQuery dataset*

The cost and time required to integrate the **Sales and Margin Plan** data into the data warehouse database are one of the reasons that the default import mode dataset was chosen for this project. The limitation of a single database within a single data source is currently one of the primary limiting factors for DirectQuery datasets. In *Figure 3.9*, an error is thrown when trying to utilize two databases from the same database server for a DirectQuery dataset:

## Apply query changes

⚠ DB DimEmployee
Connecting to tables from more than one database isn't supported in DirectQuery mode.

⚠ BI vFact_ResellerSales
Connecting to tables from more than one database isn't supported in DirectQuery mode.

*Figure 3.9: DirectQuery limitation – Single Database*

This DirectQuery limitation can be overcome by using composite data models but this adds additional complexity that is generally unwarranted in this scenario.

Let's next look at queries designed to create tables that assist with building relationships within a data model.

## Parameter tables queries

Parameter table queries are developed for usability and manageability purposes.

From a usability standpoint, the **Date Intelligence Metrics** and **Adventure Works Sales** serve to consolidate related measures in the Fields list that will be exposed to report authors and analysts such that these users don't have to scroll or hunt for measures. Additionally, the **Current Date** query is used to provide reports with a text message advising of the latest data refresh date. From a manageability standpoint, the **Measure Support** query is used to centralize intermediate or branching DAX expressions that are referenced by many DAX measures.

As shown in *Figure 3.10*, a trivial expression is used for three of the four queries since the purpose of the query is simply to provide a table name to the data model:

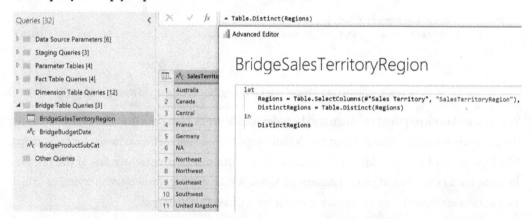

*Figure 3.10: Adventure Works Sales Parameter Tables query*

The **Date Intelligence Metrics, Adventure Works Sales**, and **Measure Support** queries all retrieve a blank value and the **Include in report refresh** property is disabled. The following two chapters demonstrate how these blank tables are utilized as data model metadata, and DAX measures are added to the dataset in *Chapter 4, Designing Import and DirectQuery Data Models*, and *Chapter 5, Developing DAX Measures and Security Roles*, respectively.

The **Current Date** query is the only parameter table query executed with each report refresh. The following M script for the **Current Date** query produces a table with one column and one record, representing the current date as of the time of execution:

```
let
    RefreshDateTime = DateTime.LocalNow(),
    TimeZoneOffset = -5,
    RefreshDateTimeAdjusted = RefreshDateTime +
#duration(0,TimeZoneOffset,0,0),
    RefreshDateAdjusted = DateTime.Date(RefreshDateTimeAdjusted),
    TableCreate = Table.FromRecords({[CurrentDate =
RefreshDateAdjusted]}),
    DateType = Table.TransformColumnTypes(TableCreate,{"CurrentDate", type
date})
in
    DateType
```

All reported times in Microsoft Azure are expressed in **Coordinated Universal Time (UTC)**. Therefore, timezone adjustment logic can be built into the M query to ensure the last refreshed date message reflects the local timezone.

In the preceding example, five hours are reduced from the DateTime.LocalNow() function, reflecting the variance between US Eastern Standard Time and UTC. The adjusted datetime value is then converted into a date value and a table is built based on this modified date value.

As shown in *Figure 3.11*, the **Current Date** query is used by a DAX measure to advise of the last refreshed date:

*Figure 3.11: Parameter Tables in Fields list and data refresh message*

Calculating the current date and time in the Power BI query captures the date and time at the time of refresh and can potentially be used as a support query for other queries within the dataset.

The `Current Date` DAX expression simply surfaces this information within the report while adding additional context for the report viewers.

The DAX expression supporting the last refreshed message is as follows:

```
Last Refresh Msg =
    VAR __CurrentDateValue = MAX('Current Date'[CurrentDate])
RETURN
    "Last Refreshed: " & __CurrentDateValue
```

An additional example of using DAX to return a string value for title or label purposes is included in the *Drill-through report pages* section of *Chapter 6, Planning Power BI Reports*.

As datasets grow larger and more complex, BI teams or dataset designers may add or revise group names to better organize M queries. For example, the four parameter group queries in this section serve three separate functions (fields list, last refreshed date, and DAX logic centralization).

To experienced Power BI and Analysis Services Tabular developers, a parameter table is understood as a custom table of parameter values loaded to a model and exposed to the reporting interface. DAX measures can be authored to detect which value (parameter) has been selected by the user (for example, 10% growth, 20% growth) and dynamically compute the corresponding result. For this dataset, the concept of parameter tables is extended to include any query that is loaded to the data model but not related to any other table in the data model.

Most large Power BI datasets include data source parameters, staging queries, fact and dimension queries, relationship table queries, and parameter tables queries. We'll next cover two optional types of queries, security table queries and custom function queries.

## Security table queries

Security table queries support the inclusion of tables for the express purpose of implementing **row-level security (RLS)** for the dataset. Such queries may be required in circumstances where each user should only see their own data. In these circumstances a security table can import the **user principal names (UPNs)** of users with access to reports built against the dataset. Typically the UPNs are the same values as user email addresses and the DAX function `USERPRINCIPALNAME()` can be used to retrieve this value for applying security or other filtering requirement in the Power BI service.

Based on the data security needs for this project described in *Chapter 1, Planning Power BI Projects*, it's not necessary to retrieve any tables for the purpose of implementing an RLS role.

As shown in the *Sample Power BI project template* section in *Chapter 1, Planning Power BI Projects*, the sales managers and associates should only have access to their **Sales Territory** groups, while the vice presidents should have global access.

With these simple requirements, the security groups of users (for example, **North America**, **Europe**, and the **Pacific region**) can be created and assigned to corresponding RLS roles defined in the data model. See *Chapter 5, Developing DAX Measures and Security Roles*, for details on implementing these security roles.

In projects with more complex or granular security requirements, it's often necessary to load additional tables to the data model such as a **Users** table and a **Permissions** table. For example, if users were to be restricted to specific postal codes rather than sales territory groups, a dynamic, table-driven approach that applies filters based on the user issuing the report request would be preferable to creating (and maintaining) a high volume of distinct RLS roles and security groups.

Given the importance of dynamic (user-based) security, particularly for large-scale datasets, detailed examples of implementing dynamic security for both import and DirectQuery datasets are included in *Chapter 5, Developing DAX Measures and Security Roles*.

We'll next look at another optional query type, custom function queries.

## Custom function queries

Since the Power Query (M) language is a functional programming language, it is possible to create custom functions as queries. These queries allow the creation of reusable code that can be used to perform repeated data transformations, such as custom parsing, or perform calculations. In the simple example below, a custom function is defined for calculating the age of customers in the **Customer** table:

```
let CalculateAge = (BirthDate as date) =>
        Date.Year(CurrentDayQuery) - Date.Year(BirthDate)
in CalculateAge
```

This custom function takes a single parameter, BirthDate, which must be a date data type. The Date.Year function is used on both the CurrentDayQuery reference and the BirthDate parameter with the latter subtracted from the former in order to return the number of years. This function can be saved as a query called GetAge and used within a custom column formula within the Customer table as follows:

```
= GetAge([BirthDate])
```

Additional examples and uses for custom functions can be found in the official Microsoft documentation at the following link: `https://bit.ly/33VJfRz`.

You should now understand all of the various types of Power Query (M) queries that can be created during dataset development. We'll next look at more specific details regarding M queries.

# Creating Power Query M queries

As mentioned, the M language is a functional programming language that includes over 700 functions. Similar to other programming languages, M has its own specific syntax, structure, operators, and data types that must be used when coding. Experienced Power Query (M) developers, for example, are very familiar with Lists, Records, and Tables and common use cases and M functions available for working with these specific types.

While a full exploration of the entire M language is beyond the scope of this book, there are a number of important subjects regarding M that we cover in the following sections as well as providing readers with examples of more complex M queries. For readers interested in fully understanding the M language, we refer them to the official *Power Query M language specification* found here: `https://bit.ly/3vmFSyr`.

We'll first take a look at numeric data types in M.

## Numeric data types

For structured data sources, such as SQL Server, the source column data types determine the data types applied in Power BI. For example, a currency or money data type in SQL Server results in a **Fixed Decimal Number** data type in Power BI. Likewise, the integer data types in SQL Server result in a **Whole Number** data type and the numeric and decimal data types in SQL Server result in **Decimal Number** data types in Power BI.

When an M query is loaded to the data model in a Power BI dataset, a **Fixed Decimal Number** data type is the equivalent of a (19,4) numeric or decimal data type in SQL Server. With four digits to the right of the decimal place, the use of the **Fixed Decimal Number** data type avoids rounding errors. The **Decimal Number** data type is equivalent to a floating point or approximate data type with a limit of 15 significant digits.

Given the potential for rounding errors with **Decimal Number** data types and the performance advantage of **Fixed Decimal Number** data types, if four digits of precision is sufficient, the **Fixed Decimal Number** data type is recommended to store numbers with fractional components. All integer or whole number numeric columns should be stored as **Whole Number** types in Power BI.

Numeric columns in M queries can be set to **Whole Number**, **Fixed Decimal Number**, and **Decimal Number** data types via the following expressions, respectively—Int64.Type, Currency.Type, and type number. The Table.TransformColumnTypes() function is used in the following M query example to convert the data types of the Discount Amount, Sales Amount, and Extended Amount columns:

```
let
    Source = AdWorksSQLServer,
    Sales = Source{[Schema = "BI", Item = "vFact_InternetSales"]}[Data],
    TypeChanges = Table.TransformColumnTypes(Sales,
        {
            {"Discount Amount", Int64.Type}, // Whole Number
            {"Sales Amount", Currency.Type}, // Fixed Decimal Number
            {"Extended Amount", type number} // Decimal Number
        })
in
    TypeChanges
```

As M is a case-sensitive language, the data type expressions must be entered in the exact case, such as type number rather than Type Number. Note that single-line and multiline comments can be included in M queries. See the *M query examples* section later in this chapter for additional details.

Given the impact on performance and the potential for rounding errors, it's important to check the numeric data types defined for each column of large fact tables. Additional details on data types are included in *Chapter 4*, *Designing Import and DirectQuery Data Models*.

Next, we'll look at item (record) access using M.

## Item access in M

Accessing records from tables, items from lists, and values from records are fundamental to M query development. In the following example, the results of the BI.vDim_Account SQL view are returned to Power BI using a slightly different M syntax than the customer dimension query from the previous section:

```
let
    Source = AdWorksSQLServer,
    AccountRecord = Source{[Name = "BI.vDim_Account"]},
    Account = AccountRecord[Data]
in
    Account
```

For this query, a record is retrieved from the `AdWorksSQLServer` staging query based only on the `Name` column. The `Data` field of this record is then accessed in a separate variable (`Account`) to return the results of the `BI.vDim_Account` SQL view to Power BI. BI teams or the dataset designer can decide on a standard method for accessing the items exposed from a data source staging query.

The following sample code retrieves the `"Cherry"` string value from an M list:

```
let
    Source = {"Apple","Banana","Cherry","Dates"},
    ItemFromList = Source{2}
in
    ItemFromList
```

M is a zero-based system such that `Source{0}` would return the `"Apple"` value and `Source{4}` would return an error since there are only four items in the list. Zero-based access also applies to extracting characters from a text value. For example, the `Text.Range("Brett",2,2)` M expression returns the et characters.

The list value type in M is an ordered sequence of values. There are many functions available for analyzing and transforming list values, such as `List.Count()` and `List.Distinct()`. List functions that aggregate the values they contain (for example, `List.Average()`) are often used within grouping queries that invoke the `Table.Group()` function. For a definitive list of all M functions, we refer the reader to the *Power Query M function reference* found here: `https://bit.ly/3bLKJ1M`.

Next we'll look at perhaps one of the most important aspects of M, query folding.

# Power Query M query examples

As demonstrated in the examples thus far, the combination of a mature data warehouse and a layer of SQL view objects within this source may eliminate any need for further data transformations. However, Power BI dataset designers should still be familiar with the fundamentals of M queries and their most common use cases, as it's often necessary to further extend and enhance source data.

The following sections demonstrate three common data transformation scenarios that can be implemented in M. Beyond retrieving the correct results, the M queries also generate SQL statements for execution by the source system via query folding, and comments are included for longer-term maintenance purposes.

If you're new to M query development, you can create a blank query from the **Other** category of data source connectors available within the **Get Data** dialog.

Alternatively, you can duplicate an existing query via the right-click context menu of a query in the **Power Query Editor** and then rename and revise the duplicate query.

## Trailing three years filter

The objective of this example is to retrieve dates from three years prior to the current year through the current date. For example, on December 30th, 2021, the query should retrieve January 1st, 2018 through December 30th, 2021. This requirement ensures that three full years of historical data, plus the current year, is always available to support reporting.

The starting date and current date values for the filter condition are computed via Date and DateTime M functions and assigned variables names (StartDate, CurrentDate). Since the starting date is always January 1st, it's only necessary to compute the starting year and pass this value to the #date constructor.

Finally, the two date variables are passed to the Table.SelectRows() function to implement the filter on the **Reseller Sales** fact table view:

```
let
//Trailing Three Year Date Values
    CurrentDate = DateTime.Date(DateTime.LocalNow()),
    StartYear = Date.Year(CurrentDate)-3,
    StartDate = #date(StartYear,1,1),
//Reseller Sales View
    Source = AdWorksSQLServer,
    ResellerSales = Source{[Schema = "BI", Item = "vFact_ResellerSales"]}
[Data],
//Trailing Three Year Filter
    FilterResellerSales =
        Table.SelectRows(ResellerSales, each Date.From([OrderDate]) >=
StartDate and Date.From([OrderDate]) <= CurrentDate)
in
    FilterResellerSales
```

As shown in the **View Native Query** dialog available in the **Applied Steps** window of the **Power Query Editor**, the custom filter condition is translated into a T-SQL statement for the source SQL Server database to execute:

```
from [BI].[vFact_ResellerSales] as [_]
where [_].[OrderDate] >= convert(datetime2, '2018-01-01 00:00:00') and
[_].[OrderDate] < convert(datetime2, '2021-12-31 00:00:00')
```

Note that the order of the variables in the expression doesn't impact the final query. For example, the two **Reseller Sales** view variables could be specified prior to the three date variables and the final `FilterResellerSales` variable would still generate the same SQL query. Additionally, be advised that M is a case-sensitive language. For example, referencing the variable defined as `StartDate` via the name `Startdate` results in a failure.

Single-line comments can be entered in M queries following the double forward slash (`//`) characters as per the trailing three years example. Multiline or delimited comments start with the (`/*`) characters and end with the (`*/`) characters, just like T-SQL queries for SQL Server.

If the requirement was only to retrieve the trailing three years of data relative to the current date (for example, December 30th, 2018 through December 30th, 2021) the `StartDate` variable could be computed via the `Date.AddYears()` function, as follows:

```
//Trailing three years (e.g. October 18th, 2018 through October 18, 2021)
    CurrentDate = DateTime.Date(DateTime.LocalNow()),
    StartDate = Date.AddYears(CurrentDate,-3)
```

Finally, note that the standard **AdventureWorksDW** database only has reseller sales through 2013 so using the `Date.AddYears()` function to subtract years from the `CurrentDate` variable calculation is necessary if you wish to display results from a standard **AdventureWorksDW** database.

In our next example, we use this trailing three years query but extend it so that in test and production environments all years are loaded.

## Combining queries

Multiple queries can be combined (appended) to one another through the use of the `Table.Combine` function. This function can be extremely useful in situations such as **Folder** queries, where multiple files with the same format need to be appended together into a single table within the data model.

In this example, a parameter called `Mode` has been created with a list of available parameter values of **Dev**, **Test**, and **Prod**. The following query checks the value of this parameter. If the parameter is set to **Dev**, then only the trailing three years are returned using the query from the previous example. Otherwise, the query from the previous example is combined with a table expression that retrieves all additional years. The two table expressions are appended to one another using the `Table.Combine` function:

```
let
//Trailing Three Year Date Values
```

```
    CurrentDate = DateTime.Date(DateTime.LocalNow()),
    StartYear = Date.Year(CurrentDate)-3,
    StartDate = #date(StartYear,1,1),
    Results =
        if Mode = "Dev"
            then Trailing3Years
            else
                Table.Combine(
                    {
                        Trailing3Years,
                        Table.SelectRows(
                            AdWorksSQLServer{[Schema = "BI", Item =
"vFact_ResellerSales"]}[Data],
                            each Date.From([OrderDate]) < StartDate)
                    }
                )
in
    Results
```

In this example, the `Trailing3Years` query would be set to not load into the data model and this query would be used as the main fact table for reseller sales. By using this approach, developers can work with a much smaller local dataset and then easily include all required data when the dataset moves from development to testing and production environments. Staging deployments in this manner is discussed in the *Staged deployments* section of *Chapter 10, Managing Workspaces and Content*.

This example also demonstrates the use of `if` statements, which have an overall format of:

```
if <true/false expression> then <expression> else <expression>
```

In this example, the use of an `if` statement prevents the query from including all rows from the vFact_ResellerSales table when the Mode is set to Dev, providing faster data loading for developers and a smaller overall dataset size.

Our next example also deals with fact tables and involves incremental refresh.

## Incremental refresh for fact tables

Incremental refresh is a power Power BI feature that can greatly decrease refresh times for extremely large fact tables.

Incremental refresh allows only part of the data (new and changed) within a table to be refreshed versus reloading all rows during every refresh cycle, which is the default refresh behavior for Power BI.

Using incremental refresh requires the use of two reserved parameters names, `RangeStart` and `RangeEnd`. These parameters must be defined as a type of date/time. In the following example, the internet sales query is modified to include filtering specific to the implementation of incremental refresh:

```
let
    Source = AdWorksSQLServer,
    InternetSales = Source{[Schema="BI",Item="vFact_InternetSales"]}
[Data],
    FilterRows = Table.SelectRows(InternetSales, each [OrderDateKey] >
ConvertDateKey(RangeStart) and [OrderDateKey] <= ConvertDateKey(RangeEnd))
in
    FilterRows
```

The code in the `FilterRows` step uses the `Table.SelectRows()` function in conjunction with the `RangeStart` and `RangeEnd` parameters as well as a custom function, `ConvertDateKey`. The `ConvertDateKey` function is necessary because the `OrderDateKey` surrogate key column is used. The `OrderDateKey` column is a surrogate key column because it stores the date as an integer value in the form of YYYYMMDD instead of as a date or date/time data type.

The `ConvertDateKey` custom function code is provided next:

```
let ConvertDateKey = (DateTime as datetime) =>
    Date.Year(DateTime) * 10000 + Date.Month(DateTime) * 100 + Date.
Day(DateTime)
in
    ConvertDateKey
```

When filtering the table using the `RangeStart` and `RangeEnd` parameters, it is important that only one of the comparison conditions contains an equal to (=) clause. Otherwise, duplicate data may result since certain rows of data may fulfill the end condition of one refresh cycle and the start condition of the next refresh cycle.

The initial refresh cycle for that dataset loads all rows of data within the dataset and the `RangeStart` parameter is set automatically by the service. The subsequent refresh cycle sets the `RangeEnd` parameter to the current date and time such that only new and updated data is added to the data table.

Next, we'll turn our attention to M query examples for dimensions, starting with the customer query.

## Customer history column

In this example, the goal is to add a column to the customer dimension table that groups the customers into four categories based on the date of their first purchase. Specifically, the new column needs to leverage the existing first purchase date column and assign the customer rows to one of the following four categories—**First Year Customer**, **Second Year Customer**, **Third Year Customer**, and **Legacy Customer**.

Since the column is computed daily with each scheduled refresh, it is used by the sales and marketing teams to focus their efforts on new and older customer segments.

A combination of date functions and conditional logic (if..then..else) is used with the Table. AddColumn() function to produce the new column:

```
let
// Customer History Date Bands
    CurrentDate = DateTime.Date(DateTime.LocalNow()),
    OneYearAgo = Date.AddYears(CurrentDate,-1),
    TwoYearsAgo = Date.AddYears(CurrentDate,-2),
    ThreeYearsAgo = Date.AddYears(CurrentDate,-3),
//Customer Dimension
    Source = AdWorksSQLServer,
    Customer = Source{[Schema = "BI", Item = "vDim_Customer"]}[Data],
    CustomerHistoryColumn = Table.AddColumn(Customer, "Customer History
Segment",
    each
    if [DateFirstPurchase] >= OneYearAgo then "First Year Customer"
    else if [DateFirstPurchase] >= TwoYearsAgo and [Customer First
Purchase Date] < OneYearAgo then "Second Year Customer"
    else if [DateFirstPurchase] >= ThreeYearsAgo and [Customer First
Purchase Date] < TwoYearsAgo then "Third Year Customer"
    else "Legacy Customer", type text)
in
    CustomerHistoryColumn
```

As shown in *Figure 3.13* from the **Power Query Editor**, the **Customer History Segment** column produces one of four text values based on the DateFirstPurchase column:

| 1²3 CustomerKey | ▼ | DateFirstPurchase | ▼ | ᴬᴮc Customer History Segment | ▼ |
|---|---|---|---|---|---|
| 382 | | 11381 | 6/12/2011 | Legacy Customer | |
| 383 | | 11382 | 11/3/2012 | Third Year Customer | |
| 384 | | 11383 | 1/1/2014 | First Year Customer | |
| 385 | | 11384 | 8/2/2013 | Second Year Customer | |

*Figure 3.12: Customer History Segment column in Power Query Editor*

Like the previous M query example of a trailing three year filter, the conditional logic for the derived customer column is also translated into T-SQL via query folding:

```
    [_].[DateFirstPurchase] as [DateFirstPurchase],
    [_].[CommuteDistance] as [CommuteDistance],
    case
        when [_].[DateFirstPurchase] >= convert(date, '2013-12-30')
        then 'First Year Customer'
        when [_].[DateFirstPurchase] >= convert(date, '2012-12-30') and
[_].[DateFirstPurchase] < convert(date, '2013-12-30')
        then 'Second Year Customer'
        when [_].[DateFirstPurchase] >= convert(date, '2011-12-30') and
[_].[DateFirstPurchase] < convert(date, '2012-12-30')
        then 'Third Year Customer'
        else 'Legacy Customer'
    end as [Customer History Segment]
from [BI].[vDim_Customer] as [_]
```

The two dynamic columns (Calendar Year Status and Calendar Month Status) included in the date dimension SQL view earlier in this chapter could also be computed via M functions.

We'll now provide additional details regarding the final parameter to the Table.AddColumn() function, in this case type text.

## Derived column data types

The final parameter to the Table.AddColumn() function is optional but should be specified to define the data type of the new column.

In the Customer History Segment column example, the new column is defined as a text data type. If a whole number column was created, an `Int64.Type` would be specified, such as the following example:

```
MyNewColumn = Table.AddColumn(Product, "My Column", each 5, Int64.Type)
```

If the data type of the column is not defined in the `Table.AddColumn()` function or later in the query via the `Table.TransformColumnTypes()` function, the new column is set as an **Any** data type, as shown in the following screenshot:

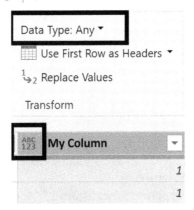

*Figure 3.13: Data Type of Any*

Columns of the **Any** data type are loaded to the data model as a text data type. Dataset designers should ensure that each column in every query has a data type specified. In other words, as a best practice, the **Any** (that is, unknown) data type should not be allowed in M queries.

We'll now move on to providing an additional M query example for the product dimension.

## Product dimension integration

The SQL view for the product dimension referenced in *Chapter 2, Preparing Data Sources*, contained the following four operations:

1. Join the `Product`, `ProductSubcategory`, and `ProductCategory` dimension tables into a single query
2. Create a custom product category group column (for example, Bikes versus Non-Bikes)
3. Apply report-friendly column names with spaces and proper casing
4. Replace any null values in the `Product  Subcategory` and `Product  Category` columns with the `'Undefined'` value

Like almost all operations available to SQL SELECT queries, the same query can also be created via M functions. If the SQL view for the product dimension cannot be created within the data source, the following M query produces the same results:

```
let
    Source = AdWorksSQLServer,
//Product Dimension Table Views
    Product = Source{[Schema = "BI", Item = "vDim_Product"]}[Data],
    ProductSubCat = Source{[Schema = "BI", Item = "vDim_
ProductSubcategory"]}[Data],
    ProductCat = Source{[Schema = "BI", Item = "vDim_ProductCategory"]}
[Data],
//Product Outer Joins
    ProductJoinSubCat = Table.
NestedJoin(Product,"ProductSubcategoryKey",ProductSubCat,
"ProductSubcategoryKey","ProductSubCatTableCol",JoinKind.LeftOuter),
    ProductJoinSubCatCol = Table.
ExpandTableColumn(ProductJoinSubCat,"ProductSubCatTableCol",
{"EnglishProductSubcategoryName",
"ProductCategoryKey"},{"Product Subcategory", "ProductCategoryKey"}),

    ProductJoinCat = Table.NestedJoin(ProductJoinSubCatCol,
"ProductCategoryKey",ProductCat,
"ProductCategoryKey","ProductCatTableCol",JoinKind.LeftOuter),
    ProductJoinCatCol = Table.ExpandTableColumn(ProductJoinCat,
"ProductCatTableCol", {"EnglishProductCategoryName"},{"Product
Category"}),
//Select and Rename Columns
    ProductDimCols = Table.SelectColumns(ProductJoinCatCol,
{"ProductKey","ProductAlternateKey",
"EnglishProductName","Product Subcategory","Product Category"}),
    ProductDimRenameCols = Table.RenameColumns(ProductDimCols,{
        {"ProductKey", "Product Key"},{"ProductAlternateKey","Product
Alternate Key"},{"EnglishProductName","Product Name"}
    }),
//Product Category Group Column
    ProductCatGroupCol = Table.AddColumn(ProductDimRenameCols,
"Product Category Group", each
        if [Product Category] = "Bikes" then "Bikes"
```

```
        else if [Product Category] = null then "Undefined"
        else "Non-Bikes"
,type text),
//Remove Null Values
    UndefinedCatAndSubcat = Table.ReplaceValue(ProductCatGroupCol,null,
"Undefined",Replacer.ReplaceValue,{"Product Subcategory","Product
Category"})
in
    UndefinedCatAndSubcat
```

The three product dimension tables in the dbo schema of the data warehouse are referenced from the AdWorksSQLServer staging query described earlier in this chapter.

The Table.NestedJoin() function is used to execute the equivalent of the LEFT JOIN operations from the SQL view, and the Table.ExpandTableColumn() function extracts and renames the required Product Subcategory and Product Category columns.

Following the selection and renaming of columns, the Product Category group column is created via a conditional expression within the Table.AddColumn() function. Finally, the Table.ReplaceValue() function replaces any null values in the Product Category and Product Subcategory columns with the 'Undefined' text string. The **Power Query Editor** provides a preview of the results as shown in *Figure 3.14*:

| ¹²₃ Product Key | A<sup>B</sup>c Product Alternate Key | A<sup>B</sup>c Product Name | A<sup>B</sup>c Product Subcategory | A<sup>B</sup>c Product Category | A<sup>B</sup>c Product Category Group |
|---|---|---|---|---|---|
| 308 | FR-M94S-38 | HL Mountain Frame - Silver, 38 | Mountain Frames | Components | Non-Bikes |
| 309 | FR-M94S-38 | HL Mountain Frame - Silver, 38 | Mountain Frames | Components | Non-Bikes |
| 310 | BK-R93R-62 | Road-150 Red, 62 | Road Bikes | Bikes | Bikes |
| 311 | BK-R93R-44 | Road-150 Red, 44 | Road Bikes | Bikes | Bikes |

*Figure 3.14: Power Query Editor preview of Product M query*

Despite the additional steps and complexity of this query relative to the previous M query examples (trailing three years filter, Customer History Segment column), the entire query is translated into a single SQL statement and executed by the source SQL Server database. The **View Native Query** option in the **Applied Steps** pane of the **Power Query Editor** reveals the specific syntax of the SQL statement generated via query folding:

```
select [_].[ProductKey] as [Product Key],
    [_].[ProductAlternateKey] as [Product Alternate Key],
    [_].[EnglishProductName] as [Product Name],
    case
        when [_].[EnglishProductSubcategoryName] is null
```

```
        then 'Undefined'
        else [_].[EnglishProductSubcategoryName]
    end as [Product Subcategory],
    case
        when [_].[EnglishProductCategoryName] is null
        then 'Undefined'
        else [_].[EnglishProductCategoryName]
    end as [Product Category],
    case
        when [_].[EnglishProductCategoryName] = 'Bikes' and [_].
[EnglishProductCategoryName] is not null
        then 'Bikes'
        when [_].[EnglishProductCategoryName] is null
        then 'Undefined'
        else 'Non-Bikes'
    end as [Product Category Group]
from
```

Note that a dedicated SQL view object in the BI schema (for example, BI.vDim_ProductSubcategory) is accessed for each of the three product dimension tables. As per the *SQL views* section of *Chapter 2, Preparing Data Sources*, it's recommended to always access SQL views from Power BI datasets, as this declares a dependency with the source tables.

Note that the Table.Join() function could not be used in this scenario given the requirement for a left outer join and the presence of common column names. With a left outer join, the presence of common column names, such as ProductSubcategoryKey or ProductCategoryKey, for the tables in the join operation would cause an error.

Although a left outer join is the default behavior of the Table.NestedJoin() function, it's recommended to explicitly specify the join kind (for example, JoinKind.Inner, JoinKind. LeftOuter, or JoinKind.LeftAnti) as per the ProductJoinSubCat and ProductJoinCat variables of the M query. As a refresher of the types of joins available in Power Query, please refer to the following link: https://bit.ly/3wWquJK.

Note that, in general, if the Table.Join function can be used then it should be preferred over Table.NestedJoin. The reason is that Table.NestedJoin uses local resources to perform the join operation while Table.Join can be folded back to the source system and is thus generally more performant. It is worth noting then that the **Merge** operation available in the **Power Query Editor graphical user interface (GUI)** performs a Table.NestedJoin by default.

Whenever any unstructured or business user-owned data sources are used as sources for a Power BI dataset, it's usually appropriate to implement additional data quality and error-handling logic within the M query.

For example, a step that invokes the `Table.Distinct()` function could be added to the **Sales and Margin Plan** query that retrieves data from the Excel workbook to remove any duplicate rows. Additionally, the third parameter of the `Table.SelectColumns()` function (for example, `MissingField.UseNull`) can be used to account for scenarios in which source columns have been renamed or removed.

While the M language provides extensive data transformation capabilities on its own, some experienced data professionals may be more comfortable with other languages like R and Python. We cover this topic in the next example.

## R and Python script transformation

It's possible to execute an R or Python script within an M query as part of a data transformation process.

As shown in *Figure 3.15*, the **Run R script** and **Run Python script** commands are available on the **Transform** tab of the **Power Query Editor** in Power BI Desktop:

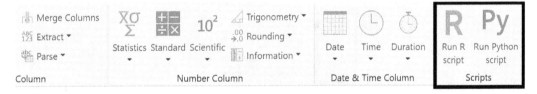

### Run R script

Enter R scripts into the editor to transform and shape your data.

Script

```
# 'dataset' holds the input data for this script
```

*Figure 3.15: Run R script and Run Python script commands in Power Query Editor*

To execute an R script or Python script in Power BI Desktop, R or Python need to be installed on the local machine as well as any packages used by the script. If the **data gateway** is used, R, Python, and appropriate packages must be installed on the server running the data gateway as well. Most importantly, for the scripts to work properly when the dataset is published to the Power BI service, the privacy levels for the data sources need to be set to **Public**.

For most organizations, this limitation rules out the use of R and Python scripts for data transformations in Power BI. Additionally, the presence of R and Python scripts adds another layer of complexity to a solution that already includes SQL, M, and DAX.

Let's next look at another way to create Power Query (M) queries using **dataflows**.

# Dataflows

Simply stated, **dataflows** are Power Query M queries created in the Power BI service. For non-My Workspace workspaces, the Power BI service provides an interface nearly identical to the **Power Query Editor** in Power BI Desktop for creating and editing Power Query queries.

Dataflows access source systems in the same manner as Power Query queries created in **Power Query Editor** within Power BI Desktop. However, the data ingested from these queries for import mode dataflows is stored in Dataverse-compliant folders within an Azure Data Lake Storage Gen2 instance. Dataflows can also be created for DirectQuery access to source systems.

There are several key advantages to the use of dataflows within enterprise BI. Chief among these advantages is reusability. Once created, a dataflow can be used as a data source within multiple different Power BI Desktop files during dataset design. Power BI dataflows are an option when using the **Get data** feature in both Power BI Desktop and **Power Query Editor** as shown in *Figure 3.16*:

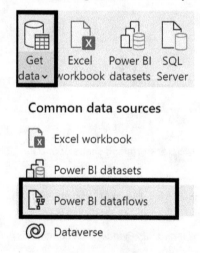

*Figure 3.16: Power BI dataflows as a data source*

This means that the data transformation logic within a query can be created once and leveraged across multiple different datasets, making the creation of datasets more efficient, more standardized, and less error-prone.

The second key advantage of dataflows for import mode datasets is that the dataflow isolates the source systems from the Power BI datasets. This means that refreshes from Power BI datasets pull from the Azure Data Lake Storage Gen2 instance instead of the source systems themselves, keeping the loading of data refreshes from multiple Power BI datasets from impacting the source systems.

The dataflow can be refreshed once, and then refreshes in all Power BI datasets utilizing the dataflow only impact the highly scalable Azure Data Lake Storage Gen2 instance and not the source systems. This is even more important if the source data system accessed by the dataflow is on-premises and requires a data gateway.

Since the data pulled by Power BI Desktop datasets is in an Azure Data Lake Storage Gen2 instance, no data gateway is required for refreshing these datasets. The data gateway is only required when refreshing the dataflow itself.

The isolation of the source data systems from the Power BI datasets also has an advantage in terms of security. Instead of providing access credentials for data source systems to multiple dataset designers, the enterprise BI team can now simply provide authorization credentials to the dataflow and not the source systems.

While an idealized state for enterprise BI would include a single data warehouse and a corresponding single Power BI dataset for reporting purposes, such an idealized state is often not possible. For example, a customized product list might be stored by the marketing team in a SharePoint site and this data is not planned to be included in the corporate data warehouse any time soon. However, this list is applicable to multiple Power BI datasets that support sales, marketing, and supply chain.

In such a situation, a single dataflow could be created that connects to this source file and applies the necessary transforms. The sales, marketing, and supply chain datasets could then all connect to this one dataflow such that any updates to this central source naturally flow to all dependent datasets.

As mentioned, dataflows provide several key advantages. When used within Power BI Premium, additional features are exposed and available for dataflows.

## Power BI Premium dataflow features

Power BI Premium supports additional dataflow features, including the **Enhanced compute engine**, **DirectQuery**, **Computed entities**, **Linked entities**, **Incremental refresh**, and machine learning capabilities in the form of **AutoML**.

The enhanced compute engine can dramatically decrease refresh speeds for complex transformations such as joins, group by, filter, and distinct operations. As previously mentioned, creating dataflows for DirectQuery sources is supported but only in Premium. It is important to note that composite models that have both import and DirectQuery sources currently do not support the inclusion of dataflows as a data source within these composite models.

Computed entities allow you to perform in-storage computations, combining data from multiple dataflows into a new, merged entity or enhancing an existing entity. For example, a Product dataflow could be enhanced by adding information from Product Category and Product Subcategory dataflows.

Similar to computed entities, linked entities allow you to reference other dataflows in order to perform calculations (computed entities) or establish a table that serves as a single source of truth for other dataflows.

Finally, AutoML automates the data science behind the creation of **machine learning (ML)** models, enabling the automatic recognition of patterns, sentiment analysis, and other ML use cases.

To wrap up this chapter, we'll explore the different editing tools used to create M queries.

# Power Query M editing tools

Similar to other languages and project types, code-editing tools are available to support the development, documentation, and version control of M queries.

In addition to the Advanced Editor within Power BI Desktop and the dataflows editing interface of the Power BI service, dataset designers can use Visual Studio or Visual Studio Code to author and manage the M queries for Power BI and other Microsoft projects. These tools include common development features, such as IntelliSense, syntax highlighting, and integrated source control.

We'll explore the different tools supporting M query development in the following sections.

## Advanced Editor

In Power BI Desktop and for dataflows in the Power BI service, the M code for each query can be accessed from the **Advanced Editor** window within the **Power Query Editor**.

With the **Power Query Editor** open, select a query of interest from the list of queries on the left and click on the **Advanced Editor** icon from the **Home** tab to access the **Advanced Editor** dialog shown in *Figure 3.17*:

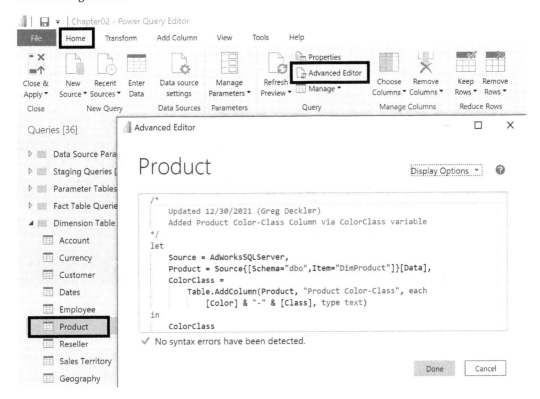

*Figure 3.17: Advanced Editor in Power BI Desktop*

Experienced M query authors often use the data transformation icons available in the **Power Query Editor** to quickly produce an initial version of one or a few of the requirements of the query. The author then uses the **Advanced Editor** or an external M editing tool to analyze the M code generated by the **Power Query Editor** and can revise or enhance this code, such as by changing variable names or utilizing optional parameters of certain M functions.

For the most common and simple data transformation tasks, such as filtering out rows based on one value of a column (for example, State = "Kansas"), the M code generated by the **Power Query Editor** usually requires minimal revision. For more complex queries with custom or less common requirements, the **Power Query Editor** graphical interface is less helpful and a greater level of direct M development is necessary.

While the Advanced Editor is convenient, it lacks proper source control integration, a deficiency that can be solved through the use of alternative tools such as Visual Studio Code.

# Visual Studio Code

Visual Studio Code is a free, lightweight code-editing tool from Microsoft that's available on all platforms (Windows, Mac, and Linux). An extension for Visual Studio Code, **Power Query / M Language**, provides code-editing support for the Power Query M language as shown in *Figure 3.18*:

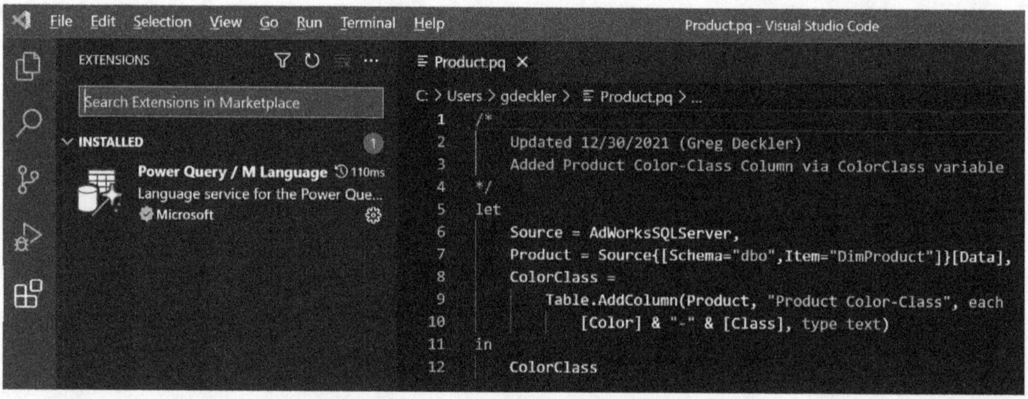

*Figure 3.18: M query in Visual Studio Code*

In this example, the same `Product` query viewed in the Advanced Editor of Power BI Desktop has been copied into a Visual Studio Code file and saved with a (.pq) file extension. Once saved with a supported file extension, code-editing features, such as colorization, auto-closing, and surrounding detection, are applied. M query files can be opened and saved with the following four file extensions—.m, .M, .pq, and .PQ.

It must be noted that M code developed in Visual Studio Code cannot be used directly by Power BI. The code must be copied from Visual Studio Code or a source control repository and pasted into Advanced Editor. However, experienced enterprise BI teams recognize the importance of proper version control, especially as it relates to changes to underlying data tables and data transformations.

Since the .pq file extension is used by the Power Query SDK for Visual Studio, this file extension is recommended for storing M queries in Visual Studio Code, as well as in Visual Studio, which we'll cover in the next section.

# Visual Studio

Visual Studio is the full-featured version of the more lightweight Visual Studio Code and is a premier **integrated development environment** (IDE) in wide use throughout the technology industry. For Visual Studio 2015 and later, the Power Query SDK can be used to create data connector and M query projects, as shown in *Figure 3.19*:

*Figure 3.19: Power Query project types in Visual Studio*

With a new PQ file solution and project in Visual Studio, the M queries of a Power BI dataset can be added as separate (.pq) files, as shown in *Figure 3.20*:

*Figure 3.20: Power Query project in Visual Studio 2019*

Unlike the extension for Visual Studio Code, the file extension type for Power Query projects is exclusively to (.pq. Most importantly, full M language IntelliSense is supported, making it dramatically easier to find M functions relevant to specific data transformation operations. IntelliSense is the general term for code-editing features such as code completion, content assist (parameter information), and code hinting.

Moreover, unlike the extension for Visual Studio Code, M queries can be executed from within Visual Studio via the Power Query SDK for Visual Studio. To execute an M query in Visual Studio, such as in the preceding example, click the **Start** button on the toolbar (green play icon) or press the *F5* key.

You can also right-click the Power Query project (for example, **AdWorks Enterprise Import**) to configure properties of the M query project, such as the maximum output rows to return and whether native queries can be executed.

To install the Power Query SDK for Visual Studio, access the **Visual Studio Marketplace (Extensions | Manage Extensions)** and search for the name of the extension (**Power Query SDK**).

The Power Query SDK for Visual Studio enables standard integration with source control and project management tools, such as Azure DevOps services (formerly Visual Studio Team Services).

This completes our exploration of connecting to sources and transforming data with M.

## Summary

In this chapter, we've covered many of the components of the data retrieval process used to support the dataset for this project as described in *Chapter 1, Planning Power BI Projects*. This included constructing a data access layer and retrieval process for a dataset and using M queries used to define and load the dimension and fact tables of the dataset.

In the next chapter, we'll leverage the M queries and design techniques described in this chapter to create import and DirectQuery data models.

## Join our community on Discord

Join our community's Discord space for discussions with the author and other readers:
https://discord.gg/q6BPbHEPXp

# 4

# Designing Import, DirectQuery, and Composite Data Models

This chapter utilizes the queries described in *Chapter 3, Connecting To Sources And Transforming Data With M*, to create import, DirectQuery, and composite data models. Relationships are created between fact and dimension tables to enable business users to analyze the fact data for both Internet Sales and Reseller Sales simultaneously by using common dimension tables and across multiple business dates. In addition, business users can compare these fact tables against the Annual Sales and Margin Plan.

This chapter also contains recommended practices for model metadata such as assigning data categories to columns and providing users with a simplified field list. Finally, we review common performance analysis tools and optimization techniques for import and DirectQuery data models.

As described in the *Dataset planning* section of *Chapter 1, Planning Power BI Projects*, data models can have modes of either import, DirectQuery, or composite. The implications of the design choices for data models significantly influence many factors of Power BI solutions including optimizations applied to source systems to support DirectQuery access and the configuration of incremental data refresh for import mode fact tables.

In this chapter, we review the following topics:

- Dataset layers
- The data model
- Relationships
- Model metadata

- Optimizing performance

We start by taking a look at the different layers within data models (datasets).

# Dataset layers

As covered in *Chapter 1, Planning Power BI Projects*, and *Chapter 3, Connecting To Sources And Transforming Data With M*, Power BI datasets are composed of three tightly integrated layers, which are all included within a Power BI Desktop file.

The first layer, the M queries described in *Chapter 2, Preparing Data Sources*, connect to data sources and optionally apply data cleansing and transformation processes to this source data to support the Data Model.

The second layer, the Data Model and the subject of this chapter, primarily involves the relationships defined between fact and dimension tables, hierarchies reflecting multiple levels of granularity of a dimension, and metadata properties such as the sort order applied to columns.

The final layer of datasets is discussed in *Chapter 5, Developing DAX Measures and Security Roles*, **Data Analysis Expressions (DAX)** measures. DAX measures leverage the Data Model to deliver analytical insights for presentation in Power BI and other tools.

The term **Data Model** is often used instead of **dataset**, particularly in the context of Analysis Services. Analysis Services Tabular models include the same three layers as Power BI datasets.

In other contexts, however, Data Model refers exclusively to the relationships, measures, and metadata, not the source queries. For this reason, and given the use of the term datasets in the Power BI service, the term dataset (and dataset designer) is recommended.

*Figure 4.1* summarizes the role of each of the three dataset layers:

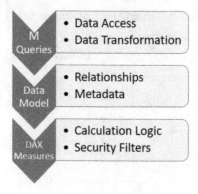

*Figure 4.1: Three layers of datasets*

At the Data Model layer, all data integration and transformations should be complete. For example, while it is certainly possible to create additional columns and tables via DAX calculated columns and tables, other tools such as data warehouse databases, SQL view objects, and M queries are almost always better suited for this need.

Ensure that each layer of the dataset is being used for its intended role. For example, DAX measures should not contain complex logic that attempts to work around data quality issues that can be addressed at the source or in a transformation within a source query. Likewise, DAX measure expressions should not be limited by incorrect data types (for example, a number stored as text) or missing columns on the date table. Dataset designers and data source owners can work together to keep the analytical layers of datasets focused exclusively on analytics.

Before diving into an exploration of the objectives for datasets, we first update the guidance from the first edition of this book.

## Power BI as a superset of Azure Analysis Services

In the first edition of this book, organizations would typically use Power BI for small and simple self-service datasets but provision **Azure Analysis Services (AAS)** or **SQL Server Analysis Services (SSAS)** resources for large models requiring enterprise features such as partitions and object-level security. Microsoft has now closed prior feature and scalability gaps with Analysis Services and added powerful modeling features exclusive to Power BI Premium-hosted datasets.

For example, only a Power BI dataset can be designed to blend import and DirectQuery data sources (composite models), to include one or multiple aggregation tables to accelerate performance over large sources, and only a Power BI dataset can have incremental refresh policies managed by the Power BI service.

Given the new modeling scenarios supported by Power BI exclusive features as well as the reduced management overhead provided by incremental refresh policies, new enterprise models are now typically deployed to Power BI Premium workspaces. Likewise, existing Analysis Services models are commonly migrated to Power BI Premium to take advantage of new enterprise modeling features and to align with Microsoft's product roadmap.

We now move on to dataset objectives.

## Dataset objectives

The intent of a Power BI dataset is to provide a central "source of truth" data source that's easy to use for report authors and analysts, applies all required security policies, and reliably delivers adequate performance at the required scale.

For both Power BI projects and longer-term deployments, it's critical to distinguish Power BI datasets from Power BI reports and dashboards. Although Power BI Desktop is used to develop both datasets and reports, a Power BI dataset is a tabular Analysis Services Data Model internally. Power BI reports, which are also saved as .pbix files, only connect to the dataset and thus exclusively leverage Power BI Desktop's visualization features, such as bookmarks and slicer visuals.

As per *Chapter 1, Planning Power BI Projects*, datasets and reports are also associated with unique technical and non-technical skills. A Power BI report developer, for example, should understand visualization standards, the essential logic and structure of the dataset, and how to distribute this content via Power BI Apps. However, the report developer doesn't necessarily need to know any programming languages and can iterate very quickly on reports and dashboards.

Given that the dataset serves as the bridge between data sources and analytical queries, it's important to proactively evaluate datasets relative to longer-term objectives. Large, consolidated datasets should be designed to support multiple teams and projects and to provide a standard version or definition of core metrics. Although organizations may enable business users to create datasets for specific use cases, corporate BI solutions should not utilize datasets like individual reports for projects or teams.

*Table 4.1* summarizes the primary objectives of datasets and identifies the questions that can be used to evaluate a dataset in relation to each objective:

| Objective | Success criteria |
| --- | --- |
| User interface | How difficult is it for business users to build a report from scratch? |
| | Are users able to easily find the measures and columns needed? |
| Version control | Do the measures align with an official, documented definition? |
| | Are the same dimensions reused across multiple business processes? |
| Data security | Have **row-level security (RLS)** roles been implemented and thoroughly tested? |
| | Are **Azure Activity Directory (AAD)** security groups used to implement security? |
| Performance | Are users able to interact with reports at the speed of thought or, at a minimum, at an acceptable level of performance? |
| | Are the base or primary DAX measures efficient? |
| | Has a repeatable, performance testing process with baseline queries been created? |

| Scalability | Can the dataset support additional business processes and/or history? |
| --- | --- |
| | Can the dataset support additional users and workloads? |
| Analytics | Does the dataset deliver advanced insights (out of the box)? |
| | Are any local (report-level) measures or complex filters being used? |
| Availability | What is the level of confidence in the data sources and the data retrieval process? |
| | Are there dependencies that can be removed or potential errors that can be trapped? |
| | Is the dataset being backed up regularly? |
| Manageability | How difficult is it to implement changes or to troubleshoot issues? |
| | Can existing data transformation and analytical logic be consolidated? |

*Table 4.1: Dataset objectives*

Several of the objectives are self-explanatory, but others, such as availability and manageability, are sometimes overlooked. For example, the same business logic may be built into many individual DAX measures, making the dataset more difficult to maintain as requirements change. Additionally, there may be certain hardcoded dependencies within the M queries that could cause a dataset refresh to fail. Dataset designers and BI teams must balance the need to deliver business value quickly while not compromising the sustainability of the solution.

To simplify individual measures and improve manageability, common logic can be built into a small subset of hidden DAX measures. The DAX measures visible in the fields list can reference these hidden measures and thus automatically update if any changes are necessary. This is very similar to parameters and data source staging queries in M as per *Chapter 3, Connecting To Sources And Transforming Data With M*. Examples of centralizing DAX logic are provided later in this chapter within the *Parameter tables* section.

Now that we have covered dataset objectives, we next consider how objectives might compete with one another.

## Competing objectives

As a dataset is expanded to support more dimension and fact tables, advanced analytics, and more business users, it may be necessary to compromise certain objectives in order to deliver others.

A common example is the desire to maintain in-memory performance over very large source tables in the hundreds of millions or even billions of rows. In this case, as it may not be technically feasible or desirable to support the scalability with in-memory import mode tables, a composite model could be created containing a DirectQuery reference to the large fact table and an import (in-memory) aggregation table designed to resolve common, summary-level report queries.

In addition to competing objectives, external factors can also influence dataset design.

## External factors

Just like any other database, a well-designed Power BI dataset may still fail to deliver its objectives due to external factors. For example, Power BI reports can be created with wide, data-extract like table visuals which result in expensive, inefficient queries given the columnar data store of Power BI datasets. Likewise, report authors may try to include 12-15 or more visualizations on the same report page resulting in throttling or performance issues as many users attempt to access this report page concurrently.

Additionally, even when the compression of an import mode dataset is maximized and the DAX measures are efficient, there may be insufficient hardware resources available to support the given reporting workload. It's the responsibility of the Power BI admin, as described in *Chapter 1, Planning Power BI Projects*, and potentially any delegated capacity administrators to utilize the monitoring capabilities of Power BI and to provision the necessary resources to ensure sufficient performance.

Now that the various design objectives, considerations, and external factors are understood, we turn our attention to the dataset or data model itself.

# The Data Model

The Data Model layer of the Power BI dataset consists of the **Model view**, the **Data view**, and the **Fields** list exposed in the **Report view**. Each of the three views in Power BI Desktop is accessible via an icon in the top-left menu below the toolbar, although the **Data view** is exclusively available to import mode and composite datasets.

Let's first take a look at the Model view.

## The Model view

The Model view provides the equivalent of a database diagram specific to the tables loaded to the dataset. The relationship lines and icons identify the cardinality of the relationship such as the parent table (1) having a one-to-many (*) relationship with the child table.

A solid line indicates that the relationship is active, while a dotted line denotes an inactive relationship that can only be activated via the USERELATIONSHIP() DAX expression.

The arrow icons on the relationship lines advise whether cross-filtering is single-directional (one arrow → one way) or bidirectional (two arrows). Composite models introduced the concept of limited or weak relationships. Weak relationships are displayed with breaks in the relationship line at either end and semi-circle line endings.

*Figure 4.2* displays an example of the Model view. In *Figure 4.2*, only the **Reseller** to **Reseller Sales** relationship is bidirectional and the relationships between all tables are active:

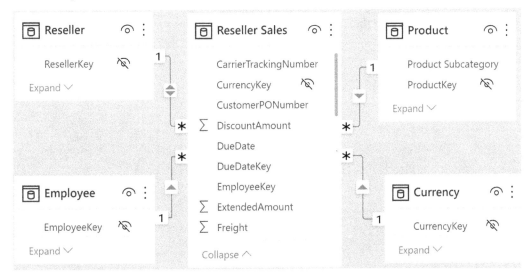

*Figure 4.2: Model view*

As shown in *Figure 4.2* referencing the **Reseller Sales** tab, multiple views or layouts for the model can be created in the Model view. Creating multiple layout diagrams such as one per fact table is a good practice similar to creating and maintaining bus matrix documentation. Particularly with larger models involving many tables, the ability to quickly view a model layout to understand the tables and relationships relevant to a given scenario such as the **Reseller Sales** table and its relationships makes the dataset more manageable.

Also shown in *Figure 4.2*, the bidirectional cross-filtering relationship between the **Reseller** table and the **Reseller Sales** table, a filter applied to the **Employee** table would filter the **Reseller Sales** table and then also filter the **Reseller** dimension table.

Any column with a slashed circle and arc icon next to it on the right indicates that the column is not visible in the Report view. For certain tables that are only used for internal logic, such as bridge tables or measure support, the entire table can be hidden by clicking the circle and arc ("eyeball") icon to the right of the table name. Certain settings, such as **Custom format strings**, can only be accessed via the Model view's **Properties** pane.

Double-clicking a relationship line, or right-clicking the relationship line and choosing **Properties**, displays the **Edit relationship** dialog which displays and allows you to modify the columns defining the relationship, the **Cardinality (One to one 1:1, One to many 1:*, Many to one *:1, Many to many *:*)**, the **Cross-filter direction (Single or Both)**, and whether the relationship is active or passive. The **Edit relationship** dialog is shown in *Figure 4.3*.

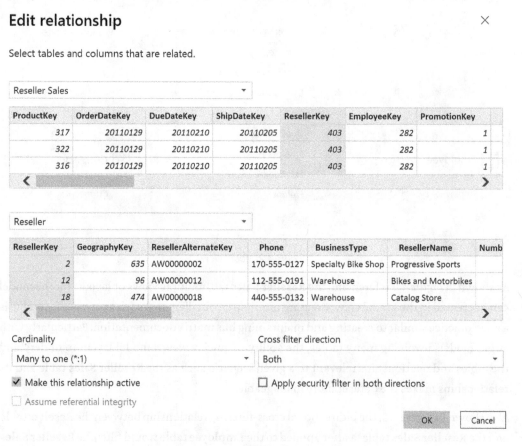

*Figure 4.3: Edit relationship dialog*

The bidirectional relationship between **Reseller** and **Reseller Sales** from this example is only intended to demonstrate the graphical representation of relationships in the Model view. Bidirectional relationships **(Both)** should only be applied in specific scenarios, as described in the *Bidirectional relationships* section later in this chapter.

*Figure 4.4* displays the Model view for a similar data model built as a composite data model.

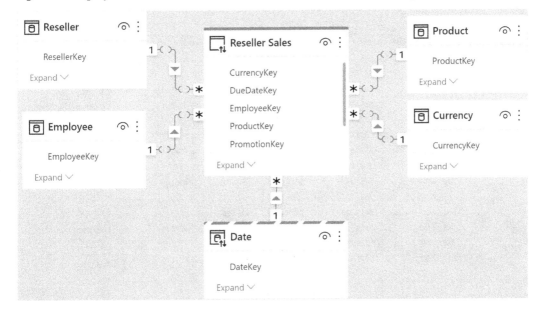

*Figure 4.4: Composite data model*

In *Figure 4.4*, the **Reseller**, **Employee**, **Product** and **Currency** tables are import mode tables. The **Reseller Sales** table is a DirectQuery mode table as designated by the solid bar above the table name. Finally, the **Date** table is a a **Dual** mode table, meaning that this table supports both import and DirectQuery. Dual mode tables have a dashed line above their table names.

Notice that the relationship lines are broken between the **Reseller Sales** table and the import mode tables. This designates a weak relationship between these tables since they are using different **Storage modes**.

However, since the **Dates** table is **Dual** mode, its relationship with **Reseller Sales** is not a weak relationship since both support DirectQuery. It is important to note that only DirectQuery tables can be switched to **Dual** mode using the **Advanced** section of the Model view's **Properties** pane.

We next explore the Data view.

# The Data view

The **Data** view provides visibility to the imported rows for each table as well as important metadata, such as the count of rows and the distinct values for columns. In *Figure 4.5*, the **Freight** column of the **Reseller Sales** table has been selected in the **Data** view, as indicated by the vertical bar to the left of the table icon at the top left:

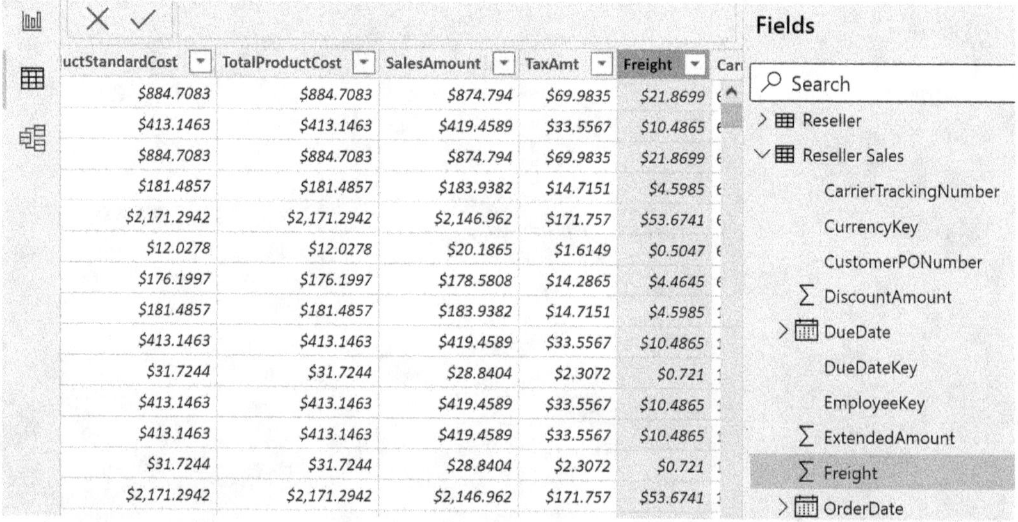

*Figure 4.5: Data view*

Metadata of the column and/or table selected is displayed at the bottom of the Data view window. For example, selecting the **Freight** column as per *Figure 4.4* results in a status message noting **60,855** rows for the **Reseller Sales** table and **1,416** distinct values for the **Freight** column. If only the table name is selected from the **Fields List**, only the count of rows imported to the table is displayed at the bottom.

The count of rows, and particularly the count of distinct values in a column, is of critical importance to import mode datasets. Columns with many unique values, such as primary keys or highly precise numeric columns (that is, 3.123456), consume much more memory than columns with many repeating values. Additionally, as a columnar database, the columns with a larger memory footprint also require more time to scan in order to resolve report queries.

DirectQuery datasets do not include the Data view and thus common modeling features, such as setting the data format of columns and measures, can only be accessed via the **Column tools** tab in the Report view. The dataset designer of a DirectQuery dataset would select the column or measure from the **Fields** list in the Report view and then access the relevant metadata property from the **Column tools** tab, such as **Data category** and **Sort by column**.

The availability of the Data view and its supporting metadata (for example, count of rows, discount count of values) is a modeling convenience of import mode datasets over DirectQuery datasets. In the absence of the Data view, DirectQuery modelers can use table report visuals on the Report view to sample or preview the values and formatting of columns and measures.

We now explore the final view, the **Report** view.

# The Report view

The **Report** view is primarily used for developing visualizations, but it also supports modeling features, such as the creation of user-defined hierarchies. *Figure 4.6* is a screenshot of a DirectQuery dataset where the **City** column of the **Customer** table is selected in the **Fields** list:

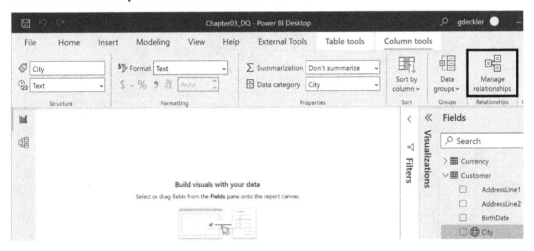

*Figure 4.6: Modeling options in Report view*

The modeling features in the **Report** view are broken up between four different tabs, the **Modeling** tab, **Table tools** tab, **Column tools** tab, and **Measure tools** tab (not shown in *Figure 4.6* but appearing instead of **Column tools** when a measure is selected).

The **Column tools** tab of the **Report** view provides access to column metadata for both import and DirectQuery tables while the **Measures tools** tab provides access to similar metadata for measures. As shown in *Figure 4.6*, the **Data Category** and **Default Summarization** metadata properties for the **City** column have been set to **City** and **Don't summarize**, respectively.

The **Modeling** tab of the Report view provides import and DirectQuery datasets access to common modeling features, such as managing relationships, creating new DAX measures and columns, and accessing RLS roles, although some of these functions are available on the **Table tools** and **Column tools** tabs as well, such as **Manage relationships**.

In terms of data modeling, the Model view and the **Manage relationships** dialog shown in *Figure 4.7* are the most fundamental interfaces as these definitions impact the behavior of DAX measures and report queries:

## Manage relationships                                                          ✕

| Active | From: Table (Column) | To: Table (Column) |
|:---:|---|---|
| ✓ | Employee (SalesTerritoryKey) | Sales Territory (SalesTerritoryKey) |
| ✓ | Internet Sales (DueDateKey) | Date (DateKey) |
| ✓ | Reseller Sales (CurrencyKey) | Currency (CurrencyKey) |
| ✓ | Reseller Sales (DueDateKey) | Date (DateKey) |
| ✓ | Reseller Sales (EmployeeKey) | Employee (EmployeeKey) |
| ✓ | Reseller Sales (ProductKey) | Product (ProductKey) |
| ✓ | Reseller Sales (ResellerKey) | Reseller (ResellerKey) |
| ✓ | Sales and Margin Plan (Sales Territory Region) | Sales Territory (SalesTerritoryRegion) |

```
  New...        Autodetect...        Edit...        Delete

                                                    Close
```

*Figure 4.7: Manage relationships dialog*

Relationships can be created, edited, and deleted from the **Manage relationships** dialog. For larger models with many tables and relationships, the dataset designer can utilize both the **Manage relationships** dialog and the Model view.

With the various different views explained, we next turn our attention to the different types of tables present in most data models, starting with fact tables.

## Fact tables

There are three fact tables for this dataset—Internet Sales, Reseller Sales, and the Sales and Margin Plan. The ability to analyze and filter two or all three of these tables concurrently via common dimensions, such as Date, Product, and Sales Territory, is what gives this dataset its analytical value to the business.

A Power BI report could contain visualizations comparing total Adventure Works Sales (Internet Sales plus Reseller Sales) to the overall Sales and Margin Plan. This same report could also include detailed visualizations that explain higher-level outcomes, such as the growth in online customers or changes in the Reseller Sales margin rates:

| BUSINESS PROCESSES | SHARED DIMENSIONS | | | | | | | |
|---|---|---|---|---|---|---|---|---|
| | Currency | Customer | Date | Employee | Product | Promotion | Reseller | Sales Territory |
| Internet Sales | ✓ | ✓ | ✓ | | ✓ | ✓ | | ✓ |
| Reseller Sales | ✓ | | ✓ | ✓ | ✓ | ✓ | ✓ | ✓ |
| Sales and Margin Plan | | | ✓ | | ✓ | | | ✓ |

*Figure 4.8: Data Warehouse Bus Matrix*

Each checkmark symbol in *Figure 4.8* represents the existence of a relationship implemented either directly between the fact and dimension tables in the Data Model or, in the case of the Sales and Margin Plan, via bridge tables. See *Chapter 1, Planning Power BI Projects*, for more details on the Data Warehouse Bus Matrix.

The Sales and Margin Plan is at a lower grain (less granular) than the Internet Sales and Reseller Sales fact tables and thus cannot be filtered directly by columns such as Product Name. For the Sales and Margin Plan fact table, an alternative model design, including bridge tables and conditional DAX measures, is used to support cross-filtering from the Product, Sales Territory, and Date dimension tables. See the *Bridge tables* section later in this chapter for more details.

We next provide more detail related to fact table columns.

## Fact table columns

Fact tables should only contain columns that are needed for relationships to dimension tables and numeric columns that are referenced by DAX measures. In some models, an additional column that isn't modeled in a dimension table and is needed for analysis, such as Sales Order Number, may also be included in a fact table.

Given their size and central role in the dataset, fact tables often receive much greater analysis to deliver optimal performance and scalability. Extremely large fact tables may be good candidates for DirectQuery mode tables within a composite model if their size exceeds the capacity of an import mode only dataset.

*Figure 4.9* shows a T-SQL query of the Reseller Sales source fact table where columns are computed that produce the same values as the ExtendedAmount, SalesAmount, and TotalProductCost columns:

```
SELECT
    FORMAT(SUM(F.ExtendedAmount),'C','en-us')[Extended Amount]
  , FORMAT(SUM(F.OrderQuantity*F.UnitPrice),'C','en-us')[Extended Amount Calc]
  , FORMAT(SUM(F.SalesAmount),'C','en-us')[Sales Amount]
  , FORMAT(SUM((F.OrderQuantity*F.UnitPrice)-F.DiscountAmount),'C','en-us')[Sales Amount Calc]
  , FORMAT(SUM(F.TotalProductCost),'C','en-us')[Total Product Cost]
  , FORMAT(SUM(F.OrderQuantity*F.ProductStandardCost),'C','en-us')[Total Prod Cost Calc]
  FROM [AdventureWorksDW2019].[dbo].[FactResellerSales] as F;
```

Results / Messages

| Extended Amount | Extended Amount Calc | Sales Amount | Sales Amount Calc | Total Product Cost | Total Prod Cost Calc |
|---|---|---|---|---|---|
| $80,978,104.87 | $80,978,104.87 | $80,450,596.98 | $80,450,596.94 | $79,980,114.38 | $79,980,114.38 |

*Figure 4.9: Reseller Sales fact column logic*

Only the UnitPrice, OrderQuantity, DiscountAmount, and ProductStandardCost columns are needed for the import mode dataset since DAX measures can be written to embed the necessary logic (for example, UnitPrice * OrderQuantity) for the ExtendedAmount, SalesAmount, and TotalProductCost columns.

By not importing these columns to the Data Model, a significant amount of data storage is saved and query performance is not compromised. Columns with few unique values, such as OrderQuantity, can be highly compressed by import mode datasets and thus are lightweight to store and fast to scan to resolve report queries.

The same three columns can also be removed from the Internet Sales fact table. The SUMX() function is used in the DAX measures and only references the source columns (OrderQuantity, UnitPrice, and ProductStandardCost).

The $0.04 difference between the sum of the Sales Amount column and the Sales Amount Calc expression is caused by the DiscountAmount column being stored as a float (approximate) data type. In almost every scenario, a variance this small ($.04 out of $80.4 M) is acceptable to obtain the scalability benefit of not importing a fact table column.

If the SQL View for the fact table is exclusively utilized by this dataset, then the three columns can be removed there. If the SQL View cannot be modified, then the three columns can be removed via an M query:

```
let
    Source = Sql.Database("localhost\MSSQLSERVERDEV",
"AdventureWorksDW2019"),
    BI_vFact_ResellerSales = Source{[Schema="BI",Item="vFact_
ResellerSales"]}[Data],
    RemoveColumns = Table.RemoveColumns(BI_vFact_
ResellerSales,{"ExtendedAmount", "TotalProductCost", "SalesAmount"})
in
    RemoveColumns
```

The `Table.RemoveColumns()` function excludes three columns from the source SQL View, as these columns only represent derived values from other columns that are included in the query. Therefore, for an import mode dataset, DAX measures can be written to efficiently implement these simple calculations via the source columns, such as `Unit Price` and `Order Quantity`.

However, for a DirectQuery dataset, these derived columns (for example, `TotalProductCost`) would not be removed due to the performance advantage of the `SUM()` SQL expressions referencing individual columns. The following chapter, *Chapter 5, Developing DAX Measures and Security Roles*, contains details on implementing these DAX measures and other measure expressions.

Along with understanding fact columns, it is also important to pay attention to fact column data types.

## Fact column data types

It's essential that the numeric columns of fact tables are assigned to the appropriate data types. All integer columns, such as `OrderQuantity`, should be stored as a **Whole number** data type, and decimal numbers are stored as either a **Fixed decimal number** or as a **Decimal number**. If four decimal places is sufficient precision, a **Fixed decimal number** type should be used to avoid rounding errors and the additional storage and performance costs of the **Decimal number** type.

In *Figure 4.10*, the Freight column is stored as a **Fixed decimal number** type and, thus, despite a format of six decimal places, only four significant digits are displayed to the right of the decimal place:

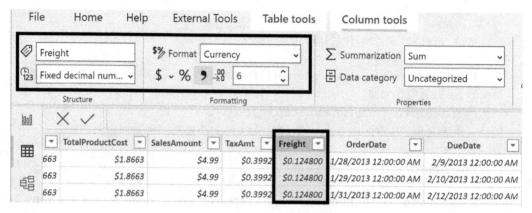

*Figure 4.10: Fixed decimal number data type*

Dataset designers should check the numeric columns of fact tables and ensure that the appropriate data type has been assigned for each column. For example, certain scientific columns may require the deep precision available for decimal number types (15 significant digits), while accounting or financial columns generally need to be exact and thus the internal (19, 4) data type of a **Fixed decimal number** type is appropriate.

Note that the result of aggregated expressions against this fixed decimal column is a number of the same type and, therefore, to avoid overflow calculation errors, also needs to fit the (19, 4) data type. The *Numeric Datatypes* section in *Chapter 3*, *Connecting to Sources and Transforming Data with M*, provides details on the relationship between M data types and data types in the Data Model, as well as the function for converting column types in M queries.

The Data view shown in *Figure 4.10* is not available for DirectQuery datasets. For DirectQuery datasets, the data types of columns should be set and managed at the data source table level such that Power BI only reflects these types. Revising data types during report query execution, either via SQL views in the data source or the M queries in Power BI, can significantly degrade the performance of DirectQuery datasets.

Finishing our exploration of fact tables, we next explain fact-to-dimension relationships.

# Fact-to-dimension relationships

Data models often follow a star schema pattern where multiple dimension tables are related to a single fact table thus forming a "star" pattern when viewed visually. An example of this "star" is shown in *Figure 4.2*.

To create the Data Model relationships identified in the Data Warehouse Bus Matrix from *Figure 4.8*, follow these steps:

1. Click **Manage Relationships** from the **Modeling** tab in the **Report** view.

2. From the **Manage relationships** dialog, click the **New...** command button at the bottom to open the **Create relationship** dialog.

3. Choose the fact table, such as Internet Sales, for the top table via the dropdown and then select the dimension table as shown in *Figure 4.11*:

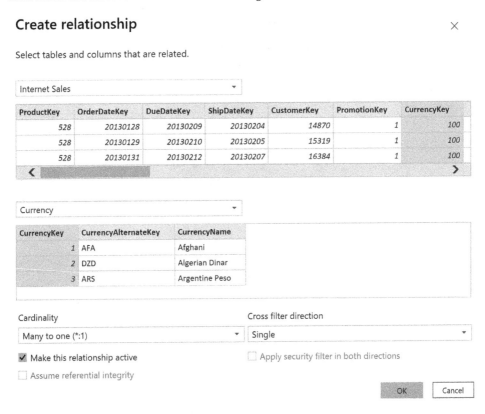

*Figure 4.11: Creating a relationship for the import mode dataset*

If the relationship columns have the same name, such as CurrencyKey in this example, Power BI automatically selects the columns to define the relationship. Almost all relationships follow this **Many to one(\*:1)** or fact-to-dimension pattern with the **Cross-filter direction** property set to **Single** and the relationship set to active.

The two columns used for defining each relationship should be of the same data type. In most relationships, both columns are of the whole number data type as only a numeric value can be used with slowly changing dimensions. For example, a ProductKey column could use the values 12, 17, and 27 to represent three time periods for a single product as certain attributes of the product changed over time.

As more relationships are created, it can be helpful to switch to the Model view and move or organize the dimension tables around the fact table. The Model view can make it clear when additional relationships need to be defined and can be useful in explaining the model to report authors and users.

4.  Click the **OK** button to create the relationship and repeat this process to build the planned star schema relationships for both the Internet Sales and Reseller Sales fact tables, as shown in *Figure 4.12*:

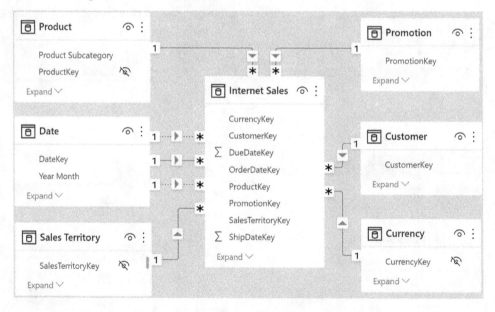

*Figure 4.12: Internet Sales relationships*

All relationships from Internet Sales to a dimension table are active (solid line) except for two additional relationships to the Date dimension table.

In this dataset, the OrderDate is used as the active relationship, but two additional inactive (dotted-line) relationships are created based on the DueDate and ShipDate columns of the fact table. DAX measures can be created to invoke these alternative relationships via the USERELATIONSHIP() DAX function, as shown in the following example:

```
Internet Net Sales (Due Date) = CALCULATE([Internet Net Sales],
USERELATIONSHIP('Internet Sales'[DueDateKey],'Date'[DateKey]))

Internet Net Sales (Ship Date) = CALCULATE([Internet Net
Sales],USERELATIONSHIP('Internet Sales'[ShipDateKey],'Date'[DateKey]))
```

The inactive relationships and their corresponding measures enable report visualizations based on a single date dimension table, such as the following table:

| | 2013-Oct | 2013-Nov | 2013-Dec | 2014-Jan | 2014-Feb | Total |
|---|---|---|---|---|---|---|
| **Internet Net Sales** | $1,673,293.41 | $1,780,920.06 | $1,874,360.29 | $45,694.72 | | **$29,358,677.22** |
| **Internet Net Sales (Due Date)** | $1,524,743.03 | $1,822,940.29 | $1,972,871.34 | $609,262.49 | $15,832.23 | **$29,358,677.22** |
| **Internet Net Sales (Ship Date)** | $1,596,816.34 | $1,835,967.41 | $2,001,722.50 | $289,446.76 | $7,716.35 | **$29,358,677.22** |

*Figure 4.13: Measures with active and inactive relationships*

In this scenario, the Internet Net Sales measure uses the active relationship based on **Order Date** by default, but the other measures override this relationship via the CALCULATE() and USERELATIONSHIP() functions.

A common alternative approach to inactive relationships is to load additional date dimension tables and create active relationships for each additional date column in the fact table (for example, DueDate, ShipDate) to these tables. The columns for these additional date tables can be named to avoid confusion with other date columns (for example, Ship Date Calendar Year) and some teams or organizations are more comfortable with table relationships than DAX measures.

Additionally, this design allows for intuitive matrix-style visualizations with two separate date dimensions (ShipDate, OrderDate) on the $x$ and $y$ axes filtering a single measure via active relationships.

For DirectQuery datasets, the **Assume referential integrity** relationship property is critical for performance as this determines whether inner- or outer-join SQL statements are generated to resolve report queries. Assume referential integrity means that the column on the one side of the relationship is never null or blank and that a corresponding value always exists on the many side of the relationship.

When enabled, as shown in *Figure 4.14*, inner-join SQL queries are passed to the source system when report queries require columns or logic from both tables of the relationship:

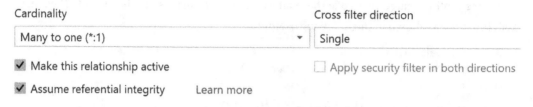

*Figure 4.14: Assume referential integrity*

If **Assume referential integrity** is not enabled, outer-join SQL queries are generated to ensure that all necessary rows from the fact table or many sides of the relationship are retrieved to resolve the report query.

The query optimizers within supported DirectQuery sources, such as SQL Server and Oracle, are able to produce much more efficient query execution plans when presented with inner-join SQL statements. Of course, improved performance is of no value if the outer join is necessary to return the correct results, thus it's essential for referential integrity violations in the source system to be addressed.

Having finished our exploration of fact tables, we next turn our attention to dimension tables.

## Dimension tables

The columns of dimension tables give the measures from the fact tables context, such as Internet Net Sales by sales territory country and calendar year. More advanced dimension columns, such as the Customer History Segment column, described in *Chapter 3, Connecting to Sources and Transforming Data with M*, can instantly give report visualizations meaning and insight.

In addition to their application within report visuals, such as the date axis of charts, dimension columns are frequently used to set the filter conditions of an entire report, a report page, or a specific visual of a report page. By default, Power BI lists dimension tables alphabetically in the **Fields** list and also lists column names of tables alphabetically.

Just as dataset designers must ensure that all common DAX measures are included in the dataset, dataset designers must also ensure that the necessary dimension columns are available to group, filter, and generally interact with the dataset.

Two of the top usability features for dimension tables include hierarchies and custom sorting. When implemented, these features enable users to explore datasets more easily, such as drilling up, down, and through the columns of a hierarchy.

Additionally, the **Sort by column** feature serves to generate logical report layouts, such as the months of the year from January through December.

Just as we provided greater detail regarding fact tables in the previous sections, additional details are provided about dimension tables in the following sections, starting with an explanation of hierarchies.

## Hierarchies

Dimension tables often contain hierarchical information where data in one column represents the parent of another column. Such constructs are referred to as hierarchies and can be seen in the **Product** dimension table where the **Product Category Group** column is the parent of the **Product Category** column, which in turn is the parent of the **Product Subcategory** column.

To create a hierarchy, select the column in the **Fields** list that represents the top level of the hierarchy and use the ellipsis to the right of the column name or right-click the column and select the **Create hierarchy** option, as shown in *Figure 4.15*:

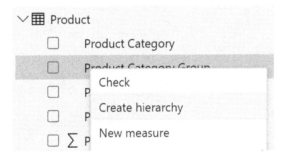

*Figure 4.15: Creating a hierarchy*

In this example, the Product Category Group column is the top level of the hierarchy and Product Category is its child or lower level. Likewise, the Product Subcategory column is a child of Product Category and the Product Name column is the lowest level of the hierarchy under Product Subcategory.

To add columns to the hierarchy, click the ellipsis to the right of the given column or use the right-click context menu to choose the **Add to hierarchy** option. Alternatively, the child columns can be dragged and dropped onto the name of the hierarchy by holding down the left mouse button when selecting the column. The levels of the columns can also be adjusted from within the hierarchy by dragging and dropping column names.

Dimension tables often contain hierarchical data, such as dates (year, quarter, month, week, day) and geographies (country, state/province, city, zip code). As shown in the *Date dimension view* section of *Chapter 2, Preparing Data Sources*, natural date hierarchies in which each column value has only one parent (for example, 2017-Sep) are strongly recommended. Unnatural date hierarchies can be confusing in reports as it isn't clear which parent value (2015, 2016, 2017?) a given child value, such as September, belongs to.

Once the hierarchy is created, a single click of the hierarchy name in the fields list adds all the columns and their respective levels to the report visualization. In *Figure 4.16*, all four columns of the Product Hierarchy are added to the **Axis** of a column chart to support drilling and interactive filter behavior in Power BI:

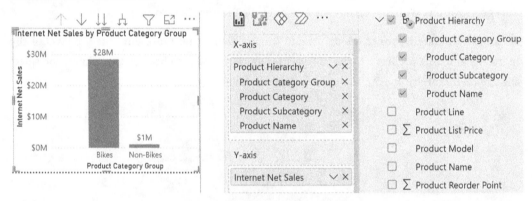

*Figure 4.16: Hierarchy in Report visual*

Certain columns or levels of the hierarchy can optionally be removed from the specific visual. For example, if the report developer only wishes to include Product Category and Product Subcategory in a particular visual, the other two columns can be removed from the **Axis** field well via the delete (**X**) icons.

The DAX language includes a set of parent and child functions, such as PATH() and PATHITEM(), that can be used to create hierarchy columns when a dimension table contains a Parent Key column. Common examples of this include an organizational structure with multiple levels of management or a chart of financial accounts. Creating these columns via DAX functions is one of the few examples when DAX-calculated columns may be preferable to other alternatives.

Another topic often related to dimension tables is custom sorting, which we explore in the next section.

# Custom sort

Most dimension columns used in reports contain text values, and, by default, Power BI sorts these values alphabetically. To ensure these columns follow their logical order (for example, Jan, Feb, Mar) in report visualizations, it's necessary to store a corresponding numeric column in the same dimension table and at the same granularity. For example, in addition to a Month Name column that contains the 12 text values for the names of the months, a Month Number column is included in the date dimension with the value of 1 for every row with the January value for Month Name, and so forth.

To set a custom sort order for a column, select the column in the **Fields** list in the **Report** view and then click the dropdown for the **Sort by column** icon under the **Column tools** tab. Choose the supporting column that contains the integer values, such as **Month Name**, as shown in the following screenshot:

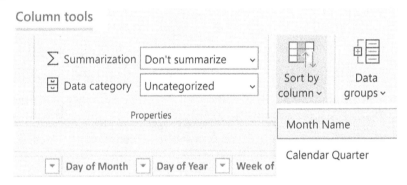

*Figure 4.17: Sort by column*

Most columns used as a **Sort by column** are not needed for report visualizations and can be hidden from the fields list. Per the *Date dimension view* section in *Chapter 2, Preparing Data Sources*, sequentially increasing integer columns are recommended for natural hierarchy columns, such as Year Month, as these columns can support both logical sorting and date intelligence calculations.

Although the Month Name and Weekday Name columns are the most common examples for custom sorting, other dimension tables may also require hidden columns to support a custom or logical sort order. In the following example, an integer column is added to the Customer dimension M query to support the logical sort order of the Customer History Segment column:

```
/*Preceding M query variables not included*/
//Customer History Segment Column
    CustomerHistoryColumn = Table.AddColumn(Customer, "Customer History
Segment",
```

```
    each
    if [DateFirstPurchase] >= OneYearAgo then "First Year Customer"
    else if [DateFirstPurchase] >= TwoYearsAgo and [DateFirstPurchase] <
OneYearAgo then "Second Year Customer"
    else if [DateFirstPurchase] >= ThreeYearsAgo and [DateFirstPurchase] <
TwoYearsAgo then "Third Year Customer"
    else "Legacy Customer", type text),
//Customer History Segment Column Sort
    CustomerHistColSort = Table.AddColumn(CustomerHistoryColumn, "Customer
History Segment Sort", each
    if [DateFirstPurchase] >= OneYearAgo then 1
    else if [DateFirstPurchase] >= TwoYearsAgo and [DateFirstPurchase] <
OneYearAgo then 2
    else if [DateFirstPurchase] >= ThreeYearsAgo and [DateFirstPurchase] <
TwoYearsAgo then 3 else 4, Int64.Type)
in
    CustomerHistColSort
```

With the integer column (Customer History Segment Sort) added to the Customer dimension table and the **Sort by column** property of the Customer History Segment column set to reference this column, Power BI reports visualize the Customer History Segment column by the logical order of the four possible values (First Year Customer, Second Year Customer, Third Year Customer, and Legacy Customer) by default.

Having covered both fact and dimension tables in detail, we next explore parameter tables.

## Parameter tables

Parameter tables are often used to store and organize measures. As such, unlike relationship tables, there are no relationships between the four parameter tables and any other tables in the model.

*Figure 4.18* shows the four parameter tables in the model:

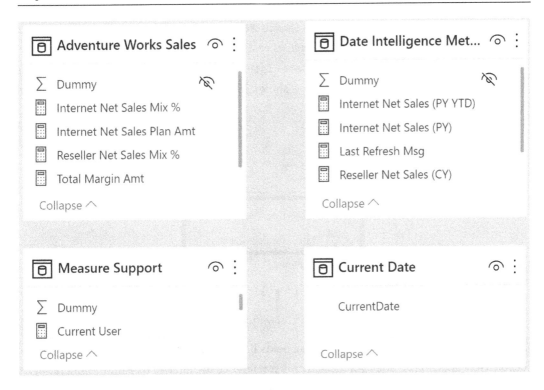

*Figure 4.18: Parameter tables*

As shown in *Figure 4.18*, the four parameter tables are Adventure Works Sales, Date Intelligence Metrics, Measure Support, and Current Date. Let's take a closer look at these different measure groups.

## Measure groups

The Date Intelligence and Adventure Works Sales tables only serve to provide an intuitive name for users to find related DAX measures. For example, several of the most important DAX measures of the dataset include both Internet Sales and Reseller Sales. It wouldn't make sense for consolidated measures, such as Total Net Sales, to be found under the Internet Sales or Reseller Sales fact tables in the field list.

For similar usability reasons, `Date Intelligence Metrics` provides an intuitive name for users and report developers to find measures, such as year-to-date, prior year-to-date, and year-over-year growth. The two parameter tables, `Date Intelligence Metrics` and `Adventure Works Sales`, effectively serve as display folders, as shown in *Figure 4.19*, a screenshot of the **Fields** list from the Report view:

*Figure 4.19: Fields list with parameter tables*

To obtain the calculator symbol icon in the fields list, all columns have to be hidden from the Report view and at least one DAX measure must reference the table in its **Home Table** property. Once these two conditions are met, the show/hide pane arrow of the fields list highlighted in the image can be clicked to refresh the **Fields** list.

In this example, the `Adventure Works Sales` and `Date Intelligence Metrics` tables both contain only a single column (named `Dummy`) that can be hidden via the right-click context menu accessible in the Model view, the **Fields** list of the **Report** view, and for import datasets the Data view as well.

The columns of the three fact tables (`Internet Sales`, `Reseller Sales`, and `Sales and Margin Plan`) are also hidden to provide users with an intuitive display of groups of measures at the top of the fields list followed by dimensions and their hierarchies.

The **Home table** for a measure can be set by selecting it from the fields list and choosing a table from the **Home table** dropdown on the **Modeling** tab in the Report view. As shown in *Figure 4.20*, the `Internet Net Sales (PY YTD)` measure is selected and `Date Intelligence Metrics` is configured as its **Home table**:

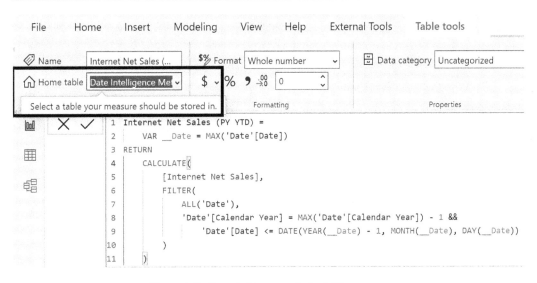

*Figure 4.20: Home table property for DAX measures*

Having explored the Adventure Works Sales and Date Intelligence Metrics parameter tables, we next explore the Current Date table.

## Last refreshed date

The Current Date table, as described in the *Data source parameters* section of *Chapter 3, Connecting to Sources and Transforming Data with M*, contains only one column and one row, representing the date at the time the source M query was executed. With this date value computed with each dataset refresh and loaded into the Data Model, a DAX measure can be written to expose the date to the Power BI report visuals. *Figure 4.21* shows a screenshot from the **Report** view. A measure named Last Refresh Msg uses a DAX variable to reference the parameter table and then passes this variable to a text string:

*Figure 4.21: Last refreshed message via the parameter table*

It's common to include a last refreshed text message on at least one report page of every published report. In the event the source dataset has failed to refresh for several days or longer, the text message advises users of the issue. See *Chapter 5*, *Developing DAX Measures and Security Roles*, for more information on DAX variables.

For DirectQuery datasets, the M query for the CurrentDate parameter table uses standard SQL syntax within the Value.NativeQuery() function, such as the following:

```
let Source = AdWorksSQLServer,
    View =   Value.NativeQuery(Source, "Select CAST(Current_Timestamp as
date) as [CurrentDate]")
in  View
```

The Source variable references the AdWorksSQLServer staging query, as described in the previous chapter. The *Data source parameters* section of *Chapter 3*, *Connecting to Sources and Transforming Data with M*, contains the M query for the CurrentDate parameter table in the import mode datasets.

Our last parameter table is the Measure Support table, which we detail in the following section.

## Measure support logic

The purpose of the Measure Support table is to centralize DAX expressions that can be reused by other measures. Since DAX variables are limited to the scope of individual measures, a set of hidden, intermediate measures avoids the need to declare variables for each measure.

The intermediate, or branching, DAX measure expressions also make it easy and less error-prone to implement a change as all dependent DAX measures are updated automatically. In this way, the Measure Support table serves a similar function to the parameter and staging query expressions, described in the previous chapter, for M queries.

For this dataset, DAX expressions containing the ISFILTERED() and ISCROSSFILTERED() functions can be used to determine the granularity of the filter context for the Product, Sales Territory, and Date dimension tables. If the user or report developer has applied a filter at a granularity not supported by the Sales and Margin Plan fact table, such as an individual product or date, a blank should be returned to avoid confusion and incorrect actual versus plan comparisons. The following DAX measure tests the filter context of the Date dimension table and returns one of two possible text values—Plan Grain or Actual Grain:

```
Date Grain Plan Filter Test =
    SWITCH(TRUE(),
```

```
        NOT(ISCROSSFILTERED('Date')),"Plan Grain",
        ISFILTERED('Date'[Week of Year]) ||
            ISFILTERED('Date'[Date]) ||
            ISFILTERED('Date'[Weekday Name]) ||
            ISFILTERED('Date'[Calendar Yr-Wk]), "Actual Grain",
        "Plan Grain"
    )
```

Similar filter test measures can be created for the Sales Territory and Product dimension tables. All such measures should be hidden from the Report view, and the **Home table** property should be set to Measure Support. Once these dimension-specific measures have been defined, a final support measure can integrate their results, as shown in the following example:

```
Plan Grain Status =
    IF(
        [Date Grain Plan Filter Test] = "Plan Grain" &&
            [Product Grain Plan Filter Test] = "Plan Grain" &&
            [Sales Territory Grain Plan Filter Test] = "Plan Grain",
        "Plan Grain",
        "Actual Grain"
    )
```

Given the logic built into the hidden measure support expressions, DAX measures can reference the results and deliver the intended conditional behavior in report visualizations, as shown in the following example of a variance-to-plan measure:

Internet Net Sales Var to Plan =

```
    IF(
        [Plan Grain Status] = "Actual Grain",
        BLANK(),
        [Internet Net Sales] - [Internet Net Sales Plan Amt]
    )
```

These support measures can be used to ensure that if users are operating at a granularity or filter not supported by the calculations that blank values are returned versus incorrect values.

With all four parameter tables explained, we next cover an alternative method of organizing measures, **Display folders**.

# Display folders

With the advent of the **Display folder** metadata property for columns and measures, it is now possible to use a single parameter table for all measures and also maintain an organized structure. As shown in *Figure 4.22*, the **Properties** pane of the Model view can be used to set the **Display folder** property:

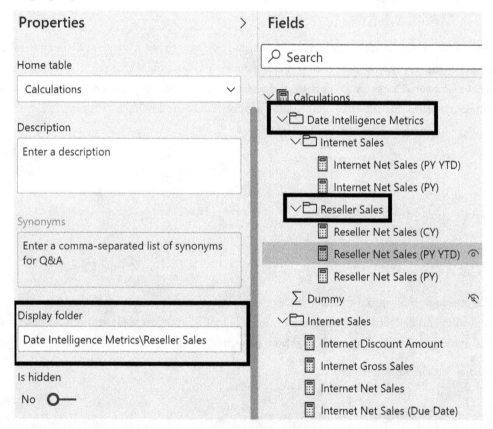

*Figure 4.22: Display folders*

In *Figure 4.22*, the **Home table** for all measures is a table called **Calculations** and the **Display folder** property for the Reseller Net Sales (PY YTD) measure has been set to **Date Intelligence Metrics\ Reseller Sales**. Thus, multiple folder levels are supported through the use of the backslash ( \ ) character to designate subfolders. Once a **Display folder** is created, measures can be organized into the display folders by dragging and dropping the measures within the **Fields** pane of the Model view.

Whether multiple parameter tables are used or display folders is a design decision and one approach may work better than another depending upon the business.

However, if display folders are used, it is recommended to keep the folder hierarchy relatively flat (only one or two levels) in order to not frustrate users by requiring them to expand many folders in order to reach a particular measure.

We have now detailed all of the different types of tables within a data model as well as alternative methods for organizing measures. The next section explores the relationships between these tables.

# Relationships

Relationships play a central role in the analytical behavior and performance of the dataset. Based on the filters applied at the report layer and the DAX expressions contained in the measures, relationships determine the set of active rows for each table of the model that must be evaluated. Therefore, it's critical that dataset designers understand how relationships drive report behavior via cross-filtering and the rules that relationships in Power BI must adhere to, such as uniqueness and non ambiguity, as discussed in the next section.

## Uniqueness

Relationships in Power BI data models are always defined between single columns in two separate tables. While Power BI does support direct many-to-many relationships, it is recommended that relationships with a cardinality of many-to-many be avoided because this implies that the related columns both contain duplicate values for the related columns. Relationships based on columns containing duplicate values on both sides of the relationship can result in poor performance and incorrect or unexpected results, and are generally indicative of poor or messy data models.

A better design practice is to instead use relationship tables with unique values in order to relate the many-to-many table relationships. Thus, a good design practice is that one of the two columns defining a relationship uniquely identifies the rows of its table, such as the CurrencyKey column from the Currency table in the *Fact-to-dimension relationships* section earlier in this chapter.

However, Power BI and Analysis Services tabular models do not enforce or require referential integrity as with relationship uniqueness. For example, a sales fact table can contain transactions for a customer that are not present in the customer dimension table. In such a circumstance, no error message is thrown and DAX measures that sum the sales table still result in the correct amount, including the new customer's transactions. Instead, a blank row is added to the customer dimension table by default for these scenarios (also known as early-arriving facts) and this row is visible when the measure is grouped by columns from the customer dimension table in report visualizations.

If missing dimensions are an issue, the dataset designer can work with the data source owner and/or the data warehouse team to apply a standard foreign key value (for example, -1) to these new dimension members within an **extract-transform-load** (**ETL**) process and a corresponding row can be added to dimensions with an unknown value for each column.

In the rare event that a text column is used for a relationship, note that DAX is not case-sensitive like the M language. For example, M functions that remove duplicates, such as `Table.Distinct()`, may result in unique text values (from M's perspective), such as **Apple** and **APPLE**. However, when these values are loaded to the data model, these values are considered duplicates.

To resolve this issue, a standard casing format can be applied to the column within a `Table.TransformColumns()` function via text functions, such as `Text.Proper()` and `Text.Upper()`. Removing duplicates after the standard casing transformation results in a column of unique values for the data model.

Along with uniqueness, another important topic related to relationships is ambiguity, which we explore in the next section.

## Ambiguity

Data model relationships must result in a single, unambiguous filter path across the tables of the model. In other words, a filter applied to one table must follow a single path to filter another table—the filter context cannot branch off into multiple intermediate tables prior to filtering a final table. In *Figure 4.23*, the Model view only shows one of the two relationships to the Auto Accidents fact table is allowed to be active (solid line) versus inactive (dashed line):

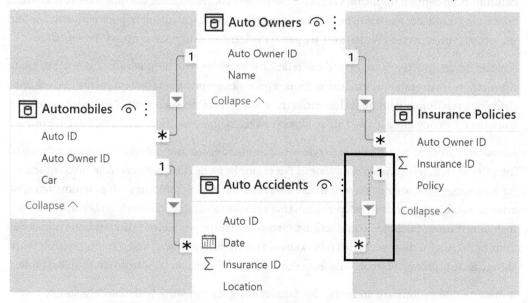

*Figure 4.23: Ambiguous relationships avoided*

When a filter is applied to the Auto Owners table, the inactive relationship between Insurance Polices and Auto Accidents provides a single, unambiguous filter path from Auto Owners to Auto Accidents via relationships with the Automobiles table. If the model author tries to set both relationships to the Auto Accidents table as active, Power BI rejects this relationship and advises of the ambiguity it would create, as shown in *Figure 4.24*:

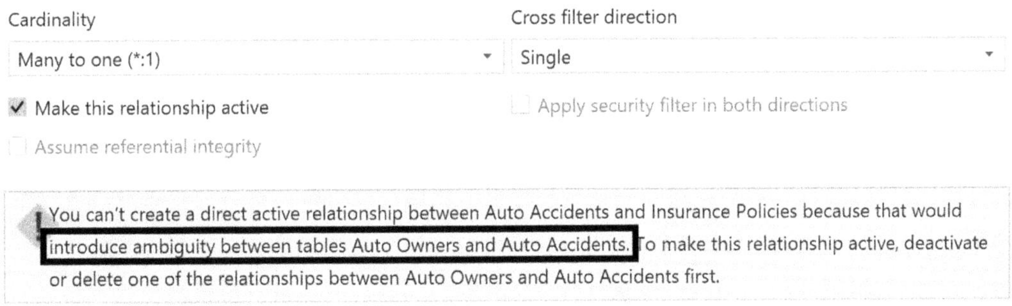

| Cardinality | Cross filter direction |
|---|---|
| Many to one (*:1)  ▾ | Single  ▾ |

☑ Make this relationship active          ☐ Apply security filter in both directions

☐ Assume referential integrity

> ▍You can't create a direct active relationship between Auto Accidents and Insurance Policies because that would introduce ambiguity between tables Auto Owners and Auto Accidents. To make this relationship active, deactivate or delete one of the relationships between Auto Owners and Auto Accidents first.

*Figure 4.24: Ambiguity error in the Edit relationship dialog*

Given the active relationship between the Automobiles and Auto Accidents tables, if the relationship between Insurance Policies and Auto Accidents was active, the Auto Owners table would have two separate paths to filter the Auto Accidents table (via Insurance Policies or via Automobiles).

With uniqueness and ambiguity understood, we now explain single-direction relationships in greater detail.

# Single-direction relationships

Single-direction cross-filtering relationships are the most common in Power BI datasets and particularly for data models with more than one fact table. In this dataset, whether import or DirectQuery, all relationships are defined with single direction cross-filtering except for the relationships from Sales Territory, Product, and Date to their corresponding bridge tables, as described in the following section on bidirectional relationships.

*Figure 4.25* shows a layout of the Model view that includes three of the seven dimension tables related to Reseller Sales:

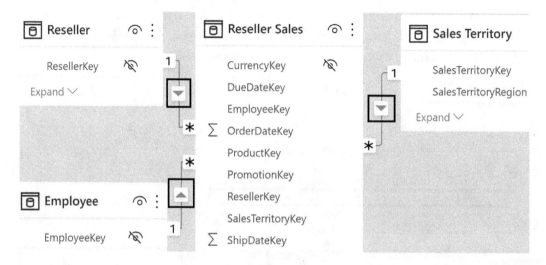

*Figure 4.25: Single-direction relationships*

As you can see from the arrow icons in the Model view shown in *Figure 4.25*, the filter context in single-direction relationships exclusively navigates from the one side of a relationship to the many side.

In the absence of any DAX expressions that override the default cross-filtering behavior, tables on the one side of single-direction relationships are not filtered or impacted by filters applied to the table on the many side of the relationship.

For example, the Employee table has 296 unique rows based on its EmployeeKey column. A measure, such as Count of Employees, that references this column always returns the 296 value regardless of any filters applied to other tables in the model.

There are, of course, valid business scenarios for allowing the filter context of the related fact table to impact dimension measures, such as the Count of Employees or the Distinct Count of Product Subcategories.

Dataset designers can support these requirements by default via bidirectional cross-filtering relationships, but in most scenarios this isn't necessary or appropriate. Instead, for these DAX measures, the CROSSFILTER() function can be applied to override the default single-direction cross-filtering. See *The CROSSFILTER Function* section for the function syntax and a use case example.

In the next section, we explore the implications of unnecessary complexity when defining relationships between tables.

## Direct flights only

For the most common and data-intensive report queries, always look to eliminate any unnecessary intermediate relationships between dimension tables and fact tables.

In *Figure 4.26*, the Reseller table must filter an intermediate table (Reseller Keys) prior to filtering the Reseller Sales fact table:

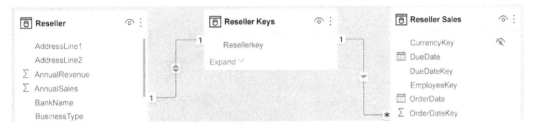

*Figure 4.26: Anti-pattern: intermediate table relationships*

Removing the intermediate table (connecting flight), Reseller Keys in this example, can significantly improve performance by reducing the scan operations required of the DAX query engine. The performance benefit is particularly acute with larger fact tables and dimensions with many unique values. For small fact tables, such as a budget or plan table of 3,000 rows, intermediate tables can be used without negatively impacting performance.

Now that we have explored single-direction relationships, we next cover bidirectional relationships.

# Bidirectional relationships

Bidirectional cross-filtering enables the filter context of a table on the many side of a relationship to flow to the one side of the relationship. A common use case for bidirectional relationships is represented in *Figure 4.27*:

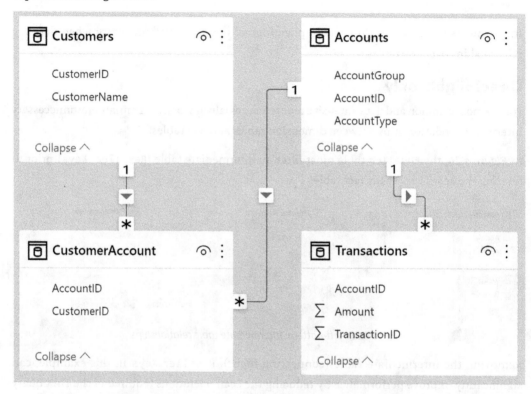

*Figure 4.27: Bidirectional cross-filtering for a many-to-many relationship*

In this model, a customer can have many accounts and an individual account can be associated with many customers. Given the many-to-many relationship between Customers and Accounts, a bridge table (CustomerAccount) is created that contains the combinations of customer and account key values.

Due to the many-to one relationship between CustomerAccount and Accounts, a filter applied to the Customers table only impacts the Transactions fact table if bidirectional cross-filtering is enabled from CustomerAccount to Accounts. Without this bidirectional relationship, a filter applied to the Customers table would only impact the CustomerAccount table as single-direction relationships only flow from the one side of the relationship to the many.

Although powerful, and preferable for certain use cases, bidirectional relationships can lead to unexpected or undesired query results. Additionally, the DAX CROSSFILTER() function makes it possible to selectively implement bidirectional relationship behavior for specific measures.

We now explore the implications of bidirectional relationships in the context of shared dimension tables.

## Shared dimensions

In this dataset, the Sales Territory, Product, Date, Currency, and Promotion dimension tables are related to both the Internet Sales and Reseller Sales fact tables. As shown in *Figure 3.28*, these relationships and the three dimension tables specific to either fact table all have single-direction cross-filtering enabled:

*Figure 4.28: Shared dimension tables*

Unlike the shared dimensions, the Reseller and Employee dimension tables are exclusively related to the Reseller Sales fact table and the Customer dimension is exclusively related to the Internet Sales fact table. This is a common scenario for larger models in that fact tables both share dimensions and maintain their own exclusive relationships to certain dimension tables.

In general, it's recommended to avoid bidirectional relationships between shared dimensions and fact tables when there are also dimension tables exclusive to certain fact tables. This is because such relationships generate filter contexts that business users often don't expect or desire and that don't add analytical value.

For example, if the relationship between Promotion and Reseller Sales was revised to allow for bidirectional cross-filtering, a report that analyzed internet sales by customers would be impacted by the filter selections of the Reseller and Employee dimension tables even though these two tables are not related to Internet Sales.

In this example, the filter context would flow from the Reseller and/or Employee tables to Reseller Sales but then, via the bidirectional relationship with Promotion, also filter the Promotion table, and finally filter the Internet Sales fact table.

In almost all scenarios, the business would expect the Reseller and Employee tables to only filter the Reseller Sales measures. For the rare cases in which this filtering behavior is useful or needed, bidirectional cross-filtering can be enabled for specific measures via the CROSSFILTER() function.

A better use case for bidirectional relationships is between the exclusive dimension tables and their fact tables, such as from Reseller to Reseller Sales or from Customer to Internet Sales. These bidirectional relationships aren't required given the CROSSFILTER() function and other options available in DAX, but they allow simple measures against these dimensions, such as the count of resellers to reflect the filter selections applied to other Reseller Sales dimensions, such as Sales Territory and Product.

Bidirectional cross-filtering is also not allowed for certain relationships due to the ambiguity this would create. In this dataset, Power BI Desktop rejects bidirectional relationships between the Sales Territory, Product, and Date dimension tables with the Internet Sales and Reseller Sales fact tables because this would create more than one filter path to the Sales and Margin Plan fact table.

For example, a bidirectional relationship between Sales Territory and Reseller Sales would allow the Product table to either filter the Sales and Margin Plan table via the Product Subcategory bridge table, or filter the Reseller Sales table and then utilize the new bidirectional relationship to filter the Sales Territory table and then its bridge table to the Sales and Margin Plan table. Rather than guess at the correct or intended filter behavior, Power BI throws an error and identifies the tables associated with the ambiguous condition.

Similar to shared dimensions, date dimensions also deserve special consideration when it comes to bidirectional relationships and we explain this in the next section.

## Date dimensions

Relationships between fact tables and date dimension tables should always use single-direction cross-filtering.

If bidirectional cross-filtering is used with date dimension tables, then filtered selections of other dimension tables related to the given fact table, such as `Promotion` or `Product`, reduce the date table rows available for date intelligence calculations.

Similar to the example with shared dimensions, although this adjusted filter context is technically correct, it often produces unexpected or undesired results, such as only the dates in which internet sales transactions were associated with a specific promotion type.

Note that the bidirectional relationship with the `Date` dimension table in this dataset is between the `Date` table and the bridge table containing unique month values. The bridge tables are hidden from the Report view and are not used to filter the `Date` table.

With the perils of bidirectional relationships understood, there are times when bidirectional filtering is appropriate. Thus, we now explain how bidirectional filtering can be implemented using the `CROSSFILTER` function.

## The CROSSFILTER function

Similar to the `USERELATIONSHIP()` function that can invoke an inactive relationship for a specific DAX measure, the `CROSSFILTER()` function can be used to implement a specific cross-filtering behavior (single, bidirectional, none) for a specific measure. The cross-filtering behavior specified in the measure overrides the default cross-filtering behavior defined for the relationship.

In *Figure 4.29*, an `Employee Count` measure only references the `Employee` dimension table and therefore is not impacted by the filter selections of the `Sales Territory Country` slicer due to the single direction relationship between `Employee` and `Reseller Sales`:

*Figure 4.29: Bidirectional cross-filtering via the DAX CROSSFILTER function*

The `Employee Count (CF)` measure, however, does adjust to reflect the `Sales Territory Country` selections as well as any other dimension table filter selections that impact the `Reseller Sales` fact table, such as the `Date`, `Product`, and `Promotion` dimension tables.

In this example, the `Reseller Sales` fact table is first filtered to the set of `Reseller Sales` rows associated with the **Germany** and **United Kingdom** sales territory countries. This filtered set of `Reseller Sales` rows is then used to filter the `Employee` table resulting in three distinct employee key values. The value of **3** represents the three salespeople associated with the `Reseller Sales` of **Germany** and **United Kingdom**.

In the absence of any filter selections in the report, the `Employee Count` and `Employee Count` (`CF`) measures return the same results (that is, 290 distinct IDs). The bidirectional cross-filtering only occurs when either a filter selection has been applied to a related dimension table in the report or within the DAX measure itself.

If the intent is to only count the distinct employee IDs associated with `Reseller Sales` and to respect filter selections on related dimensions, the DAX measure can be written as follows:

```
CALCULATE(DISTINCTCOUNT(Employee[EmployeeAlternateKey]),'Reseller Sales')
```

See the *Dimension metrics* section of *Chapter 5, Developing DAX Measures and Security Roles*, for more details.

The syntax for `CROSSFILTER()` is also very similar to `USERELATIONSHIP()`, as shown by the following code block:

```
Employee Count = DISTINCTCOUNT(('Employee'[EmployeeAlternateKey]))


Employee Count (CF) =
    CALCULATE(
        DISTINCTCOUNT('Employee'[EmployeeAlternateKey]),
        CROSSFILTER('Reseller Sales'[EmployeeKey],'Employee'[EmployeeKey],
        Both)
    )
```

The `EmployeeAlternateKey` column represents the business key or natural key of the employee. The `EmployeeKey` column uniquely identifies each row of the `Employee` table and is used in the relationship with `Reseller Sales`. Given the slowly changing dimension process, which adds a new employee row when certain attributes of an employee change, it's necessary to reference the `EmployeeAlternateKey` column in the `DISTINCTCOUNT()` measures to only count each employee once.

The third parameter to `CROSSFILTER()` can be set to `OneWay`, `Both`, or `None`. Given the potential for unexpected or undesired results when applying bidirectional cross-filtering relationships to models with multiple fact tables, it's generally recommended to selectively enable bidirectional cross-filtering per measure, such as in the preceding example.

There may be valid use cases for both single-direction and bidirectional cross-filtering relationships, such as the two measures seen here. Including these alternative measures in the dataset doesn't violate the version control objective but does entail additional user training and documentation. A report developer or business analyst can regularly provide brief tutorials or updated documents on these measures and other dataset customizations.

We have now completed our exploration of relationships. The next section covers another aspect of data models, model metadata.

# Model metadata

Metadata is simply the concept of data or information about data. In Power BI, metadata is available for tables, columns, and measures within a dataset.

The consistent and complete application of metadata properties, such as **Default summarization** and **Data category**, greatly affect the usability of a dataset. With a solid foundation of tables, column data types, and relationships in place, dataset designers and BI teams should consider all primary metadata properties and their implications for user experience as well as any additional functionality they can provide.

In the following sections, we explore many of the most important types of model metadata, starting with the visibility of tables and columns.

## Visibility

Data modelers can define the visibility of tables, columns, and measures within a dataset. In other words, each of these elements can either be visible or hidden to report authors and business users within the Report view.

Every table, column, and measure that isn't explicitly needed in the Report view should be hidden. This usually includes all relationship columns and any measure support tables and measure expressions.

If a column is rarely needed or only needed for a specific report, it can be temporarily unhidden to allow for this report to be developed and then hidden again to maximize usability. Numeric fact table columns that are referenced by DAX measures (for example, quantity) should be hidden from the fields list, as the measures can be used for visualizing this data.

As discussed in the *Parameter tables* section, when all columns of a table are hidden from the Report view and at least one DAX measure identifies the given table as its home table, a measure group icon (calculator symbol) appears in the fields list.

This clear differentiation between the `measures` and `dimension` columns (attributes) is recommended, especially if business users are developing their own reports based on the dataset.

Tables with both visible columns and measures force business users and report developers to navigate between these different elements in the fields list. This can be onerous given the volume of DAX measures for common fact tables. If it's necessary to expose one or a few fact table columns permanently, consider migrating some or all of the DAX measures for the table to a parameter table to simplify navigation.

Visibility applies to tables, columns, and measures. We next look at additional metadata available to just columns and measures.

# Column and measure metadata

Dataset designers should review the columns and measures of each table exposed to the Report view and ensure that appropriate metadata properties have been configured. These settings, including any custom sorting described earlier in the *Custom sort* section of this chapter, only need to be applied once and can significantly improve the usability of the dataset.

In the following sections, we explore some of the more important metadata settings for columns and measures. Some of these apply only to columns, such as the **Default summarization** setting explained in the next section.

## Default summarization

As mentioned, the **Default summarization** property only applies to columns and controls the default aggregation applied to a column such as sum, average, first, last, and so on.

The **Default summarization** property should be revised from Power BI's default setting to the **Do not summarize** value for all columns. Power BI applies a **Default summarization** setting of **Sum** for all columns with a numeric data type (whole number, fixed decimal number, decimal number) when a table is first loaded to the data model.

As shown in *Figure 4.30*, a summation symbol $\Sigma$ appears next to the field name in the fields list if a **Default summarization** other than **Do not Summarize** is enabled:

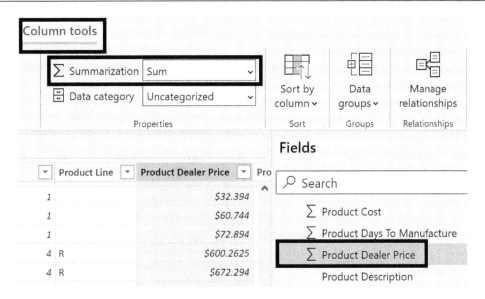

*Figure 4.30: Default summarization for numeric columns*

As illustrated in *Figure 4.30*, the **Default summarization** property for a column can be accessed via the **Column tools** tab of the Data view. Additionally, as with other metadata properties, **Default summarization** can also be accessed from the Report view.

As mentioned in the *Data view* section earlier, implementing metadata changes, such as **Default summarization** and **Data category**, via the **Column tools** tab from the Report view is the only option for DirectQuery models.

If a user selects a column with **Default summarization** enabled, the aggregation specified by the property (for example, **Sum**, **Average**) is returned rather than the grouping behavior of **Do not summarize**. In many cases, the numeric column is only used to group measures, such as `Internet Net Sales by Product Dealer Price`, and DAX measures can be written for any needed calculation logic.

Additionally, **Default summarization** can create confusion, such as when a user expects a sum aggregation based on the summation symbol but the model author has applied an alternative default summarization (for example, **Minimum**, **Average**). Alternatively, the names assigned to DAX measures, such as **Average Product Dealer Price**, make it clear which aggregation is being applied.

For these reasons, it's recommended to convert the default summarization setting to **Do not summarize**. A broader concept of this recommendation is to build essential DAX measure expressions into the dataset, as described in *Chapter 5, Developing DAX Measures and Security Roles*, to make Power BI datasets more flexible and powerful for users and report developers.

While the **Default summarization** metadata setting only applies to columns since measures inherently aggregate column information or otherwise return scalar (single) values, the **Data format** setting applies to both columns and measures as explained in the next section.

## Data format

The **Data format** setting controls how data is displayed to users when viewed in report visuals.

The default formatting Power BI applies to columns and measures should also be revised to a corporate standard or a format applicable to the column or measure. For example, the default full date format of "Friday July 1, 2011" can be revised to the more compact (mm/dd/yyyy) format of 7/1/2011. Likewise, the currency format for measures calculating financial data can be revised to display two or no decimal places and the thousands separator can also be added to numeric measures.

In addition to standard data formats such as **Whole Number**, **Currency**, **Percentage** and so on, **Custom** formats are also supported. In the **Properties** pane of the Model view under **Formatting** and then **Format**, you can choose to have a **Custom** format. Choosing a **Custom** format allows you to enter a custom display format such as `00:00:00`, for example, which can be useful for displaying duration formats such as hh:mm:ss.

Business users and report developers do not have the ability to change column and measure formatting when connecting to the published dataset from Power BI or Excel. Therefore, it's important to choose widely accepted data formats and formats that lend themselves to intuitive data visualizations.

We next explore another setting applicable to both columns and measures, the **Data category** setting.

## Data category

The **Data category** setting allows data modelers to tag columns and measures as specific types of information. Setting the data category changes the behavior of these columns and measures within Power BI.

By default, Power BI does not assign columns or measures to any of the 13 available data categories. Assigning geographic categories, such as **City**, helps Power BI determine how to display these values on map visualizations. For example, certain city names, such as **Washington**, are also associated with state or province names and without an assigned data category, map visuals would have to guess whether to plot the city or the state.

Currently 10 of the 13 column data categories are related to geography, including **County**, **Country**, **Continent**, **City**, **Latitude**, **Longitude**, **Postal code**, **Address**, **Place**, and **State or Province**.

The **Web URL Data Category** can be used to enable the initiation of emails from Power BI report visuals. In *Figure 4.31*, the **Employee Email Link** column contains mailto values (that is, mailto:// John@adworks.com) and the **URL icon** property under **Values** has been set to **On**:

| FirstName | LastName | Employee Email Link |
|---|---|---|
| Alan | Brewer | ✉ |
| Alejandro | McGuel | ✉ |
| Alex | Nayberg | ✉ |
| Alice | Ciccu | ✉ |
| Amy | Alberts | ✉ |

*Figure 4.31: Web URL data category for Employee Email Link column*

Without specifying the **Web URL** data category of the **Employee Email Link** column, the values appear as normal text. With the **Web URL** data category specified, the full mailto link is displayed in the table visual by default and this can also be used to initiate an email. Both the **Web URL** data category specification and the **URL icon** property (set to **On**) are required to display the email icon.

The **Image URL** data category can be used to expose images in report visualizations, such as with a slicer visualization set to an **Orientation** of **Horizontal** as shown in *Figure 4.32*:

*Figure 4.32: Image URL Data Category used for Chiclet slicer visual*

The **Barcode** data category, the only other non-geographic category beyond **Web URL** and **Image URL**, can be used by Power BI mobile applications to scan individual items from mobile devices.

Next, we cover another important metadata field, **Description**.

# Description

The **Description** metadata property lets data modelers provide short explanations and information about elements in the data model.

Descriptions can be added to the tables, columns, and measures of a data model to aid users during report development. Once descriptions have been applied and the dataset has been published to the Power BI service, users connected to the dataset via reports can view the descriptions as they hover over the fields in the fields list. This feature is particularly useful in communicating the business logic contained in measures, such as whether discounts are included or excluded in the Internet Net Sales measure.

Although field descriptions are recommended, particularly for measures that contain custom or complex logic, they are not a substitute for the formal documentation of a dataset. In most scenarios, the field description is only used as a convenient reminder of the essential logic or meaning and thus can be more concise than the official corporate definition of the column or measure.

In *Figure 4.33*, a report author is connected to a published Power BI dataset and has hovered over the Internet Gross Product Margin measure:

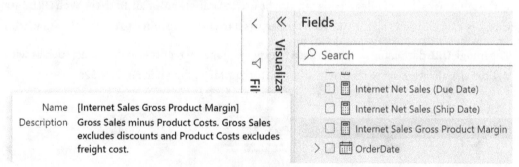

*Figure 4.33: Field descriptions as tooltips in the Fields list*

The descriptions can only be viewed from Power BI Desktop or the Power BI service. Field descriptions are exclusive to the fields list and are not displayed in visuals on the report canvas.

Descriptions can be applied by using the **Properties** pane of the Model view as shown in *Figure 4.34*:

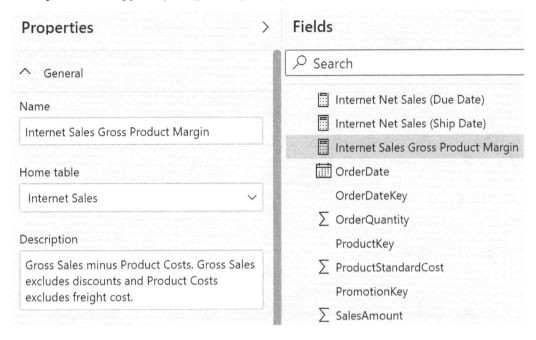

*Figure 4.34: Properties pane of the Model view*

Users connected to the dataset via Live connections can view the descriptions via the **Properties** pane. In this context, the **Name** and **Description** properties are read-only.

This completes our exploration of metadata property settings. In the following section, we provide advice around optimizing the performance of datasets.

# Optimizing data model performance

One of the main reasons for creating a dataset, particularly an import mode dataset, is to provide a performant data source for reports and dashboards. Although Power BI supports traditional reporting workloads, such as email subscriptions and view-only usage, Power BI empowers users to explore and interact with reports and datasets. The responsiveness of visuals for this self-service workload is largely driven by fundamental data model design decisions, as explained in the following subsections.

Additional performance factors outside the scope of this chapter include the hardware resources allocated to the dataset, such as with Power BI Premium capacities (v-cores, RAM), the efficiency of the DAX measures created for the dataset, the design of the Power BI reports that query the dataset, and the volume and timing of queries generated by users.

We first take a look at optimizing import mode datasets.

# Import

The performance of an import mode dataset is largely driven by fundamental design decisions, such as the granularity of fact and dimension tables. For example, large dimension tables with more than a million unique values, such as customer IDs or product IDs produce much less performant report queries than small dimensions with only 100 to 1,000 unique values.

Likewise, DAX measures that access columns containing thousands of unique values perform much more slowly than measures that reference columns with only a few unique values. A simplistic but effective understanding is that higher levels of cardinality (unique values) result in greater memory consumption via reduced compression and CPUs require additional time to scan greater amounts of memory.

An import mode designer should be cautious about the performance implications of relationships to large dimension tables. Although usability is somewhat compromised, a separate but less granular dimension containing only the most common columns can be created to drive more efficient report queries. For example, business users may rarely need to access individual product **Stock Keeping Units (SKUs)** and would prefer the performance benefit provided by a smaller dimension table that contains only product categories and product subcategories.

# Query caching

For Premium and Embedded workloads, the Power BI service supports automatic query caching that can be enabled or disabled via the **Settings** page for each dataset. When enabled, this feature automatically caches the queries associated with the initial opening of a report by each user.

Query caching is only available for import mode datasets and respects personal bookmarks, persistent filters, and security rules. The query cache resets during scheduled dataset refreshes and this can result in performance degradation in the event of multiple dataset refreshes occurring simultaneously or if the capacity is heavily loaded. While it is recommended to enable this feature, enterprise BI teams should be aware of these considerations.

We next look at another important consideration for import mode datasets, columnar compression.

# Columnar compression

Power BI uses the xVelocity In-Memory Analytics Engine (previously known as VertiPaq) for datasets. This engine applies several techniques to achieve 10X or greater data compression, thus minimizing the amount of memory required to be scanned to return query results.

To optimize columnar compression, it's important to understand the columnar layout and internal storage of import mode datasets. Power BI creates individual segments of approximately one million rows and stores separate memory structures for column data, the dictionary of unique values for columns, relationships, and hierarchies.

In *Figure 4.35*, three segments are used to store a fact table of 2.8 million rows:

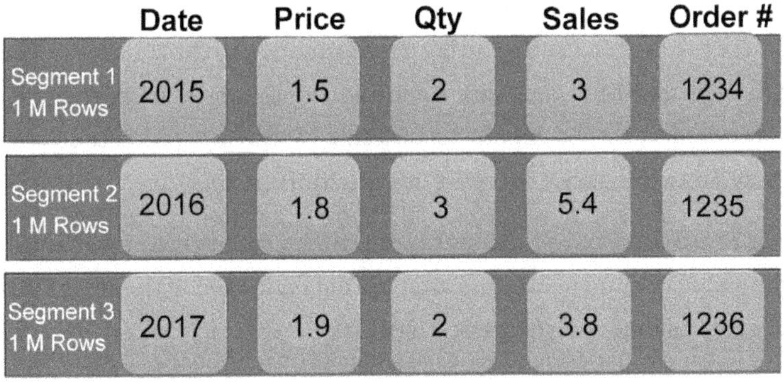

| | Date | Price | Qty | Sales | Order # |
|---|---|---|---|---|---|
| Segment 1 1 M Rows | 2015 | 1.5 | 2 | 3 | 1234 |
| Segment 2 1 M Rows | 2016 | 1.8 | 3 | 5.4 | 1235 |
| Segment 3 1 M Rows | 2017 | 1.9 | 2 | 3.8 | 1236 |

*Figure 4.35: Columnar storage of import mode datasets*

Since only the columns required for a query are scanned during query execution, a relatively expensive column in terms of memory consumption (due to many unique values), such as Order #, can be stored in the dataset without negatively impacting queries that only access other columns.

Removing fact table columns or reducing the cardinality of fact table columns that are not used in queries or relationships nonetheless benefits the storage size and resources required to refresh the dataset. Fewer fact table columns may also enable Power BI to find a more optimal sort order for compression and thus benefit the query performance.

Eliminate any DAX-calculated column on fact tables as these columns are not compressed as efficiently as imported columns. If necessary, replace DAX-calculated columns with the equivalent expression in the source M query or SQL View.

Additionally, as per the *Fact table columns* section earlier in this chapter, remove columns that can be computed within DAX measures via simple expressions (+,-,/,*). For example, the Sales column from *Figure 4.36* can be excluded from the import dataset given the Price and Qty columns.

During query execution over tables with more than one segment, one CPU thread is associated per segment. This parallelization is limited by the number of CPUs available to the dataset (for example, Power BI Premium P1 with four backend v-cores), and the number of segments required to resolve the query.

Therefore, ideally, the rows of fact tables can be ordered such that only a portion of the segments are required to resolve queries. Using the example of the 2.8M-row fact table, a query that's filtered on the year 2017 would only require one CPU thread and would only scan the required column segments within **Segment 3**.

The internal order of fact table rows cannot be dictated by the dataset designer as Power BI determines the optimal order that leads to the highest compression during dataset refreshes. However, dataset designers can add a sorting transformation to the M query of a fact table (Table. Sort()) such that Power BI, at a minimum, considers this particular order during its processing. Such a sorting operation can be expensive in terms of the time taken to refresh import mode datasets but may prove beneficial to report query performance.

Whether Power BI used the particular sort order can be determined by analyzing the memory footprint of the sorted column before and after the data is loaded. If the size of the sorted column is significantly reduced following the refresh operation, Power BI took advantage of the specified sort order.

Given the importance of columnar compression for import-mode datasets, we next explain tools and techniques for analyzing the internal workings of the xVelocity In-Memory Analytics Engine in greater detail via Data Management Views (DMVs) and the VertiPaq Analyzer.

## Memory analysis via DMVs and the VertiPaq Analyzer

DMVs are Analysis Services queries that return information about server operations, server health, and data model objects at the time the queries are run.

The same DMVs that provide information about Analysis Services tabular databases are also available for Power BI datasets. Querying these DMVs can provide schema information, such as the columns used to define relationships, the definitions of DAX measures, and the memory usage of columns and other structures.

From a memory analysis standpoint, the two most important DMVs are DISCOVER_STORAGE_ TABLE_COLUMNS and DISCOVER_STORAGE_TABLE_COLUMN_SEGMENTS.

These and other DMVs are at the heart of VertiPaq Analyzer, a set of open-source libraries that expose statistical information about tabular models. The use of VertiPaq Analyzer within DAX Studio is shown in *Figure 4.36* with the dictionary size of each column of a Power BI dataset retrieved via the DISCOVER_STORAGE_TABLE_COLUMNS DMV:

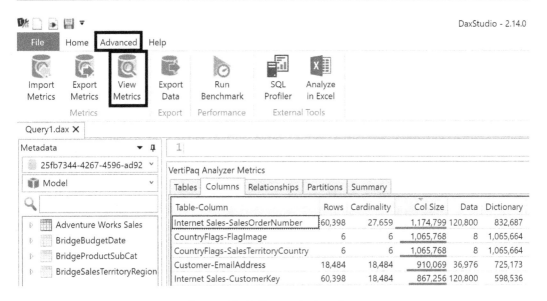

*Figure 4.36: Dictionary size by column*

The use of VertiPaq Analyzer can quickly expose columns with high **Cardinality** and large **Dictionary** sizes that may be good candidates for exclusion from the dataset.

This concludes our exploration of performance optimization for import mode datasets and we next move on to DirectQuery mode datasets.

# DirectQuery

Dataset designers have less control over the performance of pure DirectQuery datasets given that data storage and query execution is the responsibility of the source system.

However, dataset designers can ensure that the DAX functions used in measures take advantage of the source system resources and can partner with source system owners and experts to test alternative data source optimizations, such as the columnstore index for SQL Server. In SQL Server, columstore indexes use column-based data storage and query processing and can achieve gains up to 10 times the query performance and 10 times the compression versus traditional row-oriented storage and uncompressed data respectively.

Additionally, as advised earlier regarding the **Assume referential integrity** relationship property, performance can be significantly improved by generating inner-join SQL statements.

Let's now take a deeper look at optimizing DirectQuery datasets.

# Columnstore and HTAP

Business intelligence queries generated from tools such as Power BI are more suited for columnar data stores and most DirectQuery source systems offer a columnar feature to deliver improved query performance. For Microsoft SQL Server, the columnstore index is recommended for large fact tables and this index eliminates the need to maintain traditional B-tree indexes or to apply row or page compression.

Additionally, a combination of non-clustered columnstore indexes and in-memory table technologies can be used to support Hybrid Transactional and Analytical Processing (HTAP) workloads. HTAP refers to the tools and features that enable live data to be analyzed without affecting transactional operations. HTAP features include memory-optimized tables, natively compiled stored procedures, and clustered columnstore indexes.

For example, the Power BI queries against the DirectQuery dataset would utilize the columnstore index without impacting the **OnLine Transactional Processing** (**OLTP**) workload of the database. OLTP refers to the traditional transaction operations of databases that facilitate and manage transaction-oriented applications.

The details of these features and configurations are outside the scope of this book but at a minimum the owners or experts on the DirectQuery data source should be engaged on the performance of the Power BI dataset.

The following URL provides guidance on designing columnstore indexes for SQL Server database services (for example, Azure SQL Database, Azure SQL Data Warehouse) and on-premises SQL Server database environments: http://bit.ly/2EQon0q.

The *Related Tasks* section of the *Columnstore indexes – Design guidance* documentation referenced in the preceding URL contains links for the T-SQL DDL statements associated with implementing the columnstore index. In most scenarios, the dataset designer in a Power BI project or the author of an Analysis Services model is not responsible for or authorized to optimize data sources using methods such as a columnstore index.

However, the dataset designer can regularly collaborate with the responsible subject matter expert or team as the demands and requirements of the dataset change. For example, the dataset designer can use tools such as DAX Studio and SQL Server Profiler, as described in *Microsoft Power BI Cookbook 2nd Edition* (https://www.amazon.com/Microsoft-Power-Cookbook-expertise-hands/dp/1801813043), to capture the common or important SQL queries generated by Power BI reports and then share this information with the data warehouse team.

Alternatively, the database or data warehouse team can run a trace against a data source system as per the DirectQuery report execution section of *Chapter 2, Preparing Data Sources,* during a test query workload from Power BI. This trace data could be used to identify the specific columns, tables, or expressions associated with slow queries and thus inform database modification decisions.

Let's next look at automatic aggregations.

## Automatic aggregations

Automatic aggregations are a new feature (currently in preview) that uses **machine learning (ML)** to continuously train and optimize ML algorithms to intelligently cache aggregations in memory. When enabled, automatic aggregations can improve query performance by reducing DirectQuery queries against the source system.

Automatic aggregations train the ML model during scheduled refreshes of the dataset at either a **Day** or **Week** interval. The first scheduled refresh during the specified interval thus becomes a refresh of the dataset as well as a training operation for the ML model. During these training operations, Power BI evaluates the query log in order to retrain the ML algorithms regarding which aggregations are most import to cache in memory.

## Composite

Composite models, which blend import mode and DirectQuery mode tables, may be useful when dealing with extremely large fact tables with potentially trillions of rows, or even millions or billions of rows, that cannot comfortably fit into an import-only data model due to memory limitations or other constraints.

Power BI has a specific feature designed to help optimize data model performance that is specific to composite data models. Dataset designers can leverage this feature, which is specifically designed to help speed up the performance of DirectQuery tables and calculations. The feature is called aggregation tables, which we explore in the following subsection.

## Aggregation tables

Aggregation tables are a feature of composite data models specifically targeted at improving the performance of the DirectQuery components of the data model. Aggregation tables allow the dataset designer to create summary tables of pre-aggregated measures that are stored locally within the data model in either import or dual storage mode.

These aggregation tables allow simple aggregations, like sums and averages, to be retrieved from the aggregation for certain levels of granularity.

Only when the granularity of the aggregation table is exceeded, such as reporting against a particular product SKU in the case of an aggregation table grouped by product category and product subcategory, will DirectQuery operations occur. In general, filtering or displaying detail columns not included in the aggregation table will cause DirectQuery operations against the source system.

While not strictly needed given the number of rows in the Reseller Sales table, an aggregation table was created in the composite version of the data model. The aggregation table can be created using SQL or in Power Query. In this case, for demonstration purposes, we chose to use Power Query:

```
let
    Source = #"Reseller Sales",
    GroupRows = Table.Group(Source, {"OrderDateKey", "ResellerKey",
"SalesTerritoryKey"}, {{"Sum of OrderQuantity", each List.
Sum([OrderQuantity]), type nullable number}, {"Sum of Unit Price", each
List.Sum([UnitPrice]), type nullable number}, {"Sum of DiscountAmount",
each List.Sum([DiscountAmount]), type nullable number}, {"Count of Sales",
each Table.RowCount(_), Int64.Type}}),
    ChangedType = Table.TransformColumnTypes(GroupRows,{{"Sum of Unit
Price", Currency.Type}})
in
    ChangedType
```

It is critical to double-check the data types for the aggregation columns as they must have the same data type as the column on which the aggregation is based. The aggregation table, Reseller Sales Aggregation, is hidden, the storage mode set to **Import**, and relationships are created to the corresponding dimension tables, Date, Reseller, and Sales Territory, as shown in *Figure 4.37*:

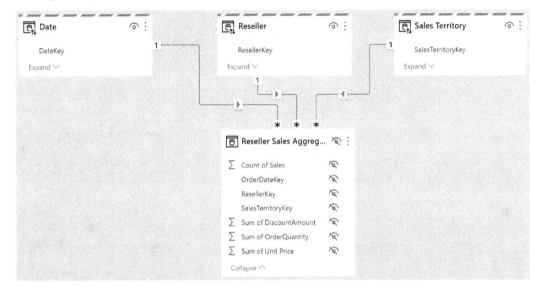

*Figure 4.37: Aggregation table relationships*

If not already, the dimension tables, Date, Reseller, and Sales Territory, should all be set to a storage mode of **Dual** as shown in *Figure 4.38*. Since these tables must operate against the DirectQuery Reseller Sales table as well as the import mode Reseller Sales Aggregation table, a storage mode of **Dual** ensures that query performance is optimized under all circumstances.

To configure aggregations, use the **Fields** pane of the Model view and either from the ellipses menu to the right of the table name or by right-clicking the table name, choose **Manage aggregations**. This opens the **Manage aggregations** dialog as shown in *Figure 4.38*:

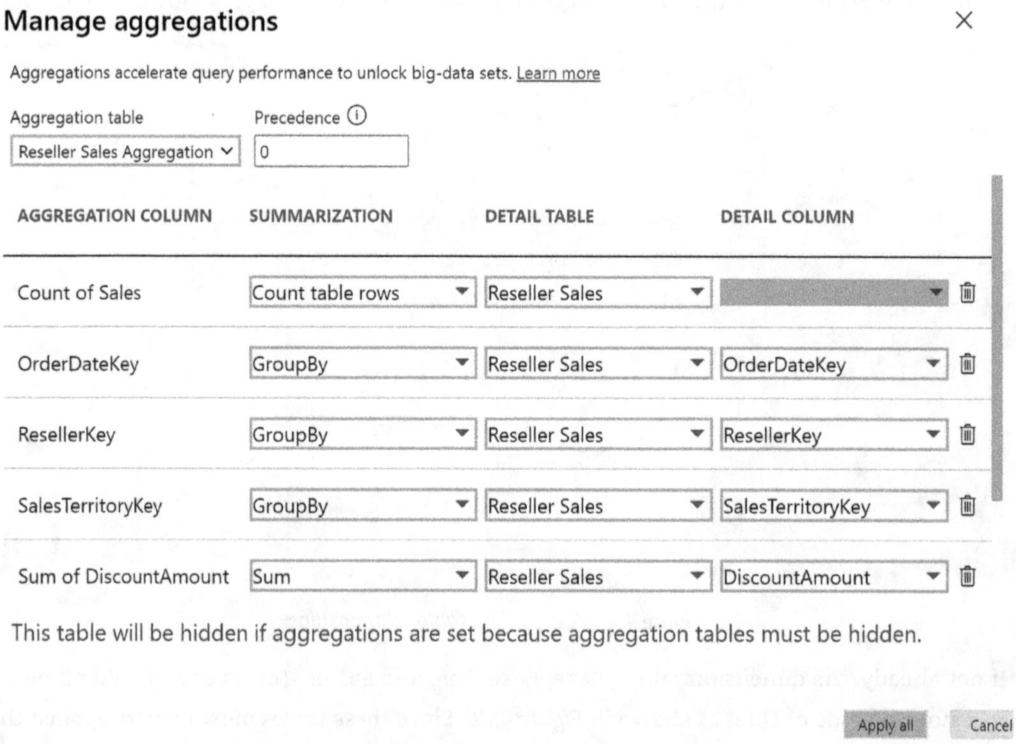

## Manage aggregations                                                                    ✕

Aggregations accelerate query performance to unlock big-data sets. Learn more

Aggregation table          Precedence ⓘ

| Reseller Sales Aggregation ∨ | | 0 | |

| AGGREGATION COLUMN | SUMMARIZATION | DETAIL TABLE | DETAIL COLUMN | |
|---|---|---|---|---|
| Count of Sales | Count table rows ▾ | Reseller Sales ▾ | ▾ | 🗑 |
| OrderDateKey | GroupBy ▾ | Reseller Sales ▾ | OrderDateKey ▾ | 🗑 |
| ResellerKey | GroupBy ▾ | Reseller Sales ▾ | ResellerKey ▾ | 🗑 |
| SalesTerritoryKey | GroupBy ▾ | Reseller Sales ▾ | SalesTerritoryKey ▾ | 🗑 |
| Sum of DiscountAmount | Sum ▾ | Reseller Sales ▾ | DiscountAmount ▾ | 🗑 |

This table will be hidden if aggregations are set because aggregation tables must be hidden.

Apply all      Cancel

*Figure 4.38: Aggregation table relationships*

As shown in *Figure 4.38*, in all cases, the **DETAIL TABLE** and **DETAIL COLUMN** settings for each aggregation table column should reflect the original source column in the corresponding fact table. Grouping columns like OrderDateKey, ResellerKey, and SalesTerritoryKey should be set to a **SUMMARIZATION** of **GroupBy** while table row counts like Count of Sales should be set to **Count table rows**. Other aggregations should be set to their designated aggregation (**Sum, Count, Max, Min**).

Once aggregations are set, you can consider the aggregation table as a sort of surrogate for the actual fact table for the designated aggregations and specified grain. Thus, queries for the aggregations contained within the local (import mode) aggregation table are used instead of querying the DirectQuery source when those aggregations are as granular as (or less than) the aggregation table.

Aggregations at a higher granularity (more granular) than the aggregation table circumvent the aggregation table and directly use the DirectQuery source instead.

This concludes our analysis and advice on optimizing data model performance. As one can see, many different features are included in Power BI that allow dataset designers to optimize the performance of datasets used for analysis and reporting.

## Summary

This chapter built on the queries from *Chapter 3, Connecting To Sources And Transforming Data With M*, to implement import, DirectQuery, and composite analytical data models. Relationships were created between fact and dimension tables as well as between bridge tables and the Sales and Margin Plan to enable actual versus plan reporting and analysis.

Additionally, the fundamentals of designing Power BI models were reviewed and detailed guidance on metadata and the DMVs available for analyzing memory usage was provided. Finally, guidance was provided for optimizing the performance of import, DirectQuery, and composite data models.

The following chapter continues to build on the dataset for this project by developing analytical measures and security models. The DAX expressions implemented in the next chapter directly leverage the relationships defined in this chapter and ultimately drive the visualizations and user experience demonstrated in later chapters.

## Join our community on Discord

Join our community's Discord space for discussions with the author and other readers: https://discord.gg/q6BPbHEPXp

# 5

# Developing DAX Measures and Security Roles

This chapter details the implementation of DAX measures and security roles for the dataset developed in the previous two chapters. We first create a set of base measures for each business process that represents business definitions such as gross and net sales, cost of sales, and margin percentages. These base measures are then leveraged in the development of date intelligence calculations including year-to-date (YTD) and year-over-year (YOY) growth. Additionally, a set of custom measures is created, including exceptions, rankings, and KPI targets, to further extract insights from the dataset and simplify report visualizations.

This chapter also contains examples of dynamic security models in which the identity of the logged-in user is used to filter the dataset. Finally, guidance is provided on testing the performance of DAX expressions with DAX Studio.

In this chapter, we'll review the following topics:

- DAX measure basics
- Base measures
- Date intelligence metrics
- Calculation groups
- Dimension metrics
- Ranking metrics
- Security roles
- Performance testing

Minimal experience or technical skill is required to grasp the essentials of star schema dimensional modeling and to create a basic Power BI dataset containing fact-to-dim relationships and a set of basic DAX measures. However, even with a well-designed data warehouse reflecting a robust data transformation process, business requirements for more complex analytical logic and security are unavoidable. To meet these requirements, it's essential to maintain a solid foundational knowledge of DAX and its concepts of filter context and row context. Thus, we start with a review of the basics concepts that underpin DAX measures.

# DAX measure basics

All analytical expressions ranging from simple sums and averages to custom, complex statistical analyses should be implemented within DAX measures. Although it's technically possible to utilize the default summarization property of columns for some basic measures, well-developed datasets should embed calculation logic into DAX measure definitions thus improving clarity and reusability.

The need for the rapid deployment of complex yet efficient and manageable DAX measures, queries, and security roles underscores earlier guidance regarding the value of an experienced Power BI dataset developer to deliver enterprise-grade solutions. Organizations are strongly advised to appreciate DAX as a functional programming language (not just Excel formulas) that is central to Power BI solutions and thus take steps to ensure that Power BI dataset developers possess the required knowledge and skills with DAX. These steps may involve certification exams, detailed technical interviews, and internal skill development and evaluation.

For example, a seasoned dataset developer should be capable of quickly translating common filtering and aggregation logic found in SQL queries and/or Excel formulas into DAX expressions that return the same numbers. Moreover, professional dataset developers utilize tools beyond Power BI Desktop such as Tabular Editor, DAX Studio, and ALM Toolkit to more productively develop, analyze, and deploy their DAX code, respectively.

Most measure expressions reference and aggregate the numeric columns of fact tables, which are hidden from the Report View, as we have seen in the previous chapter. Additional DAX measures can include filtering conditions that supplement or override any filters applied in Power BI reports, such as the net sales amount for first-year customers only.

Measures are also commonly used to count the number of dimension members that meet certain criteria such as customers who are associated with sales transactions in a given time frame. Additionally, with functions such as SELECTEDVALUE(), DAX measures are often used to display a text value or a date value such as the name of a product currently being filtered in a report or a date reflecting when the source data was refreshed.

Just like the M query language, DAX is a rich, functional language that supports variables and external expression references. Multiple variables can be defined within a DAX measure to improve readability, and the results of other measures can be referenced as well, such as the Plan Grain Status measure in *Chapter 4, Designing Import, DirectQuery, and Composite Data Models*. These layers of abstraction and the built-in code editing features of Power BI Desktop, including IntelliSense and colorization, enable dataset designers to embed powerful, yet sustainable, logic into datasets.

In addition to the DAX measures authored for a Power BI dataset, Power BI Desktop's **Analytics** pane can be used to create metrics specific to a given visual, such as a trend line, min, max, and an average of a metric on a line chart. The **Analytics** pane is reviewed in *Chapter 8, Applying Advanced Report Features*.

We now take a detailed look at perhaps the most important topic when discussing DAX measures, filter context.

## Filter context

Whenever there's a question or doubt about a certain number on a Power BI report, an early step in troubleshooting scenarios is understanding the filter context applicable to the given number. Filter context refers to the filters applied during the evaluation of a measure. The filter context limits the set of rows for each table in the data model that is available to be evaluated for each value displayed in report visualizations.

For example, each value of a Power BI chart that analyzes a sales amount measured by a Product Category column is usually unique because a different set of rows (filter context) of the sales fact table was available to the measure when calculating each value.

In *Figure 5.1*, five distinct filters representing five dimension tables have been applied to a matrix visual of the Internet Gross Sales measure:

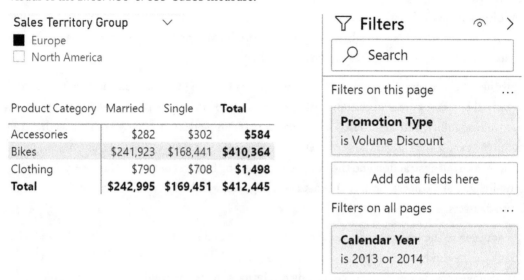

*Figure 5.1: Filtered Power BI report*

Filters applied to the Promotion, Date, Product, Customer, and Sales Territory dimension tables all flow across their relationships to filter the Internet Sales fact table. The Internet Gross Sales measure is a simple SUMX() expression described in the base measures and is thus evaluated against the Internet Sales rows remaining from these filters.

The filters applied come from external sources (those filters not applied within the visual itself such as **Product Category** and **Marital Status** in *Figure 5.1*) can be viewed by clicking on the filter icon shown when a visual is selected on the canvas, as shown in *Figure 5.2*:

*Figure 5.2: Filter icon*

Each individual value in Power BI reports is computed independently. For example, the **$242,995** subtotal value shown in *Figure 5.1* is not filtered by the Product  Category column like other values in the matrix, and it's not calculated as the sum of the three cells in the Married column.

This value is computed using the MaritalStatus column of the Customers table with a value of **Married**, as well as the other filters applied from the Sales  Territory  Group slicer and the filters in the **Filters** pane. See the *Measure evaluation process* section for details on the DAX engine's execution process.

To help better explain filter context, we now look at an equivalent SQL statement for the matrix values shown in *Figure 5.1.*

## SQL equivalent

To help understand filter context and to validate certain reports or DAX measures, it can be helpful to compare Power BI reports to SQL statements. The following SQL statement returns the same six values of the Power BI matrix (excluding the subtotals) via standard inner joins and WHERE clause conditions. Similar to the external filters for a visual, WHERE clauses in SQL statements serve to filter the base set of rows in a table available for further calculations:

```
SELECT
  P.[Product Category]
, C.[Customer Marital Status]
, FORMAT(SUM(F.[Unit Price] * F.[Order Quantity]), '$#,###') AS [Internet
Gross Sales]
FROM BI.vFact_InternetSales as F
  INNER JOIN BI.vDim_FinDate as D on F.[Order Date Key] = D.[Date Key]
  INNER JOIN BI.vDim_Promotion as Promo on F.[Promotion Key] = Promo.
[Promotion Key]
  INNER JOIN BI.vDim_Product as P on F.[Product Key] = P.[Product Key]
  INNER JOIN BI.vDim_Customer as C on F.[Customer Key] = C.[Customer Key]
  INNER JOIN BI.vDim_SalesTerritory as S on F.[Sales Territory Key] =
S.[Sales Territory Key]
WHERE D.[Calendar Year Status] in ('Prior Calendar Year', 'Current
Calendar Year')
  and S.[Sales Territory Group] = 'Europe' and
Promo.[Promotion Type] in ('Excess Inventory', 'Volume Discount')
GROUP BY
  P.[Product Category], C.[Customer Marital Status]
```

In this example, the SQL statement's WHERE clause implements the Power BI report's slicer visual filter and its report- and page-level filters. The GROUP BY clause accounts for the row and column filters of the matrix visual.

Although certain SQL concepts and examples are applicable, DAX is distinct from SQL and other languages, such as **MDX (Multi-Dimensional eXpressions)**. Additionally, since Power BI import mode datasets are stored in a columnar format, SQL developers experienced with row-based tables and B-tree indexes have to revise their design patterns in developing DAX measures and queries.

With filter context understood, another important and related topic with regard to DAX measures is the process by which measures are calculated.

## Measure evaluation process

The measure evaluation process defines how calculations are performed when computing the value of measures. Each value in *Figure 5.1*, such as the $708 from the matrix visual, is computed according to the following four-step process:

1.  Initial Filter Context

    a.  This includes all filters applied within and outside the report canvas by the report author

    b.  Selections on slicer visuals and the rows and columns of the table and matrix visuals represent on-canvas filters

    c.  Report, page, visual, and drill-through filters represent off-canvas filters that also contribute to the initial filter context

2.  Filter Context Modified via DAX

    a.  For base measures and other simplistic expressions, the initial filter context from the report is left unchanged

    b.  For more complex measures, the CALCULATE() function is invoked to further modify the initial filter context

    c.  Via CALCULATE(), the initial filter context can be removed, replaced, or supplemented with an additional filter condition

    d.  In the event of a conflict between the initial filter context from the report (for example, slicers, report-level filters) and the filter condition embedded in the DAX measure, by default, the DAX measure overrides the report filter condition

3.  Relationship Cross-Filtering

    a.  With each table filtered from steps 1 and 2, the filter context is transferred across cross-filtering relationships

    b.  In most cases, the filtered dimension tables filter the related fact tables via single direction cross-filtering

    c.  However, as described in *Chapter 4, Designing Import, DirectQuery, and Composite Data Models*, bidirectional cross-filtering allows the filter context to also transfer from the many side of a relationship to the one side

4.  Measure Logic Computation

    a.  The computation logic of the measure (for example, `DISTINCTCOUNT()`, `COUNTROWS()`) is finally evaluated against the remaining active rows for the given table or column referenced

    b.  For common and base measures, this is simply the set of remaining or active fact table rows

    c.  However, as shown in the following *Dimension metrics* section, other DAX measures reference dimension tables, and thus it's important to understand how these tables are impacted by relationship filtering and DAX expressions

This four-step process is repeated for each value of the report independently. Consequently, reports and visuals that are dense in values require more computing resources to refresh and update based on user filter selections. Large tabular report visuals with many columns and rows are particularly notorious for slow performance, as this forces the DAX engine to compute hundreds or thousands of individual values.

Although report authors and business analysts might not create DAX measures, it's important that they have a basic understanding of the filter context and measure evaluation processes. For example, the report author should understand the cross-filtering relationships of the data model (single or bidirectional) and how certain DAX measures impact the filters applied in reports. Similarly, business analysts should be able to explain to business users why certain report behaviors and results occur.

For example, since bidirectional cross-filtering relationships are generally avoided by dataset developers for performance and unexpected behavior reasons as described in *Chapter 4, Designing Import, DirectQuery, and Composite Data Models*, a common question raised by report authors and users is why a particular dimension or slicer isn't impacted by the filter selection on another dimension or slicer.

Users may expect the list of possible product names on one slicer visual to be reduced by the selection of a fiscal year on a different slicer.

The reason and explanation are simply that the two slicers reflecting different dimension tables in the model may both filter the same fact table(s) and thus impact fact table-based measure calculations but that these filters end at the fact table and there's no direct relationship between the two dimension tables.

We'll next move on to explaining an additional base concept regarding measures, row context.

## Row context

In addition to filter context, it is also important to understand the concept of row context and the ability in DAX to transition from row context to filter context. Row context is an evaluation context that always contains a single row. Row context is present for calculated columns as well as DAX iterator functions such as FILTER() and SUMX(), which execute their expressions per row of a given table.

The set of rows to evaluate from a table is always defined by the filter context, which was described earlier in this chapter. The expression parameter of iterating functions (aggregation functions ending in X such as SUMX and AVERAGEX) can aggregate the rows of a table or can invoke the filter context of the specific row being iterated upon via the CALCULATE() function or a measure reference. Evoking filter context is further explained in the following paragraphs.

Calculated DAX columns are used to illustrate row context. In *Figure 5.3*, four calculated columns have been added to a Date table and reference the Weekday Sort column:

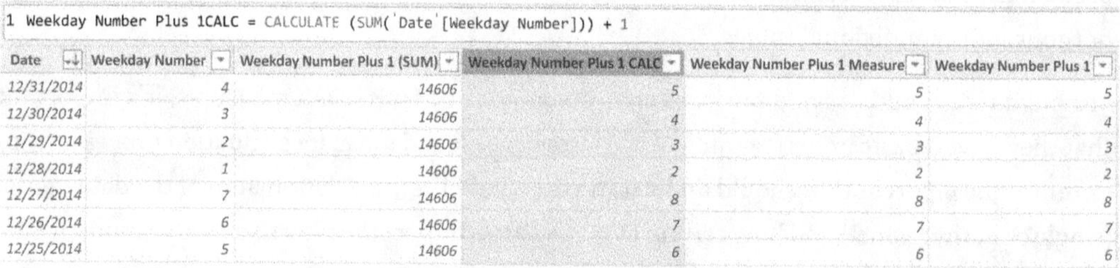

| 1 Weekday Number Plus 1CALC = CALCULATE (SUM('Date'[Weekday Number])) + 1 |||||||
| --- | --- | --- | --- | --- | --- | --- |
| Date ↴ | Weekday Number ▾ | Weekday Number Plus 1 (SUM) ▾ | Weekday Number Plus 1 CALC ▾ | Weekday Number Plus 1 Measure ▾ | Weekday Number Plus 1 ▾ |
| 12/31/2014 | 4 | 14606 | 5 | 5 | 5 |
| 12/30/2014 | 3 | 14606 | 4 | 4 | 4 |
| 12/29/2014 | 2 | 14606 | 3 | 3 | 3 |
| 12/28/2014 | 1 | 14606 | 2 | 2 | 2 |
| 12/27/2014 | 7 | 14606 | 8 | 8 | 8 |
| 12/26/2014 | 6 | 14606 | 7 | 7 | 7 |
| 12/25/2014 | 5 | 14606 | 6 | 6 | 6 |

*Figure 5.3: The row context in calculated columns*

All four calculated columns simply add the value 1 to the Weekday Number column, but achieve their results via distinct expressions:

```
Weekday Number Plus 1 (SUM) = SUM('Date'[Weekday Number]) + 1


Weekday Number Plus 1 CALC = CALCULATE(SUM('Date'[Weekday Number])) + 1
```

```
Weekday Number Plus 1 Measure = [Weekday Number Summed] + 1

Weekday Number Plus 1 = 'Date'[Weekday Number]+1
```

The Weekday Number Plus 1 CALC column and the Weekday Number Plus 1 Measure column represent the concept of context transition. These two columns invoke the filter context (context transition) of the given row via the CALCULATE() function or implicitly via the reference of an existing measure, respectively. Context transition is simply when row context is replaced with filter context. To explain this more clearly, let's expand upon how each calculation uses row and filter context:

- Weekday Number Plus 1 (SUM) is calculated using row context. However, because the SUM function evaluates all rows visible to the current filter context, this calculated column computes the sum of all rows for the Weekday Number column plus one and repeats this value for each row.

- Weekday Number Plus 1 CALC embeds a SUM() function within the CALCULATE() function prior to adding one. As explained further in the *CALCULATE() function* section in this chapter, the CALCULATE() function replaces or modifies the current filter context. In this case, since the CALCULATE() function has no filter parameter, the only purpose of the CALCULATE() function is context transition where the row context is transitioned into a filter context of a single row.

- Weekday Number Plus 1 Measure references an existing measure that sums the Weekday Number column and then adds one. Referencing a measure within a DAX calculation adds an implicit CALCULATE() and thus the same context transition occurs as with the Weekday Number Plus 1 CALC measure.

- Weekday Number Plus 1 references the Weekday Number column of the Date table and adds one. Here only row context is active and thus only the Weekday Number column value in the current row is used in the calculation.

The Weekday Number Plus 1 (SUM) expression demonstrates that aggregation functions, in the absence of CALCULATE() or the implicit CALCULATE() when invoking measures, ignore row context. The three other columns all operate on a per-row basis (row context) but achieve their results via three different methods. The Weekday Number Plus 1 column represents the default behavior of expressions executing in a row context such as calculated columns, FILTER(), and other iterating DAX functions.

To develop more complex DAX measures, it can be necessary to ignore the row context of the input table, such as the Weekday Number Plus 1 (SUM) example, or explicitly invoke the row context of the table depending upon the circumstances and desired resulting value.

Row context, filter context, and context transition can be confusing for those new to DAX and are thus important subjects to bear in mind when learning to create DAX calculated columns and measures. Similarly, another important topic is understanding the difference between DAX functions that return scalar values and tables.

## Scalar and table functions

The majority of DAX functions return a single value based on an aggregation or a logical evaluation of a table or column. For example, the COUNTROWS() and DISTINCTCOUNT() functions return individual numeric values based on a single table and a single column input parameter, respectively.

DAX functions that return individual values as their output, including information functions, such as ISBLANK() and LOOKUPVALUE(), are referred to as scalar functions. For relatively simple datasets and at early stages in projects, most DAX measures reference a single scalar function with no other modifications, such as the use of CALCULATE().

In addition to scalar functions, many DAX functions return a table as the output value. The tables returned by these functions, such as FILTER() and ALL(), are used as input parameters to other DAX measure expressions to impact the filter context under which the measure is executed via the CALCULATE() function.

The DAX language has been extended to support many powerful table functions, such as TOPN(), INTERSECT(), and UNION(), thus providing further support for authoring DAX measures. It is important to note that DAX measures cannot return a table as a value.

In addition to serving as table input parameters to DAX measures, the results of DAX table functions can be returned and exposed to client reporting tools. The most common example of this is the use of the SUMMARIZECOLUMNS() function to return a grouping of certain dataset dimension attributes and certain measures as aggregations to support a data region (e.g. table visual) in a paginated report. Paginated reports are covered in more detail in *Chapter 12, Deploying Paginated Reports*.

Additionally, DAX table functions can return a summarized or filtered table within a Power BI dataset based on the other tables in the dataset. Such DAX-created tables are known as **calculated tables**.

As models grow in complexity and as model authors become more familiar with DAX, new measures increasingly leverage a combination of scalar functions (or existing measures based on scalar functions) and table functions. As per the *DAX variables* section later in this chapter, both scalar and table values (based on scalar and table functions, respectively) can be stored as variables to further support abstraction and readability.

With scalar and table functions understood, we'll next turn our attention to an example of the use of DAX table functions with respect to related tables.

## Related tables

DAX measure calculations respect the row context formed by relationships between tables. Thus, it is possible to reference other tables in the data model from within a row context via the RELATED() and RELATEDTABLE() functions.

*Figure 5.4* shows the Data View of an import mode dataset where three calculated columns have been added to a Date dimension table with expressions referencing the Freight column of the Internet Sales fact table:

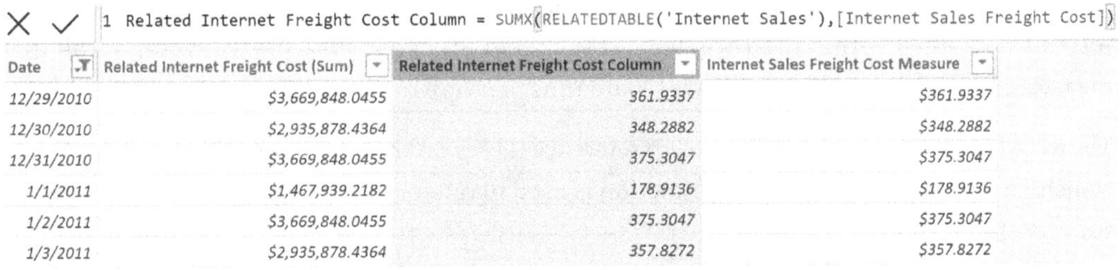

| | 1 Related Internet Freight Cost Column = SUMX(RELATEDTABLE('Internet Sales'),[Internet Sales Freight Cost]) |

| Date | Related Internet Freight Cost (Sum) | Related Internet Freight Cost Column | Internet Sales Freight Cost Measure |
|---|---|---|---|
| 12/29/2010 | $3,669,848.0455 | 361.9337 | $361.9337 |
| 12/30/2010 | $2,935,878.4364 | 348.2882 | $348.2882 |
| 12/31/2010 | $3,669,848.0455 | 375.3047 | $375.3047 |
| 1/1/2011 | $1,467,939.2182 | 178.9136 | $178.9136 |
| 1/2/2011 | $3,669,848.0455 | 375.3047 | $375.3047 |
| 1/3/2011 | $2,935,878.4364 | 357.8272 | $357.8272 |

*Figure 5.4: Row context with RELATEDTABLE()*

The DAX expressions used for each column are as follows:

```
Related Internet Freight Cost (Sum) = SUMX(RELATEDTABLE('Internet
Sales'),(SUM('Internet Sales'[Freight])))


Related Internet Freight Cost Column = SUMX(RELATEDTABLE('Internet
Sales'),[Freight])


Related Internet Freight Cost Measure = SUMX(RELATEDTABLE('Internet
Sales'),[Internet Sales Freight Cost])
```

For reference, the formula for the `Internet Sales Freight Cost` measure is simply:

```
Internet Sales Freight Cost = SUM('Internet Sales'[Freight])
```

Only `Related Internet Sales Freight Cost Column` and `Related Internet Sales Freight Cost Measure` return the correct freight cost amount for each date. The `Related Internet Freight Cost (Sum)` column computes the total freight cost on the entire `Internet Sales` table and uses this value for each related row before summing the result.

For example, five rows on the `Internet Sales` table have a date of 12/29/2010 and the sum of the `Freight` column on the `Internet Sales` table is **$733,969.61**. Given that the SUM() function ignores row context, the SUMX() function, calculates a value of **$3,669,848** for that date, which is the result of five (rows) multiplied by **$733,969.61**.

`Related Internet Freight Cost Column` returns the correct amount since the value of the `Freight` column for each row is evaluated within the row context and then the amounts in these rows are summed by the SUMX() function.

`Related Internet Sales Freight Cost Measure` also returns the correct amount, which may seem odd since `Related Internet Freight Cost (Sum)` essentially simply substitutes in the formula contained within the `Internet Sales Freight Cost` measure. However, recall that measures implicitly invoke CALCULATE() and thus preserve row context via context transition.

The RELATEDTABLE() function is used to reference tables on the many side of one-to-many relationships. Likewise, the RELATED() function is used to reference tables on the one side of many-to-one relationships.

For example, a calculated column or the row context of an iterating function such as SUMX() on the `Internet Sales` fact table would use RELATED() to access a dimension table and apply logic referencing the dimension table per row of the `Internet Sales` table.

We now turn our attention to a specific DAX function that we briefly covered in previous sections, the CALCULATE() function.

# The CALCULATE() function

The CALCULATE() function is perhaps the most important function in DAX as it enables the author to modify the filter context under which a measure is evaluated. Regardless of the fields used and filters applied in reports, the filter parameter input(s) to CALCULATE() is applied.

Specifically, the CALCULATE() function either adds a filter to a measure expression (for example, Color = "Red"), ignores the filters from a table or column (for example, ALL(Product)), or updates/overwrites the filters applied within a report to the filter parameter specified in CALCULATE().

The syntax of CALCULATE() is the following:

```
CALCULATE(<expression>, <filter1>, <filter2>, …).
```

Any number of filter parameters can be specified including no filter parameters such as CALCULATE(SUM(Sales[Sales Amount])). When multiple filter parameters are specified, the function respects all of them together as a single condition via internal AND logic. Thus, rows resulting from the specified filter context must meet the criteria of the first filter, the criteria of the second filter, and so on.

The expression parameter is evaluated based on the new and final filter context applied via the filter parameters. In the following measure, any filter applied to any column from the Product or Sales Territory tables are ignored by the calculation:

```
Internet Sales Row Count (Ignore Product and Territory) =
CALCULATE(COUNTROWS('Internet Sales'),ALL('Product'),ALL('Sales
Territory'))
```

The preceding measure represents one simple example of a table function (ALL()) being used in conjunction with a scalar function (COUNTROWS()) via CALCULATE(), as described in the previous section, *Scalar and table functions*.

There are multiple forms of the ALL() function beyond ALL(table). The ALL() function can be used to ignore the values from a single column or multiple columns, such as the following two examples: (All('Customer'[Customer City]) and ALL('Customer'[Customer City], 'Customer'[Customer Country]).

Additionally, the ALLEXCEPT() function only allows certain columns specified to impact the filter context, and the ALLSELECTED() function ignores filters from inside a query but allows filters from outside the query. Finally, the REMOVEFILTERS() function allows certain filters to be removed when executing the CALCULATE() function.

Just as the CALCULATE() function is used to modify the filter context of scalar value expressions, the CALCULATETABLE() function is used to modify the filter context of expressions that return tables. For example, the following expression returns all columns from the product dimension table and only the rows that match the two filter parameter conditions specified:

```
CALCULATETABLE('Product',
'Product'[Product Category] = "Bikes",
'Product'[Product Dealer Price] > 2100)
```

The modified table result from CALCULATETABLE() can then be used as a parameter input to another table function such as FILTER() or as a filter parameter to CALCULATE().

## The FILTER() function

The FILTER() function is one of the most important and powerful functions in DAX in that it allows complex logic to fully define the set of rows of a table. FILTER() accepts a table as an input and returns a table with each row respecting its defined condition.

The FILTER() function is almost always used as a parameter to a CALCULATE() function and can add to the existing filter context or redefine the filter context by invoking ALL(), ALLEXCEPT(), or ALLSELECTED() as its table input. The date intelligence measures described later in this chapter utilize FILTER() to fully define the set of Date rows for the filter context.

In the following DAX measure, the FILTER() function is utilized against the Date table and implements a condition based on the existing Internet Gross Sales measure:

```
Days with over 15K Gross Internet Sales =
    CALCULATE(COUNTROWS('Date'),
      FILTER('Date', [Internet Gross Sales] > 15000))
```

With respect to the use of CALCULATE, the ability to directly reference DAX measures is unique to the FILTER() function. For example, the following measure expression is not allowed by the DAX engine: CALCULATE(COUNTROWS('Date'), [Internet Gross Sales] > 15000). This is because the standard filter clause of the CALCULATE function cannot directly reference measures.

The Days with over 15K Gross Internet Sales measure and the Internet Gross Sales base measure are used to create the visuals shown in *Figure 5.5*:

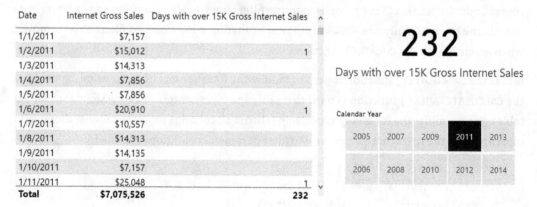

*Figure 5.5: DAX measure with FILTER*

Given that the FILTER() function simply references the Date table and does not remove any filters via ALL(), the measure executes on each date contained in the matrix visual to return a 1 or a blank. When no dates are on the visual, such as the subtotal row or the card visual, the total number of days that meet the condition (**232** for the year **2011**) is returned.

If the Internet Gross Sales measure was not included in the table visual, by default, Power BI would only display the dates with a 1 value for the Days with over a 15K Gross Internet Sales measure.

Given both its iterative (row-by-row) execution and the potential to apply complex measures to each row, it's important to use the FILTER() function carefully. For example, DAX measures should not use FILTER() directly against large fact tables since the filter condition must be evaluated for every row of the fact table, which may be millions, billions, or even trillions of rows. Additionally, FILTER() should not be used when it's not needed for simple measures such as the following two examples:

```
CALCULATE([Internet Gross Sales],'Product'[Product Category] = "Bikes")

CALCULATE([Reseller Gross Sales],'Product'[Product Color] IN {"Red",
"White"},Promotion[Discount Percentage] > .25).
```

With two of the most important DAX functions, CALCULATE() and FILTER(), explained, we'll next cover the last important base DAX concept, variables.

# DAX variables

Variables can be defined within DAX measures and primarily serve to improve the readability of DAX expressions. Rather than creating and referencing separate DAX measures, variables provide an inline option, thereby limiting the volume of distinct measures in a dataset.

As a basic example of variable syntax, the Last Refreshed measure described in the *Parameter tables queries* section of *Chapter 3, Connecting to Sources and Transforming Data with M*, uses a DAX variable in its expression, as follows:

```
Last Refresh Msg =
    VAR __CurrentDateValue = MAX('Current Date'[CurrentDate])
RETURN
    "Last Refreshed: " & __CurrentDateValue
```

The VAR function is used to name a variable and the RETURN keyword allows for the variable's result to be referenced by this name.

In this example, the `__CurrentDateValue` variable retrieves the date stored in the `CurrentDate` parameter table, and a string of text is concatenated with the variable to generate the text message.

Variables can sometimes improve the performance of slow measures. Variables are only evaluated once and their resulting values (a scalar value or a table) can be referenced multiple times within a measure.

Measures that produce fewer storage engine queries almost always execute faster and make better use of hardware resources. Therefore, any DAX measure or query that makes multiple references to the same expression logic can be a good candidate for DAX variables.

A common use case for DAX variables is to split up the components of an otherwise more complex DAX expression. In the following example, six DAX variables are used to produce a filtered distinct count of accessory products and a filtered distinct count of clothing products:

```
Reseller High Value Accessory and Clothing Products =
/*
Accessory category products with over 20K in net sales and over 32% net
margin since last year
Clothing category products with over 55K in net sales and over 28% net
margin since last year
Enable filtering from dimension tables related to Reseller Sales
*/
    VAR __AccessorySales = 30000
    VAR __AccessoryNetMargin = .32
    VAR __ClothingSales = 50000
    VAR __ClothingNetMargin = .28
//Distinct Accessory Products
    VAR __AccessoryProducts =
    CALCULATE(
        DISTINCTCOUNT('Product'[ProductAlternateKey]),
        FILTER(
            SUMMARIZE(
                CALCULATETABLE('Reseller Sales',
                    'Date'[Calendar Year] IN {2014, 2013},
                    'Product'[Product Category] = "Accessories"
                ),
                'Product'[ProductAlternateKey]
            ),
```

```
            [Reseller Net Margin %] >= __AccessoryNetMargin && [Reseller
    Net Sales] >= __AccessorySales
        )
    )
    //Distinct Clothing Products
    VAR __ClothingProducts =
    CALCULATE(
        DISTINCTCOUNT('Product'[ProductAlternateKey]),
        FILTER(
            SUMMARIZE(
                CALCULATETABLE('Reseller Sales',
                    'Date'[Calendar Year] IN {2014, 2013},
                    'Product'[Product Category] = "Clothing"
                ),
                'Product'[ProductAlternateKey]
            ),
            [Reseller Net Margin %] >= __ClothingNetMargin && [Reseller Net
    Sales] > __ClothingSales
        )
    )
RETURN
    __AccessoryProducts + __ClothingProducts
```

With the variables named and evaluated, the RETURN keyword simply adds the results of the two distinct count expressions contained within the __AccessoryProducts and __ClothingProducts variables. The multi-line comment at the top of the expression denoted by /* and */ makes the DAX measure easier to understand in the future.

Single-line comments have been added using // to precede the distinct accessory and clothing products. With the variables declared in this structure, it becomes very easy to adjust the measure to different input thresholds such as a higher or lower net sales value or net margin rates.

The most efficient filtering conditions of measures should be implemented in measures first. Efficient filter conditions are those that don't require the FILTER() function, such as the Calendar Year and Product Category filter conditions in the Reseller High Value Accessory and Clothing Products measure.

Simple filters that do not require the `FILTER()` function are known as Boolean (true/false) expressions. Boolean expressions are more efficient because import mode datasets consist of tables represented by in-memory column stores, which are explicitly optimized to efficiently filter columns based upon Boolean expressions.

However, Boolean expressions come with a number of restrictions. Namely Boolean expressions cannot:

- Compare columns to other columns
- Reference a measure
- Use nested `CALCULATE()` functions
- Use functions that scan or return a table

Once sufficient filters have been applied, more-complex but less-performant filtering conditions can operate on smaller sets of data, thus limiting their impact on query performance.

A Power BI report can leverage the measure in a visual-level filter to only display the specific products that meet the criteria of the measure. In *Figure 5.6*, only six products (two accessories, four clothing) are displayed given the filter on the `Reseller High Value Accessory and Clothing Products` measure:

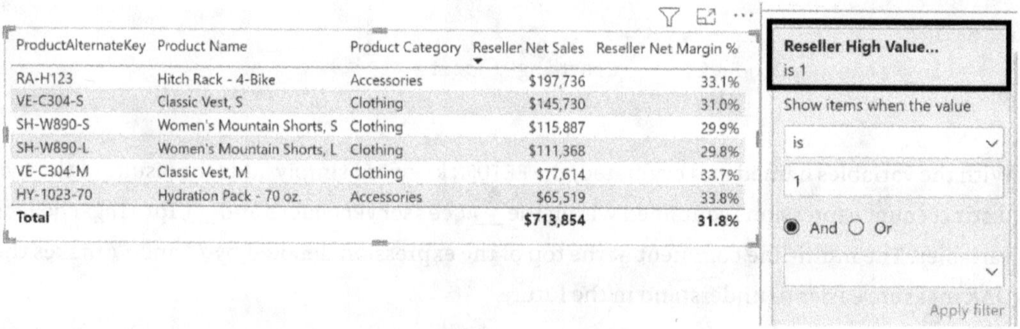

| ProductAlternateKey | Product Name | Product Category | Reseller Net Sales | Reseller Net Margin % |
|---|---|---|---|---|
| RA-H123 | Hitch Rack - 4-Bike | Accessories | $197,736 | 33.1% |
| VE-C304-S | Classic Vest, S | Clothing | $145,730 | 31.0% |
| SH-W890-S | Women's Mountain Shorts, S | Clothing | $115,887 | 29.9% |
| SH-W890-L | Women's Mountain Shorts, L | Clothing | $111,368 | 29.8% |
| VE-C304-M | Classic Vest, M | Clothing | $77,614 | 33.7% |
| HY-1023-70 | Hydration Pack - 70 oz. | Accessories | $65,519 | 33.8% |
| **Total** | | | **$713,854** | **31.8%** |

**Reseller High Value...**
is 1

Show items when the value

is

1

● And ○ Or

Apply filter

*Figure 5.6: Variable-based DAX measure as a visual-level filter*

The filter context of the `Reseller Sales` fact table is respected via the `SUMMARIZE()` function. Just like bidirectional cross-filtering via the `CROSSFILTER()` function and bidirectional relationships, other dimensions related to the `Reseller Sales` fact table can be used for filtering the measure. For example, a filter on the `SalesTerritoryCountry` column for the **United States** would result in only five products.

It's necessary to reference the alternate key of the product dimension given the implementation of slowly changing dimension logic, as described in *Chapter 1, Planning Power BI Projects*, since a single product can have multiple rows in its dimension table, reflecting various changes such as with list prices and product weight. These unique product keys would be reflected in the fact table, and so using the product key column would result in counting different versions of the same product multiple times.

In addition to scalar values like DAX measures, DAX variables can also store table values such as a specific set of customer key values or filter a set of product rows. DAX measures can then reference and apply aggregation functions against this set of tables.

In the following example, two distinct sets of customer keys (tables) are computed via variables and then combined via the UNION() function to drive the filter context of the measure:

```
Internet Sales Married and Accessory Customers =
    VAR __MarriedCustomers =
        SUMMARIZE(
            CALCULATETABLE('Internet Sales',
                'Customer'[MaritalStatus] = "Married"),
            'Customer'[CustomerAlternateKey])
    VAR __AccessoryCustomersThisYear =
        SUMMARIZE(
            CALCULATETABLE('Internet Sales',
                'Date'[Calendar Year] = 2013,'Product'[Product Category] =
"Accessories"),
            'Customer'[CustomerAlternateKey])
    VAR __TargetCustomerSet = DISTINCT(UNION(__MarriedCustomers,__
AccessoryCustomersThisYear))
RETURN
    CALCULATE(DISTINCTCOUNT('Customer'[CustomerAlternateKey]),
    __TargetCustomerSet)
```

The DISTINCT() function is applied against the result of the UNION() function since duplicate rows are retained by the UNION() function in DAX. Note that the UNION() function simply appends two or more tables together, returning a single table. The DISTINCT() function returns a table of unique values (either unique rows in a table or the unique values in a single column).

Just like the previous example with variables, the SUMMARIZE() function is used to both embed filter conditions and respect the filter context of the Internet Sales fact table. In this example, SUMMARIZE() allows selections on dimension tables related to the Internet Sales fact table, such as Sales Territory to also impact the measure.

*Figure 5.7* shows a matrix visual in a Power BI report where the Sales Territory Country column from the Sales Territory dimension is used as the column header and the results from the measure reflect each individual country:

| | United States | Australia | United Kingdom | Germany | France | Canada |
|---|---|---|---|---|---|---|
| Internet Sales Orders | 9567 | 6718 | 3031 | 2484 | 2484 | 3375 |
| Internet Sales Married and Accessory Customers | 7016 | 3217 | 1775 | 1607 | 1597 | 1382 |

*Figure 5.7: Table-valued DAX variable-based measure*

The filter context embedded into both variables (__MarriedCustomers and __AccessoryCustomersThisYear) of the measure provides the equivalent behavior of bidirectional cross-filtering between Internet Sales and the Customer dimension. The SUMMARIZE() function is used rather than CROSSFILTER() when given a performance advantage. See the *Performance testing* section later in this chapter for additional details on performance testing.

The combination of table-valued DAX variables and set-based DAX functions such as UNION(), INTERSECT(), and EXCEPT() supports a wide variety of analytical operations. Authors of DAX measures should familiarize themselves with the essentials of DAX as a query language, particularly the SUMMARIZE() and SUMMARIZECOLUMNS() functions. Custom tables resulting from DAX queries are often needed by DAX measure expressions and can also be used in other applications such as SSRS.

This completes our exploration of all of the base concepts with respect to DAX measures. Next, we use the knowledge from this section to develop the base measures for our dataset.

# Base measures

Before any custom or complex DAX measures can be developed, a set of relatively simple base measures must be implemented first. These measures represent the metrics from the *Define the facts* section of *Chapter 1, Planning Power BI Projects*, and thus contain validated and approved business definitions.

For Adventure Works, a set of base measures related to sales, cost, and margins are applicable to both the Internet Sales and Reseller Sales fact tables, such as the following:

```
Reseller Gross Sales = SUMX('Reseller Sales', 'Reseller Sales'[UnitPrice]
* 'Reseller Sales'[OrderQuantity])
Reseller Sales Discounts = SUM('Reseller Sales'[DiscountAmount])
Reseller Net Sales = [Reseller Gross Sales] - [Reseller Sales Discounts]
Reseller Sales Product Cost = SUMX('Reseller Sales', 'Reseller
Sales'[OrderQuantity] * 'Reseller Sales'[ProductStandardCost])
Reseller Sales Freight Cost = SUM('Reseller Sales'[Freight])
Reseller Cost of Sales = [Reseller Sales Product Cost] + [Reseller Sales
Freight Cost]
Reseller Gross Product Margin = [Reseller Gross Sales] - [Reseller Sales
Product Cost]
Reseller Gross Product Margin % = DIVIDE([Reseller Gross Product
Margin],[Reseller Gross Sales])
Reseller Net Product Margin = [Reseller Net Sales] - [Reseller Sales
Product Cost]
Reseller Net Product Margin % = DIVIDE([Reseller Net Product
Margin],[Reseller Net Sales])
Reseller Gross Margin = [Reseller Gross Sales] - [Reseller Cost of Sales]
Reseller Gross Margin % = DIVIDE([Reseller Gross Margin],[Reseller Gross
Sales])
Reseller Net Margin = [Reseller Net Sales] - [Reseller Cost of Sales]
Reseller Net Margin % = DIVIDE([Reseller Net Margin],[Reseller Net Sales])
```

As shown in the *Fact table columns* section from *Chapter 4, Designing Import, DirectQuery, and Composite Data Models*, three fact table columns (ExtendedAmount, SalesAmount, and TotalProductCost) were excluded from the Power BI fact table to save resources. The SUMX() function is used to compute the equivalent values from these three columns to support the Gross Sales, Net Sales, and Product Cost measures, respectively.

Sales discounts and freight costs, both simple sums of their respective fact table columns, are the two measures that create differences among the base measures. Discounts separate gross sales from net sales and freight costs separate the cost of sales from product costs only. The distinct definitions of the base measures support common analysis needs, such as the profitability (margin) of sales inclusive or exclusive of freight costs.

With base measures created for both the `Reseller Sales` and `Internet Sales` fact tables, an additional set of base measures can be created for Adventure Works as an organization. Several of these measures can simply sum the `Reseller Sales` and `Internet Sales` measures as shown in the following examples:

```
AdWorks Net Sales = [Internet Net Sales] + [Reseller Net Sales]
AdWorks Cost of Sales = [Internet Cost of Sales] + [Reseller Cost of
Sales]
AdWorks Net Margin = [AdWorks Net Sales] - [AdWorks Cost of Sales]
AdWorks Net Margin % = DIVIDE([AdWorks Net Margin],[AdWorks Net Sales])
```

Additional DAX measures with specific filtering or evaluation logic such as date intelligence metrics can reference the base measures in their expressions. Via this measure branching, any subsequent changes to the definition of the base measures are automatically reflected in other dependent measures. Additionally, the readability of the custom measures is improved, as these expressions only contain their specific logic.

With our base measures created, we can next create supporting measures.

## Measure support expressions

Large and complex Power BI datasets with many measures may have one or multiple measure support tables. As shown in the previous chapters, these hidden tables don't contain data and aren't refreshed with the dataset, but serve as the home table for commonly used DAX expressions.

Unlike DAX variables, hidden DAX measure expressions are globally available to other DAX measures and queries. Measure support expressions, therefore, serve as a staging and consolidation layer to simplify DAX measures.

The measure support table may contain any of the following types of expressions:

* KPI targets
* Current and prior periods
* Filter context information

The two measures described in the *Measure support logic* section of *Chapter 4, Designing Import, DirectQuery, and Composite Data Models*, represent the filter context information type of measure support.

These measures typically use the ISFILTERED() or ISCROSSFILTERED() functions and are referenced within conditional expressions of other measures. Additionally, the USERPRINCIPALNAME() function is a good candidate for the Measure Support table if dynamic RLS is needed, or if other, user-based functionality is built into the dataset. The USERPRINCIPALNAME() function is covered in more detail in the *Dynamic row-level security* section later in this chapter.

The ISFILTERED() function is used to test whether an individual column or a table is directly filtered only. The ISCROSSFILTERED() function, however, tests whether an individual column or a table is either directly filtered or if it's filtered via its relationship to another table in the model,

Let's now look at the first of our support measures, a target for a KPI visual.

## KPI targets

The standard **Key Performance Indicator** (**KPI**) visual in Power BI Desktop compares an indicator measure relative to a specified target value, which may also be a measure. The variance between the indicator and the target is displayed in the visual and is used to drive the color formatting (for example, red = bad; green = good).

For many measures, a corresponding target measure may need to be created that applies some calculation logic to an existing measure. The following measure is simply 10% greater than the previous year's year-to-date net sales:

```
Target: 10% Above PY YTD Internet Sales = [Internet Net Sales (PY YTD)] *
1.10
```

In a standard KPI visual, the target measure is displayed as the goal and used to calculate the variance percentage between the indicator and the target. In *Figure 5.8*, a $16.35M indicator value for Internet Net Sales (YTD) is 154.43% higher than the 10% growth target measure of $6.43M:

Internet Net Sales (YTD vs. 10) Growth)

# 16.35M˯
Goal: 6.43M (+154.43%)

*Figure 5.8: Standard KPI visual*

Several other common visuals in Power BI benefit from target measures, including the bullet chart and the gauge visual. Several of these visuals can use multiple target measures to define alternative thresholds, such as the min and max values displayed.

In certain scenarios, a dedicated table of corporate target measures can be added to a dataset. For example, a table may contain columns for expected or target customer counts, products sold, and other metrics at a given date's granularity. Target measures can be created to access the values of this table via utility functions, such as LOOKUPVALUE().

The LOOKUPVALUE() function returns a scalar value from a single column that results from filtering rows of a table based on specified criteria. In other words, LOOKUPVALUE() provides the means to return a single "cell," similar to Excel's VLOOKUP function. LOOKUPVALUE() is particularly useful because it ignores the current filter context.

As shown in the examples in the following section, the LOOKUPVALUE() function can be relied on to provide the same input value to other measures, such as a date or a number referring to specific date rows, regardless of any filters applied in the report.

Let's take a look at using the LOOKUPVALUE() function for current and prior period support measures.

## Current and prior periods

A common requirement of date intelligence metrics is to compare the YTD total for a measure versus the equivalent time period of the prior year. For example, on November 14, 2017, the visual would compare January through October of 2017 versus January through October of 2016.

Without any external filtering, however, a standard YTD measure would include the 14 days of November in 2017 and would capture the entire year of 2016 if the year 2016 was in the filter context. To deliver equivalent or apples-to-apples comparisons of equal time periods, the filter context of measures can be further customized.

The following measures retrieve the year-to-date net sales through the prior calendar month and prior calendar week. For example, throughout the month of November, the YTD Last Month measure would, at most, only retrieve the net sales through the month of October. Likewise, the YTD Last Week measure would, at most, only include the net sales through the end of the prior week of the year (45):

```
Prior Calendar Month Number =
    VAR __CurrentDay = TODAY()
RETURN
    IF (LOOKUPVALUE('Date'[Month Number],'Date'[Date],__CurrentDay) = 1,
        12,
            LOOKUPVALUE('Date'[Month Number],'Date'[Date],__CurrentDay)-1
```

```
    )
Prior Calendar Week Number =
    VAR __CurrentDay = TODAY()
RETURN
    IF(LOOKUPVALUE('Date'[Week of Year],'Date'[Date],__CurrentDay) = 1,
        CALCULATE(MAX('Date'[Week of
Year]),FILTER(ALL('Date'),'Date'[Calendar Year] = MAX('Date'[Calendar
Year]) - 1)),
        LOOKUPVALUE('Date'[Week of Year],'Date'[Date],__CurrentDay)-1
    )
Internet Net Sales (YTD Last Month) =
    IF([Prior Calendar Month Number] <> 12,
        CALCULATE([Internet Net Sales], FILTER(ALL('Date'),'Date'[Calendar
Year] = MAX('Date'[Calendar Year]) && 'Date'[Date] <= MAX('Date'[Date]) &&
'Date'[Month Number] <= [Prior Calendar Month Number])),
        CALCULATE([Internet Net Sales], FILTER(ALL('Date'),
'Date'[Calendar Year] = MAX('Date'[Calendar Year])-1 && 'Date'[Date]
<= MAX('Date'[Date]) && 'Date'[Month Number] <= [Prior Calendar Month
Number]))
    )
Internet Net Sales (YTD Last Week) =
    VAR __CurrentWeek = LOOKUPVALUE('Date'[Week of
Year],'Date'[Date],TODAY())
RETURN
    IF(__CurrentWeek <> 1,
        CALCULATE([Internet Net Sales], FILTER(ALL('Date'),'Date'[Calendar
Year] = MAX('Date'[Calendar Year]) && 'Date'[Date] <= MAX('Date'[Date]) &&
'Date'[Week of Year] <= [Prior Calendar Week Number])),
        CALCULATE([Internet Net Sales], FILTER(ALL('Date'),'Date'[Calendar
Year] = MAX('Date'[Calendar Year])-1 && 'Date'[Date] <= MAX('Date'[Date])
&& 'Date'[Week of Year] <= [Prior Calendar Week Number]))
    )
```

For any prior calendar year in the filter context, the (YTD Last Month) measure would only include January through October for this given year. Likewise, the (YTD Last Week) measure would only include weeks 1 through 45 of the given year. By embedding this dynamic filtering logic, it's possible to use these measures in report visuals without applying any additional filters.

The TODAY() function combined with the LOOKUPVALUE() function makes it possible to retrieve values at query time relative to the current date. In the previous example, the month and week number columns of the current year (for example, October = 10) are queried via LOOKUPVALUE() based on the current date.

With these values retrieved, subtracting one from the results provides the value associated with the prior month and prior week, respectively. These measures are then referenced in the FILTER() function of their respective year-to-date measures.

Similar to this simple example, dynamically computed dates and other values make it possible to create measures for the current date and yesterday:

```
Internet Net Sales (Today) = CALCULATE([Internet Net Sales],
FILTER(ALL('Date'),'Date'[Date] = TODAY()))

Internet Net Sales (Yesterday) = CALCULATE([Internet Net Sales],
FILTER(ALL('Date'),'Date'[Date] = TODAY()-1))
```

Along with the date intelligence metrics described in the following section, a rich set of date-based metrics gives users of Power BI reports and dashboards visibility for both short- and long-term results.

# Date intelligence metrics

Date intelligence metrics are typically the first set of measures to be added to a dataset following base measures. These measures reference the base measures and add a custom filtering condition to the Date dimension table, thus providing visibility to multiple distinct time intervals, such as year-to-date and the previous year-to-date.

Given their built-in date filtering logic, Power BI reports and dashboards can be developed faster and without manual maintenance costs of updating date filter conditions.

The following four measures apply custom filter contexts to either return the current year, month, and week by default, or the latest of these time intervals given the date filters applied in a report:

```
Internet Net Sales (CY) = CALCULATE([Internet Net
Sales],FILTER(ALL('Date'), 'Date'[Calendar Year] = MAX('Date'[Calendar
Year]) && 'Date'[Date] >= MIN('Date'[Date]) && 'Date'[Date] <=
MAX('Date'[Date])))

Internet Net Sales (YTD) = CALCULATE([Internet Net Sales],
```

```
FILTER(ALL('Date'),'Date'[Calendar Year] = MAX('Date'[Calendar Year]) &&
'Date'[Date] <= MAX('Date'[Date])))


Internet Net Sales (MTD) = CALCULATE([Internet Net Sales],
FILTER(ALL('Date'),'Date'[Year Month Number] = MAX('Date'[Year Month
Number]) && 'Date'[Date] <= MAX('Date'[Date])))


Internet Net Sales (WTD) = CALCULATE([Internet Net Sales],
FILTER(ALL('Date'),'Date'[Year Week Number] = MAX('Date'[Year Week
Number]) && 'Date'[Date] <= MAX('Date'[Date])))
```

As explained in the *Row context* section of this chapter, the use of the MIN( ) and MAX( ) functions within the FILTER( ) function invokes the filter context of the report query. For example, if a report page is filtered to the second quarter of 2016 (2016-Q2), the CY measure only returns the sales from these three months while the YTD measure includes both the first and second quarter of 2016. The month-to-date (MTD) and week-to-date (WTD) measures return the sales for June of 2016 and week 27 of 2016, the last month and week in the filter context.

The Date dimension table only contains rows through the current date. Therefore, in the absence of any other date filters applied in a report, these measures default to the current YTD, MTD, and WTD totals for net sales as per *Figure 5.9*:

| 5,145.91 | 1,874,360.29 | 16,351,550.34 |
|---|---|---|
| Internet Net Sales (WTD) | Internet Net Sales (MTD) | Internet Net Sales (YTD) |

*Figure 5.9: Date intelligence metrics for the last full year in the dataset (2013)*

The CY measure returns the same value as the YTD measure when no other date filters are applied.

The MTD and WTD measures both reference a numeric column on the Date table that corresponds to the given granularity. For example, December of 2013 and January of 2014 are represented by the values 108 and 109 in the Year Month Number column. As shown in the previous chapter, these sequential columns are critical for date intelligence and are also used by the Sort By column property.

The following set of DAX measures return the prior year, month, and week given the filter context of the report:

```
Internet Net Sales (PY) = CALCULATE([Internet Net
Sales],FILTER(ALL('Date'), CONTAINS(VALUES('Date'[Prior Year
Date]),'Date'[Prior Year Date],'Date'[Date])))
```

```
Internet Net Sales (PYTD) = CALCULATE([Internet Net Sales],
FILTER(ALL('Date'),'Date'[Calendar Year] = MAX('Date'[Calendar Year])-1 &&
'Date'[Date] <= MAX('Date'[Prior Year Date])))


Internet Net Sales (PMTD) = CALCULATE([Internet Net Sales],
FILTER(ALL('Date'),'Date'[Year Month Number] = MAX('Date'[Year Month
Number])-1 && 'Date'[Date] <= MAX('Date'[Prior Month Date])))


Internet Net Sales (PWTD) = CALCULATE([Internet Net Sales],
FILTER(ALL('Date'),'Date'[Year Week Number] = MAX('Date'[Year Week
Number])-1 && 'Date'[Date] <= MAX('Date'[Prior Week Date])))
```

The Calendar Year, Year Month Number, and Year Week Number columns used by the current period measures are also referenced by the prior period measures. However, the prior period measures subtract a value of one from the result of the MAX() function to navigate to the given preceding period.

In the Internet Net Sales (PY) measure, the CONTAINS() function used within the filtering parameter of the FILTER() function returns a true or false value for each prior calendar year date based on the date column. The CONTAINS() function returns true if the date column reflects the filter context of the report query and thus only the corresponding prior year dates are passed to FILTER() as the modified filter context.

DAX provides a number of functions dedicated to date intelligence, such as DATEADD() and SAMEPERIODLASTYEAR(). These functions are much less verbose than the techniques from these examples, but they're also generally limited to standard calendars. The approach described in this section leveraging DAX functions, such as FILTER() and ALL(), can also be applied to financial calendars. Additionally, the filter navigation (for example, MAX() - 1) implemented in the prior period measures is applicable to more advanced date intelligence expressions.

Each prior period measure references a column containing date values that have been adjusted relative to the date column. *Figure 5.10* of the Date dimension query in Power Query Editor highlights these three columns relative to the date column:

| Date | Prior Year Date | Prior Month Date | Prior Week Date |
|---|---|---|---|
| 1/1/2005 | 1/1/2004 | 12/1/2004 | 12/25/2004 |
| 1/2/2005 | 1/2/2004 | 12/2/2004 | 12/26/2004 |
| 1/3/2005 | 1/3/2004 | 12/3/2004 | 12/27/2004 |
| 1/4/2005 | 1/4/2004 | 12/4/2004 | 12/28/2004 |
| 1/5/2005 | 1/5/2004 | 12/5/2004 | 12/29/2004 |
| 1/6/2005 | 1/6/2004 | 12/6/2004 | 12/30/2004 |
| 1/7/2005 | 1/7/2004 | 12/7/2004 | 12/31/2004 |
| 1/8/2005 | 1/8/2004 | 12/8/2004 | 1/1/2005 |
| 1/9/2005 | 1/9/2004 | 12/9/2004 | 1/2/2005 |
| 1/10/2005 | 1/10/2004 | 12/10/2004 | 1/3/2005 |
| 1/11/2005 | 1/11/2004 | 12/11/2004 | 1/4/2005 |

*Figure 5.10: Prior date columns in the date dimension*

Given the value of date intelligence measures and the relatively static nature of the date dimension, it's recommended to develop a robust date dimension table. If the necessary columns cannot be implemented in the source database itself, the columns can be computed within the SQL view or the M query of the Date table.

Sample M query examples are available in the companion PBIX files for this book on GitHub (`https://github.com/PacktPublishing/-Mastering-Microsoft-Power-BI-Second-Edition`) and detailed instructions are provided in *Chapter 6* of *Power BI Cookbook, 2nd Edition*.

Let's now look at a different type of date intelligence measure that compares prior years.

## Current versus prior and growth rates

With date intelligence measures developed for the current and prior periods, growth or variance measures can be added to the dataset, comparing the two values. In the following example, a year-over-year (YOY) and a year-over-year year-to-date (YOY YTD) measure have been created based on the current year and prior year measures from the preceding section:

```
Internet Net Sales (YOY) = [Internet Net Sales (CY)] - [Internet Net Sales
(PY)]


Internet Net Sales (YOY YTD) = [Internet Net Sales (YTD)] - [Internet Net
Sales (PYTD)]
```

Finally, growth percentage measures can be added, which express the variance between the current and prior period measures as a percentage of the prior period. The following measures reference the above YOY measures as the numerator within a DIVIDE() function:

```
Internet Net Sales (YOY %) = DIVIDE([Internet Net Sales (YOY)],[Internet
Net Sales (PY)])


Internet Net Sales (YOY YTD %) = DIVIDE([Internet Net Sales (YOY
YTD)],[Internet Net Sales (PYTD)])
```

The DIVIDE() function returns a blank value if the denominator is zero or a blank value by default. The divide operator (/), however, returns an infinity value when dividing by zero or a blank. Given the superior error-handling behavior and performance advantages of DIVIDE(), the DIVIDE() function is recommended for computing division in DAX.

Another popular category of date intelligence measures deals with rolling date periods so let's look at those next.

## Rolling periods

Rolling periods, sometimes referred to as trailing averages, are very common in datasets, as they help to smooth out individual outliers and analyze longer-term trends. For example, a significant business event or variance 10 months ago has a relatively small impact on a trailing 12-month total. Additionally, this variance does not impact trailing 30-day or 3-, 6-, and 9-month rolling period measures.

The following two measures capture the trailing 60 days of sales history and the 60 days of history prior to the trailing 60 days:

```
Internet Net Sales (Trailing 60 Days) =
    VAR __MaxDate = MAX('Date'[Date])
    VAR __StartDate = __MaxDate - 59
RETURN
    CALCULATE([Internet Net Sales],FILTER(ALL('Date'),'Date'[Date] >= __
StartDate && 'Date'[Date] <= __MaxDate))

Internet Net Sales Trailing (60 to 120 Days) =
    VAR __MaxDate = MAX('Date'[Date])
    VAR __EndDate = __MaxDate - 60
    VAR __StartDate = __EndDate - 59
```

```
RETURN
    CALCULATE([Internet Net Sales],FILTER(ALL('Date'), 'Date'[Date] >= __
StartDate && 'Date'[Date] <= __EndDate))
```

The two 60-day measures compute the dates for the filter condition within DAX variables and then pass these values into the `FILTER()` function. The two measures help to answer the question "Is Internet sales growth accelerating?" With this logic, the value for the trailing 60 days measure on November 15th, 2013 includes Internet sales since September 17th, 2013. The 60-to-120-days measure, however, includes sales history from July 19th, 2013 through September 16th, 2013.

Rolling period or trailing average measures generally require the sequential numeric date dimension columns in the date suggested in both previous chapters. Very similar to the prior period measures from the previous section (for example, `PY YTD`), rolling period measures can reference sequential columns for the given granularity and modify the date filter by adding or subtracting values.

In the next section, we take a look at a different way to create groups of measures called *calculation groups*.

# Calculation groups

Calculation groups are a data modeling feature that enable common expression logic to be centralized and leveraged by other measures when needed in reports. In this section, we cover the creation of the same basic date intelligence from the previous section, *Date intelligence metrics*, but use calculation groups.

In the previous section, we covered the creation of basic date intelligence metrics for `Internet Net Sales`. However, supporting eight common date intelligence expressions for each of 24 base measures would imply adding 192 (8*24) distinct measures to the dataset, thus adding both development time and complexity for report authors and analysts. Calculation groups address this issue by allowing report authors to reuse common expressions such as year-to-date for whichever base measure it's needed for.

Calculation groups allow the creation of general calculation formulas that can be applied to any explicit measure within the data model. Thus, a single set of 8 basic date intelligence metrics could be created (`CY`, `YTD`, `MTD`, `WTD`, `PY`, `PYTD`, `PMTD`, `PWTD`) as a calculation group and this calculation group could be applied to all 24 base measures.

Calculation groups and certain other dataset objects such as **detail-row expressions** can only be created in external tools (outside of Power BI Desktop) such as Tabular Editor. Detail row expressions enable custom drillthrough actions in MDX-based client tools such as via PivotTables in Excel.

For example, the SELECTCOLUMNS() function could be used in a Detail Rows Expression to select the dimension attributes most valued in a drillthrough scenario such as Customer ID and Sales Order Number. Excel report users are able to simply double-click values in their Excel PivotTables to access a table containing the detail row expression attributes for the given filters applied.

*Figure 5.11* shows a calculation group being created in Tabular Editor v2:

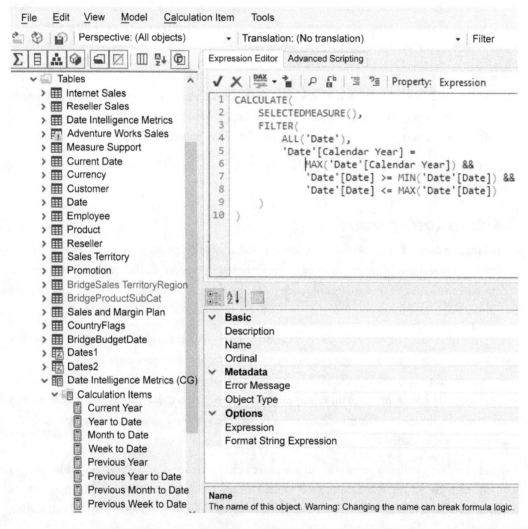

*Figure 5.11: Creating a calculation group in Tabular Editor*

Once deployed to the model, calculation groups appear as a table in the **Fields** pane with a single named column. This column represents the collection of **calculation items** defined for the calculation group.

*Figure 5.12* shows a matrix with a calculation group used with four different base measures simultaneously. In each case, the specified calculations are performed on each measure separately.

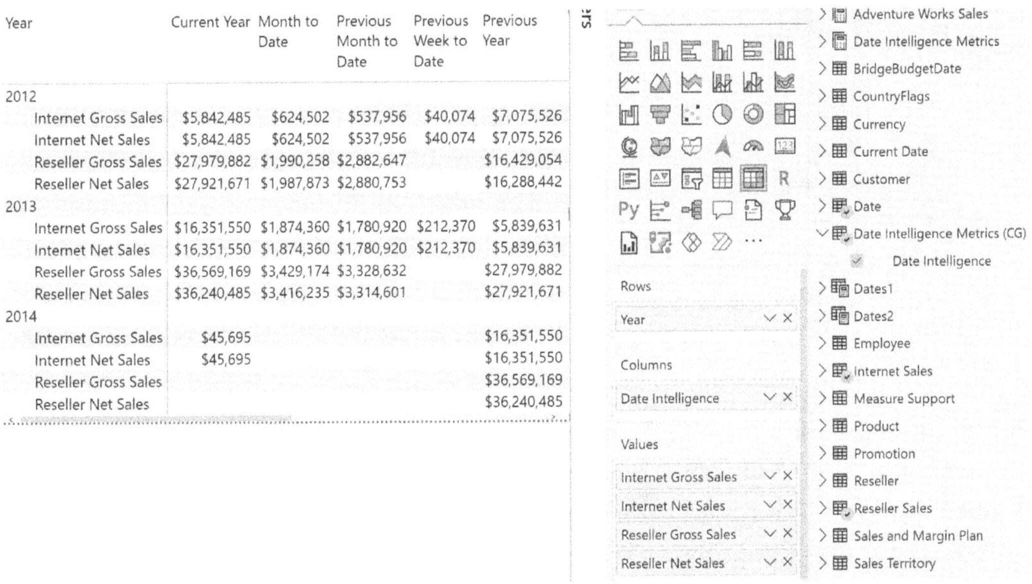
Year
Current Year
Month to Date
Previous Month to Date
Previous Week to Date
Previous Year
2012
Internet Gross Sales $5,842,485 $624,502 $537,956 $40,074 $7,075,526
Internet Net Sales $5,842,485 $624,502 $537,956 $40,074 $7,075,526
Reseller Gross Sales $27,979,882 $1,990,258 $2,882,647 $16,429,054
Reseller Net Sales $27,921,671 $1,987,873 $2,880,753 $16,288,442
2013
Internet Gross Sales $16,351,550 $1,874,360 $1,780,920 $212,370 $5,839,631
Internet Net Sales $16,351,550 $1,874,360 $1,780,920 $212,370 $5,839,631
Reseller Gross Sales $36,569,169 $3,429,174 $3,328,632 $27,979,882
Reseller Net Sales $36,240,485 $3,416,235 $3,314,601 $27,921,671
2014
Internet Gross Sales $45,695 $16,351,550
Internet Net Sales $45,695 $16,351,550
Reseller Gross Sales $36,569,169
Reseller Net Sales $36,240,485
Rows
Year
Columns
Date Intelligence
Values
Internet Gross Sales
Internet Net Sales
Reseller Gross Sales
Reseller Net Sales
Adventure Works Sales
Date Intelligence Metrics
BridgeBudgetDate
CountryFlags
Currency
Current Date
Customer
Date
Date Intelligence Metrics (CG)
Date Intelligence
Dates1
Dates2
Employee
Internet Sales
Measure Support
Product
Promotion
Reseller
Reseller Sales
Sales and Margin Plan
Sales Territory

*Figure 5.12: Calculation group used with multiple measures in a matrix*

The equivalent calculation items for the basic date intelligence metrics covered earlier in this chapter are as follows:

```
Current Year
CALCULATE(SELECTEDMEASURE(),FILTER(ALL('Date'), 'Date'[Calendar Year]
= MAX('Date'[Calendar Year]) && 'Date'[Date] >= MIN('Date'[Date]) &&
'Date'[Date] <= MAX('Date'[Date])))
Year to Date
CALCULATE(SELECTEDMEASURE(), FILTER(ALL('Date'),'Date'[Calendar Year] =
MAX('Date'[Calendar Year]) && 'Date'[Date] <= MAX('Date'[Date])))
Month to Date
CALCULATE(SELECTEDMEASURE(), FILTER(ALL('Date'),'Date'[Year Month Number]
= MAX('Date'[Year Month Number]) && 'Date'[Date] <= MAX('Date'[Date])))
Week to Date
CALCULATE(SELECTEDMEASURE(), FILTER(ALL('Date'),'Date'[Year Week Number] =
MAX('Date'[Year Week Number]) && 'Date'[Date] <= MAX('Date'[Date])))
Previous Year
CALCULATE(SELECTEDMEASURE(),FILTER(ALL('Date'),
CONTAINS(VALUES('Date'[Prior Year Date]),'Date'[Prior Year
```

```
Date],'Date'[Date])))
Previous Year to Date
CALCULATE(SELECTEDMEASURE(), FILTER(ALL('Date'),'Date'[Calendar Year] =
MAX('Date'[Calendar Year])-1 && 'Date'[Date] <= MAX('Date'[Prior Year
Date])))
Previous Month to Date
CALCULATE(SELECTEDMEASURE(), FILTER(ALL('Date'),'Date'[Year Month Number]
= MAX('Date'[Year Month Number])-1 && 'Date'[Date] <= MAX('Date'[Prior
Month Date])))
Previous Week to Date
CALCULATE(SELECTEDMEASURE(), FILTER(ALL('Date'),'Date'[Year Week Number] =
MAX('Date'[Year Week Number])-1 && 'Date'[Date] <= MAX('Date'[Prior Week
Date])))
```

As you can see, in each instance, the explicit measure such as `Internet Net Sales` has been replaced with the DAX function `SELECTEDMEASURE()`. The `SELECTEDMEASURE()` function is a placeholder that represents the current measure in the context of the calculation item. Three additional special functions are available to calculation items including `SELECTEDMEASURENAME`, `ISSELECTEDMEASURE`, and `SELECTEDMEASUREFORMATSTRING`.

`SELECTEDMEASURENAME` is used to determine the measure in context by name. `ISSELECTEDMEASURE` is used to determine if the measure in context is contained within a list of measures. `SELECTEDMEASUREFORMATSTRING` is used to retrieve the format string of the measure in context.

Each calculation item in a calculation group can only operate on a single explicit measure. In addition, calculation item formulas do not support the use of VAR and RETURN statements. That said, the YOY and YOY% calculations can be added to the calculation group with the following equations:

```
YOY
CALCULATE(SELECTEDMEASURE(),FILTER(ALL('Date'), 'Date'[Calendar Year]
= MAX('Date'[Calendar Year]) && 'Date'[Date] >= MIN('Date'[Date]) &&
'Date'[Date] <= MAX('Date'[Date])))
-
CALCULATE(SELECTEDMEASURE(),FILTER(ALL('Date'),
CONTAINS(VALUES('Date'[Prior Year Date]),'Date'[Prior Year
Date],'Date'[Date])))
YOY%
DIVIDE(CALCULATE(SELECTEDMEASURE(),FILTER(ALL('Date'),
'Date'[Calendar Year] = MAX('Date'[Calendar Year]) &&
'Date'[Date] >= MIN('Date'[Date]) && 'Date'[Date] <=
```

```
MAX('Date'[Date]))), CALCULATE(SELECTEDMEASURE(),FILTER(ALL('Date'),
CONTAINS(VALUES('Date'[Prior Year Date]),'Date'[Prior Year
Date],'Date'[Date]))))
```

Data modelers should consider calculation groups for repetitive measures such as date intelligence metrics. However, because calculation items can only refer to a single measure within their formulas, calculation groups are limited in their utility. Furthermore, the appearance of calculation groups as a table and the inability to see their formulas within Power BI Desktop or Excel can be confusing to report authors and business users unfamiliar with the functionality.

Even with calculation groups handling common expressions (YTD, YOY), given the volume of distinct business questions that datasets and specifically DAX measures are tasked with addressing, it can be challenging to avoid the development of hundreds or even thousands of DAX measures. Over time such a high volume of DAX measures can make a dataset more difficult to support and, even with a thoughtful display folder structure, can complicate the user experience of report authors and analysts.

Report-scoped measures in Power BI reports are one method that organizations can use to avoid an excessive volume of DAX measures within datasets. If a certain calculation or set of calculations is only applicable to a particular report or a few reports and isn't expected to be used in the future for self-service analysis or other reports then it may be preferable to implement these DAX measures in the report rather than the Power BI dataset.

In these instances, depending on the complexity of the measure(s) and the experience and comfort level of the report author with DAX, either the report author or the dataset developer could obtain access to the Power BI report file (.pbix) to add the measures.

This completes our exploration of calculation groups. We'll next move on to exploring measures that make calculations based upon dimension tables.

# Dimension metrics

The majority of DAX measures apply aggregating functions to numeric columns of fact tables. However, several of the most important metrics of a dataset are those that focus on dimension tables, such as the count of customers who've purchased and those who haven't.

It can also be necessary to count the distinct values of a dimension column such as the number of postal codes sold to or the number of distinct marketing promotions over a period of time.

In the dataset for this project, the customer dimension table is exclusive to the Internet Sales fact table, and the measure should only count customers with internet sales history.

Additionally, slowly changing dimension logic has been implemented so that a single customer defined by the `CustomerAlternateKey` column could have multiple rows defined by the `CustomerKey` column.

The following two DAX measures count the number of unique customers and products with internet sales history:

```
Internet Sales Customer Count =
CALCULATE(DISTINCTCOUNT('Customer'[CustomerAlternateKey]), 'Internet
Sales')


Internet Sales Products Sold Count =
CALCULATE(DISTINCTCOUNT('Product'[ProductAlternateKey]),'Internet Sales')
```

By invoking the `Internet Sales` fact table as a filtering parameter to `CALCULATE()`, any filter applied to a related dimension table such as `Sales Territory` also impacts the measure.

This behavior is the same as bidirectional cross-filtering between the `Internet Sales` and `Customer` tables. However, in the event that no filters have been applied in the reporting tool (for example, Power BI or Excel), the `Internet Sales` table filter ensures that only customers with `Internet Sales` histories are counted.

Let's next look at an additional aspect of measures focused on dimensions, missing dimensions.

## Missing dimensions

Missing dimension measures are commonly used in churn and exception reporting and analyses. Missing dimension metrics attempt to identify what dimension values are not present within a given set of fact table rows.

For example, a report may be needed that displays the specific products that haven't sold or the past customers who haven't made a purchase in a given filter context. Additionally, missing dimension measures give greater meaning to other dimension measures. For instance, the count of products sold in a period may not be as useful without knowing how many products were not sold over this same period.

The following DAX measures count the number of unique customers without `Internet Sales` history:

```
Internet Sales Customers Missing =
CALCULATE(DISTINCTCOUNT('Customer'[CustomerAlternateKey]),
FILTER(VALUES('Customer'[CustomerAlternateKey]),
```

```
      ISEMPTY(RELATEDTABLE('Internet Sales'))))


      Internet Sales Products Missing =
      CALCULATE(DISTINCTCOUNT('Product'[ProductAlternateKey]),
      FILTER(VALUES('Product'[ProductAlternateKey]),
      ISEMPTY(RELATEDTABLE('Internet Sales'))))
```

The Internet Sales Customers Missing measure references the Internet Sales fact table like the customer count measure does, but only within the ISEMPTY() function. The ISEMPTY() function operates as the filter parameter of the FILTER() function and returns a true or a false value for each distinct CustomerAlternateKey provided by the VALUES() function. Only the customer rows without any related rows in the Internet Sales fact table are marked as true and this filtered set of customer rows is passed to the DISTINCTCOUNT() function. The same methodology is applied to the Internet Sales Products Missing measure.

The following matrix visual shown in *Figure 5.13* has been filtered to five calendar quarters and broken out by the Sales Territory Group:

| SalesTerritoryGroup | 2013-Q1 | 2013-Q2 | 2013-Q3 | 2013-Q4 | 2014-Q1 | **Total** |
|---|---|---|---|---|---|---|
| Europe | | | | | | |
|    Internet Sales Customer Count | 1,097 | 1,435 | 1,575 | 1,818 | 197 | **5,427** |
|    Internet Sales Customers Missing | 17,387 | 17,049 | 16,909 | 16,666 | 18,287 | **13,057** |
| NA | | | | | | |
|    Internet Sales Customer Count | | | | | | |
|    Internet Sales Customers Missing | 18,484 | 18,484 | 18,484 | 18,484 | 18,484 | **18,484** |
| North America | | | | | | |
|    Internet Sales Customer Count | 1,663 | 2,490 | 2,514 | 2,881 | 485 | **8,928** |
|    Internet Sales Customers Missing | 16,821 | 15,994 | 15,970 | 15,603 | 17,999 | **9,556** |
| Pacific | | | | | | |
|    Internet Sales Customer Count | 763 | 1,096 | 1,223 | 1,316 | 152 | **3,580** |
|    Internet Sales Customers Missing | 17,721 | 17,388 | 17,261 | 17,168 | 18,332 | **14,904** |
| **Internet Sales Customer Count** | **3,523** | **5,021** | **5,312** | **6,015** | **834** | **17,935** |
| **Internet Sales Customers Missing** | **14,961** | **13,463** | **13,172** | **12,469** | **17,650** | **549** |

*Figure 5.13: Internet Sales Customers and Customers Missing*

Any other dimension table with a relationship to the Internet Sales fact table, such as Promotion and Product, could also be used to filter the metrics.

In this dataset, the customer dimension has 18,484 unique customers as defined by the CustomerAlternateKey. Therefore, the sum of the customer count and customers missing measures is always equal to 18,484.

As explained in the *Filter context* section of this chapter, the subtotal values execute in their own filter context. For example, only 549 customers did not make an online purchase in any of the four quarters, while over 12,000 customers did not make a purchase in each of the four quarters.

Once core dimension metrics have been established such as in the previous examples, additional metrics can be developed that leverage their logic. The following measures identify the count of first-year internet sales customers and the count of accessories products that have not sold online, respectively:

```
Internet Sales First Year Customer Count = CALCULATE([Internet Sales
Customer Count],'Customer'[Customer History Segment] = "First Year
Customer")


Internet Sales Products Missing (Accessories) = CALCULATE([Internet Sales
Products Missing],'Product'[Product Category] = "Accessories")
```

Dimension metrics, just like the base measures described earlier, may be used in reporting by themselves or may be referenced by other measures. This branching of measures underlines the importance of clearly defining, documenting, and testing the foundational measures of a dataset.

In the next section we look at another common category of measures, those that deal with ranking.

# Ranking metrics

Many reports and analyses are built around the ranking of dimensions relative to measures, such as the top 10 salespeople based on YTD sales. Ranking measures can also help deliver cleaner and more intuitive report visualizations as they substitute small integer values for large numbers and decimal places. Ranking measures can be as simple as specifying a column and a measure, or more complex with unique ranking logic applied in distinct filter contexts.

Ranking measures in DAX are implemented via the RANKX() function, which is an iterator like SUMX() and FILTER(). As an iterating function, two required input parameters include a table and the expression to be evaluated for each row of the table. The following two measures rank products based on the Internet Net Sales measure:

```
Internet Net Sales Product Rank =
RANKX(ALL('Product'[ProductAlternateKey]),[Internet Net Sales],,DESC,Skip)


Internet Net Sales Product Rank (All Products) =
    VAR __ProdRankTable =
ALL('Product'[ProductAlternateKey],'Product'[Product
```

```
Name],'Product'[Product Category Group],'Product'[Product
Category],'Product'[Product Subcategory],'Product'[Product Name])
RETURN
    RANKX(__ProdRankTable, [Internet Net Sales],,DESC,Skip)
```

As with date intelligence and other measures, `ALL()` is used to remove the filters applied to a table. The `ALL()` function both removes a filter and returns a table that can then be evaluated by other functions. `ALL()` can remove filters from an entire table, multiple columns of the same table, or a single column from a table. Additionally, the `ALLEXCEPT()` function can be used to remove filters from the current and any future columns of a table, except for one or a specific set of columns.

In the `Internet Net Sales Product Rank` measure, the `ALL()` function returns a table of the unique product's alternate key values. Since only a single column is referenced by `ALL()` in this measure, other columns from the `Product` dimension table are allowed into the filter context.

For example, in *Figure 5.14*, the `Product Category` column impacts the `Internet Net Sales Product Rank` measure so that the **HL-U509-R** product is ranked first given that it's the highest-selling product in the **Accessories** category:

| Product Category | Product Alternate Key | Internet Net Sales | Internet Net Sales Product Rank | Internet Net Sales Product Rank (All Products) |
|---|---|---|---|---|
| Bikes | BK-M38S-42 | $99,264.21 | 54 | 54 |
| Bikes | BK-M38S-40 | $98,494.72 | 55 | 55 |
| Bikes | BK-T44U-60 | $98,402.85 | 56 | 56 |
| Accessories | HL-U509-R | $78,027.70 | 1 | 57 |
| Accessories | HL-U509-B | $74,353.75 | 2 | 58 |
| Accessories | HL-U509 | $72,954.15 | 3 | 59 |
| Bikes | BK-R50B-52 | $66,917.68 | 57 | 60 |

*Figure 5.14: Ranking measures*

The `Internet Net Sales Product Rank (All Products)` measure, however, ranks the product relative to all other products including products in the `Bikes` category. The group of columns specified in the `ALL()` function (the table parameter to `RANKX()`) defines the set of rows that the ranking expression is evaluated against.

For ranking and certain other scenarios, it's necessary to apply alternative logic for subtotals. For example, the total row of the previous table visual would show a ranking value of 1 without any modification to the DAX. A common pattern to address subtotal values is to check whether an individual item of a column is in the filter context via `HASONEVALUE()`.

The following revised measure uses an `IF()` conditional function to apply the ranking for individual products, but otherwise returns a blank value:

```
Internet Net Sales Product Rank (Revised) =
IF(HASONEVALUE('Product'[ProductAlternateKey]),
RANKX(ALL('Product'[ProductAlternateKey]),[Internet Net
Sales],,DESC,Skip),BLANK())
```

As shown in this example, it's essential to understand the intended ranking logic and it may be necessary to store alternative ranking measures to suit the requirements of different reports and projects.

The `RANKX()` function has five parameters, but only the first two—the table and the expression to evaluate—are required. In this example, the third parameter is skipped via the comma and the measure is set to rank in descending order of the expression.

Additionally, the final parameter (`Skip` or `Dense`) determines how tie values are treated. For example, if two products are tied for the highest sales, both products are ranked 1, and the next-highest product is ranked 3. Descending order and the skip tie behavior are both defaults, but it's a good practice to explicitly define these settings in the measures.

We next look at a specific type of ranking measure that can dynamically calculate ranks based upon how the user interacts with the report.

## Dynamic ranking measures

The ranking measures in the previous section are specific to individual products. These measures cannot be used, for example, to rank product subcategories or product categories. Rather than develop many separate measures targeted at one specific column, logic can be embedded in DAX measures to dynamically adjust to the columns in the filter context.

In the following measure, a ranking is applied based on the filter context from three levels of a product hierarchy:

```
Internet Net Sales Product Rank (Conditional) =
    VAR __ProductFilter = ISFILTERED('Product'[Product Name])
    VAR __SubCatFilter = ISFILTERED('Product'[Product Subcategory])
    VAR __CatFilter = ISFILTERED('Product'[Product Category])
RETURN
    SWITCH(TRUE(),
    __ProductFilter = TRUE(), RANKX(ALL('Product'[Product Name]),[Internet
```

```
Net Sales],,DESC,Skip),
    __SubCatFilter = TRUE(), RANKX(ALL('Product'[Product
Subcategory]),[Internet Net Sales],,DESC,Skip),
    __CatFilter = TRUE(), RANKX(ALL('Product'[Product Category]),[Internet
Net Sales],,DESC,Skip),
    BLANK())
```

The measure checks for the existence of a filter on the Product Name, Product Subcategory, and Product Category columns within a SWITCH() function via the ISFILTERED() function. The first logical condition to evaluate as true results in the corresponding RANKX() expression being executed. If no condition is found to be true, then the BLANK() value is returned.

The dynamic ranking measure can be used in report visuals that drill up/down through the product hierarchy or in separate visuals dedicated to specific columns. Drilling within Power BI is covered in later chapters.

In *Figure 5.15*, distinct table visuals representing the three levels of the product hierarchy utilize the Internet Net Sales Product Rank (Conditional) measure:

| Product Category | Online Sales Rank | Product Subcategory | Online Sales Rank | Product Name | Online Sales Rank |
| --- | --- | --- | --- | --- | --- |
| Bikes | 1 | Road Bikes | 1 | Mountain-200 Black, 46 | 1 |
| Accessories | 2 | Mountain Bikes | 2 | Mountain-200 Black, 42 | 2 |
| Clothing | 3 | Touring Bikes | 3 | Mountain-200 Silver, 38 | 3 |
|  |  | Tires and Tubes | 4 | Mountain-200 Silver, 46 | 4 |
|  |  | Helmets | 5 | Mountain-200 Black, 38 | 5 |

*Figure 5.15: Dynamic ranking measure*

For the visuals in the preceding table, a shorter and more intuitive name was used instead of the full measure name (Internet Net Sales Product Rank (Conditional)).

To change the name of a measure or column used in a report visual, double-click the name of the measure or column in the **Values** bucket of the **Visualizations** pane. The revised name only applies to the specific visual, and hovering over the revised name identifies the source measure or column.

Similar to the Internet Net Sales Product Rank measure from the previous section, the conditional measure allows for other columns to impact the filter context. For example, if both the Product Category and Product Subcategory columns are included in the same table visual, the conditional measure ranks the subcategories relative to other subcategories of the same Product Category.

With this dataset, the **Tires and Tubes** subcategory, which is ranked fourth overall as per the above table, would be ranked number one for the **Accessories** product category. Next, we wrap up our coverage of different types of measures with a section on report-scoped measures.

# Security roles

In addition to DAX's utility for creating measures, DAX is also required when defining security roles within a dataset. Per *Chapter 1, Planning Power BI Projects*, the required data security for this project is to limit the visibility of the Adventure Works sales team users to their respective sales territory groups. There are three sales territory groups (**North America Sales Group**, **Europe Sales Group**, and **Pacific Sales Group**), and, as described in the previous chapter, cross-filtering relationships exist between the Sales Territory dimension table and all three fact tables (Internet Sales, Reseller Sales, and Sales and Margin Plan).

Therefore, security roles with a filter condition on the given sales territory group also filter the fact tables, and business users mapped to these roles only see data associated with their Sales Territory group.

Security roles are defined in Power BI Desktop via the **Manage roles** dialog of the **Modeling** tab as shown in *Figure 5.16*:

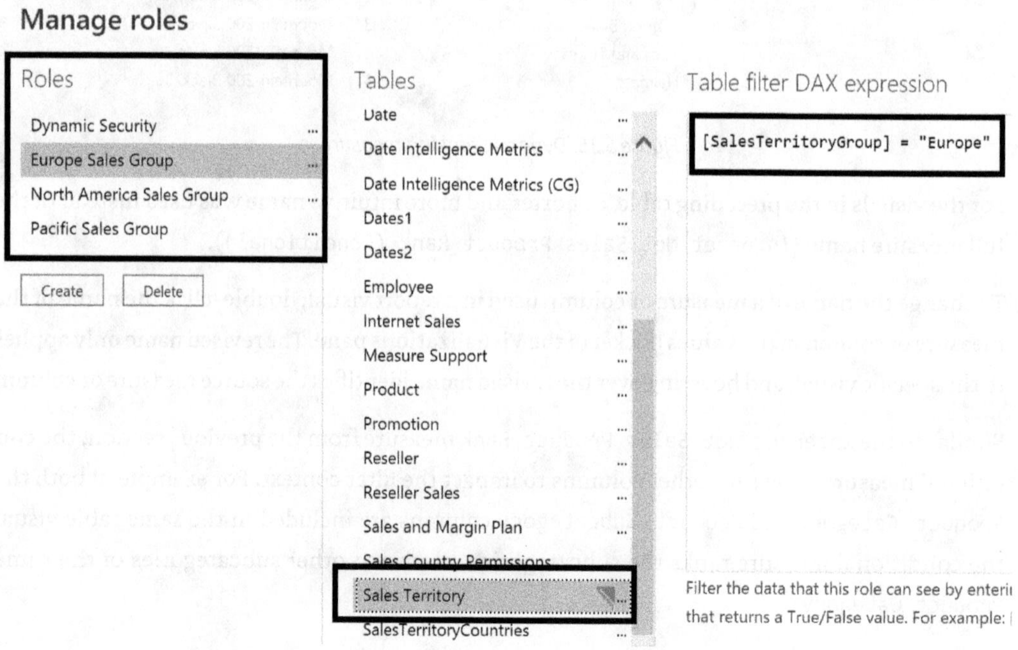

## Manage roles

*Figure 5.16: Managing security roles*

In this example model, the Sales Territory dimension table has a single-direction one-to-many relationship with the Internet Sales and Reseller Sales fact tables. For the Sales and Margin Plan fact table, the Sales Territory filter first flows to the bridge table and then uses a bidirectional cross-filtering relationship from the Sales Territory bridge to Sales and Margin Plan. Therefore, a user mapped to the **Europe Sales Group** role only has access to the Internet Sales, Reseller Sales, and Sales Plan data associated with Europe.

Just like a filter selection on a column of the Sales Territory table in a report, a security filter also flows across the cross-filtering relationships of the data model. However, unlike report filters, security filters cannot be overridden by DAX measures. Security filters are applied to all report queries for the given dataset and any additional filtering logic or DAX expression respects the security role definition.

Given the automatic filtering of security role conditions, it's important to implement efficient security filters and to test the performance of security roles. For example, a complex filter condition applied against a large dimension table could significantly degrade the performance of reports and dashboards for users or groups mapped to this security role.

In addition to defining security roles, security roles can also be tested in Power BI Desktop via the **View as roles** command on the **Modeling** tab. In *Figure 5.17*, a chart that displays sales by the sales territory country is only displaying the countries associated with the **Europe Sales Group** due to the **View as roles** selection:

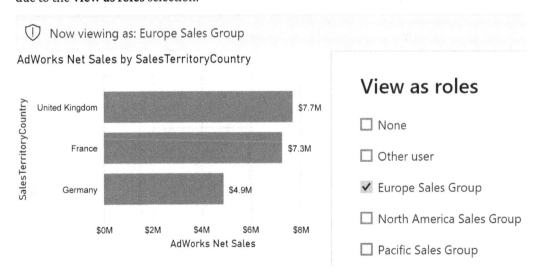

*Figure 5.17: View as roles in Power BI Desktop*

Similar to the **View as roles** feature in Power BI Desktop, a **Test as role** option is available in the Power BI service. This feature can be accessed from the ellipsis next to each **Row Level Security (RLS)** role in the **Security** dialog for the dataset.

Additionally, other users can test the security roles by connecting to published Power BI apps. In this testing scenario, the user would not be a member of the workspace, but a member of an **Azure Active Directory Security Group**, which is mapped to a security role of the dataset. The reason why test users should not be a member of a workspace is covered in detail in *Chapter 10, Managing Workspaces and Content.*

For this project, and as a strongly recommended general practice, **Azure Active Directory (AAD)** security groups should be created for the users accessing Power BI content. AAD security groups are the enterprise solution for controlling security across all systems that authenticate with AAD. While it is possible to use Microsoft 365 groups with security roles, Microsoft 365 groups are not a replacement for AAD security groups.

*Figure 5.18* displays the properties of a `North America Sales` security group:

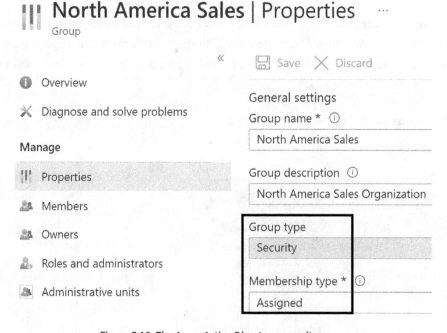

*Figure 5.18: The Azure Active Directory security group*

Users can be added or removed from AAD security groups in the Azure portal or via PowerShell scripts. PowerShell and other administration topics are covered in *Chapter 14, Administering Power BI for an Organization.*

The **Assigned** membership type can be used but alternatively, a Dynamic User membership type can be created based on a membership rule query. With Dynamic User AAD security groups, a user can be automatically added or removed from groups as their role in the organization changes.

The AAD security groups can then be mapped to their respective security roles for the published dataset in Power BI. In *Figure 5.19*, the **North America Sales** AAD security group is recognized as a potential group to be added as a member of the **North America Sales Group** RLS role:

Figure 5.19: Member assignment to row-level security roles

With the AAD security groups created and mapped to their corresponding RLS roles of the Power BI dataset, security filters are applied based on the user's membership to the AAD group. When RLS roles have been applied to a dataset, the users accessing the reports and dashboards based on that dataset need to be mapped to at least one of the roles.

For example, if a Power BI app is distributed to a user who is not included in one of the AAD security groups mapped to one of the RLS roles, and this user account is not mapped individually to one of these RLS roles, the user receives an error message in the Power BI service as shown in *Figure 5.20*:

You don't have access because row-level security (RLS) was applied.
Please contact the owner to ask for permission.

Figure 5.20: Error message: User not mapped to an RLS role

In the event that a user is mapped to multiple RLS roles, such as both the **North America Sales Group** and the **Europe Sales Group**, that user sees data for both Sales Territory groups (and not **Pacific Sales Group**). For users that require access to the entire dataset, such as administrators or executives, an RLS role can be created on the dataset that doesn't include any filters on any of the tables.

*Chapter 13, Creating Power BI Apps and Content Distribution*, and *Chapter 14, Administering Power BI for an Organization*, contain additional details on AAD's relationship to Power BI and the role of security groups in securely distributing Power BI content to users.

## Dynamic row-level security

The security model discussed thus far relies on users being a member of static groups or security roles. While appropriate for many datasets, other scenarios require a more user-specific methodology in which the identity of the report user is determined dynamically and this value is used to apply filter conditions.

Dynamic row level security implementations involve defining a single security role which uses the USERPRINCIPALNAME() DAX function to retrieve the identity (the UPN) of the connected user. This identity value is then used to filter a typically hidden table in the model which maps individuals to the dimensions they're allowed to access.

For example, a user and a permissions table could be added to the dataset (and hidden) so that the user table would first filter the permissions table, and the permissions table would then filter the dimension to be secured, such as a Sales Territory Country.

*Figure 5.21* shows an example of a permissions table where Jen Lawrence is associated with Germany, Australia, and the United States, and thus should only have visibility to these countries in any Power BI report or dashboard built on top of the dataset:

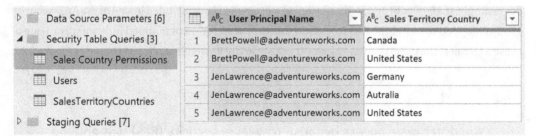

*Figure 5.21: User permissions table*

The other two tables in the Security Table Queries query group include a Users query with a distinct list of **User Principal Names** (UPNs) and a SalesTerritoryCountries query that contains a distinct list of the values in the SalesTerritoryCountry column in the Sales Territory query. The SalesTerritoryCountries table is necessary because the Sales Territory dimension table is more granular than the country one.

The SalesTerritoryCountry table receives the filter context from the permissions table and uses a simple one-to-many cross-filtering relationship with the Sales Territory dimension table to filter the fact tables.

The dynamic RLS role is defined with the User Principal Name column of the Users table equal to the USERPRINCIPALNAME() function.

```
[User Principal Name] = USERPRINCIPALNAME()
```

The relationships, and, more specifically, the cross-filtering from the Sales Country Permissions table, deliver the intended filter context for the given user.

In *Figure 5.22*, a bidirectional cross-filtering relationship is defined between Sales Country Permissions and SalesTerritoryCountries so that only the countries associated with the user filter the Sales Territory dimension table:

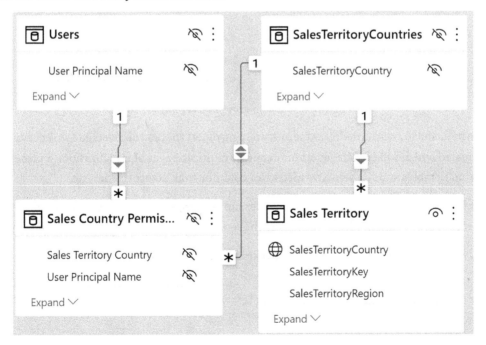

*Figure 5.22: Dynamic RLS model relationships*

The **Apply security filter in both directions** property of the bidirectional relationship between `Sales Country Permissions` and `SalesTerritoryCountries` should be enabled. This property and the relationships-based filtering design are applicable to both import and DirectQuery datasets. All three security tables should be hidden from the Report View.

With users or groups assigned to the dynamic security role in the Power BI service, the role can be tested via the **Test as role** feature in Power BI. In *Figure 5.23*, the user Brett is able to test the dynamic role as himself (**Canada, United States**), but can also view the dynamic role as though any other user is logged in, viewing the reports:

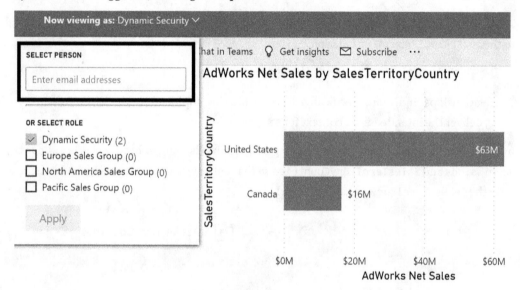

*Figure 5.23: Testing dynamic row-level security in Power BI*

It can be useful to create a dedicated security testing report that can be leveraged as security roles are created and modified. The report may contain multiple pages of visualizations representing all primary tables and any sensitive metrics or columns from across the dataset.

On this project, a business analyst or a QA tester can be mapped onto the security role and use the report to confirm that the filter context from the security role has been implemented successfully.

We'll now move on to discussing how to performance test DAX calculations.

# Performance testing

Given that DAX measures can implement complex business logic and are dynamically calculated as users interact with reports, the performance of these calculations is a critical component of providing a good user experience.

There are often many available methods of implementing business logic and custom filter contexts into DAX measures. Although these alternatives deliver the essential functional requirements, they can have very different performance characteristics, which can ultimately impact user experience and the scalability of a dataset.

When migrating a self-service dataset to a corporate solution or preparing a large and highly utilized dataset, it's always a good practice to test common queries and the DAX measures used by those queries.

For example, the same common dimension grouping (for example, Product Category and Year) and the same filter context (Year = 2018) could produce dramatically different performance results based on the measures used in the query, such as Internet Net Sales versus Count of Customers. The alternative performance statistics associated with different measures such as duration and the count of storage engine queries generated could then be used to focus performance tuning efforts.

In some cases, the DAX measures associated with slow queries cannot be significantly improved, but the data obtained from the performance testing results can drive other changes.

For example, report authors could be advised to only use certain measures in less performance-intensive visuals such as **cards**, or in reports that have been substantially filtered. In a DirectQuery model, the data source owner of the dataset may be able to implement changes to the specific columns accessed via the slow-performing measures.

Let's first look at how to use the **Performance analyzer** within Power BI Desktop in order to collect performance statistics about DAX calculations.

## Performance analyzer

The performance of DAX measures in the context of report queries reflecting Power BI visualizations is essential to the scalability of the dataset and the user experience. To assist with troubleshooting and testing performance, the Performance Analyzer has been added to Power BI Desktop thus making it easy to quickly isolate and analyze slow performing queries and metrics.

As shown in *Figure 5.24*, the **Performance analyzer** pane can be accessed from the **View** menu of the ribbon in Power BI Desktop.

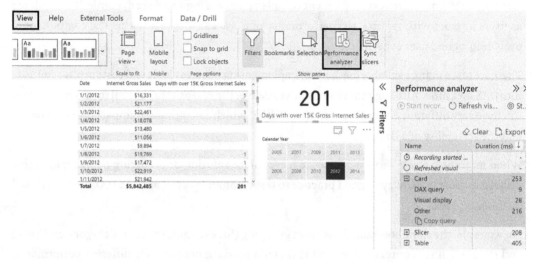

*Figure 5.24: Performance analyzer in Power BI Desktop*

As shown in *Figure 5.23*, once the **Performance analyzer** pane is activated, you can click the **Start recording** link to begin capturing performance statistics as you interact with the report. In *Figure 5.23*, performance recording was started and then the **Refresh visuals** link was pressed. The statistics for this action were recorded in the **Refreshed visual** section of the **Performance analyzer**. After that a value was selected in the slicer visual. The statistics for this action were recorded in the **Changed a slicer** section of the **Performance analyzer**.

The **Performance analyzer** logs the duration of report user interactions with the report in **milli-seconds (ms)**. Clicking on an individual performance item within the **Performance analyzer** log highlights (selects) the visual within the report. The individual item can be expanded to see more detailed statistics including the timings for the **DAX query**, **Visual display**, and **Other**. The under-lying DAX query sent to the data model can be copied to the clipboard using the **Copy query** link.

The entire **Performance analyzer** log can be exported to a JSON file by clicking the **Export** link. This exported JSON file can then be easily imported into DAX Studio via the **Load Perf Data** icon on its **Home** tab for further evaluation and testing. Once you are finished collecting performance information, you can stop recording performance statistics by clicking on the **Stop** link.

Using the **Performance analyzer** pane, data modelers and report authors can quickly understand the measures and visuals that are creating performance issues within the report including how user interactions affect performance. In addition, studying the underlying DAX queries sent to the data model is an excellent way to learn optimal DAX coding strategies.

While the Performance analyzer is powerful, there are still times when external tools such as DAX Studio provide additional performance insights.

# DAX Studio

DAX Studio is a lightweight, open source client tool for executing DAX queries against Power BI datasets and other sources that share the Microsoft Analysis Services Tabular database engine, such as SSAS in Tabular mode and Azure Analysis Services.

DAX Studio exposes the metadata of the source model (for example, tables, measures, hierarchies), includes reference panes for DAX functions and Tabular **Dynamic Management Views** (**DMVs**), and also provides query formatting, syntax highlighting, and IntelliSense for developing DAX queries.

Additionally, DAX Studio supports performance tuning as it can execute traces against its data sources and displays useful performance statistics, as well as the query plans used to execute the query.

The **Server timings** and **Query plan** panes in DAX Studio expose the **storage engine** and **formula engine** query plans, respectively. The formula engine processes data but cannot retrieve data from the tables of a dataset. Within tabular models, the storage engine is solely responsible for data retrieval.

In most performance testing scenarios, the storage engine versus formula engine results of a trace (for example, 50 ms in the storage engine, 10 ms in the formula engine) lead the user to focus on either the slowest storage engine queries or the most expensive operations in the formula engine.

For these reasons, despite improvements to DAX authoring in **SQL Server Management Studio** (**SSMS**), DAX Studio is very commonly used by Microsoft BI developers in Analysis Services and Power BI environments. Specifically, BI developers store the DAX queries created within DAX Studio as .dax or .msdax files and later open these files from DAX Studio for performance testing or troubleshooting scenarios.

For example, a team may have a DAX query that returns the count of rows for three fact tables of a data model by calendar date and use this query to troubleshoot issues related to a data-loading process. Additionally, just as M queries saved within .pq files can be added to version control systems, DAX query files can be added to version control systems, such as Azure DevOps.

DAX Studio can be downloaded from http://daxstudio.org.

# Summary

This chapter developed and described several common classes of DAX measures, including base measures, date intelligence metrics, dimension metrics, and ranking metrics. These measures utilized the fact and dimension tables developed in previous chapters.

In addition to detailed measure examples, the primary concepts of the DAX were reviewed and standard row-level security (RLS) and dynamic RLS (DRLS) models were shared. Finally, performance testing and tuning tools, including the Performance analyzer pane and DAX Studio were presented.

In the following chapter, Power BI reports are created, which leverage the dataset that has been incrementally developed since *Chapter 2* and *3*. Report-authoring features, such as the visualization types in Power BI Desktop, access the DAX measures from this chapter and the dimensions from previous chapters to deliver business insights and intuitive, self-service functionality.

# Join our community on Discord

Join our community's Discord space for discussions with the author and other readers:

`https://discord.gg/q6BPbHEPXp`

# 6

# Planning Power BI Reports

Effective and sustainable Power BI reports and Power BI solutions more generally reflect thoughtful planning and process. To this end, this chapter contains foundational concepts and features to support the design of Power BI reports including visualization best practices, report filter scopes, and Live connections to Power BI datasets.

In this chapter, we review the following topics:

- Report planning process
- Visualization best practices
- Choosing the right visual
- Visual interactions
- Drillthrough report pages
- Report filter scopes
- Bookmarks
- Live connections to Power BI datasets
- Report design summary

Before jumping into creating visuals, it is important to properly plan reports in order to ensure a good user experience and maximize the value to the business. Thus, we'll first take a look at the report planning process.

## Report planning process

Power BI reports can take on a variety of forms and use cases, ranging from executive-level dashboard layouts to highly detailed and focused reports.

Prior to designing and developing Power BI reports, some level of planning and documentation is recommended to ensure that the reports are well aligned with the needs of the users and the organization.

Effective report planning can be encapsulated in the following six steps:

1.  Identify the audience
2.  Define the business questions to answer
3.  Confirm that the dataset supports the business questions
4.  Determine interactivity
5.  Define access and distribution
6.  Sketch the report layout

Let's look at each of these steps in turn, starting with identifying report users.

## Identify the audience

When developing reports, the report author should have a clear understanding of the different consumers of the report and their priorities and use cases.

For example, analysts often place a high value on the ability of the report to help them tell a story about the data. Storytelling refers to the ability to focus on a key KPI or data element and then explain how and why that KPI is lower or higher than expected, an outlier compared to previous years, or represents a significant trend. Therefore, analysts often require significant flexibility to filter and interact with more detailed reports. Thus, reports used by analysts generally include more slicer visuals and may include table or matrix visuals as well.

Conversely, senior managers generally prefer less self-service interactivity and value simple, intuitive visuals, such as KPIs. Senior managers are less focused on storytelling and more focused on the ability to manage their business area or organization from a "single pane of glass." The term "single pane of glass" is the theoretical ability to distill and expose all of the important information regarding complex systems to a single report or tool.

Separating reports by user role or group serves to keep reports focused for users and more manageable for BI teams. In many scenarios, an organizational hierarchy provides a natural demarcation such that reports can be designed for specific roles or levels within an organization.

In the project example for the Adventure Works sales team, reports could align with the `Sales Territory` hierarchy (`SalesTerritoryGroup` | `SalesTerritoryCountry` | `SalesTerritoryRegion`).

The vice president of group sales generally values high-value corporate-wide metrics and intuitive dashboard reports. A sales analyst in the United States, however, likely needs to break out individual regions and even analyze specific ZIP codes or individual products.

We'll now move on to defining the business questions that the report should answer.

## Define the business questions to answer

In addition to knowing one's audience, it is also critical to understand the exact questions the report should be able to answer for the business.

Confirm with the business user(s) or project sponsors that the report has the correct scope and the appropriate focus. A report architecture diagram described in the subsequent section, *Report architecture diagram*, can support this communication. For example, the user could be advised that a particular business question or metric is included in a different report but featured on the same dashboard and is easily accessible within the same Power BI app.

The most important business question (for example, what were our sales?) is addressed in the top-left corner of the report, likely with a KPI or similar visual. Similar to separating reports by user role or group, a report should not attempt to resolve widely disparate business questions.

A single report certainly can contain visuals reflecting distinct fact tables and business processes such as customer service interactions, product inventories, and shipping or delivery orders. However, for most reports it's best that the visuals within the report align to the same or very similar business processes such as Internet Sales and Reseller Sales. The need to summarize and integrate visuals from multiple business processes is often best addressed by Power BI dashboards, not reports, as described in *Chapter 9, Designing Dashboards*.

Once the business questions are verified, the next step is to confirm that the dataset supports the desired questions.

## Confirm that the dataset supports the business questions

The report author should ensure that the dataset includes necessary measures such as year-over-year (YOY) sales and the dimension columns (for example, Product Category) necessary to visualize the business questions.

In order to both develop an accurate report and to support questions from consumers of the report, report authors should have a solid understanding of the Power BI dataset. This knowledge includes the logic and business definitions of DAX measures, the relationships defined between fact and dimension tables, and any data transformation logic applied to the source data.

In many projects, report authors regularly collaborate with business stakeholders or project sponsors in gathering requirements and demonstrating report iterations. Therefore, the authors need to explain the values and behaviors of Power BI reports as well as any current limitations in the dataset, such as the years of history supported and any DAX logic or measures not yet created.

If a gap exists between the dataset and the measures required for the report, the team can determine whether the dataset should be extended or whether the measure should be created local to the report. For example, with Power BI Live connections, only measures can be created within Power BI Live connection reports. Any new columns, tables, or modifications to existing tables or columns must be implemented within the source dataset.

The set of base measures described in *Chapter 5, Developing DAX Measures and Security Roles*, as well as the dynamic date dimension columns described in *Chapter 2, Connecting to Sources and Transforming Data with M* (for example, `Calendar Month Status = 'Prior Calendar Month'`), should support the most common needs of reports.

If a measure required for a report is considered to be common to other future reports, and if the measure doesn't violate the single corporate definition of an existing measure, the measure should generally be added to the dataset. However, if the report requirement is considered rare or if a measure definition has been approved only for the specific report, then the measure(s) can be created local to the report.

For version control and manageability reasons, report authors should not have to implement complex filtering logic or develop many local report measures. Report authors should communicate with dataset designers and the overall team if a significant gap exists or is developing between reports and the dataset.

Once the dataset is confirmed to support the desired business questions, the next step is to determine the report type and mobile features based on the desired report interactions and access methods.

## Determine interactivity

Although Power BI reports developed in Power BI Desktop are increasingly the default report type for new reports given their modern user experience and relative ease of development, Power BI also fully supports paginated reports, formerly **SQL Server Reporting Services (SSRS)** reports, as well as Excel-based reports.

In many instances, particularly when reports are being migrated from legacy systems and/or business processes, the features of these alternative report types more closely align with the requirements and priorities of the report users.

Choosing the incorrect report type can lead to delayed delivery timelines and frustrated stakeholders who may assume that features from current or past BI tools are supported by Power BI reports.

For example, if printing or distributing multiple pages of report data is a top priority, then a paginated report developed in Power BI Report Builder would be the appropriate report type. Similarly, if the intent is to support an existing Excel report that contains significant cell-level formatting and logic such as a financial statement, it would make sense to continue to leverage Excel but switch the data source to a Power BI dataset.

In many cases a combination of the features of multiple report types is needed or valued such as both visual interaction and exporting out multiple pages of details. In these scenarios, report authors and BI teams should consider options of providing Power BI apps containing multiple report types as well as integrated reports via the paginated report visual discussed in *Chapter 7*, *Creating and Formatting Visuals*.

Conversely, Power BI reports created in Power BI Desktop are visually interactive by default and report authors have many options to empower report users to analyze and explore the data in reports to derive their own insights. Thus, if a high degree of interactivity and exploration are the priority, then reports developed in Power BI Desktop are likely the correct choice.

Report authors and BI teams should be transparent with users and stakeholders about the differences and trade-offs between the different report types. In scenarios in which one of the three report types isn't the clear choice, the BI/IT team and the primary stakeholders can reach a consensus on the type of report to be developed. Alternatively, it can be determined that multiple report types will be required, such as an interactive Power BI report as well as a paginated report, and possibly an Excel report too.

After the interactivity of the report is determined, the next step is to define the access and distribution.

## Define access and distribution

Power BI report content can be accessed from a variety of form factors ranging from smartphones and tablets up to large screens in conference rooms and office hallways. Additionally, report content can be integrated within PowerPoint slide decks and delivered to end users via email subscriptions and data-based alerts thus limiting or avoiding the need for users to navigate to relevant content in the Power BI service.

Report authors should be familiar with the rich mobile layout features available in Power BI Desktop as well as options for email subscriptions such delivering paginated report data as attached CSV or Excel files via subscriptions.

Once the access and distribution methods are confirmed, the final step is to create a sketch of the report layout.

## Sketch the report layout

It is often beneficial to create a sketch of the basic layout of a report. Such a sketch should be completed for at least the primary page of the report and should document the position and relative size of visuals on the report canvas (page).

*Figure 6.1* shows a sample sketch created within a PowerPoint presentation file via the standard shape objects:

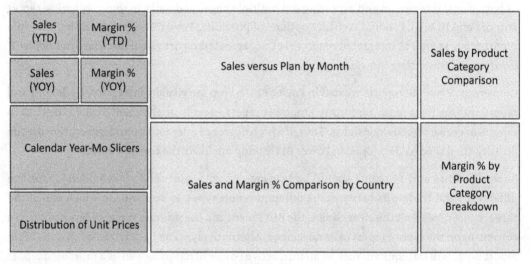

| Sales (YTD) | Margin % (YTD) | | |
| Sales (YOY) | Margin % (YOY) | Sales versus Plan by Month | Sales by Product Category Comparison |
| Calendar Year-Mo Slicers | | | |
| Distribution of Unit Prices | | Sales and Margin % Comparison by Country | Margin % by Product Category Breakdown |

*Figure 6.1: Sample report layout sketch*

As per the sample layout, the critical sales and margin measures are located in the top-left corner of the report page. Slicer (filter) visuals are planned for below these KPI or card visuals and other visuals add further context. Greater space is allocated to the two visuals in the middle of the page given their importance to the report.

The report layout sketch can be used exclusively for planning purposes or can be set as the background for a report page. For example, a PowerPoint slide of the same shapes, background shading, and borders can be saved to a network directory as a PNG file.

In Power BI Desktop, the PNG file can be imported via the **Image formatting** option under **Canvas background** on the **Format** pane or via the insert an image icon on the **Home** tab in **Report** view. Page background images with proper alignment, spacing, and colors can expedite quality report development.

Be willing to modify a report layout or even start afresh with a new layout based on user feedback. Unlike dataset development, which can require significant time and expertise (for example, DAX, M, and SQL), reports can be developed in a rapid, agile delivery methodology. Report authors can engage directly with users on these iterations and, although recommended practices and corporate standards can be communicated, ultimately, the functional value to the user is the top priority.

It's important to distinguish flexibility in report layout and visualization from the report's target users and business questions. Second and third iterations of reports should not, for example, call for fundamentally different measures or new report pages to support different user groups.

Report authors and BI teams can work with users and project sponsors to maintain the scope of IT-supported reports. The interactivity built into Power BI reports and the self-service capabilities provided by Power BI Pro licenses can broaden the reach of projects without requiring new or additional reports.

This completes the report planning process. Next, we'll look at a tool that can aid in the report planning process – a report architecture diagram.

## Report architecture diagram

Similar to the data warehouse bus matrix described in *Chapter 1, Planning Power BI Projects*, a report architecture diagram can be helpful in planning and communicating Power BI projects with both business and IT stakeholders. This diagram serves to maintain the scope and focus of individual reports.

For example, certain business questions or entities (such as Customer, Product) can be assigned to dedicated reports and the individual pages of these reports can visualize these questions or entities at varying levels of detail.

Most commonly, a single report page, such as that represented in *Figure 6.1*, addresses the top priority of a report at a summary level. This page includes cards and/or KPI visuals at the top left of the page and charts rather than tables or matrices that visualize these metrics at a high level.

Additional report pages, usually a maximum of 3-4, are designed to provide a greater level of detail supporting the summary page. With this report structure, a user can naturally start their analysis from an intuitive and visually appealing summary page and then, if necessary, navigate to pages exposing greater levels of detail.

In addition to supporting report pages with greater detail, drillthrough report pages can be designed to display the details for an individual item, such as a specific product or a combination of items, for example, the year 2018 and a specific product.

Drillthrough report pages are simply report pages that include drillthrough filters and are detailed in the *Drillthrough report pages* section of this chapter, which provides details and examples of this feature.

In the absence of a report architecture or diagram, reports can quickly become less user-friendly as many report pages are added that address unrelated business questions. Additionally, the lack of scope or focus for a report can lead to duplicated efforts with the same business question being visualized in multiple reports.

Guidance from stakeholders on the visuals to be included in or featured on a dashboard can strongly inform the report design process. For example, in the case where several dashboard tiles are closely related (such as profitability %), then it's likely that a separate report with 3-4 pages should be designed to support further analysis of each tile.

Conversely, if only one dashboard tile relates to a particular business question or entity, such as resellers, then the supporting report may only need 1-2 pages and provide relatively less detail.

In the basic example shown in *Figure 6.2*, four reports and one dashboard are planned for the German sales team:

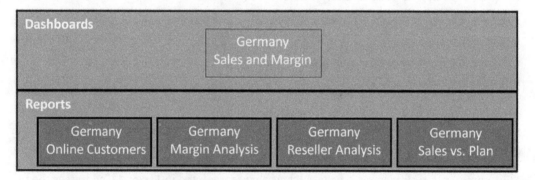

*Figure 6.2: Sample report architecture diagram*

In the example shown in *Figure 6.2*, report visuals contained in four Germany sales reports are pinned as tiles in the **Germany Sales and Margin** dashboard. By default, this would link the reports to the dashboard such that a user could access the details of any of the four reports by clicking on a related dashboard tile.

Visuals from a single report can be pinned as tiles to multiple dashboards. Additionally, a dashboard tile can be linked to a separate dashboard or to a separate report in the Power BI service. *Chapter 9, Designing Dashboards,* includes additional details and examples of Power BI report and dashboard architectures.

The four reports and the dashboard from the preceding example could be included in a dedicated app workspace for the German sales team or within a broader workspace that supports multiple sales teams and related content (for example, marketing) in the organization.

Information on workspaces and content distribution via apps is provided in *Chapter 10, Managing Application Workspaces and Content*, and *Chapter 14, Creating Power BI Apps and Content Distribution*. The following section describes Live connection reports to Power BI datasets published to the Power BI service.

It's important to understand and communicate the differences between Power BI reports and dashboards. Although Power BI report pages can appear as "dashboards" to users, dashboards created in the Power BI service serve an important and distinct role of providing a single pane of glass to highlight key performance indicators and the most important visuals for an organization.

Simply stated, dashboards are a feature of the Power BI service that allow visuals from multiple reports to be pinned to a single canvas. Dashboards are covered in detail in *Chapter 9, Designing Dashboards*.

This completes the report planning section and we'll now turn our attention to additional considerations when designing reports, starting with visualization best practices.

# Visualization best practices

Effective reports are much more than simply answering documented business questions with the available measures and columns of the dataset. Reports also need to be visually appealing and provide a logical structure that aids in navigation and readability. Business users of all backgrounds appreciate a report that is clear, concise, and aesthetically pleasing.

Now that the report planning phase described is complete, the following list of 15 visualization best practices can guide the report development process:

1.  **Avoid clutter and minimize non-essential details**: Each visual should align with the purpose of the report—to gain insight into a business question. Visualizations should not represent wild guesses or functionality that the author finds interesting.

    Eliminate report elements that aren't essential for improving understanding. Gridlines, legends, axis labels, text boxes, and images can often be limited or removed. The report should be understandable at a glance, without supporting documentation or explanation.

    A simple but helpful test is to view a Power BI report on a laptop screen from a distance of 12 to 15 feet, such as from the opposite end of a conference room.

At this distance, it is impossible to read any small text, and only the shapes, curves, and colors are useful for deriving meaning. If the report is still meaningful, this suggests the report is effectively designed visually.

2.   **Provide simple, clear titles on report pages and visuals**: Text boxes can be used to name or describe the report, report page, and provide the last-refreshed date.

3.   **For chart visuals, use the length of lines and the two-dimensional position of points to aid visual comprehension**: On line charts, users can easily perceive trends and the divergence of lines relative to each other. On column or bar charts, users can easily distinguish relative differences in the length of bars. On scatter charts, users can quickly interpret the two-dimensional position of data points relative to each other.

The purpose of these two attributes (line length and 2-D position) as the primary communication mechanism is to guide the user to an accurate assessment with minimal effort. Other visual attributes, such as color, shape, and size, can also be beneficial, particularly when these properties are driven by the data, such as with conditional formatting (data-driven colors/formatting) and KPIs.

However, line length and 2-D position (X, Y coordinates) have a natural advantage in visual perception. For example, the differences between three items on a clustered column chart are much more obvious than the same three items presented on a pie chart.

4.   **Position and group visuals to provide logical navigation across the canvas**: The most important visuals should be positioned in the top-left corner of each report page. If multiple visuals are closely related, consider grouping them within a shape object.

5.   **Use soft, natural colors for most visuals**: Avoid overwhelming users with highly saturated bright or dark colors. Only use more pronounced colors when it's necessary to make an item stand out, such as conditional formatting.

Note that some organizations may have standards that require colorblind-friendly color schemes or other color and formatting requirements for visually impaired viewers such as requiring both a symbol and a color.

6.   **Only apply distinct colors to items in chart visuals when the colors convey meaning**: For example, three colors might be useful for the data points of three separate product categories.

7. **Align visuals to common horizontal and vertical pixel positions**: For example, if a visual in the top-left corner of a page has horizontal and vertical coordinate position values of 20 and 40, respectively, then other visuals on the left side of the canvas should also have a horizontal position of 20. Likewise, the top visual(s) on the right side of the canvas should align with the left visuals at a vertical position of 40.

8. **Distribute visuals vertically and horizontally to create an equal amount of space between visuals**: The amount of spacing should be adequate to clearly distinguish the visuals as separate entities. With one or multiple visuals selected in Power BI Desktop, a **Format** tab appears on the ribbon as per *Figure 6.3*:

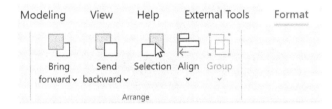

*Figure 6.3: Alignment, distribution, and Z-order format options*

The format options (**Bring forward** and **Send backward** (Z-order)), as well as the **Align** option, are consistent with common MS Office applications, such as Excel and PowerPoint. Between these formatting options and the four properties available under the **General** sub-pane of the **Visualizations** pane for all visuals (**Horizontal** position, **Vertical** position, **Width**, and **Height**), report authors can ensure that visuals are properly aligned and spaced. The **Gridlines** and **Snap to grid** options under the **View** tab also support alignment.

The **Selection** setting displays the **Selection** pane, allowing report authors to set layer order, show or hide visuals, and set the tab order. When multiple visuals are selected simultaneously (by selecting visuals while holding down the *Ctrl* key) the **Group** feature becomes active, allowing visuals to be grouped together and thereafter moved around the canvas as a single unit.

9. **Choose a page background color that naturally contrasts with visuals, such as the default white background.**

10. **For column and bar charts, sort visuals by their measure to provide an implicit ranking by the given measure**: This sorting is only applicable to nominal categories, such as product categories, when the individual items in the category don't need to follow a custom sort order.

11. **Fill the available report canvas space; avoid large blank spaces on report pages.**

12. **Provide supporting context via tooltips and additional lines in charts, such as target values and the min, max, and average:** Several measures related to a given visual can be displayed via tooltips without incurring performance penalties. The **Analytics** pane provides several support lines, including a trend line and a predictive forecast line.

13. **All report pages should follow a common design theme and color palette:** Preferably, all reports in a project and even for an organization should follow the same basic design guidelines. A **Themes** area is available on the **View** tab when in **Report** view within Power BI Desktop and exposes options for importing a report theme or customizing the current theme, as shown in *Figure 6.4*:

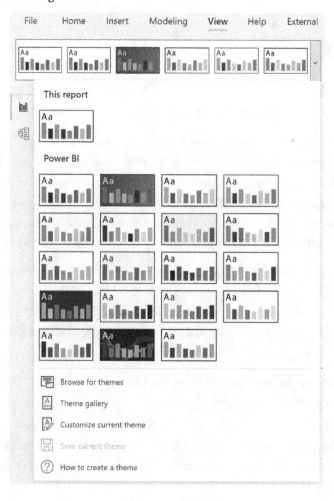

*Figure 6.4: Themes*

Custom report themes allow organizations to apply a custom set of formatting properties to Power BI reports. For example, an organization can embed its corporate colors into a report theme (a JSON file) to apply this set of colors to all Power BI reports. Additionally, more elaborate formatting properties can be specified in report themes to standardize report development, such as the font family and font sizes.

Existing report themes are available for download from the Power BI Report Theme Gallery (`http://bit.ly/2pyUKp1`). Additionally, there are other community tools for customizing themes, as covered in the article *Power BI Theme Generators* (`https://community.powerbi.com/t5/Community-Blog/Power-BI-Theme-Generators/ba-p/2265899`).

14. **The quantitative scale for column and bar charts should start at zero**: Custom quantitative scales, such as from 12% to 15%, can be applied to line, scatter, and bubble charts to emphasize specific ranges of values. However, this is generally not a good idea.

    Consider two items, Product A and Product B, of a clustered column chart with margin percentage values of 32% and 34%, respectively. With a base of zero, the two items would correctly appear similar for the given measure. However, if the base value of the visual starts at 31% and the maximum value of the scale is set to 35%, Product B would visually appear as a dramatically higher value. This distortion is the reason that quantitative scales for column and bar charts should start at zero.

15. **Lines should only be used to connect interval scale data points, such as time series and ordered bins of values**: A line should not, for example, represent the sales for different product categories. A line should, however, represent the sales of products by unit price bins (for example, $0 to $10, or $10 to $20).

In addition to visualization best practices, there are also certain practices to avoid. Thus, next, we will explore visualization anti-patterns.

# Choosing the right visual

With the report planning phase completed, an essential task of the report author is to choose the visual(s) best suited to gain insight into the particular questions within the scope of the report. The choice of the visualization type, such as a column chart or a matrix visual, should closely align with the most important use case, the message to deliver, and the data relationship to represent.

Visualization types have distinct advantages in terms of visual perception and types of data relationships such as part-to-whole and comparisons. Additionally, although several formatting options are common to all visuals, certain options such as the line style (solid, dashed, or dotted) of a line chart are exclusive to specific visuals.

A standard visual selection process is as follows:

1.  Plan and document the business question(s) and related measures and dimension columns
2.  Determine whether a table, a chart, or both are needed to best visualize this data
3.  If a chart is needed, choose the chart visual that's best aligned with the relationship (for example, trend, comparison, or correlation)

Following these three steps helps to ensure that effective reports are developed with efficient resources. Many other visualization and analysis features can be used to further enhance reports, but these should only supplement report planning and design.

Power BI currently supports 40 standard visualizations, and hundreds of custom visualizations are available in **AppSource**, Microsoft's online marketplace. The standard visuals are aligned with the most common analytical representations, including trend, rankings, part-to-whole, exceptions, geospatial, and distribution. Several of these visuals can be further enhanced via the **Analytics** pane.

Finally, advanced visualizations are included that support machine learning elements, Power Platform integration, paginated reports, Q&A capabilities, and integration with R and Python. Refer to the following chapter for additional details on basic, custom, and advanced visuals.

Let's first take a look at when to use tables and matrices versus charts.

## Tables and matrices versus charts

An initial step in the visualization selection process is to determine whether a table, a chart, or a combination of both is most appropriate. Power BI's table visual provides simple row groups of dimension values and measures, and the matrix visual supports both row and column field inputs similar to pivot tables in Excel. Both the table and matrix visuals have been significantly enhanced to provide granular controls over layouts, subtotals, field formatting, and more.

Both the table and the matrix visuals are superior to charts in enabling users to look up specific data points. However, despite conditional formatting options available to table and matrix visuals, charts are superior to table and matrix visuals in displaying trends, comparisons, and large volumes of distinct data points.

The following matrix visual shown in *Figure 6.5* breaks down the AdWorks Net Sales measure by two product dimension columns and two promotion dimension columns:

| Promotion Type | New Product | | | Volume Discount | | | | | | Total |
|---|---|---|---|---|---|---|---|---|---|---|
| Product Category Group | 15% | 20% | Total | 2% | 5% | 10% | 15% | Total | | |
| ⊟ **Bikes** | $458,091 | $612,325 | $1,070,416 | $4,412,702 | $763,929 | $69,993 | | $5,246,624 | $6,317,040 | |
| Bikes | $458,091 | $612,325 | $1,070,416 | $4,412,702 | $763,929 | $69,993 | | $5,246,624 | $6,317,040 | |
| ⊟ **Non-Bikes** | | | | $483,750 | $273,714 | $54,155 | $1,737 | $813,357 | $813,357 | |
| Accessories | | | | $83,618 | $42,347 | $3,226 | | $129,192 | $129,192 | |
| Clothing | | | | $238,480 | $194,968 | $50,930 | $1,737 | $486,114 | $486,114 | |
| Components | | | | $161,652 | $36,399 | | | $198,050 | $198,050 | |
| **Total** | $458,091 | $612,325 | $1,070,416 | $4,896,452 | $1,037,643 | $124,149 | $1,737 | $6,059,981 | $7,130,396 | |

*Figure 6.5: Matrix visual*

The product hierarchy created in *Chapter 4, Designing Import, DirectQuery, and Composite Data Models*, is used as the rows' input and a promotion table hierarchy is used as the columns' input. Via the expand all down feature for both the rows and the columns, the matrix provides easy access to specific data points, including subtotals by both product categories and promotion types.

Although it's possible to visualize the same data with a chart, a matrix visual (or a table visual) makes it easy to locate individual values and to display the exact values with no rounding.

Additionally, if a table or matrix is needed to reference individual values, but less precision is required, the field formatting card in the formatting pane allows the report author to define the display units (for example, thousands (K) or millions (M)) and the number of decimal places for the measure. The same two formatting properties (display units and value decimal places) are also accessible for chart visuals via the data labels formatting card in the formatting pane.

Matrix features, such as showing values (for example, multiple metrics) as individual rows, as a percentage of column or row totals, and full control over subtotals positions Power BI matrix visuals as an alternative to many Excel pivot tables and matrix displays in paginated reports.

Additionally, table and matrix visuals are interactive such that user selections on a row, a specific value, or a row or column header filter other visuals or can even drillthrough to other report pages.

The following line chart visual, *Figure 6.6*, breaks down the AdWorks Net Sales measure according to the calendar year week:

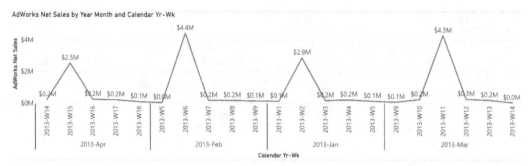

Figure 6.6: Line chart visual

With 21 different data points displayed, the periodic spikes of the line help to identify the specific weeks with relatively higher net sales. The drawback or trade-off of this visual relative to the prior matrix visual is the lack of subtotals and the loss of precision given the rounding to one decimal place.

Line charts are uniquely advantaged to call out patterns, trends, and exceptions in measures across time. More generally, chart visualizations (for example, bar, column, and scatter) are recommended over table and matrix visuals when the shape or position of the data, such as trends, comparisons, correlations, and exceptions, is more valuable than the individual values.

With a date hierarchy or the date columns in the chart axis input field, the concatenate labels property in the *x* axis formatting card should be turned off to provide the grouped layout as per the preceding line chart example. Additionally, also included in the line chart example visual, the vertical gridlines can be turned on to separate the parent values (for example, 2013-Feb).

Let's now turn our attention to chart selection.

## Chart selection

Within Power BI Desktop, there are many different types of charts, including line, column, bar, scatter, bubble, pie, doughnut, waterfall, and funnel. Different charts are better at displaying different types of information to report viewers.

Chart visuals can broadly be categorized into the following four types of data relationships:

1. **Comparison**: How items compare against each other or over time
2. **Relationship**: How items relate (or correlate) to one another across multiple variables

3. **Distribution:** The most common values for a variable and the concentration of values within a range

4. **Composition:** The portion of a total that an item represents relative to other items, possibly over time

The following table, *Table 6.1*, associates specific visuals with these categories and briefly describes their top use cases:

| Chart | Category | Notes |
|---|---|---|
| **Line** | Comparison | <ul><li>Display the fluctuation and trend of a value over time.</li><li>Compare the trends of multiple items over time.</li></ul> |
| **Column and bar** | Comparison | <ul><li>Rank items based on a value and display precise data points.</li><li>Use a bar chart if there are many items or if item data labels are long.</li></ul> |
| **Combination** | Comparison | <ul><li>Compare items against two values with different scales.</li><li>For example, display sales by country as columns across time, but also show the margin % as a line on the secondary axis.</li></ul> |
| **Scatter and bubble** | Relationship | <ul><li>Display the relative position of items (data points) on two values, such as products by sales and sales growth %.</li><li>Optionally drive the size of data points by a third variable.</li></ul> |
| **Histograms** | Distribution | <ul><li>Display a frequency distribution such as the count of items sold by different list prices or list price bins on the $x$ axis.</li><li>In Power BI, use a column chart, line chart, or custom visual.</li></ul> |
| **Pie and doughnut** | Composition | <ul><li>Commonly used for part-to-whole relationships.</li><li>Column, bar, and stacked columns and bar charts are recommended alternatives.</li></ul> |
| **Waterfall and funnel** | Composition | <ul><li>Use waterfall charts to break out the changes in a value over time by category.</li><li>Use funnel charts to display variances in the stages of a process.</li></ul> |

*Table 6.1: Chart visuals by category*

As a table of chart types, map visuals, and the three standard single number visuals provided in Power BI Desktop—Cards, Gauge, and KPI—are excluded as these visuals are generally used for different purposes. For example, single number visuals are commonly used in dashboards, mobile-optimized reports, and in the top-left section of report pages to deliver easy access to important individual metrics.

The standard single number visuals (Card, Gauge, and KPI) can also be used to create data alerts when these visuals are pinned to Power BI dashboards. Alerts can be created and managed in both the Power BI service and on the Power BI mobile application. With an alert set on a dashboard tile representing one of these visuals, whenever the number of the visual crosses a defined condition (for example, above 100), a notification is raised and optionally an email can be sent as well.

Details on standard map visuals are included in the *Map visuals* section of *Chapter 7, Creating and Formatting Visualizations*, and the ArcGIS Map visual for Power BI is reviewed in *Chapter 8, Applying Advanced Report Features*.

There are several publicly available resources on visualization practices and visual selection. The *Chart Suggestions* diagram from Extreme Presentation (`http://bit.ly/1xlXh1x`) provides additional details on the visuals and visual categories described in this section.

Additionally, the SQL BI team provides a Power BI Visuals reference (`http://bit.ly/2ndtcZj`) that categorizes visuals at a more granular level than the table in this section. Finally, Zebra BI provides an interactive Power BI report for chart selection (`https://zebrabi.com/chart-selector/`).

The next subject related to report design deals with how visuals interact with one another.

## Visualization anti-patterns

In addition to report planning and generally aligning reports with visualization best practices, it can be helpful to acknowledge and avoid several common visualization anti-patterns. Anti-patterns are common practices that negatively impact the quality, usability, performance, and other aspects of a report.

For many reports, particularly when report development time and Power BI experience are limited, simply avoiding these anti-patterns coupled with adequate planning and appropriate visual type choices is sufficient to deliver quality, sustainable content.

The most common visualization anti-patterns include the following:

1. **A cluttered interface of many visuals and report elements that are complex or difficult to interpret**: This is often the result of too many visuals per report page or too high a precision being displayed. Report visuals should be separated across distinct reports, report pages, and bookmarks to both improve usability as well as limit the volume of concurrent queries.

2. **A lack of structure, order, and consistency**: Each report page should naturally guide the user from the essential top-left visuals to the supporting visuals. A failure to align visuals or to provide proper spacing and borders can make reports appear disorganized. Mixing widely disparate grains of detail on the same report page can be disorienting to users.

3. **High-density and/or high-detail visualizations, such as large table visuals or thousands of points on a scatter chart or map**: The need for a scrollbar is a strong indication that a visual contains too many values. A table visual should not be used as a raw data extract of many columns and rows. High-density visuals, such as line and scatter charts with thousands of data points, can cause poor performance.

*Figure 6.7*, showing a table visual with seven dimension columns and three measures, is an example of a data extract anti-pattern:

| SalesTerritoryCountry | CommuteDistance | FirstName | LastName | PromotionName | Product Name | Internet Net Sales | Internet Net Product Margin | Internet Net Product Margin % |
|---|---|---|---|---|---|---|---|---|
| Australia | 0-1 Miles | Abby | Martinez | No Discount | Long-Sleeve Logo Jersey, M | $49.99 | $11.50 | $23.00% |
| Australia | 0-1 Miles | Abby | Martinez | No Discount | Water Bottle - 30 oz. | $4.99 | $3.12 | 62.60% |
| Australia | 0-1 Miles | | | | | ✕ | $15.33 | 62.60% |
| Australia | 0-1 Miles | **Data exceeds the limit** | | | | | $75.12 | 62.60% |
| Australia | 0-1 Miles | Your data is too large. Some data sampling may occur. | | | | | $1,487.84 | 43.76% |
| Australia | 0-1 Miles | | | | Continue  Cancel | | $5.63 | 62.60% |
| Australia | 0-1 Miles | | | | | | $902.13 | 37.84% |
| Australia | 0-1 Miles | Abby | Sai | No Discount | Water Bolttle - 30 oz. | $4.99 | $3.12 | 62.60% |

*Figure 6.7: Data extract anti-pattern*

The small scrollbar on the right indicates that many rows are not displayed. Additionally, the **Export data** option available from the ellipses (…) menu of the visual prompts the warning message (**Data exceeds the limit**), suggesting the visual contains too much data.

4. **The excessive use of fancy or complex visuals and images**: Reports can be aesthetic and engaging, but the priority should be to inform users, not to impress them. For example, a column chart or a stacked column chart is usually more effective than a treemap.

5. **Suboptimal visual choices such as pie charts, donut charts, and gauges**: Column or bar charts are easier to interpret than the circular shapes of pie and donut charts. KPI visuals provide more context than gauge visuals, including the trend of the indicator value. Additionally, report authors sometimes utilize table and matrix visuals when a column or line chart would better highlight the differences between items or the overall trend.

6. **The misuse of colors, such as utilizing more than five colors and overwhelming users with highly saturated colors**: Colors should be used selectively and only when the few alternative colors convey meaning.

7. **A high volume of report pages such as 10 or more**: Reports with many pages are generally less focused and more difficult to browse by end users. Report authors should consider dividing report pages into more focused or targeted reports and using bookmarks and buttons to further reduce the volume of report pages.

Just as important as following visualization best practices and avoiding visualization anti-patterns is choosing the right visualization.

# Visual interactions

Power BI reports are highly interactive by nature, allowing users to click on data points within visuals and cross-filter or highlight other filters on the page. When planning and designing reports, it is important to keep this default behavior in mind and consider whether or not the default visual interaction behavior should be changed.

By default, the filter selections applied to a single visual, such as clicking a bar on a column chart or a row on a table, impact all other data visualizations on the given report page with relationships to the selection.

In *Figure 6.8*, the bar representing the **United States** sales territory country has been selected and this causes the product category chart to highlight the portion of each product category related to the **United States** sales territory country ($45M):

*Figure 6.8: Visual interactions – Highlighting*

Multiple values from the same column can be selected (for example, **France** and **Canada**) by holding down the *Ctrl* key and the values from separate columns of the same visual, such as the dimension columns of a table visual, can also cross-filter other visuals on the report page. The ability to drive visual interactions from the selections of two or more visuals (for example, **United States** and **Bikes**) is also supported.

The highlight interaction option from the preceding example is available and enabled by default for column, bar, treemap, pie, and donut charts. Only the filter and the no interaction options are available for cards, KPIs, and line and scatter chart visuals.

As per prior chapters, the Sales Territory, Product, and Date dimension tables are related to all three fact tables—Internet Sales, Reseller Sales, and Sales and Margin Plan. Therefore, the filters and selections applied to the columns of these tables simultaneously impact measures from other fact tables.

This integration within the dataset supports robust analyses but can also require some training or explanation to users as users may not initially expect or understand the cross-filtering behavior. If this is the case, or if a different interaction between visuals is desired, report authors can modify the default behavior by editing the interactions.

## Editing interactions

Report authors can modify the visual interaction behavior such that selections (user clicks) on certain visuals don't impact other visuals or only impact certain visuals. Additionally, for the visuals set to the highlight interaction by default, report authors can revise the interaction behavior to filter.

In *Figure 6.9*, the United States selection in the middle bar chart has no impact on the multi-row car visual but causes a filter interaction (rather than highlight) on the product category chart:

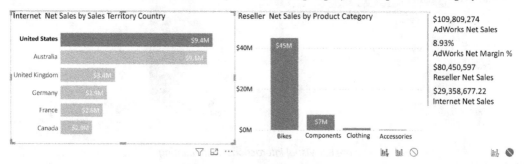

*Figure 6.9: Edit interactions in Power BI Desktop*

To edit visual interactions, select the visual that receives the selections and then enable the **Edit interactions** command under the **Format** tab in Power BI Desktop. In this example, the **None** interaction icon has been selected for the multi-row card visual as indicated by the circle with a slash through it below the visual. The **Filter** interaction icon has been selected for the **Product Category** column chart as similarly indicated by the left-most icon below the visual. To disable editing interactions, simply return to the **Format** tab and click the **Edit interactions** command again.

Like the preceding example, it's often appropriate to disable visual interactions from impacting cards or KPIs. These values can be impacted exclusively by the filters defined outside of the report canvas, such as report- and page-level filters, and do not change during user sessions like other visuals on the page.

Regardless of the design decision, if users regularly interact with reports, such as clicking on slicers and other visuals, it's important to briefly review or explain the visual interaction behavior. This is especially necessary with new users and with more customized designs, such as two or three visuals with interactions enabled and two or three visuals with interactions disabled.

In addition to interactions between visuals on the same page, visuals can also interact with one another between different report pages via drillthrough report pages.

# Drillthrough report pages

A well-designed Power BI report of summary-level visualizations may itself sufficiently address user questions. However, it's often the case that users need the ability to view the details behind particular data points of interest, such as the sales orders for a specific product, customer, or fiscal period that seems high or low relative to expectations.

Drillthrough report pages are typically hidden by default and accessed via the right-click context menu of visuals for items of interest, such as an individual bar on a bar chart. These report pages enable users to continue and often complete their own analysis at a detailed level and thus can reduce the need to create or support traditional paginated or extract-like detail reports.

As per *Figure 6.10*, a report page has been designed with a drillthrough filter set to the **Product Name** column. This drillthrough page automatically applies filters from the source report page's **Product Name** column, such as **Road-250 Black, 44**.

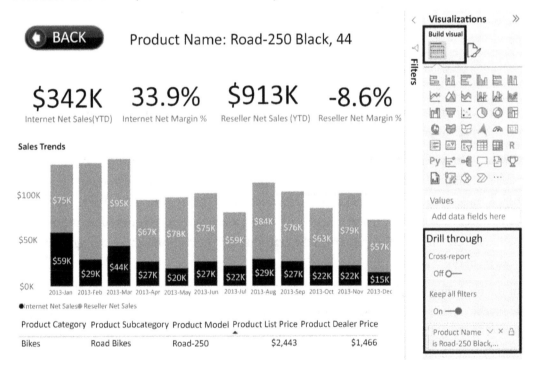

*Figure 6.10: Drillthrough report page*

Drillthrough filters are set at the bottom of the **Visualizations** pane in the **Drill through** section of the **Build visual** sub-pane, as shown in *Figure 6.10*.

With the drillthrough report page configured, when the **Product Name** column is exposed on a separate page within the report, the user has a right-click option to drill to this page as per *Figure 6.11*:

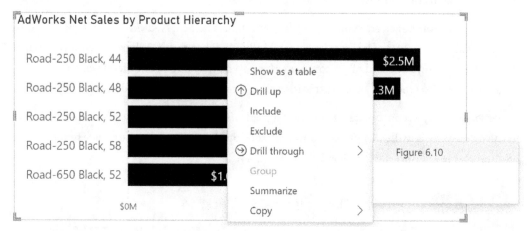

*Figure 6.11: Drillthrough source page*

Only the column or columns specified in the **Drill through** section of the **Visualizations** pane (drillthrough filters) can be used as drill columns.

For example, even if the **ProductAlternateKey** column has a 1-to-1 relationship with the **Product Name** column, the drillthrough option is not available to visuals based on the **ProductAlternateKey** column unless **ProductAlternateKey** is also specified as a drillthrough filter, like the **Product Name** column. Therefore, if some report visuals use **Product Name** and others use **ProductAlternateKey**, both columns can be configured as **Drill through** filters on the drillthrough report page to support both scenarios.

In the preceding example, the user has drilled down through the four levels of the product hierarchy created in *Chapter 4, Designing Import and DirectQuery Data Models* (Product Category Group, Product Category, Product Subcategory, and Product Name), to display a bar chart by the Product Name column.

The same right-click drillthrough option is exposed via table, matrix, and other chart visuals, including scatter charts, stacked column and bar charts, column charts, and bar charts.

The bottom-level column of a hierarchy, such as the preceding Product Name example, is often a good candidate to support a drillthrough report page.

For example, a common analysis pattern is to apply a few slicer selections and then drill down through the hierarchy levels built into chart and matrix visuals. Each level of the hierarchy provides supporting context for its parent value, but ultimately, the report user wants to investigate a specific value (for example, **Customer 123**) or a specific combination of values (**Customer 123** and **Calendar Year 2018**).

The use of drillthrough report pages can create certain challenges with regard to navigation by report viewers. In addition, users unfamiliar with Power BI Desktop may not intuitively understand the context in which they are viewing a report page. Both of these issues are addressed in the next section.

## Custom labels and the back button

Two of the most important components of the drillthrough report page shown in *Figure 6.10* include the custom **Product Name** label and back button image at the top of the report page. The **Product Name** message at the top of the page uses the following DAX measure expression:

```
Selected Product Name =
    VAR __ProdName = SELECTEDVALUE('Product'[Product Name], "Multiple
Product Names")
RETURN
    "Product Name: " & __ProdName
```

The SELECTEDVALUE() function returns either the single value currently selected for a given column or an alternative expression if multiple values have been selected. For drillthrough report pages, it's a given that the drill column only has a single value as each drillthrough column is limited to a single value.

To provide a dynamic label or title to the page, the DAX variable containing the Product Name expression is concatenated with a text string. In this example, the **Selected Product Name** measure is displayed in a card visual. Alternatively, the **Selected Product Name** measure could be used as a dynamic title for the visual. Although card visuals can be used to display text messages and dates, a text box also supports DAX measures and importantly provides much greater formatting control to define how the message appears on the canvas.

The custom back button image was added to the report via the insert image command on the **Insert** tab of **Report** view. Once positioned in the top left of the page, selecting the image exposes the image formatting cards. As per *Figure 6.12*, the **Action** card is enabled, and **Type** is set to **Back**:

*Figure 6.12: Back button image formatting*

Power BI Desktop adds a back button arrow shape by default when a drillthrough page is created, but this shape is less intuitive for users than the custom image. With the back button configured, *Ctrl +* click is used to return to the source page in Power BI Desktop. Only a single click is needed to use the back button in the Power BI service.

The single-row table at the bottom of the drillthrough report page shown in *Figure 6.10* has been filtered to only display the current, active values of the product. As described in the *Slowly changing dimensions* section of *Chapter 2, Connecting to Sources and Transforming Data with M*, the Products table contains multiple rows per product, representing different points in time.

To ensure that only one row is displayed by the table visual, a visual-level filter was applied, setting the Product Status column equal to **Current**. Alternatively, the visual-level filter condition could specify that the Product End Date column is **Blank** via an advanced filter condition.

Thus far, we have covered drillthrough report pages consisting of a single drillthrough column. However, it is possible to include multiple columns in drillthrough report pages.

## Multi-column drillthrough

In many scenarios, a more specific filter context is needed for drillthrough report pages to resolve analyses. For example, the user may be interested in one specific year for a given Product Subcategory column.

To support these needs, multiple columns can be added as drillthrough page filters. When one or both columns are exposed in a report visual on a separate page, the drillthrough right-click option can be used to apply multiple filter selections to the drillthrough page.

In the stacked column chart of **Internet Sales by Year and Product Subcategory** shown in *Figure 6.13*, right-clicking on the **Road Bikes** column for 2011 ($5.7M) exposes the **Drill through** option to the *Figure 6.13* drillthrough report page:

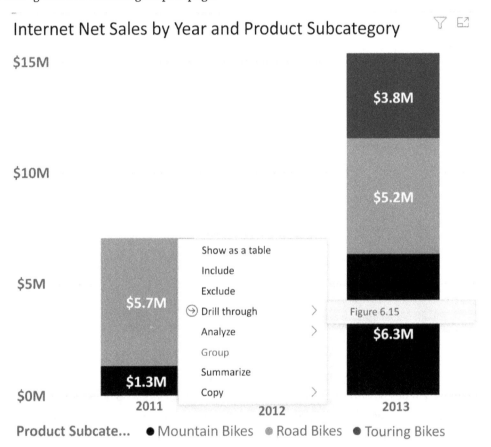

*Figure 6.13: Drillthrough by multiple columns*

The **Drill through** report page filters for both the Year and Product Subcategory columns. Report visuals that only expose one of these two columns can still drill to this multi-column drillthrough report page. In this scenario, no filter would be applied to the column not contained in the source visual.

Executing the drillthrough action from the preceding chart results in the drillthrough report page filtered for both column values. As shown in *Figure 6.14*, with **Keep all filters** toggled on, all filters from the source visual are passed to the drillthrough report page, including the most specific filters for Product Subcategory of **Road Bikes** and Year of **2011**:

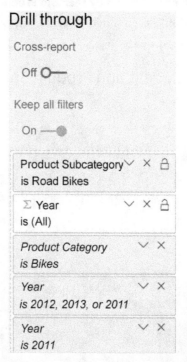

*Figure 6.14: Multi-column drillthrough report page*

The drillthrough report page in this scenario is designed to display the values of the two drill-through columns and provide supporting analysis for this given filter context. The choice to keep all filters should be considered carefully as this may confuse users who do not understand that this behavior preserves all existing source visual filters, including those outside of the specific, user-chosen context when drilling.

In *Figure 6.15*, $3M of the $5.7M of Internet Net Sales from the source page occurs in the second half of the year, as identified in a card visual and also visualized by the last 6 calendar months of **2011** in a stacked column chart to break out the product models for the **Road Bikes** subcategory:

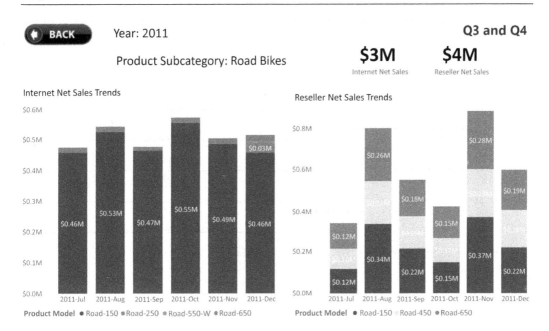

*Figure 6.15: Multi-column drillthrough report page*

In *Figure 6.15*, the user obtains details on both `Internet Net Sales` and `Reseller Net Sales` for the given `Year` and `Product Subcategory`. Visuals that utilize measures from any fact table (for example, `Sales Plan`) with a cross-filtering relationship to the drillthrough column tables can be added to the drillthrough report page to provide additional context.

In addition to stacked column charts, matrix visuals are also a common choice for initiating a drillthrough action based on two columns. For example, the `Year` column could be the columns input and the `Product Subcategory` could be the rows input for a matrix visual. Additionally, a pie chart with the two columns used in the legend and detailed input fields can also be used to drill through based on two columns.

With the concept of drillthrough filters explained, we can delve further into the subject of the different types of filters and filter scopes available in reports.

# Report filter scopes

Within Power BI Desktop, the **Filters** pane provides access to three different filter scopes, filters on all pages, filters on the current page, and filters on the current visual. In addition, a fourth filter scope can be set in the **Visualizations** pane, using drillthrough filters.

Filter scopes simply refer to what is impacted by the filter, either just the visual, the whole report page, the entire report, or only when drilling into a visual's information. A fundamental skill and practice in Power BI report development is utilizing the report filter scopes and the filter conditions available to each scope.

For example, a report intended for the European sales team can be filtered at the report level for the European sales territory group and specific report pages can be filtered for France, Germany, and the United Kingdom. Reports can be further customized by implementing filter conditions to specific visuals, applying more complex filter conditions, and providing drillthrough report pages to reflect the details of a unique item, such as a product or a customer.

Report filter scopes are defined outside of the report canvas and therefore provide report authors with the option to eliminate or reduce the need for on-canvas user selections as well as the canvas space associated with slicer visuals. This can provide a better user experience with less interaction required by users as well as larger visuals with easier-to-read font sizes.

In addition to meeting functional requirements and delivering a simplified user experience, report filter scopes can also benefit performance. Using the European sales report as an example, the simple filter conditions of **Sales Territory Group = Europe** (Report-level filter) and **Sales Territory Country = France** (Page-level filter) are efficiently implemented by the Power BI in-memory engine (import mode) and almost all the DirectQuery data sources. Even if the DAX measures used on the report page for France are complex, the report filters contribute to acceptable or good performance.

With a visual selected on the canvas in **Report** view, the **Filters** and **Visualizations** panes present the following four input field wells:

1.  **Filters on all pages**: The filter conditions defined impact all visuals on all report pages. The scope of these filters is the entire report

2.  **Filters on this page**: The filter conditions defined impact all visuals on the given report page. The scope of these filters is a single page. Report-level filter conditions are respected by the page-level filters as well. Any drillthrough filter conditions defined for the report page are also respected.

3.  **Filters on this visual**: The filter conditions defined only impact the specific visual selected. The scope of these filters is a single visual. Report- and page-level filter conditions are respected by the visual-level filters as well. Any drillthrough filter conditions defined for the report page of the given visual are also respected.

4. **Drill-through:** The filter condition, a single value from a column, impacts all visuals on the given report page. The scope of these filters is the entire page. Report-level filter conditions are respected by the drillthrough filters as well. Any page- and visual-level filter conditions are also respected.

As per prior chapters, filters are applied to Power BI visuals via the relationships defined in the dataset (via single or bidirectional cross-filtering) as well as any filtering logic embedded in DAX measures. All four of the preceding filters (**Report, Page, Visual**, and **Drill through**) contribute to the initial filter context, as described in the *Measure evaluation process section* of *Chapter 5, Developing DAX Measures and Security Roles.*

Therefore, just like filters applied on the report canvas (for example, **Slicers**), the filter logic of DAX measures can supplement, remove, or replace these filters' conditions. In the event of a conflict between any report filter and a DAX measure expression that utilizes the CALCULATE( ) function, the DAX expression supersedes or overrides the report filter.

Let's now explore the different filter conditions that can be applied to each scope.

## Report filter conditions

Different types of filter conditions can be defined for the distinct filter scopes. For example, report- and page-level filters are limited to relatively simple filter conditions that reference individual columns of a dataset. However, more complex and powerful conditions, such as filtering by the results of a DAX measure and top N filters (such as the three largest or five smallest values), can be applied via visual-level filters.

The following outline and matrix (filter conditions by filter scope) summarize the filtering functionality supported:

1. **Basic:** A single equality condition for a column to a single value or set of values, such as "is North America or Europe"; a single inequality condition for a column to a single value or set of values, such as "is not $25 or $35."

2. **Advanced:** Several condition rules per data type, such as "starts with" for text and "is greater than or equal to" for numbers; supports filtering for blank and non-blank values; optionally, apply multiple conditions per column via logical operators (and, or).

3. **Relative Date:** Supports three filter condition rules (is in this, is in the last, and is in the next) for days, weeks, months, and years. Partial period and complete period filter conditions can be defined. The same filter condition rules are available to slicers with date data type columns.

4. **Top N**: Filter a visual to a defined number of top or bottom values of a column based on their values for a measure. For example, the top 10 products based on net sales can be set as a visual-level filter condition.

5. **Filter by Measure**: Filter a visual by applying advanced filtering conditions to the results of a DAX measure. For example, greater than 45% on the **Internet Net Margin %** measure can be set as a visual-level filter condition.

*Table 6.2* summarizes the preceding filter conditions available to each of the three primary report filter scopes:

| Filter Conditions | Report Level | Page Level | Visual Level |
|---|---|---|---|
| **Basic** | Yes | Yes | Yes |
| **Advanced** | Yes | Yes | Yes |
| **Relative Date** | Yes | Yes | Yes |
| **Top N** | No | No | Yes |
| **Filter by Measure** | No | No | Yes |

*Table 6.2: Filter conditions by filter scope*

Multiple filter conditions can be defined per report filter scope. For example, a report-level filter could include two basic filter conditions and an advanced filter condition. Additionally, the same column can be used in multiple filter scopes, such as a report-level filter and a page-level filter on the product subcategory column.

All defined filter conditions are applied to the visuals within their scope provided that the DAX measures included in the visuals don't contain filtering logic in conflict with the report filter conditions. Additionally, the columns and measures referenced in the filter conditions do not need to be displayed in the report visuals. For the top N filtering condition, the column to be filtered only has to be displayed in the visual when the filter condition is initially defined.

A good indicator of Power BI development and solution-specific knowledge is the ability to accurately interpret the filters being applied to a given visual on a report page. This includes all Power BI report filters (report-level, page-level, and visual-level), any slicer selections or cross-highlighting, the filter logic of the DAX measures, the cross-filtering applied via relationships in the data model, and any filter logic built into the M queries of the dataset. Complex reports and datasets utilize all or many of these different layers in various combinations to ultimately affect the values displayed in report visuals.

BI teams generally want to limit the complexity built into reports, both for users and the report authors or developers responsible for the reports. For example, if visual-level filter conditions are applied to many visuals of a report, the filter condition for each visual must be modified if the requirement(s) of the report change or the columns or measures used by the filter condition change. Dataset designers and data warehouse teams can often implement changes or enhancements to simplify the filter conditions needed by report authors.

As one example, a filter condition implemented in multiple reports that specifies several product categories (hardcoded) could be replaced with a new column in the product dimension table. The new column would distinguish the group of product categories that meet the desired criteria relative to those that don't, and logic could be built into the data source or retrieval process to dynamically include additional product categories that later meet the given criteria.

Drillthrough filters, which are used to define drillthrough report pages as described in the previous section, are unique in that they can be used to implement basic filtering conditions at the page level as well as their more common filtering of a single column value. This can enable a report page to serve a dual purpose, both as a standard report page as well as a drillthrough page.

For example, three countries can be selected in a drillthrough filter condition and the visuals on the report page reflect these three countries. Such a page may be useful for displaying European countries such as the United Kingdom, France, and Germany.

However, a user can only drill to the report page from the context of a single column value. The source drillthrough value (for example, **Germany**), replaces the three countries in the previous filter condition on the drillthrough page when the drillthrough action is executed.

Additionally, multiple columns can be used as drillthrough filters and the values of both columns from a separate report page are applied to the drillthrough page when a drillthrough action is executed. If only one value is present from the source report page, the drillthrough action only filters this column and removes any filter defined for the other drillthrough filter column.

## Report and page filters

Report- and page-level filters (**Filters on all pages** and **Filters on this page** from the *Report filter scopes* section) are most commonly used to apply the fundamental filter context for the report. Columns with few unique values, such as SalesTerritoryCountry, are good candidates for report-level filters, while more granular columns such as SalesTerritoryRegion are better suited for page-level filters.

In *Figure 6.16*, the individual report pages are named according to the report and page filters applied:

| USA | Northeast | Northwest | Central | Southeast | Southwest |
|-----|-----------|-----------|---------|-----------|-----------|

*Figure 6.16: Power BI report pages*

In the absence of any custom DAX measures that retrieve the filter selections applied, users of the report do not typically see the applied report-, page-, and visual-level filters. Therefore, it's important to assign intuitive names to each report page as per *Figure 6.16* and to include a brief title for each report page via a text box.

*Figure 6.17* shows the **Report** and **Page** filters applied to the **Northeast** report page of a **United States** sales report:

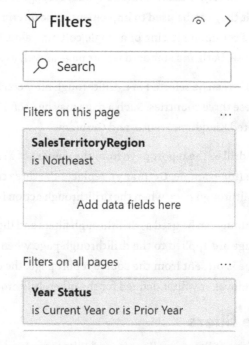

*Figure 6.17: Report- and page-level filters*

Each report page is filtered for a different sales territory region except the **USA** page, which would only contain a **Country** page filter since the USA page covers multiple sales territories (**Northeast, Northwest, Central, Southeast,** and **Southwest**).

The **Year Status** column, as described in the *Date dimension view* section of *Chapter 2, Preparing Data Sources*, restricts all visuals to only the current and prior year. One or two years of history is sufficient for many reports given the pace of change in business environments and strategies. Additionally, the report-level date filter promotes both query performance and low maintenance since the dates filtered reflect the latest dataset refresh.

Report filters are not a long-term substitute for poor data quality or a suboptimal dataset (data model or retrieval queries). If it's necessary to implement many filter conditions or complex filtering conditions within reports to return accurate results, the dataset or the source system itself should likely be revised.

Similarly, if many filter conditions or complex filter conditions are needed to retrieve the desired results, the dataset can likely be enhanced (for example, a new column, new measure) to simplify or eliminate these report filter conditions.

Power BI report authors should communicate to the dataset designer(s) and BI team whenever complex or convoluted report filters are being applied. Given limited team resources, it may be sufficient to use report filters to support rare or uncommon reports. For common reporting needs, however, it's generally appropriate to build or revise the necessary logic in the data source or dataset.

We'll now move on to exploring the use cases for relative date filtering within Power BI reports.

## Relative date filtering

Relative date filtering refers to the ability to enable date filters relative to the current date and time. Relative date filtering is available for date columns at all filter scopes (report, page, and visual) and for slicer visuals.

These dynamic filter conditions, such as the last 30 days (relative to the current date), promote both data freshness and query performance since the minimal amount of history required can be retrieved. Additionally, relative date filters can often avoid the need to add dynamically computed columns to a date dimension table or implement date filter conditions in DAX measures.

In *Figure 6.18*, five report pages are dedicated to a specific relative date filter condition:

*Figure 6.18: Relative date filter conditions per page*

A page-level filter is used for each report page with the following conditions, as per *Figure 6.19*:

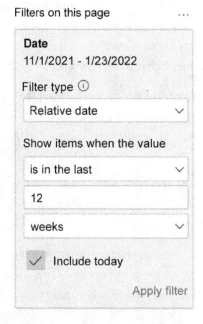

*Figure 6.19: Relative date filter condition*

As of 1/23/2022 (the current date when the report was viewed), the five report pages are filtered to the following date ranges with the **Include today** option enabled:

- Is in the last 12 months, 1/24/2021 through 1/23/2022
- Is in the last 12 weeks, 11/1/2021 through 1/23/2022
- Is in this month, 1/1/2022 through 1/31/2022
- Is in the next 12 months, 1/23/2022 through 1/22/2023
- Is in the next 12 weeks, 1/23/2022 through 4/16/2022

A report design such as this would make it simple for users to analyze immediate, near-term, and longer-term trends and issues.

Three types of relative date filter conditions can be set:

1. **is in the last**
2. **in this**
3. **is in the next**

Each of these filter conditions supports **days**, **weeks**, **months**, and **years** intervals. For the **is in the last** and **is in the next** filter conditions, **calendar weeks**, **calendar months**, and **calendar years** conditions can also be specified. These last three intervals represent full or completed calendar periods only.

For example, as of **January 23, 2022**, the last one-calendar month and last one-calendar year would include all dates of December 2021 and all dates of 2021, respectively. The week of 1/16/2022 through 1/22/2022 would represent the last one-calendar week.

In the next section, we explore filters scoped to individual visuals or visual-level filtering.

# Visual-level filtering

Visual-level filters (*Filters on this visual* from the *Report filter scopes* section) provide the most powerful filter conditions in Power BI exclusive of custom filter conditions specified in DAX expressions.

Unlike report- and page-level filters, DAX measures can be used in visual-level filter conditions, such as net sales greater than $5,000. Additionally, top N filter conditions can be implemented referencing a column and measure that are included or excluded from the visual as per the *Top N visual-level filters* section following this example.

In *Figure 6.20*, a table visual of customers has been filtered according to the **Internet Net Sales** and **Internet Sales Orders** measures:

| CustomerAlternateKey | FirstName | LastName | Internet Sales Orders | Internet Net Sales | Customer Sales Rank | | |
|---|---|---|---|---|---|---|---|
| AW00011433 | Maurice | Shan | 6 | $ 12,909.67 | 10 | **Internet Net Sales** is greater than $12,00... | |
| AW00011439 | Janet | Munoz | 6 | $ 12,489.17 | 11 | | |
| Total | | | 12 | $25,398.84 | 1 | **Internet Sales Orders** is greater than 5 | |

*Figure 6.20: Table with visual-level filters applied*

Specifically, the visual only displays items (customers) with more than $12,000 in **Internet Net Sales** and more than five **Internet Sales Orders**. As per the **Customer Sales Rank** measure, certain customers that meet the net sales condition are excluded based on the sales order condition.

Unlike the top N visual-level filter condition, filters based on measures, such as the conditions shown in *Figure 6.20*, are only applied when items (for example, customers or products) are displayed on the visual.

By removing the customer columns, the remaining measures (Internet Sales Orders and Internet Net Sales) would not be filtered by the visual-level filter conditions. In other words, the visual-level filters based on measures are only applied against the dimension column or columns in the visual, such as CustomerAlternateKey or FirstName.

Although analytically powerful, report authors should exercise caution with visual-level filters. From a usability standpoint, reports can become confusing when visuals on the same report page reflect different filter conditions. If used, report authors should include the visual-level filters as part of the visual's **Title**, such as "Customers with Internet Net Sales greater than 12K and more than 5 orders."

Additionally, executing complex filter conditions against large or dense report visuals can result in performance degradation. If a complex filter condition is repeatedly needed at the visual level, it's likely the case that the dataset should be modified to include some or all of this logic.

We complete our look at visual-level filtering with an example of the use of **Top N** filtering.

## Top N visual-level filters

In *Figure 6.21*, a table visual is filtered based on the top five products for the **Internet Net Sales (PYTD)** measure:

| Product Name | Intenet Net Sales (YTD) | Intenet Net Sales (YOY YTD) | Intenet Net Sales (YOY YTD %) |
|---|---|---|---|
| Mountain-200 Black, 42 | $970,781 | $578,419 | 147% |
| Mountain-200 Black, 46 | $947,831 | $524,241 | 124% |
| Mountain-200 Silver, 46 | $923,356 | $545,612 | 144% |
| Road-250 Black, 52 | $351,842 | ($26,353) | -7% |
| Road-250 Red, 48 | | ($388,493) | -100% |
| Total | $3,193,810 | $1,233,427 | 63% |

**Product Name**
top 5 by Internet Net Sales (PYTD)

Filter type ⓘ

Top N ⌄

Show items

Top ⌄ 5

By value

Internet Net Sales (PYTD) ✕

Apply filter

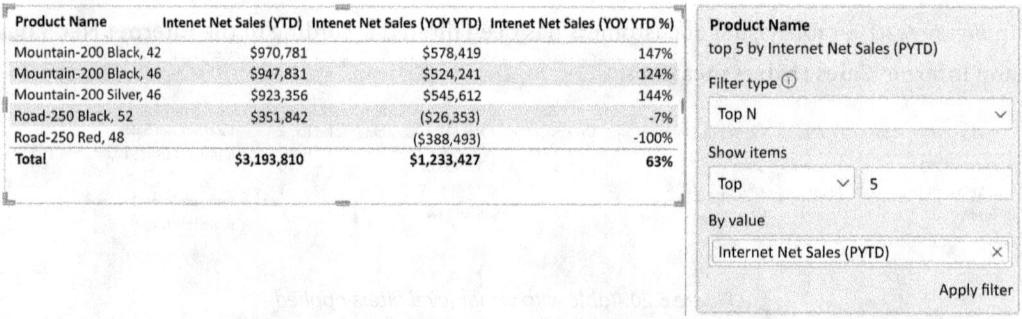

*Figure 6.21: Top N visual-level filter*

For this visual, the **Internet Net Sales (PYTD)** measure used for the filter condition is not one of the three measures displayed. Nonetheless, the **Top N** condition filters out all products, including some of the top-selling products for the current year that weren't one of the top five products in the prior year.

With a **Top N** filter defined between a column and a measure, the report author can optionally remove the column being filtered from the visual or replace it with a different column. For example, the **$3,193,810** in **Internet Net Sales** (**YTD**) associated with the top five products from the prior year could be visualized by **Occupation** instead of **Product Name**.

Alternatively, all columns except the **Internet Net Sales** (**YTD**) measure could be removed from the table visual, and a card or KPI visual could be used to visualize the **$3,193,810** value. The column referenced by the **Top N** filter condition only needs to be included in the visual when the filter condition is originally defined.

The TOPN() DAX function emulates top N filtering by returning a filtered table based on an expression (such as a net sales measure). As a table, the results of this function can be passed as a filter argument to CALCULATE() in a separate measure. For example, a measure could be created to compute the sales for the top 100 customers based on **Internet Net Sales** (**PYTD**).

In addition to filtering scopes, another report planning and design consideration involves the use of bookmarks.

# Bookmarks

**Bookmarks** enable report authors to save specific states of reports for easy access and sharing with others. For example, an important or common view of a report page that involves filter conditions across several columns can be saved as a bookmark for easy access at a later time via a command button, the bookmark navigator control, or the bookmark dropdown in the Power BI service.

By persisting the exact state of a report page, such as whether a visual is visible, bookmarks enable report authors to deliver application-like experiences for their users. For example, rather than expecting or asking users to navigate to separate report pages or to apply certain filters, bookmarks containing these different visuals and filter contexts could be readily available to the user.

By default, bookmarks represent the entire state of a report page, including all filter selections and the properties of the visuals (for example, hidden or not). However, bookmarks can also optionally be associated with only a few visuals on a report page. Additionally, report authors can choose to avoid persisting any filter or slicer selections and rather only save visual properties on the page. These granular controls, along with the **Selections** pane and linking support from images and shapes, enable report authors to create rich and compelling user experiences.

In *Figure 6.22*, 12 bookmarks have been created for a European sales report:

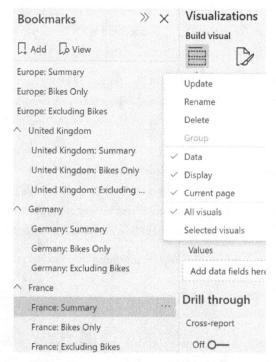

*Figure 6.22: Bookmarks pane*

Bookmarks are created via the **Add** icon at the top of the **Bookmarks** pane. With the **Bookmarks** pane visible via the **View** tab in **Report** view, a report author can develop a report page with the filters and visual layout required and then click the **Add** icon to save these settings as a bookmark. As per *Figure 6.22*, the ellipsis at the right of the bookmark's name can be used to **Update** bookmarks to reflect the current state and to **Rename** and **Delete** bookmarks. Additionally, bookmarks can be grouped together. For example, all of the **United Kingdom** bookmarks are grouped into a single folder that can be expanded or collapsed.

The second group of bookmark options, underneath the **Group** option, allows report authors to customize what is stored by the bookmark. The **Data** category includes the report-, page-, and visual-level filters, slicer selections, the drill location if a visual has been drilled into, any cross-highlighting of other visuals, and any sort of orders applied to visuals. The **Display** category includes whether a visual is hidden or not, the **Spotlight** property, **Focus mode**, and the **Show Data** view. By disabling the **Data** category for a bookmark, a user's selections on slicers or other visuals are not overridden when the bookmark is accessed. Finally, the **Current page** option determines whether the user is automatically navigated to the current page.

The third group of bookmark options, immediately beneath the **Current page** option, controls the scope of the bookmark to either apply to **All visuals** on the page or only to specific, **Selected visuals**. These options provide the report author with flexibility when creating the report and are often used in storytelling to walk others through interesting insights.

The creative use of bookmarks can help reduce the number of report pages and duplicate visuals required for reports. For example, all 12 of the bookmarks shown in *Figure 6.7* reference the same page. Thus, instead of creating 4 pages with duplicate visuals and the only difference being the country, bookmarks allow a single page to service an overall summary of all of **Europe** as well as each individual country – **France**, **Germany**, and the **United Kingdom**.

## Selection pane and the Spotlight property

The **Selection** pane and the **Spotlight** property for visuals are both closely related features to **Bookmarks**. The **Selection** pane is accessed via the **View** tab in **Report** view and displays all objects of the selected report page, including visuals, images, and shapes. Although most commonly used with **Bookmarks**, the **Selection** pane is also helpful when developing report pages that contain many visuals and objects. Selecting an object from the **Selection** pane provides access to the properties associated with that object (for example, field inputs and formatting cards) as though the object was selected on the report canvas.

In *Figure 6.23*, the **Slicer** visuals originally used to create the bookmarks are hidden for each bookmark since the bookmarks handle filtering to the correct Country and Product Category selections:

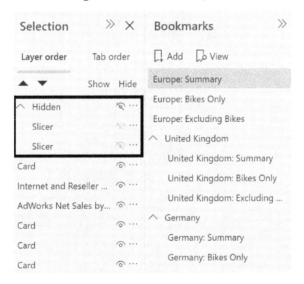

*Figure 6.23: Selection pane and the Bookmarks pane*

In the **Selection** pane, the icons next to the visuals toggle between **Show** (eye symbol) and **Hide** (eye symbol with slash). The ellipses menu next to the Show/Hide toggle icon provides the ability to **Group** visuals as well as a **Summarize** feature. Grouping allows visuals to be organized together. For example, in *Figure 6.23*, the **Slicer** visuals have been grouped into a **Hidden** group. The Show/Hide toggle can then be set for the entire group instead of each visual independently. The **Summarize** option generates a **Smart narrative** visual for the selected visual.

The **Spotlight** property, accessed via the ellipsis in the corner of any visual, draws attention to the specific visual by making all other visuals on the report page fade into the background.

**Spotlight** is particularly useful in supporting presentations via **Bookmarks**. For example, in the **View** mode described later in this section, one bookmark could display a report page of visuals normally and the following bookmark could highlight a single visual to call out a specific finding or an important trend or result. **Spotlight** may also be helpful for presenters in explaining more complex visuals with multiple metrics and/or dimension columns.

As an alternative to **Spotlight**, **Focus mode** can also be saved as a bookmark. **Focus mode** can be applied via the diagonal arrow icon in the corner of chart visuals and fills the entire report canvas with a single visual.

In *Figure 6.24*, the **Spotlight** property has been enabled for a scatter chart on the Europe report page:

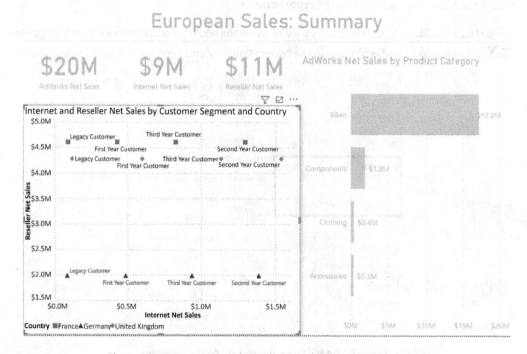

*Figure 6.24: Report page with Spotlight enabled on the scatter chart*

In *Figure 6.24,* the other visuals (four cards and a bar chart) are still visible, but the scatter chart is emphasized via the **Spotlight** property. With **Spotlight** enabled, the report author could add a bookmark with an intuitive name (for example, **Europe Summary: Customer Segment and Country Scatter**) to save this specific view. Referencing this bookmark in a meeting or presentation makes it easier to explain the meaning and insights of the scatter chart.

While bookmarks are useful on their own for preserving the state of visuals and filtering, bookmarks can also be used as an aid to navigate within a set of report pages.

## Custom report navigation

Bookmarks can also be assigned as links to shapes and images. With multiple bookmarks created across multiple report pages, a visual table of contents can be created to aid the user's navigation of a report. Rather than opening and browsing the **Bookmarks** pane, users can simply click images or shapes associated with specific bookmarks, and a back button can be used to return to the **Table of contents** page.

In *Figure 6.25,* nine images have been positioned within a rectangle shape and linked to bookmarks in the report:

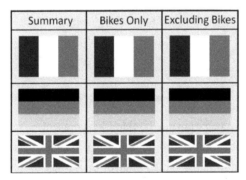

*Figure 6.25: Custom navigation to bookmarks*

Three rectangle shapes and three line shapes are used to form the matrix of icons and three text boxes display the headers. Shapes, images, and text boxes can be added from the **Insert** tab of **Report** view. With a shape, image, or text box selected, the **Format** tab appears in the ribbon, allowing the author to align and distribute the objects, as well as moving certain objects forward or backward on the canvas. Grouping similar objects within shapes is a common practice for improving usability.

In addition to the **Format** tab, when a shape, image, or text box is selected, the **Visualizations** pane is replaced with a **Format shape**, **Format image**, and **Format text box** pane, respectively.

With an image or a shape selected, an **Action** formatting card can be enabled to choose between **Back**, **Bookmark**, **Page navigation**, **Q&A**, or **Web URL** actions. In *Figure 6.26*, the France flag image positioned under the **Bikes Only** heading is linked to the **France: Bikes Only** bookmark:

*Figure 6.26: Link formatting card for images and shapes*

The combination of custom navigation and bookmarks representing many specific views or reports pages contributes to an easier, more productive experience for users. When designed properly, the user often doesn't need to know which page or bookmark to navigate to or which filters to apply as this logic is already built into the report.

In addition to using bookmarks for report navigation via images, shapes, and buttons, a special view mode exists, which is especially useful for presentations.

## View mode

The **View** icon in the **Bookmarks** pane can be used in both Power BI Desktop and in the Power BI service to navigate between visuals similar to a slideshow. When **View** mode is enabled, a navigation bar similar to that shown in *Figure 6.27* appears at the bottom of the canvas and the user can close other panes and/or launch full-screen mode in the Power BI service to further support the presentation:

Bookmark 1 of 12                          Europe: Summary                          〈  〉  ✕

*Figure 6.27: View mode navigation*

As per *Figure 6.27*, the number and order of bookmarks, bookmark names, and navigation arrows are included in the **View** mode navigation. Bookmarks are ordered based on their position in the **Bookmarks** pane from the top to the bottom. To revise the order, drag and drop bookmarks to higher or lower positions in the **Bookmarks** pane, or select a bookmark and use the up and down arrow icons to adjust the order of the bookmark.

We now consider report development using Live connections to Power BI datasets.

# Live connections to Power BI datasets

An optional but very important report planning and design decision is whether or not to develop the data model and report visuals within the same Power BI Desktop file or to separate the report from the dataset into separate files. As a general recommendation, if there's any possibility that additional reports will be needed in the future based on the same dataset, the dataset and report should be separated into separate files and likely separate workspaces as well.

With Live connections to Power BI datasets, report authors can develop reports in Power BI Desktop files containing only the visualization layer (report pages of visuals) while leveraging a single, "golden" dataset. Increasingly organizations will isolate these source datasets, which are typically maintained by an IT or BI department, into Power BI workspaces that only the IT or BI organization has edit rights to. Report authors and users of these source datasets are granted read and optionally build permission to these dataset.

The dataset (data layer) already includes the data retrieval supporting tables and columns, the data model relationships, and the DAX measures or calculations as described in previous chapters. Once the Live connection report is developed and published to Power BI, it maintains its connection to the source dataset and is refreshed with the refresh schedule configured for the dataset.

In the absence of using Live connection reports to Power BI datasets, users within teams would be forced to create multiple versions of the same dataset in order to create different reports. As both a report and a dataset, each individual report would require its own scheduled refresh process (in import mode), its own data storage, and would create version control problems as the report author could modify the underlying dataset.

Live connection reports therefore severely reduce resource requirements and promote a single version of the truth. Moreover, Live connection reports facilitate the isolation of report design and development from dataset design and development.

Most Power BI report authors are not interested in, or responsible for, dataset design topics, such as data retrieval with M queries, data modeling, and DAX measures. Likewise, a dataset designer is often less interested in, or responsible for, visualization best practices and engagement with the actual users of reports and dashboards.

As advised in *Chapter 1, Planning Power BI Projects*, the alternative roles (dataset designer and report author) need to collaborate regularly, such as identifying measures or columns that need to be added to the dataset to support reports and dashboards.

To create a Live connection report with a published Power BI dataset as the source, the report author needs a Power BI Pro license. Additionally, the tenant setting **Allow live connections** under the **Export and sharing settings** section must be enabled. Finally, if the tenant setting **Use datasets across workspaces** under the **Workspace settings** section is configured, then the Live connection reports can be published to a different workspace than where the underlying dataset is published.

In *Figure 6.28*, the report author can Live connect to datasets in many different workspaces:

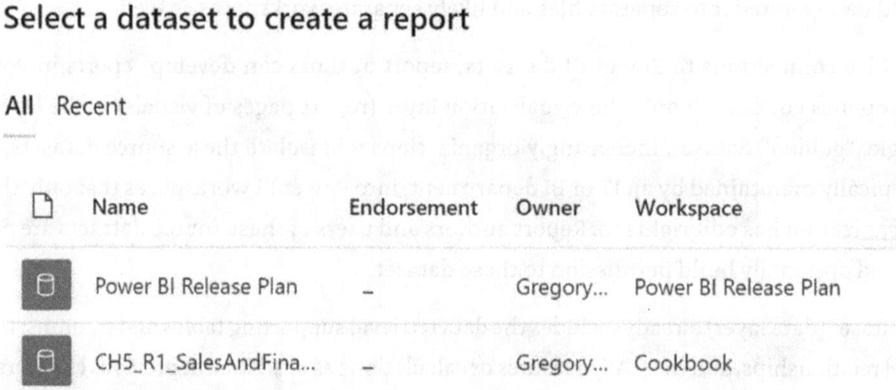

## Select a dataset to create a report

All    Recent

| | Name | Endorsement | Owner | Workspace |
|---|---|---|---|---|
| | Power BI Release Plan | – | Gregory... | Power BI Release Plan |
| | CH5_R1_SalesAndFina... | – | Gregory... | Cookbook |
| | Gaming Data | – | Gregory... | Cookbook |
| | Streaming Sensor Data | – | Gregory... | Cookbook |
| | Chapter03 | – | Gregory... | Mastering Power BI |
| | Google Analytics - Fusi... | – | Gregory... | gdeckler@fusionalliance.... |

*Figure 6.28: Creating a Live connection to the Power BI dataset*

After selecting the **Power BI datasets** from the list of **Power Platform** sources within the **Get Data** dialog, the list of the workspaces of which the report author is a member is prompted.

In this example, either double-clicking a dataset or selecting a dataset and clicking the **Create** button establishes the Live connection as per the status bar (lower right-hand corner) in Power BI Desktop, as shown in *Figure 6.29*:

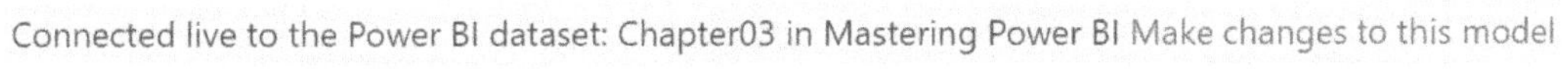

Connected live to the Power BI dataset: Chapter03 in Mastering Power BI Make changes to this model

*Figure 6.29: Live connection status bar*

When connected in Live mode, the **Fields** pane that lists the columns, measures, and tables in the dataset is exposed in **Report** view and the tables and relationships are shown in the **Relationship** view. However, the **Data** view is not available.

In the past, Live reports were always limited to a single data model as a source. However, with the advent of composite models and DirectQuery for Power BI datasets, a local model can be added to a Live connection report, as discussed in *Chapter 4, Designing Import, DirectQuery, and Composite Data Models*.

It's possible to create reports based on Power BI datasets within the Power BI online service. However, the .pbix files for these reports cannot be downloaded and thus, all edits must be implemented within the service without version history. Additionally, several important report authoring features in Power BI Desktop are not supported in the service, including the alignment of objects and local report measures.

Given these considerations, Power BI Desktop is recommended for any report development beyond personal or ad hoc use. Guidance on version history for Power BI Desktop files (reports and datasets) is included in *Chapter 10, Managing Application Workspaces and Content*.

We continue our exploration of Live connection reports by reviewing the ability to customize such reports.

## Customizing Live connection reports

Although data modeling and retrieval capabilities are removed in purely Live connection reports (non-composite model), report authors can create new measures specific to the given report via the **New measure** icon under the **Modeling** and **Table tools** tabs.

Additionally, report authors can change the names of measures and columns displayed in reports using the field wells for visualization in the **Visualizations** pane.

In *Figure 6.30*, the Internet Net Sales measure and the SalesTerritoryCountry column have been renamed to Net Sales and Country, respectively:

*Figure 6.30: Renamed measure and column in visual*

Double-clicking the name of the column or measure in the field well(s) for the visual exposes an input box for the revised name. As per the preceding diagram, the revised names appear in the report visual and the **Tooltips** in the field wells indicate the source column or measure. In this example, the Internet Net Sales measure, with a home table of the Internet Sales fact table, is the source for the Net Sales alias name.

Although the flexibility to create measures and apply names within reports is helpful and appropriate in certain scenarios, these revisions can create complexity and version control issues. For example, users can become accustomed to specific measures and names that the dataset designer is not aware of and that may conflict with other measures or names in the dataset. Therefore, it's generally recommended to incorporate the necessary measure logic and standard names into the source dataset.

Next, we look at two different scenarios involving switching between or to Live datasets, starting with switching from one Live source dataset to another.

## Switching Live source datasets

In many project scenarios, a Power BI report is initially built against a development or testing dataset. After this report has been validated or received the proper approvals, the report's source dataset can be switched to a production dataset and the report can then be published to the production workspace used for distributing Power BI content to users.

To switch the Power BI dataset of a Live connection report, click **Data Source settings** under the **Transform data** drop-down menu on the **Home** tab, as shown in *Figure 6.31*:

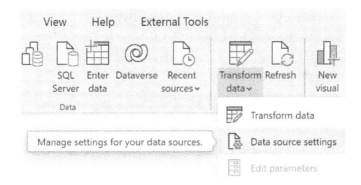

*Figure 6.31: Data source settings for a Live connection report*

The same dialog is presented as shown in *Figure 6.28*. Simply select a different dataset and click the **Create** button. See *Chapter 10*, *Managing Application Workspaces and Content*, for details on Power BI project life cycles, such as migrating from development to production environments and version control.

Next, we look at another dataset switching scenario, this time between an import mode dataset and a Live source dataset.

## Switching between import mode and Live mode datasets

Another common scenario is that report development begins with an import mode dataset for creating report visuals as a **proof-of-concept** (**POC**). Subsequently, as the project progresses, it becomes advantageous to separate data modeling from report development.

It's possible to convert an import mode dataset that contains report visuals in the same file into two separate artifacts, a dataset and a report connected to this dataset, using the following procedure:

1. Publish the dataset with the report to a workspace in the Power BI service.

2. Make a copy of the PBIX file containing the dataset and the report visuals.

3. In the copied PBIX file, open Power Query Editor and delete all source queries. Ensure that all dataset tables are removed from the file.

4. Exit Power Query Editor and return to Power BI Desktop. The report visuals should now (temporarily) return an error.

5. On the **Home** tab of **Report** view, click **Power BI Datasets** in the **Data** section of the ribbon and connect your file to the dataset published as part of *step 1*.

The report visuals should load normally as though the data was still local to the file and now the report has a Live connection to the Power BI dataset.

This concludes our advice regarding Live connections to Power BI datasets. We'll next explore the topic of some best practices with regard to visualizations.

# Report design summary

As a data visualization and analytics platform, Power BI provides a vast array of features and functionality for report authors to develop compelling content that helps users to derive insights.

Given the volume of features and possible formatting configurations, report authors and BI teams generally want to follow a set of report planning and design practices to ensure that report content of a consistent quality is delivered to stakeholders. These practices include report planning in terms of scope, users, and use cases, data visualization practices, and the selection of visuals.

The *Report planning process, Visualization best practices*, and *Choosing the right visual* sections earlier in this chapter provided details on many of the recommended practices to develop effective and sustainable report content. As a standard summary-level review of report creation, at the conclusion of a development phase and prior to deployment, the following list of questions should be asked:

1.  Does the report have a clear scope and use case?

    The report addresses specific business questions of value to specific users or teams that consume the report. The relationship and distinction between this report and other reports or dashboards that the users have access to are understood. The pages of the report naturally relate to one another to address the same or closely related business questions, perhaps at alternative levels of detail.

2.  Have standard visualization practices been followed?

    The visuals have proper spacing, alignment, and symmetry. The reports use colors selectively and there are clear titles on report pages and visuals. The report is intuitive and not cluttered with unnecessary details

3.  Have the right visuals been chosen to represent the data?

    Tables and matrices were used when cross-referencing or looking up individual values was necessary. The type of data relationship to represent (for example, comparison) and the relative advantages of the different visuals, such as line charts for the trends of a value, drove the visual choice.

4.  Does the report enable the user to easily apply filters and explore the data?

    Slicer visuals for common or important columns have been utilized and are easily accessible to users. The filtering and cross-highlighting interactions between the visuals on the report pages have been considered and configured appropriately. Hierarchies of columns have been built into certain visuals to allow a simple drill-up and drill-down experience

5.  Does the report aid the user in identifying insights or exceptions?

    Dynamic formatting, such as with KPI visuals and conditional formatting rules and techniques, has been applied. Tooltips have been added to report visuals to provide the user with additional context by hovering over the visual, such as the columns in a column chart or the data points in a line chart.

6.  Have simple and sustainable filter conditions been applied at the appropriate scope?

    Report- and page-level filter scopes have been applied to minimize the resources required by the queries generated by the report. Visual-level filters are only used when the visual needs to reflect an alternative filter context of the report- and page-level filter scopes. Report filter conditions are not being used to address issues with data quality or the source dataset. Efforts have been made (or will be made) to enhance the source dataset to better support the report. Filter conditions on the date dimension are dynamic and sustainable (for example, **Current Year** and **Prior Year**) rather than hardcoded values (for example, **2018** and **2017**).

This concludes our exploration of the report planning process and other important concepts related to report planning and design.

# Summary

In this chapter, we walked through the fundamental components of Power BI report planning and design, including visualization best practices, Live connections to Power BI datasets, and the filter scopes available in Power BI Desktop. We also reviewed the overall report planning process and introduced the report architecture diagram as a tool to aid in that planning.

The following chapter is also dedicated to report development, but goes well beyond the fundamental design concepts and features introduced in this chapter. The next chapter explores the basics of report authoring, including an exploration of the different visuals and formatting features available during report development.

# Join our community on Discord

Join our community's Discord space for discussions with the author and other readers:

https://discord.gg/q6BPbHEPXp

# 7

# Creating and Formatting Visualizations

With the report planning and design phases described in the previous chapter completed, this chapter dives into report development. This includes the creation and formatting of standard Power BI visuals such as slicers, cards, and maps as well as supporting elements such as text boxes, buttons, shapes, and images.

Visualizations are the building blocks of reports. A combination of distinct visuals, each with their own formatting and data represented at different granularities and filter contexts, enables Power BI reports to generate insights and to support data story telling. The ability to create and apply formatting to visualizations is fundamental knowledge for all report authors.

In this chapter, we review the following topics:

- The **Visualizations** pane
- Slicers
- Single-value visuals
- Map visuals
- Waterfall charts
- Power Platform visuals
- Premium visuals
- Elements
- Formatting visualizations

We start with a brief overview of the Visualizations pane.

# The Visualizations pane

While in the **Report view**, the **Visualizations** pane provides the primary interface for creating and formatting visuals. The **Visualizations** pane includes three sub-panes, the **Build visual**, **Format**, and **Analytics** panes, as shown in *Figure 7.1*:

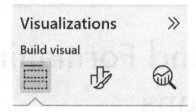

*Figure 7.1: The Visualizations pane's sub-panes*

As shown in *Figure 7.1*, the **Build visual** sub-pane is located on the left, the **Format** sub-pane in the center, and the **Analytics** sub-pane on the right. The **Analytics** sub-pane is discussed in greater depth in the next chapter.

The **Build visual** sub-pane, as its name suggests, is used for creating visuals. By default, 40 icons representing different visualization types are displayed and can be used to create visuals. In addition, when a visual is selected on the report page, the **Build visual** sub-pane presents one or more **field wells** used to configure the visual as shown in *Figure 7.2*:

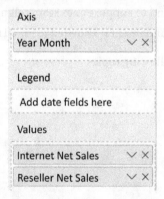

*Figure 7.2: Field wells*

Field wells are simply areas where columns and measures from the **Fields** pane can be dragged and dropped. In *Figure 7.2*, a column chart visual has three main field wells, **Axis**, **Legend**, and **Values**. Depending on the visual, field wells accept one or multiple columns and/or measures.

Once a visualization is created and selected on the report canvas, the **Format** sub-pane provides two tabs, **Visual** and **General**, used to configure various properties such as size, position, colors, and font sizes as shown in *Figure 7.3*:

Format visual

Search

Visual   General   ...

⌄ Properties

⌄ Size

Height
352

Width
813

Lock aspect ratio    Off

> Position

*Figure 7.3: Format sub-pane*

As shown in *Figure 7.3*, each tab includes multiple sections, such as the **Properties** section, and each section includes one or more format cards such as **Size** and **Position**. The **Format** sub-pane is explored in greater depth in *the Formatting visualizations* section later in this chapter.

With a basic overview of the **Visualizations** pane complete, we move on to an exploration of specific visualization types, starting with slicers.

# Slicers

Slicer visuals are interactive controls added to the report canvas to enable report users to apply their own filter selections to an individual report page. Given their power and flexible support for multiple data types, slicers have been a staple of Power BI interactive reports for years.

Slicers are a central element of self-service functionality in Power BI in addition to the visual interaction behavior described in the previous chapter. The standard slicer visual displays the unique values of a single column enabling report users to apply their own filter selections to all or some visuals on a report page.

However, although slicer visuals are still fully supported and a great addition to many reports, Power BI now also supports a **Filters** pane that can be exposed to users to deliver essential self-service filtering without requiring additional report canvas space or additional queries. Given the availability and advantages of the **Filters** pane, report authors should only use slicers for the most common or frequently used fields for filtering. Fields that are less frequently used to apply filters can be added to the **Filters** pane.

Power BI Desktop provides several formatting and filter condition options available based on the data type of the column. *Figure 7.4* contains three sample slicer visuals with each slicer representing a different data type (text, number, date):

Figure 7.4: Slicer visuals

In this example, the three slicers filter for two sales territory countries (**Australia** and **France**), a range of product list prices (**$500** to **$2,500**), and the last **30 Days** inclusive of the current date (12/25/2021 to 1/23/2022). Filter condition rules are available for numeric and date columns in slicers, such as greater than or equal to $500 and after 5/1/2021, respectively.

See the *Report filter conditions* and *Relative date filtering* sections from the previous chapter for additional details on relative date filters.

By default, **Multi-select with CTRL** is enabled on the **Selection** card of **Slicer settings**. This setting requires users to hold down the *Ctrl* key to select multiple items. For slicer visuals with many unique values, and when users regularly need to exclude only one or a few items, enabling the **Show "Select all" option** can improve usability.

Additionally, for slicers based on text data-type columns, users can search for values via the ellipsis menu (**...**) that appears at the top right or bottom right of the visual. Alternatively, a search box can be activated by toggling the **Search** settings to **On** in the **Options** card of **Slicer settings**.

To preserve space on the report canvas, the slicer visual supports a drop-down option for all column data types. In *Figure 7.5*, a single value is selected for the country and date slicers but multiple values are selected for the price slicer:

*Figure 7.5: Slicer visuals as dropdown*

The drop-down option is most applicable for columns with many unique values. In addition, it's recommended to group slicer visuals together near the edge of a report page.

Slicers are most commonly aligned on the left side of the page below the visuals in the top-left corner. If vertical canvas space is limited, slicers displayed in list format can be presented horizontally rather than vertically. The **Orientation** formatting property (**Vertical** or **Horizontal**) is available on the **General** formatting card.

One of the most powerful features of slicers is the ability to filter both the current report page and optionally other report pages from a single slicer visual. The details of utilizing this feature, referred to as **Slicer synchronization**, are included in the following section.

## Slicer synchronization

By default, slicer visuals only filter the other visuals on the same report page. However, via the **Sync slicers** pane, report designers can synchronize a slicer visual to also filter all other report pages or only specific report pages. This feature eliminates the need to include the same slicer on multiple report pages and thus simplifies the user experience.

For example, a common report may utilize three slicers (for example, Year, Product Category, Sales Country) and include four report pages. With slicer synchronization configured, the report user would only need to select values from these slicers on a single report page and the visuals from all four report pages would be updated to reflect these selections.

The **Sync slicers** pane can be accessed from the **View** tab of the ribbon in the **Report view** as shown in *Figure 7.6*:

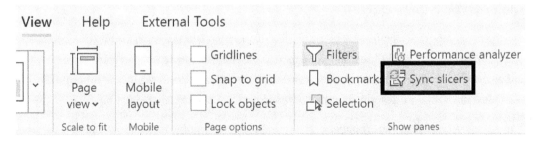

*Figure 7.6: Sync slicers pane*

Once selected as per *Figure 7.6*, the **Sync slicers** pane appears to the right of the report page. A slicer visual from the current report page can then be selected to configure its synchronization with other pages.

In *Figure 7.7*, the **SalesTerritoryGroup** slicer has been selected but has not yet been synchronized with other report pages:

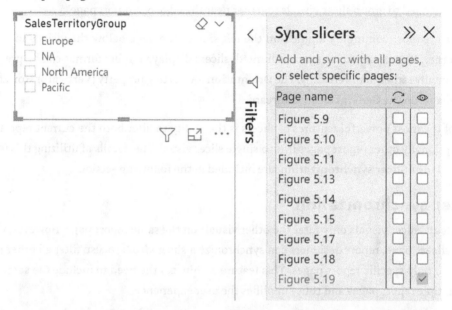

*Figure 7.7: Sync slicers pane with slicer selected*

To quickly synchronize the slicer to all other report pages, simply click the **Add and sync with all pages** link above the **Sync** (double arrows) and **Visible** (eyeball) icons. In this example, the **Add and sync with all pages** command would apply checkmarks under the **Sync** and **Visible** icons for all four report pages. You could then uncheck the **Visible** icons for the different pages. The **Sales Territory Group** slicer would now filter all report pages but would only be visible on pages where the **Visible** icon is checked.

Several other report design features are accessible from the **View** tab, such as the **Bookmarks** and **Selection** panes, show **Gridlines**, and **Snap to grid**. The **Gridlines** and **Snap to grid** features simply aid in the positioning and alignment of visuals on the report canvas while the **Bookmarks** and the **Selection** panes are described in the *Bookmarks* section of *Chapter 6, Planning Power BI Reports*.

For reports with several report pages and common slicers, a single report page can be dedicated to slicer selections and not contain any other visuals.

Report designers can configure synchronization for each slicer on this page and instruct users to only use this page for applying their filter selections for all pages on the report.

Moreover, a back button can be added to report pages allowing the user to easily navigate back to the dedicated slicer report page. An example of using a back button is included in the *Drillthrough report pages* section of *Chapter 6*, *Planning Power BI Reports*, and additional information is included in the *Embellishments* section of this chapter.

Next, we look at a distinct use case for slicers involving custom slicer parameters.

## Custom slicer parameters

A powerful use case for slicer visuals is to expose a custom list of parameter values and drive one or multiple DAX measures based on the user's selection. In the example shown in *Figure 7.8*, a slicer visual contains six date intelligence periods, and a custom DAX measure used in the central **Card** visual, **User Selected Internet Net Sales**, references the date intelligence measure corresponding to the user's selection:

$1,780,920

User Selected Internet Net Sales

$5,146
Internet Net Sales (WTD)

$1,874,360
Internet Net Sales (MTD)

$16,351,550
Internet Net Sales (YTD)

$212,370
Internet Net Sales (PWTD)

$1,780,920
Internet Net Sales (PMTD)

$5,842,485
Internet Net Sales (PYTD)

*Figure 7.8: Slicer as a measure parameter*

The table used for the slicer values could be defined within a source system and retrieved during data refresh like other tables. Alternatively, since the parameter values are unlikely to change, the table could be created within Power BI Desktop using an **Enter data** query and loaded to the model but not included in a data refresh. Like all parameter tables, no relationships would be defined with other tables.

The custom measure User Selected Internet Net Sales utilizes the SELECTEDVALUE() and SWITCH() functions to retrieve the user selection and then apply the appropriate date intelligence measure.

In this implementation, a DAX variable is used to store the period selection value, as per the following expression:

```
User Selected Internet Net Sales =
    VAR __PeriodSelection = SELECTEDVALUE('Date Parameter'[Date Period
Selection], "Year to Date")
RETURN
    SWITCH(TRUE(),
        __PeriodSelection = "Week to Date", [Internet Net Sales (WTD)],
        __PeriodSelection = "Month to Date", [Internet Net Sales (MTD)],
        __PeriodSelection = "Year to Date", [Internet Net Sales (YTD)],
        __PeriodSelection = "Prior Week to Date", [Internet Net Sales
(PWTD)],
        __PeriodSelection = "Prior Month to Date", [Internet Net Sales
(PMTD)],
        __PeriodSelection = "Prior Year to Date", [Internet Net Sales
(PYTD)]
    )
```

The second parameter to the SELECTEDVALUE() function ensures that the **Year to Date** measure is used if multiple values have been selected or if no values have been selected. In *Figure 7.8*, the radio buttons indicate that the **Single select** option has been set to **On** in the **Selection** card of the **Slicer settings** in order to avoid multiple selections. The **Single select** option disables the default behavior of allowing multiple selections within a slicer.

If several additional DAX measures are driven by the parameter selection, a dedicated measure could be created that only retrieves the selected value. This supporting measure would then eliminate the need for the variable since the support measure could be referenced directly within the SWITCH() function.

See *Chapter 5, Developing DAX Measures and Security Roles*, for example expressions of date intelligence measures as well as measure support expressions. Of course, it's possible to fully define each date intelligence expression within the parameter-driven measure but, for manageability reasons, it's almost always preferable to leverage an existing measure. This is particularly the recommendation when the required measures represent common logic, such as month-to-date.

In addition to using source system tables or **Enter data** queries to create parameter tables, Power BI provides an alternative means known as **What-if parameters**.

# What-if parameters

**What-if parameters** provide a user interface for more easily creating parameter tables than the custom slicer parameter demonstrated in the previous section. This option is currently limited to numeric parameter values but automatically creates a single-column table, slicer, and DAX measure that retrieves the slicer's input value.

In *Figure 7.9*, two **What-if parameters** are used to calculate alternative unit price and unit cost values thereby driving a hypothetical product margin % measure:

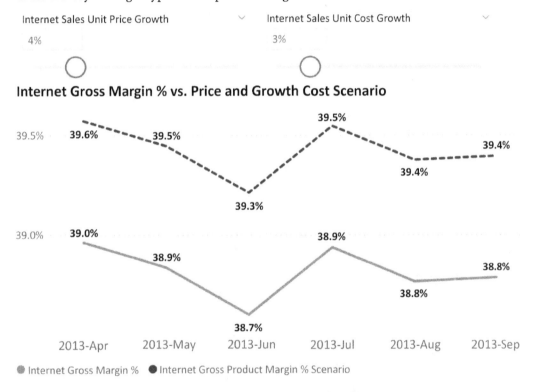

*Figure 7.9: What-if parameters applied in report visuals*

By adjusting the two slider bars, a user is able to quickly model an alternative gross product margin % scenario, as illustrated by the dotted line in *Figure 7.9*. The slider bar for modifying a single value is unique to slicers for **What-if parameter** columns.

To create a **What-if parameter**, click the **New parameter** icon on the **Modeling** tab in the **Report view** to launch the dialog shown in *Figure 7.10*:

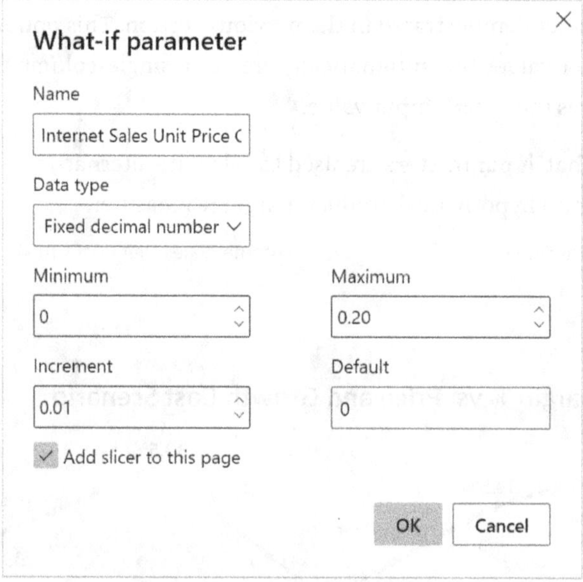

*Figure 7.10: Creating a What-if parameter*

Based on the minimum, maximum, and increment input values specified, a new table with a single column of values is created within the Power BI dataset. For the `Internet Sales Unit Price Growth` parameter, this column has 21 rows from 0 to .2 with each value representing a full percentage point (for example, 0%, 1%, 2%...20%). These tables are actually calculated tables created using DAX with formulas as follows:

```
Internet Sales Unit Price Growth = GENERATESERIES(CURRENCY(0),
CURRENCY(0.2), CURRENCY(0.01))
Internet Sales Unit Cost Growth = GENERATESERIES(CURRENCY(0),
CURRENCY(0.2), CURRENCY(0.01))
```

Additionally, a new DAX measure is created automatically to retrieve the user selection, as per the following expressions:

```
Internet Sales Unit Price Growth Value = SELECTEDVALUE('Internet Sales
Unit Price Growth'[Internet Sales Unit Price Growth], 0)
Internet Sales Unit Cost Growth Value = SELECTEDVALUE('Internet Sales Unit
Cost Growth'[Internet Sales Unit Cost Growth], 0)
```

With the second argument to both functions set to 0, both growth values return zero if a selection hasn't been made or if multiple values have been selected. The only remaining step is to create one or more measures that reference the parameter values in their calculation logic.

In this example, the **Unit Price** and **Unit Cost** growth parameters are applied to gross sales and product cost scenario measures, respectively. These two scenario measures are then used to compute a product margin scenario measure and a product margin % scenario measure, per the following expressions:

```
Internet Gross Sales Scenario = [Internet Gross Sales] * (1 + [Internet
Sales Unit Price Growth Value])

Internet Sales Product Cost Scenario = [Internet Cost of Sales] * (1 +
[Internet Sales Unit Cost Growth Value])

Internet Gross Product Margin Scenario = [Internet Gross Sales Scenario] -
[Internet Sales Product Cost Scenario]

Internet Gross Product Margin % Scenario = DIVIDE([Internet Gross Product
Margin Scenario], [Internet Gross Sales Scenario])
```

Although it's possible and sometimes necessary to create parameter columns and measures manually, the What-if parameter feature in Power BI Desktop can simplify this process for many modeling scenarios. Additionally, the slider bar slicer exclusive to the **What-if parameter** columns is the most user-friendly option for selecting parameter values.

To change the range of values available to the parameter, select the **Parameter** column in the **Fields** pane and modify the min, max, or increment arguments to the GENERATESERIES() function.

Considering that both slicers and the **Filters** pane covered in the previous chapter can both filter an entire report page, you may be curious as to when to use one or the other, so we explore that topic in the next section.

# Page filter or slicer?

Slicer visuals can serve as an alternative to distinct or dedicated report pages. With a slicer, a user has the flexibility to select one or multiple values on the same report page, such as Northeast and Southwest sales territories, without needing to navigate to a dedicated page. Additionally, by consolidating dedicated report pages, slicers can simplify report development and management.

Slicers are often the best choice when there's nothing unique to the different values of the slicer. For example, if all sales regions are always analyzed by the same measures, dimensions, and visuals, it may be unnecessary to duplicate these pages of visuals. Slicers are also very helpful or necessary when users regularly need to analyze the data by the same dimensions or by custom dimensions, such as price and date ranges.

While the **Filters** pane can be exposed to users and serve the same function as slicers, this can be less intuitive and require more training for end users. Conversely, the benefit of utilizing the **Filters** pane for this function is that more report canvas space is available for non-slicer visuals.

In general, slicer visuals that consume a small amount of canvas, such as dropdowns, are preferable for dimensions that the user is expected to regularly apply filters on. Less common or "nice to have" filters can generally be added to the filter pane rather than slicer visuals to preserve canvas space and to avoid unnecessary queries.

As shown in *Figure 7.11*, the **Filters** pane allows filters to be hidden or locked by report authors via the circle and arc (eyeball) icon and lock icon respectively:

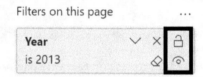

*Figure 7.11: Filter pane filter locking and hiding*

Dedicated report pages are valuable for supporting email subscriptions, data alerts, and dashboard visuals specific to a particular value such as a sales region. As shown in *Figure 7.12*, when in the Power BI service, an email subscription can be set to any of the report pages within the **USA SALES AND MARGIN** report:

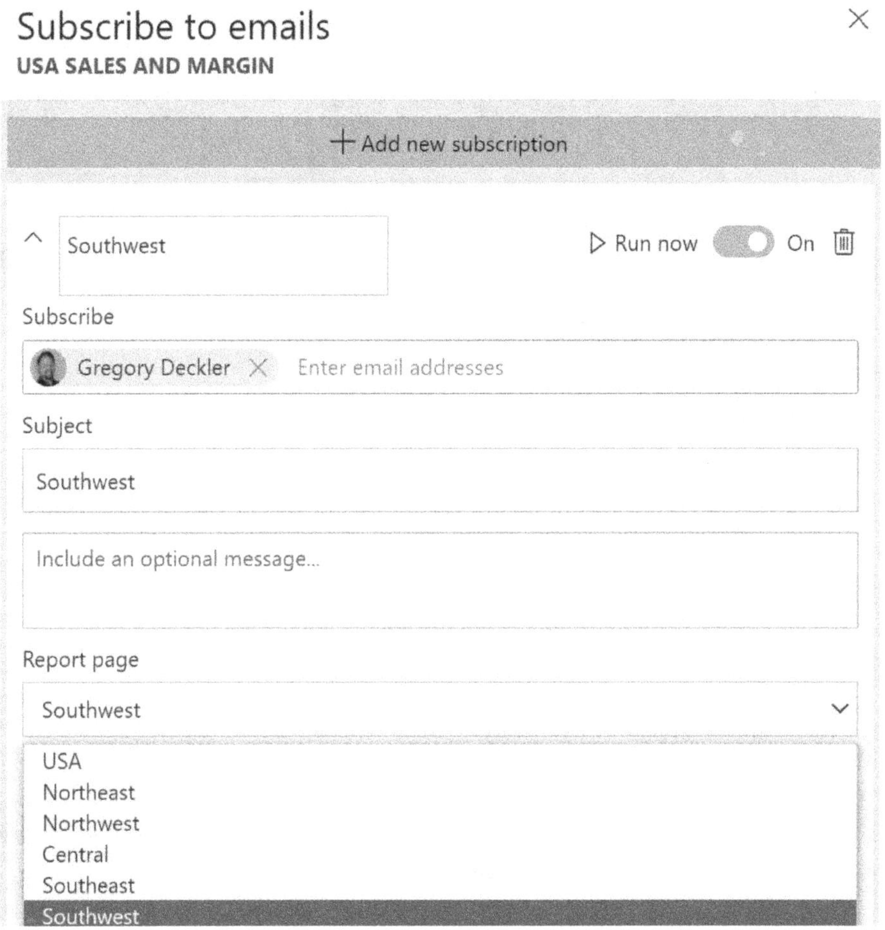

# Subscribe to emails
**USA SALES AND MARGIN**

$\times$

+ Add new subscription

∧ Southwest

▷ Run now   ⬤ On 🗑

Subscribe

🔵 Gregory Deckler ✕   Enter email addresses

Subject

Southwest

Include an optional message...

Report page

Southwest ∨

USA
Northeast
Northwest
Central
Southeast
Southwest

*Figure 7.12: Email subscription in Power BI*

As one example, the visuals from the **Northeast** report page could potentially be pinned to a **Northeast** dashboard (or another dashboard) and used in data alerts and notifications for the **Northeast** team as well. These region-specific capabilities are made possible by the distinct report pages of visuals filtered for the given sales territory region.

If using dedicated report pages, it is likely that the report author will want to hide the **Filters** pane entirely as shown in *Figure 7.13* or, alternatively, lock all of the filters within the **Filters** pane.

*Figure 7.13: Hiding the Filters pane when viewing report*

This completes our review of slicers. We next turn our attention to visuals designed to primarily feature single number values.

# Single-value visuals

Single-value visuals are a class of visuals which prominently display an important value such as the YTD Sales or the % Variance to Plan. These visuals are typically positioned at the top and left sections of report pages and are commonly pinned to dashboards in the Power BI service. Though simple relative to other visuals, single value visuals are often the first visuals users perceive and these values relative to their expectations determine whether or not other visuals in the report are analyzed.

## The Card visual

**Card** visuals present a single **Fields** field well that accepts a single column or measure. **Card** visuals are most often used to prominently display a single numeric value, such as an important business metric. While perhaps more limited and visually unappealing than the **KPI** and **Gauge** visual, **Card** visuals are valued for their simplicity and ability to drive data alerts within the Power BI service.

That said, **Card** visuals do include the ability to conditionally format the color for the displayed value and label, providing the ability to serve as a rudimentary KPI visual displaying different colors depending upon the overall health of the chosen metric.

Additionally, **Card** visuals can also display text. This is a powerful feature when combined with measures, as demonstrated in the *Drillthrough report pages* section of the previous chapter.

Note that a version of the **Card** visual exists for displaying multiple numeric or text values called the **Multi-row card** visual. The **Multi-row card** visual also includes a single **Fields** field well but accepts multiple columns and/or measures.

We now turn our attention to the standard KPI visual.

# The KPI visual

The standard KPI visual packs a tremendous amount of information within a single visual. The KPI visual is popular for displaying key business metrics given its ability to display the current value of a business metric, the metric's trend over time, and progress towards a specified goal all within a compact form factor.

As shown in *Figure 7.14*, the KPI visual presents three field wells for **Indicator**, **Trend axis**, and **Target goals**:

 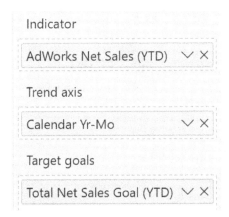

*Figure 7.14: KPI visual*

The **Indicator** field well accepts a single column or measure and is displayed as the large numeric value in the center of the visual. The **Trend axis** field well accepts a single numeric or date column and drives the shaded, sloping area behind the **Indicator** value. Both the **Indicator** and **Trend axis** field wells must be populated for the KPI visual to display.

Optionally, the **Target goals** field well accepts one or more columns and/or measures. Most often, a single goal is used. Including a **Target goal** provides conditional color formatting based on whether the current Indicator value is higher, the same as, or lower than the **Target goal**. In addition, the value of the **Target goal** is displayed beneath the **Indicator** value as well as the variance (%) between the **Indicator** and **Target goal**.

Similar to the KPI visual, we next take a look at the **Gauge** visual.

# Gauge visual

The **Gauge** visual is similar to the KPI visual in that a particular metric can be compared against a target value. The **Gauge** visual may be preferred over the KPI visual in the event that an appropriate trend axis is unavailable. However, a downside to the **Gauge** visual is that it takes up a large amount of space relative to the amount of information presented.

As shown in *Figure 7.15*, the **Gauge** visual presents five field wells:

*Figure 7.15: Gauge visual*

Of the five field wells displayed in *Figure 7.15*, only the **Value** field well is required. The column or measure in the **Value** field well is shown as the central number within the **Gauge** visual ($5.0M).

Adding a **Target value** adds a line on the gauge and displays the target value ($3.22M). Alternatively, the column or measure used as the **Target value** can instead be used as the **Maximum value** so that the gauge is completely full once the target value is reached.

Power BI automatically selects minimum and maximum values for the gauge if the **Minimum value** and **Maximum value** field wells are left unconfigured. An optional **Tooltips** field well is available for the **Gauge** visual. **Tooltips** are covered in greater detail in the *Formatting visualizations* section of this chapter.

We now move on from single number visuals to explore the various map visuals available within Power BI Desktop.

# Map visuals

Power BI currently provides five map visuals including the **Map**, **Filled map**, **Shape map** (in preview), **Azure map** (in preview), and the **ArcGIS Maps for Power BI**.

The **map visual** plots location points as bubbles over a world map and varies the size of the bubbles based on a value. The bubbles on these maps can also be broken out across a dimension to provide additional context.

The **Filled map** and **Shape map** visuals are forms of heat maps that use color and color intensity to distinguish specific areas of a map by a value, such as postal codes by population.

The **Azure map** visual is similar to the **map visual** in that it displays bubbles on a world map. The **Azure map** supports different base layers like satellite and road as well as many different settings including a display of live traffic data. While still in preview, continued enhancements to this visual could position the Azure Map as the standard for geospatial analysis in Power BI.

The **ArcGIS map** visual is the most powerful of the available geospatial visualizations and several custom map visuals are available in the App Store including the Globe Map, Flow Map, Icon Map, Mapbox Visual, Drilldown Choropleth, Drilldown Cartogram, Route map, and Google Maps for Power BI. See *Chapter 8, Applying Advanced Analytics*, for details on the **ArcGIS map** visual and using custom visuals.

The **Shape map** and **Azure map** visuals are currently still in preview and thus should only be used for testing purposes. The following URL provides documentation on the **Shape map** visual: `http://bit.ly/2zS2afU`. The following URL provides documentation on the **Azure map** visual: `https://bit.ly/3H3kEIL`.

As per the *Data category* section in *Chapter 4, Designing Import, DirectQuery, and Composite Data Models*, it's important to assign geographic data categories to columns. This information aids the map visuals in plotting the correct location when a value is associated with multiple locations (ambiguous locations).

Data categories can be assigned to columns from the **Column tools** tab in the **Data view** or the **Report view**. For DirectQuery datasets, these metadata properties can only be assigned from the **Report view**. Report authors should engage the dataset designer or BI team responsible for a dataset if data categories have not been assigned to columns needed for report development.

Additionally, for bubble and **Filled map** visuals, hierarchies can be added to the **Location** field well to avoid ambiguous results. For example, by adding the hierarchy shown in *Figure 7.16* to the **Location** field well, the map visuals only use the locations associated with their parent values, such as only the states of Australia.

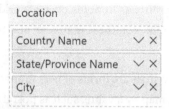

*Figure 7.16: Geographic hierarchies in map visuals*

For greater precision and performance with map visuals (excluding the **Shape map**), latitude and longitude input field wells are available as alternative inputs to **Location**.

We now take a more detailed look at the **Bubble map** visual.

## Bubble map

Bubble maps are particularly useful when embedding an additional dimension column or category to the legend input. When a geographic boundary column, such as country or postal code, is used as the location input, the added dimension converts the bubbles to pie charts of varying sizes. Larger pie charts reflect the measure used for the **Size** input field and the components of each pie are color-coded to a value from the legend column providing even greater context.

The **map visual** shown in *Figure 7.17* uses the postal code as the location input, the Internet Net Sales measure as the size input, and the Customer History Segment column as the legend input:

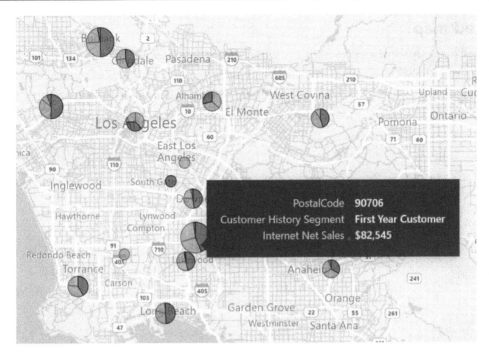

*Figure 7.17: Map visual*

For this map, the **Grayscale** theme is applied from the **Style** card in the **Map settings** category. The bubble map also includes a color saturation input to help distinguish bubbles beyond their relative sizes. This input, however, can only be used when the **legend** field well is not used.

See the *Customer history column* section of *Chapter 3, Connecting to Sources and Transforming Data with M*, for details on creating a history segment column within an M query.

Next, we explore the **Filled map** visual.

# Filled map

A **Filled map** visual includes several of the same formatting properties of a bubble map but utilizes color as its primary means to contrast locations. In the **Filled map** example shown in *Figure 7.18*, a gradient color scheme has been applied via the **Colors** card in the **Fill colors** category of the **Format** pane to highlight individual states based on the `Internet Net Sales` measure:

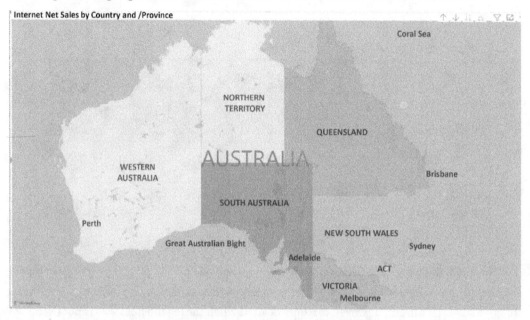

*Figure 7.18: Filled map visual with gradient colors*

Exactly like the color scheme described in the *column and line chart conditional formatting* section later in this chapter, three distinct numeric values and colors are assigned to the **Minimum**, **Center**, and **Maximum** properties. For this visual, the values of $1M, $2M, and $3M are associated with red, yellow, and green respectively; causing the **South Australia** state to appear as red (low value) while the **New South Wales** state is green (high value).

Additionally, like the previous bubble map example, a grayscale map-style theme has been applied and the auto-zoom property has been disabled.

Other map themes, such as dark, light, road, and aerial, are also available for filled and bubble maps. These alternative themes, particularly when contrasted with the bright or rich colors of a **Filled map**, can significantly add to the aesthetic appeal of a report.

As per the drill-up/down icons above the visual, a hierarchy of geographical columns (Country, State, City) has been added to the **Location** field well. These additional columns help the Bing Maps API to display the correct location, such as only Victoria in Australia. Note that whenever a hierarchy is included in an appropriate visualization's field well, the drill-up/down icons allow report viewers to move between the various levels of the hierarchy.

To ensure that Bing Maps respects the parent column (for example, Country) when plotting child locations (for example, States/Provinces), the user can enable the drill mode via the **drill-down** button in the top-right corner of the visual. With drill mode enabled, the user can click the specific parent value on the map, such as the **United States**, and Bing plots states by only searching for states within the United States.

Alternatively, with drill mode not enabled, the user can click the **expand all down one level** icon at the top left of the visual. From the initial state of the parent value (country), this also plots the states within each parent value. The other drill option at the top left of the visual, the go to the next level drill, only plots the child values without the context of the parent value.

Moving on from map visuals, we next expound upon the **Waterfall chart** visual.

# Waterfall chart

The waterfall chart is one of the most powerful standard visuals in Power BI given its ability to compute and format the variances of individual items between two periods by default.

The items representing the largest variances are displayed as columns of varying length, sorted and formatted with either an increase (green), no change (yellow), or decrease (red) color. This built-in logic and conditional formatting make waterfall charts both easy to create and intuitive for users.

In *Figure 7.19*, the `Internet Net Sales` of the last two completed months are broken down by `SalesTerritoryCountry`:

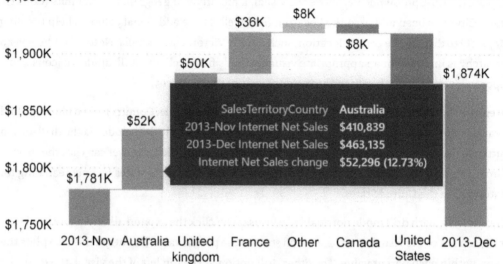

Figure 7.19: Waterfall chart with breakdown

The waterfall chart in *Figure 7.19* was created by placing the `Internet Net Sales` measure applied to the **Values** field well, and placing the `Year Month` and `SalesTerritoryCountry` columns into the **Category** and **Breakdown** input fields, respectively. The waterfall chart naturally walks the user from the starting point category on the left (2013-Nov) to the ending point category on the right (2013-Dec).

As per *Figure 7.19*, hovering the cursor over a bar results in the details for this item being displayed as a tooltip. In this example, hovering over the ($52K) green bar for Australia displays `Internet Net Sales` for both months, the variance, and the variance as a percentage. These four tooltip values are provided by default and report authors can optionally add measures to the **Tooltips** field well to deliver even greater context.

We now turn our attention to another powerful analytical visual, the **Key influencers** visualization.

# Power Platform visuals

Power BI is part of a larger suite of products known as the **Power Platform**. In addition to Power BI, the **Power Platform** is comprised of **Power Apps**, **Power Automate**, and **Power Virtual Agents**.

The **Power Platform** is designed to support low-code and no code development by business analysts familiar with MS Office tools like Excel but is also extensible to support complex, custom solutions involving application development skills and processes. **Power Automate** is used to design and run workflows and **Robotic Process Automation (RPA)**. Finally, **Power Virtual Agents** provides a platform for creating intelligent, automated agents.

Over the last few years, Microsoft has worked steadily to create seamless integration between the various **Power Platform** tools as well as **Dataverse**, Microsoft's business data object/entity store. In terms of Power BI, this has meant the introduction of standard visuals for **Power Apps** and **Power Automate**, thus enabling Power BI report users to act based on their analyses without ever leaving Power BI.

For example, after analyzing recent sales trends on one report page, a user could increase the sales budget via an integrated **Power App** that contains budget information on a separate report page. Likewise, a button could be added to a Power BI report page that enables a user to trigger a **Power Automate** workflow that refreshes a Power BI dataset.

We start by looking at an example of using the **Power Apps** visual in Power BI Desktop.

## Power Apps for Power BI

As mentioned, **Power Apps** allows for the creation of low-code/no-code applications and web portals. **Power Apps** is a cloud-first environment and the latest of a long line of forms-based collaboration technologies that include Exchange Forms, Outlook Forms, and SharePoint.

*Figure 7.20* shows the **Power Apps for Power BI** visual after being configured to have the ResellerName column from the Resellers table in the **PowerApps Data** field well within the **Visualizations** pane.

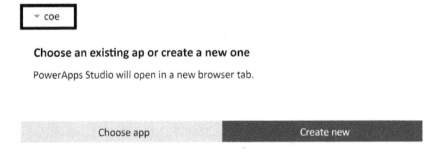

*Figure 7.20: Power Apps for Power BI visual*

As shown in *Figure 7.20*, the **Dataverse** environment for the app can be selected in the upper-right corner of the visual, in this case, the **coe** environment. Existing **Power Apps** can be chosen by clicking the **Choose app** option or a new **Power App** can be created using the **Create new** option. In either case, the data included in the **PowerApps Data** field well for the visual is available to the **Power App**.

Choosing the **Create new** option launches a browser window that navigates to the make.powerapps.com website and allows the report author to create a new **Power App**. The new **Power App** includes a default screen with a gallery control as shown in *Figure 7.21*.

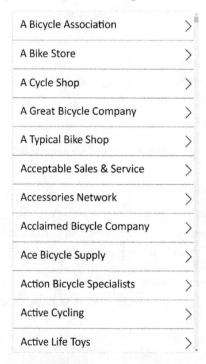

*Figure 7.21: Power app displayed in the Power Apps for Power BI visual*

Details regarding creating a **Power App** are beyond the scope of this book but *Chapter 13* of *Power BI Cookbook 2nd Edition* provides a more complete example.

Once the **Power App** is created or chosen, the **Power App** can be saved and shared with others. Once this is done, the **Power App** is displayed within the **Power App for Power BI** visual within Power BI Desktop.

Moving on, we next take a look at the **Power Automate** visual for Power BI.

## Power Automate for Power BI

**Power Automate** is Microsoft's cloud-based workflow and RPA platform. The **Power Automate for Power BI** allows **Power Automate** flows to be initiated from Power BI Desktop. These flows can utilize data from the Power BI model exposed to the **Power Automate for Power BI** visual.

*Figure 7.22* shows the **Power Automate for Power BI** visual after adding the visual to the report page and placing the EmailAddress column from the Customer table into the **Power Automate data** field well within the **Visualizations** pane.

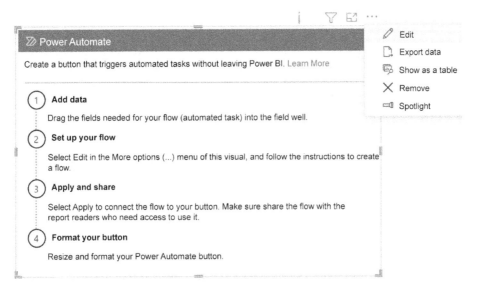

*Figure 7.22: Power Automate for Power BI visual*

As shown in *Figure 7.22*, once data fields are added to the **Power Automate data** field well, the ellipses menu is used to **Edit** the **Power Automate** flow. Choosing the **Edit** option exposes the interface shown in *Figure 7.23*, allowing the user to choose an existing flow or create an entirely new flow from a template.

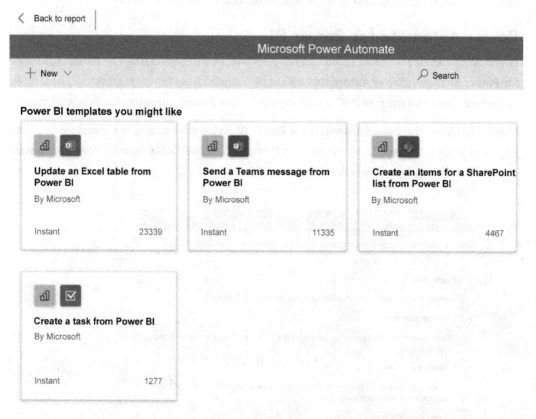

*Figure 7.23: Power Automate for Power BI visual Edit screen*

The **New** menu shown in *Figure 7.23* provides two options, **Template** and **Instant cloud flow**. In this case, the **Instant cloud flow** option was selected and a simple flow was created to send links to a web-based survey. This flow is shown in *Figure 7.24*.

*Figure 7.24: Power Automate for Power BI visual Edit screen*

In *Figure 7.24*, the `EmailAddress` data exposed to the **Power Automate for Power BI** visual via the **Power Automate data** field well is used as the **To** address for the email. Note the tooltip indicates that the email will be sent to each selected email address. The simple flow includes a **Subject** and an email **Body** that includes a link to a **survey**.

Once the flow is saved and shared, the **Power Automate for Power BI** visual displays a button that can be used by Power BI report viewers as shown in *Figure 7.25*.

*Figure 7.25: Power Automate for Power BI visual configured*

Like other Power BI visuals, the **Power Automate for Power BI** visual is interactive and filtered by other report visuals. This means that the report viewer can select data appearing in other visuals on the report page and this cross-filters the **Power Automate for Power BI** visual, meaning that upon clicking **Send Survey Email**, an email is generated for each customer email address.

In addition to integration with other Power Platform offerings, Microsoft has also introduced visuals specific to Premium (capacity-based) offerings, and we take a look at these next.

# Premium visuals

As Microsoft's Power BI Premium offering has matured, Microsoft has added two standard Power BI visuals that support features exclusive to capacity-based Power BI licenses, including Power BI **Premium and Premium Per User** (PPU). These visuals are the **Scorecard** visual and the **Paginated report** visual.

We begin by looking at the **Scorecard** visual.

## Scorecard

**Scorecards** are a relatively recent addition to Power BI that support the display and tracking of **Goals** within Power BI Premium and PPU. **Goals** allow you to create and track multiple key business metrics and objectives in a single place via a **Scorecard**. Both **Goals** and **Scorecards** are covered in more detail in later chapters.

*Figure 7.26* shows an unconfigured **Scorecard** visual added to a Power BI report page.

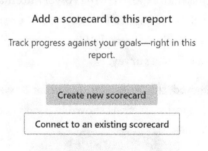

Figure 7.26: Scorecard visual

As shown in *Figure 7.26*, two options are present, **Create new scorecard** and **Connect to an existing scorecard**. *Figure 7.27* shows the same visual after being configured to **Connect to an existing scorecard**.

| Learn Power BI 2nd Edition | 2 | 0 | 0 | 0 | 1 | 1 | 0 |
|---|---|---|---|---|---|---|---|
| | Goals | Overdue | Behind | At risk | On track | Not started | Completed |

| ▽ Name | Owners | Status | Value | Progress | Due date | Notes |
|---|---|---|---|---|---|---|
| Complete 2nd Edition | 🔵 gdeckler | On track | 150.00 /100.00 % % 51.52% WoW | | Dec7, 2021 | 🖻 |
| 2nd Goal | 🔵 gdeckler | Not started | 85%/80% | | Dec7, 2021 | 🖻 |

✎ Edit  ⬡ Replace scorecard  ↗ Open in service

*Figure 7.27: Configured Scorecard visual*

As shown in *Figure 7.27*, a simple scorecard consisting of two goals is displayed in the **Scorecard** visual. The **Scorecard** visual is completely interactive, allowing the report viewer to interact with the scorecard as if viewing the scorecard in the Power BI service. Options are included to **Edit** the scorecard, **Replace scorecard**, and open the scorecard in the Power BI service.

In addition to the **Scorecard** visual, another premium visual is the **Paginated report** visual.

## Paginated reports

Paginated reports have a long and storied history at Microsoft, having first appeared in **SQL Server Reporting Services (SSRS)** in 2004. Paginated reports use an XML-based language called **Report Definition Language (RDL)**. With the paginated report visual now available in Power BI Desktop, the unique benefits of paginated reports such as exporting high volumes of data and multi-page report documents can be integrated within Power BI reports.

While Power BI reports are optimized to be highly interactive and allow self-service exploration of data by users, paginated reports allow pixel-perfect formatting that report designers can optimize for screens, printing, and PDF generation. Paginated reports are explored in greater detail in *Chapter 12, Deploying Paginated Reports*.

*Figure 7.28* shows an unconfigured **Paginated report** visual added to a Power BI Desktop report page.

All the benefits of paginated reports at
your fingertips—print with ease, maintain
a tidy layout, and more.

Connect to report

*Figure 7.28: Configured Scorecard visual*

Clicking on the **Connect to report** button within the **Paginated report** visual as shown in *Figure 7.28* opens the **Embed a paginated report** dialog shown in *Figure 7.29*.

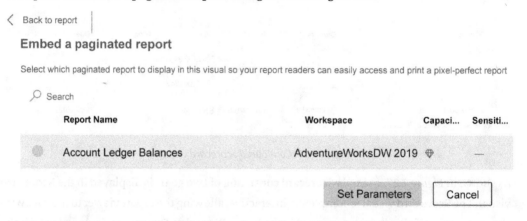

*Figure 7.29: Select paginated report*

As shown in *Figure 7.29*, any paginated reports published in the Power BI service to which the report author has permissions is displayed in the **Embed a paginated report** interface. Selecting a paginated report activates the **Set Parameters** button.

Parameters are an optional feature of paginated reports that allow a single report to display different data, such as for a specific customer or division. Once parameters, if any, are set the report can be displayed using a button.

Moving on from premium visuals, we next explore reporting elements such as text boxes, shapes, images, and buttons.

# Elements

In addition to visuals, Power BI Desktop includes the ability to add elements such as text boxes, shapes, images, and buttons to report pages.

Elements can be added to report pages using the **Insert** tab of the ribbon when in the **Report view** as shown in *Figure 7.30*:

*Figure 7.30: Select paginated report*

Elements share common traits and features. For example, buttons, shapes, and images all include the ability to activate a bookmark when clicked on as demonstrated in the *Custom labels and the back button* and *Custom report navigation* sections of the previous chapter.

In addition, selecting a text box, button, shape, or image on a report page replaces the **Visualizations** pane with a **Format text box**, **Format button**, **Format shape**, and **Format image** pane respectively. This pane works identically to the **Format** sub-pane of the **Visualizations** pane as described in the *Visualizations pane* section earlier in this chapter.

Elements are often used as navigation features between pages in a report due to the ability to configure the **Action** format card for buttons, shapes, and images for settings such as **Back**, **Bookmark**, **Drill through**, and **Page navigation** in addition to **Q&A** and **Web URL** actions.

In fact, the **Buttons** element includes a special **Navigator** feature that allows the report author to automatically add multiple buttons for each page or each bookmark in a report as shown in *Figure 7.31*:

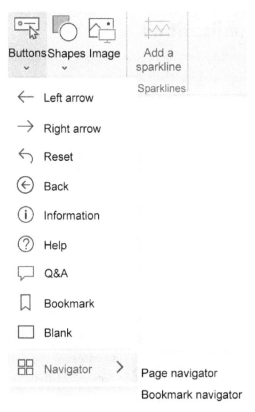

*Figure 7.31: Navigator button options*

As shown in *Figure 7.31*, there are nine different buttons available. However, realize that the only difference between these buttons is the icon and default **Action** configured, both of which can be changed after creating the button.

Other uses for elements include stylizing the report to more clearly separate report areas, such as the example from the *Custom report navigation* section of the previous chapter. In addition, text boxes are often used to display static text such as a report title or other instructional information for report viewers.

There are many other creative ways that elements can be used within Power BI reports such as referencing a DAX measure from a text box in order to display a custom message or value such as a title or date refreshed. Readers are encouraged to explore blog articles and other online materials for additional ideas and inspiration.

With many of the default visualizations and elements explained, we next discuss formatting visualizations.

# Formatting visualizations

One of the final steps in report development is configuring the formatting options for each visual. Several of these options, such as data labels, background colors, borders, and titles are common to all visuals and are often essential to aid comprehension. Several other formatting options, such as fill point for scatter charts, are exclusive to particular visuals and report authors are well served to be familiar with these features.

In addition to giving reports a professional appearance, features such as tooltips can be used to provide visuals with additional or supporting context. Furthermore, formatting features can be used to implement conditional logic to dynamically drive the color of data points by their values.

We start by exploring how **Tooltips** can aid in providing additional context and insights to report viewers.

## Tooltips

Chart and map visuals include a **Tooltips** field well in the **Visualizations** pane to allow report authors to define additional measures that display when the user hovers over the items in the visual. These tooltip values reflect the same filter context of the data labels for the visual and thus provide the user with additional context. In *Figure 7.32*, five measures have been added to the **Tooltips** field well for a column chart:

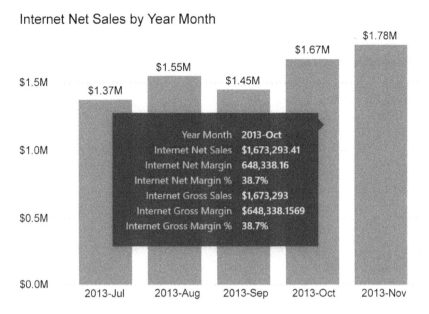

Internet Net Sales by Year Month

| Year Month | 2013-Oct |
| Internet Net Sales | $1,673,293.41 |
| Internet Net Margin | 648,338.16 |
| Internet Net Margin % | 38.7% |
| Internet Gross Sales | $1,673,293 |
| Internet Gross Margin | $648,338.1569 |
| Internet Gross Margin % | 38.7% |

*Figure 7.32: Additional measures displayed as tooltips*

By hovering over the column for online net sales in October of 2013, the tooltip is displayed, which includes both the Internet Net Sales measure used for the chart as well as the five tooltip measures. In the absence of the tooltips, the user may have to search for other reports or visuals to find this information or may miss important insights related to the visual.

Tooltips are a great way to enhance the analytical value of a visual without adding complexity or clutter. Additionally, given the features of the DAX query engine, such as **DAX fusion**, the additional measures displayed as tooltips generally do not negatively impact performance. **DAX fusion** occurs automatically when the measures displayed are based on the same fact table and the DAX query engine can optimize the query plan to generate a single storage engine query for all measures.

Next, we take a look at a special type of tooltip, report page tooltips.

## Report page tooltips

The standard tooltips described in the previous section may be sufficient for most reporting scenarios. However, Power BI Desktop also provides report page tooltips that allow report authors to display a custom page of report visuals as an alternative to the default tooltips. The following steps can be used to configure a report page tooltip:

1.  Add a new blank report page to a report.

2.  On the **Format** pane for the report page, enable the **Allow use as tooltip** property under the **Page information** formatting card.

3.  Also on the **Format** pane, specify a **Type** of **Tooltip** under **Canvas settings** as per *Figure 7.33*:

*Figure 7.33: Report page tooltip*

4.  On the tooltip page from *step 3*, set **Page view** to **Actual size** via the **Page view** icon on the **View** tab.

5.  From the **Fields** pane of the tooltip page, drag a measure or multiple measures to the tooltip **Fields** field well. Columns can also be specified as tooltip fields (for example, **Product Name**).

6.  Create report visuals on the tooltip report page that relate to the **Tooltip** field well measure(s) or column(s). For example, if the tooltip page supports a sales measure, consider building visuals that display sales versus plan, budget, or sales growth measures. Given the limited size of the tooltip report page, KPI and **Card** visuals are recommended.

By default, other visuals in the report that utilize the measure(s) or column(s) specified as tooltip fields in *step 5* display the tooltip report page when the user hovers over the items of the visual.

The **Type** of **Tooltip** from *step 3* is not required for utilizing tooltip report pages. However, this property makes the purpose of the page clear to the other report authors and has been provided by the Power BI team as a good starting point for most report page tooltips. Likewise, viewing the report page tooltip in **Actual size** as per *step 4* is technically not required but is very helpful in designing these pages as the report author can better gauge how the tooltip will be displayed to end users.

Alternatively, a **Tooltips** formatting card is available on the **General** tab of the **Format** pane for charts and map visuals. This formatting card can be used to specify a particular tooltip report page for the given visual or to disable tooltips. The **Type** of tooltip can be specified such as a **Report page** or **Default**. If **Default** is selected, the visual displays the default tooltips as described in the previous section.

We next take a closer look at formatting column and line charts.

## Column and line charts

Line, column, and bar charts are the most common chart visualization types given their advantages in visual perception, as explained in the *Visualization best practices* section of this chapter. Power BI includes clustered and stacked versions of column and bar charts in addition to two combination charts that display both a line and either a clustered or stacked column.

Note that the difference between clustered and stacked charts involves how the **Legend** impacts the columns and bars. With clustered charts, the **Legend** adds additional columns or bars to the axis within the axis groupings. Conversely, with stacked charts, the **Legend** creates groups within a single bar or column for each axis group.

The ribbon chart visualization represents a variation of the stacked column chart. Unlike the stacked column chart, the ribbon chart sorts the category items within each column based on their values and connects the items across columns with a ribbon.

*Figure 7.34* shows an example of a ribbon chart. Four product subcategories are displayed across months by `Internet Net Sales`:

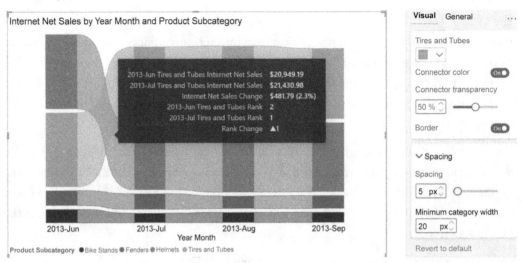

*Figure 7.34: Ribbon chart*

The **Tires and Tubes** subcategory overtook the **Helmets** subcategory in July 2013 to become the top-selling product subcategory in the visual. As per the tooltip included in the preceding image, hovering over the curved ribbon connecting the months on the X-axis displays the values for each month, the variance and percentage change between the months, and the change in rank for the given category (for example, from second to first for **Tires and Tubes**). Insights into the rankings of categories and their changes across periods wouldn't be as easily identified in a standard stacked column chart.

The ribbons formatting card allows for spacing, transparency, and a border to further aid comprehension. As shown in *Figure 7.34*, the ribbon **Border** is enabled, the **Connector transparency** of the ribbon is set to **50%**, and the ribbon **Spacing** is set to **5**. Currently, unlike the stacked column chart, the ribbon chart doesn't include a Y-axis to identify the total value of each column. Additionally, the individual ribbons are currently distinguished by color.

Let's next take a look at conditional formatting for these charts.

## Column and line chart conditional formatting

Column and line charts are two of the most common visuals in reports given their flexibility and advantages in visualizing comparisons and trends. However, these classic visuals don't have to be static or simple—report authors can embed custom rules to dynamically drive formatting properties based on source data.

Similar to tooltips, conditional formatting techniques help users more quickly derive insights from visuals without the added complexity of more data points or additional visuals, so let's start by exploring conditional formatting for column charts.

## Column chart conditional formatting

To apply conditional formatting, use the **fx** formatting option in the **Colors** format card under the **Columns** section. In *Figure 7.35*, the `Internet Net Margin %` measure is used as the **Colors** setting with a **Format** style of **Gradient**:

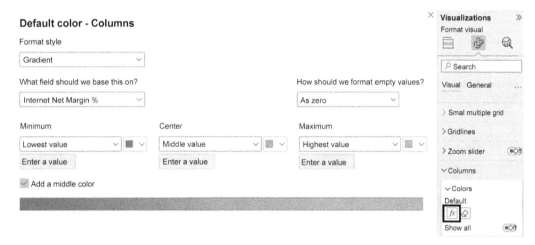

*Figure 7.35: Diverging data color formatting*

With the **Add a middle color** property enabled, this rule associates three colors (red, yellow, and green) with **Minimum**, **Middle**, and **Maximum** values. This rule makes it easy for users to distinguish the columns, such as fiscal periods or product categories, associated with low, average, and high product margins.

By switching **Format style** to **Rules**, a rule can be specified for only a minimum and a maximum value. This can be useful to change the color of a column only when a threshold is reached. In other words, the chart displays, at most, two distinct colors with one of the colors (for example, red) flagging the exceptions.

Note that the **fx** option for driving the conditional formatting for colors applies to many other visuals than just column and line charts and the interface is identical to that shown in *Figure 7.35*. However, conditional formatting for line charts works differently so let's look at that next.

## Line chart conditional formatting

Conditional formatting can be applied to line charts by applying distinct colors to separate DAX measures. In the following example, a DAX measure is created that only returns the sales per order value when its value is below $325,000:

```
Internet Net Sales Below $325K =
VAR __Sales = [Internet Net Sales]
RETURN
IF(__Sales < 325000,__Sales,BLANK())
```

Using this measure and the `Internet Net Sales` measure on the same line chart allows for separate colors to be applied as shown in *Figure 7.36*:

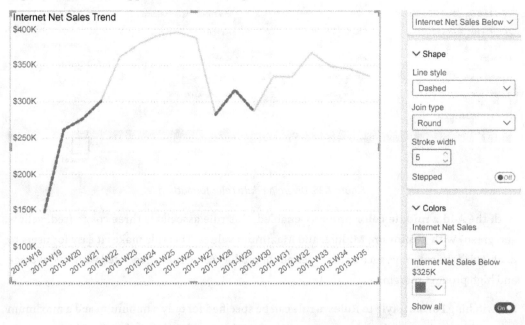

*Figure 7.36: Contrasting colors for line chart measures*

For this example, a green color is used for the Internet  Net  Sales measure and red for the Internet Net Sales Below $325K measure. Additionally, the below $325K line can be formatted with a slightly larger stroke width and a dashed line style via the **Shape** card as shown in *Figure 7.36*. The line chart appears as a single line that changes colors and styles when it goes below $325K.

The stroke width, join type, line style, and marker shape formatting properties provide a wide range of options for contrasting lines beyond their colors. These additional properties are recommended to aid general comprehension and to support users who cannot easily distinguish colors.

Let's next take a look at formatting for table and matrix visuals.

## Table and matrix visuals

As per the *Choosing the visual* section earlier in this chapter, table and matrix visuals are best suited for identifying and displaying precise values. A classic example of a matrix visual is when a user needs to view the values of a metric at multiple levels of a hierarchy such as the sales dollars for individual products, product subcategory, and category.

While Power BI reports are most known for their graphically rich visualizations, the table and matrix visuals have also received significant enhancements over the past few years to give report authors granular control over the layout and formatting of these visuals.

For example, a matrix visual can be designed in a Power BI report to generally replicate and potentially improve upon a PivotTable report in Excel or a matrix data region in a **SQL Server Reporting Services (SSRS)** report.

Table and matrix visuals also support the same **Display units** and **Value decimal places** formatting properties as other visuals. In *Figure 7.37*, both measures have been formatted to display their values in terms of millions with one decimal place:

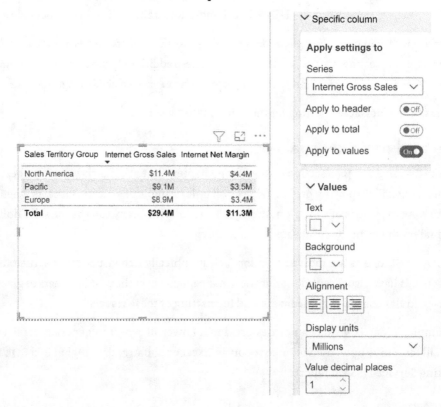

*Figure 7.37: Display units and Value decimal places for table and matrix visuals*

As shown in *Figure 7.37*, these properties are available within the **Specific column** category of the **Format** pane. **Display units** options range from **Thousands (K)** to **Trillions (T)**. By default, the **Display units** property is set to **None** for table and matrix visuals and **Value decimal places** is blank.

Prior to the availability of the **Display units** and **Value decimal places** properties, it was necessary to use the FORMAT() function in separate DAX measures to display custom formats in table or matrix visuals. The following two measures apply a custom rounded currency format to the results of the Internet Net Sales measure:

```
Internet Net Sales (Format Thousands) = FORMAT([Internet Net
Sales],"$0,.0K")
```

```
Internet Net Sales (Format Millions) = FORMAT([Internet Net
Sales],"$0,,.0M")
```

Both measures use the FORMAT() function to convert the input value (the Internet Net Sales measure) to a string in a custom, rounded format. Specifically, the comma or commas immediately to the left of the decimal are used to divide the value by 1,000 and round as necessary. The zero to the right of the decimal displays a digit or a zero. For example, the $541,613 value would be displayed as $541.6K and $0.5M by the format thousands and format millions of measures, respectively.

In addition to the visual format settings and FORMAT() function, another method is available to precisely control how values are displayed, custom format strings.

## Custom format strings

The obvious disadvantage of using the FORMAT() function is that numeric values are converted to text. However, while still an intern at Microsoft, Chelsie Eiden implemented **custom format strings**.

Custom format strings accept the same kinds of format strings as used in the FORMAT() function (such as "$0,,.0M" for millions and "mmmm" for long month names like January) but preserve the underlying data type of the column or measure.

Custom format strings can be entered into the **Format** dropdown while in the **Report view** on the **Column tools** or **Measure tools** tabs. Alternatively, while in the **Model view**, select a column or measure and in the **Properties** pane, in the **Formatting** section, set **Format** to **Custom** and then enter a **Custom format** as shown in *Figure 7.38*:

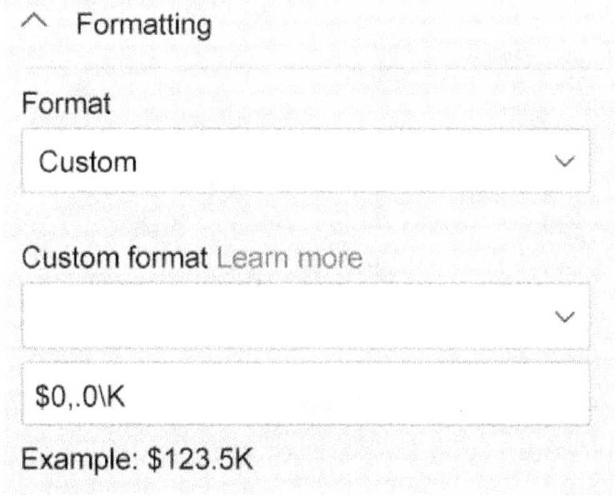

*Figure 7.38: Display units and decimal places for table and matrix visuals*

Custom format strings can be used for a variety of purposes, such as displaying numbers in duration format (hh:mm:ss). The following measure takes a column called `Duration` given in seconds and applies a transformation to locate hours, minutes, and seconds in particular orders of ten. This code can be used with a custom format string of `00:00:00` in order to display a duration in hh:mm:ss format.

```
Chelsie Eiden's Duration =
// Duration formatting
// * @konstatinos 1/25/2016
// * Given a number of seconds, returns a format of "hh:mm:ss"
//
// We start with a duration in number of seconds
VAR __SecondsDuration = SUM([Duration])
    VAR __Sign = SIGN(__SecondsDuration)
    VAR __Duration = ABS(__SecondsDuration)
// There are 3,600 seconds in an hour
VAR __Hours = INT (__Duration / 3600)
// There are 60 seconds in a minute
VAR __Minutes = INT ( MOD( __Duration - ( __Hours * 3600 ),3600 ) / 60)
// Remaining seconds are the remainder of the seconds
// divided by 60 after subtracting out the hours
// We round up here to get a whole number
VAR __Seconds = ROUNDUP(MOD ( MOD( __Duration - ( __Hours * 3600 ),3600 ),
60 ),0)
RETURN
// We put the hours, minutes and seconds into the proper "place"
(__Hours * 10000 + __Minutes * 100 + __Seconds) * __Sign
```

Additional uses of custom format strings can allow otherwise seemingly impossible things such as displaying dates and date-time values in the Y-axis of a chart. Such a chart is useful, for example, when attempting to chart at what time of day certain events occur across multiple days or on what days events occurred across years or months.

The following column definition using a `Date` column as input can be used with a custom format string of `00\/00\/0000` in order to display dates on the Y-axis.

```
DatesInY = MONTH([Date]) * 1000000 + DAY([Date]) * 10000 + YEAR([Date])
```

Since the Y-axis of charts only supports numeric values, custom format strings such as this are required in order to display dates and date times within the Y-axis.

It must be stressed that custom format strings are a general feature of columns and measures and thus can be used in all types of visuals, not just tables, matrixes, and charts.

We now turn our attention to conditional formatting for tables and matrixes.

## Table and matrix conditional formatting

As with charts, default and custom conditional formatting rules can be applied to table and matrix visuals to make it easier to identify exceptions and outlier values. Power BI currently supports **Background color**, **Font color**, **Data bars**, **Icons**, and **Web URL** conditional formatting for table and matrix visuals.

To apply conditional formatting to a table or matrix, click the drop-down arrow next to the field name of the measure or column (for example, Internet Net Sales) in the **Values** field well of the **Visualizations** pane. A **Conditional formatting** menu item appears with an arrow providing access to the different types of conditional formatting.

In *Figure 7.39*, data bar conditional formatting has been applied to four measures related to internet sales:

| Sales Territory Country | Internet Net Sales | Internet Sales Customer Count | Internet Sales Orders | Internet Net Sales (YOY YTD %) |
| --- | --- | --- | --- | --- |
| Australia | $2,128,407 | 1,127 | 1,130 | -17% |
| Canada | $307,605 | 169 | 169 | -46% |
| France | $648,066 | 356 | 359 | 58% |
| Germany | $608,658 | 335 | 339 | 17% |
| United Kingdom | $712,701 | 402 | 405 | 29% |
| United States | $1,437,049 | 866 | 867 | -42% |
| **Total** | **$5,842,485** | **3,255** | **3,269** | **-17%** |

*Figure 7.39: Data bar conditional formatting*

The length of the data bars helps to call out high or low values and alternative colors can be applied per measure. The direction of data bars is particularly helpful in distinguishing negative from positive values as per the Internet Net Sales (YOY YTD %) measure in the preceding example visual.

For large table and matrix visuals with many values, or when the relative differences between values are more important than the individual values themselves, the option to show only the data bar can be very useful.

Custom conditional formatting rules can be applied to the background and font color scales of table and matrix visual cells similar to Microsoft Excel. In *Figure 7.40*, **Rules** are defined to format the background cells of a measure as green if over 25%, yellow when between -25% and 25%, and red if the value is less than -25%:

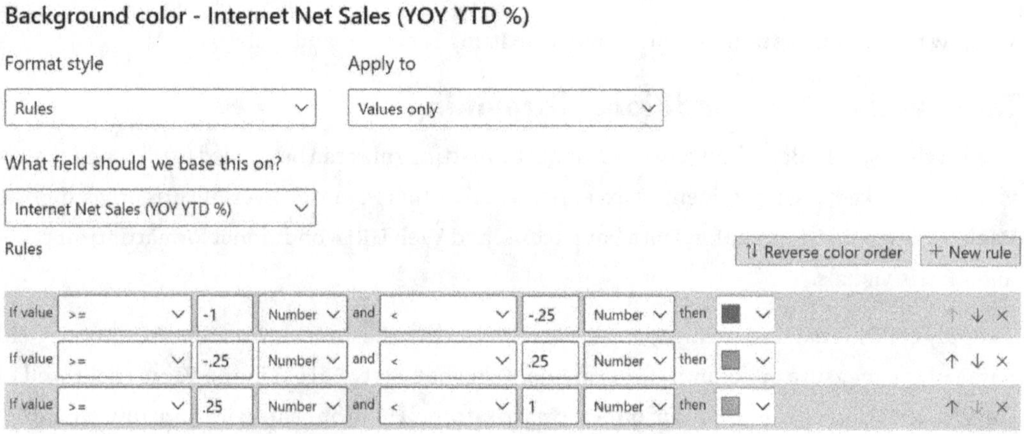

*Figure 7.40: Custom conditional formatting rules*

The conditional formatting rules are evaluated from the bottom to the top. Therefore, if a cell meets the condition of multiple rules, the lower rule is applied. The order of rules can be adjusted via the up and down arrows to the right of the color icons.

Multiple conditional formatting types can be applied against the same measure. For example, the same three conditional rules used for the background color scales in the preceding image could also be implemented as font color rules. However, the font colors specified for each rule (for example, white) could be chosen to contrast with the conditional background colors (for example, red) to further help call attention to the value.

DAX measures are also supported as inputs to conditional formatting rules. This functionality makes it easier to implement more complex rules, such as greater than the prior year-to-date sales value or a different color based upon the margin % of different product categories.

For example, the following `Internet Net Margin % Color` supporting measure can be created to return 2, 1, or 0 depending upon the `Product Category` and desired `Internet Net Margin %` measure value.

```
Internet Net Margin % Color =
    VAR __Category = MAX('Product'[Product Category])
    VAR __Margin = [Internet Net Margin %]
```

```
RETURN
    SWITCH(TRUE,
        __Category = "Bikes" && __Margin >= .40,"Green",
        __Category = "Bikes" && __Margin >= .35,"Yellow",
        __Category = "Bikes" && __Margin < .35,"Red",
        __Category = "Clothing" && __Margin >= .35,"#00ff00",
        __Category = "Clothing" && __Margin >= .30,"#ffff00",
        __Category = "Clothing" && __Margin < .30,"#ff0000",
        __Category = "Accessories" && __Margin >= .65,"Red",
        __Category = "Accessories" && __Margin >= .60,"Yellow",
        __Category = "Accessories" && __Margin < .60,"Red"
    )
```

In this example, a different target margin % is desirable for different product categories. As shown, either standard color names or hexadecimal color codes can be used as return values.

This measure can be used for field value-based background color conditional formatting as shown in *Figure 7.41*:

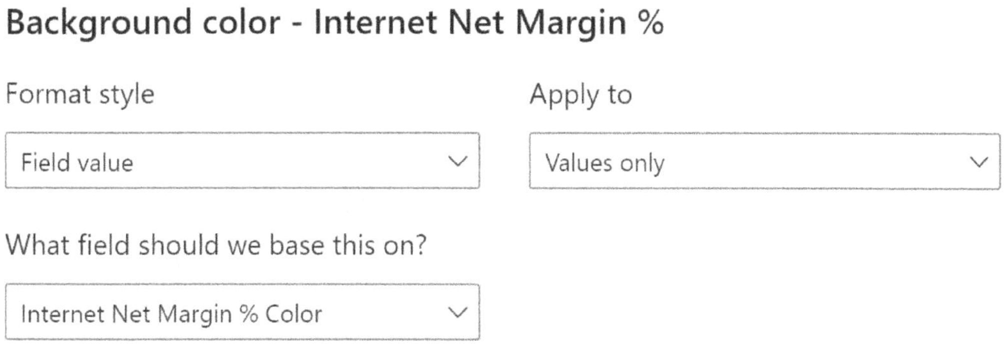

## Background color - Internet Net Margin %

Format style

| Field value                      ∨ |

Apply to

| Values only                      ∨ |

What field should we base this on?

| Internet Net Margin % Color      ∨ |

*Figure 7.41: Conditional formatting based on field values*

When applied to a simple table, the result is shown in *Figure 7.42*:

| Product Category | Internet Net Margin % |
|---|---|
| Accessories | 60.1% |
| Bikes | 38.0% |
| Clothing | 37.5% |
| **Total** | **38.9%** |

*Figure 7.42: Background conditional formatting for a table*

As shown in *Figure 7.42*, even though **Clothing** has the lowest net margin % for internet sales, the background color is green because the **37.5%** value is above the target threshold of **35%** specified in the `Internet Net Margin % Color` measure. Conversely, **Accessories** and **Bikes** are colored yellow because they do not meet the desired margin % thresholds for these categories.

Let's next look at a highly desired feature for tables and matrixes that was recently added to Power BI, **Sparklines**!

## Sparklines

**Sparklines** are small line charts drawn without axes or coordinates that help visualize the shape of variations (usually over time) of some metric. **Sparklines** have long been a staple in Excel and were one of the most requested features for Power BI Desktop, being prized for their ability to convey analytical insights with a miniscule form factor.

Recently, Microsoft added **Sparklines** to Power BI. When a table or matrix visualization is selected, the Sparkline feature becomes active on the **Insert** tab of the ribbon while in the **Report view** as shown in *Figure 7.43*:

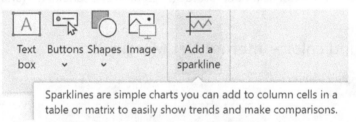

*Figure 7.43: Add a sparkline option*

Clicking on the **Add a sparkline** option shown in *Figure 7.43* presents a dialog for configuring the Sparkline as shown in *Figure 7.44*:

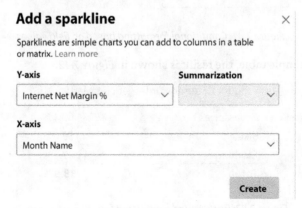

*Figure 7.44: Add a sparkline dialog*

As shown in *Figure 7.44*, the Internet Net Margin % measure is being compared across the months of the year. When added to our simple table visual from *Figure 7.42*, we can now observe the variances of the Internet Net Margin % measure over time along with our color-coded, aggregate values during that time span as shown in *Figure 7.45*:

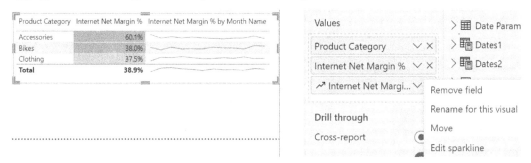

*Figure 7.45: Sparklines added to a table visual*

As shown in *Figure 7.45*, the sparkline is added to the **Values** field well of the table visualization with options available for removing, renaming, moving, and editing the sparkline.

The table visual shown in *Figure 7.45* packs a lot of analytical insights but consumes minimal report page real estate. Report viewers can observe the trend of the important metric across multiple product categories as well as easily see the health of that metric over the specified time period (in this case, the year 2013).

We next turn our attention to a feature exclusive to matrix visualizations, the ability to display measures as rows.

## Values as rows

A common form for matrix visuals is to display categories or hierarchies as rows and measures as columns. However, the reverse, displaying multiple measures as rows, particularly with one or multiple date dimension fields across the columns, is a very common layout for Excel pivot table reports.

Matrix visuals in Power BI Desktop support the important ability to show measures as rows. In *Figure 7.46*, the matrix visual breaks out six DAX measures by a date hierarchy across the columns:

| Calendar Yr-Qtr | 2013-Q1 | | | | 2013-Q2 | | | | Total |
|---|---|---|---|---|---|---|---|---|---|
| | 2013-Jan | 2013-Feb | 2013-Mar | Total | 2013-Apr | 2013-May | 2013-Jun | Total | |
| AdWorks Net Sales | $3,523,340 | $4,984,320 | $5,097,481 | **$13,605,142** | $3,328,139 | $4,767,754 | $5,154,127 | **$13,250,019** | **$26,855,162** |
| Reseller Net Sales | $2,665,651 | $4,212,972 | $4,047,574 | **$10,926,196** | $2,282,116 | $3,483,161 | $3,510,949 | **$9,276,226** | **$20,202,422** |
| Internet Net Sales | $857,690 | $771,349 | $1,049,907 | **$2,678,946** | $1,046,023 | $1,284,593 | $1,643,178 | **$3,973,793** | **$6,652,740** |
| AdWorks Net Margin % | 2.31% | -1.10% | 0.64% | **0.44%** | 10.44% | 9.12% | 11.23% | **10.27%** | **5.29%** |
| Reseller Net Margin % | -9.3% | -8.5% | -9.4% | **-9.0%** | -2.6% | -1.9% | -1.6% | **-2.0%** | **-5.8%** |
| Internet Net Margin % | 38.5% | 39.1% | 39.2% | **38.9%** | 39.0% | 38.9% | 38.7% | **38.8%** | **38.9%** |

*Figure 7.46: Values on rows in matrix visual*

To enable this feature in Power BI, simply enable the **Switch values to rows** feature within the matrix visual's **Options** card located in the **Values** section of the **Visualizations** pane's **Format** sub-pane.

## Scatter charts

Scatter charts are very effective at explaining the relationship or correlation between items against two variables. Optionally, a third variable can be used to drive the size of the data points and thereby convert the visual to a bubble chart.

In *Figure 7.47*, three countries from the **Sales Territory Country** column are used as the details input to a scatter chart:

Internet and Reseller Net Sales by Sales Territory Country and Product Subcategory

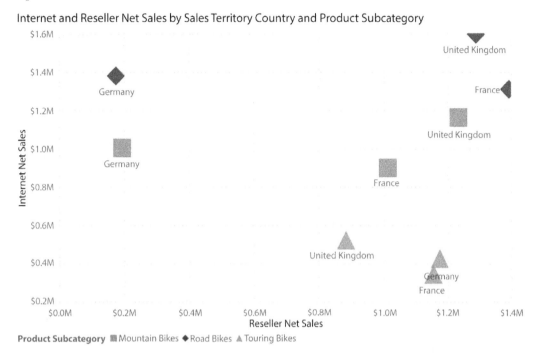

*Figure 7.47: Scatter chart*

To provide additional detail, three product subcategories are included in the legend input, such that nine total points (3 x 3) are plotted on the chart. The scatter chart naturally calls out the differences among the items based on their X position (Reseller Net Sales) and Y position (Internet Net Sales).

Moreover, to make the visual even easier to interpret, the marker shapes have been customized for each product subcategory (for example, triangles, diamonds, squares) and the size of the shapes have been increased to 40%.

By default, Power BI applies different colors to the items in the legend. If the legend is not used, the report author can customize the colors of the individual items from the details input column. Although color can be effective for differentiating values, customized marker shapes, such as this example, are helpful for users with visual disabilities.

This concludes our exploration of building and formatting visuals within Power BI. While we cannot hope to cover the myriad of formatting options available for every visual, as there are literally hundreds of available format cards, this chapter has provided a good overview of how to build and format many of the standard visualizations within Power BI Desktop.

## Summary

Building on the foundation of the previous chapter regarding Power BI report planning, this described how to create and format the basic building blocks of reports, Power BI visualizations. We initially provided an overview of the **Visualizations** pane that is foundational to building and formatting visuals, introduced the configuration and utility of numerous standard visuals and elements, and finally provided numerous examples of important formatting functionality such as conditional formatting, **Sparklines**, and custom format strings.

The following chapter builds upon the foundational knowledge of this chapter to introduce more advanced visualizations, analytics, and mobile support.

## Join our community on Discord

Join our community's Discord space for discussions with the author and other readers:
https://discord.gg/q6BPbHEPXp

# 8

# Applying Advanced Analytics

The previous two chapters focused on foundational knowledge regarding Power BI report planning, design, and how to create and format visualizations. This chapter builds upon that foundation to demonstrate how the advanced analytical capabilities of Power BI can create an even more compelling user experience and assist users in exploring data to derive insights. This includes a review of **artificial intelligence (AI)** powered visuals, custom visuals, animation, and other analytics features with Power BI Desktop and the service.

In this chapter, we will review the following topics:

- AI visuals
- ArcGIS Maps for Power BI
- R and Python visuals
- Custom visuals
- Animation and data storytelling
- Analytics pane
- Quick insights/Analyze
- Mobile-optimized report pages

## AI visuals

**Artificial intelligence (AI)** visuals incorporate aspects of machine learning such as pattern recognition and natural (human) language parsing. Machine learning is a form of AI that uses statistical models and algorithms to analyze and make inferences from complex data patterns.

In the past, the application of AI or machine learning required a data scientist, but Microsoft has made tremendous strides in democratizing machine learning within Power BI both with the **Auto ML** features of **dataflows** in the Power BI service and AI visuals within Power BI Desktop. The use of the advanced capabilities of AI visuals can add analytical punch to many reports.

Power BI Desktop contains four AI visuals as follows:

- Key influencers
- Decomposition tree
- Q&A
- Smart narrative

We explore each of these visuals in turn, starting with the **key influencers** visual.

## Key influencers

The **key influencers** visual is a powerful analytic tool included as a standard visual within Power BI Desktop. This visual can be complex to work with and is often best used by report authors to quickly identify interesting analytic insights that deserve further investigation. The report author can then create simple visuals and stories that highlight these analytical insights.

The **key influencers** visual uses machine learning algorithms to analyze and find patterns within the data. These patterns are then presented back to the report author as **key influencers** that impact a particular metric as well as clustering into **Top segments**.

In *Figure 8.1,* the **key influencers** visual has been configured to analyze the `Internet Net Sales` measure by placing numerous columns from the `Customer` table into the **Explain by** field well in order to identify what factors impact `Internet Net Sales` to be higher or lower:

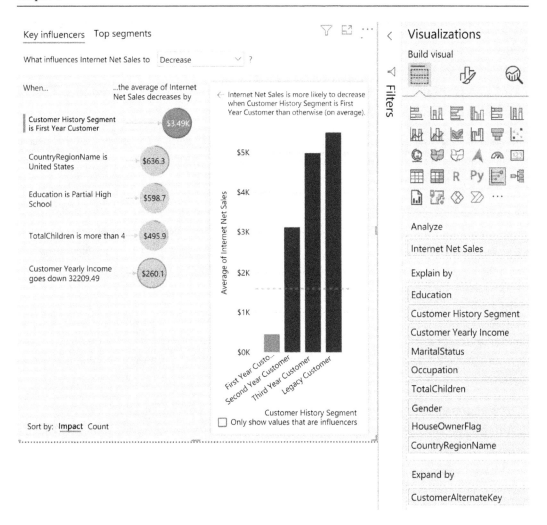

*Figure 8.1: A key influencers visual*

As shown in *Figure 8.1*, the single largest factor that impacts Internet Net Sales to **Decrease** is that the Customer History Segment column has a value of **First Year Customer**. The second most impactful factor is that the CountryRegionName of the customer is **United States**. Additional high impacts are an Education of **Partial High School**, TotalChildren of **more than 4**, and a decrease in Customer Yearly Income.

For each of these key influencers, a graphic is presented that helps explain the insight further. This visual is generally a column chart or scatter chart and includes a text narrative at the top that puts the insight into words.

In *Figure 8.1*, note that the analysis can be performed for **What influences Internet Net Sales** to either **Decrease** or **Increase**. Additionally, **Counts** have been enabled on the **Analysis** formatting card. Enabling **Counts** displays a ring around each circle that represents the count of records that form the key influencer. The key influencers can then be sorted by **Impact** or **Count** in the lower left of the visual.

Special attention should be paid to the **Expand by** field well. As shown in *Figure 8.1*, the CustomerAlternateKey field has been used in the **Expand by** field well. To understand the function of the **Expand by** field well, consider that the measure or summarized column placed in the **Analyze** field well is automatically analyzed at the detail level of the **Explain by** columns.

Depending on the data, this level may be overly summarized and thus not suitable for a machine learning regression model. Machine learning models tend to work best with more data. Thus, in order to increase the detail level analyzed, the **Expand by** field can be used. By using a unique key for each customer, this effectively forces the data to not summarize and thus the machine learning algorithm executes at the most detailed grain for the table.

In addition to the **Key influencers** tab, a **Top segments** tab is also populated by the **Key influencers** visual as shown in *Figure 8.2*:

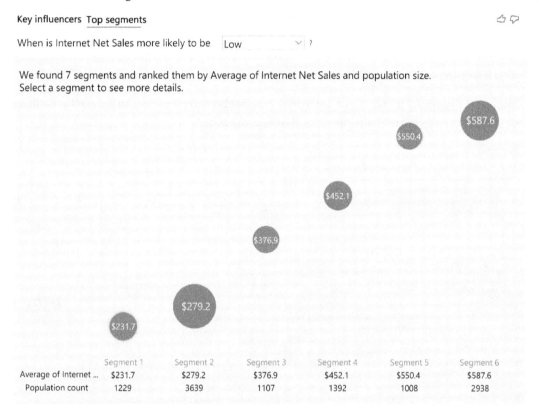

Figure 8.2: A key influencers visual, Top segments

**Top segments** use clustering algorithms to identify clusters where the **Analyze** metric is lower or higher than the average of the overall dataset. In *Figure 8.2*, six segments are presented that include the **Average of Internet Net Sales** as well as a **Population count** of the number of rows included in each segment. The size of each bubble corresponds to the **Population count**. Therefore, we can quickly see visually that **Segment 2** is more impactful than **Segment 1** since the measure value is similar, but **Segment 2** has almost 3 times the number of occurrences.

Clicking on **Segment 2** presents additional information about the segment, including the attribute values that correspond to the segment as shown in *Figure 8.3*:

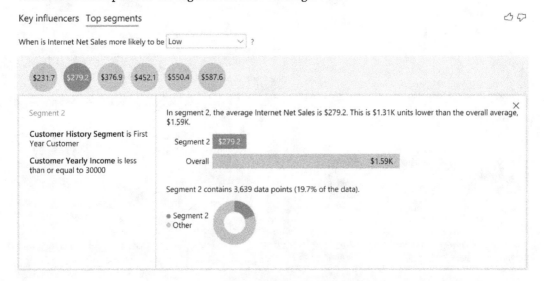

Figure 8.3: Top segments, details

As shown in *Figure 8.3*, the attributes that make up **Segment 2** are when the **Customer History Segment is First Year Customer** and the **Customer Yearly Income is less than or equal to 30000**. Clear, detailed information is presented identifying the average Internet Net Sales for the segment, the difference from the overall average, the number of data points within the segment, and the percentage of the overall data within the segment (**19.7%**).

The **key influencers** visualization is not the only Power BI visual that leverages machine learning technology. Another such visual is the **Decomposition tree** visualization that we will explore next.

# Decomposition tree

The **Decomposition tree** visual is another advanced visual that incorporates machine learning technology.

The **Decomposition tree** visual is another visual that is perhaps best used by report authors to perform ad hoc data and root cause analysis, in order to quickly gain insights into data that can then be presented to users in a more intuitive and straightforward fashion.

In *Figure 8.4*, the **key influencers** visual from *Figure 8.1* has been converted to a **Decomposition tree** visual:

*Figure 8.4: A decomposition tree visual*

As shown in *Figure 8.4*, at each level of the hierarchy data bars are displayed along with category values and amounts. A + icon is present for each category value. Clicking on this + icon allows you to manually drill into any category not already present in the visual.

In addition, you can instead choose to let the visual guide you through the analysis by displaying the next hierarchy level that has the highest or lowest value for the metric. These **High value** and **Low value** options are known as **AI splits** and can be disabled in the **Analysis** format card for the visual.

Hierarchy levels can be removed by clicking the **X** icon at the top of each column. Note also that as a hierarchy level is expanded, the sub-heading under the main column heading displays the expanded category value, which is displayed in bold within the visual itself.

Moving on from the advanced machine learning visuals, we will next explore two visuals that leverage Power BI's natural language (human language versus a constructed, artificial language) features, starting with the **Q&A** visual.

# Q&A

The Q&A visualization represents Microsoft's investments in natural language technology that can transform the user experience from selecting elements with a mouse to simply speaking or typing in their questions. Common questions and terms that business users are familiar with can be associated with metrics and attributes of the source Power BI dataset.

As with other advanced visuals such as **key influencers** and **Decomposition tree**, the **Q&A** visual is perhaps best suited for report authors attempting to quickly understand and tease out analytical insights from the data. The ability to ask natural language questions and generate visuals based upon those questions is quite powerful.

A **Q&A** visual can be added to a report page by using the **Visualizations** pane or by double-clicking the report canvas. *Figure 8.5* shows an example of an unconfigured **Q&A** visual:

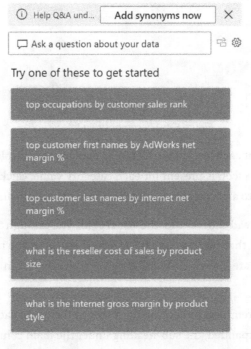

*Figure 8.5: A Q&A visual*

Selecting one of the default example questions or typing a question into the **Ask a question about your data** text box generates a visual. By default, the type of visual is most often a column or bar chart but particular visuals can be specified as part of the question. In *Figure 8.6*, the requested visual is a pie chart:

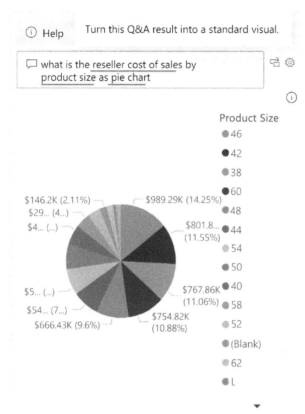

*Figure 8.6: A Q&A visual result*

As shown in *Figure 8.6*, if the report author likes the visual created, the visual can be added as a standard visual to the report page simply by clicking on the **Turn this Q&A result into a standard visual** icon to the immediate right of the question text box.

Clicking on the gear icon or clicking on the **Add synonyms now** button shown in *Figure 8.5* opens the **Q&A setup** dialog as shown in *Figure 8.7*:

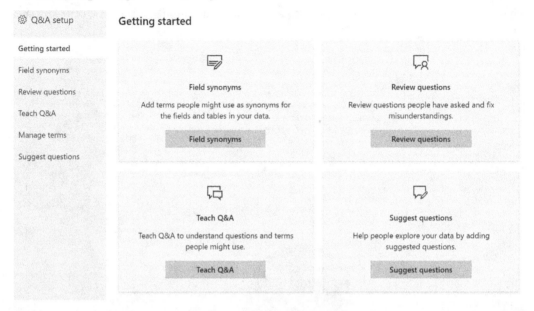

*Figure 8.7: A Q&A visual result*

As shown in *Figure 8.7*, the **Q&A setup** dialog allows the report author to create synonyms, review questions asked by report viewers, train Q&A to better understand questions, and add or remove suggested questions. A full treatment of **Q&A setup** is beyond the scope of this chapter but a detailed recipe for setting up and preparing Q&A is included in *Chapter 5* of *Power BI Cookbook, 2nd Edition*.

Enterprise business intelligence teams should consider the implications of introducing Q&A to report viewers carefully. Achieving good Q&A results depends heavily on configuring synonyms correctly.

While proper, intuitive naming of columns and measures can help, generally there are many synonyms that are required to be configured and maintained over time. In addition, it is imperative that enterprise business intelligence teams monitor the questions being asked by the business users and the results returned from those queries.

In addition to the **Q&A** visual, another visual that leverages the natural language capabilities of Power BI is the **smart narrative** visual.

# Smart narrative

The **smart narrative** visual is another impressive visualization that can save report authors a lot of time and energy. The **smart narrative** visual creates a natural language (human language) summary of an entire report page or an individual visual.

In *Figure 8.8*, the report page shown in *Figure 6.10* from *Chapter 6, Planning Power BI Reports*, was duplicated. A blank area of the canvas was clicked and then the **smart narrative** visual is chosen from the **Visualizations** pane. The **smart narrative** visual then generated the text shown in *Figure 8.8*:

*Figure 8.8: The smart narrative result*

The **smart narrative** visual can be customized by the report author to add additional text and insights. In *Figure 8.8* the custom value **Adworks net margin %** was added to the **smart narrative** visual using the **+ Value** dialog and corresponding custom text added to the visual, **AdWorks Net Margin % was**. Custom values created via the **+ Value** pane can be reviewed and removed via the **Review** pane.

**Smart narrative** visuals can also be used on individual report visuals. To create a corresponding **smart narrative** visual for an individual report visual, simply right-click the report visual and choose **Summarize**. Most standard visuals are supported such as bar, column, and line charts. However, more advanced visuals like waterfall charts and decomposition trees, for example, are not supported and have the **Summarize** option greyed out.

The **smart narrative** visual provides all of the standard text box controls for formatting text as well as all of the standard text box formatting options via the **Format text box** pane. This makes the **smart narrative** visual highly customizable. While this may make it seem like the **smart narrative** visual is just a simple text box, all of the underlined values and analysis are updated each time the report data is refreshed!

We now turn our attention to two additional visuals that integrate the powerful data analytics capabilities of the **R** and **Python** programming languages.

# R and Python visuals

The **R** and **Python** programming languages both have strong data analysis and visualization capabilities. This makes these languages a natural fit for data analysis and visualization tools such as Power BI Desktop. In addition to other integration options, such as the ability to use R and Python in Power Query, Power BI Desktop also provides standard visuals for both R and Python.

In order to use the R and Python visuals, you must first install the R and Python programming languages and ensure that the R scripting and Python scripting options are configured in the **GLOBAL** options (**File** | **Options and settings** | **Options**) as shown in *Figure 8.9*:

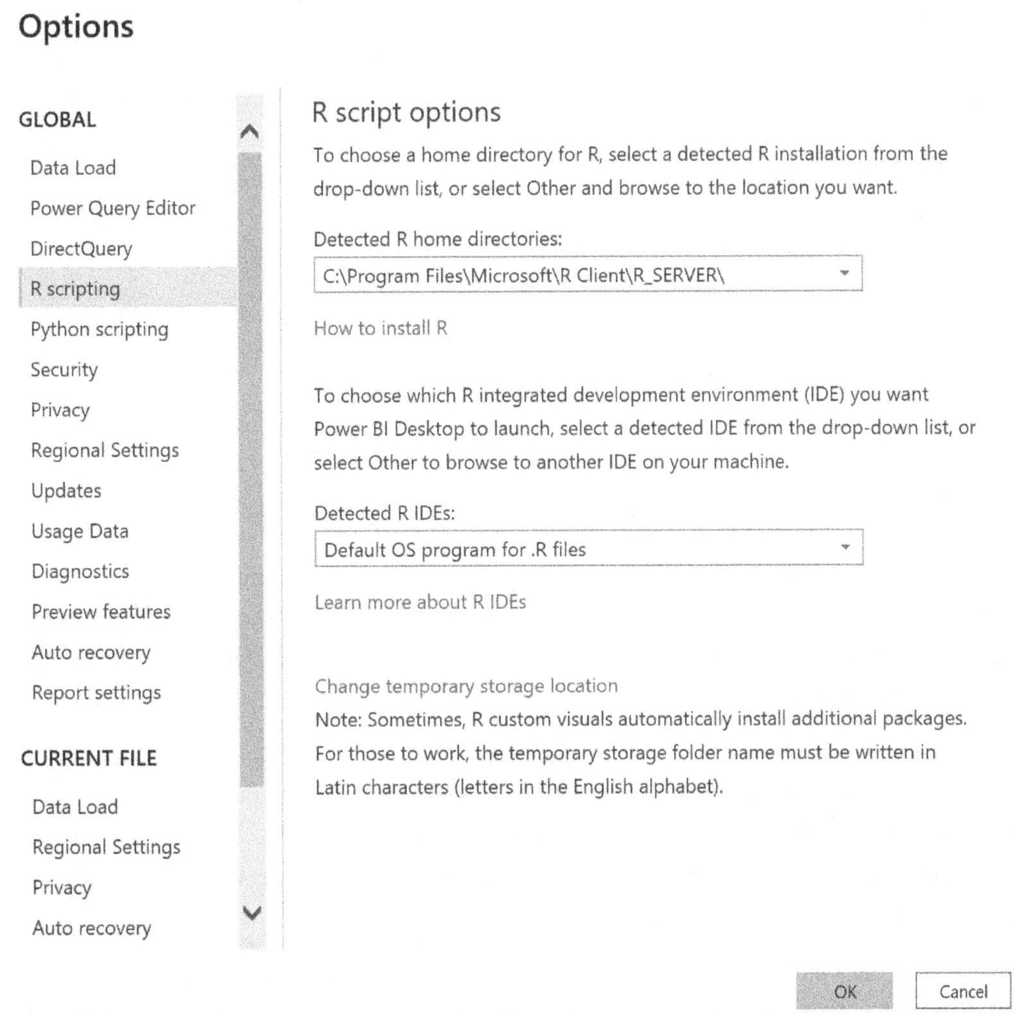
Options
GLOBAL
Data Load
Power Query Editor
DirectQuery
R scripting
Python scripting
Security
Privacy
Regional Settings
Updates
Usage Data
Diagnostics
Preview features
Auto recovery
Report settings
CURRENT FILE
Data Load
Regional Settings
Privacy
Auto recovery
R script options
To choose a home directory for R, select a detected R installation from the drop-down list, or select Other and browse to the location you want.
Detected R home directories:
C:\Program Files\Microsoft\R Client\R_SERVER\
How to install R
To choose which R integrated development environment (IDE) you want Power BI Desktop to launch, select a detected IDE from the drop-down list, or select Other to browse to another IDE on your machine.
Detected R IDEs:
Default OS program for .R files
Learn more about R IDEs
Change temporary storage location
Note: Sometimes, R custom visuals automatically install additional packages. For those to work, the temporary storage folder name must be written in Latin characters (letters in the English alphabet).
OK
Cancel

*Figure 8.9: R scripting options*

As shown in *Figure 8.9*, Power BI attempts to detect any installed R and Python program language installations and **integrated development environments (IDEs)**. Once you have the R and Python languages installed and configured, you are ready to add an R or Python visual to a report page. Adding an R or Python visual to a report page for the first time results in a security prompt as shown in *Figure 8.10*:

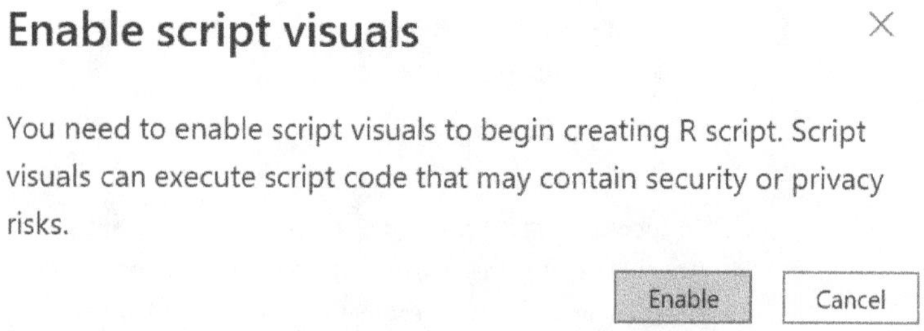

## Enable script visuals                                                  ✕

You need to enable script visuals to begin creating R script. Script visuals can execute script code that may contain security or privacy risks.

Enable      Cancel

*Figure 8.10: R and Python Enable script visuals message*

The prompt in *Figure 8.10* is displayed once per report when using R and Python visuals and is intended to alert the report author that enabling scripts has potential security and privacy risks. In addition, each time a report containing R and Python visuals is opened within Power BI Desktop the same prompt is opened.

While integration with the R and Python languages adds a tremendous amount of analytical and visual capabilities to Power BI, enterprise business intelligence teams should carefully consider the use of R and Python within their Power BI projects. While the Power BI service supports the most popular R and Python packages/modules, not every package or module is fully supported in the service.

In addition, once included in a Power BI file, other report authors or editors are required to have the R or Python language installed on their computers with the required packages and modules installed. Given the frequency of changes to both R and Python and the potential for code to work on one version of R and Python and not another, enterprise business intelligence teams that use R and Python should standardize the use of specific versions and allowed packages and modules.

We now take a closer look at using R visuals.

## R visual

The R language and runtime can be downloaded from the R Project for Statistical Computing website (`https://cran.r-project.org/bin/windows/base/`) or Microsoft (`https://www.microsoft.com/en-us/download/details.aspx?id=51205`). Once R is installed and the Power BI **R script** options configured, R visuals can be added to report pages in Power BI Desktop.

In *Figure 8.11* the Product Name column from the Products table has been added to the **Values** field well for the R visual and a word cloud has been created using the R language:

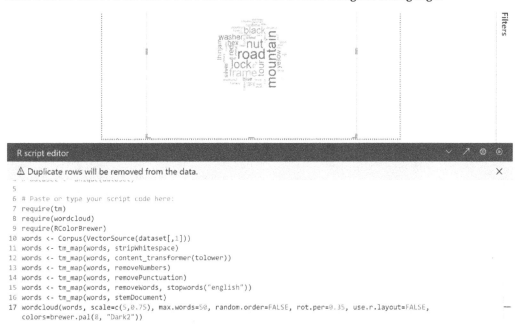

Figure 8.11: R visual

As shown in *Figure 8.11*, selecting an R visual opens an **R script editor** pane at the bottom of the canvas when in the **Report** view. This script editor allows the input of R code. Four icons are present in the upper-right corner of the R script editor. From left to right, these icons perform the following functions:

- The chevron icon expands or collapses the **R script editor** pane
- The arrow icon opens the R script in the configured IDE
- The gear icon opens the Power BI Desktop **Options (File | Options and settings | Options)**
- The run icon renders the R visual

The full code listed in the **R script editor** from *Figure 8.11* is provided here:

```
# The following code to create a dataframe and remove duplicated rows is
always executed and acts as a preamble for your script:

# dataset <- data.frame(Product Name)
# dataset <- unique(dataset)
```

```
# Paste or type your script code here:
require(tm)
require(wordcloud)
require(RColorBrewer)
words <- Corpus(VectorSource(dataset[,1]))
words <- tm_map(words, stripWhitespace)
words <- tm_map(words, content_transformer(tolower))
words <- tm_map(words, removeNumbers)
words <- tm_map(words, removePunctuation)
words <- tm_map(words, removeWords, stopwords("english"))
words <- tm_map(words, stemDocument)
wordcloud(words, scale=c(5,0.75), max.words=50, random.order=FALSE, rot.
per=0.35, use.r.layout=FALSE, colors=brewer.pal(8, "Dark2"))
```

Note the warning message displayed in *Figure 8.11*, **Duplicate rows will be removed from the data.** A similar message is repeated in the first comment within the script editor. Removing duplicate rows is done for performance reasons and cannot be overridden.

The next two comment lines display the pre-processing that occurs for the script. A **dataframe** variable called dataset is created from the columns and measures present in the **Values** field well, in this case just the Product Name column. Then, the unique function is used to return only distinct rows within the data frame. It is important to note that while these are comments within the code, these commands are in fact executed on the data prior to the rest of the script running.

The required packages, in this case **tm**, **wordcloud**, **RColorBrewer**, and **SnowballC**, were installed using the R console application outside of Power BI Desktop. While inside the R console, you can use the install.packages command to install packages:

```
install.packages("package name")
```

Since the **R script editor** lacks any real debugging features, it is often advantageous to use an external **integrated development environment** (IDE) to develop the R code. Clicking on the arrow icon in the upper-right corner of the **R script editor** pane opens the code within the configured IDE and also creates a temporary **comma-separated value** (CSV) file that holds the data configured for the visual.

The same dataset variable is initialized using the read.csv function with this temporary file specified as the source. Once you are finished debugging the R script, you must copy and paste the R code from the IDE back into the **R script editor** pane.

Using Python visual is similar to using R visual so let's look at that next.

## Python visual

Python visuals operate identically to R visuals except that the scripting language used is Python. The Python language and runtime can be downloaded from the python.org website (`https://www.python.org/downloads/windows/`) or the Microsoft Store (`https://www.microsoft.com/en-us/p/python-39/9p7qfqmjrfp7`). Once Python is installed and the Power BI **Python script** options configured, Python visuals can be added to report pages in Power BI Desktop.

In *Figure 8.12* the `CountryRegionName` column from the `Geography` table and the `Internet Sales Customer Count` measure from the `Internet Sales` table have been added to the **Values** field well for the Python visual and a simple bar chart created using the Python language.

*Figure 8.12: The Python visual*

*Figure 8.12* displays the **Python script editor** pane as collapsed. The **Python script editor** pane works identically to the **R script editor** pane. From left to right, the four icons in the upper-right corner of the **Python script editor** pane perform the following functions:

- The chevron icon expands or collapses the **Python script editor** pane
- The arrow icon opens the Python script in the configured IDE
- The gear icon opens the Power BI Desktop **Options (File | Options and settings | Options)**
- The run icon renders the Python visual

The full code listed in the **Python script editor** from *Figure 8.11* is provided here:

```
# The following code to create a dataframe and remove duplicated rows is
always executed and acts as a preamble for your script:

# dataset = pandas.DataFrame(Internet Net Sales, Product Category)
# dataset = dataset.drop_duplicates()

# Paste or type your script code here:
import matplotlib.pyplot as plt
dataset.plot(kind='barh', fontsize=6, x='CountryRegionName', y='Internet
Sales Customer Count')
plt.show()
```

As with R visuals, Python visuals remove duplicate rows within the data, creating a **dataframe** within the dataset variable.

We now turn our attention to the most powerful standard map visual for Power BI, the **ArcGIS Maps for Power BI** visual.

# ArcGIS Maps for Power BI

The ArcGIS Map visual for Power BI enables report authors to develop map visualizations far beyond the capabilities of the bubble and filled map visuals described in *Chapter 7, Creating and Formatting Visualizations*. Created by Esri, a market leader in **Geographic Information Systems (GIS)**, the ArcGIS Map supports all standard map types (for example, bubble and heatmap), but also provides many additional features including a clustering map theme for grouping individual geographic points and the ability to filter a map by the points within a geographical area.

The ArcGIS Map also enables deep control over the logic of the size and color formatting, such as the number of distinct sizes (classes) to display and the algorithm used to associate locations to these classes. Additionally, reference layers and cards of demographic and economic information are available to provide greater context and advanced analytical insights.

The ArcGIS Map visual is included in the standard visualizations pane and enabled by default in Power BI Desktop. However, the ArcGIS Map visual is not currently supported for the Power BI Report Server and thus is not available in the Power Desktop application optimized for it. Additionally, an option is available on the **Tenant settings** page of the Power BI admin portal to enable or disable the use of the ArcGIS Maps visual. Details on utilizing the Power BI admin portal to configure tenant settings and other options are included in *Chapter 14, Administering Power BI for an Organization*.

In *Figure 8.13*, customer addresses in the state of Washington have been plotted with different sizes and colors based on the Internet Net Sales measure and the Customer History Segment column, respectively:

*Figure 8.13: The ArcGIS Map visual for Power BI*

For the most visually engaging ArcGIS Map, use the **Dark Gray Canvas** base map and bright, saturated colors for the data points plotted. The **Streets** and **OpenStreetMap** base map types are practical choices whenever transportation between the data points or pinned locations is expected. In *Figure 8.13*, the **Streets** base map supports the sales team that may drive from the pinned office location on 11th street in Bremerton, Washington to the plotted customer addresses.

The visual has been zoomed into the Bremerton, Washington area near several large customers and a fictional sales office location on 11th street near downtown Bremerton. Pin locations are often used in conjunction with the **Drive Time** feature to plot an area relative to specific locations such as a group of customers who are within a 20-minute drive of an office.

To configure these options and all other layout and formatting settings, a set of icons are present in the upper left of the visual as shown in *Figure 8.13*. For this visual, the **Streets** base map type has been selected and the **Map theme** is set to **Size & Color**. The reference layer **USA Median Age** is used to distinguish areas based on age (via color intensity). A column named Full Address is used for the **Location** input field. This column includes the street address, city, state, and postal code such as the following example: 1097 Kulani Lane, Kirkland, WA, 98033.

The **Data category** for this column has been set to **Address** in Power BI Desktop to further improve the accuracy of the geocoding process in which the location input value (the address) is converted to a latitude and longitude. Latitude and longitude fields are available as well, and these inputs are recommended over street addresses for greater performance and scale.

A maximum of 3,500 street addresses can be geocoded without a Creator license. To avoid the limit of addresses geocoded and to focus the visual on more meaningful data points, a visual level filter can be applied to a measure. In this example, a visual level filter was applied to the Internet Net Sales measure to only include data points (customer addresses) with over $100. By removing the small customers, this filter reduced the count of addresses by half and still retained over 97% of the Internet Net Sales.

The **Use ArcGIS Maps for Power BI** option should be checked in the Global **Security** options of Power BI Desktop. An equivalent option is exposed in the Power BI service via the **Settings** menu **(Gear icon | Settings | ArcGIS Maps for Power BI)**, and this should be checked as well to render ArcGIS Maps in the Power BI service.

In addition, a **Use ArcGIS Maps for Power BI** setting is available in the **Tenant settings** page of the Power BI admin portal. Power BI service administrators can optionally disable this feature to prevent all users from using ArcGIS Maps for Power BI. The configuration of **Tenant settings** in the Power BI admin portal is described in *Chapter 14, Administering Power BI for an Organization*.

It should be noted that the ArcGIS Maps for Power BI visual requires additional licensing from Esri and a Pro Power BI license. The **Azure map** visual, which is currently in preview, may serve as an alternative to the **ArcGIS Map for Power BI** visual in some scenarios. The Azure map visual supports 30,000 data points, has many of the primary geospatial visualization and interactive features as the ArcGIS visual, and does not require additional licensing. More information about the Azure map visual can be found here:

https://docs.microsoft.com/en-us/azure/azure-maps/power-bi-visual-get-started

The **AI visuals**, R and Python visuals, and **ArcGIS Maps for Power BI** visual are just the tip of the iceberg when it comes to adding advanced analytical insights to Power BI. Hundreds of additional, advanced visuals developed by Microsoft and third parties are available as custom visuals.

# Custom visuals

In addition to the standard visuals included in the **Visualizations** pane of Power BI Desktop, a vast array of custom visuals can be added to reports to deliver extended functionality or to address specific use cases such as applying 'smooth lines' formatting to a line chart or displaying multiple KPIs in the same visual via the Power KPI visual by Microsoft.

These visuals, many of which have been created by Microsoft, are developed with the common framework used by the standard visuals and are approved by Microsoft prior to inclusion in Microsoft **AppSource**. Given the common framework, custom visuals can be integrated into Power BI reports with standard visuals and exhibit the same standard behaviors such as filtering via slicers and report and page filters.

Power BI report authors and BI teams are well-served to remain conscious of both the advantages and limitations of custom visuals. For example, when several measures or dimension columns need to be displayed within the same visual, custom visuals such as the **Impact Bubble Chart** and the **Dot Plot** by **Maq Software** may exclusively address this need. In other scenarios, a trade-off or compromise must be made between the incremental features provided by a custom visual and the rich controls built into a standard Power BI visual.

Additionally, performance and maintenance can be an issue with custom visuals. For example, a custom visual may generate many more queries than a similar standard visual and thus render more slowly and consume more system resources. Moreover, a Power BI environment that utilizes many custom visuals is more difficult to support as report authors are less familiar with the features and behaviors of these visuals.

Custom visuals available in **AppSource** are all approved for running in browsers and on mobile devices via the Power BI mobile apps. A subset of these visuals are certified by Microsoft and support additional Power BI features such as email subscriptions and export to PowerPoint. Additionally, certified custom visuals have met a set of code requirements and have passed strict security tests. Additional details on the certification process are available at the following link: `http://bit.ly/2AFAC9W`.

Let's now take a look at how to find and add custom visuals to a Power BI report.

# Adding a custom visual

Custom visuals can be added to Power BI reports by either downloading and importing `.pbiviz` files from Microsoft **AppSource** or directly using them within Power BI Desktop. *Figure 8.14* shows Microsoft **AppSource** filtered to **Power BI visuals**:

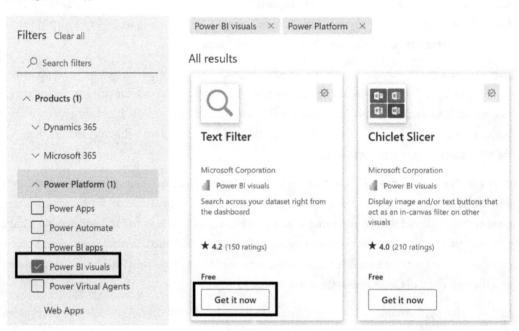

*Figure 8.14: Power BI custom visuals in AppSource*

The following link filters **AppSource** to the Power BI custom visuals per the preceding screenshot: `http://bit.ly/2BIZZbZ`.

The search bar at the top of the page and the vertical scrollbar on the right can be used to browse and identify custom visuals to download. Each custom visual tile in **AppSource** includes a **Get it now** link that, if clicked, presents the option to download the custom visual itself (the `.pbiviz` file). Clicking anywhere else in the tile other than `Get it now` displays a window with a detailed overview of the visual, ratings, support details, and the ability to download a demo `.pbix` file.

To add custom visuals directly to Power BI reports, click the **Get more visuals** option via the ellipsis of the **Visualizations** pane, as per *Figure 8.15*:

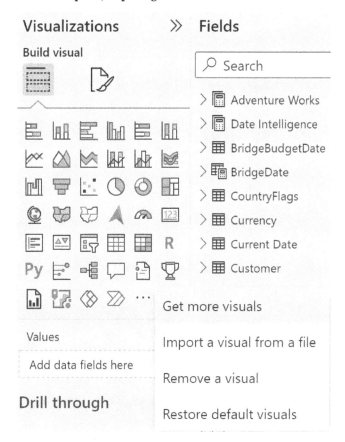

*Figure 8.15: Importing custom visuals from the store*

If a custom visual (.pbiviz file) has been downloaded from **AppSource**, the **Import a visual from a file** option can be used to import this custom visual into the report.

Selecting **Get more visuals** launches a slightly different **AppSource** experience than the website. Unlike the **AppSource** website, the visuals are assigned to categories such as **KPI**, **Maps**, and **Advanced Analytics**, making it easy to browse and compare related visuals. More importantly, utilizing the integrated **Get more visuals** avoids the need to manage .pbiviz files and allows report authors to remain focused on report development.

In *Figure 8.16*, the **KPI** category of **Power BI visuals** is selected from within **AppSource**:

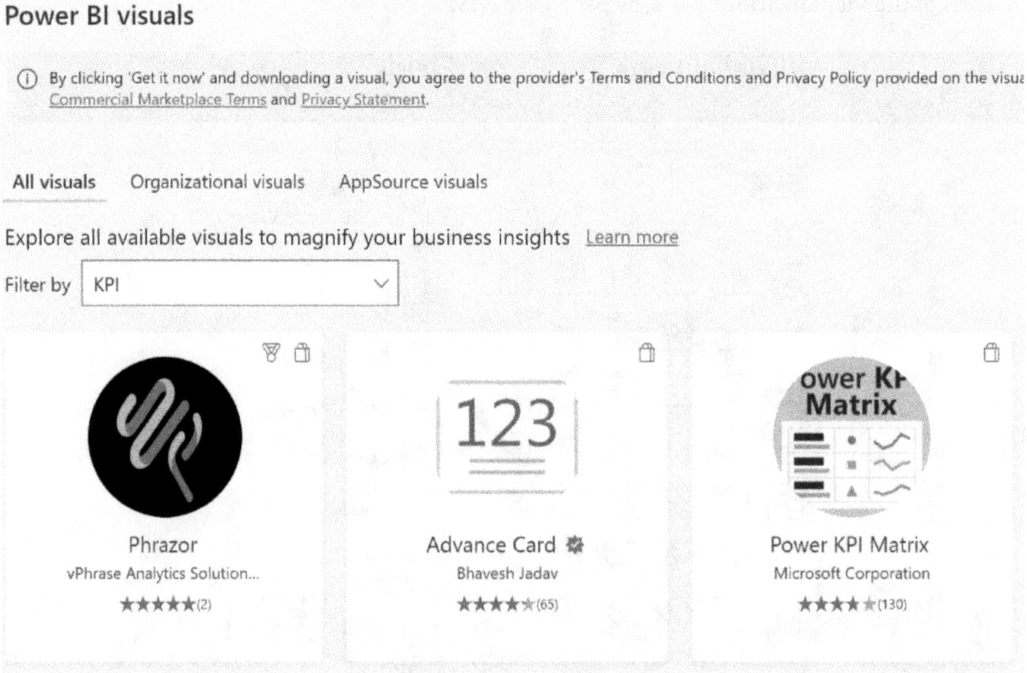

Figure 8.16: Custom visuals via the Office Store in Power BI Desktop

Selecting a custom visual's card displays the same detailed information as **AppSource** and an **Add** button directly adds the custom visual as a new icon in the **Visualizations** pane. The visual categories, customer reviews, supporting documentation, and sample reports all assist report authors in choosing the appropriate visual and using it correctly.

Organizations can also upload custom visuals to the Power BI service via the organization visuals page of the Power BI Admin portal. Once uploaded, these visuals are exposed to report authors in the **Organizational visuals** tab as shown in *Figure 8.16*.

This feature can help both organizations and report authors simplify their use of custom visuals by defining and exposing a particular set of approved custom visuals. For example, a policy could define that new Power BI reports must only utilize standard and organizational custom visuals. The list of organizational custom visuals could potentially only include a subset of the visuals that have been certified by Microsoft.

Alternatively, an approval process could be implemented so that the use case for a custom visual would have to be proven or validated prior to adding this visual to the list of organizational custom visuals. Additional details on managing organizational custom visuals are included in *Chapter 14, Administering Power BI for an Organization.*

In the next section on animation and data storytelling, we will include the use of a custom visual, the Pulse chart.

# Animation and data storytelling

A top responsibility for many data professionals is the ability to convey their findings to others in a clear and compelling fashion. Common scenarios for data storytelling include recurring performance review meetings (for example, the close of a fiscal period) and special project or ad hoc meetings with senior managers and executives. For these meetings, the data professional or team has already identified the analytical insights to highlight but must plan to properly communicate this message to the specific stakeholders or audience.

Power BI animation features, including bookmarks as described in *Chapter 6, Planning Power BI Reports*, provide powerful support for data storytelling. In addition, the play axis available in the standard **Scatter chart** visual and the animation features available in many custom visuals, such as the **Line Dot chart** and the **Pulse chart**, can also be used to deliver advanced analytical insights and data storytelling.

Let's first look at the animation features of standard **scatter charts**.

## Play axis for Scatter charts

The **Scatter** chart is the only standard visual in Power BI Desktop that supports animation. By applying a date/time series column to the **Scatter chart's Play axis** field well, animated playback and trace features are enabled.

For example, a visual can be paused at a specific point along the time series, allowing the user to provide additional context. The user can also select one or multiple items (for example, product categories) to display data points representing the previous time periods.

In *Figure 8.17*, the user has paused the animation on the month of June via the **Play axis** and selected the icon associated with the Touring Bikes product subcategory:

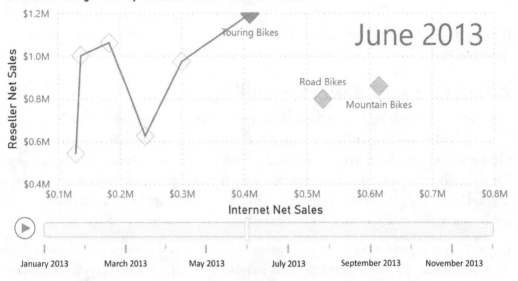

*Figure 8.17: Scatter chart with Play axis*

With the **Touring Bikes** subcategory selected, a trace line appears connecting the latest data point for this subcategory to its preceding data points. Additionally, the user can hover the cursor over the preceding data points to provide the details for these months via a tooltip.

Date, number, and text columns can be used in the **Play axis** for the **Scatter chart**. As per *Chapter 4, Designing Import and DirectQuery Data Models*, the Sort by column property can be used to define a logical sort order for text columns such as sorting a Month name column by a Month number column.

Next, we will explore similar animation capabilities of the **Pulse chart** custom visual.

## Pulse chart

The **Pulse chart** custom visual, developed by Microsoft, provides both animation and annotation features to support data storytelling. The **Pulse chart** animates the value of a single measure over time and pauses (pulses) at dates associated with events to display pop-up boxes of annotations describing these events.

During each pause, which can also be applied manually via playback buttons, other Power BI visuals on the same report page are filtered by the event date. Additionally, a second measure can be visualized as a counter at the top of the chart via the **Runner Counter** field.

In *Figure 8.18*, a **year-to-date (YTD)** internet sales measure and four events with annotations are plotted on a **Pulse chart**:

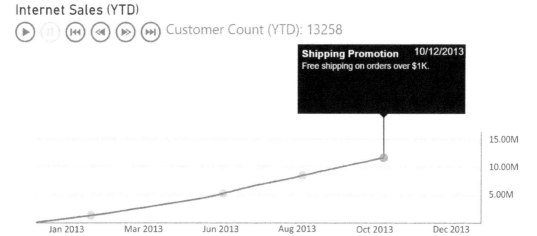

*Figure 8.18: Pulse chart*

In *Figure 8.18*, the Internet Sales (YTD) measure is visualized via the animated line (and dots) in relation to the **Y axis**. For this example, a YTD customer count measure has also been applied to the **Runner Counter** field input.

With the visual paused on the shipping promotion event of October 12, 2013, the **Y axis** indicates a sales value of approximately $12.00 M, and the **Runner Counter** displays a count of 13,258 customers.

Alternatively, the same measure can be applied to both the **Values** and **Runner Counter** fields, thus providing the precise value at each pause in addition to the trend via the line. Examples of defining YTD and customer count measures are included in *Chapter 5*, *Developing DAX Measures and Security Roles*.

If event annotations are not needed, only the **Timestamp** and **Values** input fields are required to render the **Pulse chart**. The **Event Title**, **Event Description**, and **Event Size** input fields are available to display events and annotations as pop-up boxes.

Additionally, the formatting pane provides several cards for defining the look and behavior of the **Pulse chart**, including the size and color of the pop-up text boxes and the speed of the animation. For example, white text at size 10 can be formatted against a black fill background and the pause at each event can be set to 4 seconds.

To support the **Pulse chart** in the preceding example, a separate table of events was added to the dataset as per *Figure 8.19*:

| Event Date ▼ | Event Title ▼ | Event Description ▼ |
|---|---|---|
| 2/15/2013 | New Sales Territory | Opened Southeast sales office in Atlanta, GA. |
| 6/3/2013 | Volume Discounts | Launched volume discount pricing promotion. |
| 8/7/2013 | Accessory Products | Accessories product category available online. |
| 10/12/2013 | Shipping Promotion | Free shipping on orders over $1K. |

*Figure 8.19: Events table*

The Event Date column is used to define a one-to-one relationship from the Events table to the Date dimension table. The Date column from the Date dimension table is applied to the Pulse chart's **Timestamp** input field, and the Event Title and Event Description columns from the events table are applied to their respective input fields.

The formatting options for the **X** and **Y axes** of the Pulse chart are much less robust than the standard line chart. As one example, the **Y axis** gridlines cannot be disabled. However, gridlines can be hidden by setting the axis color to match the background color. Additionally, the second and later lines of event descriptions in pop-up boxes are displayed without spaces. Report authors can adjust the width of popups or reduce the length of event descriptions to account for this.

This completes our exploration of using more complex visuals to add advanced analytics and insights to reports. We will next explore another method of adding such analytics and insights via the **Analytics** pane.

# Analytics pane

In addition to the Visualization pane's **Build visual** and **Format visual** sub-panes used to create and format report visuals discussed in the previous chapter, an **Analytics** pane is also available for certain Cartesian standard visuals such as **Line charts** and **Clustered column charts**.

The Analytics pane allows report authors to add constant and dynamic reference lines such as average, max, and min to visuals to provide greater context and analytical value. Additionally, trend and forecast lines can be added to display the results of advanced analytical techniques such as exponential smoothing to support predictive analytics.

A simple but important use case of the **Analytics** pane, exemplified in the *Trend line* section below, is to add a constant line that represents a goal or threshold to compare a measure against. Dynamic reference lines representing an aggregation (for example, a median) behave just like DAX measures and thus, in some scenarios, avoid the need to create new DAX measures in the source dataset or within the report.

The reference lines available in the **Analytics** pane depend on the type of visual. For example, reference lines are currently not supported for any custom visuals and only constant lines can be applied to the stacked column chart and stacked bar chart visuals. Additionally, the **Trend line** is exclusive to the line and clustered column chart; the forecast line is exclusive to the line chart. Moreover, a date or a numeric column is required on the **X axis** and the **X axis Type** must be set to **Continuous** in order to utilize the trend and forecast lines.

New features and capabilities are planned for the **Analytics** pane, including an expanded list of visuals supported and error bars to visualize uncertainty of the data. Similar to the **Tooltips** feature described in the previous chapter, *Chapter 7, Creating and Formatting Visualizations*, Power BI report authors should be conscious of the **Analytics** pane and its ability to enhance report visuals with additional context and insights such as the use of a **Trend line**.

# Trend line

A **Trend line** is available via the **Analytics** pane if there's time-series data for five standard visuals including the line chart, area chart, clustered column chart, scatter chart, and the combination line and clustered column chart. **Trend lines** display the general direction and slope of data points over time.

The **Trend line** is particularly valuable when a chart contains many data points and significant variation exists among the points, making it difficult to observe the trend of the metric visually.

In *Figure 8.20*, a trend line and two additional reference lines (average and constant) have been added to a clustered column chart to provide greater insight and context:

Internet Sales Unique Customers by Month and Year

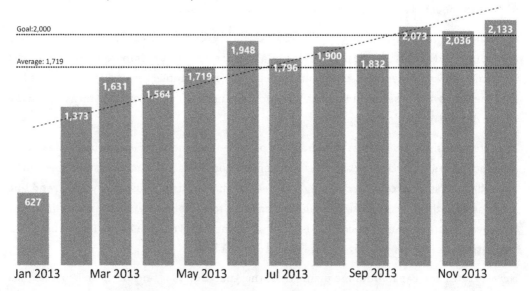

Figure 8.20: Trend, constant, and average reference lines

In *Figure 8.20*, the **Label density** property of the **Data labels** formatting card has been set to **100%** in order to ensure that all columns have a data label displayed. Additionally, the **Position** property of the data labels has been set to **Inside end** with a white color. Clear visibility of the data labels for each column, in addition to the two reference lines (**Average** and **Goal**), avoids the need to display the **Y axis** and gridlines.

Excluding the three reference lines from the **Analytics** pane, the clustered column chart simply plots the **Internet Sales Customer Count** measure against a Month Beginning Date column. The Month Beginning Date column (for example, 11/1/2013) is required for the axis input in this scenario as both the trend line and the forecast line require either a date or a number data type for the **X axis** and **Type** of **Continuous**. For example, if the Year Month column was used for the axis (for example, **2013-Nov**), both the trend line and the forecast line cards would not appear in the **Analytics** pane as the **X axis** type would be **Categorical**.

The DAX expression used for the **Internet Sales Customer Count** measure is included in the *Dimension metrics* section of *Chapter 5, Developing DAX Measures and Security Roles*. The Month Beginning Date column's formula is given below:

```
Month Beginning Date = DATE(YEAR([Date]),MONTH([Date]),1)
```

The Month Beginning Date column is used instead of a Month Ending Date column because if that was used, the **X axis** labels would be shifted to the wrong months. In other words, the **Nov 2013** label would appear under the October data. The Month Ending Date column formula is:

```
Month Ending Date = EOMONTH([Date],0)
```

With the essential column chart built, the three reference lines can be added from the **Analytics** pane as per *Figure 8.21*:

*Figure 8.21: Analytics pane*

As per *Figure 8.21*, the **Line style** of the **Trend line** is set to **Dashed** with a transparency of **0%**. This formatting ensures that the trend reference line can be easily distinguished from other data on the chart such as the other two reference lines.

The **Combine Series** property is not relevant to this visual as there is only one series and **Use Highlight Values** is the default setting for calculating the **Trend line**. The **Combine Series** property can be useful for plotting the trend of multiple, related column series.

The numeric symbols (1) next to the **Constant line** and **Average line** cards denote that a reference line of each type has also been applied to the visual. For these reference lines, a **Dotted** line style has been used, and custom names have been configured (for example, **Goal**, **Average**) to be displayed via **Data labels**. These two additional lines make it easy for users to identify the columns that are above or below the average value for the columns in the visual (**1,719**) and the constant goal value of **2,000**.

We will next look at a more advanced feature of the **Analytics** pane, **Forecasting** .

## Forecasting

The **Forecasting** feature of the **Analytics** pane is exclusive to standard line charts and utilizes predictive algorithms to generate forecasted data points as well as upper and lower boundaries.

The report author has control over the number of data points to forecast, the confidence interval (range of estimate) of the forecast (for example, 80%, 95%), and can apply formatting to distinguish the forecast from the actual data points. Additionally, the **Forecasting** feature allows authors to optionally exclude a number from the last data points. This **Ignore the last** property is useful for excluding incomplete periods as well as evaluating the accuracy of the forecast relative to recently completed periods.

In *Figure 8.22*, the clustered column chart from the **Trend lines** section has been switched to a line chart and a **Forecast** for the next two months has been added:

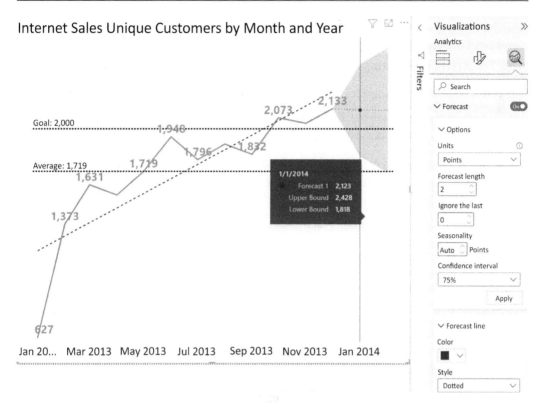

*Figure 8.22: Forecast line*

By hovering over the first forecast point, January 2014, the forecasted Internet Sales Customer Count value of **2,123** is displayed along with the upper (**2,428**) and lower (**1,818**) boundaries. The user can easily distinguish the last actual data point, **2,133** for December of 2013, from the forecast via the **Dotted** style of the forecast line and the dark fill of the **Confidence band** style. The **Trend line**, **Average**, and **Goal** reference lines applied in the previous section provide further context to the **Forecast**.

As per *Figure 8.22*, a custom **Forecast length** and **Confidence interval** have been applied to the **Forecast**. The **Seasonality** property is optional and is used to help detect seasonal variances in data. Think retail sales being seasonally impacted by holiday sales in November and December.

The **Confidence interval** property defines the distance between the upper and lower boundaries from the forecasted data points. For example, the minimum confidence interval of 75% produces a narrower range, and the maximum confidence interval of 99% produces a much wider range.

The **Ignore the last** property can be used to evaluate how accurately the forecast would've predicted recent data points. In this example, an **Ignore last value** of 2 would result in forecast values for November and December of 2013—the last two completed months. The forecast algorithm would use all available data points through October of 2013 to generate the two forecast points. If the actual data points for these two months fall outside the confidence interval (upper and lower bounds) of the forecast, the forecast may not be valid for the given data, or the **Confidence interval** may be too narrow. This testing technique is referred to as **hindcasting**.

Let's now look at one of the most advanced options for adding analytical insights to reports, the **Quick insights** or **Analyze** feature.

## Quick insights/Analyze

**Quick insights**, also known as the **Analyze** feature, is one of the most analytically advanced features in Power BI as it enables sophisticated machine learning algorithms to be executed against datasets or specific subsets of those datasets. The results of these computations automatically generate highly formatted Power BI visuals that can be integrated into reports as though they were created from scratch.

The full **Quick insights** capabilities are only generally available in the Power BI service for import mode datasets without RLS applied and with dashboard tiles reflecting those datasets. However, the essential capabilities of **Quick insights** are also available in Power BI Desktop as the **Analyze** feature.

In *Figure 8.23*, **Quick insights** has been executed against the **Chapter06_Import** dataset in the Power BI service:

Quick Insights for Chapter06_Import

A subset of your data was analyzed and the following insights were found. Learn more

*Figure 8.23: Quick insights for a dataset in the Power BI service*

To execute **Quick insights** against an entire dataset, see the **Get quick insights** option under the **Actions** ellipsis menu for a dataset in the Power BI service. Once the insights have been generated, a **View Insights** menu option replaces the **Get quick insights** option.

The visuals generated from the insights, such as the line chart on the left, advise of the algorithm used (for example, outlier, cluster, and correlation). Most importantly, the visuals can be pinned to dashboards and are displayed without the supporting text like normal dashboard tiles. In Power BI Desktop, **Quick insights** are limited to specific data points represented by report visuals.

As mentioned, **Quick insights** cannot be executed against datasets that contain row-level security roles as described in *Chapter 5*, *Designing DAX Measures and Security Roles*. Additionally, **Quick insights** cannot be executed against DirectQuery datasets, live connection datasets, or real-time streaming datasets.

In addition to the use of **Quick insights** in the Power BI service, similar capabilities are available within Power BI Desktop via the **Analyze** feature, which we will explore next.

## Explain the increase/decrease

**Quick insight** features are enabled in Power BI Desktop by default, allowing users to right-click data points in visuals and execute the relevant analysis. In *Figure 8.24* right-clicking on the data point for 2014-Feb presents an **Explain the increase** option in the **Analyze** menu:

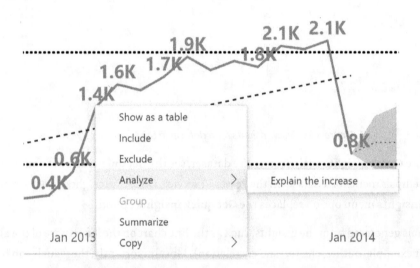

*Figure 8.24: Explaining the decrease in Power BI Desktop*

Clicking **Explain the increase** executes machine learning algorithms against the dataset and populates a window with visuals representing the insights retrieved. The user can scroll vertically to view the different insights obtained such as **Non-Bikes** accounting for all of the increase in customers, as shown in *Figure 8.25*:

# Here's the analysis of the 118.98% increase in Internet Sales Customer Count between 1/1/2013 and 2/1/2013

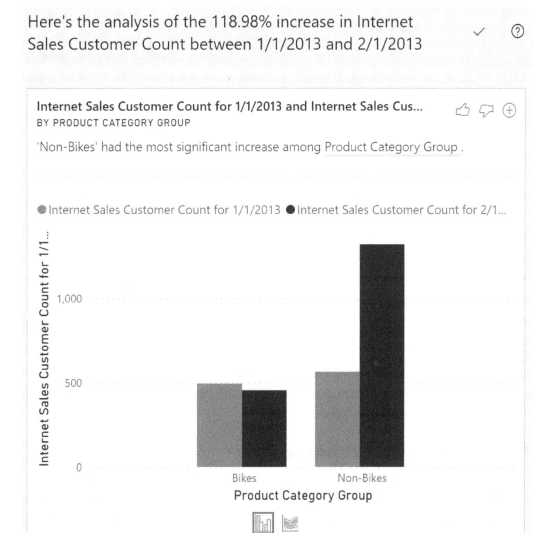

Figure 8.25: Explain the increase in Power BI Desktop

Clicking the plus sign at the top right corner of the text box explaining the insight adds the visual to the report page. Adding the visual to the report page automatically populates the associated field wells and visual level filters as though the visual was created manually. If necessary, the report author can apply further formatting to align the visual with the design and layout of the page.

The default for **Quick insight** charts is a clustered column chart but other available chart options are displayed at the bottom center of each insight card. In *Figure 8.25* a ribbon chart is also available as opposed to the clustered column chart.

Currently, **Quick insights** in Power BI Desktop is limited to the local dataset and is exclusive to import mode datasets. For example, the **Explain the decrease** option does not appear when connecting to a published Power BI dataset or an SSAS database via live connection. Given the importance of isolating reports from a central dataset as described in the previous chapter, *Chapter 6, Planning Power BI Reports*, this limitation represents a significant obstacle to utilizing this feature in corporate deployments.

Additionally, there are several limitations on the kinds of measures and filters supported. For example, measures that use the DISTINCTCOUNT() and SUMX() functions are not supported, and measures containing conditional logic (for example, IF()) are also not supported.

Just as important as delivering advanced analytics and insights to business users is the ability to deliver those such insights anytime, anywhere. Luckily, Power BI provides such capabilities through mobile-optimized report pages.

# Mobile-optimized report pages

A critical use case for many reports is access from smaller form factor devices such as phones and tablets running the iOS and Android mobile operating systems. A report that is perfectly designed for a laptop or PC monitor may be difficult to use on a tablet or mobile device, thus depriving business users of advanced analytical insights while they are traveling or otherwise on the go.

To account for multiple form factors, including both small- and large-screen phones, report authors can create mobile-optimized reports via the Phone Layout view in Power BI Desktop.

In *Figure 8.26*, the **Mobile layout** of a report page in Power BI Desktop is accessed via the **View** tab:

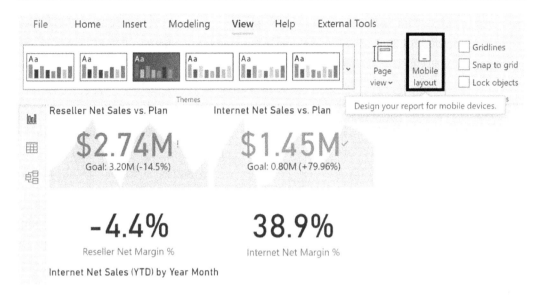

*Figure 8.26: Mobile layout in the View tab*

From the **Mobile layout** view, the visuals created and formatted for the report page can be arranged and sized on a mobile layout grid. In *Figure 8.27*, the two KPI and card visuals included in the preceding image from the **Report** view, as well as a line chart, are arranged on the mobile canvas:

*Figure 8.27: The phone layout*

Single-number visuals, such as cards and KPIs, are natural candidates for mobile-optimized layouts. More complex and data-intensive visuals, such as scatter charts and combination charts, are generally less effective choices for mobile layouts given the smaller form factor and screen resolution of mobile devices versus desktop and laptop monitors.

Given the one-to-one relationship between report pages and the phone layout, one design option is to create a dedicated report page with the visuals needed for the phone layout. This can be especially important because the font sizes and other format options for the visuals cannot be individualized for the **Mobile layout** but rather inherit the formatting of the report in the **Report** view.

The size and position of visuals can be adjusted by dragging visual icons along the **Mobile layout** grid. A mobile-optimized layout can be defined for each report page, or any number of the pages contained in a report.

The formatting and filter context of report visuals is always aligned between the **Mobile layout** and the default **Report** view. For example, to change the format or filter for a visual accessed via the **Mobile layout**, the visual can be modified from the standard **Report** view desktop layout.

When a report page is accessed from the Power BI mobile application, the **Mobile layout** created in Power BI Desktop is rendered by default in the phone report mode. If a phone-optimized layout doesn't exist, the report opens in landscape view.

Power BI dashboards can also be optimized for mobile devices. The **Mobile layout** for dashboards is implemented in the Power BI service and is reviewed in *Chapter 9, Designing Dashboards*.

This completes our exploration of applying advanced analytics to Power BI reports.

## Summary

This chapter reviewed many advanced analytical and visualization features that are available to deliver powerful and compelling report content. This included the use of more complex visuals such as the AI visuals, R and Python visuals, the ArcGIS Maps for Power BI visual, and custom visuals. Additionally, the analytical potential of animation via the standard scatter chart visual and custom Pulse chart visual was explored. Finally, the advanced analytical capabilities of the Analytics pane and the Quick insights/Analyze feature were presented.

The next chapter utilizes the report visualizations and design patterns described in this chapter as well as the previous two chapters to create Power BI dashboards.

This includes simple single dashboard projects and more elaborate multi-dashboard architectures, representing different levels of detail. Although some users may only view or interact with Power BI via dashboards, the quality and sustainability of this content, and particularly the ability to analyze the supporting details, is largely driven by the report design concepts and features from *Chapter 6, Planning Power BI Reports*.

## Join our community on Discord

Join our community's Discord space for discussions with the author and other readers:
`https://discord.gg/q6BPbHEPXp`

# 9

# Designing Dashboards

This chapter leverages the dataset and report development features and concepts from prior chapters to plan and develop Power BI dashboards and apps. Alternative dashboard architectures are described, including an organizational architecture that aligns business teams at different levels of an organization to a common set of corporate KPIs.

The design and implementation of these dashboards and apps, including layout, custom links, and mobile-optimized dashboards, are described in this chapter. Additionally, other top features and capabilities of dashboards are reviewed, including live report pages and the integration of content from other report types, including paginated reports and Microsoft Excel workbooks.

In this chapter, we will review the following topics:

- Dashboards versus reports
- Dashboard design
- Dashboard architectures
- Dashboard tiles
- Live report pages
- Mobile-optimized dashboards

## Dashboards versus reports

Executives and senior-level stakeholders require a holistic view of the top metrics or **Key Performance Indicators (KPIs)** established by their organization. While Power BI reports deliver a visually rich data analysis experience, optionally at a very detailed level, Power BI dashboards provide a simplified "single pane of glass" for viewing top metrics.

Additionally, since the tiles of dashboards can be linked to their source report visuals or other dashboards, a dashboard can serve as the starting point to optionally navigate to other dashboards and underlying reports.

From a technical standpoint, Power BI dashboards are exclusive to the Power BI online service and are primarily composed of tiles representing visuals from one or many reports. While Power BI reports are often limited to a single source dataset, a dashboard's tiles can represent multiple datasets from highly disparate sources to help provide a 360-degree view on a single canvas.

**To less experienced users and BI team members, the terms and capabilities associated with dashboards and reports can be misunderstood**. Much of this confusion stems from the fact that, in common parlance, the word dashboard is used to refer to any type of summary-level report containing multiple visualizations. However, in Power BI, dashboards and reports are two distinct types of content with their own unique capabilities and use cases.

For example, data-driven alerts are exclusive to Power BI dashboards, while embedding in SharePoint Online is only supported for Power BI reports. More fundamentally, Power BI reports deliver an interactive data exploration experience by providing many methods of filtering, cross-filtering, and drilling to different levels of detail. Power BI dashboards, with the exception of pinned live report pages, are not intended for significant user interaction but rather as a summary-level single pane of glass for displaying key performance indicators.

Although several capabilities, such as email subscriptions and printing, are common to reports and dashboards, BI teams are well served to design dashboards and reports according to their distinct roles in Power BI. For example, a dashboard should not contain granular details or complex visuals, but rather the essential metrics describing the stakeholder's area of responsibility or influence.

The following table compares dashboards to reports across 19 capabilities:

| Capability | Dashboard | Report |
|---|---|---|
| Visualization pages | One page | One or multiple pages |
| Authoring environment | Power BI service | Power BI Desktop and service |
| Viewing environment | Power BI service and mobile apps | Power Desktop, service, and mobile apps |
| Pinning | Can pin existing dashboard tiles to other dashboards in the current workspace | Can pin report visualizations and pages as tiles to dashboards |

| Email subscriptions | Supported | Supported |
|---|---|---|
| Filtering | Can only filter or interact with live report page tiles | Can filter, cross-highlight, and slice |
| Data alerts | Supported | Not supported |
| Customization | Can alter layout, tile size, names, and links | Fully customizable in **Edit** mode of the Power BI service and Power BI Desktop |
| Natural language queries (Q&A) | Available for all dataset types (import, Live, and DirectQuery) | Q&A report visual |
| Visibility to data detail | Can export data for a tile | Can export summarized and underlying data, and also the **Show Data** option to view tabular data of a visual |
| Printing | Can print current dashboard | Can print current report page |
| Featured and favorites | A dashboard can be set as featured and as a favorite | Can only be set as favorites |
| Publish to web | Not supported | Supported |
| Embed in SharePoint | Not supported | Supported in SharePoint Online via the Power BI web part |
| Mobile optimized | Supported | Supported |
| Create visuals | Can add tiles containing text, image, video, web content, and streaming data | Can create visuals using both standard and custom visuals |
| Dataset sources | Tiles pinned from Excel workbooks, PBRS, and Power BI visuals | Hundreds of supported sources |
| Datasets | Tiles can reflect one or multiple datasets | Usually a single dataset with potentially multiple data sources. Can be multiple datasets using DirectQuery for Power BI datasets and Analysis Services |
| Data caching | Tiles reflect cached query results, and the cache is updated on a schedule | Visuals generate queries against the source dataset when opened and based on user interactions |

*Table 9.1: Dashboard and report capabilities*

As per the preceding table, data-driven alerts are exclusive to Power BI dashboards in the Power BI service. Data alerts and their corresponding notifications are not available to Power BI reports, including reports published to **Power BI Report Server** (**PBRS**).

The ability to embed custom alert rules and the deep integration of data alerts with the Power BI mobile apps is a top reason to leverage dashboards in the Power BI service. Data alerts and email subscriptions to reports and dashboards in the Power BI service are reviewed in *Chapter 13, Creating Power BI Apps and Content Distribution*.

Dashboard(s) may not be necessary or appropriate for every Power BI app. If the primary use case is for users to explore and analyze data or if the desired visualizations can be developed within a report, then a dashboard may only add unnecessary time and complexity. However, if there's a need to integrate visuals from separate reports on a single canvas, or if a feature exclusive to dashboards such as data alert notifications is required, then dashboards can be an indispensable component of a solution.

The subsequent sections of this chapter describe many core dashboard features and capabilities, including dashboard tiles, mobile optimizations, and alternative sources, including Excel and paginated reports.

# Dashboard design

The design of dashboards and their relationship to both reports and other dashboards is critical to provide a consistent and robust package of information assets for an organization. Report authors and BI teams can use visual selection, layout, and supporting tiles to maximize the value and usability of dashboards.

Report authors are best positioned to produce initial drafts of dashboards based on their knowledge of the most utilized or valued report visuals. Ultimately, a well-designed dashboard delivers both at-a-glance visibility to the most important metrics for the consumer as well as accessibility to supporting and related details.

Particularly for executives and senior management, the dashboard should support all essential business questions and metrics, without requiring any user clicks.

If an executive or senior manager regularly has to access underlying reports, make filter selections on live pages, or utilize several dashboards to answer core questions, the architecture and scope of the Power BI dashboard should be reconsidered.

*Figure 9.1* shows an example dashboard organized by `Sales Territory Group`:

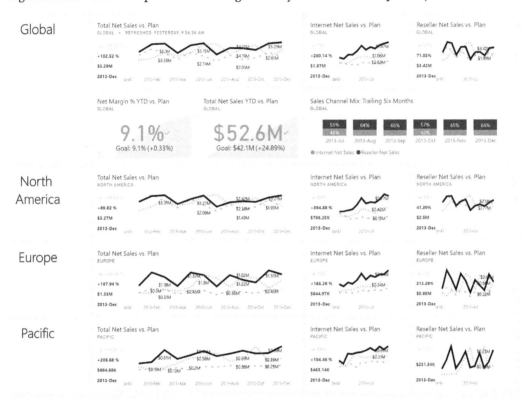

*Figure 9.1: Global sales dashboard*

In this example, three **Power KPI** custom visuals are displayed at a global level and also for each of the three sales territory groups. The Power KPI custom visual is chosen for these metrics as it presents greater detail and context than other related visuals, such as the standard KPI visual. For example, the **Total Net Sales vs. Plan** tile at the global level provides the actual value for the latest month, **$5.29M for 2013-Dec**, as well as the YOY growth for this month, **102.52%**, in addition to the ability to hover over points on the line to see individual values for particular months.

Each of the 12 Power KPI visualizations was created in the underlying report with the same basic configuration shown in *Figure 9.2*:

*Figure 9.2: Power KPI configuration*

The AdWorks Net Sales vs Plan Index measure was created using the following formula:

```
AdWorks Net Sales vs Plan Index = IF([AdWorks Sales Var to Plan %] >
0,1,2)
```

In this measure, the value 1 indicates that sales are greater than the plan, meaning that the goal has been met, while 2 indicates the opposite.

Distinct line styles are applied to each of the three lines displayed by the Power KPI visuals.

Solid, dotted, and dashed line styles are associated with the net sales, net sales plan, and net sales (PY) lines, respectively. The solid style of the net sales line and the actual KPI value helps to highlight this line relative to the two other less important lines. The distinct line styles are particularly helpful when the tile is being viewed in focus mode or the visual is being viewed with greater space in a report.

The user, such as the vice president of global sales, can quickly monitor overall performance relative to the plan via the KPI symbol icons in the top-left corner of the tiles (green caret up, red caret down). Additionally, two standard KPI visuals and a 100% stacked column chart were added specifically to the global level to deliver YTD sales and margin performance information as well as the recent mix of reseller and internet sales channels.

To view the details of a dashboard tile, such as the individual monthly values of one of the smaller tiles, a user can open the tile in **focus mode**. Focus mode fills the entire screen with a single visual and thus makes it easy to perceive differences in the length and shape of columns and lines, respectively. Focus mode can be accessed by hovering over the top-right corner of a dashboard tile and then clicking the more options ellipsis (three dots) menu. *Figure 9.3* shows the options available for the **Total Net Sales vs. Plan** dashboard tile:

*Figure 9.3: Dashboard tile options*

The 12 Power KPI dashboard tiles, combined with focus mode, provide the user with a simple interface for a robust suite of information. For a user at the global level of the sales organization, this level of detail may be more than sufficient for most scenarios, precluding the need to access other dashboards or reports.

The same three KPIs (**Total Net Sales vs. Plan**, **Reseller Net Sales vs. Plan**, **Internet Net Sales vs. Plan**) are also featured in separate, dedicated dashboards for each sales territory group. Simply clicking a tile on the **Global Sales** dashboard opens the **North America** dashboard, providing several additional visuals specific to this **Sales Territory Group**. Additionally, the **North America** sales dashboard follows the same structure as the **Global Sales** dashboard and thus contains sets of tiles dedicated to the United States and Canada.

If necessary, a third layer of dashboards could be created for each country within each sales territory group, thus enabling even greater dashboard navigation flexibility (for example, **Global | Europe | Germany**), with the same Power BI dataset being used for all reports and dashboards in the workspace. Row-level security roles described in *Chapter 5, Developing DAX Measures and Security Roles*, can ensure users do not have access to KPIs outside the scope of their assigned role. Additional details and considerations for planning multiple dashboards and creating links between dashboards and reports are described later in this chapter.

## Visual selection

Given that the primary purpose of dashboards is to provide an at-a-glance status of key business metrics, it's important to choose visuals that best fit this purpose. Too many dashboard tiles and more detailed tiles can detract from the dashboard's purpose.

Although any report visual can be pinned to a dashboard, only the visuals that either align with a corporate standard or that represent a critical insight or starting point should be represented on dashboards. Additionally, dense or relatively complex visuals, such as tables, matrices, and scatter charts, should rarely be pinned to dashboards. As per the **Global sales** dashboard, KPI visuals with built-in conditional formatting logic and supporting context are usually the best choices for dashboards given their intuitive nature and clear, concise visual display.

For example, if a table or matrix is considered to be the most valuable visual within a report, a KPI or card visual could be created targeting, but summarizing, the same business question. KPI and card visuals are more intuitive on dashboards and can be configured to provide single-click access to a report page with sufficient supporting details. Additionally, KPI or card visuals support data-driven alerts while tables, matrices, and scatter charts do not.

The visual in the top-left corner of a report page, the user's logical starting point for understanding the report, is often a good candidate to be pinned to a dashboard. Every report should have at least one summary-level visual (for example, card, KPI, or gauge) aligned to the primary business question or purpose of the report as this provides immediate context and understanding for the rest of the visuals on the report page.

Additionally, given that dashboards are limited to a single page (one canvas), visuals that provide supporting context, such as the standard KPI and the Power KPI custom visuals, should generally be favored over simple cards and gauges. The additional details provided by these visuals may not be visible in small dashboard tiles but are very valuable if additional space is allocated to the tile and when accessed in focus mode.

In *Figure 9.4*, the **Total Net Sales vs. Plan** KPI dashboard tile at the **Global** level is accessed in focus mode:

*Figure 9.4: Focus mode of dashboard tile – Power KPI custom visual*

Given the full pane of additional space provided by focus mode, the supporting metric lines of the Power KPI visual and the individual data points of those lines are exposed to the user.

Focus mode is also available in reports via the **Focus mode** icon in the corner of each report visual. This can certainly be useful as well but remember, as per *Table 1*, opening reports always results in new queries being generated. With the exception of streaming dataset tiles, dashboard tiles store the cached results of prior queries. Therefore, leveraging focus mode in dashboards, and dashboards in general (rather than reports), to address a significant portion of user analysis needs can reduce the query workload on the underlying dataset and resources (for example, the Power BI Premium capacity) and help ensure a more optimal user experience.

The Power KPI visual in the preceding example automatically adjusts to the additional space of focus mode to display data labels for all months. The distinct line styles (solid, dotted, and dot-dashed) of the actual net sales, sales plan, and prior year's sales measures are also more transparent to the user. Additionally, the three measures (net sales, sales plan, and prior year sales) and the two variances (actual versus plan and actual versus prior year) are displayed as tooltips via hovering over the data points.

These additional data details, formatting options, and other capabilities are not available in the standard KPI visual and therefore, although the Power KPI visual requires additional configuration, it ultimately delivers more analytical value and serves to reduce the need for users to search for additional visuals and reports to resolve their questions.

However, only the standard KPI, card, and gauge visuals are supported for data alerts so this could be a factor in favor of choosing the standard KPI visual. Thus, dashboard authors must carefully consider the respective tradeoffs between using custom and standard visuals. Additional details on configuring data alerts in the Power BI service are included in *Chapter 13*, *Creating Power BI Apps and Content Distribution*.

Moving on from the topic of visual selection for dashboards, another important consideration is dashboard layout.

# Layout

The position and size of dashboard tiles should align with the primary purpose or priorities of the dashboard and standard visual comprehension techniques.

For example, the **Total Net Sales vs. Plan** tile at the global level is the most important tile of the **Global Sales** dashboard. Therefore, this tile is positioned at the top-left corner of the dashboard and twice as much width is allocated to it relative to the **Reseller Sales** and **Reseller Sales** tiles.

Via this layout, the user can naturally start at the top left of the dashboard and navigate to the right (**Reseller** and **Internet Sales**) and down (**North America, Europe, and Pacific**) to add greater context to the **Total Net Sales vs. Plan** tile.

Another top consideration for layout is to maximize the available canvas space. Unlike reports, which can contain multiple pages and bookmarks, a dashboard is always a single canvas of tiles. Therefore, although a dashboard should not contain empty space, users should not have to scroll vertically or horizontally to view dashboard tiles.

Given the limited space, typically, a compromise must be made between larger tile sizes for more important visuals versus the inclusion or exclusion of tiles for less essential visuals. As one example, the trailing six-month channel mix tile (stacked column chart) in the **Global sales** dashboard could be removed, thereby allowing the **Internet Net Sales** and **Reseller Net Sales** tiles to be enlarged to the same size as the total net sales tile.

Given that space considerations are paramount to dashboard layouts, there are two techniques for adding additional space that we cover in the following two sections.

## Navigation pane

Additional space for dashboard tiles can be obtained by hiding the **navigation pane**. To toggle between hiding or showing the navigation pane, click the three lines above the **Home** icon (house symbol), as per *Figure 9.5*:

*Figure 9.5: Hidden navigation pane*

URL parameters can also be used to open dashboards with the navigation pane hidden by default. URL parameters are simply information contained within the query string of a URL. The query string is the portion of the URL that follows a question mark (?).

In the following example, a string of text from the question mark through to the `true` property has been appended to the end of the URL for a dashboard:

`https://app.powerbi.com/groups/abc123/dashboards/d8465?collapseNavigation=true`

This modified URL can be shared with users such that users of the dashboard aren't required to click on the navigation pane icon. The second technique for adding space is by using fullscreen mode, which we explore next.

## Fullscreen mode

Another technique for obtaining more space on dashboards is to utilize the fullscreen mode. The fullscreen mode can be accessed via the diagonal arrow icon in the top menu bar on the far right as per *Figure 9.6*:

*Figure 9.6: Fullscreen mode icon*

The fullscreen mode removes all of Chrome, including the navigation pane, Power BI menus, and the bars associated with the web browser (for example, tabs, address bar, and bookmarks bar). This view alone substantially increases the available space for larger tiles or a higher volume of dashboard tiles. If certain dashboard tiles are still not visible in the fullscreen mode, **Fit to Screen** and **Fit to width** options are available in the lower-right corner via the diagonal, outward-pointing arrows icon and the arrow and box icon respectively as shown in *Figure 9.7*:

Figure 9.7: Fit to Screen

The **Fit to Screen** option, exclusive to the fullscreen mode, is also referred to as TV mode and is frequently used to display Power BI dashboards on large monitors in corporate hallways. URL parameters can be used to access dashboards in fullscreen mode by default. In the following example, a text string from the question mark through to the `true` property has been appended to the URL of the dashboard such that the dashboard will be opened in fullscreen mode:

`https://app.powerbi.com/groups/abc123/dashboards/d8465?chromeless=true`

Ultimately, BI teams must align the layout of tiles with the use cases for the dashboard and the preferences of the stakeholders. For example, if a dashboard is almost exclusively going to be used in fullscreen mode, a layout that requires some level of scrolling to view all tiles outside of fullscreen mode may be acceptable.

Alternatively, if users regularly access the dashboard via the browser on their laptops or desktop monitors, they may not want to have to collapse the navigation pane or view the dashboard in fullscreen mode to see all the tiles. As the position and size of dashboard tiles can be easily adjusted via drag-and-drop handles within the Power BI service, multiple iterations of dashboard layouts can be quickly evaluated.

In addition to a dashboard's primary tiles, supporting tiles can be added to help organize and structure the dashboard.

## Supporting tiles

Supporting tiles refer to dashboard tiles used to help structure and organize the dashboard. For example, custom images and text boxes can be pinned from reports to dashboards to help structure and organize dashboards. However, shapes cannot be pinned from reports to dashboards.

While most dashboard tiles are pinned visualizations from an underlying Power BI report, additional tiles can be added via the **Add a tile** option in the Power BI service. These tiles, which can include web content, images, video, streaming data, and simple text boxes, serve to give the dashboard greater context and a more robust and finished design.

In the **Global sales** dashboard described earlier, four **Text box** tiles were used to distinguish the **Global** tiles from those associated with each of the three sales territory groups (**North America**, **Europe**, and **Pacific**). The position and size of the supporting tiles help to clarify the priority and scope of the dashboard.

For example, without any knowledge of the dashboard's title, the top position of the global tile and the additional space allocated to the global section of the dashboard help to confirm that the dashboard is primarily focused on the global level.

*Figure 9.8* shows the creation of the **Europe** text box tile, created by using the **Edit** menu and then choosing **Add a tile**.

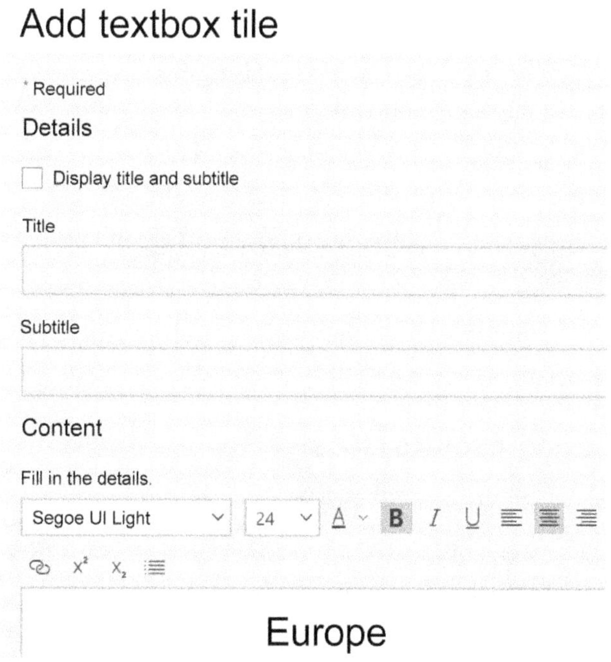

*Figure 9.8: Supporting text box tile*

Once created, the diagonal arrow handles in the lower-right corner of each supporting tile can be used to change the size of the tile. Additionally, a tile can be selected and dragged to a different location on the canvas.

# Dashboard architectures

For small projects and the early iterations of an agile BI project, a single dashboard and a few supporting reports may be sufficient. For many users, however, multiple dashboards with their own distinct reports are required. Both of these approaches, a single dashboard and multiple dashboards, are geared toward a specific stakeholder or group of consumers, such as the vice president of sales.

Although these different methodologies may meet the needs of their intended users, a potential risk is a lack of coordination across teams. For example, business units might reference distinct metrics included in their dashboard and these metrics may not be included in the dashboards of senior managers or other business units.

To promote greater consistency and coordination across groups of users, BI teams can pursue an integrated, organizational dashboard architecture. In this approach, the same metrics and KPIs considered strategic for the organization are available in multiple dashboards specific to levels in an organizational hierarchy or distinct business units.

The **Global Sales** dashboard, described earlier in this chapter, represents this methodology as separate dashboards specific to individual sales territory groups including the same KPIs as the global dashboard. This approach ensures that dashboard tiles are relevant to the specific users and make it possible to analyze up and down a natural organizational hierarchy. Additionally, a common dashboard layout with integrated KPIs makes Power BI solutions much easier to manage with limited BI resources.

In this section, we explore the single-dashboard, multi-dashboard, and organizational dashboard architectures.

## Single-dashboard architecture

A single-dashboard architecture is just that, a single dashboard supporting one or more reports.

In *Figure 9.9*, a single dashboard focused on **Reseller Sales** contains tiles representing report visuals from four separate Power BI reports:

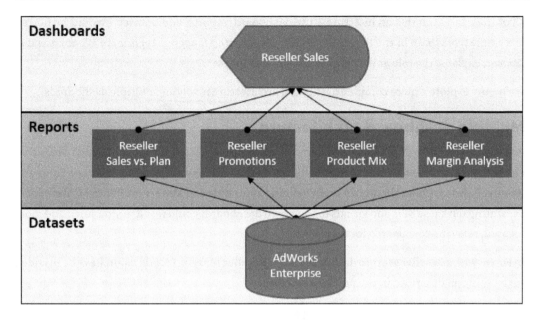

*Figure 9.9: Single-dashboard architecture*

By default, a user selection on any of the dashboard tiles opens the report page of the underlying report. For example, a dashboard tile reflecting the percentage of bike sales versus other product categories would be linked to the **Reseller Product Mix** report and the specific page of this report containing the source visual.

Each Power BI report is based on a Live connection to the **AdWorks Enterprise** dataset. As described in the *Live connections to Power BI datasets* section in *Chapter 6, Planning Power BI Reports*, leveraging this feature avoids the duplication of datasets since each Power BI Desktop report file (.pbix) only contains the visualization layer (for example, visuals and formatting).

Although relatively simple to build and support, the single **Reseller Sales** dashboard architecture provides both a summary of a diverse set of essential metrics and visuals (represented as dashboard tiles) as well as an entry point to reports containing the details supporting this dashboard. As described in the previous three chapters, Power BI reports could include multiple report pages of visuals related to the dashboard and leverage interactive features, such as slicers and bookmarks, to enable users to explore these reports more easily.

All of the content in this architecture – the dashboard, reports, and dataset – would be hosted in a single workspace in the Power BI service. *Chapter 10, Managing Application Workspaces and Content*, explains the role and configuration of workspaces.

We'll now explore a more complex dashboard architecture involving multiple dashboards.

## Multiple-dashboard architecture

Power BI solutions will often need to summarize multiple related topics or business areas that either require or benefit from having their own dashboard. As one example, **Internet Sales** and **Reseller Sales** may have slightly different definitions for **KPIs** and also serve different stakeholders. Separating out these KPIs and visuals to their own dashboards could result in simplified and more focused, relevant dashboards for their users.

In *Figure 9.10*, a **Reseller Margin** dashboard and a **Reseller Margin Trends** report have been added to the solution described in the previous section:

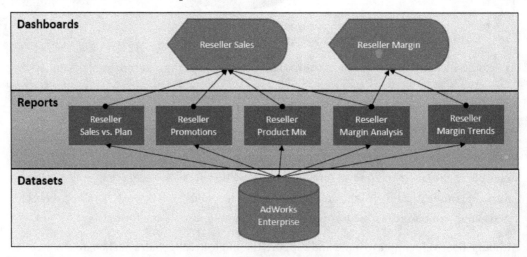

*Figure 9.10: Multiple-dashboard architecture*

In this design, a visual from the **Reseller Margin Analysis** report has been pinned to both the **Reseller Sales** and the **Reseller Margin** dashboards, as per the preceding diagram.

This is not required but is recommended for usability such that users can maintain context as they navigate between both dashboards. The new **Reseller Margin Trends** report, built via a Live connection to the published **AdWorks Enterprise** dataset, exclusively supports the **Reseller Margin** dashboard.

This architecture extends the scope of the solution to provide greater visibility to margin metrics and trends not available via the single dashboard. For example, rather than navigating through the multiple pages of the two reseller margin reports (**Reseller Margin Analysis and Reseller Margin Trends**), users could access the **Reseller Margin** dashboard for a more simplified dashboard experience. In addition to user convenience and the limited scope of a single dashboard, utilizing dashboards and their cached data helps to reduce the workload on the underlying dataset and resources.

Like the single dashboard architecture, all content (dashboards, reports, and datasets) from this multi-dashboard architecture is included in the same workspace in the Power BI service. Given this common workspace, each dashboard tile can be linked to a report or dashboard in the same workspace. For example, a margin-related tile on the sales dashboard could be linked to the margin dashboard rather than the default source report. The *Dashboard tiles* section later in this chapter contains an example of configuring custom links.

The multiple dashboard architecture described in this section focused on a specific business process, Reseller Sales. Even more complex dashboard architectures can be created when considering how to architect dashboards to service an entire organization.

# Organizational dashboard architecture

Organizational dashboard architectures are multiple-dashboard architectures designed by considering the reporting needs of an entire organization. Organizational dashboards tend to mirror the organizational hierarchy of a business in terms of its business units or departments.

In *Figure 9.11*, four dashboards contain corporate KPIs at the global level and for the three sales territory groups:

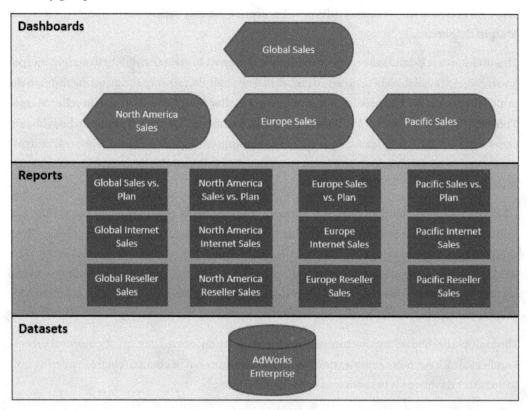

*Figure 9.11: Organizational dashboard architecture*

Since the same KPIs or metrics are included in each of the four dashboards, users of these dashboards are able to remain aligned with the same goals and can more clearly share their findings and results across teams and levels in the organization. From the perspective of an executive at the global level, the **Global Sales** dashboard provides an intuitive entry point into the individual sales territory groups and potentially further layers, if necessary.

For example, an executive could start out at the **Global Sales** dashboard and optionally click a tile related to European sales in order to access the **Europe Sales** dashboard and obtain greater detail such as the sales performance of Germany, France, and the United Kingdom. From there, even greater levels of detail from the underlying Europe reports could be accessed by clicking on tiles from the **Europe Sales** dashboard.

In *Figure 9.12*, the **Europe Sales** dashboard follows the design (layout and visual selection) of the **Global Sales** dashboard:

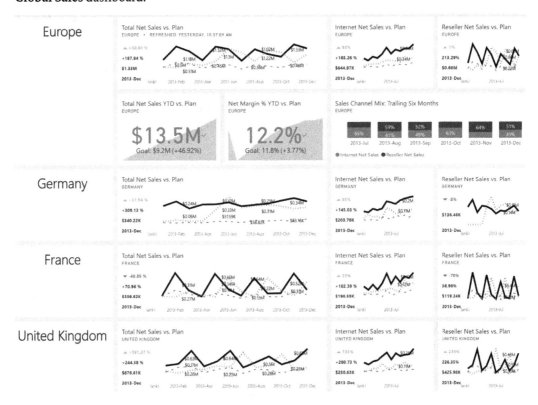

*Figure 9.12: Europe sales dashboard*

The three tiles aligned at the top of the **Europe Sales** dashboard are exactly the same tiles as presented on the **Global Sales** dashboard. The only difference is that the tiles are filtered for Europe only.

The three tiles representing the second row of the Global and **Europe Sales** dashboard (**Net Sales YTD vs. Plan, Net Margin % YTD vs. Plan, and Sales Channel Mix**) do not have to be the same across the dashboards since these are not the approved KPIs for the organization. Maintaining a 1:1 match in terms of tiles across the dashboards can be beneficial as this allows users to navigate between dashboards for further analysis of any given tile. However, in many scenarios, there are metrics or visuals that are more pertinent to the given business unit and users may rarely need to analyze non-KPIs across multiple dashboards.

As per *Figure 9.11*, a set of three dedicated European sales reports support the **Europe Sales** dashboard. The pages of these reports may provide sufficient detail or, depending on the organizational structure and requirements, an additional layer of dashboards dedicated to each sales territory country could be added.

Other forms of the organizational dashboard architecture include dedicated dashboards by product group, such as bikes, clothing, and accessories in the case of Adventure Works. Ultimately, these implementations serve to align the different business units on common corporate goals while also providing a rich set of insights relevant to each business unit or organizational level.

All of the dashboard architectures we have shown thus far have involved a single dataset. We next explore the case where multiple datasets underlie the reports and dashboards for a solution.

## Multiple datasets

The reports and dashboards that comprise a solution may be based on a single dataset or multiple datasets.

A single dataset, **AdWorks Enterprise**, was utilized to support all reports and dashboards in each of the three dashboard architectures reviewed in the previous sections. This level of integration is not technically necessary and there are valid scenarios where multiple datasets could be used in the same Power BI solution and even by the same dashboard.

Multiple datasets can quickly create problems due to separate data refresh processes, separate data source dependencies, and separate data security rules. Additionally, version control issues can arise as each dataset may include differences in the structure and definitions of tables common to both datasets. Moreover, the integration of visuals from separate datasets on a single dashboard may be insufficient to support analytical requirements.

One use case for multiple datasets is that an organization may not have a particular data source, such as an Oracle database, integrated into its data warehouse system (for example, Teradata) but still wishes to provide essential visualizations of this data in Power BI in order to supplement other reports and dashboards. In this scenario, a Power BI dataset could be built against the Oracle database, and reports utilizing this dedicated dataset could then support one or multiple dashboards. Once the necessary data warehouse integration is completed, the dedicated dataset could be retired and its reporting replaced with new reports based on an Analysis Services model (which uses Teradata as its source) that supports other Power BI reporting content for the organization.

In other scenarios, a dataset is chosen (or was already implemented) for one or a few business processes that aren't closely related to other business processes. For example, one dataset was built to include sales and marketing-related data, while a separate dataset includes inventory and shipment data. The reasoning for this isolation may have been that the users of each dataset don't need access to the other dataset or that a large, integrated dataset would be complex to develop and use. Alternatively, if Power BI Premium capacity is not available and Power BI datasets are used, the 1 GB file limit could force a team to utilize separate Power BI files to store the required data.

In general, corporate BI projects should limit the use of multiple datasets for the reasons described and the long-term value of a centralized data store. However, in environments lacking a data warehouse and other scalable resources, such as an Analysis Services instance or Power BI Premium capacity, multiple datasets can be considered an option and potentially the only option to support one or multiple dashboards in the same Power BI solution.

We'll now move on from dashboard architectures to take a closer look at working with dashboard tiles.

# Dashboard tiles

Most dashboard tiles are created in the Power BI service by pinning a visual in a report to a new or existing dashboard in the same workspace. However, dashboard tiles can also be created by adding a tile directly from the dashboard itself and by pinning from an Excel workbook or Report Server report.

With a report open in the Power BI service, hovering over the top-right corner of a visual exposes the **Pin visual** icon, as shown in *Figure 9.13*:

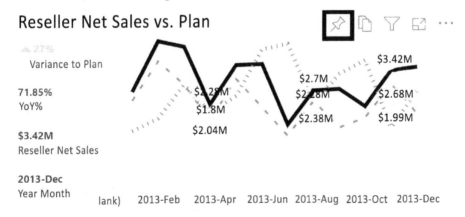

*Figure 9.13: Pin visual icon for report visual*

Once pinned to the dashboard, several options are available for configuring tiles depending on the type of tile and the content it contains. In the Global and **Europe Sales** dashboards described previously, a subtitle was added to each tile (for example, France) and custom links were applied to allow direct navigation from the Global dashboard to the Europe dashboard.

In addition, for the top, left-most visual, the **Display last refresh time** setting was enabled. This setting displays the last time the dataset completed a successful refresh. Such information is often critical to business users so that they understand how current the data is that they are viewing. For example, if a nightly refresh failed and users are looking for data that includes yesterday's data, knowing the last refresh time helps the users understand that there was an issue.

Dashboard tiles can be thought of as snapshots of a specific visual and filter context. When a visual is pinned from a report to a dashboard, the specific filter context (for example, slicers or page-level filters), visualization, and formatting at that time are captured by the dashboard. Subsequent changes to the report, such as a modified filter or a different visualization type, are not reflected by the dashboard tile. The dashboard tile will, however, continue to reflect the latest data refreshes of the underlying dataset. Additionally, by default, the dashboard tile will continue to be linked to the report from which the visual was pinned.

To maintain the synchronization between report visuals and dashboard tiles, changes to reports that impact the pinned visuals require the updated report visual to be pinned again. The existing dashboard tile, reflecting the original filter context and visualization, can be deleted.

One exception to the snapshot behavior of dashboard tiles is live report pages. When an entire report page is pinned as a single tile to a dashboard, any changes to the report page are automatically reflected on the dashboard as well. The *Live report pages* section later in this chapter includes additional details and an example.

Let's now take a deeper look at some of the additional functionality of dashboard tiles.

## Tile details and custom links

By default, pinned dashboard tiles link to the report page from which the tile was pinned. Custom links allow this default behavior to be changed to allow linking dashboard tiles to any valid URL.

Custom links are an important component of multi-dashboard architectures, and particularly the organizational dashboard architecture described previously.

As mentioned, in the absence of custom links, clicking a dashboard tile opens the report page from which the visual was pinned to the dashboard. Custom links allow BI teams to take control of the navigation experience and enable users to navigate directly to another dashboard with related information or even to an external site, such as a team site on SharePoint Online.

Tile details can be accessed by hovering over the top-right corner of a dashboard tile, clicking the ellipsis, and then selecting **Edit details**. *Figure 9.14* shows the **Tile details** pane where a **Subtitle** (**Europe**) is added to one of the **Total Net Sales vs. Plan** KPI tiles:

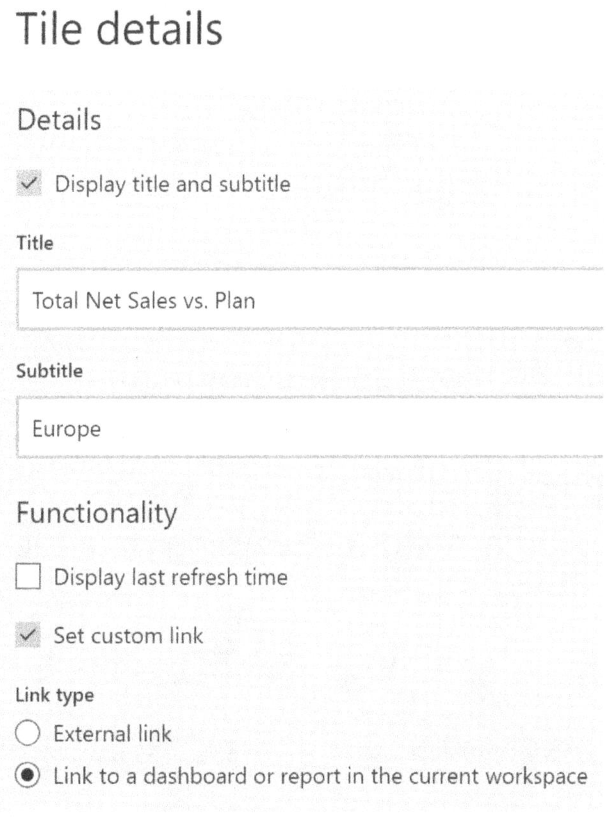

## Tile details

### Details

☑ Display title and subtitle

Title

Total Net Sales vs. Plan

Subtitle

Europe

### Functionality

☐ Display last refresh time

☑ Set custom link

Link type

◯ External link

⦿ Link to a dashboard or report in the current workspace

*Figure 9.14: Tile details*

Additionally, as shown in *Figure 9.14*, the **Set custom link** property is enabled, and the **Europe Sales** dashboard is selected for the target of the link. Clicking **Apply** at the bottom of the dialog (not included in *Figure 9.14*) confirms the selection. Different options are available in the **Tile Details** window for tiles added directly on the dashboard (not pinned), such as text boxes and images.

We next take a look at a unique aspect of dashboards, the ability to support streaming data.

## Real-time data tiles

Real-time data tiles allow streaming data from **Internet of Things (IoT)** devices and other real-time sources to be included in a dashboard. IoT is a term that refers to physical objects with sensors that connect and exchange data with other systems or devices. For example, a car battery that reports charge levels every few seconds that can then be viewed on a phone via an app.

Real-time data tiles can be added to dashboards using the **Edit** and then **Add a tile** links. One of the options when adding a tile is an option for **Custom Streaming Data** as shown in *Figure 9.15*:

REAL-TIME DATA

Custom Streaming
Data

*Figure 9.15: Custom Streaming Data tile*

Choosing this option provides the opportunity to use a current streaming dataset or add a streaming dataset as shown in *Figure 9.16*:

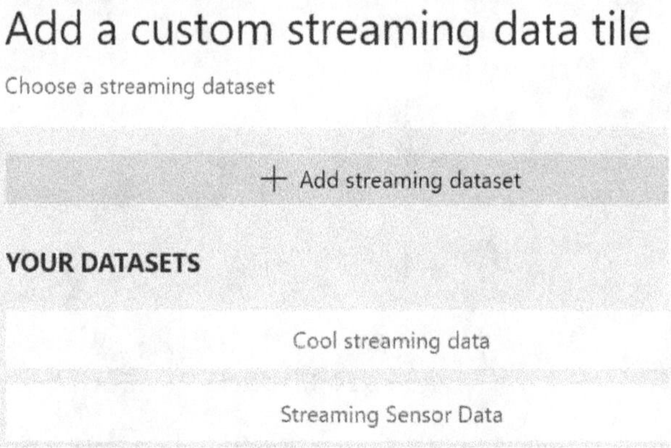

# Add a custom streaming data tile

Choose a streaming dataset

+ Add streaming dataset

**YOUR DATASETS**

Cool streaming data

Streaming Sensor Data

*Figure 9.16: Add a custom streaming data tile*

New streaming datasets can come from three sources, **API**, **Azure Stream**, and **PubNub** as shown in *Figure 9.17*:

New streaming dataset

Choose the source of your data

| API | AZURE STREAM | PUBNUB |

*Figure 9.17: Sources for new streaming datasets*

The **API** option refers to the ability of the Power BI REST API to post real-time data to a streaming dataset, referred to as **Push Datasets** in the Power BI REST API documentation. This option allows organizations to create their own applications that stream data to Power BI.

The **Azure Stream** option refers to the ability of **Azure Stream Analytics** to use Power BI as an output. **Azure Stream Analytics** is an event processing and real-time analytics engine designed to process and analyze streaming data. Integration with Azure Machine Learning allows patterns and relationships to be identified and used to trigger actions, alerts, and workflows. Business use cases for **Azure Stream Analytics** include:

- Analysis of real-time telemetry from IoT devices
- Geospatial analytics for fleet/vehicle management
- Analyzing web logs and clickstreams
- Inventory and anomaly detection for **Point of Sale (PoS)** systems
- Monitoring and predictive maintenance of remote systems

As **Azure Stream Analytics** finds patterns, these events or anomalies can be streamed in real time to a Power BI dashboard tile.

Finally, the **PubNub** option provides integration options with the third-party company PubNub. PubNub is an API platform for developers building real-time applications such as live events, online chat, remote IoT control, and geolocation.

In *Figure 9.18*, the ambient temperature from a sample PubNub streaming data source is plotted in real time:

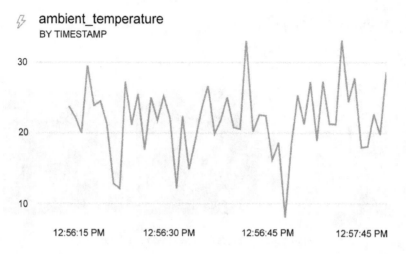

*Figure 9.18: Streaming data tile*

Next, we take a look at standardizing the look and feel of dashboards using themes.

# Dashboard themes

Similar to how Power BI Desktop supports themes for reports, as covered in the *Visualizations best practices* section of *Chapter 6, Planning Power BI Reports*, dashboards also support themes.

In *Figure 9.19*, the **Dashboard theme** dialog has been accessed by choosing **Edit** and then **Dashboard theme** from the dashboard ribbon:

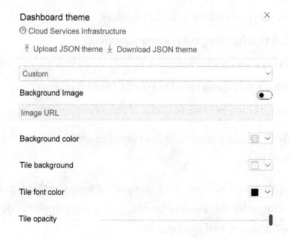

*Figure 9.19: Streaming data tile*

Three default themes, **Light**, **Dark**, and **Color-blind friendly**, are available as well as the **Custom** option shown in *Figure 9.19*.

Themes can be downloaded as JSON files, modified and uploaded back to the Power BI service. The following JSON code is an example of a Power BI dashboard theme file:

```
{
    "name":"b33fd847240881ee3107",
    "foreground":"#FFFFFF",
    "background":"#afb5b6",
    "dataColors":[
            "#01B8AA","#374649","#FD625E","#F2C80F",
            "#5F6B6D","#8AD4EB","#FE9666","#A66999"
            ],
    "tiles":{"background":"#808080","color":"#FFFFFF","opacity":1},
    "visualStyles":
        {"*":{"*":{"*":[
                {"color":{"solid":{"color":"#FFFFFF"}}},
                {"labelColor":{"solid":{"color":"#FFFFFF"}}}
                    ]}}},
    "backgroundImage":null
}
```

We now turn our attention to an additional source for dashboard tiles, paginated reports.

# Paginated reports

**SQL Server Reporting Services (SSRS)** 2016, and later versions, as well as PBRS, support integration with the Power BI service. Once integration is configured between the on-premises report server and the Power BI tenant, certain SSRS report items, such as charts and maps, can be pinned to Power BI dashboards.

Additionally, a reporting services subscription is automatically created for pinned report items, allowing report server administrators to manage the data refresh schedule of the dashboard tile. Since the source of the dashboard tile is a report published to a reporting services instance, the reporting services instance must initiate updates to the tile.

In *Figure 9.20*, showing an image of **Report Server Configuration Manager**, Power BI Report Server has been configured for **Power BI Integration:**

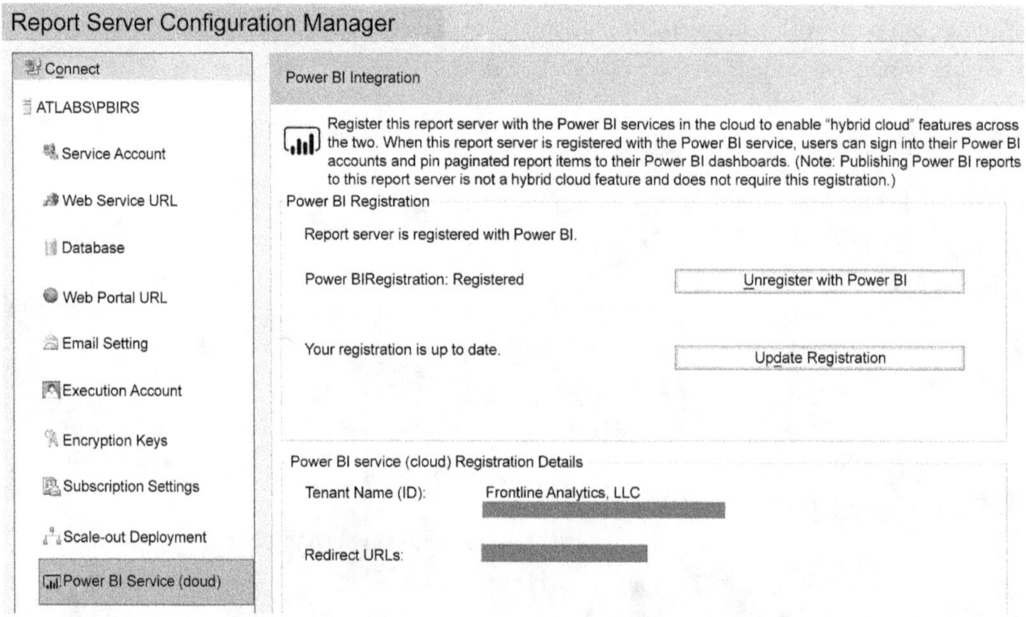

*Figure 9.20: Power BI integration with Power BI Report Server*

In *Figure 9.20*, the PBRS instance is configured for integration with the Power BI service. The same Power BI integration is available for SSRS 2016 and later via the same interface in **Report Server Configuration Manager**. The following documentation includes all the requirements for integration with the Power BI service as well as technical details on the integration and pinning process: http://bit.ly/2CnCkOU.

As described in *Chapter 12, Deploying Paginated Reports*, Power BI Report Server includes all the functionality of SSRS, including paginated (RDL) reports, report subscriptions, folder security, and the reporting services web portal. Power BI Report Server, however, provides several additional features and benefits, with the ability to view and interact with Power BI reports (PBIX files) topping this list.

In *Figure 9.21*, a paginated (RDL) report containing a map is open:

*Figure 9.21: Pin to Power BI icon in Power BI Report Server*

Selecting the **Pin to Power BI Dashboard** icon in the top-right window prompts the user to select the specific report item to pin. In this report, the map is selected, and this launches the dialog shown in *Figure 9.22* for identifying the dashboard in the Power BI service as well as defining the refresh schedule of the tile:

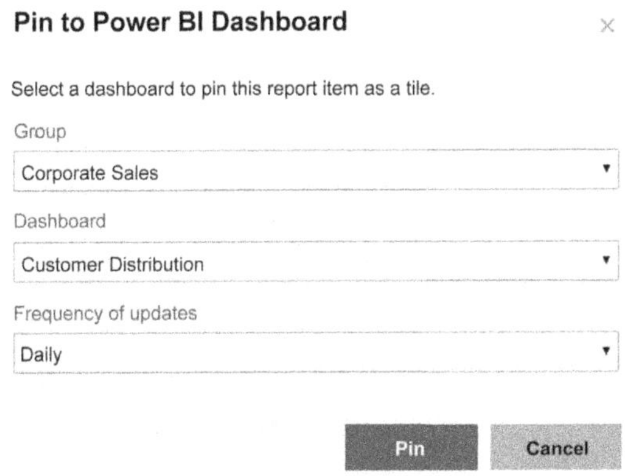

*Figure 9.22: Pin paginated report visual to Power BI dashboard*

In this example, the map is pinned to the **Customer Distribution** dashboard in the **Corporate Sales** app workspace as shown in *Figure 9.23*. The **Daily, Hourly,** and **Weekly** tile refreshes can be configured via the **Frequency of updates** drop-down menu and this setting defines the report subscription supporting the tile. Report subscriptions can be managed via the **My Subscriptions** (**Settings | My Subscriptions**) interface on the Reporting Services web portal.

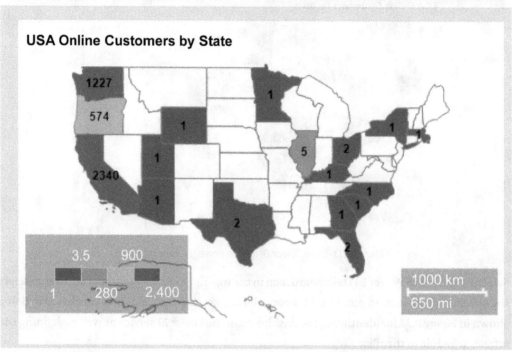

*Figure 9.23: Paginated report item as Power BI dashboard tile*

Unlike visuals from Power BI reports, which can only be pinned to dashboards in the workspace of the given report, paginated report items can be pinned to any dashboard in any workspace.

By default, the paginated report dashboard tile is linked back to the on-premises report server report. This link, as well as the title and subtitle for the tile, can be modified via the **Tile details** window just like other dashboard tiles.

Additional information on Power BI Report Server, including the deployment and scheduled refresh of Power BI reports, is included in *Chapter 12, Deploying Paginated Reports*.

# Excel workbooks

Excel workbooks containing tables and/or data models can be connected to Power BI. Once connected, users can pin Excel ranges and objects, such as pivot tables and charts. Scheduled data refreshes can be configured in the Power BI service for Excel workbooks containing data models. However, given the size limitations of Excel data models as well as the additional capabilities of Power BI reports, such as custom visuals, role security, and advanced analytics, it's generally recommended to migrate Excel data models to Power BI datasets (PBIX files).

As per *Figure 9.24*, the Power BI content contained in an Excel workbook can be imported to a Power BI Desktop file:

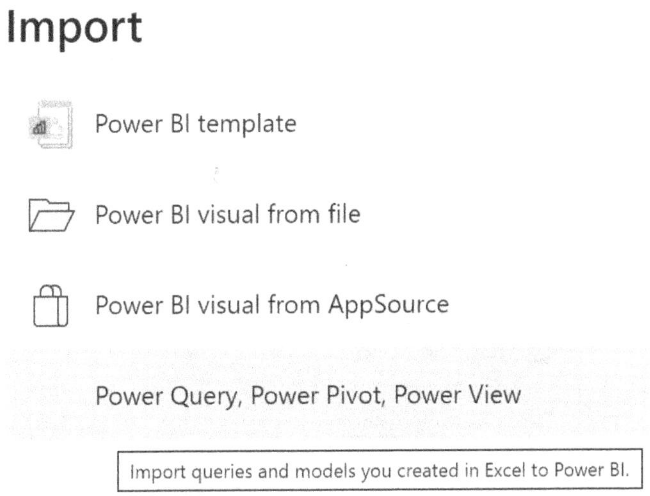

# Import

  Power BI template

  Power BI visual from file

  Power BI visual from AppSource

  Power Query, Power Pivot, Power View

   Import queries and models you created in Excel to Power BI.

*Figure 9.24: Import Excel queries and models to Power BI*

The migration process includes the data retrieval M queries, data model tables and relationships, DAX measures, and even any Power View report pages contained in the source workbook.

Only when Excel reports are deeply dependent on Excel-specific functionality, such as worksheet formulas and customized conditional formatting rules, should the model not be migrated to Power BI. Power BI Desktop's enhanced table and matrix visuals and conditional formatting options now support many of the most common Excel report use cases. Therefore, only limited effort is required to develop an equivalent Power BI Desktop relative to Excel.

In circumstances where it is not possible to migrate the Excel file to Power BI Desktop, the Excel file can be connected to Power BI using the **Get data** feature of the Power BI service. Once connected, Excel ranges, pivot tables, and charts can be pinned to Power BI dashboards. *Figure 9.25* shows a pivot table being pinned to the **Customer Distribution** dashboard in the **Corporate Sales** workspace:

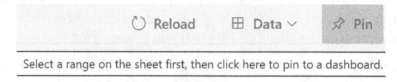

Select a range on the sheet first, then click here to pin to a dashboard.

*Figure 9.25: Pin Excel content to Power BI dashboard*

The pinning interface is the same as for Power BI report visuals, allowing the choice of pinning to an existing dashboard or a new dashboard as shown in *Figure 9.26*:

*Figure 9.26: Pin to dashboard*

Just like reporting services (SSRS and PBRS) report items, Excel content can also be pinned to any dashboard in any workspace in the Power BI service. Also, like reporting services dashboard tiles, the details of dashboard tiles containing Excel content can be configured, including the title, subtitle, and a custom link. Moreover, Excel and reporting services dashboard tiles can also be included in mobile dashboard layouts. The *Mobile-optimized dashboards* section later in this chapter describes this feature.

Although Excel and SSRS report content is not designed to be as visually engaging as Power BI visuals, the ability to leverage these common reporting tools and consolidate their distinct content on the same dashboard is a unique capability of Power BI.

The details of developing reporting services and Excel-based content as complements to a Power BI solution are beyond the scope of this chapter. However, several examples of these integrations, as well as considerations in choosing among the three tools, are included in *Microsoft Power BI Cookbook Second Edition* (`https://www.packtpub.com/product/microsoft-power-bi-cookbook-second-edition/9781801813044`).

# Live report pages

Live report pages allow entire report pages to be pinned to dashboards. This can be useful in certain situations where the interactivity of reports is desired along with the consolidation benefits of dashboards.

For some users, the self-service data exploration experience provided within Power BI report pages is the most valuable use case of Power BI content. Although a dashboard of tiles may initiate or contribute to an analysis, these users often have more complex and unpredictable analytical needs such that greater flexibility is required. Additionally, these users are generally much more comfortable and experienced in interacting with Power BI content, such as modifying slicer selections and drilling up and down through hierarchies.

To provide both the self-service experience of a report page as well as the consolidation benefits of a dashboard, an entire report page can be pinned as a single tile to a dashboard. In _Figure 9.27_, showing a dashboard for the United States, a live report page of eight visuals has been pinned to supplement the corporate standard KPI tiles:

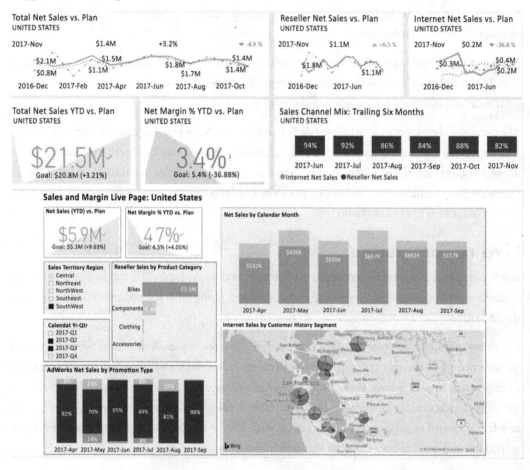

Figure 9.27: Dashboard with live report page

In the dashboard shown in _Figure 9.27_, the user can leverage the robust filtering options on the sales and margin live page to explore the dataset while maintaining visibility to standard metrics via the top six tiles. In _Figure 9.27_, the user has filtered on the **Southwest** sales territory region and also selected the **Bikes** product category via the bar chart. These selections impact the other five visuals on the page via either highlighting, in the case of the **Net Sales by Calendar Month** column chart, or filtering, in the case of the other four visuals. Filter selections on the live page do not, however, impact the dashboard tiles outside of the live page.

Like standard dashboard tiles, live page tiles are moveable on the canvas and configurable via the **Tile details** window. However, custom links cannot be configured for live report pages. In the United States dashboard example shown in *Figure 9.27*, the report page itself included a text box with a title and thus the display title and subtitle property of the dashboard tile were disabled.

Unlike the snapshot behavior of normal dashboard tiles, any saved changes to the report containing the live report page, such as a different filter condition, are automatically reflected by the live page tile on the dashboard. This automatic synchronization avoids the need to delete dashboard tiles reflecting the original state of the report and re-pinning visuals to reflect changes in the source report.

To pin an entire report page to a dashboard, when viewing or editing a report in the Power BI service, click the **More options** ellipses (**...**) menu in the report header and choose **Pin to a dashboard**. Choosing the **Pin to a dashboard** option generates the dialog shown in *Figure 9.28*:

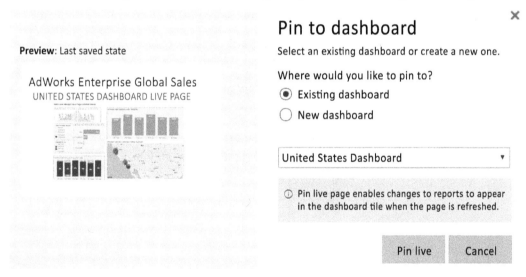

*Figure 9.28: Pin report page to a dashboard*

Live report page tiles can also be included in mobile-optimized views of dashboards. However, given their size, live pages are generally more valuable in larger form factors and with fullscreen mode.

# Mobile-optimized dashboards

Just like the mobile layout view in Power BI Desktop described in *Chapter 8, Applying Advanced Analytics*, the Power BI service provides a **Mobile layout** to customize a mobile-optimized layout for dashboards. With a **Mobile layout** configured for a dashboard, the specific tiles, sizes, and order of tiles defined for the **Mobile layout** are presented to a user when the dashboard is accessed via the Power BI mobile app.

The **Mobile layout** is accessed via the drop-down **Edit** menu in the dashboard header as shown in *Figure 9.29*:

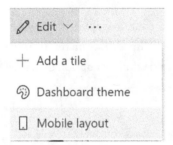

*Figure 9.29: Dashboard phone view*

The same drag and resize options available in the mobile layout for Power BI Desktop are also available for the dashboard. In *Figure 9.30*, the most important tiles from the **Global Sales** dashboard are positioned at the top and less important tiles are unpinned:

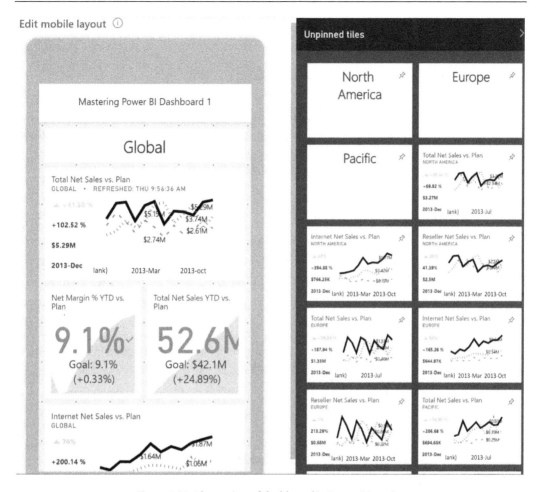

*Figure 9.30: Phone view of dashboard in Power BI service*

Power BI saves the mobile layout automatically and the defined mobile layout becomes the new default view for phones accessing the dashboard. However, the user can still turn their phone sideways to view the dashboard in the standard web view.

The subtitles applied to the dashboard tiles are particularly valuable in mobile layout. In the standard web view, the four supporting tiles with text (**Global**, **North America**, **Europe**, and **Pacific**) make it easy to determine the scope of each tile. These text box tiles are likely not, however, desired in **Mobile layout** and thus the subtitles convey the scope of each tile.

## Summary

This chapter demonstrated how dashboards are planned and developed as part of a large, integrated corporate BI solution. All essential features and processes of Power BI dashboards were highlighted, including the configuration of dashboard tiles, their links to other dashboards and reports, and mobile-optimized dashboards. Additionally, the unique capability of dashboards to integrate real-time data as well as their ability to include content from reporting services reports and Excel workbooks were reviewed.

The next chapter transitions from the development of Power BI content to the management of Power BI content. This includes the application of version control to Power BI Desktop files and the migration of content across test and production environments using workspaces.

## Join our community on Discord

Join our community's Discord space for discussions with the author and other readers:
`https://discord.gg/q6BPbHEPXp`

# 10
# Managing Workspaces and Content

The preceding six chapters have focused on the design and development of Power BI datasets, reports, and dashboards. While the creation of impactful and sustainable content is essential, this chapter reviews the processes and features IT organizations can leverage to manage and govern this content through project life cycles and ongoing operational support.

These features include the planning and use of workspaces in the Power BI service, staged deployments between test and production environments, and maintaining version control of Power BI Desktop files. Additional features and practices highlighted in this chapter include data classification for dashboards, documenting Power BI datasets, and utilizing the Power BI REST API to automate and manage common processes.

In this chapter, we will review the following topics:

- Workspaces
- Staged deployments
- Dashboard data classifications
- Version control
- Metadata management
- Metadata reporting

We'll first take a look at one of the fundamental building blocks of Power BI content, workspaces.

# Workspaces

**Workspaces** are containers in the Power BI service of related content (reports, dashboards, and scorecards) as well as datasets. As discussed in the *Power BI licenses* section of *Chapter 1, Planning Power BI Projects*, members of workspaces are able to create and test content, such as new dashboards and changes to reports, without impacting the content being accessed by users outside of the workspace.

Once the new or revised content in the workspace is deemed ready for consumption, the workspace is published or updated as a Power BI **app**. Apps are collections of dashboards, reports, and datasets and are described in detail in *Chapter 13, Creating Power BI Apps and Content Distribution*.

> *"We intend workspaces just for creation...it's the place where content gets created in Power BI."*
>
> *— Ajay Anandan, Senior Program Manager.*

In addition to the default isolation or staging between content creation (workspaces) and content consumption (apps), BI teams can utilize multiple workspaces to stage their deployments as per the *Staged deployments* section later in this chapter. For example, reports and dashboards can be initially created in a development workspace, evaluated against requirements in a test workspace, and finally deployed to a production workspace.

The production workspace supports the app. If large numbers of business users access the Power BI content via the app, the production workspace could be assigned to Power BI Premium capacity to provide dependable performance and the flexibility to scale resources according to the needs of the workload.

*Chapter 15, Building Enterprise BI with Power BI Premium*, provides details on the features and benefits of Power BI Premium. This includes the cost advantage of capacity-based pricing versus per-user licensing for large-scale deployments, managing Premium capacities (hardware), such as scaling up or out, and assigning workspaces to Premium capacities.

Additional capabilities exclusive to content stored in Premium capacity, such as larger Power BI datasets, more frequent scheduled data refreshes (for example, every 30 minutes), deployment pipelines, scorecards, and goals, are also described in *Chapter 15, Building Enterprise BI with Power BI Premium*.

*Figure 10.1* depicts the four-step process showing the essential role of workspaces in the life cycle of Power BI content:

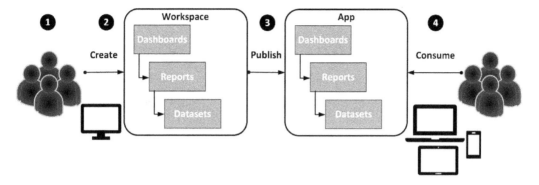

*Figure 10.1: Workspaces and apps*

1. A Power BI Pro user creates a workspace and adds other Power BI Pro users as members with edit rights. Workspaces are created in the Power BI service by clicking the **Workspaces** option in the left navigation menu and then clicking the **Create a workspace** button at the bottom of the fly-out panel. Additional users can also be added as Admin users. Only Admins can add members with edit rights to a workspace as explained in the *Workspace roles and rights* section of this chapter.

2. The members of the workspace publish reports to the workspace and create dashboards in the workspace.

3. All content or a subset of the content in the workspace is published as a Power BI app.

4. Users or groups of users access content in the published app from any device.

All users within the workspace need a Power BI Pro license. All users consuming the published Power BI app also need a Power BI Pro license unless the workspace is assigned to Power BI Premium capacity. If the workspace is assigned to Power BI Premium capacity, users with Power BI (free) licenses and, optionally, external guest users from outside the organization with free licenses can read or consume the Power BI app.

In small team scenarios (5–15 users) where maximum self-service flexibility is needed, all users can be assigned Pro or PPU licenses and collaborate on content within the workspace. This approach negates the isolation benefit of workspaces from apps but provides immediate visibility to the latest versions of the content. Additionally, Power BI users within the workspace can create their own Power BI and Excel reports based on connections to the published dataset in the workspace.

Opening a workspace within the Power BI service presents an interface similar to that shown in *Figure 10.2*:

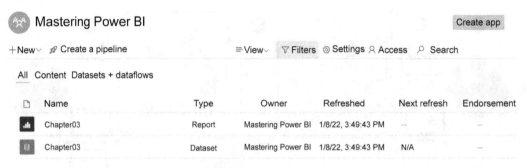

Figure 10.2: Workspace

As shown in *Figure 10.2*, the workspace dialog presents a header for accessing the workspace's **Settings** and controlling **Access**, as well as the ability to create or update an associated app. Furthermore, content within the workspace such as dashboards, reports, and datasets are shown.

It is highly recommended that the creation of workspaces be controlled by enterprise BI and IT teams. Workspace creation can be restricted to specific users or groups of users via tenant settings as discussed in *Chapter 14, Administering Power BI for an Organization*. A simple workflow process can govern the workspace creation process as part of the overall Power BI project planning and execution.

In addition to serving as containers of content, workspaces also provide a logical security context where specific users and groups can be provided different roles and rights within the workspace.

## Workspace roles and rights

Workspace roles are used to provide access to all content within a workspace. Both **Azure Active Directory** (**AAD**) users and groups can be assigned to one of four roles:

1. **Viewer**
2. **Contributor**
3. **Member**
4. **Admin**

It's strongly recommended to assign groups to workspace roles and thus manage workspace permissions by adding or removing users to or from these groups. Azure Active Directory security groups as well as Microsoft 365 groups and distribution lists are all supported for workspace roles.

Manually mapping individual user accounts to various workspace roles is both difficult to main-tain and could introduce a security risk with a user getting more access than required. Power BI administrators should partner with both the business and IT to decide on an appropriate and efficient process for approving membership and adding/removing users to/from groups.

It is important to understand that users or all users within a group added to a workspace role gain access to all content within the workspace regardless of whether specific content is shared with those users. In addition, the Admin, Member, and Contributor roles override **row-level security** (**RLS**) for content in the workspace. Thus, workspace roles are fundamentally different than individually sharing workspace content with specific users or via links.

To assign users to roles, use the **Access** option in the workspace header as shown in *Figure 10.2*. Choosing the **Access** option opens the **Access** dialog shown in *Figure 10.3*:

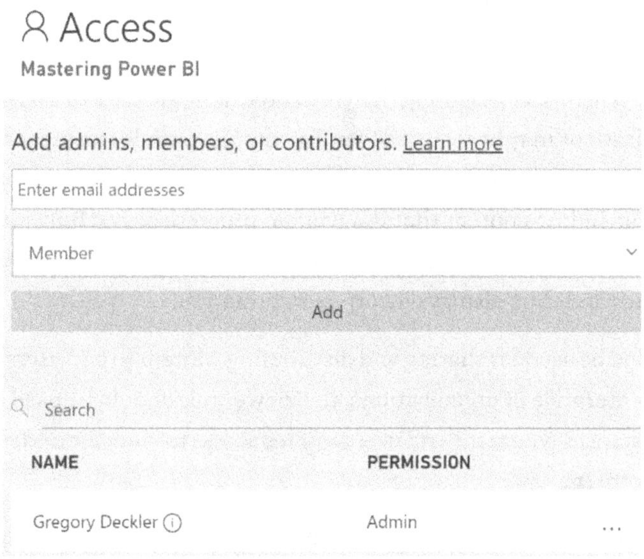

*Figure 10.3: Workspace Access dialog*

Depending on the specific role assigned, members can view content, edit content, create new content, and publish content from the workspace to a Power BI app. The specific capabilities and features available for each role are explained in the following sections, starting with the least privileged, the **Viewer** role.

# Viewer role

The **Viewer** role provides read only access to workspaces. Users assigned to the Viewer role can view and interact with all content within the workspace as well as read data stored in workspace dataflows. Importantly, the Viewer role does not override RLS for content within the workspace. It is imperative to remember that every other role other than the Viewer role overrides RLS. Every other workspace role is effectively an administrator of the Power BI datasets in a workspace and thus this permission overrides RLS roles. Thus, users that should not see data restricted by RLS should never be added to any role other than Viewer.

While limited to read access to workspace content, the Viewer role is well suited for certain QA/Test or "early look" scenarios. For example, if a workspace is hosted on Premium capacity, a team's primary QA/Test user or a key stakeholder who only has a Power BI Free license could be assigned the Viewer role in order to access new reports and dashboards that haven't yet been published to a Power BI app.

Because of the convenience of assigning the Viewer role a single time to a user or group within a workspace, organizations may be tempted to utilize the Viewer role as a means of sharing content with end users (report consumers). This is best avoided as the Viewer role is able to see all content in the workspace including content that is a work in progress or not fully ready for production. This can lead to confusion by end users or, worse, incorrect decisions being made by viewing a report that has bugs and thus displays incorrect information.

Instead, apps should be used for sharing and distributing content to end users and offer the same convenience. For enterprise BI organizations, the Viewer role should be used sparingly and only in specific circumstances where the end user requires access to view the underlying datasets and other workspace content.

Viewers can also reshare content if the **Add reshare** option is selected for specific content. To add resharing capabilities for users with the Viewer role, users in the Member or Admin role can access the permissions for specific content. This is done by accessing the **More options** menu (three vertical dots) for specific content in the workspace as shown in *Figure 10.4*:

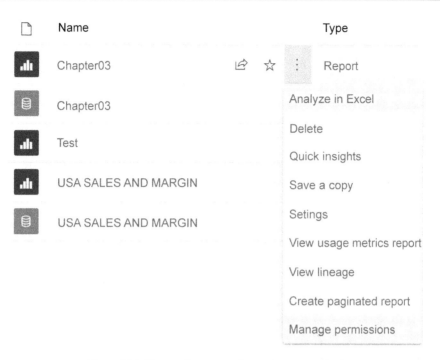

*Figure 10.4: More options menu for workspace content*

Once within the **Manage permissions** dialog for the dashboard, report, or dataset, users assigned to workspace roles are listed under the **Direct access** tab. Accessing the **More options** menu (three horizontal dots) for a particular user assigned to the Viewer role provides the option to **Add reshare** rights as shown in *Figure 10.5*:

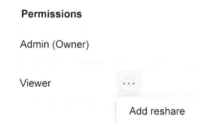

*Figure 10.5: More options menu user with Viewer role*

The same **Add reshare** option is also displayed for users assigned to the Contributor role, which we detail in the next section.

## Contributor role

The Contributor role has create and edit permissions to content in the Workspace but by default lacks the sharing and publishing permissions of the Member and Admin roles. For example, a BI developer could be granted the Contributor role to publish a new report to the workspace but a user with higher privileges would be required to publish or update a Power BI app containing this report to end users. In addition, the Contributor role provides the ability to schedule dataset refreshes and modify data gateway connection settings.

The Contributor role is a natural fit for report authors and dataset developers within a corporate BI organization. These users can perform their work within Power BI Desktop and publish to the workspace but are prevented from managing permissions for the workspace's content or sharing it unless specifically granted reshare rights.

As mentioned, the Contributor role overrides RLS for content in the workspace. Thus, never assign users to the Contributor role that should not see data protected by RLS. In addition, Contributors can also be granted the ability to update the app for the workspace. This setting is accessed by choosing the **Settings** option in the workspace header as shown in *Figure 10.2*. This opens the **Settings** pane. Expanding the **Advanced** section, the option to **Allow contributors to update the app for this workspace** setting is displayed at the bottom of the **Settings** pane as shown in *Figure 10.6*:

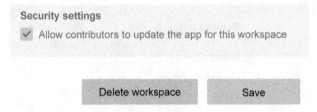

*Figure 10.6: More options menu user with Viewer role*

The ability to set the **Allow contributors to update the app for this workspace** setting is exclusive to the Admin role. Users in the Member role cannot configure this setting, as we detail in the next section.

# Member role

The Member role provides full workspace functionality, features, and access, save for a few permissions exclusive to the Admin role, such as the ability to allow Contributors to update the app for a workspace, mentioned previously. This role includes all of the permissions of the Contributor roles plus the ability to add members with lower permission roles, publish, unpublish, and change permissions for apps and content, update apps, and share content.

The Member role is best suited to the business owner of the app or, in more restrictive environments, personnel specifically responsible for defining permissions and security. Less restrictive environments are likely happy to offload the sharing and permission requirements from IT to the business since the business is generally more in tune with the personnel that require access to the workspace content.

We'll now cover the final workspace role, the Admin role.

# Admin role

Every workspace has one or multiple administrators who manage the access of other Power BI users to the workspace. The user that initially creates the workspace is the workspace admin by default.

The admin role is the highest security role for workspaces and includes all of the rights and permissions of the Member role. In addition, only workspace Admins can add other users as Admins to the workspace. As already mentioned, only Admins can grant Contributors the right to update the associated app. Finally, Admins also have the exclusive right to update a workspace's settings or delete a workspace, thus removing all of its content (dashboards, reports, and datasets) from the Power BI service.

Prior to deleting a workspace, check to see if an app is published from the workspace. If an app is published, unpublish the app via the ellipsis (three dots) next to the **Access** option in the header of the workspace. If the workspace is deleted but the published app is not unpublished, users of the published app will see errors when attempting to access or refresh its content.

If Power BI Premium capacity is provisioned for the organization and if the workspace Admin is granted assignment permissions to Premium capacity, they can assign the workspace to a Premium capacity. This action moves the content in the workspace to dedicated hardware (capacity) exclusive to the organization and enables many additional features, such as the distribution of apps to Power BI Free users.

Further information on the assignment of app workspaces to Power BI Premium capacity is included in *Chapter 15, Building Enterprise BI with Power BI Premium*. The additional capabilities provided by Power BI Premium and considerations in allocating Premium capacity are also included in *Chapter 15, Building Enterprise BI with Power BI Premium*.

Now that workspace roles and rights are understood, we'll next consider a common workspace configuration in enterprise deployments, the use of datasets across workspaces.

## Datasets across workspaces

A common deployment pattern for enterprise BI teams is to separate the dataset development from the report development. In this pattern, data modelers focus on dataset development and report authors connect live to this dataset when creating reports. This separates the duties of data modelers and report authors and enables a single dataset to service multiple audiences.

Taking this a step further, datasets can be published to dedicated dataset-only workspaces that only dataset authors and admins can access. Report authors and end users are granted read or read and build permissions to these datasets thus ensuring that the datasets will only be modified by dataset authors. Additional, content-only workspaces can then be created and used for content development such as reports, dashboards, and scorecards. With the proper tenant settings configured as discussed in *Chapter 14, Administering Power BI for an Organization*, the datasets in the separate workspace can be accessed by report authors and used when building content.

Separating the concerns of data modelers and report developers using workspaces provides a least-privileges security model, meaning that only the least amount of permissions required to perform a task are granted. As opposed to report authors being made Contributors or Members of a workspace, which grants them the ability to modify existing datasets in that workspace, this pattern secures the datasets such that only approved data models can modify published datasets.

Using datasets across workspaces requires that the datasets be shared with users and groups that require access to build content using those datasets. Sharing content is discussed in the *Sharing content* section of *Chapter 13, Creating Power BI Apps and Content Distribution*. However, specifically for this scenario of using datasets across workspaces, the **Allow recipients to build content with the data associated with this dataset** checkbox must be checked. This setting is sometimes referred to as the **Build** permission.

We'll now consider the default **My workspace** provisioned for every Power BI user.

# My workspace

All Power BI users, including those with free licenses, are assigned a **My workspace** in the Power BI service. This workspace should only be used and thought of as a private scratchpad for content specific to the individual user. For those familiar with SharePoint My Sites or OneDrive, the concept is similar. By default, only each individual user has permissions to see and access content within their **My workspace**, including even Global administrators and Power BI administrators.

**My workspace** is accessed via the same **Workspaces** menu as other workspaces, as shown in *Figure 10.7*:

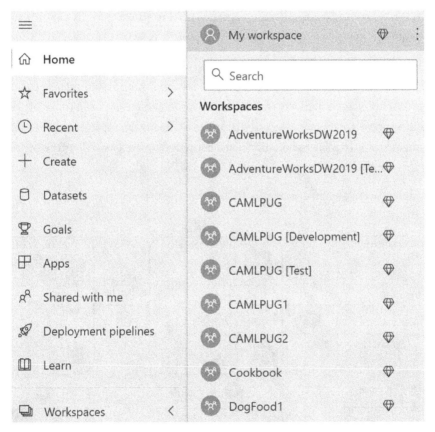

*Figure 10.7: My workspace*

Any Power BI content that requires access by other users should be stored in a different workspace and distributed as an app. Although **My workspace** can host the same content types as other workspaces, with the exception of dataflows, any content shared and distributed from **My workspace** is dependent on the individual user's account.

Armed with a basic understanding of workspaces, we next turn our attention to how workspaces can be used in staged deployments.

# Staged deployments

Staged deployments are a familiar process to technical IT teams involved with application development and the creation of data assets. Quite simply, staged deployments provide separate environments for different life cycle stages such as development, test, and production. Each stage of the life cycle is designed to accomplish specific tasks and ensure quality. Development stages are for work-in-progress content and are solely used by report authors and other content developers. Test is for users to perform **user acceptance testing** (**UAT**) to verify that the reports and other content function as desired. The production stage is only for content that has passed UAT.

Multiple workspaces and their corresponding apps are used to stage and manage the life cycle of Power BI content. Similar to the development, test, and production release cycles familiar to IT professionals, staged deployments in the Power BI service are used to isolate data, users, and content appropriate to each stage of the process. Effectively implementing a staged Power BI deployment serves to raise the quality of the content delivered as well as the productivity of project team members.

The nine-step process depicted in Figure 10.8 shows the primary elements of a staged deployment life cycle:

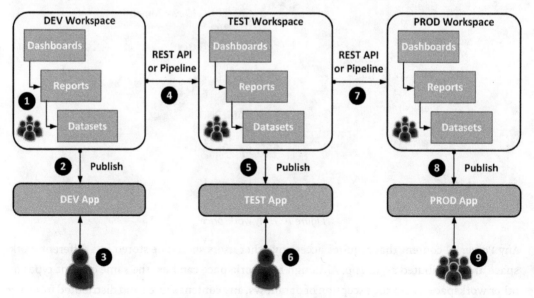

*Figure 10.8: Staged deployment life cycle*

An explanation of the various numbered steps of the staged deployment life cycle process is provided here:

1. A development workspace is created. A Power BI Desktop file containing the dataset is published to the development workspace. Reports are developed in Power BI Desktop based on live connections to the development workspace dataset and published to the workspace. Dashboards are created within the development workspace in the Power BI service.

2. An app is published or updated and made available to a small number of users for their review.

3. The BI manager or project lead reviews the status of content being developed and provides feedback to the developers. As purely a preference, in some scenarios, certain business stakeholders are allowed early access to content under development.

4. The Power BI REST API, Power BI PowerShell module, or a pipeline is used to migrate completed content from the development workspace to the test workspace. The Power BI REST API operations are called via PowerShell scripts. The Power BI REST API, Power BI PowerShell module, and pipelines are explained in the following sections.

5. A TEST app is published or updated and made available to a small number of users for their review.

6. A UAT user or team reviews the content relative to requirements and provides feedback. If necessary, revisions are implemented in the TEST workspace and the TEST app is updated for further review.

7. The Power BI REST API, Power BI PowerShell module, or pipeline is used to migrate approved content from the TEST workspace to the production workspace. Supported REST API operations, such as a clone report and rebind report, are called via PowerShell scripts.

8. A production app is published or updated and made available to groups of users for their consumption. Publishing and accessing apps is described in *Chapter 13, Creating Power BI Apps and Content Distribution.*

9. Groups of business users access and consume the dashboards and reports via the production app from any device. Measuring and monitoring the usage of the published app is also described in *Chapter 13, Creating Power BI Apps and Content Distribution.*

Creating and managing workspaces as well as publishing apps for testing or consumption are all simple processes handled via the user interface in the Power BI service.

Properly utilizing the Power BI REST API or Power BI PowerShell module to copy or migrate content across workspaces, however, requires some level of custom scripting, usually performed via Windows PowerShell. Organizations using Power BI Premium can instead leverage deployment pipelines instead of relying on the Power BI REST API and/or PowerShell scripts.

Before delving into either the Power BI REST API, PowerShell, or deployment pipelines, however, we'll consider the management of datasets during the staged deployment process.

## Workspace datasets

As per *Figure 10.8*, this architecture requires distinct Power BI datasets per workspace. To minimize resource usage and for data security reasons, the development workspace dataset could include the minimal amount of data necessary and exclude all sensitive data. This would allow the organization to comfortably provide development access to teams of content developers, potentially from outside of the organization.

Access to the test workspace could be limited to a small number of trusted or approved users within the organization and thus could include sensitive data. Finally, the production workspace dataset would have the same schema as the other datasets but include the full volume of data as well as sensitive data.

If a common schema exists between the different datasets in each workspace, the source dataset of a Power BI Desktop report file can be revised to a dataset in a separate workspace as per the *Switching source datasets* section in *Chapter 6, Planning Power BI Reports*.

For example, the report file (which has an extension of .pbix) approved for migration from the development workspace to the test workspace could be opened, modified to reference the test workspace dataset, and then published to the test workspace. This approach represents a manual alternative to the Power BI REST API described in the following section.

The ability to use datasets across workspaces can help eliminate the resource cost and manageability issues of duplicated datasets across multiple app workspaces. This functionality can be turned on within **Tenant settings** of the **Admin portal** in the Power BI service. This setting is explained in more detail in *Chapter 14, Administering Power BI for an Organization*.

For example, distinct Power BI apps developed for the finance, sales, and marketing teams could all leverage a single production dataset in a dedicated workspace rather than individual datasets within each workspace. That said, the development of the dataset itself should also follow a staged deployment life cycle similar to that shown in *Figure 10.8*.

Let's now explore how the Power BI REST API and Power BI PowerShell module can be used to implement a staged deployment.

# Power BI REST API and PowerShell module

The Power BI REST API provides programmatic access to resources in the Power BI service including content (datasets, reports, and dashboards), workspaces, and the users of these resources. This access enables organizations to automate common workflows, such as cloning a report to a different workspace or triggering a dataset refresh operation via familiar tools, such as Windows PowerShell.

The goal of the REST API is to fully support all functionality available in the Power BI service, including capabilities exclusive to the Power BI Admin portal, thus providing complete administrative and automation capabilities. The following URL provides updated documentation on the REST API including the request syntax and a sample result set for each operation: `http://bit.ly/2AIkJyF`.

Windows PowerShell is a task-based command-line shell and scripting language. It's primarily used by system administrators to automate administrative tasks. For example, PowerShell script files, having an extension of `.ps1`, are commonly used in scheduled data refresh processes for Analysis Services models.

PowerShell can use the Power BI REST APIs directly or alternatively use the Power BI PowerShell module. Both approaches are covered in the following sections and additional documentation can be found here: `https://bit.ly/3vDJ5qc`. We'll first investigate the Power BI REST API.

## Power BI REST API

To use the Power BI REST API in a custom .NET program, the application must be registered with Azure Active Directory. This registration is performed in the Azure portal application and specifically here: `https://bit.ly/3C04EG2`.

1.  Sign in with the Azure Active Directory account and provide a name for the application. Sign in with the account used for logging into the Power BI service. Once complete, the **App registrations** dialog is displayed as shown in *Figure 10.9*.

Home > App registrations >

🖫 **Test Power BI App**  📌  ⋯

| 🔍 Search (Ctrl+/) | « | 🗑 Delete | ⊕ Endpoints | ⊡ Preview features |

🟦 Overview

🐬 Quickstart

🚀 Integration assistant

**Manage**

🗔 Branding & properties

🔃 Authentication

🔑 Certificates & secrets

⫼ Token configuration

⦿ API permissions

ℹ️ Got a second? We would love your feedback on M

∧ **Essentials**

Display name
Test Power BI App

Application (client) ID

Object ID

Directory (tenant) ID

Supported account types

*Figure 10.9: App registration in Azure Active Directory portal*

2.  Select **API permissions** under the **Manage** heading as shown in *Figure 10.9*. On the **API permission** page, select **Add a permission**. Scroll down until you find **Power BI Service** as shown in *Figure 10.10* and select it.

# Request API permissions

| 📄 **Office 365 Management APIs** | 📒 **OneNote** | 📊 **Power BI Service** |
|---|---|---|
| Retrieve information about user, admin, syste, and policy actions and events from Office 365 and Azure AD activity logs | Create and manage notes, lists, pictures, files, and more in OneNote notebooks | Programmatic access to Dashboard resources such as Datasets, Tables, and Rows in Power BI |

*Figure 10.10: Request API permissions*

3. In the **Request API permissions** dialog, choose **Delegated permissions**. Under **Select permissions**, expand all sections and check all checkboxes as shown in *Figure 10.11*.

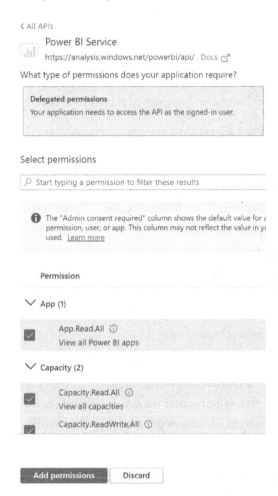

*Figure 10.11: Adding Request API permissions*

4. When finished, click the **Add permissions** button shown in *Figure 10.11*.

Once an application is registered in Azure Active Directory with the correct permissions, the client ID created for the application can be used within .NET applications to perform actions in the Power BI service. Next, we'll look at the Power BI PowerShell module.

# Power BI PowerShell module

The **Power BI PowerShell module** was created to simplify the scripting of Power BI tasks from within PowerShell. Scripting operations via the Power BI PowerShell module is significantly easier than using the Power BI REST API directly and does not require application registration as covered in the previous section. However, the Power BI PowerShell module does not necessarily include all of the operations available via the Power BI REST API.

To use the Power BI PowerShell module, ensure that you are a Power BI administrator or otherwise have appropriate permissions to the Power BI service, and then follow these steps:

1.  Open a **Windows PowerShell** session as administrator by right-clicking the Windows PowerShell app and then choosing **Run as administrator**.

2.  Set the execution policy to **RemoteSigned** by entering the following command:

    ```
    Set-ExecutionPolicy RemoteSigned
    ```

3.  Answer **Y** when prompted.

4.  Run the following command to install the Power BI PowerShell module:

    ```
    Install-Module MicrosoftPowerBIMgmt -Force
    ```

5.  Log in to the Power BI service using the `Connect-PowerBIServiceAccount` command or its alias `Login-PowerBI`.

The Windows PowerShell session is now ready to start interacting with the Power BI service via function calls called **Cmdlets**. However, using either the Power BI REST API or the Power BI PowerShell module often requires that the unique identifiers for content objects such as workspaces, dashboards, reports, and datasets are known. Thus, we'll next cover how to identify these unique identifiers.

# Workspace and content identifiers

All workspaces and content within those workspaces are provided a **globally unique identifier** (**GUID**). A GUID is simply a unique ID that adheres to RFC 4122. These GUID values must be known in order to perform most operations within the Power BI service using PowerShell or a .NET program.

For example, in order to clone a report to a separate workspace and then bind the report to a dataset in the new workspace, GUID values associated with the report, the source and target workspace, and the dataset must be obtained.

Once known, these GUID values can be passed into the variables of PowerShell script files and executed on demand or as part of a scheduled process, such as with dataset refresh operations.

The GUIDs for Power BI objects can be obtained by executing scripts that reference the appropriate REST API, such as **Get Reports** (GET `https://api.powerbi.com/v1.0/myorg/reports`). Alternatively, the necessary GUIDs can be found by navigating to the specific object or collection of objects in the Power BI service and noting the URL.

For example, to retrieve both the workspace GUID and the dataset GUID, navigate to **Workspace** and open the **Settings** menu for a report. This is the same menu displayed in *Figure 10.4* previously.

In this example, opening the **Settings** menu for the AdWorks Enterprise dataset of the Ad-Works Global Sales workspace results in the following URL in the address bar of the browser: `https://app.powerbi.com/groups/c738f14c-648d-47f5-91d2-ad8ef234f49c/settings/datasets/61e21466-a3eb-45e9-b8f3-c015d7165e57`.

Based on this URL, the following two GUIDs can be used in PowerShell scripts:

- AdWorks Global Sales (workspace): `c738f14c-648d-47f5-91d2-ad8ef234f49c`
- AdWorks Enterprise (dataset): `61e21466-a3eb-45e9-b8f3-c015d7165e57`

The GUIDs for reports and dashboards can similarly be found by simply navigating to them within the Power BI service. With GUIDs in hand, we are now ready to present information regarding available sample PowerShell scripts.

## PowerShell sample scripts

Several self-documenting sample PowerShell scripts that leverage the Power BI REST API are available at the following GitHub repository: `https://github.com/Azure-Samples/powerbi-powershell`. This repository includes PowerShell scripts (`.ps1` files) for the refresh of a dataset, the rebinding of a report (to a dataset), and other common use cases.

A similar GitHub repository for PowerShell scripts that utilize the Power BI PowerShell module is available here: `https://github.com/Microsoft/powerbi-powershell`. This repository is even more extensive.

**CopyWorkspace.ps1** and **CopyWorkspaceSampleScript.ps1** from their respective repositories can be used to perform the staged deployment steps between workspaces shown in *Figure 10.8* (*steps 4* and *7*).

The use of PowerShell scripts, either via the Power BI REST API or the Power BI PowerShell module, can help automate the implementation of a staged deployment life cycle for all paid licensing scenarios. We'll next take a look at an even easier method of implementing staged deployments available to Premium capacities and PPU users, Power BI deployment pipelines.

# Power BI deployment pipelines

**Power BI deployment pipelines**, or simply **Pipelines**, are a Premium (Premium and PPU) feature specifically designed to support staged deployment life cycles. Pipelines provide a simple user interface within the Power BI service that move content between workspaces with the click of a button.

Pipelines are created in the Power BI service using the **Deployment pipelines** tab in the left navigation pane or from a workspace using the **Create a pipeline** option in the workspace header as shown in *Figure 10.2*.

Pipelines are the recommended method for executing staged deployment life cycle processes in Power BI. Pipelines do not require any custom scripting and are fully supported by Microsoft as part of the Power BI service.

Once created, pipelines allow workspaces to be assigned to three different deployment stages: **Development**, **Test**, and **Production**, as shown in *Figure 10.12*:

*Figure 10.12: Power BI deployment pipeline*

Alternatively, clicking the **Deploy to ...** button in **Development** or **Test** can automatically create a workspace for the next stage if no workspace is currently assigned.

The **Show more** option enables granular control over exactly what content is deployed to the next stage and the three vertical dots menu provides options for publishing the app for the workspace, modifying access to the workspace and workspace settings as shown in *Figure 10.13*:

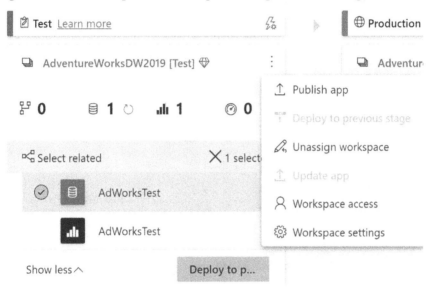

*Figure 10.13: Pipeline options*

Pipelines also provide automation via rules. Clicking on the lightning bolt icon in the stage header as shown in *Figure 10.13* opens the **Deployment settings** panel. Subsequently clicking on a dataset within the **Deployment settings** panel allows **Data source rules** and **Parameter rules** to be defined as shown in *Figure 10.14*:

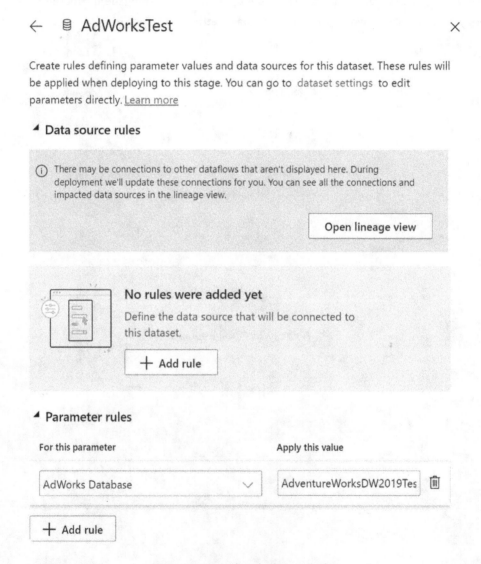

Figure 10.14: Pipeline deployment rules

In *Figure 10.14*, a parameter rule is defined to update the **AdWorks Database** query parameter to point to a different database, **AdventureWorksDW2019Test**, instead of the original value from the development stage, **AdventureWorksDW2019Dev**.

Pipelines greatly simplify the deployment of content between the stages of a staged deployment life cycle, eliminating the need for scripting and the identification of GUIDs.

Moving on from staged deployments, we'll next consider another important topic with respect to managing workspaces and content within Power BI, content sensitivity and protection.

# Content sensitivity and protection

A key advantage of Power BI is its native integration with Microsoft 365. This integration is perhaps most evident when it comes to securing and sharing content. Power BI uses AAD for assigning permissions to content as well as authenticating users. However, the integration with the security features of Microsoft 365 runs much deeper to include the integration of **information protection** and **data loss prevention** policies.

In the following sections, we explore this deeper integration with the security and compliance features of Microsoft 365 since the subjects of information protection and data loss prevention are often prominent in the minds of enterprise BI and information security teams.

## Information protection

The **Microsoft Information Protection** solution involves the creation and application of sensitivity labels to emails, files, and content containers such as Microsoft Teams, Microsoft 365 Groups, and SharePoint sites.

Sensitivity labels serve to alert end users to the privacy level of the information they are viewing and can also include protection settings to encrypt the content. For example, sensitivity labels of "Internal Only" or "Confidential" help alert end users that the content they are viewing should not be shared outside of the organization.

Using Microsoft Information Protection requires an Azure Information Protection license, which can be purchased separately or via licensing suites such as Microsoft 365 Enterprise plans, Microsoft 365 Business, and Enterprise Mobility + Security plans. In addition to licensing, there are a number of steps required to activate the information protection capabilities within Power BI.

The first step is to use the **Microsoft 365 admin center** (`https://admin.microsoft.com`) to create a sensitivity label. Within the admin center, use the **Compliance** left navigation option under **Admin centers** to open the **Microsoft 365 compliance** portal (`https://compliance.microsoft.com`).

Within the Microsoft 365 compliance portal, choose **Information protection** in the left navigation pane as shown in *Figure 10.15*:

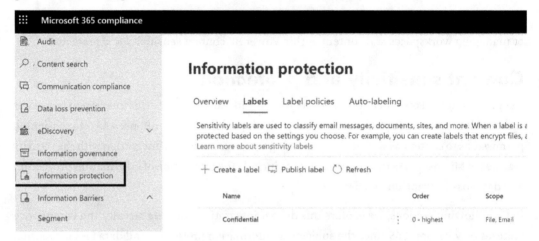

*Figure 10.15: Information protection label*

In *Figure 10.15*, an **Information protection** label has been created called **Confidential** with a **Scope** of **File, Email**.

Once **Information protection** labels are created, the next step is to turn on **Information protection** for the Power BI tenant. This is done using the tenant settings of the Power BI **Admin portal** in the service as shown in *Figure 10.16*. More information about using the Power BI Admin portal and tenant settings is provided in *Chapter 12, Administering Power BI for an Organization*.

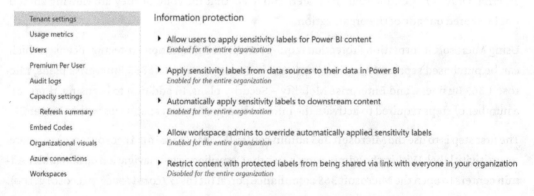

*Figure 10.16: Information protection tenant settings*

In *Figure 10.16*, four of the five information protection settings have been enabled for the entire organization.

Once the **Information protection** settings are enabled, users are able to apply sensitivity labels to content within the Power BI service using the settings for dashboards, reports, and datasets as shown in *Figure 10.17*:

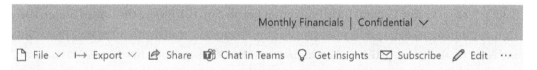

Figure 10.17: Sensitivity labels in the Power BI service

In *Figure 10.17*, the **Confidential** sensitivity label is applied to the Monthly Financials report. Once applied, the sensitivity label is displayed next to the report title as shown in *Figure 10.18*:

Figure 10.18: Sensitivity labels displayed for a report

In addition to setting sensitivity labels in the Power BI service, sensitivity labels can also be applied within Power BI Desktop from the **Home** tab of the ribbon, as shown in *Figure 10.19*:

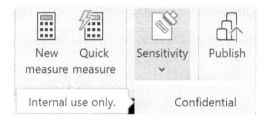

Figure 10.19: Sensitivity labels in Power BI Desktop

When **Sensitivity** labels are applied within Power BI Desktop, publishing to the Power BI service automatically marks the dataset, as well as the report, with the applied **Sensitivity** label.

Information protection sensitivity labels can be useful in alerting end users about the privileged nature of the content of Power BI reports and dashboards and enterprise BI teams are encouraged to work with information security and compliance teams to enable and use clear, consistent labeling policies. For example, reports developed for human resources often include sensitive or personally identifiable information that should not be shared outside of the organization.

Next, we'll take a look at Power BI's integration with Microsoft's data loss prevention solution.

## Data loss prevention

Microsoft's **data loss prevention (DLP)** solution assists organizations in detecting and protecting sensitive (private) data such as United States **Social Security Numbers (SSNs)** and other **personally identifiable information (PII)**. The ability to detect and respond to potential breaches of privacy is an important component in maintaining compliance with many different government regulations.

Privacy and compliance are important topics within almost all organizations, particularly when dealing with information about employees and customers. In the **European Union (EU)**, the main privacy act is the **General Data Protection Regulation (GDPR)**. In the United States, there are many different federal privacy laws such as the Privacy Act, the **Health Insurance Portability and Accountability Act (HIPAA)**, the **Children's Online Privacy Protection Act (COPPA)**, as well as individual state laws.

Tracking and maintaining compliance with so many different regulations is complex and time-consuming and violations can be costly. Microsoft's data loss prevention solution assists with compliance through the use of built-in DLP policy templates that implement the privacy rules of the most prominent government privacy regulations throughout the world.

*Figure 10.20* shows the policy templates available in the Microsoft 365 compliance portal for medical and health information.

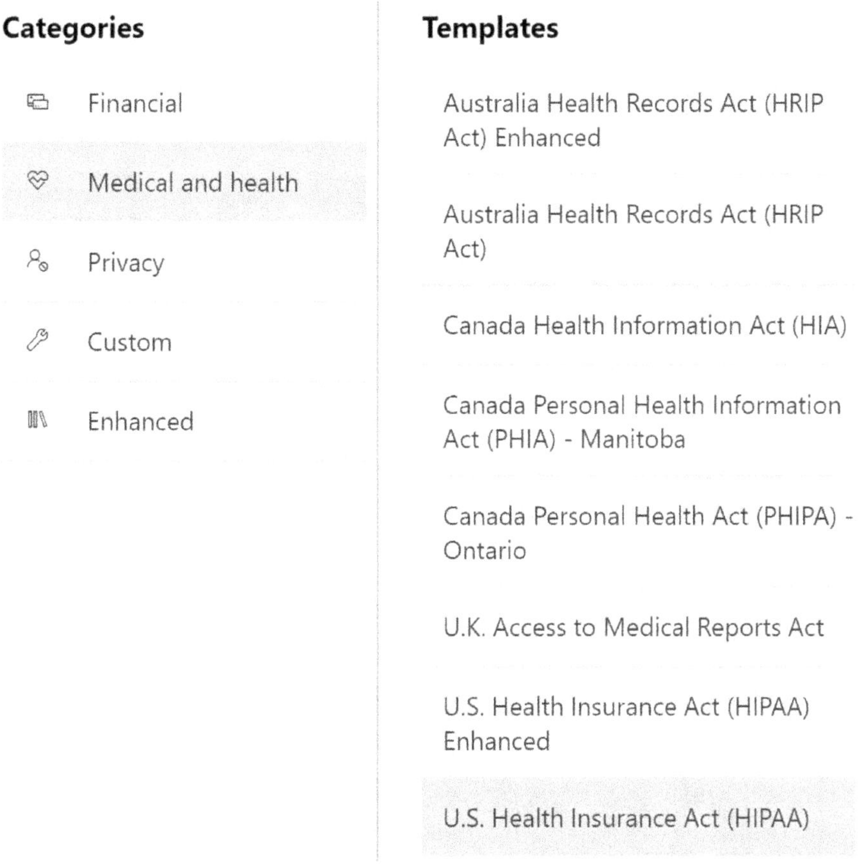

## Categories

🖾  Financial

♥  Medical and health

👤  Privacy

✎  Custom

▥  Enhanced

## Templates

Australia Health Records Act (HRIP Act) Enhanced

Australia Health Records Act (HRIP Act)

Canada Health Information Act (HIA)

Canada Personal Health Information Act (PHIA) - Manitoba

Canada Personal Health Act (PHIPA) - Ontario

U.K. Access to Medical Reports Act

U.S. Health Insurance Act (HIPAA) Enhanced

U.S. Health Insurance Act (HIPAA)

*Figure 10.20: Sensitivity labels in Power BI Desktop*

As shown in *Figure 10.20*, templates are available for medical and health regulations enacted in Australia, Canada, the United Kingdom, and the United States. These policy templates are maintained by Microsoft and updated to reflect changes in regulations such as the **Enhanced** version of the **Australia Health Records Act (HRIP Act)**.

DLP policies can identify over 250 standard types of PII such as Australia Tax File Number, Belgium Driver's License Number, IP Address, and U.S. / U.K. Passport Number. In addition, DLP rules can include custom rules identifying organizationally sensitive information. These policies can be applied to many different Microsoft 365 systems, including Power BI, as shown in *Figure 10.21.*

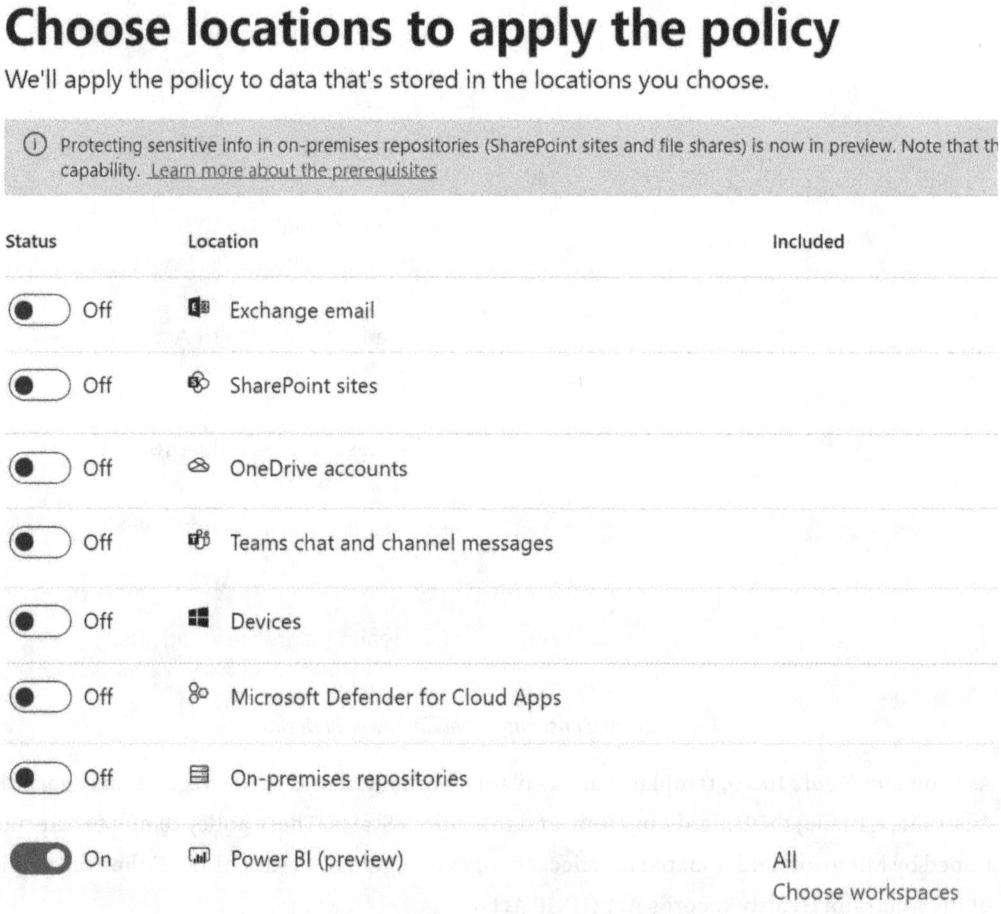

# Choose locations to apply the policy

We'll apply the policy to data that's stored in the locations you choose.

(i) Protecting sensitive info in on-premises repositories (SharePoint sites and file shares) is now in preview. Note that th capability. Learn more about the prerequisites

| Status | Location | Included |
|---|---|---|
| Off | Exchange email | |
| Off | SharePoint sites | |
| Off | OneDrive accounts | |
| Off | Teams chat and channel messages | |
| Off | Devices | |
| Off | Microsoft Defender for Cloud Apps | |
| Off | On-premises repositories | |
| On | Power BI (preview) | All<br>Choose workspaces |

*Figure 10.21: Sensitivity labels in Power BI Desktop*

When turned on, DLP policies targeting Power BI are evaluated whenever content is published or refreshed. If a potential violation is identified, the user can be notified via a policy tip. In addition, alerts can be sent to administrators and users via email and alerts also appear in the Microsoft 365 compliance center. DLP policies can thus help prevent the publishing of sensitive information that may violate government regulations such as the HIPAA or GDPR.

It should be clear now that the ability to leverage pre-built and custom DLP policies across emails, files, devices, and data assets both on-premises and in Microsoft 365 is a significant differentiator for Power BI in the enterprise BI software market.

Moving on, another top concern regarding the management of workspaces and content is version control.

# Version control

Version history and source control are essential elements of an IT organization's **application life cycle management** (**ALM**) processes and policies. Power BI files that are used in any production sense should be stored in a system such as Azure DevOps that provides version control features for tracking who made changes when and the ability to restore or recover files from their previous states.

For example, changes to an Analysis Services data model, such as new DAX measures, are typically committed to a source control repository, and tools such as Azure DevOps Services, formerly known as **Visual Studio Team Services** (**VSTS**), provide features for teams to manage and collaborate on these changes. Perhaps most importantly, these tools enable teams to view and revert back to prior versions.

Power BI Desktop files (.pbix and .pbit) do not integrate with these robust systems in the same manner as code (text) files. That said, Power BI files can be included in Azure DevOps, Git, or other version control repositories with support for common commit and pull operations. For example, a team of BI developers could all stay synchronized to a set of Power BI files in a Git repository via their local/remote repository. Additionally, a team could enforce a pull request process and review changes to Power BI files before approving the merging of developer branches to a master branch.

Alternatively, Microsoft recommends **OneDrive for Business**, given its support for version history and large file size limit. Additionally, for longer-term and larger-scale projects, BI teams can optionally persist the core DAX and M code contained in a dataset into a structure suitable for implementing source control.

## OneDrive for Business

OneDrive for Business is Microsoft's cloud-based file storage platform. It supports large files, version history, and other features such as sharing, synchronization to desktop systems, and automation via integration with Microsoft Power Automate. OneDrive for Business features are built into SharePoint Team sites, which are also used by Teams, Microsoft's collaboration software. Thus a business unit that uses Teams could keep their Power BI files on the Teams site and synchronize those files to their local device.

In *Figure 10.22*, a **Power BI template file** (.pbit) has been uploaded to a OneDrive for Business folder. A template file can be created from a Power BI Desktop file (.pbix) by selecting **File** and then **Save as** and setting **Save as type** to **Power BI template files (.pbix)**. Template files preserve all of a report's queries, DAX measures, and visualizations but do not contain any data. Thus, while the full .pbix file could also be uploaded, .pbit files are significantly smaller in size and thus are excellent candidates for version control.

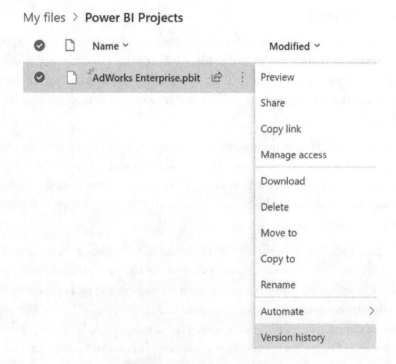

*Figure 10.22: OneDrive for Business file options*

Selecting the three vertical dots exposes several file options including **Version history**. As changes are implemented and saved in the .pbix file, such as a revised DAX measure or a new M query, the updated .pbix or an updated .pbit template file is uploaded to OneDrive for Business.

As shown in *Figure 10.23*, the **Version History** pane makes it easy to view the history of changes to a file and to restore an earlier version.

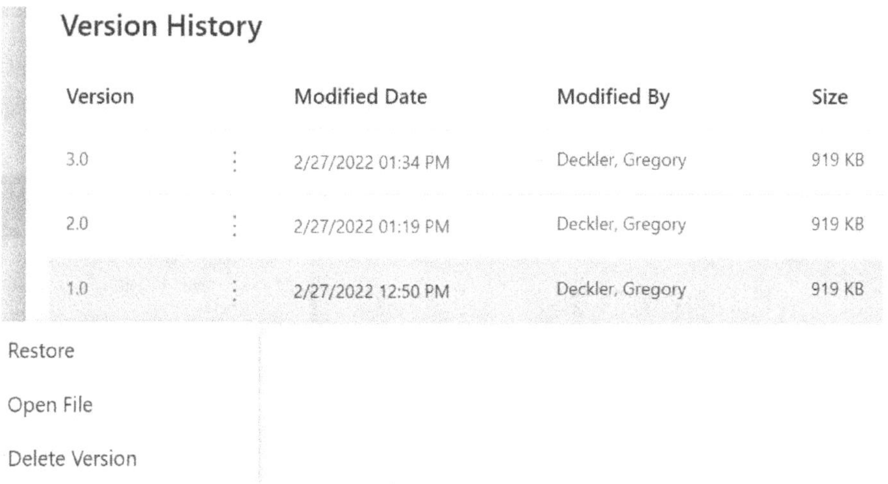

## Version History

| Version | | Modified Date | Modified By | Size |
|---------|---|--------------|-------------|------|
| 3.0 | ⋮ | 2/27/2022 01:34 PM | Deckler, Gregory | 919 KB |
| 2.0 | ⋮ | 2/27/2022 01:19 PM | Deckler, Gregory | 919 KB |
| 1.0 | ⋮ | 2/27/2022 12:50 PM | Deckler, Gregory | 919 KB |

Restore

Open File

Delete Version

*Figure 10.23: File options in Version History*

As shown in *Figure 10.23*, selecting the three vertical dots for the **Version 1.0** row exposes three file options, including **Restore**. Selecting **Restore** creates a new version (Version 4.0), which is an exact copy of the file restored. This restored file replaces the current file accessible in the OneDrive for Business folder.

As described in the *Live connections to Power BI datasets* section in *Chapter 6, Planning Power BI Reports*, reports should be created with Power BI Desktop files rather than within the Power BI service to enable version history. However, since dashboards are created exclusively within the Power BI service, version history is currently not possible for dashboards.

With version control for entire Power BI files covered, we'll next explore version control for M and DAX code.

## Source control for M and DAX code

Although the version history of M and DAX code within Power BI Desktop files is technically available via OneDrive for Business, some BI organizations may also choose to utilize more robust version control tools on essential queries and measures. With this approach, it is easier to manage complex code, as well as reusing code across solutions.

For example, an M query can be saved as a .pq file and synchronized with a team project code repository in Azure DevOps services or a private GitHub repository. In *Figure 10.24*, a Power Query project containing multiple folders of PQ files (M queries) has been added to a solution in Visual Studio and synchronized with a Git repository in an Azure DevOps project:

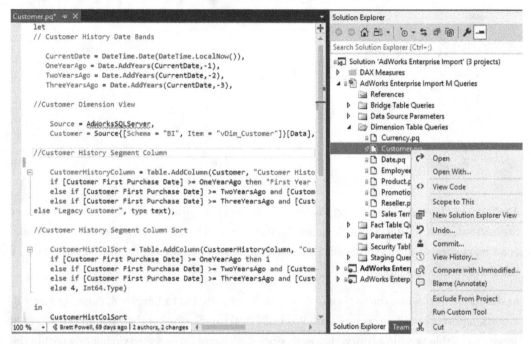

*Figure 10.24: Power Query project in Visual Studio*

In this example, all M queries (.pq files) are checked into source control as indicated by the lock icon in the Solution Explorer window, except for the **Customer** query, which is pending an edit (checkmark icon). The revised **Customer** dimension table query would be implemented within the Power BI Desktop file first but also saved within the Power Query project in Visual Studio.

As an enterprise tool, many version control options are available in Visual Studio, including **Compare with Unmodified...** and **Blame (Annotate)**. By clicking **Commit**, a message describing the change can be entered and the updated file can be synced to the source control repository in Azure DevOps Services.

Given the additional maintenance overhead, enterprise source control tools may not be suitable for smaller, simpler Power BI projects or the very early stages of projects. In addition to sound requirement gathering efforts, teams can minimize the maintenance effort required of the version control project by only including the essential M queries and DAX measures.

For example, only the DAX measures containing fundamental business logic, such as the base measures described in *Chapter 4*, *Designing Import, DirectQuery, and Composite Data Models*, could be saved as .msdax files.

In addition to OneDrive for Business, Visual Studio, and Azure DevOps Services, there are several external tools that can be leveraged for code maintenance purposes, such as the oddly named external tool MSHGQM.

## MSHGQM

MSHGQM is a free external tool for Power BI Desktop used for the creation of DAX measures and columns as well as measure and column definitions that can be reused between multiple datasets. MSHGQM includes over 200 DAX calculation definitions, including all of Power BI Desktop's built-in quick measures.

MSHGQM allows measure and column formulas to be created using replaceable parameters, as shown in *Figure 10.25*. These definitions can then be used to create measures and columns within datasets.

*Figure 10.25: Power Query project in Visual Studio*

In addition to using the built-in calculation definitions, users can create their own custom calculation definitions. MSHGQM stores custom calculation definitions within a JSON file and includes the ability to store pre-defined labels, tooltips, default values, and even custom format strings.

Using MSHGQM, enterprise BI teams can create a single measure definition for key metrics and share the measure definitions among team members by distributing the JSON file. This ensures that all team members are using the same calculations for such things as date intelligence measures, enabling consistency and repeatability across different data modelers, and speeding up the data model development process.

MSHGQM can be downloaded from the following GitHub repository (`https://bit.ly/3HlkjRa`), which includes documentation on its installation and use. Additional information and demonstrations are provided via a dedicated YouTube channel: `https://bit.ly/3M9QsPp`.

This concludes our explanation of various version control options for Power BI. We'll next turn our attention to the subject of metadata management.

# Metadata management

Metadata is simply data about data. While often overlooked, metadata management is an important aspect of properly managed content within Power BI.

Power BI datasets support metadata capabilities with the ability to include descriptions and other metadata about tables, columns, and measures found within the dataset. The information provided by metadata can become important as it's common for hundreds of DAX measures to be built into datasets over time to support advanced analytics and address new requirements.

In addition, content published to the Power BI service also allows metadata to be set via the **Settings** pane as shown in *Figure 10.26*:

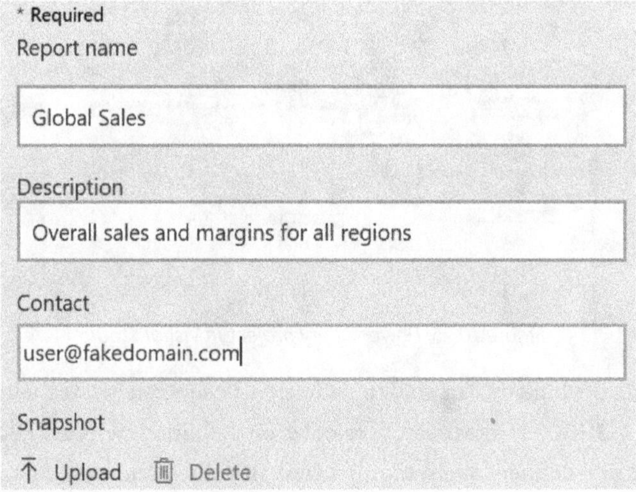

*Figure 10.26: Metadata settings for a report in the Power BI service*

Consider that as Power BI projects grow to support more teams and business processes, the dataset(s) supporting the reports and dashboards for these projects also grows. In addition, the number of reports, dashboards, and other content is also likely to increase. For example, integrating the general ledger into the existing AdWorks Enterprise dataset would require new fact and dimension tables, new relationships, and additional measures with their own unique business rules or definitions.

Given this added complexity, BI teams and specifically the dataset designer described in *Chapter 1*, *Planning Power BI Projects*, can embed descriptions to aid report authors in correctly utilizing the data model. Additionally, the **dynamic management views (DMVs)** for Analysis Services models can be leveraged to generate metadata reports providing detailed visibility of all essential objects of the dataset. DMVs are simply Analysis Services queries that return information about server health, server operations, and model objects.

The combination of field descriptions and metadata reporting can help drive consistent report development, as well as facilitating effective collaboration within the project team and between the project team and other stakeholders. In addition, the consistent application of metadata for content published to the Power BI service can also help users search for and find content, as well as understanding the intent and purpose of that content.

In addition to field descriptions, properties such as synonyms, display folders, and custom format strings are additional examples of metadata. Let's take a closer look at field descriptions.

## Field descriptions

A **Properties** pane in the **Model** view of Power BI Desktop allows dataset designers to enter descriptions and other metadata for the measures, columns, and tables of a dataset. The description metadata is then exposed to report authors who connect to this dataset as they hover over these objects in the **Fields** list of the **Report** view and within the input field wells of visualizations.

Although field descriptions are not a full substitute for formal documentation, descriptions of the logic, definition, or calculation of various objects enable report authors to develop content more efficiently. For example, rather than searching an external resource such as a data dictionary or contacting the dataset designer, the report author could simply hover over measures and column names from within Power BI Desktop.

Creating and viewing field descriptions is relatively simple, as explained in the following sections, starting with how to create field descriptions.

## Creating descriptions

To create a description, open the Power BI Desktop file containing the dataset and navigate to the **Model** view. By default, both the **Properties** pane and **Fields** pane are expanded as shown in *Figure 10.27*.

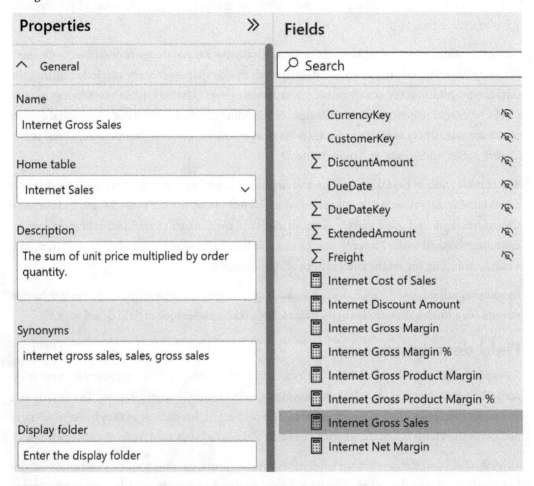

*Figure 10.27: Power Query project in Visual Studio*

As shown in *Figure 10.27*, the **Internet Gross Sales** measure is selected on the **Fields** pane and a sentence is entered into the **Description** box. Additional metadata such as **Synonyms** is also displayed.

Just like the preceding example with measures, selecting a table or a column in the **Fields** pane exposes similar metadata, including a **Description** box. Table and column descriptions can be valuable, but measures are likely the best use case for this feature given the volume of measures in a dataset and the variety of calculations or logic they can contain.

Identify the most important measures in a dataset and apply concise, consistent descriptions using business-friendly terms. The set of measures described in the *Base measures* section of *Chapter 5, Developing DAX Measures and Security Roles*, represents good candidates for descriptions since they are reused in many other measures, including the date intelligence measures. For example, it's essential that the report author knows that the net sales measure includes discounts while the gross sales measure does not.

Next, we'll look at how to view field descriptions.

## View field descriptions

The descriptions included in Power BI datasets can be viewed in the **Fields** pane, the input field wells of visualizations, and the **Properties** pane (for import and composite mode datasets).

In *Figure 10.28*, the report author built a simple visual using the Customer History Segment column and Internet Gross Sales measure. Hovering the mouse cursor over the Customer History Segment column in the visual's **Values** field well exposes the description in the tooltip along with the table and column name.

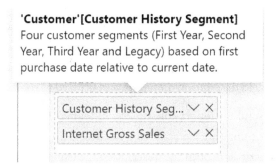

*Figure 10.28: Field description via visualization field wells*

As shown in *Figure 10.27*, the report author can view the description of the field (column or measure) via the tooltip to understand the essential definition, such as the first purchase date relative to the current date in this example.

Likewise, the author can also hover over the `Internet Gross Sales` measure in the **Values** field well to view this description or hover over other measure, column, and table names in the **Fields** pane, as shown in *Figure 10.29*:

*Figure 10.29: Description of measure via the Fields pane*

For the **Internet Gross Product Margin** measure and other measures in the dataset, the description applied uses proper casing when referring to DAX measures. This approach helps to keep each description concise and advises the user of the other measures they may need to review.

Field descriptions cannot be viewed by hovering over names or values in the visuals themselves on the report canvas. However, as per the *Visualization formatting* section of *Chapter 6, Planning Power BI Reports*, chart visuals contain a **Tooltips** input field well that provides a very similar experience to viewing field descriptions.

Tooltips are typically used to display DAX measures related to the measures in the visual, such as the net margin percentage for a chart that visualizes net sales. However, measures can also return text strings and, thus, if necessary, to aid the users viewing the reports, measures can be created containing the field description metadata and utilized as tooltips.

Although potentially useful for report consumers, BI teams should be cautious that the DAX measures used for descriptions are isolated from the actual field descriptions. Therefore, in the event of a change in description, both the description measure and the field description would need to be updated.

Additionally, if description measures are used extensively, a dedicated measure support table, as described in *Chapter 3, Transforming Data with M*, and *Chapter 4, Designing Import, DirectQuery, and Composite Data Models*, may be necessary to organize these measures. Alternatively, they could be organized into display folders.

Field descriptions applied to Analysis Services data models also flow through to Power BI reports just like the examples in this section with a Power BI dataset.

However, field descriptions applied to Power BI datasets are not visible when connecting via Microsoft Excel.

Managing metadata such as descriptions for all tables, columns, and measures within a dataset can be burdensome and time-consuming. Additionally, for datasets with many tables, columns, and measures, it is easy to miss setting the metadata for particular items. Thus, we'll next briefly explore an external tool for Power BI that helps make the management of metadata easier.

## Metadata Mechanic

Metadata Mechanic is a free, external tool for Power BI Desktop specifically designed to make the management and setting of metadata easier and faster. Using Metadata Mechanic, the metadata for all tables, columns, and measures within a data model can be retrieved and updated as shown in *Figure 10.30*:

*Figure 10.30: Metadata Mechanic*

Metadata Mechanic includes the ability to automatically mass configure displayed metadata, such as hiding all columns in a table, moving all measures to another table, or setting the thousands separator for all whole number columns and measures.

Metadata Mechanic can be downloaded from the following GitHub repository (`https://bit.ly/3HlkjRa`), which includes documentation on its installation and use.

Additional information and demonstrations are provided via a YouTube channel: `https://bit.ly/3M9QsPp`. We'll now turn our attention to reporting on this metadata.

# Metadata reporting

Analysis Services DMVs are available to retrieve the descriptions applied to datasets and related information. These DMVs can be leveraged for both simple, ad hoc extracts via common dataset tools, such as DAX Studio, as well as more robust and standardized reports in Power BI or Excel.

Official documentation of Analysis Services DMVs, including a reference and description of each DMV, query syntax, and client-tool access, is available via the following link: `http://bit.ly/2A81lek`.

The following query can be used to retrieve the measures in a dataset with descriptions as well as their DAX expression:

```
SELECT
        [Name] as [Measure Name]
    ,   [Description] as [Measure Description]
    ,   [Expression] as [DAX Expression]
FROM
$SYSTEM.TMSCHEMA_MEASURES
WHERE LEN([Description]) > 1
ORDER BY [NAME];
```

The `WHERE` clause in this query ensures that only measures with a description applied are returned. Removing or commenting out this clause (for example, `--WHERE LEN([Description]) > 1`) returns all measures whether or not they have a description. Additionally, column aliases of `Measure Name`, `Measure Description`, and `DAX Expression` improve the usability of the DMV columns.

As shown in *Figure 10.31*, the query can be executed from DAX Studio against the open Power BI Desktop file:

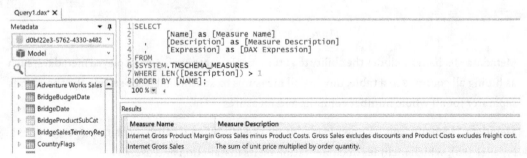

*Figure 10.31: Measure descriptions via a DMV query in DAX Studio*

Just as measure descriptions can be retrieved via the TMSCHEMA_MEASURES DMV, the following query retrieves the column descriptions from the TMSCHEMA_COLUMNS DMV:

```
SELECT
        [ExplicitName] as [Column Name]
    ,   [Description] as [Column Description]
FROM $SYSTEM.TMSCHEMA_COLUMNS
WHERE LEN([Description]) > 1
ORDER BY [ExplicitName];
```

As per the official documentation referenced earlier in this section, the query engine for DMVs is the **Data Mining parser** and the DMV query syntax is based on the SELECT (DMX) statement. Therefore, although the queries appear to be standard SQL statements, the full SQL SELECT syntax is not supported, including the JOIN and GROUP BY clauses.

For example, it's not possible to join the TMSCHEMA_COLUMNS DMV with the TMSCHEMA_TABLES DMV within the same SELECT statement to retrieve columns from both DMVs. Given these limitations, it can be helpful to build lightweight data transformation processes on top of DMVs, as described in the following section.

## Standard metadata reports

For larger datasets with many measures, relationships, and tables, a dedicated metadata report can be constructed using Power BI. In this approach, the Analysis Services data connector is used to access the DMVs of the Power BI dataset and this data is transformed via M queries.

A set of report pages can be created to visualize the primary objects of the model and support common ad hoc questions, such as which relationships use bidirectional cross-filtering? Implementing the DMV-based Power BI report consists of the following four steps:

1. Obtain the server and database parameter values of the Power BI dataset
2. Query the DMVs of the Power BI dataset from a separate Power BI Desktop file
3. Integrate and enhance the DMV data to support the visualization layer
4. Develop the report pages

Each of these steps is explained in the following sections starting with obtaining the server and database parameters.

## Server and database parameters

The server value of the Power BI dataset is visible in the status bar (bottom-right corner) when connected to the dataset from DAX Studio, as shown in *Figure 10.32*:

Ln 9, Col 1     localhost:59910    16.0.15.15    1125    2 rows    00:00.0

*Figure 10.32: Server value of Power BI dataset via DAX Studio*

In *Figure 10.31*, the server parameter is **localhost:59910**. To obtain the database parameter, run the following query in DAX Studio:

```
SELECT
    [CATALOG_NAME]
,   [DATABASE_ID]
FROM $SYSTEM.DBSCHEMA_CATALOGS
```

Both columns retrieve the same GUID value, which can be used as the database parameter.

There are other methods of obtaining the server parameter, such as finding the **process ID (PID)** in **Task Manager** and then running netstat -anop tcp from **Command Prompt** to find the port associated with the PID. However, connecting to the dataset from DAX Studio is more straightforward and it's assumed that experienced Power BI dataset designers will have at least a basic familiarity with DAX Studio.

The server parameter (for example, **localhost:59910**) can also be used to connect to the running Power BI dataset via **SQL Server Profiler**. This can be useful for identifying the DAX queries generated by report visuals and user interactions. Alternatively, Power BI Desktop can generate a trace file via the **Enable tracing** setting within the **Diagnostics** tab (**File | Options and Settings | Diagnostics**).

## Querying the DMVs from Power BI

With the server and database known, parameters and queries can be created in Power BI Desktop to stage the DMV data for further transformations. In *Figure 10.33*, showing the Power Query Editor, three query groups are used to organize the parameters, the DMV queries, and the enhanced queries (**Metadata Report Tables**) used by the report:

Queries [11]                          Advanced Editor

▲ ▦ Data Model Parameters
    ▤ *AnalysisServicesServer*        # TablesDMV
    ▤ *AnalysisServicesDatabo*

▲ ▦ DMV Queries [4]                   ```
                                      let
    ▦ *TablesDMV*                         TablesDMV = AnalysisServices.Database
    ▦ *ColumnsDMV*                        (
                                          AnalysisServicesServer, AnalysisServicesDatabase,
    ▦ *RelationshipsDMV*                  [Query="select * from $SYSTEM.TMSCHEMA_TABLES"]
    ▦ *MeasuresDMV*                       )
                                      in
▲ ▦ Metadata Report Tables                TablesDMV
                                      ```
    ▦ Columns

    ▦ Tables
                                      ✓ No syntax errors have been detected.
    ▦ Relationships

    ▦ Metrics

    ▦ CurrentDate

    ▦ Other Queries

*Figure 10.33: Power Query Editor in Power BI Desktop*

As per the `TablesDMV` query, the two parameters (`AnalysisServicesServer` and `AnalysisServicesDatabase`) are passed to the `AnalysisServices.Database()` function for each DMV query. As indicated by the gray font of the DMV queries and the parameters, these queries are not loaded to the data model layer.

To update the metadata report in a future session to reflect changes to the dataset, the server and database parameter values would need to be retrieved again. These values could then be passed to the data model parameters, thus allowing all queries to update. This manual update process is necessary with Power BI Desktop files, given changes to the port and database ID, but is not necessary for metadata reports based on Analysis Services models.

Given the small size of the DMV data and the limitations of SQL `SELECT` queries against DMV data, a simple `SELECT *` is used to expose all columns and rows. The **Metadata Report Table** queries contain all the joins and transformations to prepare the data for reporting.
                                      ```

## Integrating and enhancing DMV data

The following M query produces the Relationships table by implementing joins to retrieve the table and column names on each side of each relationship:

```
let
    FromTableJoin = Table.NestedJoin(
        RelationshipsDMV,{"FromTableID"},TablesDMV,{"ID"},"TableDMVColumns",
JoinKind.Inner),
    FromTable = Table.ExpandTableColumn(FromTableJoin, "TableDMVColumns",
{"Name"}, {"From Table"}),
    ToTableJoin = Table.NestedJoin(
        FromTable,{"ToTableID"},TablesDMV,{"ID"},"TableDMVColumns",
JoinKind.Inner),
    ToTable = Table.ExpandTableColumn(ToTableJoin, "TableDMVColumns",
{"Name"}, {"To Table"}),
    FromColumnJoin = Table.NestedJoin(
        ToTable,{"FromColumnID"},ColumnsDMV,{"ID"},"ColumnsDMVColumns",
JoinKind.Inner),
    FromColumn = Table.ExpandTableColumn(FromColumnJoin,
"ColumnsDMVColumns",
        {"ExplicitName"}, {"From Column"}),
    ToColumnJoin = Table.NestedJoin(
        FromColumn,{"ToColumnID"},ColumnsDMV,{"ID"},"ColumnsDMVColumns",
JoinKind.Inner),
    ToColumn = Table.ExpandTableColumn(ToColumnJoin, "ColumnsDMVColumns",
        {"ExplicitName"}, {"To Column"}),
    CrossFilteringColumn = Table.AddColumn(ToColumn, "Cross-Filtering
Behavior", each
        if [CrossFilteringBehavior] = 1 then "Single Direction"
        else if [CrossFilteringBehavior] = 2 then "Bidirectional" else
"Other", type text),
    RenameActiveFlag = Table.
RenameColumns(CrossFilteringColumn,{{"IsActive", "Active Flag"}})
in
    RenameActiveFlag
```

The **Relationships** DMV (TMSCHEMA_RELATIONSHIPS) includes table and column ID columns, which are used for the joins to the tables (TMSCHEMA_TABLES) and columns (TMSCHEMA_COLUMNS) DMVs, respectively. Additionally, a more intuitive cross-filtering behavior column is added based on a conditional (if..then) expression.

## Metadata report pages

With the enhanced DMV data loaded, report pages can be created, visualizing the most import-ant columns. In *Figure 10.34*, the table and column names retrieved via the M query joins in the previous section, *Integrating and enhancing DMV data*, are included in a simple table visual:

**Dataset: Adventure Works Enterprise**
**Report Page: Relationships Metadata**

Last Refreshed: 1/3/2018

| From Table | | From Table | From Column | To Table | To Column | Active Flag | Cross-Filtering Behavior |
|---|---|---|---|---|---|---|---|
| ☐ Date | | Internet Sales | Currency Key | Currency | Currency Key | True | Single Direction |
| ■ Internet Sales | | Internet Sales | Customer Key | Customer | Customer Key | True | Single Direction |
| ■ Product | | Internet Sales | Due Date | Date | Date | False | Single Direction |
| ☐ Reseller Sales | | Internet Sales | Order Date | Date | Date | True | Single Direction |
| ☐ Sales and Margin Plan | | Internet Sales | Product Key | Product | Product Key | True | Single Direction |
| ☐ Sales Territory | | Internet Sales | Promotion Key | Promotion | Promotion Key | True | Single Direction |
| | | Internet Sales | Sales Territory Key | Sales Territory | Sales Territory Key | True | Single Direction |
| **Cross-Filtering Behavior** | | Internet Sales | Ship Date | Date | Date | False | Single Direction |
| ☐ Bidirectional | | Product | Product Subcategory | BridgeProductSubCat | Product Subcategory | True | Bidirectional |
| ☐ Single Direction | | | | | | | |

*Figure 10.34: Metadata report page*

A Power BI Desktop file containing the M queries and report pages from this example is included with the code bundle for this book. Additionally, *Chapter 3, Transforming Data with M*, and *Chapter 4, Designing Import, DirectQuery, and Composite Data Models*, describe the essential concepts of M queries and relationships contained in this section, respectively.

This concludes our exploration of metadata management and reporting.

# Summary

This chapter introduced workspaces and their fundamental role in managing and delivering Power BI content to groups of users in the Power BI service. A staged deployment architecture across development, test, and production workspaces was described and implementation guidance was provided. Additionally, several features and processes related to content management and governance were reviewed, including content sensitivity and protection, version history, and metadata management and reporting.

The next chapter examines the on-premises data gateway and the configuration of data refresh processes in the Power BI service. This includes the administration of the gateway, such as authorizing users and data sources, as well as monitoring gateway resource utilization.

## Join our community on Discord

Join our community's Discord space for discussions with the author and other readers: https://discord.gg/q6BPbHEPXp

# 11

# Managing the On-Premises Data Gateway

For many organizations, the data sources for Power BI datasets or reports are located in on-premises environments. The **on-premises data gateway** (gateway) serves as a bridge between the Power BI service and on-premises data sources, providing a means to securely connect to these sources to support scheduled data refreshes. In the case of DirectQuery and Analysis Services Live connections, the gateway is used to return the results of queries requested by users in the Power BI service.

As a critical component of many Power BI solutions and potentially other solutions utilizing Microsoft cloud services, such as Azure Analysis Services, Power Automate, and Power Apps, a sound understanding of the data gateway is essential.

This chapter reviews the architecture and behavior of the On-premises data gateway in the context of Power BI. End-to-end guidance and best practices are provided across the primary stages of deployment, from planning to installation, and setting up to management and monitoring.

In this chapter, we review the following topics:

- On-premises data gateway planning
- Gateway concepts
- Gateway installation and configuration
- Managing gateway clusters
- Troubleshooting and monitoring gateways
- Data refresh

We start with planning for the implementation of the On-premises data gateway.

# On-premises data gateway planning

Planning for the On-premises data gateway involves considerations for infrastructure/resources and networking, data governance, and the administration of the gateway itself. Before committing to a gateway, an organization can determine if BI solutions should be developed against data sources that require a gateway such as legacy on-premises databases or if this data should be loaded/centralized in a source that doesn't require a gateway such as Azure Synapse or Azure SQL Database.

For example, a BI team could determine that a gateway will only be used for a particular on-premises SQL Server database and any other on-premises sources such as files on network file shares and other databases will either not be supported or will require its own gateway in the future.

After determining that a gateway or cluster of gateways will indeed be a required component of the Power BI architecture, more detailed considerations can be reviewed such as the resources this gateway will need to support its expected workload, who will be responsible for administering this gateway, and who will be granted permissions to use the gateway.

One such detailed consideration is identifying which data sources require a gateway and understanding the role of the gateway in each deployment scenario. Recall from previous chapters that datasets support import, DirectQuery, and composite storage modes. In addition, reports can connect Live to Power BI datasets published to the Power BI service.

For example, if an import mode Power BI dataset or an import mode Azure Analysis Services model simply needs to be refreshed with on-premises data every night, then gateway resources (hardware) should be provisioned to support this specific nightly workload. This deployment scenario, with the refreshed and in-memory data model hosted in the cloud, is preferable from a user experience or query performance standpoint, as the report queries generated in the Power BI service do not have to access the on-premises source via the On-premises data gateway.

Alternatively, when the data model or data source accessed directly by Power BI reports is located in an on-premises environment, the On-premises data gateway is used to facilitate data transfer between the data source and the report queries from the Power BI service.

For example, a DirectQuery Power BI dataset built against an on-premises Teradata database results in report queries being sent from the Power BI service to the Teradata database via the On-premises data gateway and the results of those queries being returned to the Power BI service via the On-premises data gateway.

This deployment scenario can naturally require alternative gateway resources, such as additional CPU cores, given the potentially high volume of queries being generated dynamically based on user activity.

In addition to on-premises data sources, data sources residing in **Infrastructure-as-a-Service (IaaS) virtual machines (VMs)** also require a data gateway. This is an important exception as cloud data sources generally do not require a gateway. For example, **Platform-as-a-Service (PaaS)** sources, such as Azure SQL Database, and **Software-as-a-Service (SaaS)** solutions, such as Google Analytics, do not require a gateway.

The following two sets of questions address essential, high-level planning topics including the administration of the installed gateway. The following section, *Top gateway planning tasks*, as well as the *Gateway architectures* section later in this chapter, contain greater detail to support gateway deployment:

1. Where is the data being used by the Power BI dataset?

   Confirm that a gateway is needed to access the data source from Power BI. This access includes both scheduled data refresh and any DirectQuery or Live connections to the data source. Additional details on sources requiring a gateway are provided in the next section, *Top gateway planning tasks*.

2. If a gateway is needed, is the data source supported with a **generally available (GA)** data connector?

   If a source-specific connector is not available, the gateway supports **Open Database Connectivity (ODBC)** and **Object Linking and Embedding Database (OLE DB)** connections as well. The current list of supported data sources is available at https://bit.ly/30N5ofG. Data connectors labeled as (Beta) in the **Get Data** window of Power BI Desktop should only be used for testing for stability reasons and the fact that functionality may change.

3. Is the on-premises data or the IaaS data being imported to the Power BI dataset(s) or an Azure Analysis Services model?

   If yes, the gateway supports the scheduled refresh/processing activities for these datasets. If no, the gateway supports user report queries of the data source via DirectQuery or Live connections.

4. Will a standard On-premises data gateway be used or will a personal gateway (personal mode) be used?

In all corporate BI deployments, the default and recommended on-premises gateway is installed by the IT organization on IT-owned and maintained servers.

However, in certain business-led self-service projects or in scenarios in which an IT-owned gateway server is not available, the personal gateway could be installed on a business user's machine, allowing that user to configure scheduled refreshes of import mode datasets.

A single gateway can be used to support multiple datasets, and both import and DirectQuery modes. However, it can be advantageous to isolate the alternative Power BI workloads across distinct gateway clusters (discussed later in this chapter), such as with an import gateway cluster and a DirectQuery or Live connection gateway cluster.

Without this isolation, the scheduled refresh activities of import mode datasets (Power BI or Azure Analysis Services) could potentially impact the performance of user queries submitted via DirectQuery and Live connection datasets. Additionally, as mentioned earlier, scheduled refresh activities can require far different gateway resources (for example, memory) than the queries generated via DirectQuery datasets or Live connections to on-premises **SQL Server Analysis Services (SSAS)**.

In addition to provisioning hardware and installing the gateway(s) for each scenario, BI teams must also plan for the administration and management of the gateway. Answering the following five questions contributes to planning the implementation:

1. Which users will administer the gateway in Power BI?

   This should be more than one user. Preferably, an **Azure Active Directory (AAD)** security group of multiple gateway admins can be configured. These users do not need Power BI Pro licenses if they're only administering gateway clusters.

   In larger Power BI deployments, distinct users or security groups could be assigned as administrators of different gateways. For example, two users could administer a gateway cluster utilized by enterprise or corporate-owned BI content while two other users could administer a gateway cluster used to support self-service BI content and projects.

   This isolation of hardware resources between corporate and self-service BI (that is, business user/team owned) can also be implemented with Power BI Premium capacities, as described in *Chapter 15, Building Enterprise BI with Power BI Premium*. The essential goal of this isolation is to provide the self-service projects with resources aligned to these needs while ensuring that high priority and widely utilized corporate BI assets are not impacted by self-service content or activities.

2. Which authentication credentials or method will be used to configure the gateway data sources?

   For SSAS and Azure Analysis Services, this should be a server administrator of the Analysis Services instance. For certain DirectQuery data sources, a **single sign-on (SSO)** option is supported in which the Power BI user's identity is passed to the source system, thus leveraging the source system's security. The *DirectQuery datasets* section later in this chapter contains details of this configuration.

3. Which users will be authorized to use the gateway?

   Users or security groups of users must be mapped to the data source of a gateway. These are usually report authors with Power BI Pro licenses.

4. Where will the gateway recovery key be stored?

   Recovery keys are necessary for migrating, restoring, or taking over an existing gateway.

5. Who will be responsible for updating the On-premises data gateway as new versions are released?

   Just like Power BI Desktop, new versions of the On-premises data gateway are frequently released. This release schedule is as frequent as once a month. New versions include new features and improvements, such as the support for datasets with both cloud and on-premises data sources and/or new and updated connector support.

   The Power BI team recommends staying up to date with new releases and will not support old gateway versions. Each new gateway version includes the same M Query engine utilized by the corresponding release of Power BI Desktop. Examples and considerations for M Queries were described in *Chapter 3, Connecting to Sources and Transforming Data with M.*

With the essential questions answered regarding gateway planning, we next take a closer look at the most important gateway planning tasks.

# Top gateway planning tasks

Since the gateway relates to different areas of IT, including infrastructure, networking, and data security, subject matter experts in these areas often inquire about the technical requirements of the gateway and its functionality. Additionally, business intelligence teams want to ensure that the gateway doesn't become a bottleneck to query performance and that dependencies on an individual gateway are avoided.

BI/IT teams responsible for deploying Power BI solutions with on-premises data (or IaaS data) must partner with these other IT stakeholders to resolve questions and provision the appropriate resources for the On-premises data gateway. This section addresses four of the most common gateway planning tasks. Information related to high availability and security is included in the gateway clusters and architectures, and gateway security sections, respectively.

Let's now address the first gateway planning task, determining whether a gateway is needed.

## Determining whether a gateway is needed

As one would expect, an On-premises data gateway is usually not required for connectivity to cloud data sources. PaaS offerings, such as Azure SQL, and SaaS solutions, such as Salesforce, do not require a gateway. In addition, a virtual network data gateway is available for securely connecting to resources provisioned within the same virtual network in Azure such as Azure table and blob storage, Cosmos DB, and Snowflake.

However, data sources that reside in an IaaS VM do require a gateway. Additionally, the Web. Page() function used in M Queries also requires a gateway. This function is used by the **Web Data Connector (WDC) (Get Data | Web)** to return the contents of an HTML web page as a table, as shown in the following M Query:

```
// Retrieve table of data access M functions and their descriptions
let
    Source = Web.Page(Web.Contents("https://msdn.microsoft.com/en-US/
library/mt296615.aspx")),
    PageToTable = Source{0}[Data],
    ChangedType = Table.TransformColumnTypes(PageToTable,
        {{"Function", type text}, {"Description", type text}})
in
    ChangedType
```

In the preceding example, a two-column table (Function, Description) of M functions is retrieved from an MSDN web page and imported into a table in Power BI.

Additionally, all data sources for a dataset that accesses an on-premises data source must be added to the list of data sources in the gateway management portal. For example, if a dataset uses both SharePoint (on-premises) and an Azure SQL database, the URL for the Azure SQL database must also be added as a data source (via the SQL Server data source type) in the gateway management portal. If one of the data sources for the dataset is not configured for the gateway, the gateway will not appear in the dataset settings to support a refresh.

Assuming that a gateway is needed, the next task is to identify where to install the gateway.

## Identifying where the gateway should be installed

Gateways should be installed in locations that minimize the latency between the Power BI service tenant, the gateway server, and the on-premises data source. Reduced latency between these three points results in improved query performance.

Minimizing this latency is especially important when the gateway is used to support interactive report queries from Power BI to on-premises DirectQuery sources and Live connections to on-premises SSAS models. Network latency from an IP location to Azure data regions can be tested at http://azurespeed.com.

For example, via this free tool, it can quickly be determined that the average latency to the West US region is 100 ms while the East US region is only 37 ms. The lower latency of the East US region is due to the physical proximity of this region to the source IP location (near Columbus, OH). It is most often the case that reduced physical distance results in lower network latency.

For example, if the Power BI tenant for your organization is located in the North Central US (Illinois) region in Microsoft Azure and your on-premises data source (for example, Oracle) is also located in the upper Midwest region of the United States, then the gateway should be installed on a server near or between these two locations.

The location of a Power BI tenant can be found by clicking the **About Power BI** menu item via the question mark (?) icon in the top-right corner of the Power BI service. Performing this action displays a dialog similar to *Figure 11.1*.

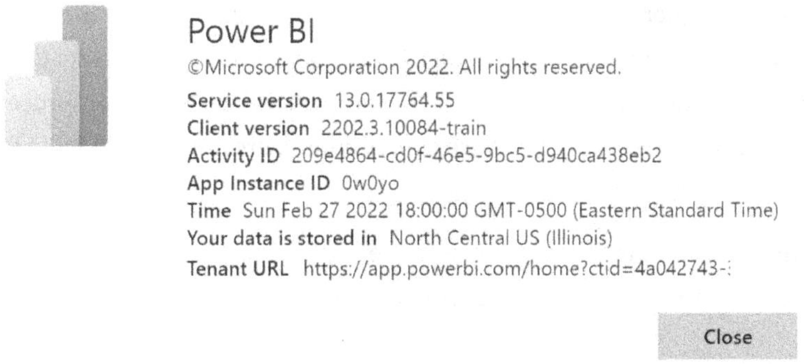

Power BI
©Microsoft Corporation 2022. All rights reserved.
Service version  13.0.17764.55
Client version  2202.3.10084-train
Activity ID  209e4864-cd0f-46e5-9bc5-d940ca438eb2
App Instance ID  0w0yo
Time  Sun Feb 27 2022 18:00:00 GMT-0500 (Eastern Standard Time)
Your data is stored in  North Central US (Illinois)
Tenant URL  https://app.powerbi.com/home?ctid=4a042743-:

Close

*Figure 11.1: About Power BI: tenant location*

In this example, the Power BI content for the organization is being stored in the **North Central US (Illinois)** Azure region.

Therefore, the gateway should be installed on a location that minimizes the distance between Illinois and the location of the data source.

One example of this would be to install the gateway on the same subnet of the production data source server. It's not necessary, or recommended, to install the gateway on the same server as the production data source given that the data gateway service will consume memory and processor resources that may impact the performance of the source system.

Alternatively, assuming the on-premises data center is hybridized with Azure via a **virtual private network (VPN)** connection such as Azure **ExpressRoute**, the gateway could be installed as an IaaS VM in the North Central US (Illinois) Azure region. ExpressRoute extends on-premises networks to Microsoft Azure via a private connection.

Currently, there are 66 Azure regions globally with 12 new regions planned. This link identifies the Azure regions and the criteria for choosing a specific region: http://bit.ly/2B598tD.

Once a location is identified, the next task is to determine the hardware resources required for the gateway.

## Defining the gateway infrastructure and hardware requirements

The recommended starting point for a server that hosts the gateway is eight CPU cores, 8 GB of memory, at least 4 GB of **solid-state drives (SSD)**, the 64-bit version of Windows 2012 R2 (or later), and .NET Framework 4.8 (for gateway version February 2021 or later). However, hardware requirements for the gateway server vary significantly based on the type of dataset supported (import versus DirectQuery/Live connection), the volume of concurrent users, and the queries requested.

For example, if an M query or part of an M query is not folded back to the source system, as described in *Chapter 3, Connecting to Sources and Transforming Data with M*, the gateway server must execute the non-folded M expressions during the scheduled refresh (import) process. Depending on the volume of data and the logic of these expressions, a greater amount of RAM would better support these local operations.

Similarly, if many users are interacting with reports based on a DirectQuery dataset or a Live connection to an SSAS model (on-premises), additional CPU cores would provide better performance.

The gateway installs on any domain-joined machine and cannot be installed on a domain controller. Additionally, only one gateway can be installed per computer per gateway mode (enterprise versus personal). Therefore, it's possible to have both an enterprise mode and a personal mode gateway running on the same machine.

It's strongly recommended to avoid a single point of failure by installing instances of the gateway on separate servers. These multiple instances can serve as a single gateway cluster of resources available to support data refreshes and queries against on-premises data sources. Gateway clusters and architectures consisting of separate gateway clusters are described in the *Gateway clusters* and *Gateway architectures* of this chapter.

Performance logging associated with the gateway and the gateway server can be used to determine whether adjustments in available resources (RAM and CPU) are necessary. Guidance on interpreting reporting on and interpreting these logs is included in the *Troubleshooting and monitoring gateways* section later in this chapter.

In terms of network configuration, the gateway creates an outbound connection to Azure Service Bus and does not require inbound ports. The gateway communicates on the following outbound ports: TCP 443 (default), 5671, 5672, and 9350 through 9354.

It's recommended that organizations whitelist the IP addresses for the data region of their Power BI tenant (for example, North Central US) within their firewall. The list of IP addresses for the Azure data centers can be downloaded via the following URL: https://bit.ly/3vqg6JQ.

The downloaded list of Azure IP addresses is contained within a JSON file which can be easily accessed via Power BI Desktop via an M Query similar to the following:

```
let
    Source = Json.Document(File.Contents("C:\Users\gdeckler\Downloads\
ServiceTags_Public_20220221.json")),
    #"Converted to Table" = Table.FromRecords({Source}),
    #"Expanded values" = Table.ExpandListColumn(#"Converted to Table",
"values"),
    #"Expanded values1" = Table.ExpandRecordColumn(#"Expanded values",
"values", {"name", "id", "properties"}, {"values.name", "values.id",
"values.properties"}),
    #"Expanded values.properties" = Table.ExpandRecordColumn(#"Expanded
values1", "values.properties", {"changeNumber", "region", "regionId",
"platform", "systemService", "addressPrefixes", "networkFeatures"},
{"values.properties.changeNumber", "values.properties.region", "values.
properties.regionId", "values.properties.platform", "values.properties.
systemService", "values.properties.addressPrefixes", "values.properties.
networkFeatures"}),
    #"Changed Type" = Table.TransformColumnTypes(#"Expanded values.
properties",{{"changeNumber", Int64.Type}, {"cloud", type text}, {"values.
```

```
name", type text}, {"values.id", type text}, {"values.properties.
changeNumber", Int64.Type}, {"values.properties.region", type any},
{"values.properties.regionId", Int64.Type}, {"values.properties.
platform", type text}, {"values.properties.systemService", type text},
{"values.properties.addressPrefixes", type any}, {"values.properties.
networkFeatures", type any}}),
    #"Expanded values.properties.addressPrefixes" = Table.
ExpandListColumn(#"Changed Type", "values.properties.addressPrefixes"),
    #"Extracted Values" = Table.TransformColumns(#"Expanded values.
properties.addressPrefixes", {"values.properties.networkFeatures", each
Text.Combine(List.Transform(_, Text.From), ","), type text}),
    #"Filtered Rows" = Table.SelectRows(#"Extracted Values", each true)
in
    #"Filtered Rows"
```

Once the infrastructure and hardware are configured and provisioned, the next task is to define gateway roles and permissions.

## Defining gateway roles and permissions

Similar to Power BI workspace roles described in the previous chapter, different roles are available for the on-premises data gateway and organizations should plan for which users and/or groups should be assigned to which roles.

There are three security roles for gateways, Admin, Connection creator, and Connection creator with sharing. The Admin role has full control of the gateway including the ability to fully manage data sources (connections), users and permissions. In contrast, the Connection creator role is limited to only creating connections (data sources) on the gateway. The Connection creator with sharing provides the additional ability to share the gateway with users.

There are also three connection security roles, Owner, User and User with sharing. The Owner role can fully manage the connection including the ability to delete the connection, update data source credentials and manage permissions. In contrast, the User role can simply use the connection and the User with sharing adds the ability to share the connection with others.

For example, a small team of IT admins may be assigned the gateway Admin role and be responsible for keeping the gateway updated to the latest version and granting required access to other users. Additionally, certain dataset authors or BI teams could be identified as valid users of the gateway or for only certain data sources configured on the gateway.

Some BI teams might prefer to use the User with sharing role, assigning this to a small group within the business. As these users are closer to the needs and requirements for the business these users would then have the necessary knowledge to know who else within the business requires access to the data source connection.

As with the Power BI workspace roles described in the previous chapter, groups should be used in role assignments and then users assigned to those groups. Assigning users and/or groups to gateways, as well as managing data sources, is done within the Power Platform Admin Center (`https://admin.powerplatform.microsoft.com/`) using the Data page.

With roles and permissions assigned, the next task is to plan for the creation and management of recovery keys.

## Planning for recovery keys

Recovery keys (essentially a password) are a critical security component of Power BI gateways. Recovery keys are used to generate encryption keys used to encrypt data source credentials. Recovery keys are also required to move gateways from one server to another and when adding gateway instances to gateway clusters. These subjects are explained in greater detail later in this chapter.

A recovery key is entered when installing a new gateway instance. This key is not shown when entered and must be confirmed. This original key must be known in order to set a different key. Given the importance of recovery keys, it is imperative that enterprise BI teams properly plan for their creation and management.

Once entered and the gateway installation is complete, loss of the recovery key may mean that the entire gateway or even an entire gateway cluster must be removed and rebuilt. Therefore, enterprise BI teams should agree upon and pre-generate an alphanumeric key consisting of at least 8 characters/numbers. This key should then be stored in password vault software or otherwise treated as a highly valuable, highly confidential enterprise password.

Because the requirement to enter a recovery key during gateway installation often comes as a surprise to those unfamiliar with Power BI and because recovery keys are often not needed for extended periods of time, more than one gateway has had to be rebuilt because of the loss of the recovery key. With the importance of recovery keys understood, the next decision to make is deciding between installing the gateway in standard or personal mode.

# Standard versus personal mode

There are two separate downloads for the On-premises data gateway, one for **standard mode** and one for **personal mode**. The recommended gateway mode, standard mode, provides all the functionality of the personal mode plus many more features and management capabilities.

The additional features include support for DirectQuery and Live connection datasets, several other Azure services, such as Power Automate, and the management capabilities described in the *Managing gateway clusters* section later in this chapter.

Who can install gateways can be managed within the **Power Platform admin center**. The Data page of the Power Platform Admin Center provides an option to Manage gateway installers where administrators can specify which users are authorized to install standard mode gateways. Personal gateways can only be disabled or managed by PowerShell scripts that utilize the `DataGateway` module and specifically the `Set-DataGatewayTenantPolicy`.

A single personal mode gateway can be installed per Power BI user account and can only be used for the on-demand or scheduled refresh of the import mode Power BI datasets. Most importantly, the personal mode gateway is completely tied to the individual user and cannot be shared.

For example, if the gateway is installed in personal mode on a user's laptop, that laptop will need to be on and connected to the internet to support any scheduled data refreshes. Additionally, unlike the administrators of a standard mode gateway, a personal mode user cannot authorize other users to leverage the personal mode gateway and its configured data sources.

In *Figure 11.2*, both a personal mode gateway and a standard gateway are available to refresh a dataset.

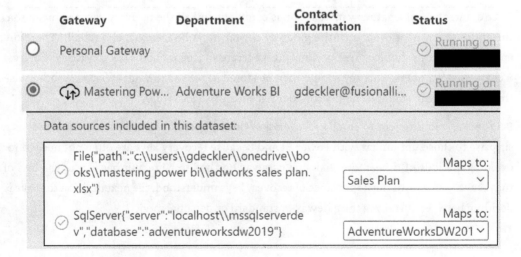

*Figure 11.2: Dataset gateway connection*

In *Figure 11.2* the various data source connections within the dataset are mapped to configured data sources available in the standard gateway cluster. If the user was not authorized to use the On-premises data gateway (**Mastering Power BI**), the personal mode gateway could be used to complete the refresh assuming the user has the necessary privileges to the on-premises data sources of the import mode dataset.

The personal mode gateway is not intended for large datasets or datasets supporting reports and dashboards that many users depend on. The personal mode gateways should only be considered for enabling individual business users to work on personal or proof-of-concept projects.

For example, the business user may have several Excel workbooks and other frequently changing local files that are not configured as data sources on a standard gateway. If the user has been assigned a Power BI Pro license, the personal mode gateway allows the user to keep Power BI reports and dashboards based on these sources updated for review by colleagues.

In the event that the user's content requires reliable, longer-term support, the BI/IT organization can add the data sources to a standard gateway thus removing the dependency on the user's machine. All the remaining sections of this chapter are exclusively focused on the standard data gateway.

With reliability and supportability in mind, we now look at some important concepts related to gateways.

# Gateway concepts

There are a number of different concepts and designs enterprise BI teams should be familiar with when it comes to the On-premises data gateway. These include the concept of gateway clusters, different gateway architecture designs, and security. Each of these subjects is explored in detail in the following sections.

## Gateway clusters

Gateways natively support clustering. Clustering is when independent software systems, called instances or nodes, work together as a unified resource to provide greater scalability and reliability. Each Power BI dataset is associated with a single gateway cluster, which is composed of one or more standard gateway instances.

For example, if a Power BI dataset imports data from both a SQL Server database and an Excel file, the same gateway cluster is responsible for the import from both sources.

Likewise, if hundreds of business users interact with reports based on the same DirectQuery dataset or a Live connection to an on-premises SSAS instance, these user interactions generate query requests to the same gateway cluster.

Gateway clusters representing multiple standard gateway instances (for example, primary and secondary) provide both high availability and load balancing. Each instance must be installed on a separate machine as per the *Defining the gateway infrastructure and hardware requirements* section.

From an availability standpoint, if an individual gateway instance within a cluster is not running, the data refresh and user query requests from the Power BI service are routed to the other gateway instance(s) within the cluster. In terms of query performance and scalability, the Power BI service can automatically distribute (load balance) the query requests across the multiple gateway instances within the cluster.

Data source configurations for the primary gateway of the cluster, which is the first gateway installed for the cluster, are leveraged by any additional gateways added to the cluster. In *Figure 11.3* from the gateway installer application, a new gateway is added to an existing gateway cluster:

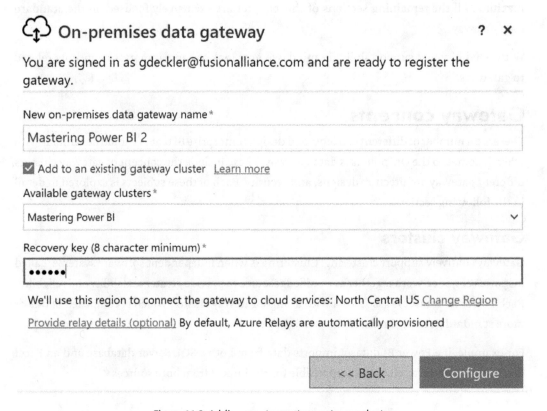

*Figure 11.3: Adding a gateway to a gateway cluster*

In this example, the new gateway (**Mastering Power BI 2**) is added to the **Mastering Power BI** gateway cluster as per the **Add to an existing gateway cluster** checkbox and **Available gateway clusters** selection. Note that the **Recovery key** for the primary gateway instance, which was created when the first gateway instance of the cluster was installed, is required to add a gateway to a cluster.

Be aware that the gateway management portal in the Power BI service only displays the gateway clusters, not the individual gateways within each cluster. Both the gateway clusters and the individual gateways within each cluster can be accessed and managed via PowerShell scripts as per the *Managing gateway clusters* section.

Before adding a gateway to a cluster, ensure that the new gateway instance is able to connect to the same data sources configured for the cluster. As described in the *Top gateway planning tasks* section, the additional gateways added to gateway clusters should also be installed in locations that minimize the distance between the gateway server, the Power BI service tenant, and the data source(s).

Let's now turn our attention to some different architectures for gateways within an enterprise configuration.

## Gateway architectures

For large-scale deployments of Power BI in which multiple types of datasets and workloads are supported (such as import, DirectQuery, and Live connection queries), BI teams can consider multiple gateway clusters. In this approach, each gateway cluster is tailored to meet the specific resource needs (RAM and CPU) of the different workloads, such as large nightly refreshes or high volumes of concurrent queries in the early mornings.

For example, one gateway cluster could be composed of two gateway instances with a relatively high amount of available RAM on each gateway server. This cluster would have resources available during the most intensive scheduled refresh operations (for example, 4 A.M. to 6 A.M.) and would be exclusively used by import mode Power BI datasets and any Azure Analysis Services models that also regularly import data from on-premises sources.

A separate gateway cluster would be created based on two gateway instances with a relatively high number of CPU cores on each gateway server. This gateway cluster would be used exclusively by DirectQuery Power BI datasets and any reports based on Live connection to an on-premises SQL Server Analysis Services instance.

A third gateway cluster, in addition to an import and a DirectQuery/Live connection cluster, could be dedicated to business-led BI projects. For example, as described in the *Standard versus personal mode* section earlier in this chapter, certain data sources maintained by business teams (for example, Excel workbooks) may require the high availability and management benefits of the On-premises data gateway.

Generally, this self-service cluster would be oriented toward scheduled refresh operations, but organizations may also want to empower business users to create DirectQuery datasets or reports based on Live connections to SSAS instances (on-premises).

In *Figure 11.4* from the **Manage gateways** portal in the Power BI service, two gateway clusters have been configured:

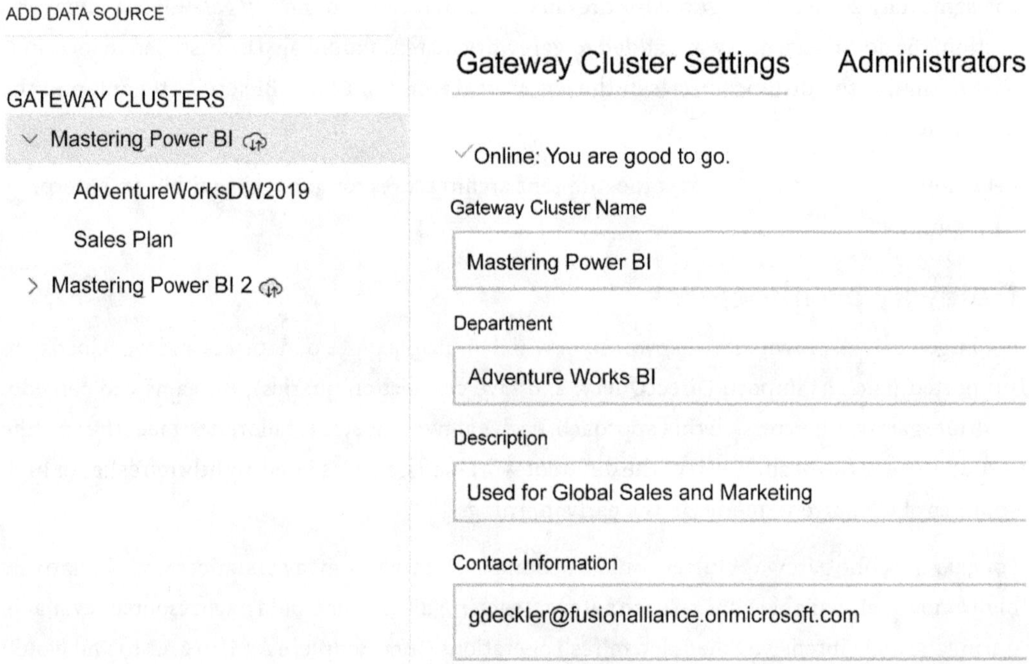

ADD DATA SOURCE

GATEWAY CLUSTERS

∨ Mastering Power BI ☁

    AdventureWorksDW2019

    Sales Plan

> Mastering Power BI 2 ☁

Gateway Cluster Settings       Administrators

∨ Online: You are good to go.

Gateway Cluster Name

Mastering Power BI

Department

Adventure Works BI

Description

Used for Global Sales and Marketing

Contact Information

gdeckler@fusionalliance.onmicrosoft.com

*Figure 11.4: Manage gateways in the Power BI service*

If gateway clusters are created for specific workloads (for example, import versus DirectQuery), it can be helpful to note this both in the **Gateway Cluster Name** and in its **Description**. It's not recommended to allow a single point of failure but if only one gateway server is used in a cluster then the name of this server can be included in the cluster name and description.

*Figure 11.5* depicts a gateway cluster that supports scheduled refreshes of datasets:

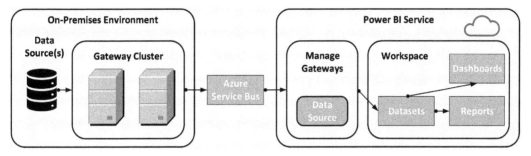

*Figure 11.5: Scheduled data refresh via gateway cluster*

With the data source(s) configured in the **Manage Gateways** portal in the Power BI service, a scheduled data refresh for an import mode dataset can be configured to use the **Gateway Cluster**. The **Gateway Cluster** receives the query request at the scheduled time and is responsible for connecting to the data source(s) and executing the queries that load/refresh the tables of the Power BI dataset.

Once the dataset in the Power BI service is refreshed, dashboard tiles based on the dataset are also refreshed. Given that report queries are local to the refreshed dataset within the same Power BI service tenant, and given the performance optimizations of the engine running within import mode Power BI datasets (that is, columnar compression, in-memory), query performance is usually very good with this deployment.

*Figure 11.6* depicts two gateway clusters being used to support both the scheduled refresh of an import mode dataset and a Live connection to an SSAS tabular instance:

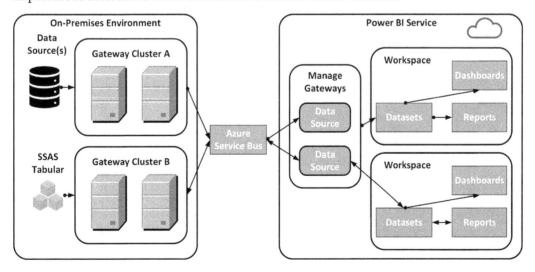

*Figure 11.6: Multiple gateway clusters*

**Gateway Cluster A** in the preceding diagram functions just like *Figure 11.5* in supporting scheduled refreshes of import mode datasets. **Gateway Cluster B** has been created to exclusively support queries requested via Live connections to an on-premises SSAS database—an SSAS tabular model in this scenario.

Given the high volume of query requests generated by users interacting with Power BI reports based on the SSAS model, the servers used in **Gateway Cluster B** can be provisioned with additional CPU cores and actively monitored via performance counters for changes in utilization.

In addition to the interactive query requests from Live connection reports, owners of datasets can configure a scheduled refresh for the cache supporting dashboard tiles based on Live connection reports. Guidance on configuring this feature is included in the *Dashboard cache refresh* section at the end of this chapter.

The description of **Gateway Cluster B** is also generally applicable to DirectQuery datasets based on supported sources, such as SQL Server, Oracle, and Teradata. Just like Live connections to SSAS, DirectQuery reports built against these datasets also generate high volumes of queries that must go through the gateway cluster and be returned to the Power BI service tenant.

Given the additional latency created by the requests for queries and the transfer of query results back to the Power BI service, it's especially important to develop and provision efficient data sources for DirectQuery and Live connection reports. Two examples of this include using the clustered columnstore index for SQL Server and optimizing the DAX expressions used for measures of an SSAS model.

Additionally, organizations can consider Azure ExpressRoute to create a fast, private connection between on-premises infrastructure and Azure. The following URL provides documentation on this service: `http://bit.ly/2tCCwEv`.

With alternative gateway architectures understood, let's next explore how gateways implement security.

## Gateway security

Given that potentially sensitive data can flow back and forth between the cloud and on-premises environments, Microsoft has designed the On-premises data gateway to be extremely secure.

Administrators of the On-premises data gateway are responsible for configuring the data sources that can be used with each gateway cluster. As shown in *Figure 11.7* from the **Manage gateways** portal in the Power BI service, credentials entered for data sources are encrypted:

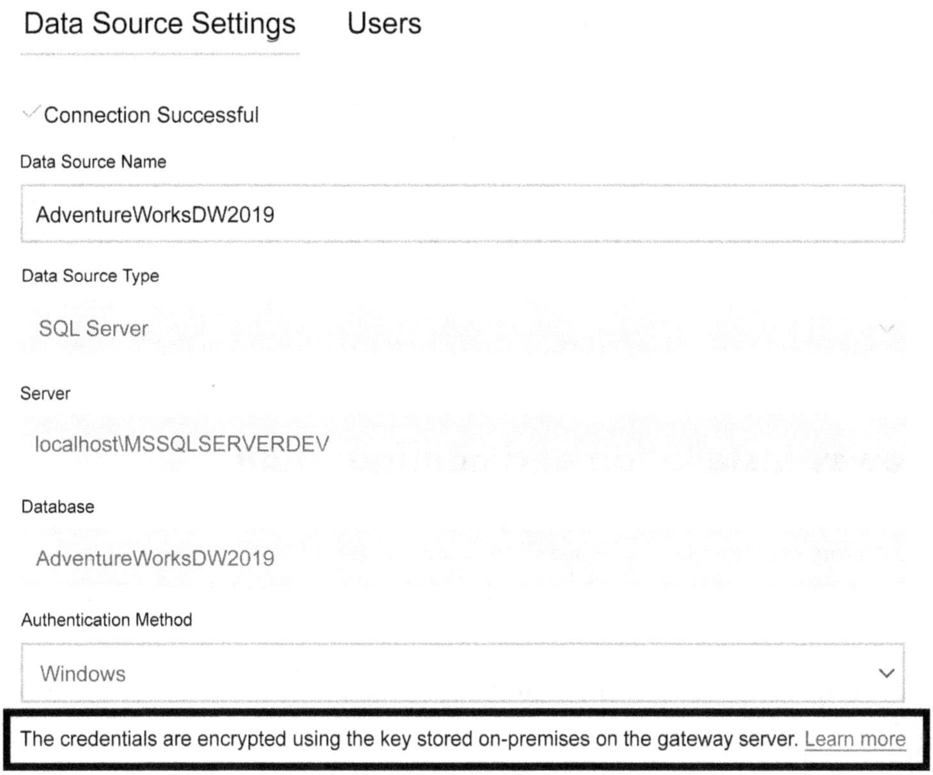

## Data Source Settings　　Users

---

✓ Connection Successful

Data Source Name

> AdventureWorksDW2019

Data Source Type

> SQL Server ⌄

Server

> localhost\MSSQLSERVERDEV

Database

> AdventureWorksDW2019

Authentication Method

> Windows ⌄

The credentials are encrypted using the key stored on-premises on the gateway server. Learn more

*Figure 11.7: Encrypted data source credentials*

As mentioned, the recovery key entered during gateway installation is used to encrypt these credentials. The data source credentials are only decrypted once the query request reaches the on-premises gateway cluster within the corporate network.

The gateway decrypts the credentials needed for query requests and, once the query has executed, it encrypts the results of these query requests prior to pushing this data to the Power BI service. The Power BI service never knows the on-premises credential values.

Technically, the following four-step process occurs to facilitate communication and data transfer between the Power BI service and the on-premises sources:

1. The Power BI service initiates a scheduled refresh or a user interacts with a DirectQuery or a Live connection report.

2. In either event, a query request is created and analyzed by the data movement service in Power BI.

3.  The data movement service determines the appropriate Azure Service Bus communication channel for the given query.

4.  A distinct service bus instance is configured per gateway.

Obviously, all of this complexity is hidden from the end users and even administrators and all network traffic is encrypted. For more information regarding the specifics of security for the gateway and Power BI in general, see the Power BI security whitepaper found here: `https://bit.ly/3tmJJJ3`.

With the important concepts of clustering, architectures, and security understood, we next look at installing and configuring gateways.

## Gateway installation and configuration

Once the gateway scenario and architecture are planned as per the previous sections, BI or IT administrators can download and install the gateway (or multiple gateways) on the chosen server(s). The gateway installation file to be downloaded is small and the installation process is quick and straightforward.

The gateway installer application is obtained via the **Download** (down arrow) dropdown in the Power BI service, as shown in *Figure 11.8*.

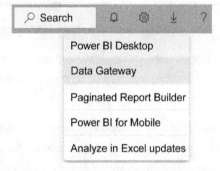

*Figure 11.8: Download in Power BI service*

The **Data Gateway** item from the download menu shown in *Figure 11.8* currently links to a Power BI Gateway page with two large buttons near the top for downloading either the standard or personal mode gateway installers.

Selecting either button downloads the installer file (`GatewayInstall.exe` or on-premises data gateway (`personal mode`).exe) locally. The installation and configuration process via the installer application is very straightforward.

Step-by-step instructions have been documented here (see *Install the gateway* section): https://bit.ly/3C71AYo. As noted in the *Planning for recovery keys* section, the most critical step in this process is entering and securely storing the recovery key used during installation.

Once the installation and configuration are complete, an On-premises data gateway application is available on the server to help manage the gateway, as shown in *Figure 11.9*.

On-premises data gateway — 1.53 GB — 11/7/2021

*Figure 11.9: On-premises data gateway application*

Details on the settings available via this application are included in the *Troubleshooting and monitoring gateways* section later in this chapter. When first getting started with the gateway, you can launch the application after configuration and sign in with a Power BI service account to check the status of the gateway and to get familiar with the tool.

The same installation software can be downloaded and run to update an existing On-premises data gateway to the latest version. The update process is very quick to complete and the On-premises data gateway application reflects the new version number on the **Status** page, as shown in *Figure 11.10*.

## On-premises data gateway

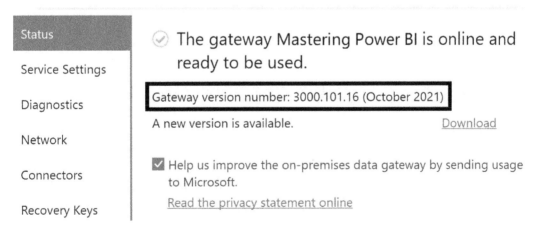

*Figure 11.10: On-premises data gateway Status*

It's strongly recommended to regularly update the On-premises data gateway to the latest version. An out-of-date gateway is flagged for updating on the **Status** page of the On-premises data gateway and may result in data refresh or connectivity issues.

Additionally, administrators should be aware of the following two XML configuration files for the gateway:

```
C:\Program Files\On-premises data gateway\EnterpriseGatewayConfigurator.
exe.config
```

```
C:\Program Files\On-premises data gateway\Microsoft.PowerBI.
EnterpriseGateway.exe.config
```

The `EnterpriseGatewayConfigurator.exe.config` file relates to the installation screens that configure the gateway. The `Microsoft.PowerBI.EnterpriseGateway.exe.config` file is for the actual Windows service that handles the query requests from the Power BI service. This Windows service runs under a default service account, as explained in the next section.

## The gateway service account

By default, the gateway runs under the **NT SERVICE\PBIEgwService** Windows service account. However, as shown in *Figure 11.11*, this account can be changed via the **Service Settings** tab of the On-premises data gateway desktop application.

 On-premises data gateway

*Figure 11.11: On-premises data gateway Service Settings*

In *Figure 11.11*, a user has opened the gateway application from the server on which a gateway instance has been installed. Additionally, in order to change the service account, the user has signed in to Power BI from the gateway application with the email address used to log in to the Power BI service.

If the default account (**NT SERVICE\PBIEgwService**) is able to access the internet and thus Azure Service Bus, ensure that the account can also authenticate to the required on-premises data sources, such as the production SQL Server instance. In some environments, the default account cannot access the internet as it is not an authenticated domain user.

In this scenario, the service account can be revised to a domain user account within the Active Directory domain. To avoid the need to routinely reset the password for the Active Directory account, it's recommended that a managed service account is created in Active Directory and used by the gateway service.

We next take a more detailed look at the network communication used by the gateway.

## TCP versus HTTPS mode

As shown in *Figure 11.12*, the **Network** tab of the On-premises data gateway desktop application displays the network settings for a gateway. By default, the gateway uses **HTTPS** network communication. However, as shown in *Figure 11.12*, the gateway can be forced to exclusively use direct **Transmission Control Protocol (TCP)** instead.

*Figure 11.12: On-premises data gateway application Network settings*

A restart of the gateway is required to apply a change in network communication mode and thus this modification should only be implemented when minimal or no query requests are being processed.

When originally released, the gateway defaulted to direct TCP with HTTPS provided as an option. HTTPS is now the default as this requires fewer network ports to be opened in firewalls and overall less configuration.

We next look at the subject of custom connectors.

## Connectors

The gateway supports custom connectors not included with Power BI Desktop. Custom connectors are optional and may be developed by third parties or internally by organizations.

As shown in *Figure 11.13*, the **Connectors** tab is used to configure **Custom data connectors** in the On-premises data gateway desktop application.

*Figure 11.13: On-premises data gateway application Connectors settings*

As shown in *Figure 11.13*, the gateway provides a suggested folder path:

```
C:\WINDOWS\ServiceProfiles\PBIEgwService\Documents\Power  BI  Desktop\Custom
Connectors
```

This folder path may or may not exist and may not be the desired folder for custom connectors. Regardless of the folder path chosen, it is recommended that all gateways have a consistent path for custom connectors and that gateway administrators verify that the folder exists and the service account has the appropriate permissions on each gateway.

More information about creating custom connectors for Power BI can be found here: `https://github.com/Microsoft/DataConnectors`.

Let us now turn our attention to the subject of recovery key configuration.

# Recovery Keys

The **Recovery Keys** tab in the On-premises data gateway desktop application provides a single option to **Set new recovery key.** Clicking this link opens up the **Add new recovery key** dialog shown in *Figure 11.14*.

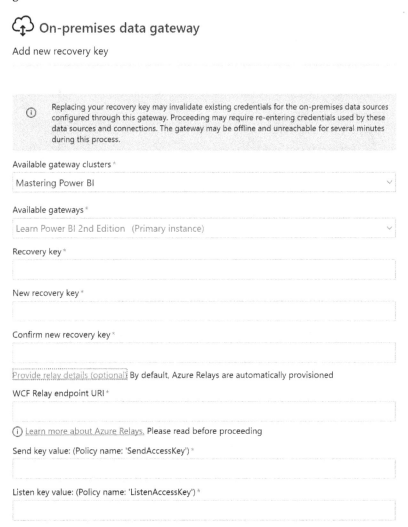

*Figure 11.14: On-premises data gateway application Connectors settings*

As indicated by the information displayed in the text box at the top of the page, changing the recovery key should only be done when the gateway is not being used as the change requires that the gateway restart and that data credentials need to be reentered.

Changing recovery keys should be a rare event and only entertained if the security of the recovery key has been compromised, such as someone that had access to the recovery key leaving the organization.

Also notice in *Figure 11.14* that it is possible to configure the **Azure Relays** used by the gateway by clicking the **Provide relay details (optional)** link. Azure Relays enable the ability to securely expose services running on-premises to Azure without opening firewall ports or otherwise changing network infrastructure. More information about this option can be found here: `https://bit.ly/35FUeis`.

This completes our exploration of gateway installation and configuration. We next turn our attention to managing gateway clusters.

## Managing gateway clusters

Once a gateway is installed, the Power BI account used to register the gateway during installation can access the **Manage gateways** portal in the Power BI service to assign administrators for the gateway.

The **Manage gateways** portal is available via the gear icon in the top-right corner of the Power BI service, as shown in *Figure 11.15*:

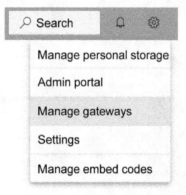

*Figure 11.15: Manage gateways*

The **Manage gateways** portal exposes all gateway clusters where the user is assigned as an administrator. The following sections describe the management of gateways within the Power BI Service. However, it is important to note that certain essential gateway management features have been moved to the Power Platform Admin Center.

Specifically, the gateway security roles and permissions described in the *Defining gateway roles and permissions* section of this chapter are only available in the Power Platform Admin Center. In addition, the Power Platform Admin Center also provides the ability to specify which users are authorized to install standard mode gateways as described in the *Standard versus personal mode* section of this chapter.

Moving forward, it is likely that additional gateway management functionality will be introduced within the Power Platform Admin Center given that on-premises data gateways are used across multiple Power Platform products including Power BI, Power Apps and Power Automate.

Let's now explore the primary functionality and tasks of gateway administrators in the following sections.

# Gateway administrators

Administrators of gateway clusters have the ability to add or remove data sources, modify the authentication to those sources, and enable or disable users or groups of users from utilizing the cluster.

Given the importance of these responsibilities, assigning more than one gateway administrator, such as a security group of administrators, is strongly recommended. In the event that the credentials for a data source need to be revised or when a data source needs to reference a different database, only an admin for the gateway is able to implement these changes in the **Manage gateways** portal.

In *Figure 11.16* from the **Manage gateways** portal in Power BI, a single security group (**IT Administration**) is added as the administrator of the **Mastering Power BI** cluster.

*Figure 11.16: Power BI gateway administrators*

The primary job of administrators added to gateway clusters is to manage data sources and users for the gateway as we see in the next section.

## Gateway data sources and users

The primary role of gateway administrators is to add data sources as per the gateway cluster and to authorize (or remove) users or groups of users. Both of these duties are performed in the **Manage gateways** portal.

With the gateway cluster selected within the **Manage gateways** portal, clicking **ADD DATA SOURCE** from the list of gateway clusters creates a blank new data source, as shown in *Figure 11.17*.

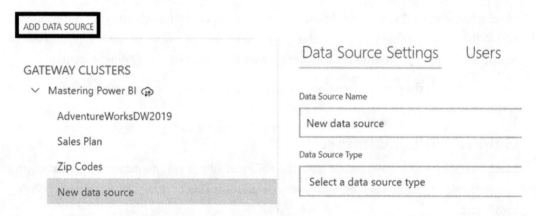

*Figure 11.17: Adding a data source to a gateway cluster*

New data sources can also be added via the ellipsis (three dots) to the right of each cluster name in the **Manage gateways** portal as shown in *Figure 11.18*. This menu is notoriously hard to find as the ellipses only appear if hovered over with the mouse cursor.

*Figure 11.18: The hidden ellipsis menu for gateway clusters*

As shown in *Figure 11.18*, this menu is the only way in which a gateway cluster can be removed from within the Power BI service.

Once data sources have been added, the users who publish reports and/or schedule data refreshes via the gateway can be added to the data source. This is done via the **Users** tab as shown in *Figure 11.19*.

Figure 11.19: Adding a security group of users to the gateway data source

In *Figure 11.19*, a security group of users is added to the data source of the gateway cluster. The users included in the security group will see the option to use the gateway cluster when scheduling refreshes for datasets.

As shown, the most critical administration functions are performed manually within the Power BI service. However, a PowerShell module is also available for the administration of gateway clusters as covered in the next section.

## PowerShell support for gateway clusters

A PowerShell module is available to support the management of gateway clusters. This module is named **DataGateway** and requires PowerShell 7.0.0 or higher. This means that the standard Windows PowerShell app is unable to successfully use this module. Instead, the cross-platform version of PowerShell referred to as PowerShell Core must be used instead. PowerShell Core can be downloaded from the following link: https://bit.ly/3IAxhvT.

Once installed, PowerShell can be run as Administrator and the following command can be used to install the DataGateway module:

```
Install-Module -Name DataGateway
```

Once the DataGateway module is installed, future sessions of PowerShell can import the module via the Install-Module command:

```
Import-Module -Name DataGateway
```

Once the module is installed and/or imported to a session of PowerShell in which the user has administrator privileges, a login command (`Login-DataGatewayServiceAccount`) must be executed to enable other gateway management commands.

Unlike the **Manage gateways** portal in the Power BI service, the PowerShell commands provide access to the specific gateway instances configured for each cluster. For example, properties of a specific gateway within an instance can be modified or a gateway instance can be removed from a cluster altogether.

Once authenticated, the `Get-DataGatewayCluster` command is used to retrieve the list of gateway clusters in which the logged-in user is an administrator along with the gateway clusters' unique IDs. These IDs can then be used to get information about the individual gateway instances for the cluster, including the server names where these instances are installed. The following command exposes the information about gateway instances for a cluster:

```
Get-DataGatewayCluster -GatewayClusterId ID | Select -ExpandProperty
Permissions
```

In the example given, ID would be replaced with the actual ID of the gateway cluster, such as dc8f2c49-5731-4b27-966b-3db5094c2e77. The full list of available gateway cluster PowerShell commands and their parameters can be found here: https://bit.ly/3Izft48.

This section has covered the overall management of gateway clusters within the Power BI service and via PowerShell. We next look at troubleshooting and monitoring gateways.

# Troubleshooting and monitoring gateways

For organizations with significant dependencies on the On-premises data gateway, it's important to plan for administration scenarios, such as migrating or restoring a gateway to a different machine. Administrators should also be familiar with accessing and analyzing the gateway log files and related settings to troubleshoot data refresh issues. Finally, gateway throughput and resource availability can be monitored using Power BI template files provided by Microsoft.

In this section, we investigate each of these topics in turn.

## Restoring, migrating, and taking over a gateway

Sometimes it is necessary to migrate or restore a gateway to a separate server. For example, a gateway may have initially been installed on a server with insufficient resources to support the current workload. In other cases, a hardware failure may have occurred on a gateway's server and thus it's necessary to quickly restore connectivity.

Using the recovery key created when a gateway is first installed and configured, the data sources and their associated settings (authentication and credentials) can be restored on a new server. In *Figure 11.20*, during gateway installation on a different server, the option is given to **Migrate, restore, or takeover an existing gateway** rather than register a new gateway.

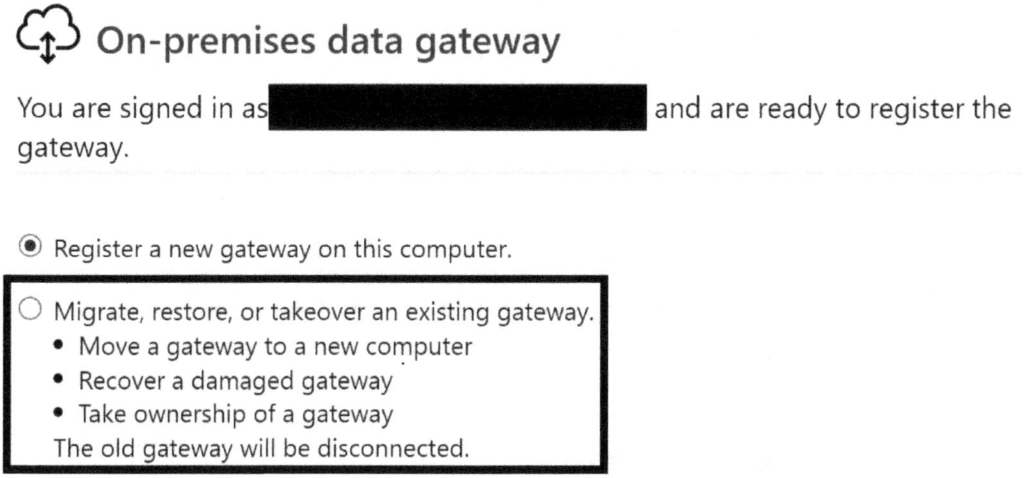

## ☁ On-premises data gateway

You are signed in as █████████████████████ and are ready to register the gateway.

⦿ Register a new gateway on this computer.

○ Migrate, restore, or takeover an existing gateway.
- Move a gateway to a new computer
- Recover a damaged gateway
- Take ownership of a gateway
The old gateway will be disconnected.

*Figure 11.20: Gateway setup options*

Choosing to **Migrate, restore, or takeover an existing gateway** requires the recovery key that is created when a gateway is originally configured. If this key is not available, the only option is to install a new gateway and manually add the data sources and authorized users for that gateway.

This again speaks to the importance of properly securing and managing recover keys as covered in the section *Planning for recovery keys* earlier in this chapter. Also, only an administrator of a gateway cluster can use the recovery key to restore a gateway to a different server.

Next, we take a closer look at the diagnostic and logging capabilities for gateway instances.

# Gateway diagnostics

The On-premises data gateway desktop application makes it easy for gateway administrators to analyze gateway request activity. As shown in *Figure 11.21*, the **Diagnostics** tab allows admins to record additional details in the gateway log files, export these files for analysis, and even test network port connectivity.

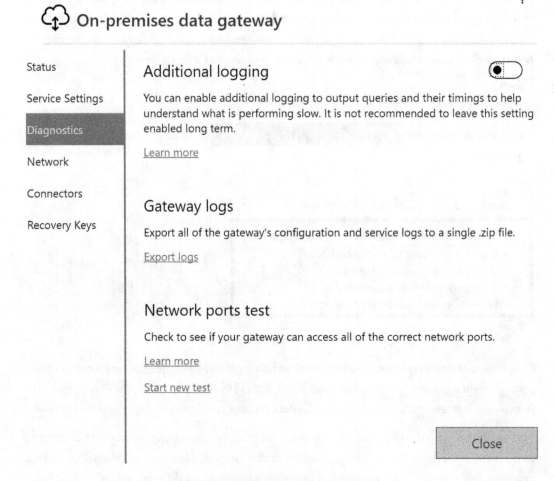

*Figure 11.21: Diagnostics settings*

Applying the additional logging setting requires the gateway to be restarted but provides visibility to the specific queries requested and the duration of their execution.

In a typical troubleshooting or analysis scenario, a gateway admin would temporarily enable additional logging, execute a data refresh or query from the Power BI service, and then export the gateway log files to analyze this activity. Once the log files have been exported, additional logging should be disabled to avoid reduced query throughput.

Technically, the additional logging setting modifies the `EmitQueryTraces` and `TracingVerbosity` properties of the following two XML configuration files, respectively:

`Microsoft.PowerBI.DataMovement.Pipeline.GatewayCore.dll.config`

`Microsoft.PowerBI.DataMovement.Pipeline.Diagnostics.dll.config`

As an alternative to the gateway application setting, both configuration files can be accessed and modified at the installation location of the gateway, such as `C:\Program Files\On-premises data gateway`.

Log files for gateway instances are stored in the `AppData` folder for the account running the **On-premises data gateway service**. For example, if using the default **PBIEgwService** account, the log files are stored in the following location depending on the version of the operating system:

`C:\Windows\ServiceProfiles\PBIEgwService\AppData\Local\Microsoft\On-premises data gateway`

`C:\Users\PBIEgwService\AppData\Local\Microsoft\On-premises data gateway`

With the essentials of gateway logs understood, we next explain how to easily explore and gain insights from these logs.

## Gateway monitoring reports

A recent addition to gateway logging and diagnostics are special log files that can be used in conjunction with a Power BI template file to easily visualize log performance. Prior to these new gateway log files and template, it was necessary to configure Windows performance monitor counters and create custom monitoring reports from scratch.

The special log files are stored within a `Report` directory of the log file directory identified in the previous section. The Power BI report template can be downloaded here: `https://bit.ly/3nffIJQ`.

Opening the template file opens Power BI Desktop and prompts for the **Folder Path** to the Report directory as shown in *Figure 11.22*.

**GatewayPerformanceMonitoring**

Folder Path

C:\Windows\ServiceProfiles\PBIEgwService\AppData\Loca ▼

Load ▼      Cancel

*Figure 11.22: GatewayPerformanceMonitoring Power BI template*

Entering the **Folder Path** and clicking the **Load** button loads the report data and visuals. Using the generated reports, gateway administrators can easily observe the volume of queries, identify slow queries, and break out queries by source system.

The combination of gateway diagnostics, logging, and pre-built Power BI reports greatly eases the burden of troubleshooting and monitoring gateway instances. We next explore data refresh in more detail.

# Data refresh

The configuration of gateways and their role during data refresh varies depending upon the mode of the dataset, such as import, DirectQuery, or Live. In this section, we explore the gateway's role, additional configuration steps, and technical nuances of each of these modes.

## Scheduled data refresh

Scheduled data refreshes allow Power BI datasets to be updated with the latest data on a preset schedule. The scheduled refresh for an import or composite mode dataset is configured on the **Settings** page for each dataset in the Power BI service.

The **Settings** option is found by clicking the three vertical dots displayed next to datasets listed in the Power BI service, either in the left navigation pane or the **Datasets + dataflows** tab of a workspace. Once on the **Settings** page, the **Schedule refresh** section can be expanded as shown in *Figure 11.23*.

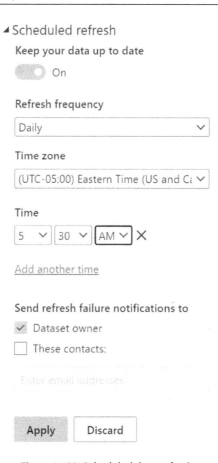

*Figure 11.23: Scheduled data refresh*

In *Figure 11.23*, a **Daily** refresh at 5:30 A.M. **Eastern Time** is set.

Import mode datasets hosted in a shared capacity (non-premium) are currently limited to eight scheduled refreshes per day. Import datasets hosted in Power BI Premium capacity, however, can be refreshed up to 48 times per day. Each scheduled refresh for both Power BI Premium and the shared capacity dataset is separated by a minimum of 30 minutes.

Non-premium refreshes must complete in 2 hours while refreshes for Premium capacities must complete in 5 hours. In addition, any dataset whose dashboards and reports have not been viewed in 2 months automatically has the scheduled refresh suspended.

In addition to the scheduled refreshes configured in the Power BI service interface, Power Automate can also be used to initiate refreshes. Finally, the **Settings** page for each dataset contains a **Refresh history** link that can be used to help troubleshoot refresh issues.

As mentioned, scheduled refreshes are for import mode datasets and composite mode datasets only since DirectQuery and Live datasets do not contain a local data model. Next, we consider the gateway's role and configuration for DirectQuery and Live datasets.

## DirectQuery datasets

When publishing DirectQuery datasets, it's essential that the data source settings (for example, server name, database name) configured for the gateway data source exactly match the entries used for the Power BI Desktop file. The Power BI service automatically matches these settings to available data sources in gateway clusters.

Many organizations have made significant investments in scalable on-premises data sources and have implemented user security rules/conditions in these sources. For these organizations, it's often preferable to use DirectQuery data connections that leverage both the resources of the source and the custom security rules.

To address this scenario, the On-premises data gateway supports a single sign-on feature that passes the identity of the Power BI user to the data source via **Kerberos constrained delegation** as shown in *Figure 11.26*.

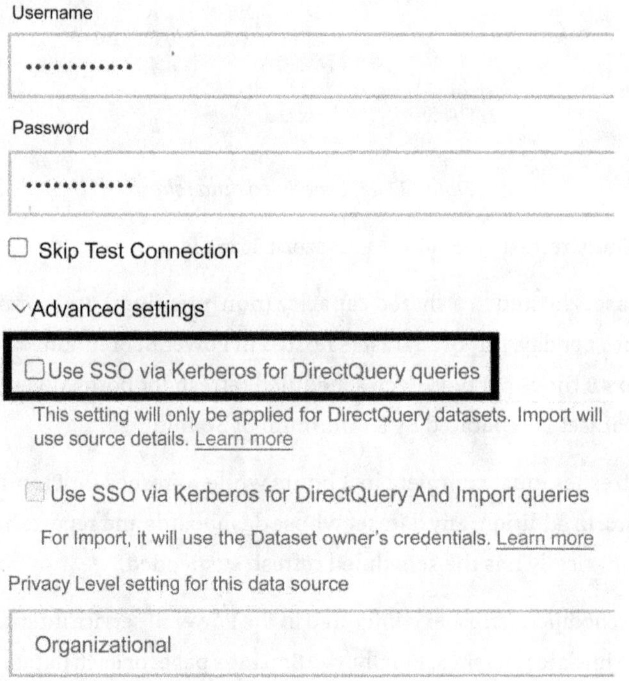

Username

••••••••••••

Password

••••••••••••

☐  Skip Test Connection

∨ Advanced settings

☐ Use SSO via Kerberos for DirectQuery queries

This setting will only be applied for DirectQuery datasets. Import will
use source details. Learn more

☐ Use SSO via Kerberos for DirectQuery And Import queries

For Import, it will use the Dataset owner's credentials. Learn more

Privacy Level setting for this data source

Organizational

*Figure 11.24: Single sign-on for DirectQuery*

*Figure 11.23* shows a portion of the dialog when creating a new data source in the Power BI service via the **Manage gateways** portal.

By default, the **single sign-on (SSO)** feature is not enabled, and thus all DirectQuery queries (from any user) execute via the credentials specified in the source. If enabled, the **user principal name (UPN)** of the user viewing content in the Power BI service is mapped to a local Active Directory identity by the gateway. The gateway service then impersonates this local user when querying the data source.

Kerberos constrained delegation must be configured for the gateway and data source to properly use the SSO for DirectQuery feature. This involves changing the service account of the gateway to a domain account, as discussed in the *Gateway installation and configuration* section earlier in this chapter.

Additionally, a **Service Principal Name (SPN)** may be needed for the domain account used by the gateway service and delegation settings must be configured for this account as well. SPNs and detailed instructions on configuring Kerberos constrained delegation can be found here: `https://bit.ly/3Mqas0i`.

## Live connections to Analysis Services models

For on-premises **SQL Server Analysis Services (SSAS)** models that Power BI users access via Live connections, an SSAS data source must be added in the **Manage gateways** portal. Critically, the credentials entered for this data source in the **Manage gateways** portal must match an account that has server administrator permissions for the SSAS instance.

**SQL Server Management Studio (SSMS)** can be used to determine the server administrators for both SSAS and Azure Analysis Services by right-clicking the instance name, choosing **Properties**, and then the **Security** tab. Identification of the Power BI user by SSAS only works if a server administrator account is specified and used when opening connections from the gateway.

User authentication to SSAS is based on the **EffectiveUserName** property of SSAS. Specifically, the user principal name (for example, `user@company.onmicrosoft.com`) of the Power BI user is passed into this property and this email address must match a UPN within the local Active Directory. This allows the SSAS model to apply any row-level security roles built into the model for the given Power BI user.

# Dashboard cache refresh

Dashboard tiles based on import/composite mode datasets are refreshed when the dataset itself is refreshed in the Power BI service. For dashboard tiles based on DirectQuery or Live connection datasets, however, the Power BI service maintains a scheduled cache refresh process for updating dashboard tiles. The purpose of this cache is to ensure dashboards are loaded extremely quickly since, as described in *Chapter 9, Designing Dashboards*, many users, such as executives, exclusively rely on dashboards.

For DirectQuery and Live datasets, the **Scheduled refresh** section of a dataset's **Settings** page, as described in the *Scheduled data refresh* section, controls the dashboard cache refresh instead of how frequently data is imported and refreshed. By default, the dashboard tile cache is refreshed once every hour but as shown in *Figure 11.24*, owners of these datasets can configure this refresh process to occur as frequently as every 15 minutes or as infrequently as once per week:

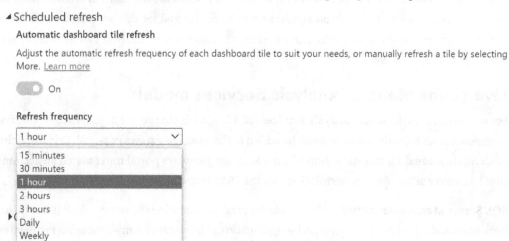

*Figure 11.24: Scheduled cache refresh*

Switching **Refresh frequency** to 15 minutes causes the queries associated with each dashboard tile dependent on the DirectQuery dataset to be submitted at 15-minute intervals. Users can also manually refresh dashboard tiles via the **Refresh dashboard tiles** menu option. This option, exposed via the ellipsis in the top-right corner of dashboards, also sends queries to the DirectQuery or Live connection data source like the scheduled cache refresh.

Power BI reports containing either a Live connection or a DirectQuery connection to the data source are represented as distinct datasets in the Power BI service. Power BI reports created based on these published datasets utilize the scheduled dashboard cache refresh configured for the given source dataset.

The optimal cache refresh frequency depends on the business requirements for data freshness, the frequency with which the source database is updated, and the available resources of the source system.

For example, if the top priority of the source system is **OnLine Transaction Processing** (**OLTP**) transactions and the dashboard queries are resource-intensive, it may be preferable to limit the refresh frequency to once a day. However, if the very latest data updates are of top value to the business users and ample resources are available to the source system, a 15-minute cache refresh schedule may be appropriate.

## Summary

This chapter reviewed the primary planning and management scenarios for the On-premises data gateway. This included alternative-solution architectures, methods for distributing workloads across multiple gateways, and ensuring high availability via gateway clusters. Additionally, this chapter described the process of administering a gateway, including the configuration of data sources and the authorization of users or groups to utilize the gateway per source. Finally, the primary tools and processes for troubleshooting and monitoring the gateway were reviewed.

While this chapter focused on using the Power BI service with on-premises data and traditional Power BI datasets and reports, the following chapter highlights paginated reports and the option to deploy Power BI exclusively on-premises via Power BI Report Server. This includes the publication, refresh, and management of Power BI reports on-premises and within the Power BI service as well as the primary differences between Power BI Report Server and the Power BI service.

## Join our community on Discord

Join our community's Discord space for discussions with the author and other readers:
https://discord.gg/q6BPbHEPXp

# 12

# Deploying Paginated Reports

Paginated reports are **eXtensible Markup Language** (**XML**)-based report definitions that were first introduced in **SQL Server Reporting Services** (**SSRS**). Unlike Power BI reports, which deliver highly interactive visualization experiences on a single page, paginated reports provide richly formatted multi-page documents optimized for printing, exporting, and automated delivery.

As a Power BI Premium feature, paginated reports provide organizations with a mature and robust option for migrating existing SSRS and other similar operational reports to Power BI without the need to manage report server infrastructure. Additionally, for organizations that require an on-premises solution, the **Power BI Report Server** (**PBRS**) continues to be enhanced and also supports both paginated and Power BI reports.

This chapter reviews the primary considerations in migrating paginated reports to Power BI as well as planning and deploying the PBRS. This includes feature compatibility with the Power BI service, licensing and configuration details, and an example deployment topology. Additionally, management and administration topics are reviewed, including the scheduled data refresh of Power BI reports and monitoring server usage via execution log data.

In this chapter, we will review the following topics:

- Paginated reports in the Power BI service
- Migrating reports to the Power BI service
- Planning the **Power BI Report Server** (**PBRS**)
- Installing and upgrading PBRS
- PBRS client applications

We begin by looking at using paginated reports within the Power BI service.

# Paginated reports in the Power BI service

So far, this book has primarily focused on the Power BI reports created in Power BI Desktop. While these reports are increasingly the de facto standard, given their ability to quickly generate insights and the speed with which these reports can be developed, paginated reports uniquely address several important use cases such as the need to email, print, or export report data that spans multiple pages.

As explained in the *Paginated reports* section of *Chapter 7, Creating and Formatting Visualizations*, paginated reports are optimized for printing and PDF generation. These reports have a long and storied history at Microsoft, having first appeared in SSRS in 2004.

In contrast to Power BI reports, which are highly interactive, paginated reports have limited user interactivity via the use of parameters, which filter the entire report page. However, unlike Power BI reports, which can only present a single report page at a time, paginated reports can display multiple pages.

Paginated reports are only supported in the Power BI service in Premium workspaces, specifically, those workspaces running on embedded capacity, Premium capacity, or created using a **Premium Per User (PPU)** license. To be clear, environments using only pro licenses do not have access to paginated report features.

In addition, paginated reports do not import data, but rather use dataset connections that query the underlying data sources when reports are rendered. This is similar to how DirectQuery or live reports operate. Thus, reports published to the Power BI service that use on-premises data sources must always use a standard mode data gateway, as discussed in *Chapter 11, Managing the On-Premises Data Gateway*.

Before building a paginated report, it is important to determine whether the paginated report is a good fit for the intended purpose.

## Planning paginated reports

Before building a paginated report, it is helpful to confirm whether or not a paginated report is suitable or appropriate. The following possible requirements can help confirm that a paginated report is indeed required:

1.  The report is primarily intended for printing.
2.  The report is primarily intended for printing or exporting simple table(s) of data to standard document formats such as Excel (.xlsx) or PDF.

3. The report needs to be printed across multiple pages of data.

4. Users of the report do not require or expect any significant level of interaction beyond possibly making a few filter selections.

5. The report needs to render a very specific and detailed document template layout such as an invoice or a job application form.

6. The report requires a significant amount of custom logic or source data that's not available in an existing Power BI dataset. For example, a paginated report could be built with SQL statements or stored procedures directly against a SQL Server or Azure SQL database system.

7. Users of the report need the ability to export large amounts of data beyond the limit of Power BI reports (150,000 rows).

8. The report data itself needs to be delivered to people in a file format such as CSV or Excel via an email subscription.

9. The report data needs to be able to be exported in XML, Microsoft Word, or **Multipurpose Internet Mail Extension (MIME) HyperText Markup Language (HTML)** format, otherwise known as **MHTML**.

For example, consider a simple report that lists a table of product categories, product subcategories and individual product SKU sales amounts, tax costs, and freight costs. The report needs to report on all products across multiple pages, while additional pages are desired for each individual product category and/or product subcategory. The report is designed to be printed and used in board meetings. Such a report is a good candidate for a paginated report. In contrast, a report that shows a single report page at a time, features interactions between the visuals, and supports drillthrough between the report pages would not be a good candidate for paginated reports and should be created as a Power BI desktop report.

Once paginated reports are identified as a good fit for the specified requirements, the next step is to build and publish the paginated report.

## Building and publishing paginated reports

Paginated reports use an XML-based language called **Report Definition Language** (RDL). RDL is traditionally written in **Visual Studio** or **Report Builder**, but a specific **Power BI Report Builder** application is available and should be used when building paginated reports for publication with the Power BI service. Visual Studio Code and Power BI Report Builder can be freely downloaded, but recall that a Premium capacity is required to use paginated reports in the Power BI service.

Power BI Report Builder requires Windows 7 or higher, Microsoft .NET Framework 4.7.2, 80 MB of disk space, and 512 MB of RAM. To download Power BI Report Builder, use the following link: `https://bit.ly/3rM6P9k`.

Designing and creating reports in Power BI Report Builder is an extremely different process and experience from creating reports in Power BI Desktop. *Figure 12.1* shows the **Design** view of a simple report containing a single matrix visual:

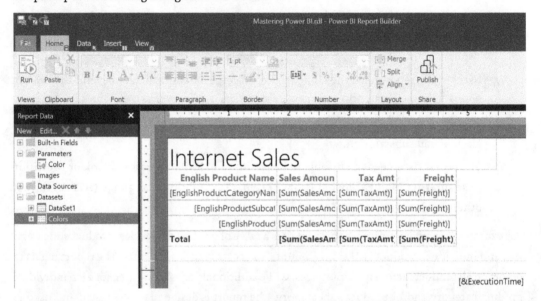

*Figure 12.1: Design view of a paginated report*

As shown in *Figure 12.1*, the report contains two **Datasets**, **Dataset1** and **Colors**, as well as a single **Parameter**, **Color**.

Both datasets, which should be thought of as tables, pull from the same SQL Server **data source**. Data sources are simply defined connections to source systems. Power BI Report Builder supports eleven different data sources including Power BI Dataset, Dataverse, Azure SQL Database, Azure Analysis Services, and Azure Synapse, as shown in *Figure 12.2*:

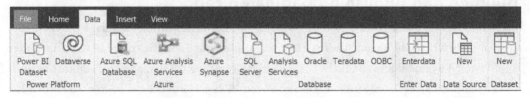

*Figure 12.2: Available data sources in Power BI Report Builder*

The data source, in this case, is a SQL Server hosting the AdventureWorksDW2019 database. An important question in the real world is whether the paginated report should be built against a Power BI dataset or a source system like Azure SQL. There are important security implications such as the ability to leverage any row-level security roles in the Power BI dataset or if security needs to be applied to the SQL database system. There are also often performance implications, as the paginated report may require a query that involves many columns and, thus, doesn't perform well against a columnar system like import mode Power BI datasets.

In this example, the SQL query defined for **DataSet1** is the following:

```
SELECT
  BI.vDim_Product.ProductKey AS [vDim_Product ProductKey]
  ,BI.vDim_Product.ProductSubcategoryKey AS [vDim_Product
ProductSubcategoryKey]
  ,BI.vDim_Product.DaysToManufacture
  ,BI.vDim_Product.Color
  ,BI.vDim_ProductCategory.ProductCategoryKey AS [vDim_ProductCategory
ProductCategoryKey]
  ,BI.vDim_ProductCategory.EnglishProductCategoryName
  ,BI.vDim_ProductSubcategory.ProductSubcategoryKey AS [vDim_
ProductSubcategory ProductSubcategoryKey]
  ,BI.vDim_ProductSubcategory.EnglishProductSubcategoryName
  ,BI.vFact_InternetSales.ProductKey AS [vFact_InternetSales ProductKey]
  ,BI.vFact_InternetSales.OrderQuantity
  ,BI.vFact_InternetSales.UnitPrice
  ,BI.vFact_InternetSales.DiscountAmount
  ,BI.vFact_InternetSales.TaxAmt
  ,BI.vFact_InternetSales.SalesAmount
  ,BI.vFact_InternetSales.Freight
  ,BI.vFact_InternetSales.OrderDate
  ,BI.vDim_ProductSubcategory.ProductCategoryKey AS [vDim_
ProductSubcategory ProductCategoryKey]
  ,BI.vDim_Product.EnglishProductName
FROM
  BI.vDim_Product
  LEFT OUTER JOIN BI.vFact_InternetSales
    ON BI.vDim_Product.ProductKey = BI.vFact_InternetSales.ProductKey
  LEFT OUTER JOIN BI.vDim_ProductSubcategory
```

```
   ON BI.vDim_Product.ProductSubcategoryKey = BI.vDim_ProductSubcategory.
ProductSubcategoryKey
  LEFT OUTER JOIN BI.vDim_ProductCategory
   ON BI.vDim_ProductSubcategory.ProductCategoryKey = BI.vDim_
ProductCategory.ProductCategoryKey
```

This query pulls information from four different SQL views, vFact_InternetSales, vDim_Product, vDim_ProductCategory, and vDim_ProductSubcategory. Relationships between these tables are defined using key columns to form the following relationships:

- A left outer join between vDim_Product and vFact_InternetSales in the ProductKey columns of each table
- A left outer join between vDim_Product and vDim_ProductSubcategory in the ProductSubcategoryKey columns of each table
- A left outer join between vDim_ProductSubcategory and vDim_ProductCategory in the ProductCategoryKey columns of each table

Particularly for critical production environment reports, some organizations require report dataset queries to be created as database objects such as stored procedures or views in the data source system. Similar to creating view objects for each Power BI dataset table, this policy helps to promote transparency between the BI/reporting layer teams and the data warehouse or data engineering teams. Additionally, it reduces the number of scenarios in which source data or objects used in Power BI solutions are altered or removed.

In either case, whether writing the query in the report or as a database object, the query returns a table or a dataset for the report. Then, this query is executed against the SQL Server, with possible filtering, each time the matrix visual in the report is rendered. *Figure 12.3* shows such a filter:

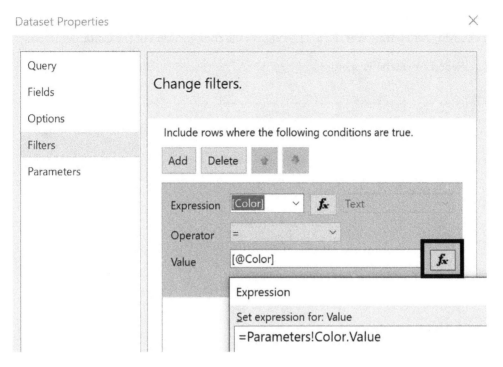

*Figure 12.3: Dataset filter*

As shown in *Figure 12.3*, the **Color** column from the vFact_InternetSales table is selected for the **Expression** value, and the value in this column must equal (=) the **Value** of the report parameter **Color**. This **Color** parameter is defined for the **Value** by choosing the **fx** button and specifying the code =Parameters!Color.Value, which returns the current value of the report parameter.

Report parameters can be added by right-clicking the **Parameters** folder, as shown in *Figure 12.1*, and choosing **Add parameter**. *Figure 12.4* shows the configuration of the **Color** parameter:

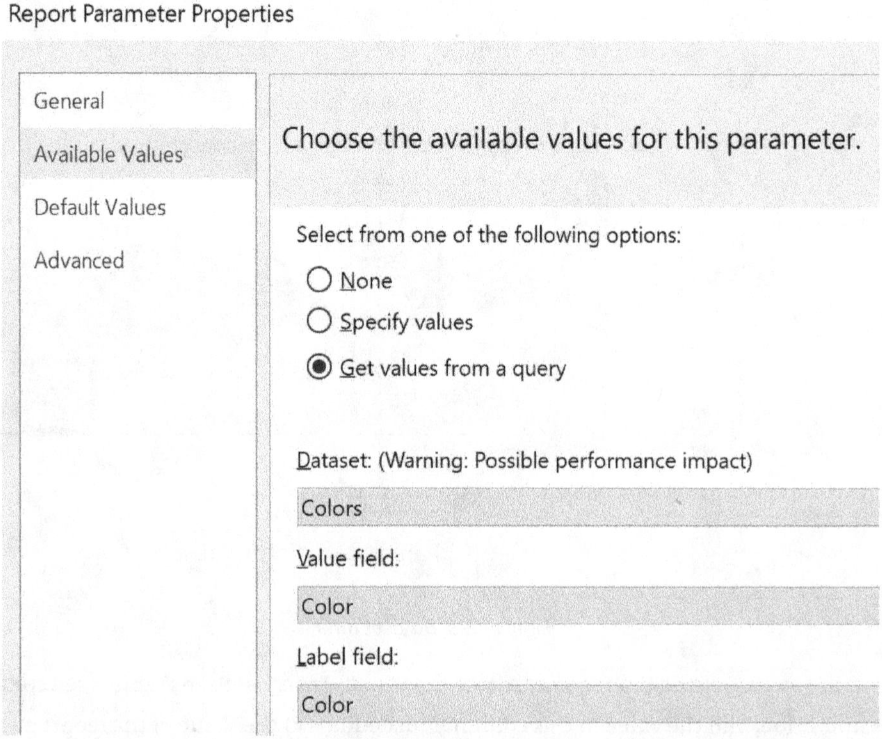

Report Parameter Properties

*Figure 12.4: Dataset filter*

As shown in *Figure 12.4*, the **Color** parameter gets the available values using the **Colors** dataset, from the **Color** field/column for both the **Label field** and **Value field** of the listed items. The **Colors** dataset is another simple SQL query that simply gets the DISTINCT values of the Color column in the vDim_Product view, as shown here:

```
SELECT DISTINCT
   BI.vDim_Product.Color
FROM
   BI.vDim_Product
```

Additional charts and report elements can be added to a report via the **Insert** menu. In *Figure 12.5*, a **Header** has been added to the report and an image placed within the header:

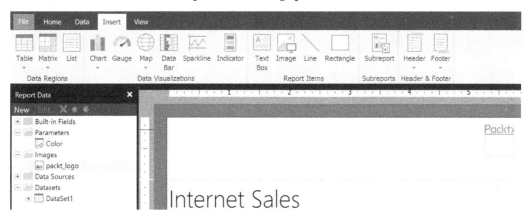

*Figure 12.5: Additional report elements including a header and an image*

Because the image has been added to the header section of the report, the image will appear on every page of the report in the event that the report spans multiple pages. Similarly, footers are also available and printed on every page of the report. Both headers and footers can include built-in fields such as PageNumber, TotalPages, and ExecutionTime that return the current page number, the total number of pages in the report, and the date and time the report was rendered respectively.

As shown in *Figure 12.5*, Power BI Report Builder supports many common visuals and report elements such as lines and rectangles, although not nearly the number of visuals and report elements available in Power BI Desktop.

Once the report design is complete, the report can be previewed using the **Run** button found on the **Home** tab, as shown in *Figure 12.6*:

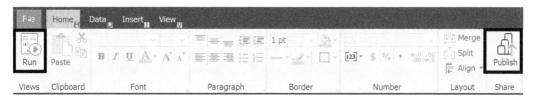

*Figure 12.6: The Run and Publish buttons on the Home tab*

A preview of the report is shown in *Figure 12.7*:

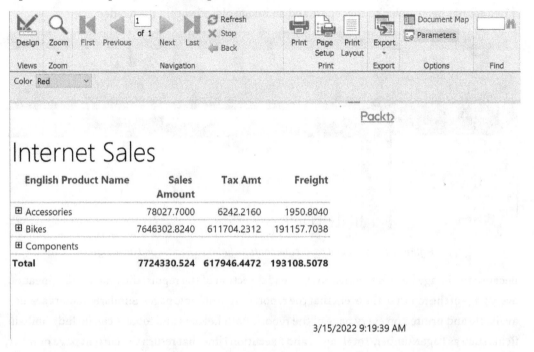

*Figure 12.7: Report preview*

Returning to the design view via the **Design** button, as shown in the upper-left corner of *Figure 12.7*, the report can be published to the Power BI service via the **Publish** button shown in *Figure 12.6*.

Clicking the **Publish** button allows the user to choose a workspace for the report, as shown in *Figure 12.8*:

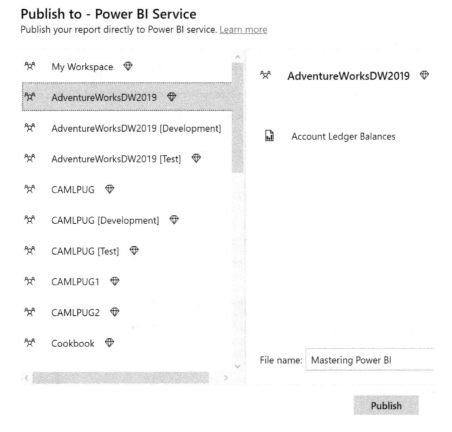

*Figure 12.8: Report publishing*

It is important to keep in mind that paginated reports are only supported in the Power BI service via a dedicated capacity such as Premium and PPU workspaces. Therefore, only workspaces using a dedicated capacity, denoted by the diamond icon, appear in the list of available workspaces.

Once published to the Power BI service, we can now view and interact with the report in a web browser.

## Identifying and interacting with paginated reports

With the report published to the Power BI service, you can now log in and view the report. Paginated reports can be identified in the Power BI service via a different icon, as shown in *Figure 12.9*:

*Figure 12.9: Paginated report icon in the Power BI service*

Once opened, paginated reports can appear blank in the Power BI service if parameters are required to be set prior to running the report. If the report is blank, click the **Parameters** button in the ribbon to display the parameters of the report. Set the parameters and then click the **View report** button, as shown in *Figure 12.10*:

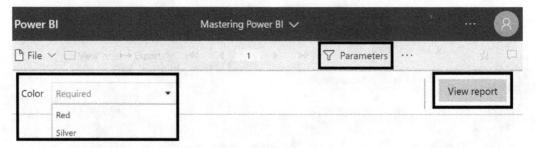

*Figure 12.10: Paginated report parameters in the Power BI service*

Interactivity with paginated reports is limited to setting the report parameters and then re-rendering the report. Paginated report visuals are not interactive in the same manner as reports created in Power BI Desktop, meaning that report visuals are static once rendered and cannot interact with one another such as via cross-filtering or highlighting.

If multiple pages are generated by the report, these pages can be navigated to and displayed using the paging controls located to the left of the **Parameters** button, as shown in *Figure 12.10*.

While users like the robust interactivity of Power BI Desktop reports, paginated reports do offer more export options as well as different printing options.

## Printing, exporting, subscribing, and sharing

The paginated report printing options are slightly different from Power BI Desktop reports. Choosing **File** and then **Print** from the report ribbon presents the dialog shown in *Figure 12.11*:

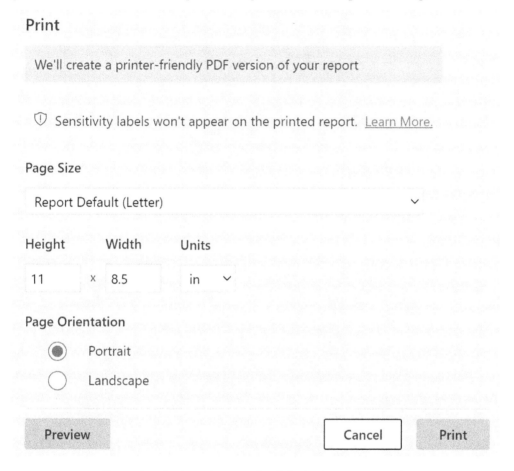

Figure 12.11: Paginated report print dialog in the Power BI service

Unlike Power BI Desktop reports, paginated reports offer the ability to specify the exact **Height** and **Width** of the printed pages in addition to a **Preview** ability.

In addition to the different printing capabilities, paginated reports offer additional export options in the **Export** menu, as shown in *Figure 12.12*:

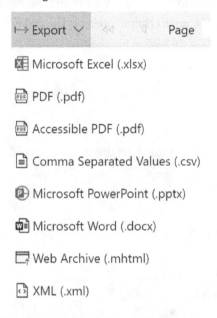

*Figure 12.12: Paginated report Export menu in the Power BI service*

As shown in *Figure 12.12*, additional export options include the XML (.xml), Microsoft Word (.docx), and Web Archive (.mhtml) formats.

While printing and exporting are different for paginated reports, the ability to Subscribe and Share is the same as Power BI Desktop reports and provides the exact same interface. Subscribing and sharing are covered in the next chapter, *Chapter 12, Creating Apps and Content Distribution*.

While new reports can be created and published using Power BI Report Builder, it is likely that organizations interested in paginated reports in the Power BI service already have existing paginated reports. Migrating existing paginated reports to the Power BI service comes with certain considerations that we explore in the next section.

## Migrating reports to the Power BI service

Given their long and successful history in the competitive enterprise reporting platform market, many organizations continue to support hundreds and even thousands of paginated or SSRS reports. Additionally, existing reports built with other common BI tools such as Cognos, MicroStrategy, and Crystal Reports are usually more easily re-produced in paginated reports than Power BI reports.

A key question to answer is whether the existing or legacy reports should be maintained going forward or if they can be replaced (or perhaps supplemented) with a more modern and interactive experience offered by Power BI reports. In somes cases, users would prefer a well developed Power BI report and the existing reports merely reflect the functionality that was available years ago in SSRS or another similar tool. This section covers the steps and considerations organizations should bear in mind when migrating existing RDL reports to paginated reports for Power BI.

Assuming the organization has already determined that they wish to use paginated reports in the Power BI service, the migration of reports to Power BI includes the following phases:

1. Inventory

2. Assess

3. Plan

4. Migrate

5. **User Acceptance Testing (UAT)**

Each of these phases is discussed in the following sections.

## Inventory

Before migrating reports, it is important to understand the size and scope of the effort required. This means creating an inventory of all the report servers and reports within the environment.

Creating an inventory of all reports should begin with identifying all the SSRS and PBRS servers within the environment. The **Microsoft Assessment and Planning Toolkit (MAP Toolkit)** is useful in discovering the SQL Server instances within the environment, including identifying the versions and installed features of those SQL instances. The MAP Toolkit can be downloaded at the following link: `https://bit.ly/3KSBoUG`.

Once SQL Server instances have been identified, the following versions of SQL Server can have their reports migrated to the Power BI service:

- SQL Server 2012

- SQL Server 2014

- SQL Server 2016

- SQL Server 2017

- SQL Server 2019

- Power BI Report Server

The final step in creating the inventory of reports is to understand the reports present on each SQL Server. This can be done with a simple SQL query run within **SQL Server Management Studio (SSMS)** such as this:

```
SELECT
      ,[Path]
      ,[Name]
      ,[Description]
      ,[CreatedByID]
      ,[CreationDate]
      ,[ModifiedByID]
      ,[ModifiedDate]
    FROM [ReportServer].[dbo].[Catalog]
```

Here, ReportServer can be replaced with the name of the reporting server database. Once the results are obtained, right-click the results in SSMS and choose **Save Results As...** to save the list of reports in a **comma-separated value (CSV)** file.

With our inventory complete, we should now assess our inventory of reports in order to determine which, if any, reports should be migrated.

## Assess

The next step in migrating paginated reports to the Power BI service involves assessing the reports in our inventory. It is common for reports to be created and then slowly fall out of use over time. We can determine if reports are no longer being used using a simple SQL query run from SSMS such as the following:

```
USE ReportServer
GO
DECLARE @Days INT
    SET @Days = 365
SELECT
    [Path],
    [Name],
    [DateLastViewed]
  FROM dbo.catalog [cat]
  INNER JOIN (SELECT [ReportID],[DateLastViewed] = MAX([TimeStart])
        FROM dbo.[ExecutionLog] GROUP BY [ReportID]) [exe]
        ON [cat].[ItemID] = [exe].[ReportID]
```

```
WHERE DATEDIFF(day, [DateLastViewed], GETDATE()) <= @Days
ORDER BY [DateLastViewed] DESC
```

Here, ReportServer should be changed to the name of the reporting services database, and the number of days, 365, should be adjusted according to business preferences. The preceding query returns all the reports that have been executed within @Days number of days, in this case, 365.

The results of this query can be compared to the inventory, and those reports not included in the results of reports that have been executed in the last year can be removed from the list of reports to be migrated.

The next step in assessing reports involves determining if the reports include any features that are not supported by the Power BI service. The Power BI service does not support the following features of RDL reports:

1. Shared data sources and shared datasets

2. Resources, like image files

3. KPIs and mobile reports (SSRS 2016, or later—Enterprise Edition only)

4. Report models and report parts (deprecated)

5. Map visuals (not supported by the data gateway)

The **RDL Migration Tool** that is available on GitHub, `https://github.com/microsoft/RdlMigration`, can be used to test reports for incompatibility with any of the four identified unsupported features identified previously.

It should be noted that the RDL Migration Tool must be compiled locally within Visual Studio Code or a similar **integrated development environment (IDE)**. After compiling, the tool is run from a command line and instructions for its use are available on the GitHub repository.

BI teams and the business should work in coordination when assessing reports to further refine the list of reports to be migrated. Teams using paginated reports should be encouraged to consider redeveloping those reports in Power BI Desktop, if possible, in order to potentially modernize the reports.

For example, mobile reports or reports using KPI visuals can be redeveloped in Power BI Desktop. Similarly, reports using on-premises data sources and map visuals are good candidates to be redeveloped in Power BI Desktop since the data gateway does not support complex data types such as geographic spatial data types.

Once an acceptable list of paginated reports has been identified, the next step is to plan the migration of these reports to Power BI.

## Plan

The Plan phase ensures that the necessary infrastructure and other components are in place to facilitate running paginated reports within the Power BI service. In addition, the Plan phase helps identify how security will be implemented.

First, since paginated reports are a premium feature, the BI team needs to ensure that an appropriate dedicated capacity or PPU workspaces have been created and defined within the Power BI service. Second, since paginated reports that access on-premises resources must use a data gateway, BI teams should ensure that such gateways are present and functioning prior to migration.

Perhaps the most important element of planning the migration of paginated reports is security. The Power BI service and SSRS use very different security models; thus, it is important to understand these differences when planning to migrate reports.

SSRS uses folders and permissions to secure content while the Power BI service uses workspaces, as covered in the *Workspace roles and rights* section of *Chapter 9, Managing Workspaces and Content*. BI teams need to understand how SSRS folders and permissions work and then create a plan to map these permissions to one or more workspaces.

BI teams should also consider the use of the built-in report field, **UserID**. In the Power BI service, this field returns the User Principal Name (user@domain.com) instead of the Active Directory account name (domain\user). Thus, if using the **UserID** field to secure content within the report, the dataset definitions and possibly the source systems will need to be revised.

Special consideration should also be given to the use of the built-in field **ExecutionTime**. In the Power BI service, this returns a date/time in Coordinate **Universal Time (UTC)** versus the local time zone of the report server. This may cause confusion among report viewers.

Finally, while the RDL Migration Tool is capable of converting shared data sources and shared datasets into local data sources and local datasets, BI teams may wish to consider migrating shared data sources to shared Power BI datasets published within the Service.

With a plan in place for the migration, the next step is to actually migrate the paginated reports.

## Migrate

With an appropriate plan in place, the next step is to actually migrate the selected reports. This can be done manually or automatically.

To migrate reports manually, simply download the RDL files from the reporting services instances within the environment. Open these RDL files in Power BI Report Builder, as described in the *Building and publishing paginated reports* section of this chapter. Make any necessary modifications and then publish to the Power BI service.

Alternatively, the migration of reports can be automated by using the **RDL Migration Tool**. Instructions for using the RDL Migration Tool can be found on the GitHub page here: `https://github.com/microsoft/RdlMigration`.

It is also possible to create a custom migration tool or script using the Power BI REST APIs and the SSRS REST APIs. More information on the Power BI REST APIs can be found in the *Power BI REST API and PowerShell Module* section of *Chapter 10, Managing Workspaces and Content*.

The choice of which approach to use when migrating reports is highly situational and may even require a combination of approaches. For example, the RDL Migration Tool might be used to migrate the majority of reports. The remaining reports that the RDL Migration Tool cannot successfully migrate could then be processed manually. However, if there are hundreds of reports that the RDL Migration Tool cannot successfully process, it might be necessary to create a custom migration script using the APIs.

With reports migrated to the Power BI service, the final step is UAT and final deployment.

## User Acceptance Testing and final deployment

Migrated paginated reports should follow the same life cycle as Power BI Desktop reports, such as the process described in the *Power BI deployment pipelines* section of *Chapter 10, Managing Workspaces and Content*. This means that migrated reports should first be published to a **Development** workspace to allow the report developers to verify that the report operates and renders in the Power BI service.

Once published to the Development workspace and checked for basic functionality by the BI team, the reports should then be promoted to the **Test** workspace for UAT. UAT includes the business users running the reports and ensures that the reports still function and return the correct results.

Once users have signed off on UAT, the BI team can then promote the reports that pass UAT to the **Production** workspace. Reports that do not pass can be revised by the BI team and sent through the process again as needed.

This completes our exploration of paginated reports in the Power BI service. Next, we will look at Power BI's support for continuing to use paginated reports on-premises using PBRS.

# Planning the Power BI Report Server (PBRS)

PBRS is a modern enterprise-reporting platform that allows organizations to deploy, manage, and view Power BI reports, in addition to other report types, internally. PBRS renders Power BI reports (.PBIX files) for data visualization and exploration, just like the Power BI web service.

PBRS allows large numbers of users to view and interact with the same reports created in Power BI Desktop in a modern web portal and via the same Power BI mobile applications used with the Power BI cloud service. PBRS addresses a current and sometimes long-term need to maintain a fully on-premises BI solution that includes both data sources and reports. Additionally, PBRS can be used in combination with the Power BI service to support scenarios in which only certain reports need to remain on-premises.

PBRS is built on top of SSRS; therefore, organizations can continue to utilize existing paginated SSRS reports and familiar management skills to easily migrate to PBRS. In addition to Power BI and paginated reports, the **Office Online Server (OOS)** can be configured to allow for viewing and interacting with Excel reports in the same report server portal, thus providing a consolidated hub of BI reporting and analysis.

Moreover, when provisioned with the Power BI Premium capacity, organizations can later choose to migrate on-premises Power BI reports to a dedicated capacity in the Power BI service, without incurring an additional cost.

> *Power BI Report Server is extending our journey of giving customers more flexibility in terms of being able to deploy some of their workloads on-premises behind their firewall.*
>
> *– Riccardo Muti, Group Program Manager*

Prior to any licensing or deployment planning, an organization should be very clear on the capabilities of PBRS in relation to the Power BI cloud service. PBRS does not include many of the features provided by the Power BI cloud service, such as the dashboards described in *Chapter 9, Designing Dashboards*, or the apps, email subscriptions, Analyze in Excel, and data alert features reviewed in *Chapter 13, Creating Power BI Apps and Content Distribution*.

Although new features are included with new releases of PBRS, PBRS is not intended or planned to support the features provided in the Power BI cloud service.

Additionally, for organizations using SSRS, it's important to understand the differences between the PBRS and SSRS, such as the upgrade and support life cycle. Mapping the capabilities and the longer-term role of the PBRS in relation to a current and a longer-term BI architecture and cloud strategy is helpful to plan the PBRS.

The following list of five questions can help guide the decision to deploy the PBRS:

1. **Do some or all reports currently need to stay on-premises and behind a corporate firewall?**

   PBRS is a fully on-premises solution designed to meet this specific scenario. Alternatively, organizations can deploy PBRS to virtual machines provisioned in Azure.

2. **Is SSRS currently being used?**

   PBRS includes SSRS and, thus, allows seamless migration from an existing SSRS server.

3. **Are the primary data sources for reports located on-premises and expected to remain on-premises?**

   As an on-premises solution, the on-premises data gateway is not required to connect to on-premises sources. As discussed in the previous chapter, some degree of query latency, hardware, and administrative costs are incurred by using on-premises data sources with the Power BI service.

4. **Are there features exclusive to the Power BI service that are needed?**

   PBRS is limited to rendering paginated reports and Power BI Report (.PBIX) files, as will be discussed in the following section.

5. **Will large import mode Power BI datasets be needed, or will the Power BI reports use DirectQuery and Live connections?**

   The size of the files that can be uploaded to PBRS for Scheduled refresh is limited to 2 GB. Additionally, unlike the Power BI service, a single Power BI dataset cannot be used as a source for other reports. With Power BI Premium capacity in the Power BI service, 10 GB and larger files (datasets) are supported.

Given these considerations, organizations with significant on-premises investments or requirements may wish to consider PBRS as at least part of their BI architecture. One example of this is a large on-premises data warehouse with many existing paginated (.RDL) SSRS reports built against it.

As described in the *Migrating reports* section from earlier in this chapter, new Power BI reports deployed to PBRS can later be migrated to the Power BI cloud service via the same licenses.

For example, a group of related Power BI reports initially published to a folder on PBRS could later be uploaded to a workspace in the Power BI service. The app workspace could be assigned a Power BI Premium capacity; thus, the reports could be distributed to all users, including Power BI Free users, via an app, as per *Chapter 13, Creating Power BI Apps and Content Distribution*.

Prior to deciding on the use of PBRS, it is important to understand the key feature differences between PBRS and the Power BI service.

## Feature differences with the Power BI service

The PBRS renders Power BI reports (.pbix files) similar to the Power BI service, but it is not intended to deliver other features found in the Power BI service such as dashboards and data alerts.

For users or organizations inexperienced with Power BI concepts (datasets, reports, and dashboards) and the Power BI service, these reports may be considered to be dashboards, and many of the additional features provided by the Power BI service, such as dashboards, workspaces, and apps, may not be known or utilized.

Although viewing and interacting with Power BI reports is clearly central to Power BI, Power BI as a **Platform-as-a-Service (PaaS)** and **Software-as-a-Service (SaaS)** cloud offering provides many additional benefits beyond the standard infrastructure cost and maintenance benefits of a cloud solution. These additional features support content management, collaboration, and the managed distribution of content throughout the organization.

Prior to committing to PBRS, it's recommended that you understand the role and benefit of features exclusive to the Power BI service such as the following:

- Dashboards
- Data alerts and notifications
- Email subscriptions to dashboards and reports
- Workspaces and apps
- Quick insights
- Natural Language Query (Q&A)
- Analyze in Excel
- Streaming datasets
- R and Python custom visuals

- Composite datasets
- Many-to-many relationships
- Cross-report drillthrough
- Full-screen mode
- Advanced Microsoft 365 collaboration
- Template apps
- Shared Power BI datasets

Several of the Power BI Service features not available on the PBRS have been reviewed in earlier chapters, such as dashboards (*Chapter 9, Designing Dashboards*, and *Chapter 10, Managing Workspaces and Content*).

Other features exclusive to the Power BI service, including email subscriptions to dashboards and reports, Power BI apps, and data alerts, are reviewed in *Chapter 13, Creating Power BI Apps and Content Distribution*.

While PBRS does not include certain features of the Power BI service, PBRS does have full feature parity with SSRS.

## Parity with SQL Server Reporting Services

PBRS is 100% compatible with SSRS. In fact, PBRS can be thought of as a superset of an SSRS server in the sense that both modern Power BI reports and all SSRS features up to the latest release of SSRS are included.

Therefore, it's not necessary to deploy both an SSRS report server and PBRS to support existing SSRS workloads.

> *There is no reason, except in some edge cases, for you to be running both SSRS and Power BI Report Server.*
>
> *– Christopher Finlan, Senior Program Manager for Power BI Report Server*

It's certainly possible to deploy PBRS along with an instance of SSRS. For example, a PBRS instance could be dedicated to self-service BI reports built with Power BI Desktop, while the SSRS instance could be dedicated to IT-developed paginated (.RDL) reports.

For the majority of organizations, however, PBRS and its modern web portal should be used to consolidate all report types.

There are three main differences between PBRS and SSRS:

1.  Power BI Report (.PBIX) files can only be viewed from the PBRS web portal.

2.  Excel workbooks (.XLSX) can only be viewed from the PBRS web portal although this requires the OOS.

3.  The upgrade and support cycles are significantly shorter for the PBRS. A new version of PBRS is released approximately every 4 months in January, May, and September.

New versions of SSRS continue to be tied to the release of SQL Server. For example, SSRS 2017 was made **generally available (GA)** on October 2, 2017, along with SQL Server 2017. Although the upgrade cycle has shortened for SQL Server, it doesn't match the pace of innovation of Power BI's monthly release cycles. Therefore, to make new Power BI features available to customers with on-premises deployments, a new PBRS is released approximately every 4 months.

Unlike versions of SSRS, which continue to receive support such as cumulative updates for years following their release, support for each PBRS release ends after one year. Therefore, while upgrading to each new version of PBRS every 4 months is not required, organizations should plan to upgrade within one year of each version's release to maintain support. Additional information and considerations on upgrade cycles are included in the *Upgrade cycles* section later in this chapter.

Support for multiple instances per server represents one additional difference between PBRS and SSRS. Currently, only one instance of PBRS can be installed per server. Therefore, unlike SSRS, virtual machines need to be configured if multiple instances are required for the same server.

There are no plans to deprecate SSRS or replace it with PBRS. However, given the additional features exclusive to PBRS and the more frequent release cycles, there are strong reasons to choose PBRS over SSRS going forward. Additionally, an existing SSRS server can be easily migrated to PBRS.

BI teams who are familiar with SSRS can quickly take advantage of the mature features, such as report subscription schedules and role-based user permissions. For organizations running older versions of SSRS, the significant features introduced in SSRS 2016, including the modern web portal and KPIs, can further supplement their BI solution.

In summary, PBRS allows organizations to continue to fully support existing and new SSRS reports, while also enabling the self-service and data visualization features of Power BI reports.

Let's review the data sources and connectivity options for PBRS next.

# Data sources and connectivity options

All three main connectivity options for Power BI Reports (import, DirectQuery, and Live connection) are supported by PBRS. However, composite datasets are not supported.

For example, corporate BI teams could develop DirectQuery and Live connection reports based on a Teradata database and a **SQL Server Analysis Services** (**SSAS**) model, respectively. Business users with Power BI Pro licenses can also import data from Excel and other sources to the Power BI Desktop version optimized for the PBRS and publish those reports to the PBRS.

Power BI reports deployed to PBRS cannot currently utilize a single Power BI dataset (.PBIX file) as their data source, as described in the *Live connections to the Power BI datasets* section of *Chapter 6, Planning Power BI Reports*. Given the resource limitations of the report server and the important goals of reusability and version control, this implies that DirectQuery and Live connection reports are strongly preferred for the current version of PBRS.

Imported Power BI datasets are currently limited to 2 GB file sizes. This compares to the 10 GB file size limit of Power BI datasets published to the Premium capacity in the Power BI server. Therefore, if it's necessary to import data to a Power BI report for deployment to the PBRS, only include the minimal amount of data needed for the specific report.

Avoid duplicating imported data across many reports by leveraging report pages, slicer visuals, and bookmarks. If import mode reports are required, such as when data integration is needed or when an Analysis Services model is not available, look for opportunities to consolidate report requests into a few .PBIX reports that can be shared.

One advantage of PBRS is that, as an on-premises solution, the on-premises data gateway section described in *Chapter 11, Managing the On-Premises Data Gateway* is not needed. The report server service account, running either as the Virtual Service Account or as a domain user account within the local Active Directory, is used to connect to data sources.

We will now turn our attention to hardware and user licensing.

# Hardware and user licensing

The rights to deploy PBRS to a production environment can be obtained by purchasing Power BI Premium capacity or via SQL Server Enterprise Edition with a Software Assurance agreement.

Power BI Premium is the primary and recommended method as this includes both a Power BI service (cloud) dedicated capacity and PBRS at the same cost. By licensing PBRS via Power BI Premium capacity, an organization can choose to migrate Power BI reports to the Power BI service (cloud) at a future date.

For example, a Power BI Premium P2 SKU includes 16 v-cores of dedicated capacity in the Power BI service, as well as the right to deploy PBRS to 16 processor cores on-premises. Furthermore, the cores provisioned via Power BI Premium can be allocated to on-premises hardware as needed by the organization, such as one PBRS with all 16 cores or two PBRS instances with eight cores each.

Once Power BI Premium capacity has been purchased, a product key required to install the report server becomes available in the Power BI admin portal. The details of Power BI Premium including the management of Premium (dedicated) capacities and the additional capabilities enabled by Premium capacities for deployments to the Power BI service are included in *Chapter 15, Building Enterprise BI with Power BI Premium*.

As an alternative to licensing via Power BI Premium, organizations with SQL Server Enterprise Edition with Software Assurance can use their existing SQL Server licenses to deploy PBRS.

One of the benefits of the Software Assurance program has been to provide access to new versions of SQL Server as they're released, and this benefit has been extended to include PBRS. For example, if an organization has already licensed 24 cores to run SQL Server Enterprise Edition with a Software Assurance agreement, they could allocate 8 of those 24 cores to a server for running PBRS. Just like current SQL Server licensing, additional SQL Server products (such as SQL Server Integration Services) could also be deployed on the same eight-core server. It's essential to realize that, unlike Power BI Premium, this licensing method does not provide access to the many additional features exclusive to the Power BI (cloud) service, as described earlier in this chapter.

## Pro licenses for report authors

In addition to licensing for PBRS, each user who publishes Power BI reports (.PBIX files) to the report server's web portal requires a Power BI Pro license. In most large deployments, these are typically a small number of BI report developers and self-service BI power users, as described in the *Power BI licenses* section of *Chapter 1, Planning Power BI Projects*.

Users who only view and optionally interact with reports published to PBRS do not require Power BI Pro licenses or even Power BI Free licenses. This licensing structure (Premium Capacity + Pro licenses for report authors) further aligns PBRS with the Power BI service.

Let's now take a look at the various ways PBRS can be deployed within an organization.

## Alternative and hybrid deployment models

PBRS, along with the ability to embed Power BI content into custom applications, gives organizations the option to choose a single deployment model (such as PBRS only) or a combination of deployment models in which both PBRS and the Power BI service are utilized for distinct scenarios or content.

With both the Power BI service and the PBRS available via Power BI Premium capacity, an organization could choose to match the deployment model to the unique needs of a given project, such as by using the PBRS if traditional paginated reports are needed, or if the reports need to remain on-premises for regulatory reasons.

For example, one Power BI solution for the marketing organization could be completely cloud-based, such as using Azure SQL Database as the source for Power BI reports and dashboards hosted in the Power BI service.

A different solution for the sales organization could use the on-premises data gateway to query a SSAS model (on-premises) from the Power BI service, as described in *Chapter 11, Managing the On-Premises Data Gateway*.

Finally, it could be used for scenarios in which both the data source(s) and the report/visualization layer must remain on-premises, such as for sensitive reports used by the human resources organization. Power BI reports developed against on-premises sources could be deployed to the PBRS.

*Figure 12.13* shows the essential architecture of three distinct Power BI solutions: cloud-only, cloud and on-premises, and on-premises only:

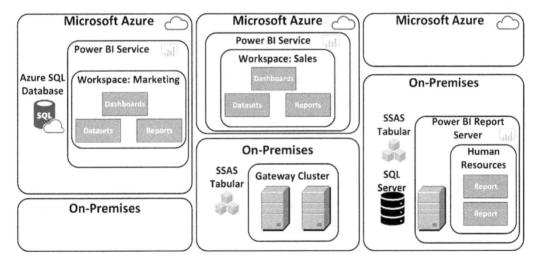

*Figure 12.13: Power BI solutions by deployment model*

In this example, Power BI reports and dashboards developed for the marketing department are hosted in the Power BI service and based on an Azure SQL database. The sales team also has access to dashboards and reports in the Power BI service, but the queries for this content utilize a Live connection to an on-premises SSAS model via the on-premises data gateway.

Finally, Power BI reports developed for the human resources department based on on-premises data sources are deployed to the PBRS.

BI solutions that utilize PaaS and SaaS cloud offerings generally deliver reduced overall cost of ownership, greater flexibility (such as scaling up/down), and more rapid access to new features. For these reasons, plans and strategies to migrate on-premises data sources to equivalent or superior cloud solutions, such as Azure Synapse and Azure Analysis Services, are recommended.

If multiple Power BI deployment models are chosen, BI teams should understand and plan to manage the different components utilized in different models. For example, identify the administrators, hardware, and users of the on-premises data gateway.

Likewise, identify the Power BI service administrators and the tenant settings to apply, as described in *Chapter 14, Administering Power BI for an Organization*. Additionally, as discussed in the *Upgrade cycles* section later in this chapter, organizations can choose either a single Power BI Desktop version to utilize for both PBRS and the Power BI service, or run separate versions of Power BI Desktop side by side.

BI teams responsible for managing these more complex deployments should have monitoring in place to understand the utilization and available resources of the alternative deployment models.

For example, rather than adding resources to a PBRS or adding another report server in a scale-out deployment, certain Power BI reports could be migrated to available Premium capacity in the Power BI service. The Power BI Premium capacities section in *Chapter 14, Administering Power BI for an Organization*, includes details on the Premium capacity monitoring provided in the Power BI service.

We will now take a closer look at a reference topology for PBRS.

## PBRS reference topology

The four main components of a PBRS deployment include the report server instance, the Report Server Database, Active Directory, and the data sources used by the reports. The Active Directory domain controller is needed to securely authenticate requests by both the data sources and the report server.

In *Figure 12.14*, a SQL Server database and an SSAS Tabular model are used as data sources by the report server:

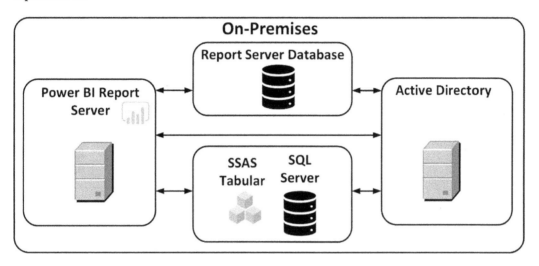

*Figure 12.14: PBRS reference topology*

In *Figure 12.14*, the Report Server Database is hosted on a separate server from the PBRS. This is recommended to avoid competition for resources (the CPU, memory, and network) between the PBRS and the SQL Server database engine instance required for the Report Server Database.

Let's take a look at how to scale out the reference architecture next.

## Scale PBRS

Both scale-up and scale-out options are available for PBRS deployments. In a scale-up scenario, additional CPU cores can be provisioned via Power BI Premium capacity or an existing SQL Server Enterprise Edition with Software Assurance agreement.

For example, if 16 cores were obtained via Power BI Premium P2 SKU, an additional 8 cores could be purchased via a P1 SKU. Additionally, particularly if import mode Power BI datasets are used, additional RAM can be installed on the report servers.

In a scale-out deployment, multiple instances of PBRS are installed on separate machines. These instances share the same Report Server Database and serve as a single logical unit exposed to business users via the web portal.

*Figure 12.15* shows a diagram of a scale-out deployment. Business user report requests are distributed between two different instances of PBRS via a network load balancer:

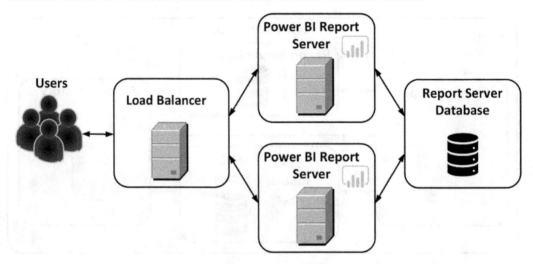

Figure 12.15: Scale-out PBRSes

Servers can be added or removed from a scale-out deployment. In addition to supporting more users and greater usage, scale-out deployments also increase the resiliency of the deployment.

To avoid a single point of failure, the scale-out deployment of the report servers can be coupled with high availability features for the Report Server Database, such as SQL Server Always On availability groups or a failover cluster. Additional information on configuring Always On availability groups with a Report Server Database is available via the following URL: http://bit.ly/2rLtSqY.

We will now cover the basics of installing PBRS.

# Installing and upgrading PBRS

Once capacity (cores) to deploy PBRS have been obtained, teams can prepare to install and configure the environment by downloading the report server software and the version of Power BI Desktop optimized for PBRS.

Both the report server installation software and the report server version of Power BI Desktop can be downloaded from Microsoft at the following link: https://powerbi.microsoft.com/en-us/report-server/. Clicking the **Advanced download options** link on that page transports the user to the most current release of PBRS available in the Microsoft Download Center.

Clicking the large **Download** button presents the option to download three different files, as shown in *Figure 12.16*:

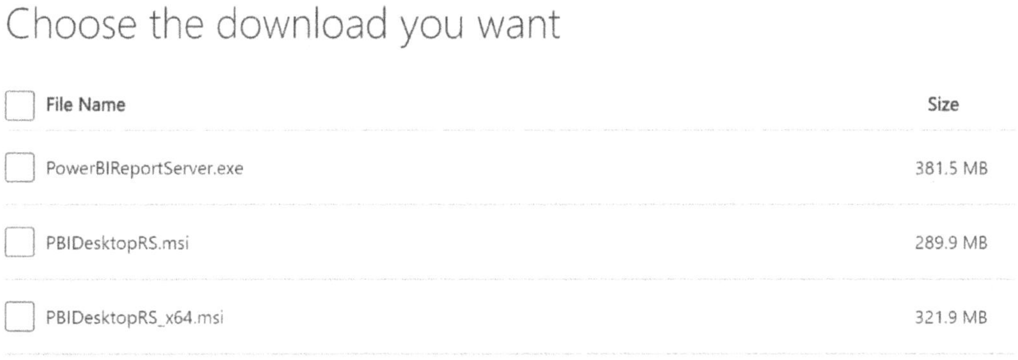

## Choose the download you want

| File Name | Size |
| --- | --- |
| PowerBIReportServer.exe | 381.5 MB |
| PBIDesktopRS.msi | 289.9 MB |
| PBIDesktopRS_x64.msi | 321.9 MB |

*Figure 12.16: Downloading PBRSes*

Referring to *Figure 12.16*, the **PowerBIReportServer.exe** file is the file for installing PBRS, while the **PBIDesktopRS.msi** and **PBIDesktopRS_x64.msi** files are for downloading the Power BI Desktop application optimized for PBRS (either 32-bit or 64-bit respectively).

System requirements for running PBRS can change over time, so it is recommended that you expand the **System Requirements** section and ensure that the target system meets the necessary minimum requirements for running PBRS.

For PBRS, an operating system of Windows Server 2016 or later is required, as is 1 GB of RAM, 1 GB of available hard-disk space, and a 64-bit processor with a clock speed of 1.4 GHz or higher. 4 GB of RAM and a 64-bit processor with a 2.0 GHz or a faster clock speed is recommended. Additional hard disk space is required on the database server hosting the Report Server Database.

Detailed instructions for installing and configuring PBRS can be found here: `https://bit. ly/36uTWLS`. However, prior to installing PBRS, you must have the necessary installation key, which we will cover next.

## Retrieve the PBRS product key

If a Power Premium capacity has been purchased, the PBRS product key can be retrieved from the Power BI admin portal. The Power BI admin portal can be accessed by either an Office 365 global administrator or a user assigned to the Power BI service administrator role.

For these users, a link to the **Admin portal** is exposed from the gear icon in the top-right corner of the Power BI service, as shown in *Figure 12.17*:

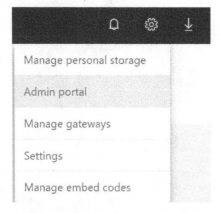

*Figure 12.17: Admin portal*

Note that depending on the browser display settings and window size, three dots (**...**) may be displayed next to the user's profile image in the upper-right corner of the window. Clicking the ellipsis exposes a **Settings** menu, which in turn displays the Admin portal link, as shown in *Figure 12.18*:

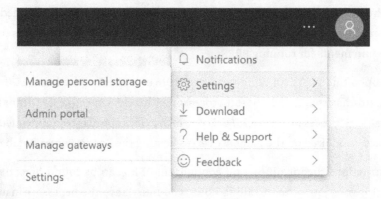

*Figure 12.18: Admin portal alternate path*

Once in the **Admin portal**, choose **Capacity settings** and then click on the **Power BI Report Server key** link, as shown in *Figure 12.19*:

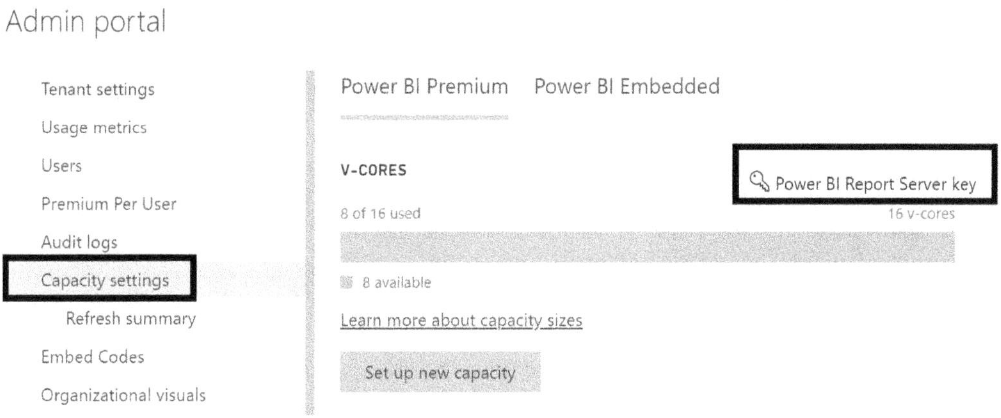

## Admin portal

| Tenant settings | Power BI Premium    Power BI Embedded |
|---|---|
| Usage metrics | |
| Users | **V-CORES** |
| Premium Per User | 8 of 16 used |
| Audit logs | |
| **Capacity settings** | 8 available |
| Refresh summary | Learn more about capacity sizes |
| Embed Codes | Set up new capacity |
| Organizational visuals | |

Power BI Report Server key

16 v-cores

*Figure 12.19: Admin portal alternate path*

Once your PBRS instance has been installed and configured, the PBRS instance needs to be maintained over time as new PBRS versions are released approximately every 4 months. Thus, we will look at considerations regarding upgrade cycles next.

## Upgrade cycles

A new version of the PBRS is released approximately every 4 months with release months typically being January, May, and September.

For example, the May 2021 release was followed by a September 2021 version, which in turn was followed by a January 2022 release. Security and critical updates are available for the prior version until the next release. After the next release, security updates are only provided for prior versions and only for 1 year after the initial release. In other words, for the three releases cited previously, their support end dates will be May 2022, September 2022, and January 2023 respectively.

Therefore, enterprise organizations wishing to remain compliant with Microsoft support would be required to update their PBRS instances a minimum of once a year. The upgrade cycle is one of the reasons for choosing the Power BI service since this process is managed by Microsoft within the Power BI service.

For example, new features are automatically added to the Power BI service each month, and users can update to the latest release of Power BI Desktop automatically via the Windows Store in Windows 10 operating systems.

The main reason PBRS is not released more frequently, such as every 2 months, is that most IT organizations will not want to upgrade their BI environments more than three to four times per year. Some organizations are expected to skip one or two of the releases per year to coincide with their internal upgrade policies and schedules.

With each release of PBRS, a new version of the Power BI Desktop optimized for this version of the PBRS is also released. This is a distinct application from the Power BI Desktop application, which can be downloaded directly from PowerBI.com and is described more fully in the following section.

To avoid report rendering errors, it's strongly recommended that you synchronize the deployment of the PBRS with its associated version of the Power BI Desktop. For example, once an upgrade to the January 2022 version of PBRS is complete, the January 2022 version of Power BI Desktop optimized for the PBRS should be installed on users' machines.

We will now look at the Power BI Desktop application optimized for PBRS.

## PBRS client applications

As mentioned in the previous section, a version of the Power BI Desktop application optimized for PBRS is made available with each release of PBRS.

As shown in the *Installing and upgrading PBRS* section earlier, a **PowerBIDesktopRS_x64.msi** file is also available for download when downloading PBRS. This is the application used to create the Power BI reports to be published to that specific version of PBRS.

When running the report server optimized version of Power BI Desktop, the version is displayed in the title bar in parentheses, such as **(January 2022)**. In addition, the **Save as** menu displays an option for PBRS, as shown in *Figure 12.20*:

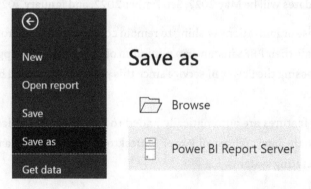

*Figure 12.20: Power BI Desktop optimized for PBRS*

As suggested by the **Save as** menu in the preceding screenshot, a report created via the PBRS optimized application can be saved directly to the report server. In other words, a .PBIX file doesn't necessarily have to be saved to a user's machine—the PBRS can serve as a network file share. If a report needs to be modified, the user (with a Power BI Pro license) could open the file directly from the web portal and save their changes back to the report server.

It is possible to run both the regular Power BI Desktop application and the optimized report server version at the same time.

## Running desktop versions side by side

It's possible to install and run both versions of Power BI Desktop (the standard and Report Server optimized) on the same machine. This can be useful in organizations deploying reports to both the Power BI service and PBRS.

For example, the standard Power BI Desktop application could be used to create a new report for a workspace in the Power BI service, which utilizes the very latest features. The report server optimized version, however, would be used to create or edit reports that are deployed to a PBRS instance.

As an alternative to running both applications side by side, an organization could choose to exclusively use the PBRS-optimized version of Power BI Desktop for reports published to both the Power BI service and PBRS. This single-application approach could simplify the management of the overall deployment but would prevent the utilization of the latest features available in the standard version of Power BI Desktop.

Next, we will look at the mobile version of Power BI and how it can be used with PBRS.

## Power BI mobile applications

The same Power BI mobile applications for the iOS, Android, and Windows platforms, which are used to access content published to the Power BI service, can also be used with PBRS. As shown in *Figure 12.21*, the user has opened the **Settings** menu via the global navigation button (≡) to connect to a report server:

*Figure 12.21: Power BI mobile app: Settings*

Referring to *Figure 12.21*, clicking **Connect to server** opens a page to enter the report server address and optionally provide a friendly name for the server, such as **AdWorks Report Server**. The server address entered should follow one of two formats:

```
http://<servername>/reports
```

```
https://<servername>/reports
```

The connection between the mobile application and the report server can be created by opening a port in the firewall, being on the same network (or VPN), or through a Web Application Proxy from outside the organization. Information on how to configure OAuth authentication via Web Application Proxy is available at the following URL http://bit.ly/2EepW4J.

Regardless of the platform (iOS or Android), up to five concurrent connections can be created for different report servers. Each report server connection appears in the **Settings** menu. Additionally, the **Favorites** menu displays reports and content marked as favorites, whether that content is hosted on PBRS or in the Power BI service.

From a business user or consumption standpoint, the mobile layout and mobile optimizations described in the *Mobile optimized reports* section of *Chapter 8, Applying Advanced Analytics,* are reflected in Power BI reports accessed from the Power BI mobile app.

## Summary

This chapter introduced paginated reports for Power BI both within the Power BI service and on-premises only via the PBRS. While the support of paginated reports in the Power BI service has greatly reduced the need for PBRS in many organizations, there are still use cases where a fully on-premises solution for reporting is required.

Key topics covered in this chapter were migrating **Report Description Language** (RDL) files to the Power BI service, the feature differences between PBRS and the Power BI service, and the overall planning, scaling, and upgrading of PBRS.

In the next chapter, we focus on the distribution of published content to end users. This includes the delivery and management of packages of related Power BI content to large groups of users via Power BI Apps as well as other content delivery capabilities of the Power BI service such as data-driven alerts and scheduled email subscriptions.

## Join our community on Discord

Join our community's Discord space for discussions with the author and other readers:

`https://discord.gg/q6BPbHEPXp`

# 13

# Creating Power BI Apps and Content Distribution

This chapter walks through all facets of Power BI apps as the primary method for distributing content to groups of users. Given the current one-to-one relationship between apps and workspaces, you are advised to review *Chapter 10, Managing Application Workspaces and Power BI Content*, prior to this chapter.

Additional content distribution and consumption methods including email subscriptions, SharePoint Online embedding, data-driven alerts, and Analyze in Excel are also described in this chapter. The distribution methods available in Power BI Report Server and the technical details of integrating Power BI content into custom applications are outside the scope of this chapter.

In this chapter, we will review the following topics:

- Content distribution methods
- Power BI apps
- Sharing content
- Embedding
- Data alerts
- Email subscriptions
- Analyze in Excel
- Self-service BI workspaces

We'll start with an overview of methods for distributing content in Power BI.

# Content distribution methods

Content distribution refers to the sharing and distribution of artifacts that result from Power BI projects. Sharing reporting artifacts is a balance of ease of access, discoverability, security, and general data governance.

As a result, there are multiple different ways to share reports, datasets, and other content. Some of these methods, like Power BI apps, focus heavily on read-only reports and centralization. Others, like self-service workspaces, focus more on collaboration and editing. In fact, one of the main value propositions of Power BI is the ability of users to access relevant analytical content in a manner and context that's best suited to their needs.

For example, many read-only users may log in to the Power BI service to view dashboards or reports contained within Power BI apps that are specific to their role or department. Other users, however, may only receive snapshot images of reports and dashboards via email subscriptions or respond to data alert notifications on their mobile devices. In other scenarios, certain users may analyze a dataset hosted in Power BI from an Excel workbook, while other users could observe a Power BI report embedded within a SharePoint team site.

Organizations can choose to distribute or expose their Power BI content hosted in the Power BI service via a single method or a combination of various different methods. The following table summarizes eleven different methods of content distribution and data access:

| # | Method | Summary |
|---|--------|---------|
| 1 | Power BI apps | • A group of related dashboards, scorecards, Power BI reports, paginated reports, and Excel reports within a workspace<br>• The app can be published to the security groups of users, enabling wide distribution |
| 2 | Embed in custom applications | • Power BI content is embedded in a custom application or a separate service from Power BI<br>• Dedicated capacity is required to host embedded content (Power BI Premium or embedded) |
| 3 | Share reports and dashboards | • An individual report or paginated report can be shared with a user or a group of users<br>• A dashboard and its underlying reports are shared with a user or a group of users |

| 4 | Embed in SharePoint Online | • A Power BI report is embedded in a SharePoint Online site page via the Power BI web part<br>• Power BI Pro licenses, the Power BI Premium capacity, or embed licenses can be used to license site users |
|---|---|---|
| 5 | Email subscriptions | • Subscriptions are configured for dashboards or individual pages of reports<br>• Users receive recurring emails with snapshot images of updated dashboards or report pages |
| 6 | Data alerts | • Alerts are configured for dashboard tiles in the Power BI service or mobile applications<br>• Users receive notifications when the alert conditions are triggered |
| 7 | Publish to web | • A report is made available via a publicly accessible URL or embedding in a website<br>• Insecure; anyone with the URL can view the report |
| 8 | Analyze in Excel | • Users with Power BI Pro licenses can connect to Power BI datasets via Excel |
| 9 | Live connections in Power BI Desktop | • Users with Power BI Pro licenses can connect to Power BI datasets from Power BI Desktop<br>• Users have the option of publishing new report files back to the Power BI service |
| 10 | Microsoft Teams integration | • A Power BI report is added as a tab in Microsoft Teams<br>• Power BI Pro licenses, the Power BI Premium capacity, or embedded licenses can be used to license site users |

*Table 13.1: Power BI content distribution methods*

The most common corporate BI distribution methods for supporting large numbers of users are the first two methods listed in *Table 13.1*: Power BI apps and embedding Power BI content into custom applications. Several other methods, however, are useful for small-scale and self-service scenarios, such as Analyze in Excel as well as supplements to larger Power BI solutions. Additionally, email subscriptions, data alerts, and embedding options for SharePoint Online and Microsoft Teams help bring analytical data to wherever the user works.

The Power BI mobile application aligns with and supports several of the primary distribution methods, including Power BI apps, the sharing of dashboards and reports, and data alerts. Examples of the relationship between the Power BI service, Power BI mobile, and other Microsoft applications and services are included in the following sections.

Let's now take a closer look at Power BI apps.

# Power BI apps

A Power BI app is a published collection of content from a workspace. An app can include all or a subset of the dashboards, scorecards, reports, and Excel workbooks within a single workspace.

There is currently a one-to-one relationship between apps and workspaces such that each workspace can only have a single associated app, and an app's content can only come from a single workspace. This limitation has caused organizations to create and manage more workspaces than they would like in order to isolate app content to different groups. Given the customer feedback for this issue, a new feature is planned for later in 2022 that will allow a single workspace to support multiple app versions for different consumer groups.

Just as workspaces are intended for the creation and management of Power BI content, apps are intended for the distribution of that content to groups of users. Once granted permission to an app, users can view the contents of the app within the Power BI service or via Power BI mobile applications.

Power BI apps should be the primary method of content consumption within organizations, so let's discuss how apps are licensed.

## Licensing apps

Apps are particularly well suited to large, corporate BI deployments that support the reporting and analysis needs of many users. This is because apps provide a centralized method of content distribution for a workspace where app creators can customize the navigation of content, as well as including additional links and information, such as links to supporting information and contacts for questions about the app. In addition, apps also provide a superior user interface and user experience versus navigating to and viewing many different individual reports, dashboards, and other content.

There are three primary mechanisms for licensing apps:

- Power BI Pro
- Power BI **Premium Per User (PPU)**

- Power BI Premium capacity

In most of these scenarios, the great majority of users only need to view certain reports or dashboards and don't require the ability to edit or create any content like Power BI Pro users.

For example, a salesperson within the northwest region of the United States may only briefly access a few dashboards or reports 2–3 times per week and occasionally interact with this content, such as via slicer visuals. With the source workspace of the app hosted in the Power BI Premium capacity, these read-only users can be assigned Power BI Free licenses yet still be allowed to access and view published apps. Additionally, Power BI Free licensed users can be granted the ability to connect to the datasets used by the reports in the published app from client applications like Power BI Desktop and Excel.

In the absence of the Power BI Premium capacity, a Power BI Pro license is required for each user that needs to access the app. In small-scale scenarios, such as when organizations are just getting started with Power BI, purchasing Power BI Pro licenses for all users can be more cost-effective than Power BI Premium capacities.

However, at a certain volume of users, the Power BI Premium capacity becomes a much more cost-efficient licensing model. For example, once an organization exceeds approximately 500 Power BI Pro licenses, the Power BI Premium capacity should be considered as a potential way to save on licensing costs.

For organizations that desire some of the additional features of Premium capacities, Power BI PPU licenses can also be an alternative to the Premium capacity. However, once an organization exceeds approximately 250 PPU licenses, the Power BI Premium capacity can potentially save those organizations money.

The same licensing considerations apply to users outside of the organization. If the Premium capacity is used, these external users do not require a Pro or PPU license to view the content. However, if the Premium capacity is not used, these external users require a Pro or PPU license assigned by their organization.

Power BI Premium and PPU licenses enable many additional features intended to support enterprise deployments. The details of provisioning and managing Power BI Premium capacity are described in *Chapter 15, Scaling with Power BI Premium*.

Let's look at the deployment process for Power BI apps next.

# App deployment process

The app deployment process simply refers to the manner in which an app is created and distributed to users. A Power BI app is published from a workspace and inherits the name of its source workspace.

As mentioned previously, an app can only contain content from its source workspace. However, an app does not have to expose all the content of its source workspace. The members of the workspace responsible for publishing and updating the app can utilize the **Include in app** toggle switch to selectively exclude certain dashboards or reports.

For example, two new reports that have yet to be validated or tested could be excluded from the app in its initial deployment. Following the validation and testing, the **Include in app** property (on the far right of each report and dashboard when viewing a workspace, as shown in *Figure 13.1*) can be enabled and the app can be updated, thus allowing users access to the new reports:

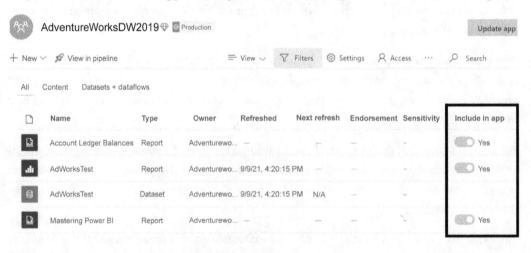

*Figure 13.1: Include in app property*

The one-to-one relationship between workspaces and apps underscores the importance of planning for the scope of a workspace and providing a user-friendly name aligned with this scope. Too narrow a scope could lead to users needing to access many different apps for relevant reports and dashboards. Alternatively, too broad a scope could make it more difficult for users to find the reports and dashboards they need within the app. Additionally, the workspace and app-update process could become less manageable.

A simple publish (or update) process is available within the workspace for defining the users or groups who can access the app as well as adding a description and custom navigation, and choosing a default landing page for users of the app. The details of the publish process are included in the *Publishing apps* section.

*Figure 13.2* and the supporting five-step process describe the essential architecture of apps and workspaces:

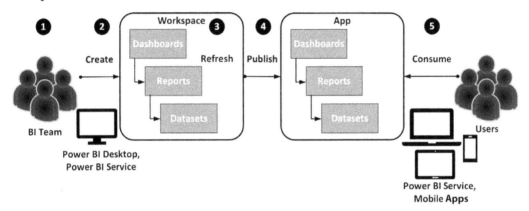

*Figure 13.2: App deployment process*

An example of using this deployment process is a Global Sales app being accessed by a sales team consisting of 200 users, as per the *Sample Power BI project template* section of *Chapter 1, Planning Power BI Projects*. Additionally, the row-level security roles described in *Chapter 5, Developing DAX Measures and Security Roles*, and the organizational dashboard architecture reviewed in *Chapter 9, Designing Dashboards*, would be utilized by such an app.

The deployment process involves five steps, as noted in *Figure 13.2* and described below:

1. One or more workspaces are created in the Power BI service, and dataset modelers and report designers are added as workspace members with edit rights to the workspace(s). Individual members and Microsoft 365 groups can be added to workspaces.

2. Members of the workspace publish datasets, scorecards, reports, and Excel workbooks to the given workspace and create dashboards based on the reports. Power BI Desktop is used to author and publish datasets and reports based on a Live connection to the published datasets. Visuals from the published reports are pinned to dashboards, such as European Sales. However, dashboards are not required to publish an app and neither are scorecards or Excel workbooks.

It should be noted that Power BI reports can access datasets via Live connections even if those datasets are contained in a separate workspace, which is often a best practice employed by organizations to maintain security and the separation of duties. This requires a specific Power BI tenant setting to be enabled, which is discussed in further detail in *Chapter 14, Administering Power BI for an Organization*.

3.  Scheduled data refresh or dashboard cache refresh schedules are configured, and the workspace content is validated. In this example, an import mode dataset is used, and thus, the dashboards and reports are updated when the scheduled refresh completes.

4.  A workspace administrator or a member with edit rights publishes an app from the workspace. The app is distributed to one or multiple users and/or Microsoft 365 groups, Azure AD security groups, or Azure AD mail-enabled security groups.

5.  Members of the sales team view and optionally interact with the content in the Power BI service and/or Power BI mobile applications. The dashboards and reports reflect the row-level security roles configured in the dataset.

Certain sales team users requiring Power BI Pro features, such as Analyze in Excel, could utilize the Power BI app as well. Additional content access methods exclusive to Power BI Pro users, such as email subscriptions to dashboards and reports, are described later in this chapter.

As organizations are generally keen on making certain that sensitive business information is secure, let's take a closer look at the security and user permissions for apps.

## User permissions and security

BI teams distributing Power BI content via apps have three layers of control for granting users permission to view the app's dashboards and reports. The first layer is control over which users or groups of users should be able to access the app after publishing in the Power BI service. Remember that Microsoft 365 groups, Azure AD security groups, and mail-enabled Azure AD security groups can all be assigned access to apps.

In *Figure 13.3*, a security group from Azure AD (**Sales**) is specified when publishing the workspace as an app:

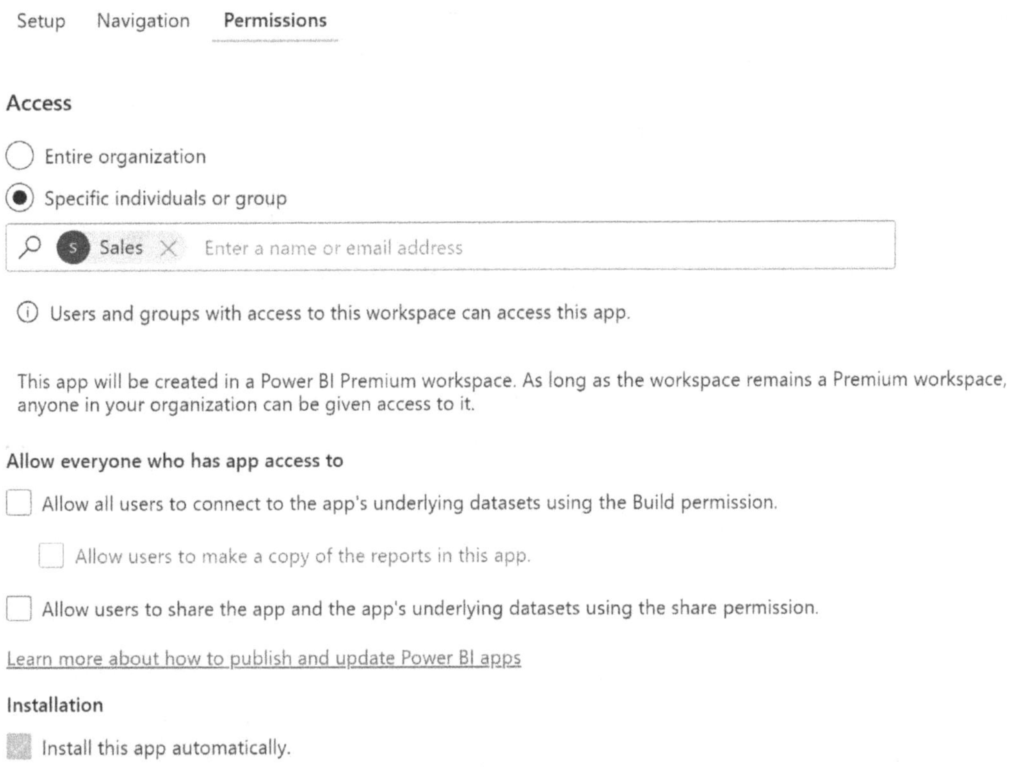

Setup    Navigation    **Permissions**

### Access

○ Entire organization

◉ Specific individuals or group

| 🔍 **S** **Sales** ✕   Enter a name or email address |
| --- |

ⓘ Users and groups with access to this workspace can access this app.

This app will be created in a Power BI Premium workspace. As long as the workspace remains a Premium workspace, anyone in your organization can be given access to it.

**Allow everyone who has app access to**

☐ Allow all users to connect to the app's underlying datasets using the Build permission.

    ☐ Allow users to make a copy of the reports in this app.

☐ Allow users to share the app and the app's underlying datasets using the share permission.

Learn more about how to publish and update Power BI apps

Installation

☐ Install this app automatically.

*Figure 13.3: Publishing an app to a security group*

In this example, a Power BI user must be included in the **Sales** security group to see and access the app. The user who published the app is also automatically granted permission to the app.

Additionally, as per the **Install this app automatically** checkmark, the published app will be automatically installed for members of the **Sales** security group. These users will be able to access the installed app via the **Apps** menu item in the left navigation menu of the Power BI service.

The **Install this app automatically** option, as well as the option to grant access to the **Entire organization,** only appears if specific tenant settings are enabled in the Power BI **Admin portal.** Specifically, a Power BI admin can enable the **Push apps to end users** setting and/or **Publish content packs and apps to the entire organization**, respectively, in the **Tenant settings** page for an entire organization or for specific security groups of users.

Microsoft recommends that apps should only be pushed to users during off-hours and that teams should verify the availability of the app prior to communicating to a team that the published app is available. The configuration of **Tenant settings** in the Power BI admin portal is described in *Chapter 14, Administering Power BI for an Organization*.

The second layer of control is the available options shown under the **Allow everyone who has app access to** heading. Here, app publishers can control whether or not app users have the ability to build new reports from the underlying datasets of the app, copy reports within the app, and share the app with other users. In most enterprise scenarios, all three of these options should be disabled in order to prevent unintended individuals from accessing the app as well as the creation of unofficial reports. Build permission, which is the ability to create new reports against an existing dataset, can be granted to report authors and self-service report authors via the **Manage Permissions** page for the source dataset in the workspace of the source dataset.

The third layer of control is the **row-level security (RLS)** roles configured for the dataset supporting the reports and dashboards. If RLS is defined within the dataset, all users accessing the app should be mapped to one of the RLS roles in the Power BI service.

Included in this third layer is **object-level security (OLS)**. Since RLS simply filters data rows, users without access can still potentially see that certain tables and columns exist in the dataset. In contrast, OLS completely hides the tables and columns from users that do not have access to this information.

Note that OLS cannot be configured within Power BI Desktop, but rather must be implemented using tools such as Tabular Editor. Also, be aware that using columns secured by OLS directly in visualizations will break those visuals for users that do not have access to those columns.

In *Figure 13.4*, another Azure AD security group (**Admin**) is being mapped to the **Europe Sales Group** RLS role:

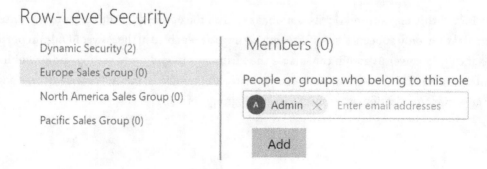

*Figure 13.4: Dataset security role assignment*

This dialog is accessed via a dataset's **Security** setting, which is accessed from the three vertical dots menu when viewing the content of a workspace, as shown in *Figure 13.5*:

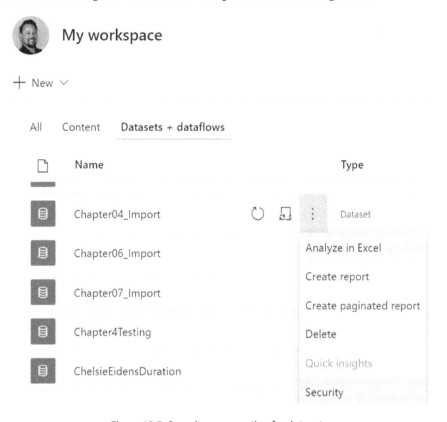

*Figure 13.5: Security menu option for datasets*

Thus, in this example, the user accessing and consuming the app must be a member of both the **Sales** security group and one or more of the security groups assigned to an RLS role. If the user is only a member of the **Sales** security group, the visuals of the dashboard and report will not render.

With the three distinct levels of security and permission controls understood, let's take a look at actually publishing an app next.

## Publishing apps

Apps are published from app workspaces in the following way:

1.  A workspace member with edit rights clicks the **Create app** button in the top-right corner of the workspace. Three pages are launched for configuring the app: **Setup**, **Navigation**, and **Permissions**.

2. On the **Setup** page, an **App name** and a short **Description** of the app are entered, such as in the following example:

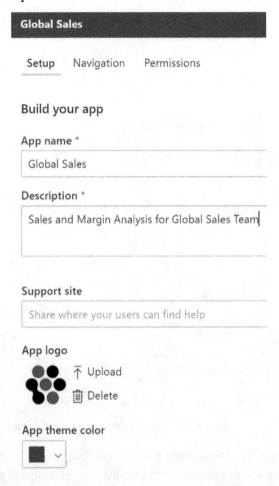

*Figure 13.6: Setup page when publishing an app*

3. As shown in *Figure 13.6*, in addition to the **App name** and **Description**, the **Support site**, **App logo**, **App theme color**, and **Contact Information** (not shown) properties can also be configured for the app.

4. On the **Navigation** page, customize the navigation with custom sections and links to dashboards, reports, scorecards, and Excel workbooks:

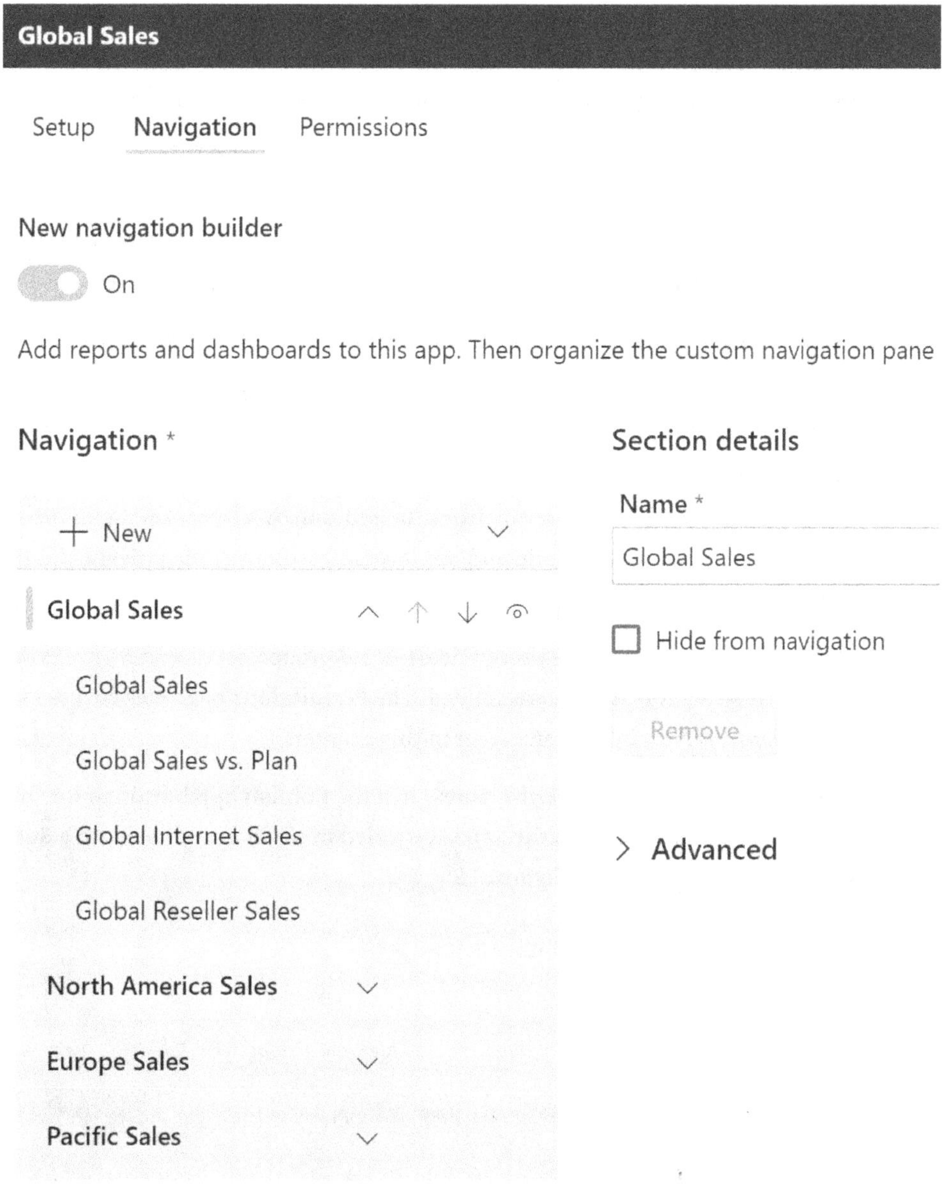

**Global Sales**

Setup    Navigation    Permissions

## New navigation builder

⬤◯ On

Add reports and dashboards to this app. Then organize the custom navigation pane

### Navigation *

| + New | ⌄ |

| Global Sales | ∧  ↑  ↓  ⊙ |

  Global Sales

  Global Sales vs. Plan

  Global Internet Sales

  Global Reseller Sales

North America Sales    ⌄

Europe Sales    ⌄

Pacific Sales    ⌄

### Section details

Name *

Global Sales

☐ Hide from navigation

Remove

> Advanced

*Figure 13.7: App Navigation page*

In *Figure 13.7*, four sections (**Global Sales, North America Sales, Europe Sales**, and **Pacific Sales**) have been created to group the different sections of the app and help users more easily navigate to content. In this example, users accessing the **Global Sales** app will land on the **Global Sales** (dashboard) by default since this is first in the **Navigation** list.

The **Navigation** page also provides a consolidated view of the dashboards, reports, scorecards, and Excel workbooks that are included in the app given the current settings. In the event that any content has been included that shouldn't be, the user can navigate to this item in the workspace and disable the **Include in app** property.

By default, the **Include in app** property for new dashboards, reports, scorecards, and Excel workbooks is enabled. Therefore, prior to publishing the app, ensure that this property has been disabled for any internal testing or development content.

In addition to creating custom sections, the **New** button also allows the creation of custom links. Custom links can be useful to direct viewers of the app to such things as the external support pages or other content that is not stored in Power BI.

Individual navigation items or entire sections can be moved up and down in the **Navigation** list using the up and down arrow icons. In addition, list items can be hidden from the **Navigation** list using the circle and arc (eyeball) icon or, alternatively, the **Hide from navigation** checkbox.

5.  On the **Permissions** page, the users, Microsoft 365 groups, and security groups that should have permission for the app are defined. The **Permissions** page was covered in the *User permissions and security* section earlier in this chapter.

    Once finished configuring permissions, click the **Publish app** button in the lower-right corner of the page. A URL to the app is provided in a window along with a **Successfully published** message, as per *Figure 13.8*:

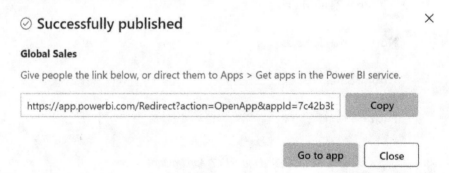

*Figure 13.8: Published app*

The published app can now be accessed by the users or groups of users defined on the **Permissions** page. If the **Install this app automatically** option was used, the user or team publishing the app can verify with a few users that the app is now installed and available.

Depending on the number of items (dashboards, reports, scorecards, and Excel workbooks) included in the app, the automatic installation could take some time. Once the automatic installation is confirmed, an email or other communication can then be sent to advise users of the availability of the published app.

Viewing the app is an immersive experience. As shown in *Figure 13.9*, much of Power BI chrome, such as the left navigation, is replaced with app elements, such as the **Navigation** list for the app. The user experience feels very much like the app is a standalone web application versus a page within the Power BI service. This is beneficial as it allows app viewers to focus on the content without distractions or confusion regarding the standard Power BI service features and functionality:

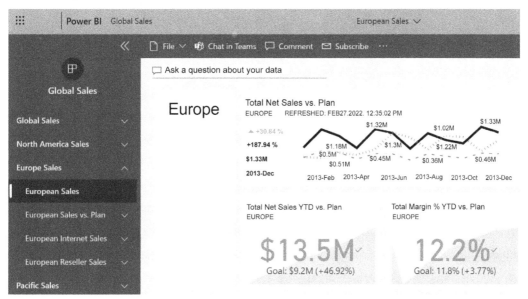

*Figure 13.9: App*

The following section describes the installation of an app if the **Install this app automatically** (push apps to end users) feature was not used.

## Installing apps

When an app is published and not pushed to end users via the **Install this app automatically** feature described in the previous section, a one-time install per user is necessary. This install can be completed by either sharing the URL for the app with users or by instructing users to add the app to the Power BI service.

In *Figure 13.10*, a user has logged into the Power BI service and clicked **Get apps** from the **Apps** menu to observe the **Global Sales** app:

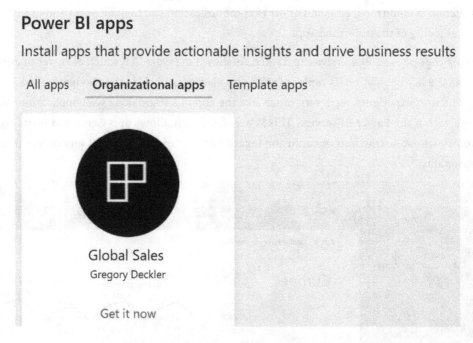

*Figure 13.10: Installing a Power BI app manually*

Clicking the **Get it now** link installs the app for the user.

The **Apps** menu can be found in the left navigation pane of the Power BI service. Once on the **Apps** menu page, all installed apps are listed. Users can hover over an app, to either mark the app as a favorite or remove the app via the **More options** menu, as shown in *Figure 13.11*:

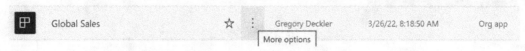

*Figure 13.11: Installed app*

A second option to install the app is to share the URL to the app provided in the Power BI service. As per the *Publishing apps* section, this URL is provided in a dialog (*Figure 13.8*) when the app is first published. Additionally, this URL can be obtained from the **Permissions** page when publishing or updating the app, as shown in *Figure 13.12*:

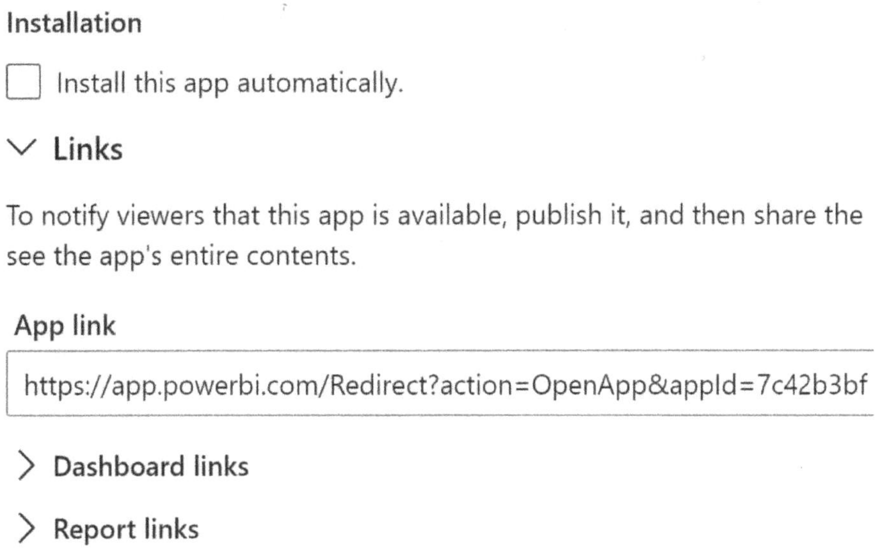

Installation

☐  Install this app automatically.

∨  **Links**

To notify viewers that this app is available, publish it, and then share the
see the app's entire contents.

App link
_____

| https://app.powerbi.com/Redirect?action=OpenApp&appId=7c42b3bf |

⟩  **Dashboard links**

⟩  **Report links**

*Figure 13.12: App link*

In the preceding example, a member of the Global Sales app workspace has clicked **Update app**
from the top-right corner of the workspace and navigated to the **Permissions** page. The **App link**,
as well as other URLs specific to dashboards and reports within the app, is located in the **Links**
section at the bottom of the page.

Once the apps are installed and are being used within the organization, it may be necessary to
update the app with additional content.

# App updates

As new content becomes available within a workspace, it may be necessary to update an app with
this new content or remove certain content that has become outdated.

One of the main advantages of Power BI apps is their isolation from workspaces. The members
of the workspace can continue to develop, test, and modify content in the app workspace while
users only view the latest published app.

This single level of built-in staging could be a sufficient alternative for some teams and projects
relative to the multiple workspaces (Dev, Test, and Prod) involved in a staged deployment life
cycle, as described in *Chapter 10, Managing Application Workspaces and Content*.

After an app has been published, the **Publish app** icon in the top-right corner of the workspace is changed to an **Update app** icon, as shown in *Figure 13.13*:

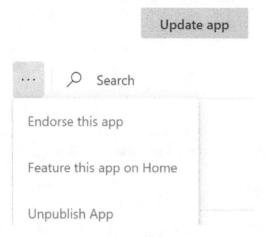

Figure 13.13: Update app

In *Figure 13.13*, the ellipsis (**...**) to the left of the **Update app** icon has been selected. As shown, three options exist to **Endorse this app**, **Feature this app on Home**, and **Unpublish App**.

Endorsing apps promotes or certifies an app and can help other users find useful organizational apps. Enterprise BI teams may also wish to feature certain apps on the Power BI service **Home** page for users in order to promote and encourage the use of the app. Finally, there may be times when an app should be unpublished and, thus, made unavailable.

Clicking **Update app** launches the same three pages (**Setup**, **Navigation**, and **Permissions**) described in the *Publishing apps* section. In the most common update scenarios, such as adding a new report or modifying a dashboard, it's unnecessary to change any of these settings, and the **Update app** icon in the lower-right corner of the page can be clicked a second time. However, these pages enable fundamental modifications to be implemented, including the users or groups with permission to access the app and the **Navigation** for the app.

As previously mentioned, users can view the contents of apps within the Power BI service or via Power BI mobile applications, so let's look at how apps can be viewed on mobile devices next.

## Apps on Power BI mobile

Just like the **Apps** menu item in the Power BI service, users can access published Power BI apps from the main menu within Power BI mobile applications. In *Figure 13.14*, a user has accessed the **Global Sales** app on the Power BI mobile application for Android devices:

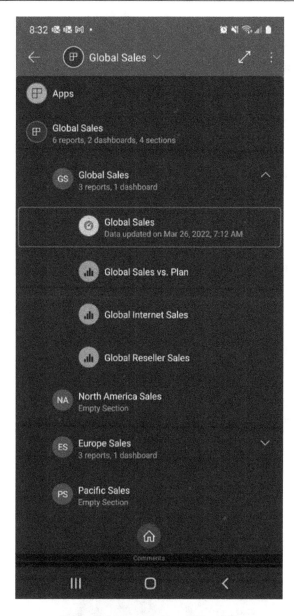

*Figure 13.14: Apps on Power BI mobile*

The user can easily navigate to the dashboards and reports contained within the app and take advantage of all the standard mobile features, such as the exclusive ability of the Power BI mobile apps to annotate and share both the annotations and the content with colleagues. Additionally, any mobile optimizations configured by the report authors for the reports and dashboards are also reflected through apps.

Overall, mobile applications provide the benefit of accessing Power BI content from anywhere using just about any mobile device such as iOS, Android, or Windows phones and tablets. This is important for executives, salespeople, and other consumers that are constantly on the move and require timely analytics.

Moving on from apps, we can now explore additional content distribution methods, starting with another common distribution method – the direct sharing of content.

## Sharing content

In addition to Power BI apps, Power BI Pro users can share individual dashboards, reports, scorecards, and Excel workbooks directly with users, groups, and even guest users from outside the organization.

For example, unlike a Power BI app built for the sales organization containing several dashboards and many reports, a single dashboard or report could be shared with two or three users in the customer service department. In this scenario, the few customer service department users may have limited or undefined reporting needs, or the corporate BI team may not have a full Power BI app for their department prepared yet.

Recipients of directly shared content receive the same essential benefits of Power BI apps in terms of easy access as well as the latest updates and modifications to the content. In terms of user access, the **Shared with me** menu in the left navigation of the Power BI service provides easy access. The **Shared with me** menu option is also available within Power BI mobile applications.

In *Figure 13.15*, the user has accessed the **More pages** dialog via the three vertical dots at the bottom of the mobile application:

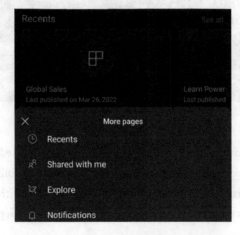

*Figure 13.15: Power BI mobile More pages menu*

Recipients of shared content can also add this content to their list of **Favorites** just like Power BI apps.

The Power BI service gives content owners a properties pane to define the recipients of the shared content and whether the recipients will also be allowed to share the content. This pane can be accessed via the **Share** icon in the ribbon menu when viewing the content in the Power BI service.

Alternatively, as shown in *Figure 13.16*, a share icon is also available when viewing the content list of a workspace:

*Figure 13.16: Sharing action in Power BI service*

The same sharing icon from *Figure 13.16* is available for dashboards and scorecards.

Excel workbooks published to the Power BI service cannot be shared directly. To share a published Excel workbook (indirectly), a dashboard can be shared containing a tile that was pinned to the Excel workbook. The user receiving the shared dashboard can access the workbook via the dashboard tile, just like accessing a Power BI report based on a pinned report visual.

Once the sharing action has been selected, a **Send link** dialog is launched to define the recipients who will receive access as well as their permissions. In *Figure 13.17*, the **European Reseller Sales** report is being shared with specific people, Pamela Hagely and Mike Laning:

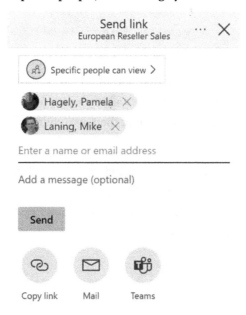

*Figure 13.17: Sharing the report*

Three options exist regarding who content can be shared with. In *Figure 13.18*, the **Specific people can view** link from *Figure 13.17* has been clicked to reveal the three options:

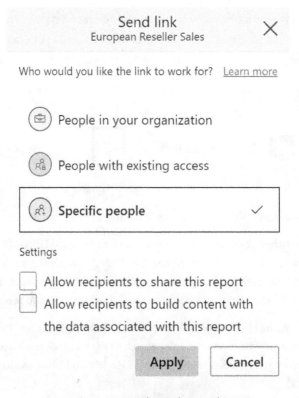

*Figure 13.18: Who to share with*

As shown in *Figure 13.18*, the sharing link can work for everyone in the organization, those users with existing access, or specific people that you specify. In addition, as per the checkboxes in *Figure 13.18*, the content owner has the option to allow sharing recipients to also share the content with others or allow sharing recipients to build their own content from the underlying dataset. If these boxes are not checked, sharing recipients can only view the content.

In addition to the **Send link** dialog, clicking the ellipses (three dots) shown in the upper-right corner of *Figure 13.17* provides access to a **Manage permissions** pane. This pane, as shown in *Figure 13.19*, displays all the sharing links created for the content as well as those users with direct access to the content via their workspace membership:

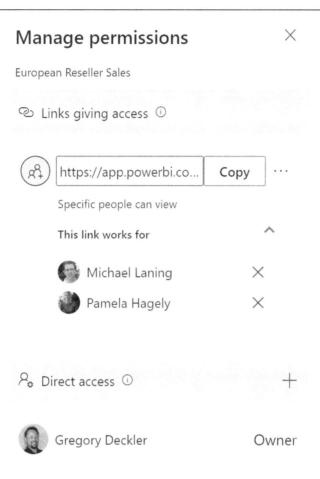

*Figure 13.19: Manage permissions pane*

The **Links giving access** can be edited using the ellipses menu to the right of the **Copy** button. Members with edit rights to the workspace containing the shared dashboard or report can manage user access by utilizing the **Manage permissions** pane. For example, several days after the report was shared, it may be necessary to add or remove users from the share. Additionally, the ability of recipients to reshare the content can be revoked if this was enabled originally.

Sharing dashboards and reports should only be generated from workspaces and not from a user's private **My Workspace**. The workspace allows the workspace members to manage both the content and its distribution and, thus, eliminates a dependency on a single user.

If content is shared from a user's **My Workspace**, or if the user leaves the organization and their account is removed, their **My Workspace** is also removed. This can mean the potential loss of important information and useful analytics. A possible exception to this may be the solicitation of feedback from others on a personal analytics project.

Let's now dive a little deeper into how sharing works, starting with an explanation of sharing scopes.

## Sharing scopes

When a dashboard is shared, the reports containing the visuals pinned to that dashboard are shared as well. The recipient of the shared dashboard can, therefore, access and interact with the underlying reports by clicking the linked dashboard tile(s).

The ability to share a report directly eliminates the need for the owners of a report to create a dashboard and for the recipients to leverage this dashboard when they only need to access the report. However, recipients of a shared dashboard can still add one or more of the underlying reports as favorites, thus providing the same ease of access as a shared report. Although a single report may be all that's needed currently, sharing a dashboard provides greater scalability because of the caching of dashboard tiles.

For example, a shared dashboard may begin with only one report, but visuals from two or three new reports could be pinned to the dashboard, thus granting access to these additional reports. This would negate the need to share each new report individually, and the dashboard could help summarize the reports for the user. When a report is shared, the only option for adding content is to add report pages to the existing report, and this can reduce the usability of the report.

Let's now look at the similarities and differences between direct sharing and the use of Power BI apps.

## Sharing versus Power BI apps

Just like Power BI apps, either the Power BI Pro or PPU licenses, as well as the Power BI Premium capacity, can be used to enable user access. In the example from this section, both Pam and Mike could be assigned Power BI Pro licenses to allow both users to view the shared content.

Alternatively, the workspace of the shared content could be assigned to a Power BI Premium capacity, thus allowing Power BI Free users to access the content. The same licensing considerations for external guest users described in the *Licensing apps* section apply to sharing dashboards and reports.

Also, like Power BI apps, the recipients of the shared content need to be mapped to an RLS role if RLS has been configured on the source dataset. Otherwise, the users attempting to access the shared content receive an error message if this mapping is not implemented within the security settings of the dataset, as described in the *User permissions and security* section earlier in this chapter.

Ultimately, Power BI apps provide the best long-term solution for content distribution, particularly for groups of users. Unlike sharing content, any number of new dashboards and reports can be added to Power BI apps as needs grow and change.

Additionally, as described earlier in this chapter, owners of the workspace can stage and test content prior to republishing the app via the app update process. In the case of shared dashboards and reports, any revision to the shared content is immediately visible to the user(s).

Let's move on to the options for distributing content via embedding next.

# Embedding

Embedding refers to the distribution of Power BI content outside of the Power BI service and mobile applications such as SharePoint Online, Microsoft Teams, custom applications, and the public internet. In this section, we will cover the separate licensing considerations for embedding as well as four embedding scenarios:

- Publish to web
- Secure URL embedding
- Microsoft 365 apps
- Custom applications

In addition to the embedding options covered in this section, it is worth noting that other Microsoft applications also include the ability to embed Power BI content, including Dynamics 365 and Power Apps. Many of these additional embedding scenarios are covered in *Chapter 13* of *Microsoft Power BI Cookbook, Second Edition*.

Before diving into the four embedding scenarios, it is first important to understand how Power BI content embedding is licensed.

## Licensing embedding

Power BI Premium capacity isn't required for embedding reports into SharePoint Online or MS Teams. If the content is not in a Premium workspace, the SharePoint users would need to have Power BI Pro or **PPU** licenses. If the content is in a Premium workspace, the SharePoint users only need a fee license.

Embedding content from Power BI into other applications requires the use of at least one of three different **stock-keeping units (SKUs)**. These SKUs are referred to as P, EM, and A SKUs.

P SKUs (P1–P5) are Premium capacity SKUs primarily intended for enterprises to cost-effectively license large numbers of view-only Power BI users. However, these SKUs also grant the ability to embed Power BI content into Microsoft 365 apps such as SharePoint Online and Microsoft Teams and even custom applications developed by the business for both internal and external use. P SKUs are billed monthly, and the commitment is either monthly or yearly.

EM SKUs (EM1–EM3) are specifically designed for smaller organizations using Pro licenses to add embedding capabilities. EM SKUs have lower amounts of memory and processor cores than P SKUs, but they include the same functionality and are also billed monthly although they require a yearly commitment.

It is a common misconception that EM SKUs do not grant the ability to embed Power BI content for external customers. The only differences in terms of embedding between P SKUs and EM SKUs are the cost of the license, commitment length, and resources provisioned.

A SKUs (A1–A8) are specifically designed for **independent software vendors (ISVs)** to include Power BI content within their custom applications. As such, the A SKUs do not grant the right to embed content within the organization, in Microsoft 365 apps, or via secure URL embedding. A SKUs also differ in that they are billed hourly and can be paused and resumed to avoid charges.

While additional licensing is required for most embedding scenarios, it is not required for **Publish to web**.

## Publish to web

If enabled by the Power BI administrator, reports in the Power BI service can be embedded on any website and shared via a URL to the public internet. The **Publish to web** feature provides an embed code for the Power BI report, including an HTML iFrame markup and a report URL. iFrames are inline HTML elements for embedding nested content within a web page.

Organizations can utilize **Publish to web** to expose non-confidential or publicly available information on their public-facing corporate website. In *Figure 13.20*, a **Publish to web** embed code has been obtained in the Power BI service:

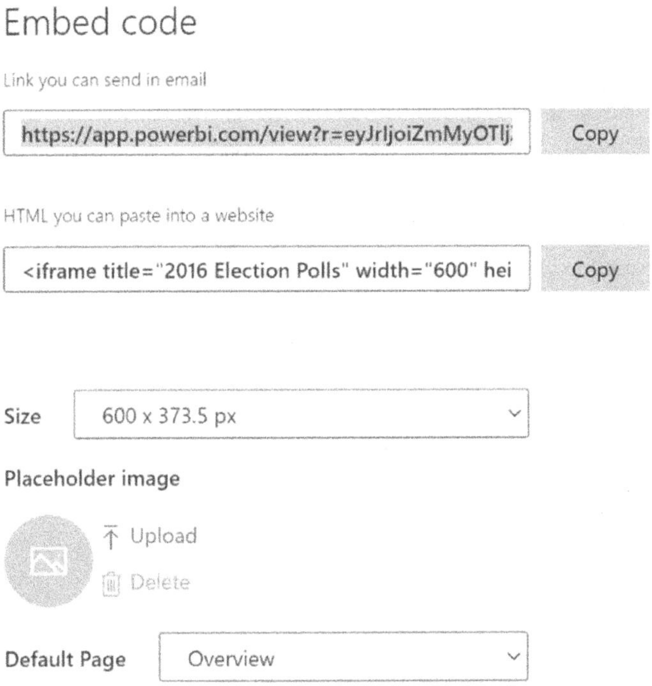

# Embed code

Link you can send in email

| https://app.powerbi.com/view?r=eyJrIjoiZmMyOTlj. | Copy |

HTML you can paste into a website

| <iframe title="2016 Election Polls" width="600" hei | Copy |

Size | 600 x 373.5 px ⌄ |

Placeholder image

↑ Upload
🗑 Delete

Default Page | Overview ⌄ |

*Figure 13.20: Publish to web embed code*

The **Publish to web** feature is accessed via the **File** menu dropdown for a report, then accessing the **Embed report** option, and finally selecting **Publish to web (public)**. Members of a workspace with edit rights can use the settings menu (the gear icon) to access the **Manage embed codes** page. This page allows the user to retrieve or delete any embedded codes for the given workspace.

With the exception of R and Python visuals, all standard and custom visuals are supported in publish-to-web reports. However, there are many other limitations to the **Publish to web** feature including not supporting reports using RLS, any Live connection, shared and certified datasets, and Q&A.

Given the obvious potential risk of users accidentally sharing confidential or protected information over the public internet, Power BI administrators have granular controls over this feature including the ability to disable it for the entire organization. Details of these administrative settings are included in *Chapter 14, Administering Power BI for an Organization*.

Power BI reports accessed via embed codes reflect the latest data refresh of the source dataset within approximately one hour of its completion. Additional documentation on **Publish to web**, including tips for fitting the iFrame into websites, is available at `http://bit.ly/2s2aJkL`.

Let's now look at a method of securely embedding Power BI content into web pages.

## Secure URL embedding

Just as workspace members can easily use the **Publish to web** feature to embed Power BI reports in web pages available on the public internet, workspace members can also securely embed Power BI reports onto any web page by using the **Secure URL embedding** feature.

Securely embedding Power BI content into a web page works almost identically to **Publish to web,** but it requires the viewer to have been authenticated to Power BI and granted access to the content either via their workspace membership or direct sharing.

To securely embed Power BI reports, view the report in the Power BI service. Then, access the **File** menu, the **Embed report** option, and finally **Website or portal**. *Figure 13.21* shows the dialog for creating a secure embed code:

Securely embed this report in a website or portal                                  ✕

Here's a link you can use to embed this content.

https://app.powerbi.com/reportEmbed?reportId=54▇▇▇▇▇▇▇▇▇▇▇▇▇▇▇▇▇▇▇▇▇▇

HTML you can paste into a website

<iframe title="anonymous" width="1140" height="541.25" src="https://app.powerbi.com/r

Explore more embedding options in our Power BI embedded analytics playground          Close

*Figure 13.21: Secure embed code*

Unlike **Publish to web** embed codes, secure embed codes are not stored or managed via the **Manage embed codes** page, which is available to workspace members, or the **Embed code** page, which is available to Power BI administrators within the **Admin portal**. In addition, secure URL embedding requires a Power BI Pro or PPU license, or the content must be in a workspace assigned to the Premium capacity (a P or EM SKU).

Let's now turn our attention to embedding Power BI content within Microsoft 365 apps such as Teams and SharePoint Online.

# Microsoft 365 apps

Microsoft 365 consists of many different apps such as Outlook, OneDrive, Power Apps, and Power Automate. Two of these apps, Teams and SharePoint Online, are natively integrated with Power BI. Thus, organizations that obtain a P or EM SKU can embed content from Power BI into these apps, or alternatively, all users must have a Pro or PPU license.

Let's first take a look at how embedding works for Teams.

## Teams

Teams is Microsoft's popular real-time collaboration, communication, meeting, file, and app sharing app. Within Teams, users can create team workspaces for sharing and collaborating on content as well as conducting audio and video meetings.

Once a team is created, multiple channels can be created to organize content. Each channel can have multiple tabs. Each tab represents a particular app used by the channel, such as OneDrive for file sharing, a Wiki, a Whiteboard, or even YouTube. One of the available apps is Power BI.

*Figure 13.22* shows a team member adding the **Global Internet Sales** report from the **Global Sales** Power BI app as a tab called **Global Internet Sales**:

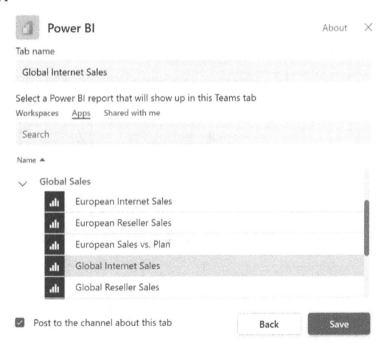

*Figure 13.22: Adding a Power BI tab to a Teams channel*

The ability to surface content from a variety of different apps is a strength of Teams. Distributing content via a central collaboration space such as Teams eases the user experience since important content is directly available within users' primary collaboration workspaces without requiring those users to switch back and forth between separate applications.

While Teams has, in many respects, supplanted SharePoint in terms of collaboration and content sharing, many organizations still cling to SharePoint as their primary means of information sharing. Thus, let's look at embedding in SharePoint Online next.

## SharePoint Online

As mentioned, while the importance and utility of SharePoint as a collaboration platform has diminished over the years to the point where SharePoint is primarily used as a backend document repository for apps such as OneDrive and Teams or as a rudimentary intranet/extranet, there are instances where organizations still wish to distribute Power BI content within SharePoint.

Distributing content to SharePoint Online is actually a two-step process, requiring actions in both the Power BI service and within SharePoint Online. The first step is to generate an embed code in the Power BI service. This step is similar to generating embed codes for **Publish to web** and **Secure URL embedding**.

In fact, the same basic steps are necessary: view the report in the Power BI service, then access the **File** menu, the **Embed report** option, and finally **SharePoint online,** as shown in *Figure 13.23*:

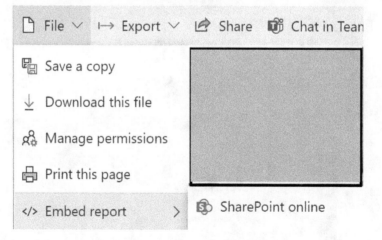

*Figure 13.23: Adding a Power BI tab to a Teams channel*

Choosing this option generates an embed code similar to the one shown in *Figure 13.24*:

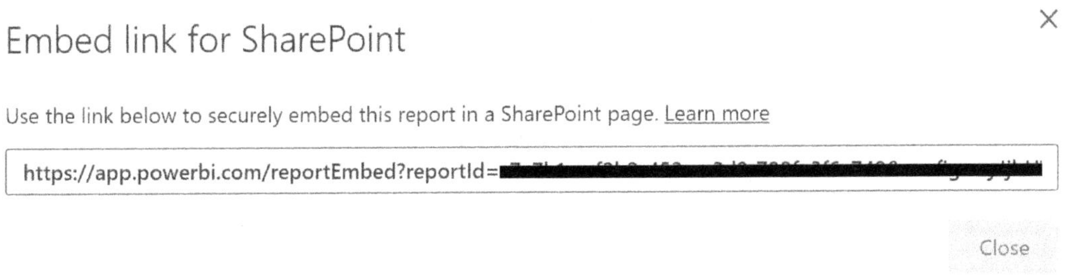

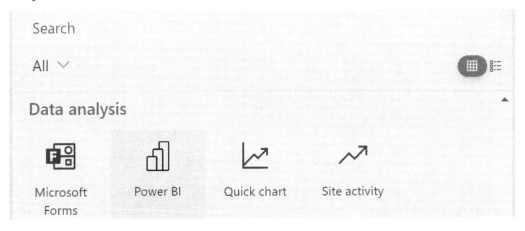

## Embed link for SharePoint ✕

Use the link below to securely embed this report in a SharePoint page. Learn more

https://app.powerbi.com/reportEmbed?reportId=▒▒▒▒▒▒▒▒▒▒▒▒▒▒▒▒▒▒▒▒▒▒▒

Close

*Figure 13.24: Adding a Power BI tab to a Teams channel*

This embed code must be copied. Similar to secure URL embedding, this code is not stored or managed via the **Manage embed codes** page, which is available to workspace members, or the **Embed code** page, which is available to Power BI administrators within the **Admin portal**.

The second step requires editing a SharePoint Online page. In *Figure 13.25*, the + icon for a section of a SharePoint Online page in edit mode has been selected, allowing the insertion of a Power BI web part:

Search

All ⌄

Data analysis

Microsoft Forms     Power BI     Quick chart     Site activity

*Figure 13.25: Adding a Power BI web part to a SharePoint Online page*

Adding the Power BI web part to the page enables the configuration options to paste the embedding link from the first step in **Power BI report link**, as shown in *Figure 13.26*:

*Figure 13.26: Configuring a Power BI web part*

Once the Power BI report web part has been added and configured, republish the SharePoint Online page.

We will now look at our last embedding scenario, embedding Power BI content into custom applications.

## Custom applications

In addition to the embedding options covered so far, Power BI embedded analytics enables the ability to embed reports, dashboards, and individual dashboard tiles into any custom application provided that a P, EM, or A SKU is purchased.

As opposed to embedding within an organization, otherwise known as **user owns data**, Power BI embedded analytics are known as **app owns data**. The terms user owns data and app owns data simply refer to how authentication is handled, either by the user or by the app respectively.

Power BI embedded analytics work very differently from the link embedding solutions such as **Publish to web**, **Secure URL embedding**, and **SharePoint Online** embedding. One of the differences is with regard to authentication. **Publish to web** uses anonymous authentication, while organizational embedding uses interactive authentication to Azure AD. In contrast, embedded analytics uses non-interactive authentication where the custom application uses a service principal or master user for authentication.

Using a service principal is the recommended method for authentication when using Power BI embedded analytics. A service principal is simply an application whose security tokens can be used to authenticate Azure resources from a service, tool, or user app.

With service principals, tokens can either be an application secret or a certificate. Application secrets are simply strings of letters, numbers, and special characters unique to that application. Information about creating and registering Azure service principals can be found here: `https://bit.ly/3tGVag7`.

In contrast, the master user approach uses an actual username and password. This approach is sometimes referred to as "fake user" since the user ID is not tied to a physical individual but rather exists solely to facilitate application authentication. As mentioned, the use of service principals is preferred over the master user approach.

Once an authentication method has been selected, the next step is to register the Azure AD application. Registering the Azure AD application allows access to the Power BI REST APIs and establishes permissions for the Power BI REST resources. Additional information about registering Azure AD applications to use Power BI can be found at the following link: `https://bit.ly/3DgKc41`.

Once the Azure AD application has been properly registered, the next step is to create a Power BI workspace and publish content within this workspace. This is the same process as described throughout this book.

With a workspace created and content published, the next step is to obtain a number of embedding parameters. For service principals, embedding requires the following embedding parameters:

- Client ID
- Workspace ID
- Report or dashboard ID

- Client secret
- Tenant ID

If using the master user approach instead, then the embedding parameters required are the client ID, workspace ID, and report or dashboard ID as well as the chosen username and password for the "fake" Power BI user.

The workspace ID as well as the report or dashboard ID can be obtained by viewing content within the Power BI service. Workspace IDs are the unique ID appearing just after the /groups/ portion of a Power BI service URL. Similarly, report and dashboard IDs appear just after the /reports/ or /dashboards/ portion of such URLs.

The client ID, client secret, and tenant ID parameters are obtained within the Microsoft Azure portal when viewing the app registration for the application registered previously. In the Azure portal, select **App registrations** and then the registered app. From the **Overview** section, copy the **Application (client) ID**. Also in the **Overview** section, copy the **Directory (tenant) ID**. On the same page, under **Manage**, select **Certificates & secrets**. Under **Client secrets**, select **New client secret**, and, once created, copy the string in the **Value** column of the newly created secret.

The next step is to ensure that service principals are allowed to access your Power BI tenant. This is done in the **Tenant settings** of the Power BI **Admin portal** and specifically the **Allow service principals to use Power BI APIs** setting. More information about the Power BI **Admin portal** and **Tenant settings** is included in *Chapter 14, Administering Power BI for an Organization*.

Once service principals are granted the ability to use the Power BI APIs for the tenant, the service principal must be given access to the workspace. This is done by adding the service principal as a member of the workspace. This is the same as adding any other user as a member of a workspace and is covered in *Chapter 10, Managing Application Workspaces and Content*.

Once access has been granted, it is time to embed your content. While developing a full-blown application that embeds Power BI content is beyond the scope of this book, Microsoft provides code samples for .NET Core, .NET Framework, Java, Node.js, PowerShell, Python, and React-TS in a GitHub repository: https://github.com/microsoft/PowerBI-Developer-Samples.

In addition, a Power BI embedded analytics playground is available for developers to test embedding code. This playground can be accessed at http://playground.powerbi.com/. For example, the following simple code embeds a Power BI report:

```
let loadedResolve, reportLoaded = new Promise((res, rej) => {
loadedResolve = res; });
```

```
let renderedResolve, reportRendered = new Promise((res, rej) => {
renderedResolve = res; });
models = window['powerbi-client'].models;
function embedPowerBIReport() {
    let accessToken = EMBED_ACCESS_TOKEN;
    let embedUrl = EMBED_URL;
    let embedReportId = REPORT_ID;
    let tokenType = TOKEN_TYPE;
    let permissions = models.Permissions.All;
    let config = {
        type: 'report',
        tokenType: tokenType == '0' ? models.TokenType.Aad : models.
TokenType.Embed,
        accessToken: accessToken,
        embedUrl: embedUrl,
        id: embedReportId,
        permissions: permissions,
        settings: {
            panes: {
                filters: {
                    visible: true
                },
                pageNavigation: {
                    visible: true
                }
            }
        }
    };
    let embedContainer = $('#embedContainer')[0];
    report = powerbi.embed(embedContainer, config);
    report.off("loaded");
    report.on("loaded", function () {
        loadedResolve();
        report.off("loaded");
    });
    report.off("error");
    report.on("error", function (event) {
        console.log(event.detail);
```

```
    });
    report.off("rendered");
    report.on("rendered", function () {
        renderedResolve();
        report.off("rendered");
    });
}
embedPowerBIReport();
await reportLoaded;
await reportRendered;
```

We have now covered all four embedding scenarios, so let's move on to data alerts.

# Data alerts

Data-driven alerts are email notifications and one of the top capabilities exclusive to dashboards in the Power BI service. For many users and business scenarios, data-driven alerts are a high-value complement, or even a substitute, to dashboards and reports as they help to avoid frequently accessing Power BI to search for actionable information.

For example, rather than opening Power BI in the browser or on a phone every morning and looking for red colors or certain KPI symbols, users could view certain dashboards or reports less frequently and only respond to data-driven alert notifications sent via email.

With a standard card, KPI, or gauge visual pinned to a dashboard, a data-driven alert can be configured either in the Power BI service or via the Power BI mobile app. In *Figure 13.27*, the ellipses (**...**) of a KPI visual are clicked, exposing the **Manage alerts** option:

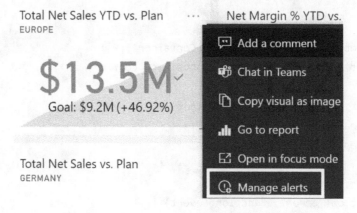

*Figure 13.27: Manage alerts in Power BI service*

Choosing **Manage alerts** from the menu displays the **Manage alerts** pane, allowing one or multiple alert rules to be added, as shown in *Figure 13.28*:

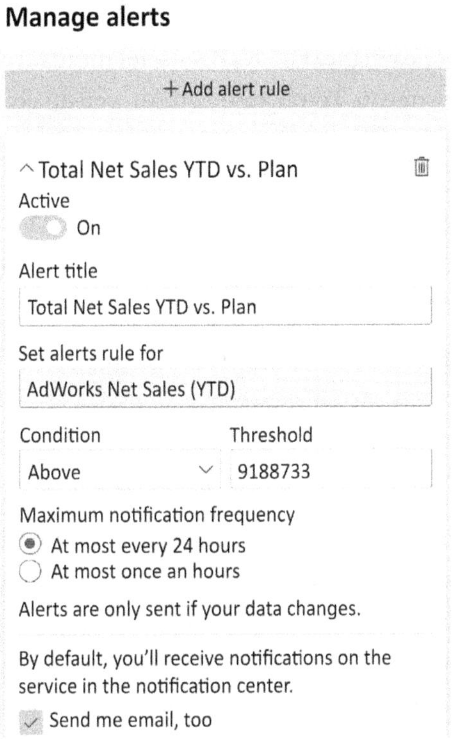

## Manage alerts

| + Add alert rule |
| --- |

∧ Total Net Sales YTD vs. Plan 🗑

Active

⬤ On

Alert title

| Total Net Sales YTD vs. Plan |
| --- |

Set alerts rule for

| AdWorks Net Sales (YTD) |
| --- |

Condition        Threshold

| Above         ∨ | 9188733 |
| --- | --- |

Maximum notification frequency

⬤ At most every 24 hours
◯ At most once an hours

Alerts are only sent if your data changes.

By default, you'll receive notifications on the service in the notification center.

☑ Send me email, too

*Figure 13.28: Setting an alert rule*

Each alert rule is limited to a single condition and, thus, additional alert rules can be configured for the same dashboard tile to provide notifications for multiple conditions. For example, a separate alert rule could be configured for the gauge tile with a condition of **Above 15,000,000**. When the underlying dataset of the dashboard tile is refreshed, a value for **Total Net Sales YTD** above that threshold will trigger an alert notification. Notifications appear in the Power BI service as a counter next to the bell icon in the upper-right corner of all the Power BI service pages, as shown in *Figure 13.29*:

*Figure 13.29: Notifications in the Power BI service*

Data alerts and notifications are deeply integrated with Power BI mobile applications. Between the mobile alert notifications, the notifications within the Power BI service, and the optional email delivery of the notification, users are able to respond quickly as significant data changes occur.

While data alerts are easy to configure and highly useful for many users, if organizations have more complex alerting requirements, Power Automate can potentially be used to fulfill those needs.

## Power Automate integration

Currently, the alert notification emails from Power BI are limited to the user who configured the data alert. In many scenarios, however, several users or a group email account should receive the notification email, as it's not practical for each user to individually configure the data alerts.

Power Automate provides a powerful but easy-to-use alternative to the standard Power BI alert email. For example, without any custom data connections or code, it enables a single user to fully define one or multiple email recipients of an alert notification and to customize the content of an email message.

Power Automate is an online service that enables the automation of workflows between applications and services. Since each Power Automate flow is fundamentally composed of a trigger (starting action) and one or more corresponding actions, a top use case for Power Automate is to send custom email messages based on various trigger events. For example, when a sales lead is added in Dynamics 365 **Customer Experience (CE)**, an email could be automatically sent to a sales team member via Power Automate.

Several pre-built Power Automate templates are available that leverage the Power BI data alert as a trigger. These templates make it easy to get started and to customize details, such as email addresses and the data from the alert to include. In the following Power Automate flow, the **Total Net Sales YTD** alert, as described in the *Data alerts* section, is used to trigger a customized email message, as shown in *Figure 13.30*:

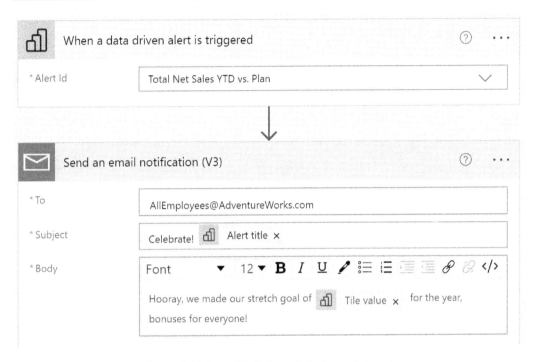

*Figure 13.30: Power BI alert email via Power Automate*

Dynamic content from Power BI is available for the **Subject** and **Body** of the email. In the subject, the alert title would be replaced by the title of the alert – in this case, **Total Net Sales YTD vs. Plan**. In the body, the tile value placeholder would be replaced by the actual value for the KPI dashboard tile.

Power Automate provides a rich platform for building both simple and complex workflows to obtain greater value from Power BI assets. Other common Power Automate and Power BI integrations, beyond custom email notifications, include posting messages to a Slack channel and triggering an alert in Microsoft Teams based on an alert in Power BI.

# Email subscriptions

Power BI also provides email subscriptions for Power BI Pro users of both reports and dashboards as well as users with Free licenses if the content is hosted in a Premium capacity workspace (a P or EM SKU). With email subscriptions configured in the Power BI service, a user is sent a snapshot of either the report page or the dashboard canvas as well as an optional link to the content in the Power BI service.

In *Figure 13.31*, a user with a Power BI Pro license has accessed **European Sales** (dashboard), as described earlier in this chapter, from within a Power BI app:

*Figure 13.31: Subscribe to the dashboard*

Clicking the **Subscribe** icon, as shown in *Figure 13.31*, opens the **Subscribe to emails** pane to configure and confirm the email subscription, as shown in *Figure 13.32*:

*Figure 13.32: Subscribe to emails pane*

With the yellow slider set to **On**, selecting the **Save and close** button (not shown) at the bottom of the pane enables the email subscription to the dashboard with the configured settings. An email containing an image of the current state of the dashboard and a link to the dashboard in Power BI is sent at the scheduled **Frequency** and **Scheduled time**.

A very similar subscription icon and dialog is also available for Power BI reports. The only significant difference with report subscriptions is that each subscription is associated with a single page. Therefore, the Power BI Pro user must choose the page for each subscription and configure multiple subscriptions to the same report if multiple pages of the report need to be emailed.

A common scenario for subscriptions is for the report data, which may consist of thousands of rows and many report pages, to be distributed in standard file formats such as Excel or CSV. For example, an accounting department team may utilize the data from a weekly or monthly report to help analyze recently closed financial periods. Paginated report subscriptions can be configured to deliver report data in seven different common file formats as email attachments and, thus, are the correct report type for these scenarios.

Unlike data alerts, subscriptions can be set for other users using the **Subscribe** field. Additionally, subscriptions are currently sent with the report's default filter and slicer states.

Subscriptions do not support most custom visuals. However, certified custom visuals, such as the Power KPI visual used in **European Sales** (dashboard), are supported.

Let's now look at Power BI's Analyze in Excel functionality.

# Analyze in Excel

Users with Power BI Pro licenses can connect to datasets hosted in the Power BI service from both Power BI Desktop and Microsoft Excel. Either of these tools displays the tables, columns, and measures for the dataset and, based on the report visuals created (for example, pivot tables), sends queries to Power BI for execution by the source dataset.

In the case of Power BI Desktop, these reports can be published back to the Power BI service and retain their connection to the dataset, as recommended in the *Live connections to Power BI datasets* section of *Chapter 6, Planning Power BI Reports*.

Prior to broadly recommending Excel as a client-reporting tool, consider whether Power BI Desktop isn't better suited to common use cases, such as pivot tables. As the adoption of Power BI increases, Power BI reports that are built in Power BI Desktop provide a richer and more familiar user experience.

The Analyze in Excel feature is exposed as an action for Power BI reports and datasets in the Power BI service. The action is accessible for Power BI Pro and PPU users in both workspaces as well as when viewing the report or dataset and in published apps.

In addition, connecting to a Power BI dataset is an option when using the **Get Data** dropdown in Excel.

In the following example from a workspace, the option to analyze the **European Internet Sales** report in Excel is available on the right-hand side after clicking the three vertical dots menu:

*Figure 13.33: Analyze in Excel icon*

Clicking the **Analyze in Excel** icon provides a Microsoft Excel (.xlsx) file that can be saved to the local machine. This file contains a default pivot table tied to the live Power BI dataset that supports the report.

For example, even though the **European Internet Sales** report may only utilize a few measures and columns of the dataset, the entire fields list of the dataset is exposed with a pivot table connection in Excel, as shown in *Figure 13.34*:

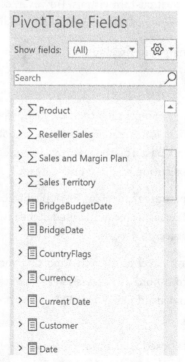

*Figure 13.34: Excel connection to the Power BI dataset*

Similar to the fields list in Power BI Desktop, Excel positions tables with only measures visible at the top of the list preceding the tables. Just like standard Excel pivot tables, users can drag measures and columns to the field wells to structure each pivot table report. Right-clicking a column name presents the option to add the column as a slicer.

Just like interacting with a Power BI report, any RLS roles applied on the source dataset are enforced on the user's report queries generated from Excel. The Excel workbook and any reports created based on the connection can be saved and shared like other Excel workbooks. However, for other users to refresh and query the source dataset from Excel, they require access to the app or workspace, a Power BI Pro license, and must be mapped to a security role if RLS is configured.

We now turn our attention to self-service BI workspaces.

# Self-service BI workspaces

As part of an organization's effort to empower users and drive a data culture, some workspaces are often created for the purpose of enabling business users and their teams to create and manage their own content.

For example, although other workspaces and apps containing financial reporting could be wholly owned by the BI/IT team, a workspace could be created for certain members of the finance and accounting department, and a few authors could be assigned Power BI Pro licenses and some training and documentation on data sources.

Such a self-service BI workspace allows business users, versus the enterprise BI team, to create and share content. As per the Power BI deployment modes section of *Chapter 1, Planning Power BI Projects*, some organizations may choose to empower certain business users to create and manage the visualization layer (**Self-Service Visualization**).

This hybrid approach gives business users more flexibility to address rapidly changing analytical needs, yet leverages IT-supported and validated data sources and resources. When even greater business user flexibility is required, or when IT resources are not available, the self-service BI mode can be implemented via Power BI Pro licenses and a self-service BI workspace.

In the Self-Service BI deployment model, several business users (for example, between five and ten) who regularly collaborate within a team or department are assigned Power BI Pro licenses. One of these users then creates a workspace in the Power BI service and adds the other users as members.

The BI/IT team typically requires that at least one member of the BI organization be added as a workspace administrator. Additionally, if applicable, the BI/IT team would authorize a few business users in the workspace to utilize an on-premises data gateway for their required data sources.

Once enabled, the business users can begin creating content and publishing the content to their self-service BI workspace. These users can then begin to distribute that content, as we will cover in the following section.

## Self-service content distribution

Given that each user has a Pro license, members of the Self-Service BI workspace (for example, the finance team), a user has the full flexibility to view content in the Power BI service or mobile app, as well as utilizing Pro features, such as Analyze in Excel and email subscriptions.

The users could choose to publish an app from the app workspace and advise workspace members to only use the published app for any production scenarios, such as printing reports or dashboards or referencing this content in meetings. As a small team, the users could delegate the responsibilities for creating and testing the dataset(s), reports, dashboards, scorecards, and any Excel workbooks hosted within the workspace.

A typical example of Self-Service BI is with advanced power users within finance and accounting functions. These users often have sophisticated and rapidly changing analytical needs that can't easily be translated into corporate BI-owned solutions.

Additionally, the managers or stakeholders of this team's work may not require access to this content themselves. For example, the analyst team could produce a monthly financial close package (that is, a PowerPoint deck) or a project analysis and either present this content in person or distribute printed materials.

If it has been determined that the business team requires additional resources, such as support for greater scale or sharing their content with users outside the workspace, the BI/IT team can consider assigning the workspace to the Power BI Premium capacity.

Additionally, if the needs or the value of the workspace grows, the project could be migrated from Self-Service BI to one of the other deployment modes. For example, the Power BI dataset created by the business team could be migrated to an Analysis Services model maintained by the BI team.

Self-service BI can help address certain business issues such as rapidly changing analytical needs. However, self-service BI is not without its risks.

# Risks of self-service BI

Perhaps no greater risk exists in BI than the potential to motivate or drive an incorrect decision. Several of the earlier chapters in this book, particularly *Chapter 1, Planning Power BI Projects*, through *Chapter 5, Developing DAX Measures and Security Roles*, are dedicated to topics and practices that aim to reduce that risk.

Although business users and analysts are often comfortable with the visualization layer given their familiarity with Microsoft 365 apps, the quality and sustainability of this content rests on the planning, testing, and skills (for example, M queries and DAX measures) applied to the source dataset. A severe risk, therefore, to Self-Service BI projects is whether the business user(s) can build and maintain a source dataset that provides consistent, accurate information.

For example, a self-service BI author may not fully understand what definitions are used in a measure or how filters in a measure and filters in the report interact to produce the numbers in the report. Thus, the self-service author and users of the self-service content could incorrectly interpret the meaning of the report.

Another significant risk is a loss of version control and change management. Although business users may have access to version control systems, such as OneDrive or SharePoint document libraries, they may not be required to use these systems or appreciate the value of version control.

It's not uncommon for "self-service" BI solutions to result in a significant level of management overhead for the BI/IT team, as business users struggle to effectively build and manage their own content. For example, the business team could submit requests or help desk tickets for IT to help them write certain DAX measures or to integrate certain sources. Likewise, the reports business teams create may result in a very high volume of queries or slow, expensive queries.

A final risk is that the self-service solution created may ultimately need to be discarded rather than migrated. For example, to quickly respond to new and changing analytical needs, the source dataset and reports may include many inefficient customizations and design patterns.

These customizations can render the solution difficult to support and potentially consume unnecessary system resources. As more users and reports become dependent on these designs or anti-patterns, it can be more difficult and costly to migrate to a more sustainable solution.

# Summary

This chapter provided a broad overview of Power BI's different content distribution and data access methods. Power BI apps were particularly emphasized as they represent the primary distribution mechanism supporting large groups of users.

The essential details of utilizing other distribution methods, such as email subscriptions, data alerts, and sharing reports and dashboards, were also reviewed. Furthermore, guidance was provided on analyzing datasets in Excel as well as utilizing Power Automate to drive custom email alerts.

The following chapter looks at Power BI deployments from an administration perspective. This includes the Power BI service administrator role and the controls available for administrators to define and manage authentication, monitor user activities, and limit or disable various features.

## Join our community on Discord

Join our community's Discord space for discussions with the author and other readers:

`https://discord.gg/q6BPbHEPXp`

# 14

# Administering Power BI for an Organization

The management and administrative processes described in previous chapters have primarily reflected the role of corporate business intelligence teams and BI professionals. In this chapter, the features and processes relevant to IT administrators are reviewed. These features and processes help organizations deploy and manage Power BI according to their policies and preferences. This includes data governance in the context of both self-service BI and corporate BI, the Power BI admin portal, monitoring user activity and adoption, and the administration of Power BI Premium capacity.

As in the previous chapter, this chapter exclusively covers the Power BI service. Administrative topics relevant to on-premises deployments were included in *Chapter 12, Deploying the Power BI Report Server*. Additionally, although data governance concepts and implementation guidance are included, readers are encouraged to review Microsoft documentation for further details on implementing data governance as part of Power BI deployments.

In this chapter, we will review the following topics:

- The Power BI administrator role
- Data governance for Power BI
- Azure Active Directory
- The Power BI admin portal
- Using metrics reports

- Audit logs
- The Power BI REST API for admins

We start with an overview of the Power BI administrator role.

# Power BI administrator role

Within organizations, one or more Power BI administrators are responsible for the overall monitoring, configuration, and management of the Power BI tenant. This role was covered briefly in the *Power BI admin* section of *Chapter 1, Planning Power BI Projects*.

As explained in that chapter, Power BI administrators are focused on the overall deployment of Power BI within an organization in terms of security, governance, and resource utilization. It is the Power BI administrator's job to understand the overall organizational policies and governance regarding data security and management and then implement those policies and governance within Power BI.

Similar to a **database administrator (DBA)**, a Power BI administrator regularly fields questions and issues related to stability, performance, and permissions/access. Effective Power BI admins are therefore fully knowledgeable of the roles, permissions, and licensing in Power BI as well as tools and techniques for analyzing and troubleshooting performance issues.

**Azure Active Directory (AAD)** includes a built-in role, Power BI administrator, that can be assigned to certain users, typically senior administrators and/or Power BI architects who are tasked with implementing tenant-level policies and configurations. Users assigned the Power BI admin role can manage all aspects of Power BI, including Premium capacities, workspaces, audit and activity logs, feature access, and more.

Assigning roles is performed within the Azure portal (`https://portal.azure.com`). Once in the portal, select **Azure Active Directory**. Select **Users** under the **Manage** heading in the left navigation pane, select a user, and then choose **Assigned roles** as shown in *Figure 14.1*:

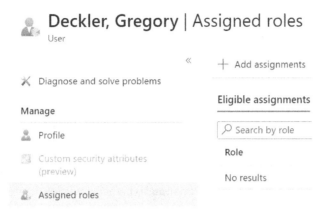

*Figure 14.1: Assigned roles in the Azure portal*

As shown in *Figure 14.1*, you can then click the **Add assignments** link to add a role for the user. The Power BI administrator role is available in the **Select role** dropdown as shown in *Figure 14.2*.

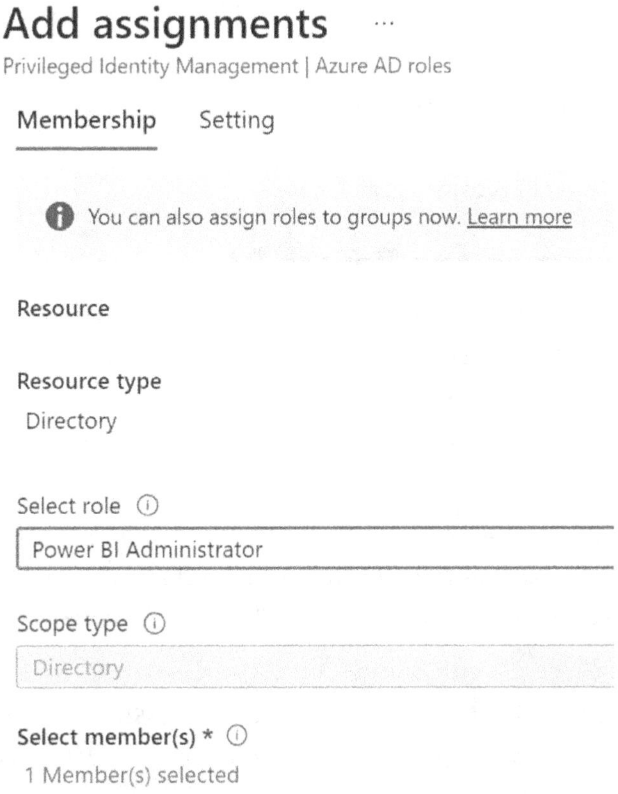

# Add assignments ···

Privileged Identity Management | Azure AD roles

**Membership**     Setting

ℹ️ You can also assign roles to groups now. Learn more

**Resource**

**Resource type**
Directory

Select role ⓘ

Power BI Administrator

Scope type ⓘ

Directory

**Select member(s) \*** ⓘ
1 Member(s) selected

*Figure 14.2: Assigning the Power BI Administrator role*

Smaller organizations and organizations getting started with Power BI may not require a dedicated Power BI administrator as there's limited content or resources to monitor and manage. Larger organizations with hundreds or thousands of Power BI users and workspaces, however, may find a Power BI administrator indispensable. Here are some of the most common tasks assigned to Power BI administrators:

- Monitor resources such as Power BI Premium capacity, any critical source systems of Power BI such as an Azure SQL database, any on-premises data gateways, and license availability

- Monitor usage and content such as determining which reports and dashboards are most heavily accessed across the organization and whether Power BI adoption is increasing or not

- Create and manage workspaces such as assigning or removing groups/users from workspace roles and assigning or moving workspaces to Premium capacities

- Grant or revoke access to groups to certain Power BI features such as the ability to create workspaces and use custom visuals

- Troubleshoot issues such as dataset refresh failures, user access/licensing issues, performance problems, etc.

A number of different tools are available to Power BI administrators to meet these different tasks, including the Power BI admin portal, the Power BI Premium Metrics app, the Power Platform admin center, the Power BI activity log, and more.

# Data governance for Power BI

Data governance is defined as a set of policies used to secure an organization's data, ensure consistent and accurate decision making, and manage access to data. In general, data governance is applicable to all types of **business intelligence** (**BI**), but organizations investing in Power BI for the long term should consider their data governance strategy and policies in the specific context of Power BI.

A central component of data governance relates to the three deployment modes described at the beginning of *Chapter 1, Planning Power BI Projects*, and seeks to address the following question: *"How can we ensure our data is secure and accurate while still providing the business with the access and flexibility it needs?"*

It's generally understood that some level of **self-service BI** (**SSBI**) is appropriate and beneficial to empower business users to explore and discover insights into data. Tools, such as Power BI Desktop, and features in the Power BI service, such as apps, make it easier than ever for business users to independently analyze data and potentially create and distribute content.

However, experience with enterprise SSBI projects also strongly suggests that IT-owned and managed administrative controls, enterprise-grade BI tools, and data assets, such as data warehouses, are still very much necessary. In response to the strengths and weaknesses of both traditional IT-led BI and business-led SSBI, Microsoft has suggested and internally implemented a managed, self-service approach to data governance.

From a BI architecture standpoint, managed SSBI represents a hybrid approach between the corporate (enterprise) BI and self-service visualization modes introduced in *Chapter 1, Planning Power BI Projects*. As shown in *Figure 14.3*, certain projects are carried out by the BI/IT department, while business users have the flexibility to analyze data and create their own reporting:

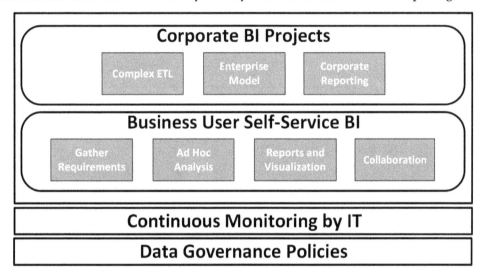

*Figure 14.3: Multi-mode Power BI deployments*

The three capabilities of corporate BI projects identified in *Figure 14.3* address the limitations or weaknesses of SSBI projects and tools. These limitations include data accuracy, scalability, complex data integration processes, and custom distributions of reports to groups of users.

Certain projects requiring these skills and tools such as the integration of multiple source systems and the scheduled distribution of user-specific reports could be exclusively developed and managed by IT. Additionally, the business stakeholders for certain projects may prefer or insist that certain projects are wholly owned by IT.

However, as shown in the **Business User Self-Service BI** part of *Figure 14.3*, business users are still empowered to leverage SSBI tools, such as Power BI Desktop, to conduct their own analysis and to internally determine requirements within their business unit.

Most commonly, business users can leverage an IT-owned asset, such as an Analysis Services model, thus avoiding the data preparation and modeling components while retaining flexibility on the visualization layer. This self-service visualization model is very popular and particularly effective when combined with Excel report connections.

Note that continuous monitoring and data governance policies are in effect across the organization regardless of corporate BI or business user SSBI. This is very important to detect any anomalies in user activity and is a first step in migrating a business-developed solution to a corporate BI solution.

For example, monitoring the Microsoft 365 Audit Log data for Power BI may indicate high and growing adoption of particular reports and dashboards based on a particular Power BI dataset. Given this query workload, or possibly other future needs for the dataset, such as advanced DAX measures, it may be appropriate to migrate this dataset to an Analysis Services model maintained by IT or move the dataset to Premium capacity. An example of this migration process to an Azure Analysis Services model is included in *Chapter 15, Scaling with Premium and Analysis Services*.

Let's now look at how to implement data governance within Power BI deployments.

## Implementing data governance

With an overarching strategy in place for deploying Power BI, as shown in the previous section, concrete tasks can be defined for implementing data governance. These tasks include the following:

1.  **Identify all data sources and tag sources containing sensitive data**

    Additional access and oversight policies should be applied to data sources containing sensitive or protected data. The labels assigned to content in the *Information protection* section of *Chapter 10, Managing Application Workspaces and Content*, is an example of data tagging.

2.  **Determine where critical data sources will be stored**

    For example, determine whether the data warehouse will be hosted on-premises or in the cloud. Power BI reporting can be deployed fully on-premises via Power BI Report Server, fully in the cloud, or organizations can pursue hybrid deployment models.

    Additionally, determine whether analytical (OLAP) BI tools such as Analysis Services and SAP BW will be used with these data sources and whether those tools will be stored on-premises or in the cloud.

3.  **Define who can access which data and how this access can be implemented**

Defining and managing Microsoft 365 groups or security groups in **Azure Active Directory (AAD)** or **Active Directory (AD)** is strongly recommended. Determine whether data security roles will be implemented in a data warehouse source such as Teradata or if row-level security roles will be implemented in analytical models such as Analysis Services.

4.  **Develop or obtain monitoring solutions to continuously monitor activities**

    Visibility to the Microsoft 365 audit log data, as described later in this chapter, is an essential part of this task. Any high-risk or undesired activities should be automatically detected, enabling swift action.

5.  **Train business users on data governance and security**

    This is particularly relevant for any dataset designers within business units who will leverage Power BI Desktop to access shape and model data.

The extent of data governance policies is driven by the size of the organization, its industry and associated regulations, and the desired data culture. For example, a large healthcare provider that wishes to pursue a more conservative data culture will implement many data governance policies to eliminate security risks and promote data quality and accuracy. However, a small to mid-sized company in a less regulated industry, and perhaps with fewer IT resources available, will likely implement less dense governance policies to promote flexibility.

For example, with Power BI Desktop and Power BI Premium capacity, a large analysis model containing complex M queries and DAX expressions could potentially be created and supported by a business user or team. However, the dataset designer of this model will need to be familiar with both the governance policy determining the level of visibility users of the dataset will have, as well as how to implement the corresponding row-level security roles.

Additionally, business users with Power BI Pro licenses responsible for distributing content such as via Power BI apps will need to know the security groups that should have access to the app.

Let's next look at another important component of all Power BI deployments, Azure Active Directory.

# Azure Active Directory

As with other Microsoft Azure services, Power BI relies on **Azure Active Directory (AAD)** to authenticate and authorize users. Therefore, even if Power BI is the only service being utilized, organizations can leverage AAD's rich set of identity management and governance features, such as conditional access policies, **multi-factor authentication (MFA)**, and business-to-business collaboration.

For example, a conditional access policy can be defined within the Azure portal that blocks access to Power BI based on the user's network location, or that requires MFA given the location and the security group of the user. Instructions for creating conditional access policies are covered in the *Conditional access policies* section later in this chapter.

Additionally, organizations can invite external users as guest users within their AAD tenant to allow for seamless distribution of Power BI content to external parties, such as suppliers or customers. This subject is covered in the next section, *AAD B2B collaboration*.

Guidance on configuring AAD security groups to support **row-level security** (**RLS**) is included in the *Security roles* section of *Chapter 5, Developing DAX Measures and Security Roles*. This section reviews other top features of AAD in the context of Power BI deployments.

## AAD B2B collaboration

AAD **business-to-business** (**B2B**) collaboration enables organizations using AAD to work securely with users from any organization. Invitations can be sent to external users, whether the user's organization uses AAD or not, and once accepted the guest user can leverage their own credentials to access resources, such as dashboards and reports contained in a Power BI app.

Just like users within the organization, guest users can be added to security groups and these groups can be referenced in the Power BI service. Prior to the existence of AAD B2B, it was necessary to create identities within AAD for external guest users, or even develop an application with custom authentication.

A guest user can be added to AAD by sending an invitation from AAD and by sharing content with the external user from the Power BI service. The first method, referred to as the planned invite method, involves adding a guest user from within AAD and sending an invitation to the user's email address.

In *Figure 14.4* from the Azure portal (`portal.azure.com`), **Azure Active Directory** has been selected and the **Users | All users** page has been accessed:

*Figure 14.4: Add a guest user in AAD*

As shown in *Figure 14.4*, the administrator can click **New guest user** to add the user, and enter an invitation message, such as in *Figure 14.5*:

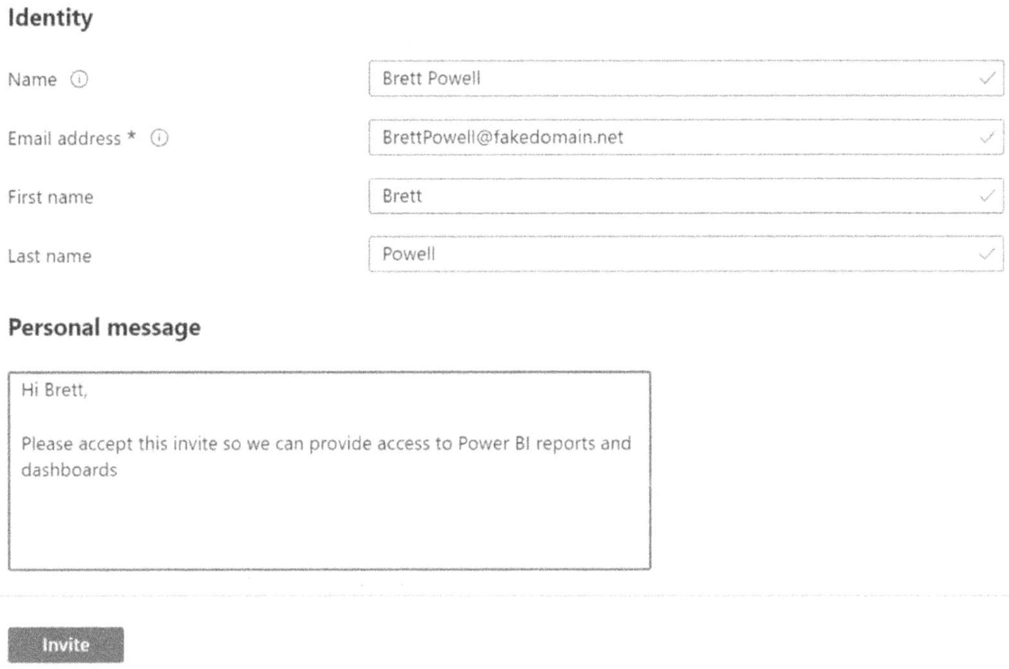

## Identity

| | |
|---|---|
| Name ⓘ | Brett Powell ✓ |
| Email address * ⓘ | BrettPowell@fakedomain.net ✓ |
| First name | Brett ✓ |
| Last name | Powell ✓ |

## Personal message

Hi Brett,

Please accept this invite so we can provide access to Power BI reports and dashboards

**Invite**

*Figure 14.5: Invite a guest user to AAD*

Once the **Invite** button is clicked, the guest or external user is sent an invitation via email containing the personal message. The user must accept the invitation and, once accepted, the guest user can be managed and added to security groups for use in Power BI. Adding users to security groups provides authorization to perform certain activities within the organization or can be used to exclude groups of users from using certain features as explained in the *Tenant settings* section later in this chapter. Guest users are identified in AAD with a **User type** of **Guest**.

As an alternative to the planned invite method via AAD just described, an invite to an external user can also be generated from the Power BI service directly. In this method, commonly referred to as ad hoc invites, a guest user's email address is specified when publishing or updating a Power BI app or when directly sharing Power BI content.

The external user would then receive an email invite to the specific content. Upon accepting this invite, the external user would be added as a guest user in AAD. Details on distributing content to users via apps and other methods are included in *Chapter 13, Creating Power BI Apps and Content Distribution*.

Organizations have the option to completely block sharing with external users via the **External sharing** tenant setting in the Power BI admin portal. As shown in *Figure 14.6*, this setting can be enabled or disabled for an entire organization, or limited to certain security groups:

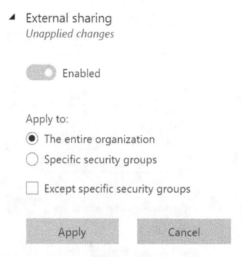

Figure 14.6: External sharing tenant setting in Power BI admin portal

In addition to the Power BI admin portal, additional management options for external guest users are available in AAD. These settings, including whether members in the organization (non-admins) can invite guest users, are available on the **External collaboration settings** page of AAD.

External B2B users are limited to consuming content that has been shared or distributed to them. For example, they can view apps, export data (if allowed by the organization), and create email subscriptions, but they cannot access workspaces or create and publish their own content. Additionally, external users cannot currently access shared content via Power BI mobile apps. The exact permissions and rights for external users depend upon each organization's security policies.

## Licensing external users

In addition to authentication to the Power BI content, either a Power BI Pro license or Power Premium capacity is needed to allow the guest user to view the content. The following three licensing scenarios are supported:

- The app workspace of the Power BI app can be assigned to Power BI Premium capacity
- The guest user can be assigned a Power BI Pro or PPU license by the guest user's organization

- A Power BI Pro license can be assigned to the guest user by the sharing organization

In the case of the third option, the Power BI Pro license only allows the user to access content within the sharing organization. Assigning licenses for guest users is identical to assigning licenses for organizational users and is performed in the Microsoft 365 portal. Additional information on licensing is covered in the *Power BI licensing* section of *Chapter 1, Planning Power BI Projects*.

Let's now look at securing access through the use of conditional access policies.

## Conditional access policies

Administrators of AAD can configure conditional access policies to restrict user access to Power BI based on the user or security group, the IP address of the user sign-in attempt, the device platform of the user, and other factors.

A common scenario supported by conditional access policies is to either block access to Power BI from outside the corporate network or to require **multi-factor authentication** (**MFA**) for these external sign-in attempts. As a robust, enterprise-grade feature, organizations can use conditional access policies in conjunction with security groups to implement specific data governance policies.

Each AAD conditional access policy is composed of one or more conditions and one or more controls. The conditions define the context of the sign-in attempt such as the security group of the user and the user's IP address, while the controls determine the action to take given the context.

For example, a policy could be configured for the entire organization and all non-trusted IP addresses (the conditions) that requires MFA to access Power BI (the control). The Azure portal provides a simple user interface for configuring the conditions and controls of each conditional access policy.

The following steps and supporting screenshots describe the creation of an AAD conditional access policy that requires MFA for users from the sales team accessing Power BI from outside the corporate network:

1. Log in to the Azure portal (`portal.azure.com`) and select **Azure Active Directory** from the main menu.

2. In the left-hand navigation under the **Manage** section, select **Security** and then select **Conditional Access**, as shown *Figure 14.7*:

*Figure 14.7: Conditional access in AAD*

3. Select the **New policy** icon at the top, select **Create new policy**, and enter a name for the policy, such as Sales Team External Access MFA.

4. Under **Assignments**, set the **Users or workload identities** property to **Include** an Azure AD security group (such as AdWorks DW Sales Team).

5. Under **Assignments**, set the **Cloud apps or actions** property to **Power BI Service**.

6. Under **Assignments**, set the **Conditions** property and configure the **Locations** to **Include** locations of **Any location** and **Exclude** locations of **All trusted locations**. With this definition, the policy will apply to all IP addresses not defined as trusted locations in AAD.

7. Under **Access controls**, set the **Grant** property and select the checkbox to require MFA.

8. Finally, set the **Enable policy** property at the bottom to **On** and click the **Create** command button:

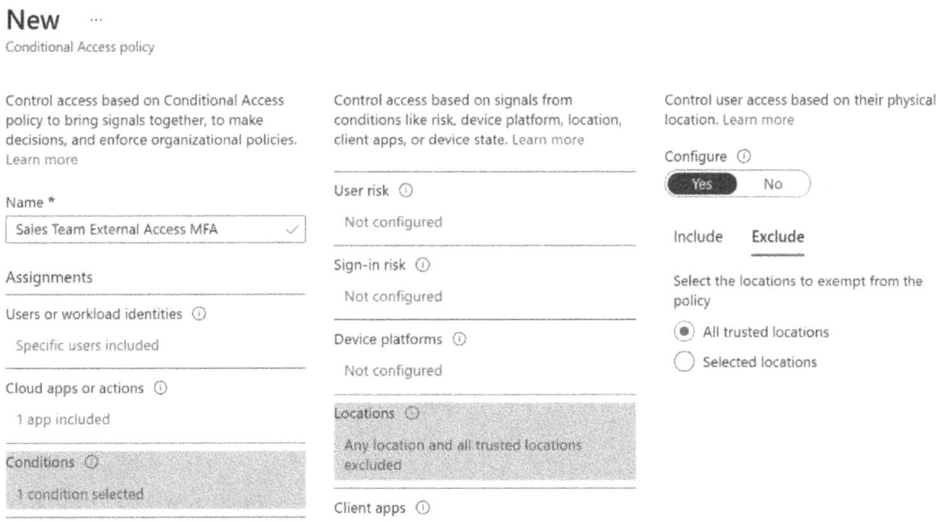

## New ...
Conditional Access policy

Control access based on Conditional Access policy to bring signals together, to make decisions, and enforce organizational policies. Learn more

**Name ***

Sales Team External Access MFA               ✓

**Assignments**

Users or workload identities  ⓘ

Specific users included

Cloud apps or actions  ⓘ

1 app included

Conditions  ⓘ

1 condition selected

Control access based on signals from conditions like risk, device platform, location, client apps, or device state. Learn more

User risk  ⓘ

Not configured

Sign-in risk  ⓘ

Not configured

Device platforms  ⓘ

Not configured

Locations  ⓘ

Any location and all trusted locations excluded

Client apps  ⓘ

Control user access based on their physical location. Learn more

Configure  ⓘ

Yes    No

Include    **Exclude**

Select the locations to exempt from the policy

⦿ All trusted locations

◯ Selected locations

*Figure 14.8: Configure a new Azure AD conditional access policy*

The minimum requirements to create new conditional access policies are the **Users or workload identities** property, the **Cloud apps or actions** property (Power BI service), and at least one access control. As with all security implementations, conditional access policies should be tested and validated.

In *Figure 14.8*, a user within the AdWorks DW Sales Team could attempt to log in to Power BI from outside the corporate network. The user should be prompted (challenged) to authenticate by providing a mobile device number and entering an access code sent via text message.

It's important to remember that conditional access policies are in addition to the user permissions defined in the Power BI service and the RLS roles created in Power BI datasets or Analysis Services data models. The *User permissions and security* section in *Chapter 13, Creating Power BI Apps and Content Distribution*, contains additional information on these security layers.

AAD conditional access policies require either an Enterprise Mobility and Security E5 license or Azure AD Premium P2 license. **Enterprise Mobility and Security (EMS)** E5 licenses include Azure AD Premium P2 as well as Microsoft Intune, Microsoft's mobile device management service. Additional information on features, licensing, and pricing for EMS is available at the following URL: `http://bit.ly/21mHDZt`.

Let's now look specifically at administering Power BI via the **admin portal**.

# Power BI admin portal

The Power BI **admin portal** provides controls for administrators to manage the Power BI tenant for their organization. This includes settings governing who in the organization can utilize which features, how Power BI Premium capacity is allocated, and other settings such as embed codes and custom visuals.

The admin portal is accessible to Microsoft 365 **global administrators** and users mapped to the **Power BI administrator** role. The **Power BI administrator** role and the assignment of a user to this role in Microsoft 365 were described in the *Power BI project roles* section of *Chapter 1, Planning Power BI Projects*.

To open the admin portal, log in to the Power BI service and select the **Admin portal** item from the **Settings** (gear icon) menu in the top right, as shown in *Figure 14.9*:

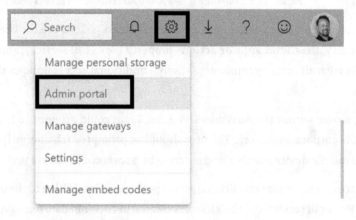

*Figure 14.9: Admin portal in the Settings menu*

Note that depending on screen resolution and zoom settings, the gear, bell, and other icons may not appear and instead be replaced by ellipses (**...**). In this case, click the ellipses, then choose **Settings** and then **Admin portal**.

All Power BI users, including Power BI free users, are able to access the admin portal. However, users who are not admins can only view the **Capacity settings** page. Power BI administrators and Microsoft 365 global administrators have view and edit access to all of the pages shown in *Figure 14.10*:

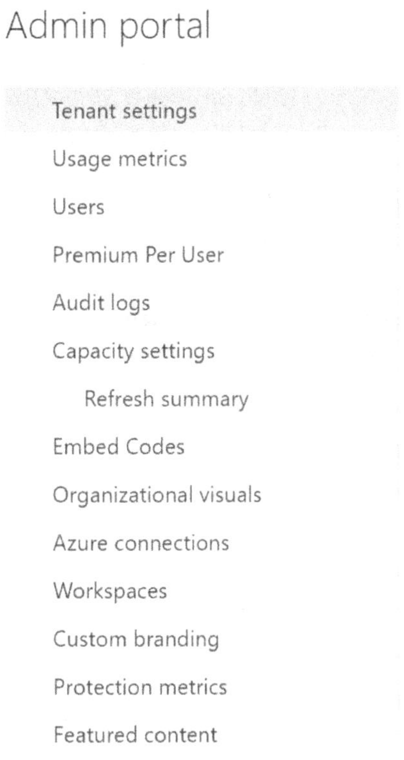

# Admin portal

Tenant settings

Usage metrics

Users

Premium Per User

Audit logs

Capacity settings

   Refresh summary

Embed Codes

Organizational visuals

Azure connections

Workspaces

Custom branding

Protection metrics

Featured content

*Figure 14.10: Admin portal pages*

Administrators of Power BI most commonly utilize the **Tenant settings** and **Capacity settings** as described in the *Tenant settings* and *Power BI Premium capacities* sections later in this chapter. However, the admin portal can also be used to manage any approved custom visuals for the organization, as well as any embed codes associated with the **Publish to web** feature described in *Chapter 13, Creating Power BI Apps and Content Distribution*.

Let's take a look at the pages of the **admin portal**, starting with **Tenant settings**.

## Tenant settings

The **Tenant settings** page of the **admin portal** allows administrators to enable or disable various features of the Power BI service. For example, an administrator could disable the **Publish to web** feature described in *Chapter 13, Creating Power BI Apps and Content Distribution*, for the entire organization. Likewise, the administrator could allow only a certain security group to embed Power BI content in **Software as a Service (SaaS)** applications such as SharePoint Online.

There are over 80 tenant settings currently available in the admin portal and more settings are continually added on a consistent basis. While a detailed explanation of each of these settings is beyond the scope of this book, *Chapter 12* of *Learn Power BI, 2nd Edition* contains a comprehensive list and explanation of all tenant settings present at the time of publication (February 2022).

All of the tenant settings provide certain controls while certain tenant settings also provide controls specific to the particular tenant setting. For example, all tenant settings provide a control to enable or disable the tenant setting (feature) within the Power BI tenant. If **Disabled**, the feature is not available within the Power BI tenant. If **Enabled**, the feature can be applied to **The entire organization** or to **Specific security groups**. In addition, the option is provided to **Except specific security groups** as shown in *Figure 14.11*:

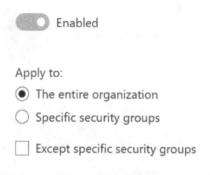

*Figure 14.11: Common tenant setting controls*

If a tenant setting is **Enabled**, as shown in *Figure 14.11*, it is recommended that the feature be relegated to **Specific security groups** unless it is deemed appropriate to allow the tenant setting for **The entire organization**. Power BI administrators should consult with their enterprise network and security teams regarding whether each tenant setting should be enabled and for which security groups.

For example, a common scenario is that only specific security groups should be allowed to export data. In this case, the **Specific security groups** radio button can be selected, and the security groups selected that should be able to export data.

In other scenarios, the feature should apply to the whole organization except certain groups of users. For example, the organization may want to enable a feature for all internal users but exclude external users. In this case, external users could be added to an **External users** security group. The radio button for **The entire organization** would be selected and then the checkbox for **Except specific security groups** would be checked. Finally, the **External users** security group could be selected to be excluded.

Tenant settings are broken down into the following 23 groups:

1. **Help and support settings**
2. **Workspace settings**
3. **Information protection**
4. **Export and sharing settings**
5. **Discovery settings**
6. **Content pack and app settings**
7. **Integration settings**
8. **Power BI visuals**
9. **R and Python visuals settings**
10. **Audit and usage settings**
11. **Dashboard settings**
12. **Developer settings**
13. **Admin API settings**
14. **Dataflow settings**
15. **Template app settings**
16. **Q&A settings**
17. **Dataset Security**
18. **Advanced networking**
19. **Goals settings**
20. **User experience experiments**
21. **Share data with your Microsoft 365 services**
22. **Insights settings**
23. **Quick measure suggestions**

Seven of these groups, **R and Python visuals settings**, **Dashboard settings**, **Dataflow settings**, **Dataset Security**, **Goals settings**, **User experience experiments**, and **Share data with your Microsoft 365 services**, only contain a single setting that essentially enables or disables the feature. For example, the single settings for **R and Python visuals settings**, **Dataflow settings**, and **Goals settings** simply either allow or disallow the use of R and Python visuals, dataflows, and goals respectively.

The **Help and support settings** group controls custom support links, email notifications of outages, whether users are allowed to try paid features, and whether a custom message is shown when users publish reports. These settings should be reviewed carefully and in coordination with IT administration and help desk resources.

The **Workspace settings** group enables or disables users to create workspaces, use datasets across workspaces, and configure how workspace upgrades are performed. Of particular interest are the **Create workspaces** and **Use datasets across workspaces** settings. The **Create workspaces** setting should only be enabled for the enterprise BI team and those users trusted and authorized by that team. Enabling the ability to use datasets across workspaces is also the preferred setting for enterprises as this allows greater security and separation of concerns between data modelers and report authors.

The **Information protection** settings impact the use of sensitivity labels within the tenant. Sensitivity labels were discussed in the *Information protection* section of *Chapter 10, Managing Workspaces and Content*, and these settings should be reviewed carefully if using **Microsoft Information Protection**.

From a data security perspective, the **Export and sharing settings** group is perhaps most important. The settings in this group provide granular control over export formats such as downloading report (.pbix) files or exporting to Excel or CSV files.

In addition, the **Allow Azure Active Directory guest users to access Power BI**, **Invite external users to your organization**, **Allow Azure Active Directory guest users to edit and manage content in the organization**, **Show Azure Active Directory guests in lists of suggested people**, and **External sharing** settings provide granular control over if and how external users can access the Power BI tenant. Obviously, the first setting regarding AAD guest users would need to be enabled for the AAD B2B scenario discussed earlier in this chapter.

The **Export and sharing settings** group also includes other critical settings such as **Publish to web**, **Printing**, **Email subscriptions** and **Microsoft Teams integration** settings. Many organizations choose to disable the **Publish to web** feature for the entire organization. Additionally, only certain security groups may be allowed to share content in Teams or to print hard copies of reports and dashboards.

The **Discovery settings** group controls whether content that users do not have access to can be returned in search results or otherwise discovered by users. Enabling discoverability can help promote a data culture where users can find and request access to interesting content.

The **Content pack and app settings** group is another important group of tenant settings. The settings in this group control whether apps can be published to the entire organization and whether apps can be pushed to end users. The impact of these settings being enabled or disabled was discussed in the *App deployment process* section of *Chapter 13, Creating Power BI Apps and Content Distribution*.

The **Integration settings** group controls whether certain visuals can be used as well as **single sign-on (SSO)** integration for Snowflake, Redshift, and the data gateway. Settings are available to enable or disable the ArcGIS Maps for Power BI, Azure Maps, and other map visuals. These visuals were discussed in *Chapter 7* and *Chapter 8*. Also, importantly, this group contains a setting to enable **Analyze in Excel** for on-premises datasets. Analyze in Excel was discussed in *Chapter 13, Creating Power BI Apps and Content Distribution*.

The **Power BI visuals** group controls the use of custom visuals within the organization. Notably, visuals added to **Organizational visuals** (discussed later in this chapter) are generally not impacted by these settings.

The **Audit and usage settings** group controls the creation of audit logs and usage metrics within the tenant. For example, the collection of **Per-user data in usage metrics for content creators** can be enabled or disabled. It is highly recommended to enable the **Create audit logs for internal activity auditing and compliance** setting.

There are four settings available in the **Developer settings** group that control the embedding of content in apps as well as the use of service principals. Recall that the use of service principals for embedding was discussed the *Custom applications* section of *Chapter 13, Creating Power BI Apps and Content Distribution*.

The **Admin API settings** group controls whether service principals can use the Power BI admin APIs as well as the content of API responses.

The **Template app settings** group controls the use and availability of template apps. Template apps are intended for partners and ISVs to easily create Power BI apps and then deploy those apps to any Power BI customer. Template apps can be published to the Power BI Apps marketplace and to Microsoft AppSource. More information about template apps can be found at the following link: `https://bit.ly/36yntoj`.

There are two settings in the **Q&A settings** group. The first setting, **Review questions**, allows dataset owners to review questions asked via Q&A within the Power BI service.

Enabling this feature helps dataset owners tune their synonyms and data model to provide more relevant answers to users. The second setting, **Synonym sharing**, allows Q&A synonyms to be shared within the organization. **Synonym sharing** can reduce the time required to configure synonyms within a data model by leveraging previous work by colleagues.

The **Advanced networking** group allows blocking public internet access as well as the ability to configure a Private Link. Azure Private Link enables accessing Azure **Platform as a Service (PaaS)** applications like Power BI over a private endpoint on your virtual network. More information about Azure Private Link can be found here: `https://bit.ly/3NqqHec`.

The **Insights settings** and **Quick measure suggestions** groups are currently in preview. These settings deal with the ability to request insights within a report as well as the ability to use natural language to write DAX measures.

Moving on from tenant settings, we next explore the **Usage metrics** page.

## Usage metrics

The **Usage metrics** page of the **admin portal** provides admins with a Power BI dashboard of several top metrics, such as the most viewed dashboards and the most viewed dashboards by workspace.

However, the dashboard cannot be modified, and the tiles of the dashboard are not linked to any underlying reports or separate dashboards to support further analysis. Given these limitations, alternative monitoring solutions are recommended, such as the Microsoft 365 audit logs and usage metric datasets specific to Power BI apps. Details of both monitoring options are included in the *Usage metrics reports* section as well as the following section discussing the **Users** and **Audit logs** pages.

# Users and Audit logs

The **Users** and **Audit logs** pages simply provide links to the Microsoft 365 admin center. In the Microsoft 365 admin center, Power BI users can be added, removed, and managed. Audit logs record activity that occurs within the Power BI service such as publishing reports, sharing reports, and viewing dashboards.

Audit logging is important to organizations and can greatly benefit security and governance. For example, audit logs may be regularly reviewed to identify potentially high-risk activities such as sharing with external users, data exports, or logins from odd locations or at odd times (such as 3 AM).

In addition, audit logs can help identify users and content that is potentially important for the business intelligence team to be aware of and possibly move to a more managed solution. For example, the audit logs could reveal that a report in a single user's My Workspace is being shared with a large audience and that the report is regularly viewed by many important business users within the organization. In such a circumstance, it would be advisable for the business intelligence team to contact the user regarding the report and determine if it is a candidate to be moved to a workspace under the control of the BI team.

If audit logging is enabled for the organization via the **Create audit logs for internal activity and auditing and compliance** tenant setting discussed earlier in the *Tenant settings* section of this chapter, then this audit log data can be retrieved from the Microsoft 365 Security & Compliance Center or via PowerShell. Additional information regarding audit logs is included in the *Audit logs* section of this chapter.

We now take a look at the Premium Per User settings.

## Premium Per User

**Premium Per User (PPU)** licensing is the licensing method that grants features previously relegated to Premium capacities to individual users on a per user basis. The **Premium Per User** page contains the settings shown in *Figure 14.12*:

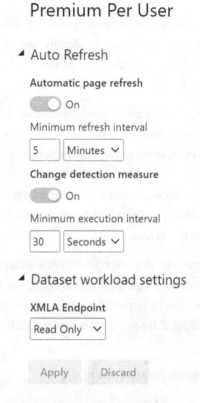

*Figure 14.12: Premium Per User settings*

Two of the Premium rights granted by PPU licensing include automatic page refresh and the XMLA endpoint.

Automatic page refresh allows a web browser viewing a dashboard or report page to automatically refresh after a certain amount of time. This capability is often used to display a dashboard of information on a large screen for the purposes of monitoring critical events.

For example, such a solution might be used within a warehouse for monitoring the shipping and receiving of goods or within a manufacturing facility to monitor the status of machines.

The XMLA endpoint is what enables connectivity between tabular data models and other tools and services. Here, the XMLA endpoint can be set to **Off**, **Read Only**, or **Read Write**.

Some organizations might consider the ability to access their Power BI datasets from a tool external to the Power BI service a security risk and thus set this setting to **Off**. However, this disables certain functionality, such as Analyze in Excel. At a minimum, the **XMLA Endpoint** must be set to **Read Only** for Analyze in Excel to function. If using the ALM Toolkit for deployments of dataset changes, as explained in the *ALM Toolkit Deployment* section of *Chapter 15, Building Enterprise BI with Power BI Premium*, the **XMLA Endpoint** would need to be set to **Read Write** since the ALM Toolkit writes updates to datasets.

We now look at capacity settings.

## Capacity settings

Capacity settings control dedicated capacities within the Power BI service. Microsoft 365 global admins and Power BI administrators can view, create, and manage all Power BI Premium capacities from the **Capacity settings** page. This includes the ability to create, resize, and monitor capacities as well as bulk assign workspaces to capacities.

Capacity settings are discussed in detail in the *Create, size, and monitor capacities* section of *Chapter 15, Scaling with Power BI Premium*.

We now turn our attention to the **Embed Codes** page.

## Embed codes

Embed codes are created and stored in the Power BI service when the **Publish to web** feature is utilized. As described in the *Publish to web* section of *Chapter 13, Creating Power BI Apps and Content Distribution*, this feature allows a Power BI report to be embedded in any website or shared via URL on the public internet.

Users with edit rights to the workspace of the **Publish to web** content are able to manage the embed codes themselves from within the workspace. However, the **admin portal** provides visibility and access to embed codes across all workspaces, as shown in *Figure 14.13*:

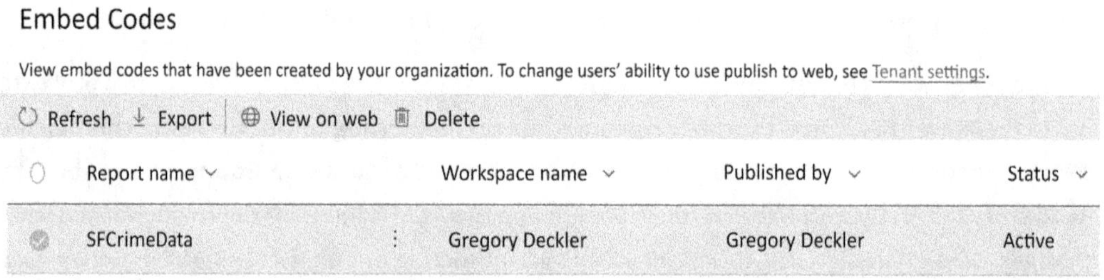

## Embed Codes

View embed codes that have been created by your organization. To change users' ability to use publish to web, see Tenant settings.

| | Report name ⌄ | | Workspace name ⌄ | Published by ⌄ | Status ⌄ |
|---|---|---|---|---|---|
| ✔ | SFCrimeData | ⋮ | Gregory Deckler | Gregory Deckler | Active |

⟳ Refresh   ⤓ Export   ⊕ View on web   🗑 Delete

*Figure 14.13: Embed Codes in Power BI admin portal*

Once an embed code is selected, the Power BI admin can view the report in a browser or remove the embed code via the **View on web** and **Delete** actions in the header. The **Embed Codes** page can be helpful to periodically monitor the usage of the **Publish to web** feature and for scenarios in which data was included in a **Publish to web** report that shouldn't have been, and thus needs to be removed.

Next, we explore the **Organizational visuals** page.

# Organizational visuals

The **Organizational visuals** page allows admins to upload and manage custom visuals (`.pbiviz` files) that have been approved for use within the organization. Organizations can enforce that only custom visuals included within the organizational visuals list can be used in reports published to their Power BI tenant using tenant settings in the **Power BI visuals** group.

For example, an organization may have proprietary custom visuals developed internally, which it wishes to expose to business users. Alternatively, the organization may wish to define a set of approved custom visuals, such as only the custom visuals that have been certified by Microsoft. The process of obtaining custom visuals via Microsoft AppSource and the details of certified custom visuals are included in the *Custom visuals* section of *Chapter 8, Applying Advanced Analytics*.

In *Figure 14.14*, the Pulse Chart custom visual has been added as a custom organizational visual from the **Organizational visuals** page of the Power BI **admin portal**:

## Organizational visuals

Add and manage power BI visuals for your organization. Learn more

| + Add visual ˅ | ○ Refresh | ↓ Export | ≡ Details | 🗑 Delete | ◉ Enable for Visualization Pane | | |
|---|---|---|---|---|---|---|---|
| 🗋 From a file | | | Source ˅ | | Changed ˅ | | Visualization Pane |
| 🗋 From AppSource | ⚙ | | AppSource | | Mar 28, 2022 | | Disabled |
| ⊘ ⌇ Pulse Chart ⚙ | | ⋮ | AppSource | | Mar 28, 2022 | | Disabled |

*Figure 14.14: Add organizational custom visual*

As shown in *Figure 14.14*, visuals can be added from AppSource or from a file (`.pbiviz`). In addition, organizational visuals can be automatically configured to appear in the **Visualization** pane of Power BI Desktop users by selecting a visual and clicking the **Enable for Visualization Pane** link in the header. The **Visualization Pane** property column shows whether or not this setting is enabled for each visual.

In *Figure 14.15*, the **Visualization Pane** property has been enabled for the Pulse Chart visual and thus the Pulse Chart visual is listed in the default list of visualizations available for report creation:

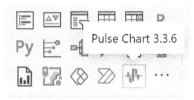

*Figure 14.15: Organizational visual enabled for the Visualization pane in Power BI Desktop*

Organizational visuals not enabled with the **Visualization Pane** setting can still be accessed and used by Power BI Desktop users.

Once the custom visual has been uploaded as an organizational custom visual, it will be accessible to users in Power BI Desktop. In *Figure 14.16*, when adding a custom visual as described in the *Adding a custom visual* section of *Chapter 8, Applying Advanced Analytics*, the user has selected the **Organizational visuals** tab:

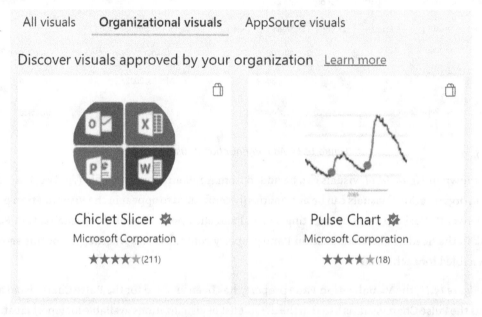

*Figure 14.16: Organizational visuals in Power BI Desktop*

Notably, adding an organizational visual in this manner does not add the custom visual as part of the default set of visuals but rather below a faint, dotted line as is usually the case when adding custom visuals. This is shown in *Figure 14.17*:

*Figure 14.17: Organizational visual not enabled for the Visualization pane in Power BI Desktop*

Overall, it is generally a good idea for organizations to standardize on a set of allowed custom visuals and to then disable the **Allow visuals created using the Power BI SDK** and **Add and use certified visuals only (block uncertified)** tenant settings found in the Power BI visuals group.

A business process can be developed to request, certify, and add additional visuals as necessary. The Power BI administrator would participate in this process and ultimately be the individual that adds the visual to the list of approved organizational visuals.

Such standardization ensures that reports remain similarly designed and that business users are appropriately aware and understand how to interpret and use visuals found in reports. In addition, this rigor can help ensure that security and compliance concerns are also addressed to prevent unintended data loss.

We next look at the Azure connections page.

## Azure connections

The Azure connections page contains three settings related to using your own Azure storage accounts for Power BI as shown in *Figure 14.18*:

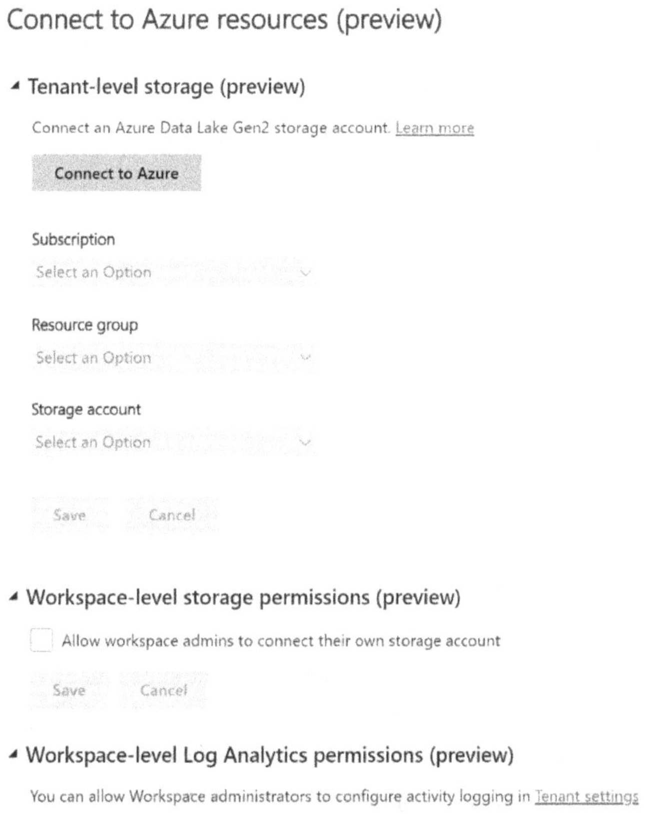

### Connect to Azure resources (preview)

▲ Tenant-level storage (preview)

Connect an Azure Data Lake Gen2 storage account. Learn more

    Connect to Azure

Subscription

Select an Option ∨

Resource group

Select an Option ∨

Storage account

Select an Option ∨

    Save    Cancel

▲ Workspace-level storage permissions (preview)

☐ Allow workspace admins to connect their own storage account

    Save    Cancel

▲ Workspace-level Log Analytics permissions (preview)

You can allow Workspace administrators to configure activity logging in Tenant settings

*Figure 14.18: Azure connections page*

By default, data used in Power BI is stored internally by the Power BI service. However, with the implementation of dataflows to use Azure Data Lake Storage Gen2 (ADLS Gen2), it is now possible to store your dataflows within your own ADLS Gen2 storage accounts versus default internal Power BI provisioned storage.

Using your own ADLS Gen2 storage account can be beneficial. Power BI stores dataflow data in **Common Data Model (CDM)** format. This format captures metadata about the data created by dataflows. This can be useful in scenarios involving automation, monitoring, extensibility, and backups. In addition, this can help ensure that multiple roles within the organization such as analysts, data scientists, and other data professionals are working with and reusing the same set of curated data.

Let's now turn our attention to the **Workspaces** page of the **admin portal**.

## Workspaces

The **Workspaces** page provides a centralized view of all workspaces provisioned within the Power BI tenant, providing administrators a central hub for managing these workspaces.

For example, in *Figure 14.19*, an administrator is using the **Workspaces** page to **Recover** an **Orphaned** workspace:

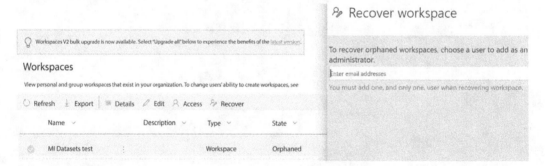

*Figure 14.19: Recover orphaned workspace*

Orphaned workspaces are workspaces that have no active AAD user as a member or administrator. This can happen if the user who created the workspace subsequently left the organization. Workspace recovery allows an administrator to be assigned so that the workspace content can be inspected and a decision made whether to assign a new owner to the workspace, migrate the content to a different workspace, or simply remove the workspace entirely.

As shown in *Figure 14.19*, administrators can also view users assigned to workspaces and even add and remove admins, members, and contributors of workspaces via the **Access** menu option. The **Details** and **Edit** menu options provide information such as the workspace ID and the ability to edit the name and description of the workspace respectively.

We now look at the **Custom branding** page.

## Custom branding

The **Custom branding** page can be used to customize the look and feel of the Power BI service. Only three customizations are possible, adding a **Logo**, a **Cover image**, and a **Theme color**, as shown in *Figure 14.20*:

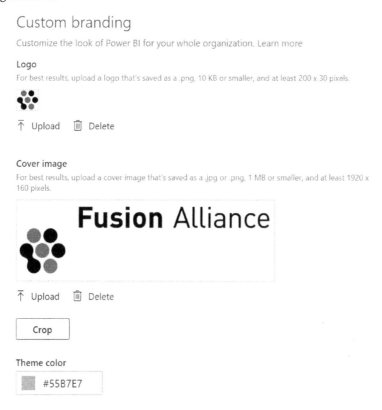

*Figure 14.20: Recover orphaned workspace*

The **Logo** and **Theme color** affect the very top of Power BI service pages with the chosen logo image displayed at the top left of the page and the background color of the entire header bar set to the chosen **Theme color**. If configured, the **Cover image** is displayed as a banner image on the **Home** page of the Power BI service.

Let's next look at the **Protection metrics** page.

## Protection metrics

The **Protection metrics** page displays a simple report that graphs how sensitivity labels are applied to content and is most useful if the organization has deployed sensitivity labels and associated information policies as described in the *Information protection* section of *Chapter 10, Managing Workspaces and Content.*

As discussed in that chapter, sensitivity labels serve to alert end users to the privacy level of the information they are viewing and can also include protection settings to encrypt the content. The page also includes a link to open the **Microsoft Defender for Cloud Apps** portal for additional metrics and reporting.

The final page available in the **admin portal** is the **Featured content** page, so let's finish this section by looking at it now.

## Featured content

The **Featured content** page provides a centralized view of all content that has been set to be featured on the Power BI **Home** page. Reports, dashboards, and other content can be set as **Feature on Home** via their **Settings** panes as shown in *Figure 14.21*:

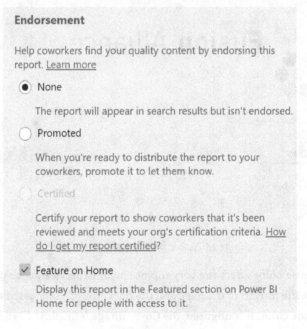

*Figure 14.21: Feature on Home*

In this example, the **Utilization** report has been set to **Feature on Home** and appears on the Power BI **Home** page in the **Featured** section as shown in *Figure 14.22*.

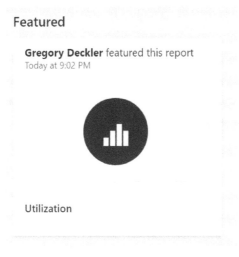

*Figure 14.22: Featured report tile*

Note that if no content is featured, then the **Featured** section of the **Home** page does not appear. Also, who can feature content within the Power BI tenant is controlled by the **Featured content** tenant setting found in the **Export and sharing settings** group.

This completes our tour of the Power BI admin portal. We now provide additional information regarding usage metric reports.

# Usage metrics reports

The Power BI service provides standard usage metrics reports for both dashboards and reports. These reports, which themselves are Power BI reports, provide quick insights into fundamental user adoption questions, such as how often the published content is being viewed and which users are viewing the content the most.

These read-only reports can be generated for specific dashboards and reports and can also be personalized (edited) by saving a copy. Once a copy of a usage metrics report has been saved, a Power BI dataset of usage metrics is created for either all the dashboards or all the reports in the workspace. The usage metrics datasets, which are updated by the Power BI service for the last 90 days of activity, and the saved usage reports can then serve as a foundation for a lightweight but robust monitoring solution for the workspace.

For example, the Global Sales app described in the previous chapter contains several dashboards and reports, with some of the reports containing multiple report pages. The following process and supporting images detail the creation and viewing of usage metrics reports:

1. Access the workspace in the Power BI service containing the content to monitor. A Power BI Pro license and edit rights to the workspace are required to access usage metrics data.

2. From the **Content** page, select **View usage metrics report** from the three vertical dots menu for a report, dashboard, or scorecard as shown in *Figure 14.23*:

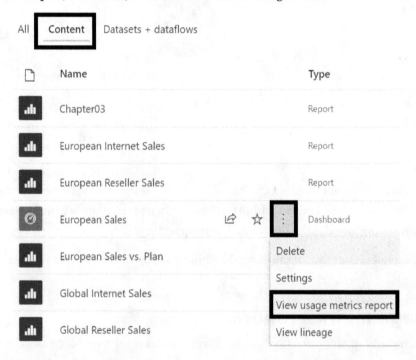

*Figure 14.23: View usage metrics report*

3. Once prompted that the usage metrics are ready, click the **View usage metrics** report button as shown in *Figure 14.24*. Alternatively, click the **View usage metrics report** icon again for any of the dashboards or reports in the workspace.

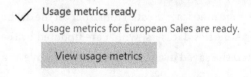

*Figure 14.24: Usage metrics ready*

4.  A Power BI report containing usage metrics for the selected dashboard or report is displayed, such as the report shown in *Figure 14.25*:

*Figure 14.25: Report usage metrics report*

5.  *Figure 14.25* shows a usage metrics report for a report. Four report pages are included.

6.  The **Report usage** page includes information such as report views, unique viewers, and trends over time. In addition, information regarding how the report is distributed and what platforms users are using to view the report is included as well as individual user statistics. The **Per-user data in usage metrics for content creators** tenant setting in the **Audit and usage settings** group is enabled.

7.  The **Report performance** page includes information regarding how fast the report opens for users. The report list provides statistics regarding all reports in the workspace including report usage across the entire workspace as well as individual report usage statistics. The **FAQ** page simply provides definitions for the different metrics and answers to other frequently asked questions.

8.  At this point, usage metrics reports specific to either all reports, all dashboards or all scorecards in the workspace will be accessible on demand via the **View usage metrics report** action depending upon the content type chosen in *step 2*.

9. Repeat *step 2* for the other types of content in the workspace but note that paginated reports do not support usage metrics. Usage metrics reports look different depending upon the content type. For example, *Figure 14.26* shows a portion of a dashboard's usage metrics report.

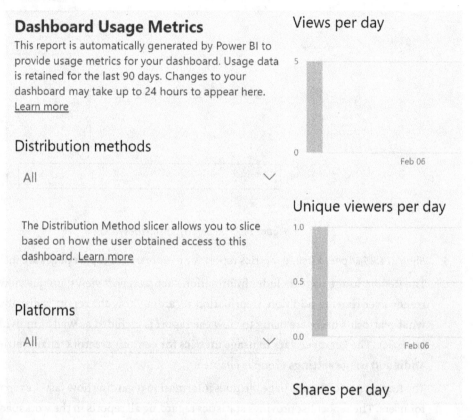

Figure 14.26: Dashboard usage metrics report

With the usage metrics report opened, the **Filters** pane can be used to adjust the reports, dashboards, and scorecards included in the report although these are identified by their *globally unique identifiers (GUIDs)* and not their names. These are the same GUIDs as discussed in the *Workspace and content identifiers* section of *Chapter 10, Managing Workspaces and Content*.

Usage metrics reports are an effective way to monitor the adoption of Power BI content within the enterprise and identify performance issues. Although useful for workspaces that support many users or important scenarios (such as executive dashboards), usage metrics reports are ultimately limited to individual workspaces.

Additionally, the usage metrics don't include other activities of interest to administrators, such as when the newly scheduled refresh is configured or when a data source from a gateway is removed. A more comprehensive monitoring dataset inclusive of all workspaces and all Power BI activities is available via the Microsoft 365 audit logs for Power BI, as described in the following section.

# Audit logs

Power BI activities stored in the Microsoft 365 audit logs provide administrators with a complete view of user activities in the Power BI service. Each log event record identifies the user, the date and time of the activity, the type of activity, such as the printing of a report page, and the item in Power BI, such as the report that was printed. This level of detail at the tenant level across all primary activities helps administrators answer both high-level usage and adoption questions, as well as targeted compliance questions.

For example, the audit logs could prove that the volume of users and their level of engagement with Power BI reports and dashboards is increasing and thus that additional capacity is required or that the organization might benefit from a move to Premium capacity. Alternatively, an administrator could investigate the activities of just a few users to ensure they're only engaging in activities aligned with their role.

As explained in the *User and audit logs* section of this chapter, audit logs should be regularly reviewed to identify potentially high-risk activities such as sharing with external users, data exports, or logins from odd locations and times. In addition, audit logs can help identify users and content that is potentially important for the business intelligence team to be aware of and possibly move to a more managed solution.

Because Power BI uses the centralized Microsoft 365 audit logs, Power BI activities can leverage other integrated solutions within Microsoft 365 and Azure. For example, Azure Sentinel can be used to identify anomalous activities within Power BI via machine learning/artificial intelligence, thus automating the process of regularly reviewing the audit log.

Perhaps most importantly, by using audit logs, an IT organization can understand what Power BI content is being utilized by the business. In the event that a few reports or dashboards become very popular, some level of engagement may be appropriate to ensure the underlying dataset is accurate and secure or the content migrated to an IT-supported solution.

Once enabled in the Power BI admin portal, the audit log data can be retrieved on an ad hoc basis or, more commonly, retrieved on a recurring basis as part of a continuous monitoring and governance solution. To minimize the setup and maintenance of these monitoring solutions, Microsoft has made available PowerShell scripts that export Power BI audit log data to a CSV file format.

The first step in utilizing the audit logs is to enable audit log searching within the Microsoft 365 Compliance Center. This can be done at the following link: `https://compliance.microsoft.com/auditlogsearch`. If auditing is not turned on for the tenant, a link is present to **Start recording user and admin activity**. Click that link and after approximately one hour, activity will start being recorded.

Next, enable the **Create audit logs for internal activity auditing and compliance** setting in the Power BI admin portal. This setting is in the **Audit and usage settings** group of the **Tenant settings** page.

Once the audit log setting is enabled, user activities start to be recorded in the audit logs with a delay of 12 hours or less from their occurrence and will be stored for 90 days. This log data can be accessed directly from the Microsoft 365 Compliance Center or remotely via PowerShell scripts. In terms of direct or ad hoc access, a Microsoft 365 global administrator or a user with permission to the Compliance Center can log in to Microsoft 365 and navigate to the URL, `https://compliance.microsoft.com/auditlogsearch`.

Alternatively, a link to the Microsoft 365 admin center is provided on the **Audit logs** page of the Power BI admin portal. This links directly to the audit log search interface of the Compliance Center.

From the audit log search page, users can configure a search for a **Date and time range**, specific **Activities**, and specific **Users**, as shown in *Figure 14.27*:

*Figure 14.27: Audit log search configuration*

Once configured, clicking the **Search** button returns audit log activities that meet the specified criteria as shown in *Figure 14.28*:

Audit > Audit search

Tuesday, Mar 22, 2022 12:00:00 AM to Tuesday, Mar 29, 2022 6:00:00 PM, Viewed Power BI report,Deleted Power BI report,Printed Power BI report page

| ↓ Export ∨ | | | | 150 items |
| --- | --- | --- | --- | --- |
| Date ↓ | IP Address | User | Activity | Item |
| Mar 29, 2022 3:17 PM | | ▇▇▇▇▇▇▇ | Viewed Power BI report | Utilization |
| Mar 29, 2022 2:36 PM | ▇▇▇▇▇ | ▇▇▇▇▇▇▇ | Viewed Power BI report | Utilization |
| Mar 29, 2022 1:43 PM | ▇▇▇▇▇ | ▇▇▇▇▇▇▇ | Viewed Power BI report | GitHub |
| Mar 29, 2022 1:25 PM | | ▇▇▇▇▇▇▇ | Viewed Power BI report | Microsoft 365 Usage |

*Figure 14.28: Audit log search in Security & Compliance Center*

Click the **Export** dropdown and then **Download all results** in order to download a CSV file of the audit log search results. The CSV file contains four columns, **CreationDate**, **UserIds**, **Operations**, and **AuditData**.

The **CreationDate** column is a date and time stamp for the activity in **Coordinated Universal Time (UTC)** format, while the **UserIds** column contains the UPN of the user performing the activity shown in the **Operations** column, such as ViewReport.

The **AuditData** column contains additional information in JSON format, such as the following:

```
{
"Id":"0c20ca7f-24b5-48df-bbd6-94e1b9d4a7e4",
"RecordType":20,
"CreationTime":"2022-03-29T17:43:55",
"Operation":"ViewReport",
"OrganizationId":"xxxxxxxx-xxxx-xxxx-xxxx-xxxxxxxxxxxx",
"UserType":0,
"UserKey":"10030000819AD21A",
"Workload":"PowerBI",
"UserId":"user@fakedomain.com",
"ClientIP":"xx.xxx.xxx.xxx",
"UserAgent":"Mozilla\/5.0 (Windows NT 10.0; Win64; x64)
AppleWebKit\/537.36 (KHTML, like Gecko) Chrome\/99.0.4844.74
Safari\/537.36 Edg\/99.0.1150.55",
```

```
"Activity":"ViewReport",
"ItemName":"GitHub",
"WorkSpaceName":"Github",
"DatasetName":"GitHub",
"ReportName":"GitHub",
"WorkspaceId":"xxxxxxxx-xxxx-xxxx-xxxx-xxxxxxxxxxxx",
"AppName":"Github",
"ObjectId":"GitHub",
"DatasetId":" xxxxxxxx-xxxx-xxxx-xxxx-xxxxxxxxxxxx ",
"ReportId":" xxxxxxxx-xxxx-xxxx-xxxx-xxxxxxxxxxxx ",
"IsSuccess":true,
"ReportType":"PowerBIReport",
"RequestId":" xxxxxxxx-xxxx-xxxx-xxxx-xxxxxxxxxxxx ",
"ActivityId":" xxxxxxxx-xxxx-xxxx-xxxx-xxxxxxxxxxxx ",
"AppReportId":" xxxxxxxx-xxxx-xxxx-xxxx-xxxxxxxxxxxx ",
"DistributionMethod":"Apps",
"ConsumptionMethod":"Power BI Web"
}
```

As shown in the preceding activity record associated with viewing a report via an app, many more attributes of the activity are available in the audit logs that aren't displayed from the main audit log search results interface. To view these additional details from the audit log search page, click on a specific activity.

Object IDs such as **WorkspaceID** and **DatasetID** can be used to programmatically manage Power BI content via the Power BI REST API, as described in the *Staged deployments* section of *Chapter 10, Managing Application Workspaces and Content*.

A BI team would expect the creation and deletion of datasets and gateways to be infrequent activities relative to the creation and deletion of reports and dashboards. If many datasets are being created, this could be a sign of inefficient resource utilization and version control issues.

For example, rather than four reports using live connections to a single published dataset, each report may have its own dataset that requires its own resources and data refresh schedule (if import mode).

Excluding global admins, an Exchange Online license is required to access the auditing section of the Microsoft 365 Compliance Center. Additionally, administrators who are not global admins need to be mapped to a role that provides access to the audit log. This is done on the **Permissions & roles** page of the Compliance Center.

There are currently hundreds of distinct Power BI activities tracked in the audit logs, including the sharing of dashboards and reports, any updates to an organization's Power BI settings (tenant settings), and activities related to the management of Power BI Premium capacities. The list of Power BI activities audited and their descriptions is available and kept updated at the following URL: `http://bit.ly/2skXjAB`.

The maximum date range for an audit log search is 90 days and the date/time of each activity is presented in UTC format. Additionally, a maximum of 50,000 events can be displayed per audit log search. Given these limitations and the manual nature of audit log searches, a scheduled log retrieval process is necessary to support a more robust monitoring solution.

## Audit log monitoring solution

To internally develop a monitoring solution based on the audit log data, a PowerShell script that searches and exports the audit log data to a CSV file can be scheduled. This CSV file is then used as the source of an **extract-transform-load** (ETL) or **extract-load-transform** (ELT) process to persist the log data in a source system, such as a SQL Server database or, on a small scale, a Power BI dataset using a **Folder** query. Finally, Power BI Desktop can be used to implement remaining lightweight transformations, create DAX measures, and develop monitoring reports.

When developing an audit log monitoring solution for Power BI, the first step is to choose between the **Unified Audit Log** (all Microsoft 365 audit activities) and the **Power BI Activity Log**. While both log sources contain all Power BI auditing activities, it is highly recommended to use the Power BI Activity Log since this log only contains Power BI activities and does not require a global administrator role to access. In the example that follows, we use the Power BI Activity Log.

To use the PowerShell script, you must install the **MicrosoftPowerBIMgmt** PowerShell module. This can be done by opening PowerShell and running the following command:

```
Install-Module -Name MicrosoftPowerBIMgmt -Scope CurrentUser
```

The `Scope` parameter is highly recommended as the module should only be accessible to and used by the Power BI administrator. To export the last 12 hours of data, the following PowerShell script can be used to export the audit log data to a CSV file in the `C:\PowerBIAuditLogs` directory:

```
Login-PowerBI
$Current = Get-Date
$Begin = $CurrentDate.AddHours(-12)
$dateString = $CurrentDate.ToString("yyyy_MM_dd_HH_mm")
$csvFile = "C:\PowerBIAuditLogs\" + $dateString + ".csv"
```

```
$StartTime = $Begin.ToUniversal().ToString("yyyy-MM-ddTHH:mm:ss")
$EndTime = $CurrentDate.ToUniversal().ToString("yyyy-MM-ddTHH:mm:ss")
$activities = Get-PowerBIActivityEvent -StartDateTime $StartTime
 -EndDateTime $EndTime | ConvertFrom-Json | Export-Csv $csvFile
```

This PowerShell script (.ps1 file) can be executed on a schedule of every 12 hours. An ETL (or ELT) process could then be executed to access the CSV file and load the new data to a data source such as an Azure SQL database. The import and transformation could be done using **Azure Data Factory**. Alternatively, Power BI Desktop could use a **Folder** query to import all files within the C:\PowerBIAuditLogs folder.

The results of each audit log search can contain duplicate rows. However, the **Id** column included in the search results can be used to eliminate these duplicate rows. 24 columns of information are available in the CSV file.

With a sound data retrieval process in place, DAX measures could be authored, such as the count of active users, the average number of users per day and per month, and the count of created reports or dashboards.

To support security and compliance, measures and visualizations could be created targeting high-risk or undesirable activities, such as exporting report visual data or publishing reports to the web. For example, a card visual representing the count of data export activities could be pinned to a Power BI dashboard and a data alert could be configured against this dashboard tile.

An out-of-the-box Power BI monitoring solution is expected later this year that could potentially eliminate the need to develop and support a custom monitoring solution from scratch. Nonetheless, as every organization and Power BI environment is unique, administrators may evaluate whether this new solution provides sufficient flexibility and control to serve as an alternative to an internally developed and maintained monitoring solution.

Note that in addition to the **MicrosoftPowerBIMgmt** PowerShell module, administrative actions are also available via the Power BI REST API and supporting .NET Client library for Microsoft Power BI public REST endpoints.

# The Power BI REST API for admins

Although the Power BI admin portal and the Power Platform Admin Center portal provide easy graphical tools for common and simple administrative tasks, the Power BI REST APIs provide programmatic access to many administration-focused endpoints, such as for retrieving artifact access for a given user, restoring deleted workspaces, and rotating encrypting keys.

Power BI administrators and BI/IT managers are therefore encouraged to review the documentation on the Power BI REST APIs (`https://docs.microsoft.com/en-us/rest/api/power-bi`) and to consider incorporating these APIs into standard admin processes.

One relatively new and very powerful admin API is **GetGroupsAsAdmin**. This API can be called to retrieve up to 5,000 workspaces and include the users, reports, dashboards, datasets, dataflows, and workbooks associated with each given workspace. The JSON output of this single API call can then be loaded to a monitoring SQL database or potentially directly to a monitoring reporting solution to provide easy, centralized visibility to all the primary artifacts within a Power BI environment.

There are several methods for calling the Power BI REST APIs but perhaps the most familiar and straightforward option is to use the `Invoke-PowerBIRestMethod` cmdlet included with the Power BI Management PowerShell module. With this cmdlet, the admin can simply pass a text string variable to the URL parameter and specify the appropriate API method for the `Method` parameter (`GET`, `POST`, `PUT`, `DELETE`).

In the following snippet from a PowerShell script, a custom URL text string is created and passed to the `Invoke-PowerBIRestMethod` cmdlet in order to retrieve up to 5,000 active workspaces along with their associated dashboards, reports, datasets, and users:

```
$PBIGroupsFile = "C:\Users\bpowell\Admin\BIAdminArtifacts\
PowerBIWorkspaces.json"
$ActiveGroupsURLExPersonal = '/admin/groups?$top=5000&' +
'$filter=type eq' + " 'Workspace'" + ' and state eq' + " 'Active'" +
'&$expand=dashboards,reports,datasets,users'
#Retrieve workspace data (with expanded values) and write to the JSON file
Invoke-PowerBIRestMethod -Url $ActiveGroupsURLExPersonal -Method Get |
Out-File $PBIGroupsFile
```

This completes our review of activities related to administering Power BI for an organization.

# Summary

This chapter reviewed the features and processes applicable to administering Power BI for an organization. These included the configuration of tenant settings in the Power BI admin portal, analyzing the usage of Power BI assets, and monitoring overall user activity via the Microsoft 365 audit logs. Additionally, important administrative capabilities of Azure Active Directory, such as conditional access policies and external guest users, were also described.

The following chapter looks at the options for scaling Power BI to support increased user adoption, larger datasets, and enterprise BI solutions through the use of Premium capacities. This includes methodologies for allocating Power BI Premium capacity to workloads, leveraging the additional benefits of Power BI Premium, and other activities related to using Power BI at scale.

# Join our community on Discord

Join our community's Discord space for discussions with the author and other readers:

https://discord.gg/q6BPbHEPXp

# 15
# Building Enterprise BI with Power BI Premium

For many organizations, the deployment of Power BI entails surfacing mission-critical KPIs over vast sets of data as well as empowering business users as part of a data culture. Power BI Premium is designed to meet these needs via a workload-based pricing model and scalable, enterprise-grade semantic modeling and reporting features.

While Power BI projects may begin as a proof-of-concept or as a self-service solution developed by a business analyst, the features exclusive to Power BI Premium capacity, such as large datasets, paginated reports, and the XMLA endpoint are often necessary to meet performance, scalability, and application life cycle needs of enterprise solutions.

Power BI Premium represents Microsoft's flagship business intelligence suite, including a superset of Analysis Services semantic modeling features, a paginated reporting service offering the pixel-perfect enterprise reporting features of Reporting Services, and additional workloads including artificial intelligence and dataflows.

This chapter focuses on a review of the capabilities enabled by Power BI Premium capacities and the top considerations in provisioning and using this capacity. In addition, subjects such as life cycle management, data management, and disaster recovery are also addressed.

In this chapter, we will review the following topics:

- Power BI Premium
- Premium capacity nodes
- Premium capacity estimations

- Premium capacity administration and allocation
- Premium capacity resource optimization
- Life cycle management with Premium

# Power BI Premium

Power BI Premium consists of dedicated capacity (hardware) that an organization can provision to host some or all of its Power BI content (datasets, reports, scorecards, and dashboards). As an alternative to the free clusters of capacity provided by Microsoft and shared by many organizations, Premium capacities are isolated to a specific organization and thus are not impacted by the use of Power BI by other organizations.

As flexible platform and **software as a service (SaaS)** architectures become the norm, organizations increasingly value the ability to focus their efforts on building the right solutions for their stakeholders with the appropriate amount of resources and with minimal to no infrastructure maintenance. Power BI Premium capacity aligns well with these new expectations as it enables an organization to provision and deploy enterprise-scale resources it requires in seconds and avoids the need to configure or maintain the underlying hardware

With Power BI Premium, organizations can utilize their provisioned capacity as needed and are not constrained by the limits imposed on shared (free) capacity, such as a max of 1 GB dataset sizes and eight (8) refreshes per day. Additionally, as a cloud service managed by Microsoft, organizations have great flexibility to scale, allocate, and manage Premium resources according to their preferred allocation methodology and changing requirements.

The top benefit of Power BI Premium is the ability to provide read-only access to Power BI Free users and thus cost-effectively scale Power BI deployments based on workloads rather than individual user accounts. This is particularly essential for large organizations with thousands of users, the majority of which only need the ability to infrequently view and optionally interact with content. Thus, an IT organization can assign a Power BI Free license to all users and decide which relatively small group of users should be assigned Power BI Pro licenses for developing and publishing content.

When Power BI content is hosted in a Premium capacity, the users consuming content such as via Power BI apps can view and interact with the content, such as making filter selections on a report or viewing a mobile-optimized dashboard on Power BI mobile applications without requiring a paid license. Thus, Power BI Premium enables organizations to limit the assignment of Power BI Pro users to those who create and distribute content.

Additionally, Power BI Premium capacity can be used to deliver Power BI content to users in applications and environments outside of the Power BI service. For example, Premium capacity can be used to embed Power BI visuals in custom applications, in other SaaS applications such as SharePoint Online, and to license **Power BI Report Server (PBRS)**. Details regarding PBRS and alternative content distribution methods are included in *Chapter 12, Deploying Paginated Reports*, and *Chapter 13, Creating Power BI Apps and Content Distribution*, respectively.

The Premium capacity-based licensing model, which currently starts at $4,995 per month for a P1 SKU, implies the following three fundamental questions:

1.  How much Premium capacity should be provisioned?
2.  How should provisioned capacity be allocated?
3.  What can be done to minimize capacity utilization and thus resource costs?

Guidance and consideration of these questions are included in the following sections.

Premium **Embedded (EM)** SKUs, which are exclusive to embedding Power BI content in applications or services such as SharePoint Online, have a lower starting price point and fewer resources. EM SKUs were discussed in the *Embedding* section of *Chapter 13, Creating Power BI Apps and Content Distribution*. As most organizations will leverage the Power BI service and mobile apps for large-scale deployments, Power BI Premium P SKUs are the focus of this chapter.

## Power BI Premium capabilities

Power BI Premium provides many additional capabilities beyond the ability to distribute content to read-only Power BI Free users. For example, Premium capacity or **Premium Per User (PPU)** licensing would be required to migrate SSRS, Cognos, or other similar types of reports to paginated reports in the Power BI service. Likewise, the limits of 1 GB of in-memory dataset size and only 8 refreshes per day may not be sufficient for many scenarios. Power BI Premium unlocks these resource limitations and exposes many other features, including artificial intelligence, and a rich suite of tool support via the XMLA endpoint.

*Table 15.1* identifies additional features of Premium capacities as well as **Premium Per User (PPU)** licenses:

| # | Feature | License Type |
|---|---------|--------------|
| 1 | Enable Power BI users to view content without a license | Premium |
| 2 | Licensing for Power BI Report Server (PBRS) | Premium |
| 3 | Multi-geo deployment | Premium |

Building Enterprise BI with Power BI Premium

| 4 | **Bring your own key (BYOK)** | Premium |
| 5 | Autoscale add-on | Premium |
| 6 | Increased model size limit of 100 GB (PPU) and 400 GB (Premium) | Premium and PPU |
| 7 | Paginated reports in the Power BI service | Premium and PPU |
| 8 | Advanced AI (AutoML and Azure Cognitive Services) | Premium and PPU |
| 9 | XMLA endpoint (read/write) | Premium and PPU |
| 10 | Enhanced dataflow functionality (enhanced compute engine, DirectQuery, linked, and computed entities) | Premium and PPU |
| 11 | Application life cycle management (pipelines) | Premium and PPU |
| 12 | 100 TB maximum storage | Premium and PPU |
| 13 | Maximum scheduled refreshes of 48 times per day (note: refreshes can be more frequent using the API endpoint) | Premium and PPU |
| 14 | Backup and restore datasets | Premium and PPU |

*Table 15.1: Power BI Premium features*

Some of the capabilities identified in this table enable completely new scenarios for projects involving Power BI datasets created with Power BI Desktop. For example, up to 400 GB datasets can be hosted in Premium capacity. Likewise, a dataset can be configured to refresh every 30 minutes in Premium capacity.

The integration of advanced artificial intelligence enables organizations to apply machine learning and other cognitive services models to their datasets, enabling predictive capabilities for categorization and regression as well as sentiment analysis, text analytics, and vision capabilities.

The ability to publish **SQL Server Reporting Services (SSRS)** reports, also referred to as paginated reports (RDL reports), to the Power BI service is especially valuable for organizations with significant SSRS investments. Without this capability, these organizations were previously required to deploy the Power BI Report Server (or an SSRS server), as described in *Chapter 12, Deploying Paginated Reports*.

Additionally, connectivity parity with Analysis Services, as provided by the XMLA endpoint, allows BI developers to utilize rich and familiar model development and management tools, including **SQL Server Management Studio (SSMS)**, Tabular Editor, ALM Toolkit, DAX Studio, and Visual Studio, as they would with Analysis Services models. Additionally, the standard XMLA protocol allows for other popular BI reporting tools such as Tableau to leverage a Power BI dataset as a data source.

The dataflow capabilities enabled by the enhanced compute engine allow the use of DirectQuery in dataflows as well as incremental refreshes. The enhanced compute engine also drastically improves data refresh speeds when performing costly data transformation operations such as joins, distinct rows, and grouping. Finally, linked and computed entities enable the reuse of dataflows within other dataflows as well as the pre-aggregation of data into new tables, respectively.

To support the largest Power BI deployments, the multi-geo feature of Power BI Premium allows Premium capacities to be assigned to different regions, allowing datasets and reports to be located closer to users in different geographies and thus achieve a better overall performance.

Note that BYOK allows organizations to use their own encryption keys, making it easier to meet compliance requirements and exercise more control over their data assets, and that the 100 TB storage limit for Premium capacities is a per-capacity node.

Finally, the autoscale feature allows additional processing power to be added temporarily depending upon the load within the Premium capacity. Autoscaling allows Premium capacities to remain performant during peak load times.

Let's now take a closer look at Power BI Premium capacities.

# Premium capacity nodes

A Premium capacity node can be thought of as a fully managed server in the Azure cloud that runs the Power BI service, including all frontend and backend operations such as loading a report and refreshing a dataset, respectively. The capacity node is dedicated and isolated to the organization that provisioned the capacity, and the same user experience and functionality are delivered as the shared (free) capacity provided by the Power BI Service.

Each capacity node has a set of processing and memory resources (v-cores and RAM), bandwidth limits, and a cost that aligns with these resources. For example, a P1 capacity node includes 8 v-cores and 25 GB of RAM at a cost of $4,995 per month, while a P2 capacity includes 16 v-cores and 50 GB of RAM at a cost of $9,995 per month.

When workspaces containing Power BI content (datasets, reports, and dashboards) are assigned to Premium capacity nodes, the resources of the given capacity node are used to execute Power BI activities associated with this content, such as query processing and data refresh operations. Depending upon how Power BI datasets and results are architected, different resources are more important than others.

For example, if Power BI reports utilize a DirectQuery dataset or a live connection to an Analysis Services model, then the amount of RAM provided per capacity is much less important than the limits on the number of connections and the max page renders at peak times. In such deployments, the resources provisioned for the data source system (CPU cores, clock speed, and RAM), as well as the latency and bandwidth of the connection between the source system and the data center region of the Power BI tenant, would largely drive query performance.

The following table identifies the resources associated with the eight EM and P Premium capacity nodes currently available as well as their equivalent A capacities:

| Capacity SKUs | Total v-cores | Backend v-cores | Frontend v-cores | RAM (GB) | DirectQuery/ Live connections (per second) | Max memory per query (GB) | Model refresh parallelism |
|---|---|---|---|---|---|---|---|
| EM1/A1 | 1 | 0.5 | 0.5 | 3 | 3.75 | 1 | 5 |
| EM2/A2 | 2 | 1 | 1 | 5 | 7.5 | 2 | 10 |
| EM3/A3 | 4 | 2 | 2 | 10 | 15 | 2 | 20 |
| P1/A4 | 8 | 4 | 4 | 25 | 30 | 6 | 40 |
| P2/A5 | 16 | 8 | 8 | 50 | 60 | 6 | 80 |
| P3/A6 | 32 | 16 | 16 | 100 | 120 | 10 | 160 |
| P4/A7 | 64 | 32 | 32 | 200 | 240 | 10 | 320 |
| P5/A8 | 128 | 64 | 64 | 400 | 480 | 10 | 640 |

*Table 15.2: Premium capacity nodes*

The differences between P, EM, and A SKUs were discussed in the *Embedding* section of *Chapter 13, Creating Power BI Apps and Content Distribution.* As mentioned there, EM SKUs are exclusive to embedding Power BI content in external applications (custom, Teams, SharePoint) and do not support viewing the content in the Power BI service or Power BI mobile apps without a license.

Given their more limited workloads, EM SKUs have significantly fewer resources and cost less to provision. Premium P SKUs (P1, P2, P3, P4, P5), however, support both embedding content in applications and the usage of the Power BI Service. As shown in *Table 15.2*, the largest Premium capacity node (P5) includes 128 v-cores and 400 GB of RAM.

The dataset size limitation for Power BI Premium of 400 GB reflects the maximum amount of memory available within Premium capacity nodes. In other words, dataset sizes are limited based on the maximum amount of memory available within the capacity. For example, a P2 Premium capacity could support several 45 GB datasets but would not support a 55 GB dataset given its 50 GB limit.

This per-dataset limit associated with Premium Capacity Generation 2 represents a dramatic leap in scalability relative to the per-capacity limits of the first generation of Premium capacity. Keep in mind that some memory must be reserved for dataset refreshes and queries, and thus the maximum permitted dataset size may be smaller than the total amount of memory for the capacity.

Some of the limits in *Table 15.2* only apply to certain dataset modes. For example, the DirectQuery/ Live connections (per second), and Max memory per query (GB) are applicable to DirectQuery/ Live mode connections, while Model refresh parallelism applies to import mode datasets. Model refresh parallelism refers to the number of objects (tables) that can be refreshed at the same time.

We now further explain additional columns in *Table 15.2*, specifically, the differences between frontend and backend resources.

## Frontend versus backend resources

It's important to understand the composition of frontend and backend resources in relation to Power BI workloads. For example, although a P2 capacity provides 16 total v-cores, only 8 backend cores are dedicated to processing queries, refreshing datasets, and the server-side rendering of reports.

Additionally, only the backend of a Premium capacity node, such as the 50 GB of RAM for a P2 capacity, is exclusive to the provisioning organization. If Power BI is only being used to create reports and dashboards against DirectQuery or Live connection sources, then these backend resources are less important and the connection limit (60 per second for a P2 capacity) would be the most relevant resource to understand and monitor.

The frontend cores (8 for a P2) are shared with other organizations in a pool of servers responsible for the web service, the management of reports and dashboards, uploads/downloads, and the user experience in navigating the Power BI service. Organizations that utilize Power BI datasets in the default import (in-memory) mode will want to ensure that sufficient RAM and backend cores are available to support both the data refresh process and the query workloads.

*Figure 15.1* illustrates the distribution of frontend and backend resources for a Premium capacity node (P2):

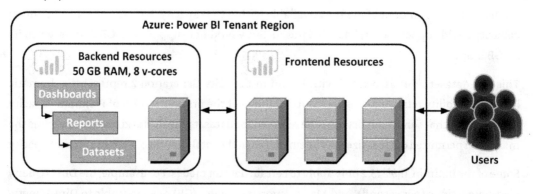

*Figure 15.1: Power BI Premium capacity node*

As shown in *Figure 15.1*, the backend of a capacity node can be thought of as a dedicated server or virtual machine with a fixed amount of CPU and RAM. It's the backend server that is responsible for the most resource-intensive or heavy lifting operations and thus should always be considered in relation to the resource needs of import mode datasets assigned to the given capacity.

In Power BI Premium Generation 1 (Gen1), the backend v-cores were reserved physical computing nodes dedicated to a particular Power BI Premium capacity. However, in Power BI Generation 2 (Gen2), these backend resources are physical nodes within regional clusters that service all Premium capacities within that region. This new architecture has significant advantages in terms of performance and monitoring.

For example, because the limitations of different capacity SKUs listed in *Table 15.2* are no longer based on physical constraints, as they were in Gen1, but rather a set of rules that the Power BI service enforces, administrators no longer need to monitor their capacities as closely as before. Instead of monitoring capacities to observe whether the capacity was approaching the limits of its resources, administrators are instead simply notified when capacity limits have been reached, thus significantly reducing the overhead required by administrators to maintain optimal performance.

A factor of 2.5X (times) is generally used to size the RAM requirements of in-memory Power BI datasets. For example, a 10 GB Power BI dataset (.PBIX), would require 25 GB of RAM (10 * 2.5 = 25). This estimate is based on 10 GB to store the dataset in-memory, another 10 GB for a copy of the dataset that is created during full refresh/processing operations, and an extra 5 GB to support temporary memory structures that can be required to resolve user queries.

Note that this example is exclusive to import mode datasets hosted in the Power BI Premium capacity (the backend resources). A separate architecture and considerations for capacity nodes apply when query requests are routed to Analysis Services models via Live connection or a DirectQuery data source such as Teradata or SAP HANA.

From a Premium capacity perspective, in these scenarios, the BI team would need to determine via load testing and the usage metrics described in the *Monitoring Premium capacities* section later in this chapter whether the query throughput limit (DirectQuery/Live connections per second from *Table 15.2*) to these sources is sufficient. If this throughput level is sufficient, yet performance is still unacceptable, several other components of the overall solution could represent the performance bottleneck and could be evaluated separately.

The other components or factors impacting performance include the design of the data model, the efficiency or complexity of DAX measures, the design of the data source, the design of Power BI reports (for example, quantity and type of visuals), the resources and performance of the gateway server(s) if applicable, the network connection between the Power BI service and the data source, and the level of user interactivity with reports.

Techniques and practices to optimize data models and the visualization layer in Power BI are provided in the *Data model optimizations* and *Report and visualization optimizations* sections later in this chapter, respectively.

With the basics of Premium capacities understood, we next turn our attention to answering one of the three primary questions regarding Premium capacities introduced at the beginning of this chapter: how much Premium capacity should be provisioned?

# Premium capacity estimations

The volume of factors involved in Premium capacity utilization makes it difficult to forecast the amount of Premium capacity (and thus cost) required. This complexity is particularly acute for large deployments with diverse use cases to support.

Additionally, for organizations relatively new to Power BI, the level and growth of user adoption, as well as the requirements for future projects, can be unclear. In the past, Microsoft provided an online tool to estimate which capacities would be needed for estimated workloads. However, that online tool no longer exists. Instead, use the guidance in this section to estimate Premium capacity requirements and then use the *Monitoring Premium capacities* section later in this chapter to determine whether additional resources are necessary.

Recall from the previous section that the important capacity limits from *Table 15.2* vary per dataset storage mode and usage. Available RAM is highly important to import mode datasets while somewhat less important for DirectQuery/Live datasets. Also, consider that resource requirements are not simply defined based on the number of concurrent users.

For example, 1,000 users viewing a single report with one visual is vastly different from 1,000 users viewing 100 reports, each with 10 different visuals. Add to this the variability of resource requirements based upon the complexity and efficiency of data transformation operations and/ or DAX calculations as well as RLS rules and it is easy to understand the complexity of providing clear estimates in all circumstances.

For import models, it is important to realize that these models must be fully loaded into available memory in order to facilitate refreshing and querying. In addition to the size of these data models, it is important to consider how many active, heavily used, data models will exist within the capacity. Enough memory should be available to allow all such datasets to be loaded into memory at the same time in order to maximize performance.

Referencing the 2.5X factor mentioned in the last section, thus, if two 10 GB datasets are heavily used by the organization, then this would require a total of 50 GB or a P2 node. Alternatively, organizations may instead choose to deploy two P1 nodes and dedicate a dataset to each node. By using multiple capacities, organizations can isolate workloads and thereby guarantee resources for priority datasets and reports.

Import mode datasets are also constrained by the model refresh parallelism (how many models can be refreshed simultaneously), but in Gen2 are no longer constrained by the number of concurrent refreshes. In Gen1, the maximum number of concurrent refreshes was 1.5X the number of backend v-cores, rounded up.

For DirectQuery and Live connection datasets, the DirectQuery/Live connections per second and maximum memory per query are two primary constraints, but also consider that these datasets can require significant v-core resources and even memory when evaluating complex RLS rules and DAX measure calculations.

Finally, dataflows and paginated reports.

Given the complexity of estimating required capacity sizes, a fiscally conservative approach would be to develop initial assets as part of shared capacity. Subsequently, the organization could purchase equivalent A SKUs for test purposes, which is why the A SKUs were included in *Table 15.2*.

A SKUs are charged on an hourly basis and require no minimum commitment. These A SKUs are thus an inexpensive way to load test workloads. Load testing can be executed using a PowerShell script or, for more complex scenarios, performed within Visual Studio. The Power BI Dedicated Capacity Load Assessment Tool can be downloaded from the following link: `https://bit.ly/3tG66aR`.

Power BI Embedded A SKUs can be purchased within the Azure portal, while Power BI EM and P SKUs are purchased within the Microsoft 365 Admin Center under the Billing section.

With an approach to capacity estimation provided, we next turn our attention to capacity administration and the second of the three primary questions regarding Premium capacities introduced at the beginning of this chapter: how should provisioned capacity be allocated?

# Premium capacity administration and allocation

One of the most important responsibilities of a Power BI administrator is the management of Power BI Premium capacities. From a Power BI administration perspective, Power BI Premium can be thought of as an organization's dedicated hardware resources to support the use of the Power BI service.

Not all of an organization's content needs to be hosted in Premium capacity. However, these resources enable the distribution of content to read-only Power BI Free users and they provide more consistent performance, among other scalability and management benefits.

Microsoft 365 global administrators and users assigned to the Power BI service administrator role automatically have the right to administer Premium capacities in the Power BI admin portal. An administrator's role in relation to Premium capacity is to ensure that the provisioned resources are utilized according to the organization's policies, and that sufficient resources are available to support the existing workload.

Power BI Premium administrators should be familiar with the following list of responsibilities:

1. **Create a new capacity with the available (purchased) v-cores**

   An organization may choose to dedicate a Premium capacity to a specific project or application. In other scenarios, one capacity could be dedicated to self-service projects while another capacity could be used by corporate BI projects.

2. **Grant capacity assignment permissions to users or security groups of users**

This enables Power BI Pro users who are also administrators of workspaces to assign their workspaces to Premium capacity. This setting can also be disabled or enabled for the entire organization.

3. **Assign workspaces to Premium capacity, or remove a workspace from Premium capacity, in the Power BI admin portal**

   This is an alternative and complementary approach to capacity assignment permissions. Power BI service administrators can manage existing capacities and assign workspaces in bulk. These bulk assignments can be by user, by a security group of users, or for the entire organization.

4. **Monitor the usage metrics of Premium capacities to ensure sufficient resources are available**

   An app is available for monitoring Premium capacities. More information about this app can be found at the following link: `https://bit.ly/3EmzbPu`.

5. **Change the size of an existing capacity to a larger (scale up) or smaller (scale down) capacity node**

   As more users and content utilize a specific capacity, it may be necessary to scale up or allocate certain workspaces to a different Premium capacity or shared (free) capacity.

6. **Assign a user or group of users as capacity administrators for a capacity**

   This can be appropriate to support large, enterprise deployments with multiple capacities and many app workspaces.

Given the importance of performance to any BI project, as well as the cost of Power BI Premium capacities, BI/IT teams need to plan for an efficient, manageable allocation of Premium capacity. This allocation plan and any project-specific decisions need to be communicated to the Premium administrator(s) for implementation. The following sections describe the responsibilities identified here and related considerations in greater detail.

## Capacity allocation

Power BI Premium provides organizations with significant flexibility for both allocating their resources to Premium capacities, as well as assigning Power BI content to those capacities.

Although it's possible to broadly assign all workspaces (and thus all content) of an organization to a single Premium capacity, most organizations will want to efficiently allocate and manage these resources.

For example, certain Power BI reports and dashboards that are utilized by executives or which contribute to important business processes might be identified and prioritized for Premium capacity. In an initial deployment of a Premium capacity, a BI/IT team may exclusively assign the workspaces associated with content considered mission-critical to this capacity. This capacity may remain isolated to the specific workload(s) or, based on testing and monitoring, the BI team may determine that sufficient resources are available to support additional workspaces and their associated resource requirements.

Similar to provisioning a Premium capacity exclusive to high-value content, a Premium capacity may be provisioned due to the unique requirements of a particular solution. As one example, a new Power BI dataset may be developed that represents a data source or business process not currently supported in the data warehouse. In this scenario, a large import mode Power BI dataset, perhaps initially developed by the business team, would serve as the source for reports and dashboards that require distribution to many Power BI Free users or even the entire organization. Given these characteristics, a Premium capacity node could be provisioned and dedicated to the app workspace hosting this dataset and its visualizations so that no other solution could impact its performance.

A single Premium capacity can be provisioned and created for an organization, or, for larger and more diverse deployments, multiple Premium capacities can be created with different sizes (CPU, memory, bandwidth) appropriate for their specific workloads.

In terms of allocating resources to Premium capacities, an organization is only limited by the number of **virtual cores (v-cores)** that have been purchased. For example, an organization could initially purchase a P2 capacity, which includes 16 v-cores. Once purchased, a P2 capacity could be created in the Capacity settings page of the Admin portal that utilizes all of these cores. However, at some later date, this capacity could be changed to a P1 capacity that only uses 8 v-cores. This would allow the organization to create a second P1 capacity given the 8 remaining v-cores available. Alternatively, a second P2 capacity could be purchased, providing another 16 v-cores. With 32 total v-cores purchased by the organization, an existing P2 capacity could be increased to a P3 capacity (32 v-cores).

*Figure 15.2* illustrates this example of capacity allocation:

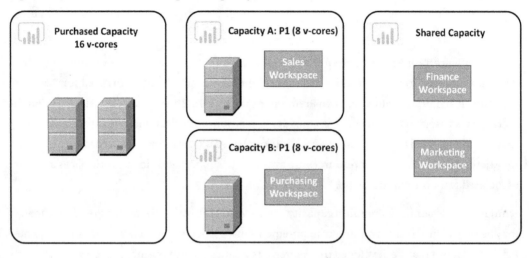

Figure 15.2: Power BI Premium capacity allocation

Regardless of the Premium SKU (P1, P2, P3, P4, or P5), the combination of SKUs purchased in the Microsoft 365 admin center, or the number of specific SKUs (instances), an organization can use the total number of v-cores purchased as it wishes. For example, purchasing a P3 SKU provides 32 v-cores, the same as purchasing four instances of a P1 SKU (8 X 4 = 32).

For organizations getting started with Power BI and that are comfortable with actively managing their Premium capacities, individual instances of the P1 SKU with no annual commitment (month-to-month) could make sense. For example, a single P1 instance could be purchased to start and then, if it's determined that more resources are needed, a second P1 instance could be purchased, making 16 cores available for either a P2 capacity or two P1 capacities.

In this diagram, an organization has chosen to isolate the sales and purchasing workspaces to their own P1 capacities with eight v-cores each. This isolation ensures that the resources required for one workspace, such as the user's connection to the Sales app, do not impact the other workspace (Purchasing). Additionally, the Finance and Marketing workspaces have been left in shared (free) capacity for now but could later be assigned to Capacity A or Capacity B if sufficient resources are available.

Whether Power BI workspaces are allocated to Premium capacity or shared capacity is transparent to end users. For example, the same login and content navigation experience in the Power BI service and Power BI mobile apps applies to both Premium and shared capacity. Therefore, organizations can selectively allocate certain workspaces, such as production workspaces accessed by many Power BI Free users, to Premium capacity while allowing other small or team workspaces to remain in the shared capacity.

The following section describes a capacity planning method.

## Corporate and Self-Service BI capacity

As described in the *Data governance for Power BI* section of *Chapter 14, Administering Power BI for an Organization*, certain projects will likely be wholly owned by the BI/IT team, including the report and visualization layer. Other projects, however, may be owned by business units or teams but still require or benefit from IT-provided resources, such as the on-premises data gateway and Premium capacity.

The BI team can manage a continuous life cycle over both project types (Corporate BI, Self-Service BI) by validating use cases or requirements for Premium capacity. Additionally, the migration of Power BI content across distinct Premium capacities could become part of a standard migration process from a self-service solution to a corporate BI-owned solution.

The provisioning and allocation of Power BI Premium capacity can further reflect an organization's support for both Corporate and Self-Service BI solutions. Typically, the Power BI content created and managed by IT is considered mission-critical to the organization or is accessed by a high volume of users. Self-service BI solutions, however, tend to utilize smaller datasets and usually need to be accessible to a smaller group of users.

In the following example shown in *Figure 15.3*, the allocation includes two Premium capacities, a P3, and a P2, dedicated to Corporate BI Capacity and Self-Service BI Capacity content, respectively:

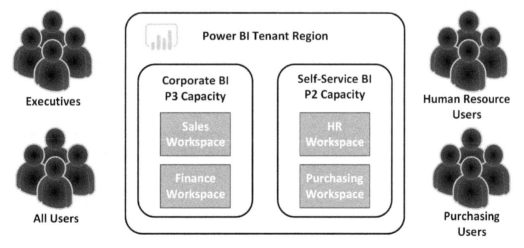

*Figure 15.3: Power BI Premium Capacity allocation: Corporate and Self-Service BI*

As shown in *Figure 15.3*, the Sales and Finance workspaces have been assigned to a P3 capacity dedicated to corporate BI solutions.

The Human Resources and Purchasing workspaces, however, have been assigned to a P2 Premium capacity dedicated to self-service BI projects. For example, certain Power BI Pro users in these departments have developed datasets and reports that have proven to be valuable to several stakeholders. The assignment of these workspaces to Premium capacity enables these users to make this content accessible to a wider audience, such as the 20 Power BI Free users in the Purchasing department.

Remember that not all workspaces need to consume Premium capacity resources. A team of Power BI Pro users may collaborate within a workspace and still be effective with the content hosted in shared capacity. Premium capacity is only needed in scenarios requiring broad distribution to read-only Power BI Free users or when the additional capabilities (for example, large datasets) identified in the Power BI Premium capabilities section earlier in this chapter are required.

In the event that one of the self-service solutions needs to be migrated to the corporate BI team, the BI team could re-assign the workspace to the existing P3 capacity. Alternatively, to avoid consuming any additional resources of the existing P3 capacity and potentially impacting these workloads, a new corporate BI capacity could be created for the workspace or the capacity expanded to a P4.

BI teams consistently need to evaluate the trade-offs involved with isolating projects/solutions to specific Premium capacities. Assigning a single workspace or multiple related workspaces to a dedicated capacity ensures that no other project or activity impacts performances. However, many dedicated Premium capacities may become onerous to manage and could be an inefficient use of resources if the Power BI workload doesn't fully utilize the resources.

Ultimately, teams will need to monitor capacity resource utilization and either re-allocate and re-assign capacities and workspaces, respectively, or provision additional Premium resources (v-cores) and scale up existing capacities. Scaling up and scaling out activities are discussed in the next section, which covers creating, sizing, and monitoring capacities.

# Create, size, and monitor capacities

Microsoft 365 global admins and Power BI service administrators can view, create, and manage all Power BI Premium capacities via the Admin portal, as discussed in *Chapter 14, Administering Power BI for an Organization*.

In *Figure 15.4*, the **Capacity settings** page from the Admin portal is shown:

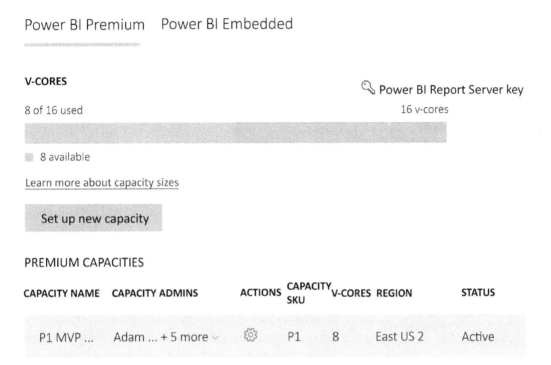

Figure 15.4: Admin portal's Capacity settings page

As shown in *Figure 5.4*, 16 v-cores have been provisioned for the organization and a single P1 capacity has been created, which consumes half of these cores.

A **Set up new capacity** button is located above the list of Premium capacities that have been configured. Clicking the **Set up new capacity** button launches a setup window, as shown in *Figure 15.5*:

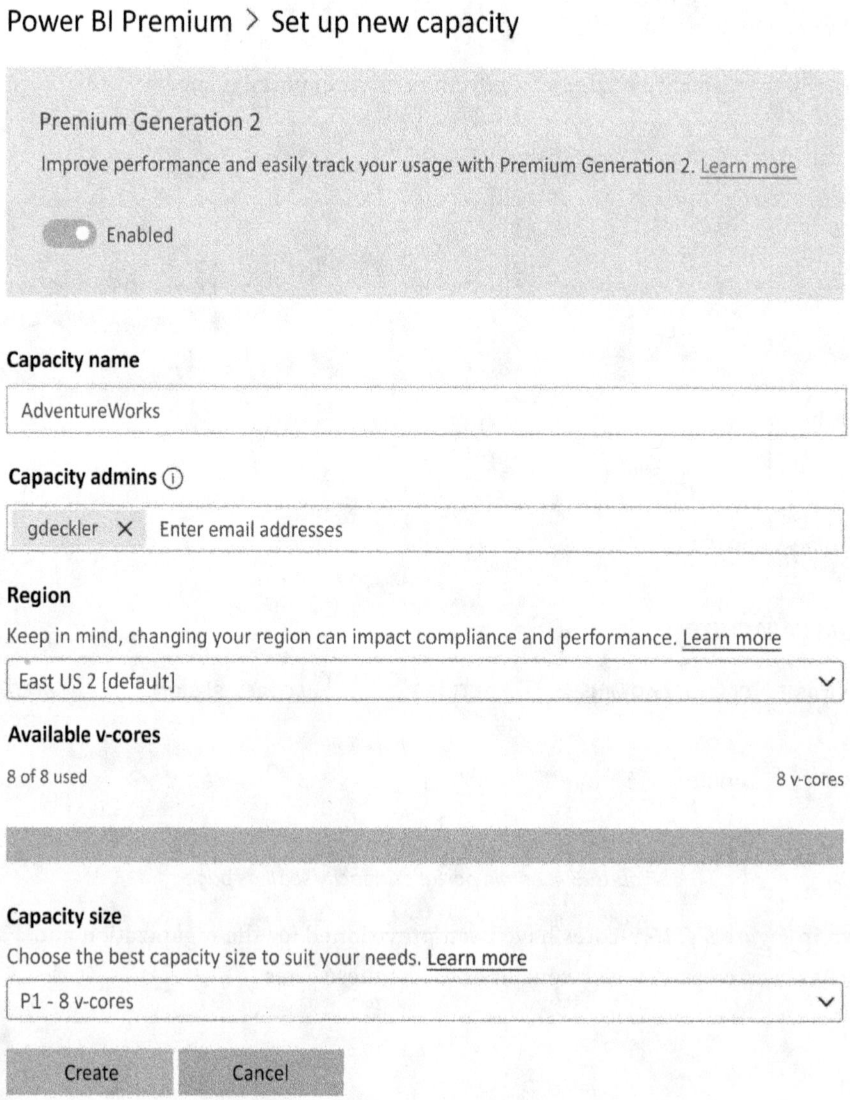

Power BI Premium > Set up new capacity

Premium Generation 2

Improve performance and easily track your usage with Premium Generation 2. Learn more

⬤◯  Enabled

**Capacity name**

AdventureWorks

**Capacity admins** ⓘ

gdeckler ✕    Enter email addresses

**Region**

Keep in mind, changing your region can impact compliance and performance. Learn more

East US 2 [default]                                                                    ⌄

**Available v-cores**

8 of 8 used                                                                          8 v-cores

**Capacity size**

Choose the best capacity size to suit your needs. Learn more

P1 - 8 v-cores                                                                        ⌄

Create          Cancel

*Figure 15.5: Set up new Premium capacity*

In this example, eight v-cores are available for the new capacity, and thus a P1 capacity requiring eight v-cores can be created. The capacity is named and the capacity administrator(s) for the new capacity are defined.

The **Capacity size** dropdown exposes all capacity sizes, but sizes requiring more v-cores than the volume of v-cores currently available cannot be selected. Once these properties are configured, click the **Create** button to complete the process.

Note that the **Capacity size** and **Capacity admins** properties are required to set up the new capacity. Each capacity must have at least one capacity admin, who has full administrative rights to the given capacity. These users do not have to be a Microsoft 365 global admin or a Power BI service administrator. Users assigned as capacity administrators have the same administrative rights to the given capacity as Power BI service administrators, such as the ability to change capacity sizes, assigning workspaces to the capacity as well as user assignment permissions.

For example, a Power BI Pro user could be assigned as a capacity admin and could access this capacity via the Admin portal just like a Power BI admin. However, only the capacities for which the user is a capacity admin would appear on the **Capacity settings** page. Additionally, other pages of the Admin portal, such as Tenant settings, would not be visible or accessible to the capacity admin.

As mentioned, capacity admins are capable of changing capacity sizes and settings, so let's look at those topics next.

## Changing capacity size

At some point after a capacity has been created, it may be necessary to change the size of the capacity. For example, given the increased adoption of Power BI, the P1 SKU may be insufficient to support the current workload, and thus an additional eight v-cores could be purchased with the intent to scale up the existing capacity to a P2 capacity size (16 v-cores). Alternatively, an administrator may wish to view the recent utilization of a Premium capacity to help determine whether additional app workspaces can be assigned to the capacity.

To change a capacity size and to view the utilization for a capacity, click the name of the capacity from the **Capacity settings** page shown in *Figure 15.4*. In *Figure 15.6*, a capacity was selected and then the **Change size** button clicked in order to expose the **Change size** pane:

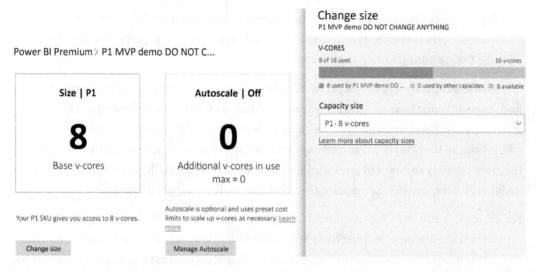

*Figure 15.6: Changing the capacity size*

The **Change size** pane contains a dropdown used for setting the capacity size. In this scenario, eight additional v-cores are available, meaning that the P1 capacity could be changed to a P2 capacity in just a few clicks.

Alternatively, instead of changing sizes manually, as shown in *Figure 15.6*, an option exists to autoscale Premium capacities. Autoscaling is an optional feature with an additional cost that allows capacities to automatically scale up by adding additional v-cores once certain thresholds are exceeded. Using autoscale can help ensure optimal performance during peak hours. Additional information about autoscale can be found at the following link: `https://bit.ly/3J2bb4S`.

With the creation and sizing of capacities understood, we next look at monitoring Premium capacities.

## Monitoring Premium capacities

As mentioned previously, Gen2 of Power BI Premium capacities has reduced the need to constantly monitor capacity nodes since the performance of backend resources are no longer physically constrained.

That said, it is still important to monitor capacities in order to identify problematic queries or datasets and reports receiving increased traffic.

An app is available for monitoring all capacities to which a user is a capacity admin. This app is available in AppSource as the Power BI Premium Capacity Utilization and Metrics app, as shown in *Figure 15.7*:

Apps > **Power BI Premium Capacity Utilization and Metrics**

# Power BI Premium Capacity Utilization and Metrics

by Microsoft

Applicable to:  Power BI apps

★ 1.8 (37 AppSource ratings)

Pricing **Free**     Get it now     ☆ Save to my list

Overview    Ratings + reviews    Details + support

**Premium capacity admins can gain visibility into the resources utilized by their PBI items**

This app enables admins to see how much CPU utilization, processing time and memory is utilized by datasets, paginated reports, dataflows, and other artifacts in Power BI Premium Gen2 (Preview) workspaces. Gain visibility into overload causes, peak demand times, resource consumption and more, and easily identify the most demanding or most popular Power BI artifacts.

*Figure 15.7: Changing capacity size*

This app allows capacity admins to understand the usage of datasets, dataflows, paginated reports, and other content within Power BI Premium Gen2 capacities, as well as important metrics such as memory utilization and v-core processing time. A link to the app is included under the **Capacity usage report** section of the settings for a capacity. Additional information about this app is available at the following link: `https://bit.ly/377d0Qu`.

In addition to the monitoring of utilization and metrics, Premium capacities also include the ability to send notifications when certain important metrics have been reached or exceeded. This is done in the notifications section after clicking on a specific capacity from the **Capacity settings** page of the Admin portal, as shown in *Figure 15.8*:

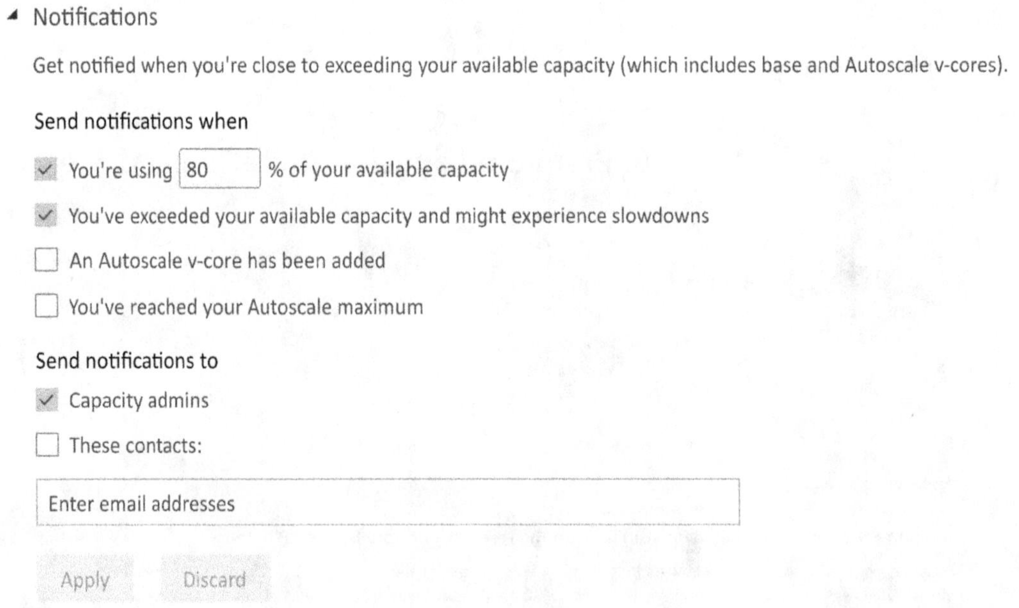

◢ Notifications

   Get notified when you're close to exceeding your available capacity (which includes base and Autoscale v-cores).

   **Send notifications when**

   ☑ You're using | 80        | % of your available capacity

   ☑ You've exceeded your available capacity and might experience slowdowns

   ☐ An Autoscale v-core has been added

   ☐ You've reached your Autoscale maximum

   **Send notifications to**

   ☑ Capacity admins

   ☐ These contacts:

   | Enter email addresses                                              |

   Apply          Discard

*Figure 15.8: Notification settings*

As shown in *Figure 15.8*, instead of the constant need to monitor capacities typical of Gen1, Gen2 allows for less rigorous monitoring via notifications. Capacity admins can choose thresholds for notifications as well as for important events such as autoscaling.

Let's next take a look at assigning workspaces to capacities.

# Workspace assignment

Just as organizations have the flexibility to allocate their purchased v-cores across one or multiple Premium capacities, there are also multiple options for assigning workspaces to Premium capacity.

To bulk assign multiple workspaces to a capacity within the Admin portal, navigate to a specific capacity by clicking on the capacity name from the **Capacity settings** page of the Admin portal, expand the **Workspaces assigned to this capacity** section, and then click the **Assign workspaces** link, as shown in *Figure 15.9*:

◢ Workspaces assigned to this capacity

    Search for, add, or remove workspaces assigned to this capacity

    🔍 Search workspaces            ✕ Remove all    ＋ Assign workspaces

*Figure 15.9: Assigning workspaces*

Clicking this link exposes the **Assign workspaces** pane as shown in *Figure 15.10*:

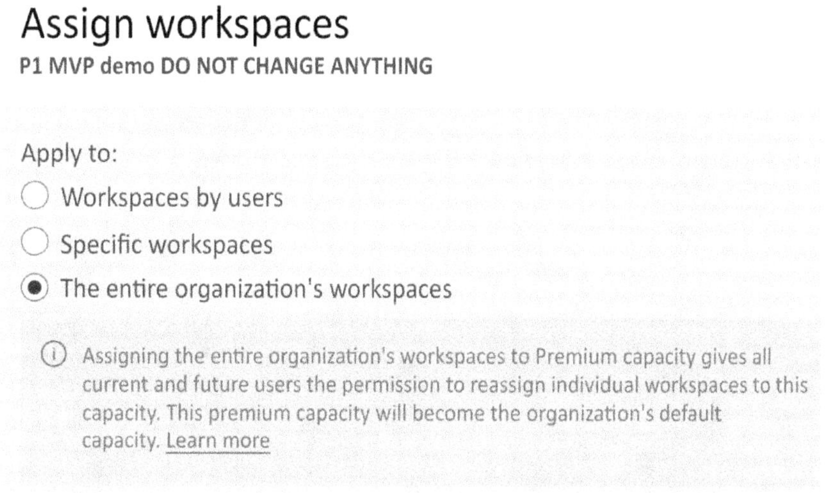

## Assign workspaces
**P1 MVP demo DO NOT CHANGE ANYTHING**

Apply to:

◯ Workspaces by users

◯ Specific workspaces

◉ The entire organization's workspaces

    ⓘ Assigning the entire organization's workspaces to Premium capacity gives all current and future users the permission to reassign individual workspaces to this capacity. This premium capacity will become the organization's default capacity. Learn more

*Figure 15.10: Assign workspaces pane*

As shown in *Figure 15.10*, all workspaces for the entire organization can be bulk assigned to the capacity. In addition, specific workspaces or all workspaces created by specific users can also be assigned. If applied to specific users, any existing workspaces assigned to those users, including workspaces already in a separate capacity, will be moved to the capacity assigned.

As an alternative or complementary approach to assigning workspaces in the Admin portal, administrators of a capacity can also grant users or groups of users permission to assign workspaces to Premium capacity. This is done in the **Contributor permissions** section for a capacity. In *Figure 15.11*, a user (gdeckler) is granted contributor permissions to a Premium capacity:

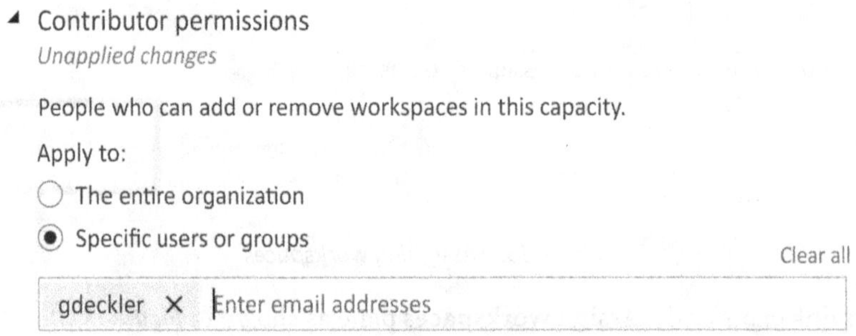

◢ Contributor permissions
*Unapplied changes*

People who can add or remove workspaces in this capacity.

Apply to:

◯ The entire organization

◉ Specific users or groups

Clear all

| gdeckler ✕ | Enter email addresses |

*Figure 15.11: Contributor permissions*

Users granted this permission will also require administrative rights to any workspace they wish to assign to Premium capacity. Workspace assignment is performed by workspace administrators via the **Premium** tab of the **Setting** pane for a workspace, as shown in *Figure 15.12*:

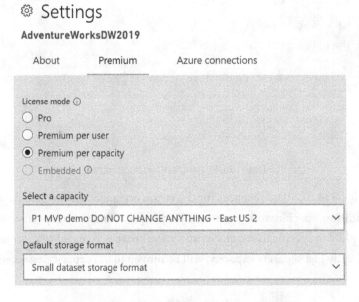

*Figure 15.12: Assigning to Premium per capacity*

The differences between workspace administrators and members were described in the *Workspace roles and rights* section of *Chapter 10*, *Managing Workspaces and Content*.

This completes our coverage of the administration and allocation tasks for Premium capacities. We now turn our attention to the final primary question regarding Premium capacities introduced at the beginning of this chapter: what can be done to minimize capacity utilization and, thus, resource costs?

# Premium capacity resource optimization

Given the cost of Premium capacity, BI teams will want to follow practices to ensure that these resources are actually required and not being used inefficiently. For example, with large import mode datasets, a simple design change such as the removal of unused columns from a fact table can significantly reduce the size of the dataset and, hence, the amount of memory needed.

By following a series of recommended practices in terms of both modeling and report design, fewer Premium capacity resources will be required to deliver the same query performance and scale. With small-scale self-service BI datasets and reports, performance tuning and optimization are usually not necessary. Nonetheless, as these models and reports can later take on greater scale and importance, a basic review of the solution can be applied before the content is assigned to Premium capacity.

The following two sections identify several of the top data modeling and report design practices to efficiently utilize Premium capacity resources.

## Data model optimizations

For many data models, particularly those that were developed as part of pilot projects or by business users, a number of modifications can be implemented to reduce resource requirements or improve query performance. Therefore, prior to concluding that a certain amount of Premium capacity is required, data models can be evaluated against a number of standard design practices and optimization techniques such as the following:

1. **Avoid duplicate or near-duplicate data models**

   Design and maintain a consolidated, standardized dataset (data model) of fact and dimension tables that can support many reports. Multiple datasets that represent near duplicates of the same source data and logic will require their own resources for refreshes and will also be difficult to manage and maintain version control.

2.  **Remove tables and columns that aren't needed by the model**

    For import mode models, columns with unique values (cardinality) will be the most expensive to store and scan at query time. The *Fact table columns* section of *Chapter 4, Designing Import, DirectQuery, and Composite Data Models* provides examples of avoiding derived columns that, for import mode models, can be efficiently implemented via DAX measures.

3.  **Reduce the precision and cardinality of columns when possible**

    If four digits to the right of the decimal place are sufficient precision, revise a column's data type from a Decimal number to a Fixed decimal number (19, 4). Apply rounding if even less precision is required. Split columns containing multiple values, such as a datetime column, into separate columns (date and time).

4.  **Limit or avoid high cardinality relationships, such as dimension tables with over 1.5 million rows**

    Consider splitting very large dimension tables into two tables and defining relationships between these tables and the fact table. The less granular table (such as Product Subcategory grain) could support most reports while the more granular table (such as Product) could be used only when this granularity is required.

5.  **Avoid expensive DAX measures**

    Avoid measures that require a high volume of context transitions (from row to filter context) or that cause an unnecessary number of evaluations. For example, only define DAX variables that will always be required for the expression and that can be used to replace other expressions. Additionally, rather than embedding complex logic in measures, particularly logic that involves materializing large temporary tables or iterating over large tables, look for opportunities to revise the model such as with new attributes to keep the DAX measures simple and efficient.

6.  **Use whole number (integer) data types instead of text data types whenever possible**

7.  **If the data model uses a DirectQuery data source, optimize this source**

    For example, implement indexes or columnar technologies available, such as the Clustered Columnstore Index for SQL Server. Additionally, ensure that the source database supports referential integrity and that the DirectQuery model assumes referential integrity in its defined relationships. This will result in inner join queries to the source. Additionally, consider whether an in-memory or even a DirectQuery aggregation table could be used to improve the performance of common or high priority report queries.

8. **Avoid or limit DISTINCTCOUNT() measures against high cardinality columns**

For example, create the `DISTINCTCOUNT()` measure expression against the natural key or business key column identifying the dimension member (such as Customer ABC), rather than the columns used in the fact-to-dimension relationship. With slowly changing dimension processes, the relationship columns could store many more unique values per dimension member and thus reduce performance. Additionally, if a slight deviation from the exact result is tolerable, the `APPROXIMATEDISTINCTCOUNT()` function can be considered a more performant alternative to `DISTINCTCOUNT()`.

9. **Avoid the use of calculated DAX columns on fact tables**

Create these columns in the source system or in the queries used to load the model to allow for better data compression. For DirectQuery models, avoid the use of DAX calculated columns for all tables.

In addition to dataset optimizations, it is also important to consider report and visualization optimizations.

# Report and visualization optimizations

A well-designed analytical model with ample resources can still struggle to produce adequate performance due to an inefficient visualization layer. The following list of techniques can be applied to Power BI reports and dashboards to reduce the query workload and avoid slower resource-intensive queries:

1. **Create dashboards on top of reports to leverage cached query results representing the latest data refresh**

Unlike dashboards, report queries are sent and executed on the fly when Power BI reports are loaded. Multiple dashboards can be linked together as described in *Chapter 9, Designing Dashboards*. If the dataset uses a DirectQuery or Live connection, take advantage of the scheduled cache refresh, as described in the *Dashboard cache refresh* section of *Chapter 11, Managing the On-Premises Data Gateway*.

2. **Avoid report visuals that return large amounts of data such as tables with thousands of rows and many columns**

Report visuals that require scrolling or which represent a data extract format should be filtered and summarized. Report visuals that return more data points than necessary to address their business question can be modified to a lower granularity.

For example, a dense scatter chart of individual products could be modified to use the less granular product subcategories column.

3. **Ensure that filters are being applied to reports so that only the required data is returned**

   Apply report-level filters to only return the time periods needed (such as current year and last year). Use visual-level filters such as a top N filter, as described in the *Visual-level filtering* section of *Chapter 8, Creating and Formatting Visualizations*.

4. **Limit the volume of visuals used on a given report page**

   Optionally, remove the interactions between visuals (cross-highlighting) to further reduce report queries.

5. **Understand which DAX measures are less performant and only use these measures when required**

   For example, only use expensive measures in card visuals or within highly filtered visuals exposing only a few distinct numbers.

Following these best practices for reports will help optimize the use of Premium capacity resources. In addition, the capacity settings themselves can be tuned in order to optimize resource workloads.

# Workloads

Power BI Premium was originally exclusive to datasets but has been expanded to include three additional workloads: Paginated Reports, AI, and Dataflows. Power BI administrators have the option of configuring settings specific to each of these workloads. Workloads settings are available for Premium capacities in the **Workloads** section after navigating to a specific capacity from the **Capacity settings** page of the Admin portal. These settings are shown in *Figure 15.13*:

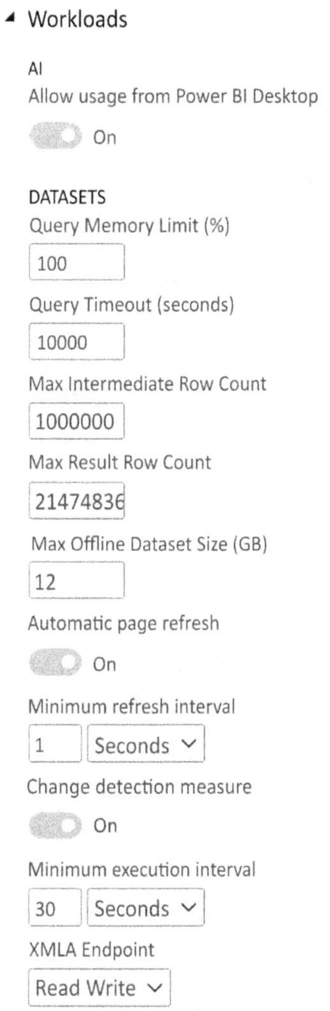

◢ Workloads

AI
Allow usage from Power BI Desktop

⬤◯ On

DATASETS
Query Memory Limit (%)

| 100 |

Query Timeout (seconds)

| 10000 |

Max Intermediate Row Count

| 1000000 |

Max Result Row Count

| 21474836 |

Max Offline Dataset Size (GB)

| 12 |

Automatic page refresh

⬤◯ On

Minimum refresh interval

| 1 | | Seconds ∨ |

Change detection measure

⬤◯ On

Minimum execution interval

| 30 | | Seconds ∨ |

XMLA Endpoint

| Read Write ∨ |

*Figure 15.13: Workloads settings*

Configuring Premium capacity workload settings is an important tool for ensuring that Premium capacity resources are being allocated to the highest priority workloads and to avoid or mitigate the impact of inefficient or resource-intensive queries and artifacts on the overall Premium capacity.

For example, setting threshold values for both **the Query Memory Limit %** and the **Max Result Row Set Count** dataset settings can help avoid capacity resources being allocated to poorly designed queries or 'data extract' style reports. Likewise, the **Minimum refresh interval** dataset setting can be used to avoid report authors from configuring reports that would generate a high and unnecessary volume of queries against a DirectQuery source system. Additional information on **Workloads** can be found at the following link: https://bit.ly/379PEK3.

The three primary questions regarding Premiums capacities have now been covered. However, there are additional secondary considerations for Premium capacities, such as life cycle management.

# Life cycle management with Premium

In addition to the enhanced life cycle management capabilities of Power BI Premium described in the *Power BI deployment pipelines* section of *Chapter 10, Managing Workspaces and Content*, the write capabilities of the XMLA endpoint enable additional capabilities with regard to life cycle management of datasets assigned to Premium capacities.

Specifically, given the write capabilities of the XMLA endpoint, the recommended tool for deploying incremental changes to datasets becomes the ALM Toolkit from MAQ Software, which is based on the BISM Normalizer by Christian Wade.

## ALM Toolkit deployment

ALM Toolkit is a free, open source tool that enables the object-level comparison of source and target datasets and the incremental deployment of changes such as new or revised DAX measures. ALM Toolkit can be downloaded from http://alm-toolkit.com.

Once downloaded, simply run the .msi installer file to install. After installation, ALM Toolkit is available from the **External tools** tab of Power BI Desktop, as shown in *Figure 15.14*:

*Figure 15.14: ALM Toolkit as available through External Tools*

Open a Power BI Desktop file and then launch ALM Toolkit from the ribbon on the **External tools** tab. Once opened, click the **Compare** button to display the **Connections** dialog shown in *Figure 15.15*:

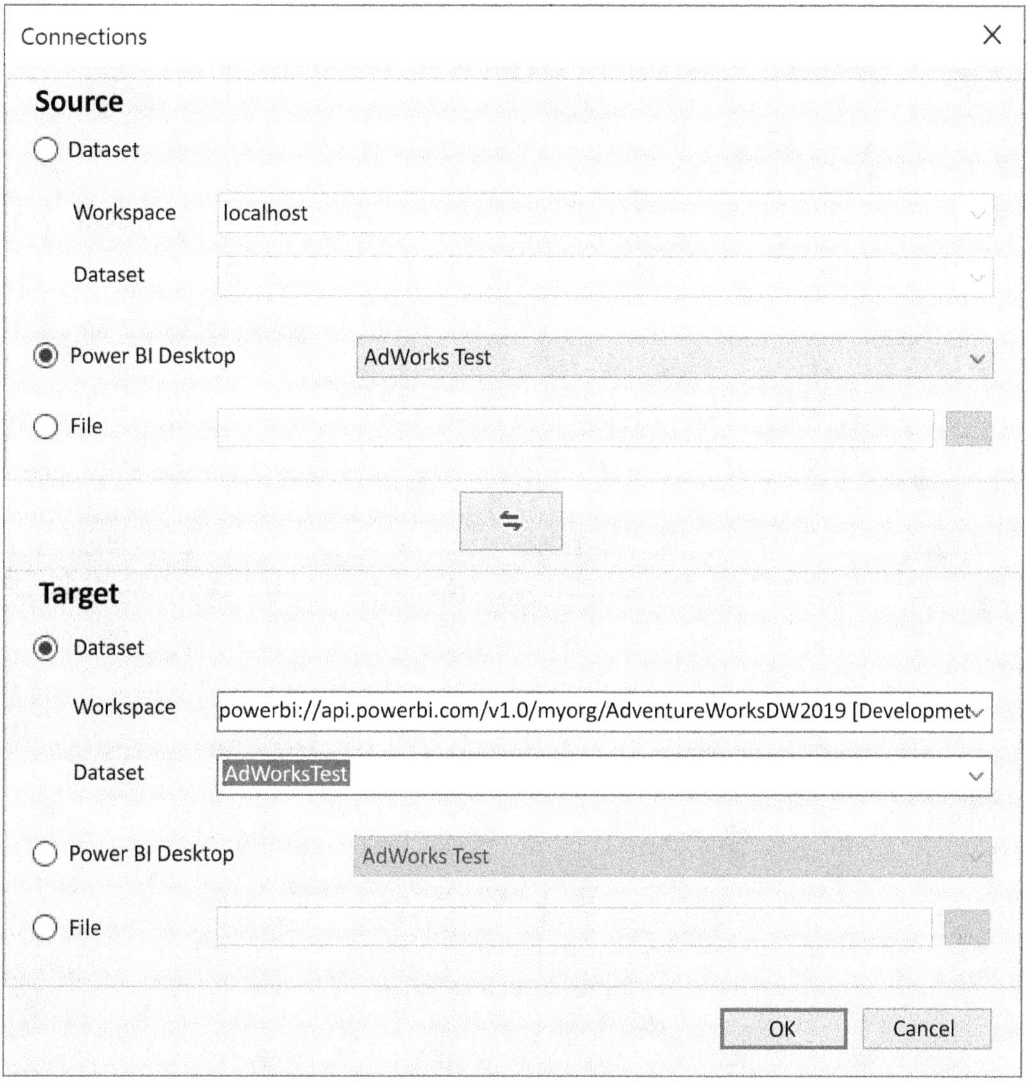

| Connections | ✕ |
|---|---|
| **Source** | |
| ◯ Dataset | |
| Workspace | localhost ⌄ |
| Dataset | ⌄ |
| ⦿ Power BI Desktop | AdWorks Test ⌄ |
| ◯ File | |
| | ⇆ |
| **Target** | |
| ⦿ Dataset | |
| Workspace | powerbi://api.powerbi.com/v1.0/myorg/AdventureWorksDW2019 [Developmet ⌄ |
| Dataset | AdWorksTest ⌄ |
| ◯ Power BI Desktop | AdWorks Test ⌄ |
| ◯ File | |
| | OK    Cancel |

*Figure 15.15: ALM Toolkit Connections dialog*

As shown in *Figure 15.15*, the local dataset open in Power BI Desktop serves as the **Source** and is compared with a **Target** dataset in the Power BI service. Clicking the **OK** button compares the **Target** with the **Source** in order to ascertain any differences between the data models.

As shown in *Figure 15.16*, a new measure, **New Account Measure**, has been added to the local data model but does not exist in the **Target** dataset published to the Power BI service.

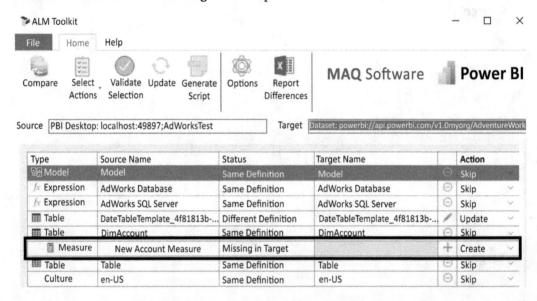

| Type | Source Name | Status | Target Name | | Action |
|---|---|---|---|---|---|
| Model | Model | Same Definition | Model | ⊖ | Skip |
| *fx* Expression | AdWorks Database | Same Definition | AdWorks Database | ⊖ | Skip |
| *fx* Expression | AdWorks SQL Server | Same Definition | AdWorks SQL Server | ⊖ | Skip |
| Table | DateTableTemplate_4f81813b-... | Different Definition | DateTableTemplate_4f81813b-... | ✎ | Update |
| Table | DimAccount | Same Definition | DimAccount | ⊖ | Skip |
| Measure | New Account Measure | Missing in Target | | + | Create |
| Table | Table | Same Definition | Table | ⊖ | Skip |
| Culture | en-US | Same Definition | en-US | ⊖ | Skip |

*Figure 15.16: ALM Toolkit comparison of data models*

Use the **Select Actions** dropdown shown in *Figure 15.16* to select **Create all objects Missing in Target**, as shown in *Figure 15.17*:

*Figure 15.17: ALM Toolkit Select Actions dropdown*

Next, click the **Validate Selection** button and, once validated, click the **OK** button. Finally, click the **Update** button to deploy the changes to the published dataset in the Power BI service.

In this example, changes made by a developer to a local copy of the Power BI Desktop (.pbix) file were deployed to a workspace assigned to the **Development** stage of a Power BI Deployment pipeline. As discussed in the *Power BI deployment pipelines* section of *Chapter 10, Managing Workspaces and Content*, these changes could then be promoted to the workspace assigned to the **Test** stage and finally, to the **Production** stage.

Using ALM Toolkit to deploy changes to Power BI datasets is particularly important when using incremental refresh. Incremental refresh creates an additional partition within the dataset for each incremental refresh cycle. In addition, because of this, datasets using incremental refresh cannot be downloaded from the Power BI service.

Without the use of ALM Toolkit, if model changes are required, the local Power BI Desktop file would need to be fully refreshed and then republished to the Power BI service, removing all incremental refresh partitions and effectively "starting over" with regard to incremental refreshes. For large, complex data models, this could be a costly and time-consuming exercise, especially if only minor changes have been made.

Additionally, there's often a scenario in which certain objects in the source dataset, such as query parameters, need to remain different than the target dataset. ALM Toolkit makes it easy to exclude certain differences and deploy only the changes required.

Documentation for ALM Toolkit can be found at the following link: https://bit.ly/3f95oDQ.

We next take a look at another life cycle scenario enabled by the XMLA endpoint.

## Dataset management with SSMS

With the XMLA endpoint feature of Power BI Premium, it is possible to connect to datasets published to the Power BI service from within **SQL Server Management Studio** (**SSMS**). To accomplish this, follow these steps:

1.  First, open **Settings** for a workspace and navigate to the **Premium** tab, as shown in *Figure 15.18*:

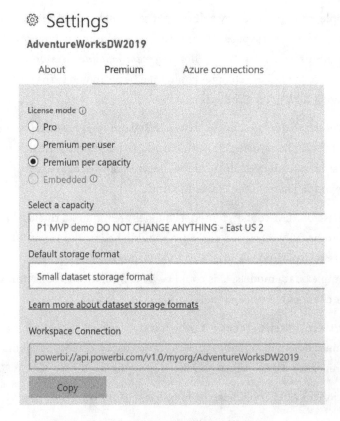

*Figure 15.18: Premium Workspace Connection*

2.  Use the **Copy** button to copy the workspace connection

3.  Open SSMS

4.  In the **Connect to Server** dialog, choose **Analysis Services** in the **Server type** field and paste the copied connection string into the **Server name** field, as shown in *Figure 15.19*:

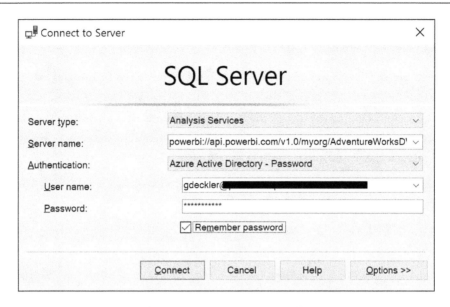

*Figure 15.19: SQL Server Connection*

5.   As shown in *Figure 15.19*, choose **Azure Active Directory - Password** in the **Authentication** field, enter a username and password, and then click the **Connect** button

6.   The datasets published to the workspace are available in the **Object Explorer** pane of SSMS, as shown in *Figure 15.20*:

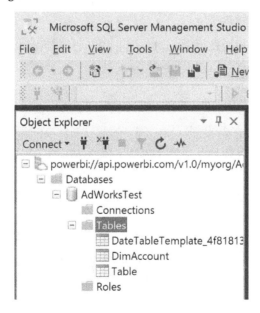

*Figure 15.20: SSMS Object Explorer*

The datasets within the workspace can now be managed within SSMS as if they were any other Analysis Services tabular cube.

For example, the data warehouse team might need to reload the entire sales history for the past 5 years to correct an issue found by an external audit. However, the incremental refresh policy in Power BI is only loading the last 1-2 months' worth of data. Using SSMS via the XMLA endpoint, the older partitions can be manually refreshed for the historical data by viewing the partitions for the dataset, as shown in *Figure 15.21*:

*Figure 15.21: Partitions within SSMS*

Note that PowerShell scripts and the SqlServer PowerShell module can also be used as a means to handle these custom refresh scenarios and to potentially supplement incremental refresh policies managed by Power BI.

We will now look at a final topic regarding the life cycle of Premium capacity datasets – backup and restoration.

## Backing up Premium capacities

The release to **general availability (GA)** support for backing up and restoring Power BI Premium and PPU datasets closed an important gap with Analysis Services and also provides a mechanism for migration from an Analysis Services model to Power BI Premium.

Either SSMS or the Analysis Services cmdlets for PowerShell can be used to back up and restore datasets published to the Power BI service using the XMLA endpoints. For example, once connected to a Power BI workspace, as explained in the previous section, the **Back Up** and **Restore** options become available for datasets published to Premium capacities, including PPU workspaces, as shown in *Figure 15.22*:

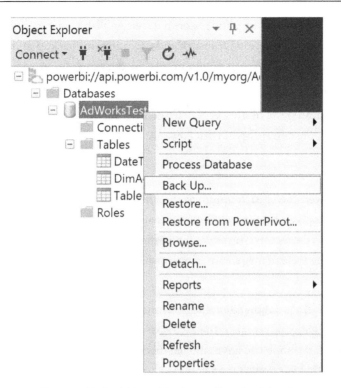

*Figure 15.22: Back Up and Restore options for datasets*

To use the **Back Up** and **Restore** features, you must register an **Azure Data Lake Gen2 (ADLS Gen2)** storage account for the tenant or at the workspace level. These settings were discussed in the Azure connections section of *Chapter 14, Administering Power BI for an Organization*. Offline backups can be obtained by using Azure Storage Explorer to download backup files from the connected ADLS Gen2 storage.

Backups performed place backup files (.abf files) into a power-bi-backup container within the ADLS Gen2 storage container. A folder is created in this container with the same name as the workspace. In the event that a workspace is renamed, the corresponding backup folder is also automatically renamed to match. To conduct a restore, the backup files must also be placed in that same folder.

Workspace users who have write or administrator permissions can perform backups of datasets within that workspace. This includes users who are members of the admin, member, and contributor roles discussed in the *Workspace roles and rights* section of *Chapter 10, Managing Workspaces and Content*. In addition, users with direct write permissions to a dataset can back up that dataset. Only workspace admins, members, and contributors can restore a dataset.

As mentioned, the ability to back up and restore datasets published to the Power BI service enables a migration path for Analysis Services workloads. In addition, backup and restore operations might be undertaken in the event of tenant migration, data corruption, or for regulatory-based data retention requirements.

This concludes our analysis of life cycle management for Premium capacities as well as our exploration of building enterprise BI with Power BI Premium.

## Summary

This chapter reviewed Power BI Premium as the primary means to deploy Power BI at scale and with enterprise BI tools and controls. The features and administration of Power BI Premium were described, as well as the factors to account for inefficiently provisioning and allocating Premium capacity. Finally, life cycle management concerns particular to Premium capacity features were explored.

This book has been all about how to enable enterprise-level business intelligence using Power BI, and this chapter highlighted some of the exclusive features that Power BI Premium provides in pursuit of this goal. We hope you have enjoyed this book and are now confident in how to apply this knowledge within your own organization.

## Join our community on Discord

Join our community's Discord space for discussions with the author and other readers:
https://discord.gg/q6BPbHEPXp

# Other Books
# You May Enjoy

If you enjoyed this book, you may be interested in these other books by Packt:

**Learn Power BI**

Greg Deckler

ISBN: 9781801811958

- Get up and running quickly with Power BI
- Understand and plan your business intelligence projects
- Connect to and transform data using Power Query
- Create data models optimized for analysis and reporting
- Perform simple and complex DAX calculations to enhance analysis
- Discover business insights and create professional reports
- Collaborate via Power BI dashboards, apps, goals, and scorecards
- Deploy and govern Power BI, including using deployment pipelines

**Microsoft Power BI Cookbook**

Greg Deckler

Brett Powell

ISBN: 9781801813044

- Cleanse, stage, and integrate your data sources with Power Query (M)
- Remove data complexities and provide users with intuitive, self-service BI capabilities
- Build business logic and analysis into your solutions via the DAX programming language and dashboard-ready calculations
- Implement aggregation tables to accelerate query performance over large data sources
- Create and integrate paginated reports
- Understand the differences and implications of DirectQuery, live connections, Import, and Composite model datasets
- Integrate other Microsoft data tools into your Power BI solution

# Packt is searching for authors like you

If you're interested in becoming an author for Packt, please visit authors.packtpub.com and apply today. We have worked with thousands of developers and tech professionals, just like you, to help them share their insight with the global tech community. You can make a general application, apply for a specific hot topic that we are recruiting an author for, or submit your own idea.

# Share your thoughts

Now you've finished *Mastering Microsoft Power BI, Second Edition*, we'd love to hear your thoughts! Scan the QR code below to go straight to the Amazon review page for this book and share your feedback or leave a review on the site that you purchased it from.

*https://packt.link/r/1801811482*

Your review is important to us and the tech community and will help us make sure we're delivering excellent quality content.

# Index

# R

**ranking metrics 214-216**
dynamic ranking measures 216, 217

**RColorBrewer package 346**

**RDL Migration Tool**
reference link 513

**related tables 187, 188**

**relationships 149**
ambiguity 150, 151
bidirectional relationships 154, 155
single-direction relationships 151-153
uniqueness 149, 150

**relative date filtering 263, 264**

**Report Definition Language (RDL) 309, 310, 499**

**report design**
summarizing 278, 279

**report filter scopes 257, 259**
filter conditions, applying 259-261
relative date filtering 263, 264
report- and page-level filters 261-263
visual-level filtering 265

**reporting elements**
exploring 310-312

**report planning process 229**
access and distribution, defining 233
audience, identifying 230, 231
business questions, defining to answer 231
dataset support to business questions, checking 231, 232
interactivity, determining 232, 233
report architecture diagram 235-237
report layout, sketching 234, 235
steps 230

**reports**
versus dashboard 373, 374, 376

**Report Server Database**
reference link 526

**Report view 124, 129, 130**

**rolling periods 206, 207**

**row context 184-186**

**Row Level Security (RLS) 64, 220, 415, 544**

**R visual 342, 344-346**
download link 344

# S

**sample project analysis 44, 45**

**scalar function 186, 187**

**Scatter charts 328, 330**
Play axis 355, 356

**scheduled data refresh 490-492**

**Scorecard 308, 309**

**Secure URL embedding 562**

**security roles 218-222**
dynamic row-level security 222-224

**Selection pane, bookmarks 269**

**Self-Service 3**

**self-service BI workspaces 577**
content distribution 578
risks 579

**Server Management Studio (SSMS)**
dataset management 655-658

**Service Principal Name (SPN) 493**

**Shape map visuals**
reference link 297

**shared capacity, Power BI licenses 18**
Free licensing 18-20
Pro licensing 20, 21

# Download a free PDF copy of this book

Thanks for purchasing this book!

Do you like to read on the go but are unable to carry your print books everywhere? Is your eBook purchase not compatible with the device of your choice?

Don't worry, now with every Packt book you get a DRM-free PDF version of that book at no cost.

Read anywhere, any place, on any device. Search, copy, and paste code from your favorite technical books directly into your application.

The perks don't stop there, you can get exclusive access to discounts, newsletters, and great free content in your inbox daily

Follow these simple steps to get the benefits:

1.  Scan the QR code or visit the link below

https://packt.link/free-ebook/9781801811484

2.  Submit your proof of purchase
3.  That's it! We'll send your free PDF and other benefits to your email directly

Printed in the USA
CPSIA information can be obtained
at www.ICGtesting.com
LVHW080915051223
765725LV00044B/923